FROMMER'S
DOLLARWISE
SOUTHWEST

INCLUDING NEW MEXICO, ARIZONA, AND COLORADO

ROY BONGARTZ

□

1989–1990

Published by Prentice Hall Trade Division
A Division of Simon & Schuster, Inc.
Gulf + Western Building
One Gulf + Western Plaza
New York, NY 10023

ISBN 0-13-048554-3
ISSN 0899-3335

Text design: Levavi & Levavi, Inc.

Manufactured in the United States of America

*Although every effort was made to ensure the accuracy of price
information in this book, it should be kept in mind that prices can
and do fluctuate in the course of time.*

CONTENTS

MAPS

ACKNOWLEDGMENTS

Special thanks for providing information and other services useful in the preparation of this guide go to: Mary K. Cline of the Albuquerque Convention & Visitors Bureau; Marsha Eckstrom of the Taos County Chamber of Commerce; Richard Grant of the Denver Metro Convention & Visitors Bureau; Michael E. Pitel of the New Mexico Tourism Department; and Sally Hankin, Maria Vigil, and Maria Anderson of the Metropolitan Tucson Convention & Visitors Bureau.

INFLATION ALERT: I don't have to tell you that inflation has hit the United States as it has everywhere else. In researching this book I have made every effort to obtain up-to-the-minute prices, but even the most conscientious researcher cannot keep up with the current pace of inflation. As we go to press, I believe I have obtained the most reliable data possible. Nonetheless, in the lifetime of this edition—particularly its second year (1990)—the wise traveler will add 15% to 20% to the prices quoted throughout these pages.

A DISCLAIMER: Although every effort was made to ensure the accuracy of the prices and travel information appearing in this book, it should be kept in mind that prices do fluctuate in the course of time, and that information does change under the impact of the varied and volatile factors that affect the travel industry.

CHAPTER I

THE SOUTHWEST: AN INTRODUCTION

□ □ □

The Southwest of the Upper Rio Grande owes its unique character to a dual heritage: the Pueblo Indian civilizations reaching back into prehistory and the Spanish colonization that began in the 16th century. Add to this historic base the boom-and-bust gold and silver rushes in the mountains of the Southwest during the last half of the past century and you have the makings of the somewhat-elusive culture called the West.

This partly real, partly imaginary realm that challenged pioneers with its temptations of virgin frontier lands still captures our imaginations even as the placeless urban sprawl spills out across Phoenix and its Valley of the Sun and a dozen other cities that draw northerners down to the year-round blue skies. In spite of the sameness of those new building developments, condominium complexes, and mobile-home parks that are the newest towns and cities of our land, the country here has the oldest communities too: cliff dwellings abandoned in the 13th century that look as if they might have been lived in yesterday, and—more remarkable—the Indian pueblos where people have been living since prehistoric times.

Newcomers to the Southwest find a complex population: aboriginal Indians, including 150,000 Navajos and Pueblo groups, each different from the other in language and culture; Hispanics descended from original colonists or more recently come in from Mexico; and the locally termed "Anglos," from the term Anglo-Saxon, who include everybody neither Hispanic nor Indian—that is, an Anglo may be a black person, or a Slav or Italian by descent. Among Anglos a particular influence in the Southwest has come from the Mormons.

Visitors to the oldest continuously inhabited communities in the U.S. such as the Hopi capital of Oraibi ("the center of the universe") or Acoma (the Sky City of the Acoma people) learn a new perspective on what is old and what is new in the U.S. Old-style Spanish weaving still carried on in the mountains around Taos and Santa Fe also steps back in time in villages clustered around the adobe church facing the plaza. A restored Mormon ranch in the wilderness north of the Grand Canyon, now a national monument, can take us back to the time of the pioneers. Descendants of all these people populate the Southwest, some of them, such as the Pueblo Indians and many of the Hopi and Navajo, and some of the Hispanics in the mountain villages, keeping to the old ways. Others blend with the leveling forces of booming urban populations swelled by sun-belt retirees from every part of the U.S. that make Sun City a sort of over-60 microcosm of the American scene. The very oldest in our country, from dinosaur fossils and mysteriously designed petroglyphs to cliff dwellings and those still-inhabited pueblos, comes right beside the newest in the land in the Southwest. A particular aim of this guide is to make it easy to learn about what is old and permanent, and to help visitors enjoy the experience of touring these sites.

Ten years before the Pilgrims arrived in Massachusetts, the Spanish were already building their new Palace of Governors in Santa Fe, and today Spanish is still an official language of the state of New Mexico. Reaching back beyond the time of written history in the Southwest are the 19 pueblos in New Mexico that are still inhabited (the largest, Zuni pueblo, famous for its silversmiths). But nearby is Albuquerque, booming with aerospace industry, and in nearby Los Alamos a colony of scientists gives the town the U.S.'s highest per capita rate of PhDs. To the southwest near Alamogordo is a reminder to the world of the power of nuclear explosions, the crater left by the world's first.

What is probably the country's greatest natural wonder gives Arizona its nickname, the Grand Canyon State. Of the millions of visitors to the south and north rims every year who peer down at what seems a trickle of water a mile below, there are a few hundred who actually make the trek down the precipitous switchback trail, either on foot or muleback, to find that there is really a wide, fast-flowing river, the Colorado, down there. A series of dams farther downstream not only serves seven states with irrigation and other water supplies, and hydroelectric power, but also has made recreation areas in reservoirs in the hottest parts of the desert. Around Tucson especially, and scattered widely elsewhere in the Southwest, are successors to the old dude ranches, now called guest ranches, a great favorite of European visitors and also of families who like vacationing with horseback riding and all-you-can-eat ranch food included.

Colorado calls itself the Top of the Nation and has a cool climate on its 8,000-foot-high plateaus altogether different from that in the desert lowlands, drawing outdoor lovers to its hiking trails, forests, lakes, and streams in the summertime, while in winter the surrounding mountain peaks provide the continent's best skiing to some eight million enthusiasts each year. Again we see the new and the old—the booming resort of Vail that a generation ago was only a bright idea in the mind of an enterprising ski buff, and Mesa Verde, the nation's most extensive prehistoric ruins visible in ancient villages built in caves in the sides of cliffs. The lure of the great gold and silver strikes of the past century is still strong in the Southwest, especially in such old Colorado mining camps as Cripple Creek and Victor, and even today there is the occasional visitor who leaves the region richer than when he got here, simply by panning for gold.

1. DOLLARWISE—WHAT IT MEANS

In brief, this is a guidebook giving specific details—including prices—about the Southwest's hotels, motels, restaurants, bars, cafés, sightseeing attractions, nightlife, and tours. Establishments in many price ranges have been documented and described. No restaurant, hotel, motel, nightclub, store, or café paid to be mentioned in this book.

Unfortunately, although every effort was made to be as accurate as possible, remember that prices do change, and they rarely go downward. When checking into a hotel, always inquire about the rate and agree on it. That policy can save much embarrassment and disappointment when it comes time to settle the tab. If the prices quoted are not the same as those mentioned in this book, remember that my prices reflect those in effect at the time this edition was researched.

This guide is revised cover to cover every other year. But even in a book that appears with such frequency, establishments do change their décor, their name, their management, their type of service, a fact in our fast-moving world that leads up to the next major point—

AN INVITATION TO READERS: Like all the books in the "Dollarwise" series, *Dollarwise Southwest* hopes to maintain a continuing dialogue between its author and its readers, for your comments and suggestions can be a great aid to other readers.

Therefore, if you come across a particularly appealing accommodation, restaurant, store, or bargain, please don't keep it to yourself. Comments about existing listings are also very helpful. So send your comments or finds—and yes, those inevitable complaints that always arise—to Roy Bongartz, c/o Frommer Books, Prentice Hall Press, Gulf + Western Building, One Gulf + Western Plaza, New York, NY 10023.

FROMMER'S™ DOLLARWISE® TRAVEL CLUB— HOW TO SAVE MONEY ON ALL YOUR TRAVELS

In this book we'll be looking at how to get your money's worth in the Southwest, but there is a "device" for saving money and determining value on *all* your trips. It's the popular, international Frommer's Dollarwise Travel Club, now in its 28th successful year of operation. The club was formed at the urging of numerous readers of the $-A-Day and Dollarwise Guides, who felt that such an organization could provide continuing travel information and a sense of community to value-minded travelers in all parts of the world. And so it does!

In keeping with the budget concept, the annual membership fee is low and is immediately exceeded by the value of your benefits. Upon receipt of $18 (U.S. residents), or $20 U.S. by check drawn on a U.S. bank or via international postal money order in U.S. funds (Canadian, Mexican, and other foreign residents) to cover one year's membership, we will send all new members the following items:

(1) Any *two* of the following books

Please designate in your letter which two you wish to receive:

Frommer's™ $-A-Day® Guides
Europe on $30 a Day
Australia on $30 a Day
Eastern Europe on $25 a Day
England on $40 a Day
Greece (including Istanbul and Turkey's Aegean Coast) on $30 a Day
Hawaii on $50 a Day
India on $25 a Day
Ireland on $30 a Day
Israel on $30 & $35 a Day
Mexico (plus Belize and Guatemala) on $25 a Day
New York on $50 a Day
New Zealand on $40 a Day
Scandinavia on $50 a Day
Scotland and Wales on $40 a Day
South America on $30 a Day
Spain and Morocco (plus the Canary Is.) on $40 a Day
Turkey on $25 a Day
Washington, D.C., & Historic Virginia on $40 a Day

Frommer's™ Dollarwise® Guides
Austria and Hungary
Belgium, Holland, & Luxembourg
Bermuda and The Bahamas
Brazil
Canada
Caribbean
Egypt
England and Scotland
France
Germany
Italy
Japan and Hong Kong
Portugal, Madeira, and the Azores
South Pacific
Switzerland and Liechtenstein
Alaska
California and Las Vegas
Florida
Mid-Atlantic States
New England
New York State
Northwest
Skiing USA—East
Skiing USA—West
Southeast and New Orleans
Southwest
Texas
USA

(Dollarwise Guides discuss accommodations and facilities in all price ranges, with emphasis on the medium-priced.)

Frommer's™ Touring Guides
Australia
Egypt
Florence
London
Paris
Thailand
Venice

(These new, color illustrated guides include walking tours, cultural and historic sites, and other vital travel information.)

Gault Millau
Chicago (avail. April 1989)
France (avail. July 1989)
Italy (avail. July 1989)
Los Angeles
New England (avail. April 1989)
New York
San Francisco
Washington, D.C.

(Irreverent, savvy, and comprehensive, each of these renowned guides candidly reviews over 1,000 restaurants, hotels, shops, nightspots, museums, and sights.)

Serious Shopper's Guides
Italy
London
Los Angeles
Paris
(Practical and comprehensive, each of these handsomely illustrated guides lists hundreds of stores, selling everything from antiques to wine, conveniently organized alphabetically by category.)

A Shopper's Guide to the Caribbean
(Two experienced Caribbean hands guide you through this shopper's paradise, offering witty insights and helpful tips on the wares and emporia of more than 25 islands.)

Beat the High Cost of Travel
(This practical guide details how to save money on absolutely all travel items—accommodations, transportation, dining, sightseeing, shopping, taxes, and more. Includes special budget information for seniors, students, singles, and families.)

Bed & Breakfast—North America
(This guide contains a directory of over 150 organizations that offer bed & breakfast referrals and reservations throughout North America. The scenic attractions, and major schools and universities near the homes of each are also listed.)

Dollarwise Cruises
(This complete guide covers all the basics of cruising—ports of call, costs, fly-cruise package bargains, cabin selection booking, embarkation and debarkation and describes in detail over 60 or so ships cruising the waters of Alaska, the Caribbean, Mexico, Hawaii, Panama, Canada, and the United States.)

Dollarwise Skiing Europe
(Describes top ski resorts in Austria, France, Italy, and Switzerland. Illustrated with maps of each resort area. Includes supplement on Argentinian resorts.)

Guide to Honeymoon Destinations
(A special guide for that most romantic trip of your life, with full details on planning and choosing the destination that will be just right in the U.S. [California, New England, Hawaii, Florida, New York, South Carolina, etc.], Canada, Mexico, and the Caribbean.)

Marilyn Wood's Wonderful Weekends
(This very selective guide covers the best mini-vacation destinations within a 200-mile radius of New York City. It describes special country inns and other accommodations, restaurants, picnic spots, sights, and activities—all the information needed for a two- or three-day stay.)

Manhattan's Outdoor Sculpture
(A total guide, fully illustrated with black and white photos, to more than 300 sculptures and monuments that grace Manhattan's plazas, parks, and other public spaces.)

Motorist's Phrase Book
(A practical phrase book in French, German, and Spanish designed specifically for the English-speaking motorist touring abroad.)

Paris Rendez-Vous
(An amusing and *au courant* guide to the best meeting places in Paris, organized for hour-to-hour use: from power breakfasts and fun brunches, through tea at four or cocktails at five, to romantic dinners and dancing 'til dawn.)

Swap and Go—Home Exchanging Made Easy
(Two veteran home exchangers explain in detail all the money-saving benefits of a home exchange, and then describe precisely how to do it. Also includes information on home rentals and many tips on low-cost travel.)

The Candy Apple: New York for Kids
(A spirited guide to the wonders of the Big Apple by a savvy New York grandmother with a kid's-eye view to fun. Indispensable for visitors and residents alike.)

The New World of Travel
(From America's #1 travel expert, Arthur Frommer, an annual sourcebook with the hottest news and latest trends that's guaranteed to change the way you travel —and save you hundreds of dollars. Jam-packed with alternative new modes of travel that will lead you to vacations that cater to the mind, the spirit, and a sense of thrift.)

Travel Diary and Record Book
(A 96-page diary for personal travel notes plus a section for such vital data as passport and traveler's check numbers, itinerary, postcard list, special people and places to visit, and a reference section with temperature and conversion charts, and world maps with distance zones.)

Where to Stay USA
(By the Council on International Educational Exchange, this extraordinary guide is the first to list accommodations in all 50 states that cost anywhere from $3 to $30 per night.)

(2) Any one of Frommer's™ City Guides
Amsterdam
Athens
Atlantic City and Cape May
Boston
Cancún, Cozumel, and the Yucatán
Dublin and Ireland
Hawaii
Las Vegas
Lisbon, Madrid, and Costa del Sol
London
Los Angeles
Mexico City and Acapulco
Minneapolis and St. Paul
Montréal and Québec City
New Orleans
New York

Orlando, Disney World, and EPCOT
Paris
Philadelphia
Rio
Rome
San Francisco
Santa Fe and Taos (avail. Mar. 1989)
Sydney (avail. Feb. 1989)
Washington, D.C.
(Pocket-size guides to hotels, restaurants, nightspots, and sightseeing attractions covering all price ranges.)

(3) A one-year subscription to *The Dollarwise® Traveler*

This quarterly eight-page tabloid newspaper keeps you up to date on fast-breaking developments in low-cost travel in all parts of the world bringing you the latest money-saving information—the kind of information you'd have to pay $35 a year to obtain elsewhere. This consumer-conscious publication also features columns of special interest to readers: **Hospitality Exchange** (members all over the world who are willing to provide hospitality to other members as they pass through their home cities); **Share-a-Trip** (offers and requests from members for travel companions who can share costs and help avoid the burdensome single supplement); and **Readers Ask . . . Readers Reply** (travel questions from members to which other members reply with authentic firsthand information).

(4) Your personal membership card

Membership entitles you to purchase through the club all Frommer publications for a third to a half off their regular retail prices during the term of your membership.

So why not join this hardy band of international budgeteers and participate in its exchange of travel information and hospitality? Simply send your name and address, together with your annual membership fee of $18 (U.S. residents) or $20 U.S. (Canadian, Mexican, and other foreign residents), by check drawn on a U.S. bank or via international postal money order in U.S. funds to: Frommer's Dollarwise Travel Club, Inc., Gulf + Western Building, One Gulf + Western Plaza, New York, NY 10023. And please remember to specify which *two* of the books in section (1) and which *one* in section (2) you wish to receive in your initial package of members' benefits. Or, if you prefer, use the order form at the end of the book and enclose $18 or $20 in U.S. currency.

Once you are a member, there is no obligation to buy additional books. No books will be mailed to you without your specific order.

CHAPTER II

INTRODUCING NEW MEXICO

□ □ □

New Mexico is a vast, varied landscape with many wild areas barely explored even today, covering 121,000 square miles between Texas and Arizona to the east and west, Colorado to the north, and more of Texas and part of the Mexican state of Chihuahua to the south. From the east the approach is into a flat prairie called the llano that a third of the way across to the west rises into a series of mountains, beyond which are wonderlands of valleys, more ranges, canyons, and the fabulous mesa country. Six of the earth's seven life zones are represented in New Mexico, from the bleak tundra levels of northern peaks to the subtropical temperatures of the Sonoran desert. Brightening the sandy, rocky landscape in a north-south run through the western half of the state is the Rio Grande, whose banks attracted many of the prehistoric Indian pueblos still visible—some in ruins, some still occupied by descendants of those earlier populations. The river draws fishermen and irrigates cotton fields and pecan orchards, and gives white-water rafting enthusiasts big thrills in the spring thaws.

The natural beauties of the state have drawn many artists to live and work here, particularly in **Santa Fe** and in Taos. Dating from the turn of the century, the art colony of **Taos** is one of the oldest in the country and is thriving today with literally hundreds of members, many of whom are in allied fields in various crafts. The life around the old-style Spanish plazas of both Taos and Santa Fe is much involved with arts and crafts, many of the old adobe structures housing working studios or galleries where works of art are sold.

The one big city in the state, **Albuquerque,** enjoying such a dry, sunny climate that it has been a health center for a century, is well into a population boom that is bringing Americans from all points of the compass into the Southwest to live—there are over half a million within the sprawling city limits. The city let the sprawl grow uncontrolled until recently, but nevertheless there are two important signs here: first, many historic buildings were saved from the bulldozers, and second, an overall civic plan is now in force to ensure that green areas are preserved, and new ones established. The city has its plaza to compare with those of Taos and Santa Fe in Old Town, also the center of an area devoted to shops and galleries purveying arts and crafts produced in the region.

Most of the Indians of New Mexico live in 19 **pueblos,** the Spanish word for village. The Indians differ from most other Native Americans in that they have lived in these pueblos since prehistoric times. When King Philip of Spain first sent explorers into their lands he recognized their sovereignty as individual self-governing communities, the Indians have held onto this right throughout the centuries and in almost every pueblo have kept their cultural and ethnic individuality; the various languages and customs, their celebrations and dances, their art and their particular craft designs, are uniquely their own. The 19 pueblos of New Mexico, with their adobe apartment buildings built to two and three stories, make a world apart from any other—different, too, from the civilizations of the nomadic Indians elsewhere. Although there is the unmistakable feeling of entering a foreign land when you go to a pueblo, if you mind the various rules against taking pictures or drawing or painting without permission, you'll feel a quiet welcome. The experience of attending one of the Indian ceremonies, with various dances celebrating feast days at different times depending on the pueblo, is alone worth a trip to New Mexico.

The ruins of cliff dwellers and pueblo builders dating back 1,000 to 2,000 years are another prime attraction to visitors at several national monuments and other areas under government protection. The intricate masonry work shows sophisticated craftsmanship also visible in such artifacts as pottery or baskets recovered from these sites. Numerous exhibits in museums on the sites as well as in Santa Fe and Albuquerque are so fascinating they may make a casual visitor into a would-be archeologist. Isolated sites such as Chaco Canyon in the northwestern part of the state or the Gila Cliff Dwellings to the south blend with the beauties of the land and make visual experiences that are unforgettable.

Vast national **forest lands** that occupy a quarter of the state offer so much variety in outdoor attractions that nobody could visit all the fishing sites, ponds, trails, and campsites in a lifetime. Some of the best trout fishing in the West is within the state, and there are hunting seasons on game birds and certain mammals, including bear, deer, bighorn sheep, and elk. The state has a dozen ski areas too, some in the north vying with the best in the country; others, farther south, within a short car drive to hot weather in the valleys below them.

Another major attraction, of course, is **Carlsbad Caverns National Park,** which has drawn 17 million visitors since its opening half a century ago. Visitors will discover nearby areas of almost equal interest: the incredibly white vistas of **White Sands National Monument** over near Alamogordo; or the majestic multicolored cliffs of **Guadalupe Mountains National Park** just south across the Texas line.

HOW TO GET THERE: Albuquerque, roughly in the center of the state and the only large city, has the one airport serving national and international flights into New Mexico. Connections can be made to other destinations within the state by local carriers. National airlines serving Albuquerque are **American, America West, Continental, Delta, Eastern, Pacific Southwest, Southwest, Trans World,** and **United.** Distances run from 800 miles to Los Angeles and 1,350 to Chicago to 670 from Dallas and 2,000 to New York.

Airlines serving other New Mexico airports include **Mesa Airlines,** flying to Carlsbad, Hobbs, Roswell, Clovis, Alamogordo, and Silver City. **Ross Aviation** provides commuter service to Los Alamos.

Amtrak, the National Railroad Passenger Corporation, provides inter-city service through north-central and southwest areas of New Mexico. The *Southwest Limited,* which runs from Los Angeles to Chicago, links Raton, Las Vegas, Lamy (ten miles south of Santa Fe), Albuquerque, Grants, and Gallup. The *Sunset Limited* links Lordsburg, Deming, and El Paso, Tex., on its run from Los Angeles to New Orleans. In cooperation with Trailways bus system, Amtrak offers through-ticketing between El Paso and Albuquerque. For information within New Mexico call toll free 800/421-8320 (in Albuquerque, 242-7816); from elsewhere call the local Amtrak information office.

There is **taxi** service in the following locations: Carlsbad, Clovis, Deming, Farmington, Gallup, Grants, Hobbs, Las Cruces, Las Vegas, Roswell, Ruidoso, Socorro, Alamagordo, Taos, as well as in Albuquerque and Santa Fe. Car rentals are available in Alamogordo, Albuquerque, Carlsbad, Clovis, Farmington, Gallup, Hobbs, Las Cruces, Roswell, Ruidoso, Santa Fe, Socorro, and Taos.

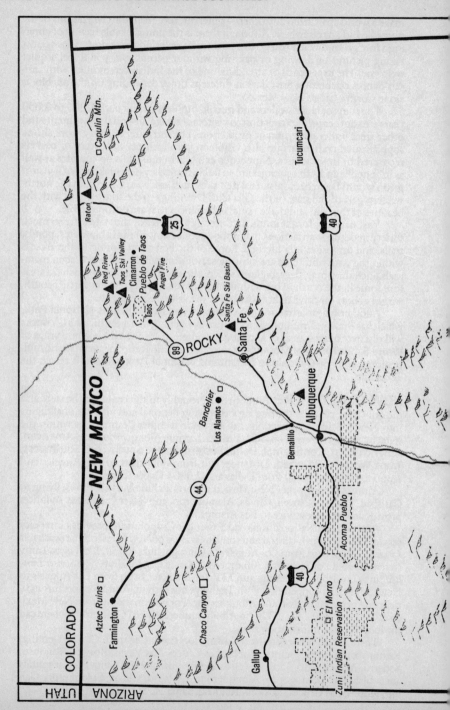

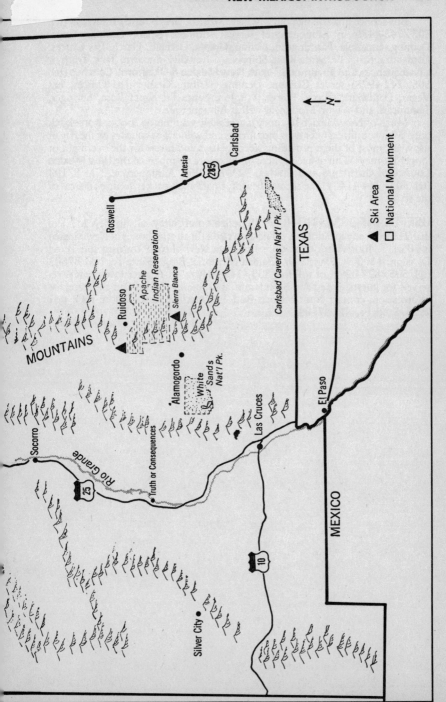

Bus service links many points in New Mexico. **Greyhound/Trailways** (tel. 505/243-4435 in Albuquerque) serves Anthony, Belen, Costilla, Cuba, Deming, Española, Farmington, Gallup, Grants, Garfield, Hatch, Las Cruces, Lordsburg, Santa Fe, Santa Rosa, Shiprock, Silver City, Socorro, Taos, Truth or Consequences, and Tucumcari. **Texas, New Mexico & Oklahoma Coaches** (tel. 505/242-4998) serves Clayton, Deming, Gallup, Grants, Las Cruces, Las Vegas, Lordsburg, Pecos, Raton, San Jon, Santa Fe, Santa Rosa, Springer, Tucumcari, and Wagon Mound, as well as Albuquerque.

Much of New Mexico territory is accessible via trails on foot or **horseback** only. Many outfitters offer trips into forests and wilderness country by the day or the week, most of them providing sleeping bags and meals for the overnight or longer journeys. Thirty-five of these outfitters are members of the **New Mexico Council of Outfitters and Guides,** P.O. Box 952, Albuquerque, NM 87103 (tel. 505/344-4143). The council has information on pack trips into all areas of the state.

USEFUL INFORMATION: For all **police emergency** calls in New Mexico, dial 911 from any location. . . . The **area code** for all telephones in New Mexico is 505. . . . **Tourist information** is had from New Mexico Tourism and Travel Division, 1100 St. Francis Dr., Bataan Memorial Bldg., Santa Fe, NM 87503 (tel. 505/827-0291, or toll free 800/545-2040). . . . A special welcome is reserved for guests in bed-and-breakfast establishments throughout the state; for information, contact **New Mexico Bed & Breakfast Association,** P.O. Box 2925, Santa Fe, NM 87504.

CHAPTER III

SANTA FE AND SURROUNDING COUNTRY

□ □ □

Founded in 1610, Santa Fe, the oldest U.S. state capital, was the administrative center of the Spanish "Kingdom of New Mexico." When the Pueblo Indians revolted in 1680 and routed the Spanish from their colony, the city was abandoned for 12 years. In 1692 it was retaken by the Spanish, led by one Diego de Vargas. An annual fiesta commemorating this event began in 1712 and continues to be celebrated every summer.

At an altitude of 7,000 feet, the small city, with a population of 75,000, lies at the foot of the Sangre de Cristo range. Although it enjoys a mild climate year round, there is a good skiing area close by in those mountains. The city is striking for its low skyline of Spanish/Indian-style buidings. A city ordinance prohibits structures over three stories tall. An architecture unique to the area grew out of a combination of Spanish designs, Indian pueblo construction, and available materials. Originally all the buildings were of adobe, with thick walls, small windows, and flat roofs. Today much of the construction is an imitation of the original style, but the character of the city seems to remain untroubled.

The Spanish governor, Don Pedro de Peralta, who founded the city as his capital, originally named it Villa Real de la Santa Fé de San Francisco de Asis—Royal City of the Holy Faith of St. Francis of Assisi. He built the Palace of Governors in 1610 along one side of the central Plaza, where it stands today as an excellent museum of the four centuries of history that has involved the lives and fates of Indians, Spaniards, Mexicans, and Americans. It is one of the major attractions in the Southwest, and under the portal across its façade Indians still sell their foods and crafts as they have for hundreds of years.

The Plaza was the scene of festivities of the annual fiesta, as it still is today, and was also the terminus of the Santa Fe Trail, from the states back east, as well as of the earlier Camino Real—the Royal Road—up from Mexico, when the city thrived on the wool and fur of the Chihuahua trade. When the U.S. took over the territory from Mexico in 1846 and trade began flowing from the eastern states, new tools and materials began to change the face of the city. The old adobe took on brick façades and roof decoration in what became known as the Territorial style. But the flat roofs were in the main retained so that the city never lost its unique, low profile, giving a serenity to be found in no other American city, and only in a few of the smaller towns in the Southwest, such as Taos.

Bishop John B. Lamy, the inspiration for the character of Bishop Latour in Willa Cather's *Death Comes to the Archbishop,* was appointed in 1851 and built the French Romanesque St. Francis Cathedral. Older structures are still standing, including what is claimed as the oldest house in the U.S., built of adobe by Indians 800 years ago. The San Miguel Mission is the oldest mission church in the country, while the state capital, built in the circular form of a ceremonial Indian *kiva,* a place set aside for religious rites, is the newest in the country.

Although the population of Santa Fe, like that of the entire Southwest, is growing at a rate of about 10% a year, mainly with newcomers from the North who share neither the region's Indian nor Hispanic traditions, Santa Fe has kept much of its ethnic legacy, and not merely in its street names or its architecture. There are real Indians from the pueblos out in front of the Palace of Governors every morning, real Hispanics taking part in the annual Spanish Market or preparing authentic specialties in the unique New Mexico–style restaurants. Of the 19 Indian Pueblos in New Mexico, eight of them banded together as the Eight Northern Pueblos, and market Indian-made crafts here (the eight are all within easy motoring distance of the city). In mountain villages in the Sangre de Cristos there are also Hispanic craftspeople, particularly weavers, in such rustic communities as Chimayo or Truchas, and Santa Fe is where these people bring their wares, as well.

Santa Fe has become a major art center, with a so-called art "colony" like that of Taos farther north, but whether the major gains have been commercial rather than esthetic remains a topic of discussion among many of the artists themselves. There is a question as to whether local artists are passed by for famous names, and other questions as to the esthetic influence of the proliferating galleries in the city: whether they tend to stifle originality and stick to the conservative or realistic styles.

One artist says of the city: "It's not an art center. It's an art market for traditional Indian and Western art." Nevertheless a visitor with enough patience to search for the art quality he may be hoping to find will likely succeed somewhere in the wide variety of work shown in the scores of galleries all over the city.

A couple of dozen registered Indian traders also bring in retail customers interested in Indian crafts, jewelry, and art, most of it the product of Pueblo Indians of New Mexico. It is possible to find lower prices in the tiny shops in the pueblos themselves—usually in the house of the craftsperson—but there the selection is small and the Indians do not always answer the door when you knock, even when there's an "open" sign on their window. The greatest Indian market in the Southwest is held annually in Santa Fe, in late August. Only authentic Indian-made wares are allowed, and Indian craftspeople show up from all over the country for the festive outdoor sale.

Santa Fe, then, is a great center for arts and crafts, and for historic walks, or just plain pleasurable walks on quiet streets where buildings the same color as the earth look as if they might have been there forever. It is a center for trips to mountain villages, Indian pueblos, and such great outdoors destinations as state parks, prehistoric ruins, and the forest wilderness of high country lakes, streams, hiking, trails, and campsites.

Because it is a state capital the city has a busy air even when the tourist flow is not at its peak. Summertime and the height of winter bring in the most visitors, and there are good lodging places, many in the attractive southwestern style of building and decorating that pretty well originated here in the city. Santa Fe is also known for its good restaurants, both those making New Mexico specialties and others that purvey American or other cuisines. It makes a likely center for the study of prehistoric archeology and the culture of the Pueblo Indians, subjects that go together automatically. There is even a good ski resort just above the town—you can see the crest of the mountain it's on right from the Plaza. Santa Fe is small enough to visit most of its points of interest on foot—or a bicycle is perfect. The weather is almost always clear through the year, a bright sun and blue sky outside your window nearly every morning.

1. ORIENTATION

Santa Fe lies at the center of the northern half of New Mexico, its eastern city limits nudging up against the foothills of the Sangre de Cristo mountains in Carson National Forest, a woodland of over a million and a half acres that in two divisions reaches 100 miles north to the Colorado line. The state's largest city, Albuquerque, is 50 miles distant, reached by superhighway, while the once-secret "Atomic City" of Los Alamos is 40 miles to the northwest in the Jemez mountains. Some 75 miles to the north is the art-colony and Indian-pueblo town of Taos. Because of its 7,000-foot elevation and its dry air the Santa Fe nights can be chilly even in summer, but the sun, visible on most days of the year, makes for comfortable days even in wintertime.

GETTING TO AND FROM SANTA FE: Santa Fe is reached from the east and west by car via I-40, the improved version of the famous old highway U.S. 66; from the east motorists turn north off I-40 at Clines and continue 52 miles into the city via U.S. 285. From the west motorists leave I-40 in Albuquerque to follow I-25 northeast 50 miles into Santa Fe. I-25 is also the route for travelers from El Paso and southern New Mexico (Las Cruces, Socorro). For travelers from the northwest the best route is through Farmington via U.S. routes 64 and 84 through the town of Española to Santa Fe. From the northeast a good entry point into the state is Raton, over Raton pass, continuing to Santa Fe all the way on I-25 traveling southwest.

Air service to Santa Fe is via **Albuquerque International Airport** and either a shuttle or scheduled bus trip to the city. Airlines serving Albuquerque include TWA, Delta, United, Eastern, America West, Western, Continental, Pacific, Southwest, and American. For **airline information** from Albuquerque airport, call 842-4366.

Shuttlejack (tel. 982-4311 in Santa Fe, or 243-3244 in Albuquerque) runs seven round trips daily from 7:30 a.m. to 7:30 p.m. between the airport and the Hilton Inn or the Inn at Loretto (both downtown in Santa Fe) for a fare of $20. **Greyhound** bus lines also run two round trips daily between the airport and the

Santa Fe bus station at 858 St. Michaels Dr. (tel. 471-0008). Regular daily service north to Taos and Denver and to other parts of the state and the U.S. via Albuquerque is available on Greyhound.

The **Amtrak** (tel. 505/988-4511, or toll free 800/421-8320) *Southwest Limited* running between Los Angeles and Chicago makes a stop at Lamy, 14 miles south of Santa Fe, but there is no scheduled transport to the city.

Two taxi companies serving Santa Fe are **24-Hour Taxi** (tel. 982-9990), and **Capital City Cab** (tel. 988-1211). Cars may be rented from **Hertz** (tel. 982-1844) and **Avis** (tel. 982-4361).

GETTING AROUND SANTA FE: A loop encloses the central part of Santa Fe, a thoroughfare called the **Paseo de Peralta,** and most of the city's historic structures, churches, museums, restaurants, and hotels lie within it. The Plaza is the geographical and spiritual center of the town, and the best way to get around this part of the city, including the capitol building and its associated office structures south of the Plaza, is on foot. The Chile Line (see below) runs "trolleys" and a number of tour buses operate, some only in the summer.

The most popular summertime tour is a **Roadrunner bus** around downtown and along nearby Canyon Road, a street of restaurants and arts-and-crafts shops. It leaves from under the Spitz clock on the Plaza every two hours from 9 a.m. to 4 p.m. For information call 983-6565. The charge is $8 for adults, $5 for children under 12.

Historical Walking Tours of Santa Fe depart at 9:30 a.m. and 1:30 p.m. Monday through Saturday, organized by Santa Fe natives Kathy and Frank Montoya. Departure point is Las Tres Gentes market center, 418 Cerrillos Rd. (tel. 984-8235). The three-hour tours cost $8.50.

Free walking-tour maps for going on your own are among useful folders available at the **Santa Fe Convention and Visitors Bureau,** west of the Plaza at 201 W. Marcy St. (tel. 984-6760, or toll free 800/528-5369).

Street parking is difficult to find during the summer months. There is a parking lot near the Federal Courthouse, one block east of the Plaza, another behind Santa Fe Village near the Plaza, and a third at Water and Sandoval Streets.

For visitors staying at hotels it is a simple matter to leave the car behind and ride on the **"trolleys"** of the Chile Line (tel. 989-8595)—they are actually buses, decked out to resemble old-style trolley cars, that circulate hourly on three routes departing from and returning to the Plaza. Among direct stops at hotels are the Ramada, the El Rey Inn, the Santa Fe Budget Inn, the Hotel St. Francis, the Residence Inn, the Inn of the Governors, the Eldorado Hotel, the Sheraton, the Inn of Alameda, and La Fonda. Service runs daily except Sunday from 8 a.m. to 5:35 p.m. at a nominal fare of 50¢, with free transfers. The name of the line is taken from a narrow-gauge railroad that a century ago ran between Santa Fe and Española to the north. You can get maps and schedules aboard the trolleys.

USEFUL INFORMATION: The **ZIP Code** for central Santa Fe is 87501. . . . The **post office** is on South Federal Street two blocks north of the Plaza. . . . **St. Vincent's Hospital,** 455 St. Michaels Dr., has a 24-hour emergency room (tel. 983-3361). For **police emergency,** dial 911, or for fast advice on any kind of difficulty, call the **Crisis Intervention Center** at 982-2771. . . . Emergency **lodging assistance**—particularly helpful around Fiesta time in September—is available free after 4 p.m. daily at 988-4252. . . . Information on **road conditions** in the Santa Fe area can be had by calling 983-0120, and for weather forecasts, call 988-3437. . . . There are 24-hour taped reports on snow conditions up

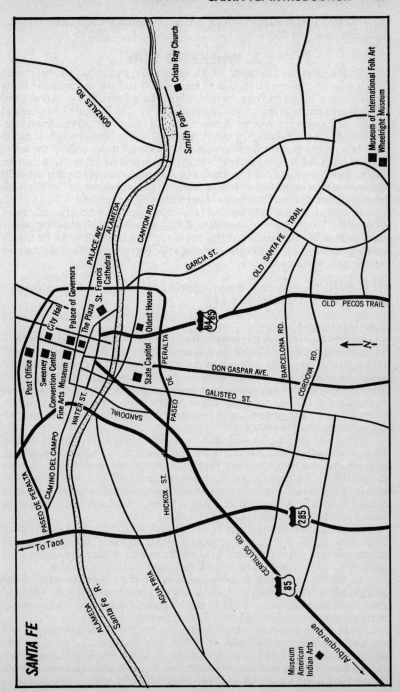

SANTA FE

To Taos →

← -N-

Cristo Ray Church
Smith Park
GONZALES RD.
PALACE AVE.
ALAMEDA
CANYON RD.
GARCIA ST.
OLD SANTA FE TRAIL
OLD PECOS TRAIL
Museum of International Folk Art
Wheelright Museum
St. Francis Cathedral
Palace of Governors
City Hall
The Plaza
Post Office
Sweeney Convention Center
Fine Arts Museum
Oldest House
State Capitol
WATER ST.
SANDOVAL
PASEO DE PERALTA
BARCELONA RD.
CORDOVA RD.
DON GASPAR AVE.
GALISTEO ST.
PASEO DE PERALTA
CAMINO DEL CAMPO
HICKOX ST.
AGUA FRIA
ALAMEDA
Santa Fe R.
CERRILLOS RD.
Museum American Indian Arts
Albuquerque →

at the **Santa Fe Ski Area** at 983-9155. The **New Mexico Snowphone** gives state-wide reports at 984-0606.

2. WHERE TO STAY

Of the two dozen inns and motels in Santa Fe, nearly half are within easy walking distance of the Plaza. Like all traditionally laid-out Spanish cities Santa Fe focuses its life on its Plaza, so that visitors staying for a few days find a real advantage to this proximity to the center of activity. The Plaza, with its trees and flowers and inviting iron benches, makes an ideal spot to take a break from touring or walking around town or gallery hopping. If your hotel is nearby it makes the Plaza easy to become familiar with. The modest, human scale of the town, with its restricted skyline height and its streets made more for strolling than for traffic, makes it one of the few remaining American cities where staying right downtown is an important advantage. But even the motels out on Cerillos Road are not all that far from the center—five minutes by car.

In contrast to these are a handful of so-called guest resorts that partake more of the Wild West scenery of mountain, fishing stream, and horse-riding trail—these used to be called dude ranches, but the present establishments are mostly much more luxurious than that term suggests. The latter are all some distance outside the city limits.

IN TOWN: The following are my suggestions for accommodations downtown near the Plaza and on Cerillos Road.

The Top Hotels

La Fonda, 100 E. San Francisco St., Santa Fe, NM 87504 (tel. 505/982-5511, or toll free 800/523-5002), is known as "the inn at the end of the trail" because the street on the west side of the hotel comprised the last few hundred yards of the Santa Fe Trail. The street is officially named, in fact, Old Santa Fe Trail. A hotel on this site dating back to the early days of the last century was demolished in 1919 to make way for the present three-story rambling structure of brown adobe-like concrete, with wooden balconies, and beam ends protruding over the tops of windows.

While the original inn had such illustrious guests as Kit Carson, Bishop Lamy, and the brothers Charles and William Bent, among many personages out of Territorial New Mexico history, the present inn has accommodated such modern notables as Anthony Quinn, James Stewart, and Paul Newman. A big attraction is La Plazuela, an indoor patio restaurant with natural overhead light, solid Spanish colonial chairs and tables, hanging plants, tiled floors, and waitresses in traditional Spanish colonial skirts and blouses.

The Old Spain theme is carried out throughout the inn. Rooms have great beds with spindle posts and marvelously ornate folkloric painted designs in bright reds and golds on carved headboards, as well as chests of drawers and wooden foot-of-the-bed trunks in similar traditional Hispanic designs.

La Fonda has 165 bedrooms and suites, nightly entertainment in the lounge, a heated swimming pool, and a shopping arcade with a beauty shop and newsstand. Rates are $85 to $100 for double rooms (children under 12 can stay in the same room free), and $130 to $295 for suites.

Nearby, also within a minute or two of the Plaza, is the recently opened luxury establishment, the **Eldorado,** at 309 W. San Francisco St., Santa Fe, NM 87501 (tel. 505/988-4455, or toll free 800/CLARION). The 218 rooms include 26 suites, most with fireplaces, wet bars, Jacuzzis, and balconies. Two restaurants are open for guests and the public: the Old House, specializing in Mexican and continental cooking, and the sunlit Eldorado Court, for casual lunches and dining. There is also what is called a "Southwestern/New York deli," Big Jo's, named for the lumber company that owned the land here. *Vigas* —hand-hewn ceiling beams—are used in making the construction traditional to the region, and there is a lush courtyard with fountain, not to mention a rooftop swimming pool, plus entertainment in the Lobby Lounge nightly beginning at 7 p.m.

Rates for a double room range from $100 to $125.

Moderately Priced Hotels

Three blocks from the Plaza is **La Posada de Santa Fe,** 330 E. Palace Ave., Santa Fe, NM 87501 (tel. 505/983-6351), offering both regular hotel rooms and separate adobe cottages on a 5½-acre estate around the Abraham Staab mansion, built in 1882. The 111-room hotel has been recently refurbished so as, according to general manager Dottie Reed, to "upgrade everything and keep the old and not lose the charm of Santa Fe." Among major changes is the addition of five new suites with slate floors and viga and latilla ceilings.

But the traditional Victorian rooms keep their style, as does the southwestern décor of the public areas. There are deep-walled windows, hand-cut wooden ceilings, and Indian rugs and wall hangings. The leather chairs are just right on the red-tile floor of the lobby; the chic bar has a crystal chandelier out of the last century. A drawing room has low marble tables, pink and green upholstered chairs, and a love seat. The Rose Room, just inside the entrance, now has its original parquet flooring exposed, set off by a marble fireplace. Even the original steam radiators have been sandblasted free of many layers of paint to reveal their good utilitarian lines. Many of the cottages have kiva fireplaces supplied with piñon firewood; the surrounding gardens are set off by venerable pear trees illuminated at night. The inn is the base for many state legislators when the House and Senate are in session; a New Mexico governor lived here for years. Author Oliver LaFarge used the place as the setting for his book *The Quarter Given;* another resident was Lew Wallace, author of *Ben-Hur.*

Rates are $48 to $83 for double rooms, $72 to $202 for casitas.

On a hillside a couple of miles south of the Plaza, the **Residence Inn,** 1698 Galisteo St., Santa Fe, NM 87501 (tel. 505/988-7300, or toll free 800/552-0070), one of a national chain, offers suites-only accommodations with separate kitchen and dining areas, and working fireplaces—there is free wood in a shed outside, or you can simply call room service and have some brought in. The most modest spaces here are "studio" suites, half again as large as the usual hotel room. The "penthouse" suites are duplexes with separate bedrooms and bathrooms on each level.

The décor makes good use of locally made drawings and watercolors along with traditional Spanish-style details like the rosettes hand-carved into wooden benches and chests. Indeed it blends well with the region's desert and mountain country, using, as manager Dave Brazda jokes, "every shade of tan and brown known to man"—combined with light pinks and faint yellows. In the lobby, Pueblo Indian rugs and blankets hang on the walls, along with decorative bunches of Indian corn emphasizing the New Mexican atmosphere. Twice a week guests are invited to meet here before dinner for free drinks and hot hors d'oeuvres—a nice friendly touch.

Kitchens come fully equipped with pots, pans, and dishes—and maid service takes care of doing those dishes too. Like all Residence Inns, this one provides a number of extra services for guests: a free breakfast of juice, fresh rolls and pastry, cereals, and coffee, in a sunlit dining room in the Gatehouse; and free grocery-shopping service for stocking your kitchen. A few staple items are also available from a deli cooler in the Gatehouse. The nearest supermarket is three blocks west, on St. Michaels Drive. There are free morning copies of Santa Fe or Albuquerque newspapers, *USA Today,* or the *Wall Street Journal;* and satellite television programs at no charge. The kitchen counter makes a fine dining or working table; suites are well soundproofed, and there's plenty of storage space.

Every house in the Residence village contains four suites, each with its own entrance. Outside are a swimming pool, heated whirlpool, racquetball and volleyball courts, and gas-operated barbecue grills for free use. Guests may use washers and dryers at the Gatehouse.

Rates, depending on season, are $60 to $95 for a studio suite, $80 to $120 for a two-room penthouse suite. Long stays are encouraged; rates are cut after seven days in residence.

Some 6½ miles south of the Plaza, **La Quinta Inn,** 4298 Cerrillos Rd., Santa Fe, NM 87501 (tel. 505/471-1142, or toll free 800/531-5900), is owned by a chain that is highly rated for good value by *Consumer Reports* magazine. Extra facilities include a clock-radio and remote-control television, extra-big towels, two telephones with unlimited free local calls, and free morning coffee served in the sunny lobby. Half the rooms in the motel are for nonsmokers, and there are free copies of the current *Newsweek* in every room. Senior citizens get a 15% discount; for families there's a special plan. Besides the usual swimming pool, the motel offers one-day laundry service or a coin laundry on the premises. The motel has rates of $40 to $45 in winter, $45 to $50 in the busier summer season.

Hidden in the center of town, the **Preston House,** 106 Faithway St., Santa Fe, NM 87501 (tel. 505/982-3465), is an elegant bed-and-breakfast inn occupying a century-old Queen Anne–style house. Though it's only three blocks to the Plaza, its location on a short side street ignored by most Santa Feans gives it a secluded feeling. On the National Register of Historic Places, the inn is shaded by ancient elms over a garden where guests relax at redwood tables and chairs. Inside is an ornate, Oriental-style curving staircase built by Chinese artisans, and stained-glass windows embellish the parlor and dining room. The house has four Edwardian tiled fireplaces. In addition to the six bedrooms in the house, two cottages, connected by a walkway, were built in 1987, each equipped with telephone, television, fireplace, and bath. Breakfast includes homemade muffins and bread, fresh fruit, yogurt, cereal, and coffee; and tea and cookies are served in the afternoon. Rates are $45 for a room with shared bath, $95 for the master bedroom with private bath, and $110 for a cottage.

Still another in-town lodging, this one a block from the Plaza, is **Garrett's Desert Inn,** 311 Old Santa Fe Trail, Santa Fe, NM 87501 (tel. 505/982-1851, or toll free 800/552-0070), with a terrace overlooking the Santa Fe River (the walkway along the river is part of a tiny state park). Again the dining room is decorated in Southwest style, with a big white beehive fireplace as the centerpiece —this is the Prime Rib Room, specializing in prime ribs and western-style charcoal-broiled steaks. There is the obligatory kidney-shaped pool for this sort of digs, surrounded by artificial turf on which white metal tables invite guests to relax under the tilted parasols.

Room décor is a sort of luxurious utilitarian, with restful green-patterned bedspreads on the queen- or king-size beds and blending wallpapers, carpets, and wall-width curtains over the picture window—one of the few such motels that relaxes the ranch-and-adobe motif a trifle. Besides cable television and free movies, Garrett's offers free local telephone calls, room service, and dressing areas in each room.

Rates for a double room are $49 to $69.

Right on the diminutive Santa Fe River, the **Inn of the Governors,** at Alameda and Don Gaspar Avenue, Santa Fe, NM 87501 (tel. 505/982-4333), has 99 modern rooms. A rustic-style cocktail lounge has a ceiling paneled in deep-toned woods and barrel ends on the wall, the shadows dispelled by a bright fire in a modern fireplace. The inn combines a modern touch with the spirit of the old Santa Fe that seems to pervade every structure in town. A dining room with white linen and a red carpet is particularly inviting—this is the Forge (see my restaurant recommendations). A heated pool draws guests to splash or lounge along an adobe wall where cottonwoods form a backdrop along the river just beyond. Many rooms have the rounded white southwestern-style fireplaces that are a treat on chilly nights at this height.

Double rates are $85 to $115.

Budget Accommodations

Among numerous moderate and budget-priced motels along Cerrillos Road, a good choice is the **El Rey Inn,** 1862 Cerrillos Rd., Santa Fe, NM 87504 (tel. 505/982-1931). Built in the Spanish style, with red-tile roofs, it is on two levels overlooking a spacious pool surrounded by white lawn tables and by chaise longues. The lobby has a bright fire in its Spanish-style fireplace under authentic Spanish-American beams, and outside there's a playground for the kids on the 3½-acre grounds.

Besides the usual amenities, such as air conditioning, free coffee goes with rooms at $37 to $47 double. Some of the rooms offer vigas and latilla ceilings, while others have beams and rough-hewn wood. Adobe nichos, tile murals, and kiva fireplaces are admired in many units, and there are southwestern-style rugs and hand-carved headboards.

A LUXURY GUEST RANCH OUTSIDE SANTA FE: Just north of Santa

Fe is the **Bishop's Lodge,** on Bishop's Lodge Road, Santa Fe, NM 87504 (tel. 505/983-6377), five miles north of the city. A popular area guest ranch for over 60 years, the lodge is welcoming some fourth-generation young people who are following their families' traditional vacation here. The ranch had its origin as a retreat for Bishop Lamy in the middle of the 19th century. The adobe house he used was purchased, after Lamy's death, by newspaperman Joseph Pulitzer, who made a summer place of it, adding some structures. These were purchased in 1918 by James R. Thorpe, and became the base of the present lodge, still owned and operated by the Thorpe family. On the premises is a tiny chapel built by Lamy during his residence here.

Lavish indoor buffets and outdoor barbecues compete with such activities as traditional dude-ranch trail riding, tennis on five courts, and a swimming pool. Each room is decorated differently, most in the southwestern tradition and many with working fireplaces. A lively lounge, the El Charro, draws both guests and outside visitors during the evenings. A special treat is a range breakfast, served in the open at the end of an early horseback ride.

Bishop's Lodge is closed in winter, from November through February. American Plan rates, in the summer only, include three meals daily: $170 to $295 for two. In spring and fall European Plan rates are available, at $95 to $210 double. With advance notice, arriving and departing guests are given free transportation to and from downtown Santa Fe.

3. WHERE TO EAT

A comment of Santa Feans about the wide variety of restaurants in their city is that the fancy décor, mostly in the traditional Southwest style, outdoes the cooking. The fact is that transients do make up much of the restaurant trade, especially in summertime in Santa Fe, and thus it may be that more attention has gone into catching their eye than appealing to their palate once seated in some luxurious setting, conquistador helmets gleaming on the walls, and reflecting off their sparkling table setting. Nevertheless a growing local pride in regional dishes is gradually widening choices in dining both in style and content.

LUXURY DINING IN SANTA FE: The **Staab House,** at La Posada, 330 E. Palace Ave. (tel. 983-6351), serves a variety of continental dishes such as three-wine veal. A specialty is roast duckling with tart red raspberry sauce at $14. Other choices are carne escarchada and shrimp and scallop de Jonghe. The restaurant is open daily for breakfast, lunch, and dinner (to 9:30 p.m.), and all wines and drinks are available with dinner or at the classy Victorian Bar, where merely standing around for a few minutes makes you feel an aristocrat. Don't miss the especially good salad bar. The 1882 Staab House is the focal point of La Posada de Santa Fe and has been restored to its original Victorian opulence. Luncheon fajitas are a favorite, and there are free drinks with the Sunday brunch.

La Plazuela, at La Fonda Hotel, 100 E. San Francisco St. (tel. 982-5511), is a delightful indoor patio with bright skylights, colorful tiled floors and columns, Spanish Colonial tables and chairs, and serving people in regional Hispanic costumes. Open daily for lunch and dinner to 9 p.m., the restaurant offers such specialties as lobster Delamar or roast duck, along with excellent prime rib and chateaubriand. Entrees are priced from $6.25 to $16, and all drinks and wines are at hand. The establishment also continues an old Santa Fe tradition taken from the Spain of long ago, the "afternoon luncheon" served after regular lunch hours, from 2:30 to 5 p.m., when you might be tempted to try the oysters Rockefeller or a poached salmon, with perhaps a Belgian waffle for dessert.

The Compound, 653 Canyon Rd. (tel. 982-4353), has daily specials in the continental mode, including seafood delivered fresh, and fresh vegetables as well, with bread and pastries baked on the premises fresh every day. Entrees begin at $18, and there is a full wine list. Reservations are required. Open from noon for lunch, from 6:30 to 9:30 p.m. for dinner Tuesday through Sunday. Specialties are Dover sole, peppersteak, and lamb and veal dishes. There's space for 85 diners inside and another 20 at patio tables. The owner notes: "We are a dressy restaurant."

Comme Chez Vous, 116 W. San Francisco St. (tel. 984-0004), is probably the best French restaurant in Santa Fe, now located in a luxurious setting in the Plaza Mercado. Specialties include veal medallions in cream sauce with tomatoes and tarragon, seafood en casserole, and duck, quail, and rack of lamb. A sheltered outdoors balcony invites diners in warm weather. Hot appetizers are available at the bar all day. Open for lunch Monday through Saturday from 11:30 a.m. to 2 p.m. Dinner is served Sunday through Thursday from 6 to 9 p.m., on Friday and Saturday until 10 p.m. Special opera dinners on opera nights begin at 5:30 p.m., and Sunday brunch begins at 11:30 a.m. Dinner entrees are priced from $13 to $20, and there is an excellent wine list.

The **Pink Adobe,** 406 Old Santa Fe Trail (tel. 983-7712), is a likely spot for leisurely dining—the somewhat slow service is in fact made up for because the food is well worth the wait. You'll have plenty of time for a cocktail or two after ordering. With a traditional décor, the small restaurant is cheerful and its Dragon Lounge makes a pleasant stop before dining on what some locals aver is the best New Mexico–style cuisine in the city. But the Pink Adobe also has such excellent continental dishes as porc Napoléon, steak Dunnigan, and poulet Marengo, with entrees priced from $8 to $16. Lunch is served daily except Saturday and Sunday; dinner, daily from 5:30 to 10 p.m. The Dragon Lounge, incidentally, is one of the most popular meeting places in town for after-office-hours drinks and talk.

REGIONAL NEW MEXICO CUISINE IN SANTA FE: The basic ingredients of New Mexico cuisine are three locally grown vegetables—chiles, beans, and corn. Certain Santa Fe restaurants have glamorized the traditional recipes using these ingredients and have created new recipes where attractive colors vie in importance with good, harmonizing flavors. This is the basis of an emerging style called the Santa Fe Cuisine.

Perhaps most crucial here is the *chile,* which has come a long way from its origins as a small, shriveled vegetable of inconsistent taste. Today, because of research carried out over many years at the University of New Mexico, chiles are large, meaty, brilliant red or green, with various levels of spicy bite to them. The green chiles are fresh off the vine, and must be roasted, peeled, and deseeded before use (if the seeds are left in they are hotter). They are cooked whole, chopped up, and become a central ingredient in most of these regional dishes. Chiles can be frozen easily and they defrost quickly. A red chile is the same green chile at its ripe stage. Strung together like a garland to dry in the sun, they make the base for the red sauce known everywhere in the Southwest as salsa. When dried, they are washed, cleaned of seeds, rehydrated in hot water, and blended with other seasonings. There are both red and green salsas in most restaurants—the red is usually the hotter of the two.

The *beans* must be spotted or painted pinto beans with the nutty taste—high in both fiber and protein. They are simmered with garlic, onion, and red chile powder to be served as a side dish. They can then be mashed and refried in oil to become frijoles refritos. The *corn* supplies the vital dough called masa for the tortillas, which, when filled with peppers or other foods, become enchiladas. New Mexico corn comes in six colors, of which the blue, white, and yellow are the most common; a regional favorite, for example, is the blue corn tortilla enchilada.

A few delicacies you will find on restaurant menus in places specializing in regional food include: *biscochito,* a cookie with anise; *burrito,* a bean and sauce concoction in a tortilla; *chile con carne,* peppers and meat; *chile relleno,* green stuffed pepper, usually containing cheese and chicken, the whole thing deepfried; *empanada,* fried pie with nuts and currants; *enchilada,* a tortilla variously stuffed and covered with red or green peppers; *nachos,* crisp cornmeal wafers served with cheese and pepper; *posole,* a stew of hominy and pork with peppers; *sopaipilla,* a deep-fried bread; *taco,* a tortilla folded over various fillings; and *tamale,* cornmeal stuffed with shredded meats and red peppers wrapped in husks and steamed.

Among eating places specializing in this regional fare are the following:

Cordelia's, 1601 Berry Ave. (tel. 988-1303), has a number of traditional New Mexican specialties, including a hearty sampler, a $9 combination plate. There are a number of entrees for no more than $5 at both lunch and dinner, served daily except Sunday. There is a pleasant indoor patio, and on weekends a guitarist entertains. Beer and wines are served.

La Tertulia, 416 Agua Fria (tel. 988-2769), occupies several small rooms of a century-old adobe house and is popular not only for regional foods but also for steaks; without a reservation you may not get a table. In the summer there is dining in a garden outside as well. There is full bar service. Open for lunch and dinner every day except Monday. Specialties include chalupas, carne adovada, and chile relleno. Entrees range from $8 to $17.

Josie's Casa de Comida, 225 E. Marcy St. (tel. 983-5311), is renowned for its enchiladas, made with blue-corn tortillas—the traditional Indian blue corn still grown in small quantities in New Mexico. Longhorn cheese and ground beef in red or green chile make the filling. If you want half red and half green chiles, your order is called out as "a Christmas tree"! The Mexican dinner at $6.50 is the highest-priced item on the menu: rolled enchilada, a tamale without its husk, a taco, lettuce, beans, and a tortilla. Homemade mocha cake, fresh pear pie, baked apples with whipped cream, or lemon soufflé, among 22 homemade desserts, are extra. Open for lunch only, from 11 a.m. to 4 p.m.

Maria's New Mexican Kitchen, 555 W. Cordoba Rd. (tel. 983-7929), has been a tradition for regional foods since it was opened in the 1940s by Maria and Gilbert Lopez. Now the restaurant has been bought, and according to one local critic, "brought back to life," by a local television executive and his wife, Al and Laurie Lucero, whose aim is to stick to New Mexican traditional cuisine while making various improvements in the restaurant as they go along. Since their take-over in 1985 business has been booming, due partly to $200,000 worth of re-modeling, but mainly to the introduction of fajitas—beef, chicken, shrimp, and vegetarian fajitas. Basically consisting of light, stir-fried ingredients, fajitas are a regional specialty that has become widely popular in the past few years. Laurie Lucero's fajitas have already won "Best of Show" at one Santa Fe restaurant com-petition called Cuisines of Santa Fe, and grand prize at another contest called Taste of Santa Fe. "We take extra steps in preparation," says Lucero, "like hand-mashing our avocados for the guacamole. We make our tortillas by hand, too, right in front of you." There is in fact a tortilla booth in which a cook prepares the tortillas before your eyes.

Demand is high for the blue-corn enchiladas with either red or green chile. Tamales are made daily in the kitchen, each hand-tied with a corn husk and stuffed either with pork and red chile filling, or with cheddar cheese, piñon nuts, corn, and green chile. The corn dough—masa—is made fresh too. Also popular is the chile relleno, a green pepper filled with creamy cheese, coated in egg batter, and deep-fried; it is served covered in green chile sauce. Lucero says, "We use only chiles grown in the state of New Mexico and prepare it the way the old Span-ish settlers have prepared it for years. Chile is like wine. You can take grapevine cuttings from the Napa Valley and plant them in Santa Fe and you'll get an en-tirely different-tasting wine. By the same token, plant our chile in the Napa Val-ley and you'll get a completely different-tasting chile. You must use New Mexico-grown chile or you don't have New Mexican food." Lucero says that sometimes he has to explain to newcomers that by "New Mexican," what is meant is cuisine of the state of New Mexico—*"not* a new way of fixing Mexican food."

Lucero says that visitors soon learn to follow local people's tastes in regional foods, including the "picoso" level—the peppery hotness—of the chiles. In serving beans, he has returned to an earlier tradition, explaining: "I noticed that New Mexican restaurants had compromised by using whole beans and posole corn with the caldo [broth] drained off, as a garnish. Beans and posole are a soup, or could even be called a stew, and are served in bowls, so you can savor all the delicious broth that's created in their slow cooking." These "soupy beans," or posole, can be ordered as a side dish; it is rarely found elsewhere in Santa Fe.

New Mexican fried bread, the sopaipilla, is often used like ordinary bread to go with food, but, says Laurie Lucero, "I love 'em with both butter and honey, when they're piping hot." Customers here have them either way. Traditional des-serts include natillas, a bread pudding called sopa, flan, and chocolate mousse; in addition there is cheesecake imported from San Francisco. Also new is a selection of steaks (to go with an expanded wine list, Lucero explains), but staple items known here for 40 years still grace the menu: barbecued pork ribs, for example.

The dining booths are built out of bricks from an old prison that was torn down across the street; the beer is kept in a cooler adapted from a century-old icebox out of a New Mexico mining town. There is full bar service, and hand-shaken margaritas made with fresh lime juice is the specialty. Salient in setting the atmosphere of the cantina is an array of southwestern murals painted years ago by Santa Fe artist Alfred Morang that have been painstakingly restored. An adobe patio invites diners outdoors in warm weather. Entrees cost $7 to $11. Open every day for lunch and dinner.

MODERATELY PRICED RESTAURANTS: At **Vanessie of Santa Fe**, 434 W. San Francisco (tel. 982-9966), the attraction is good fresh entrees prepared with care and served up in copious portions at fair prices, to be enjoyed in a bright décor accented by vast abstract artworks. Wooden tables and canvas-backed director's chairs, with great overhead vigas and pine-board floors, complete the scene. Vanessie, a voluble blonde woman originally from Hawaii, prides herself on the selection of fresh fish, certified black Angus beef (served in New York cuts or filets), and roast chicken, priced from $8 to $11. Big helpings of vegetables, ample for two persons, are served separately—baked potato, Saratoga chips, lettuce-and-tomato salad, or onion loaf (a house specialty). Each vegetable adds $1.50 to the tab. Among several desserts, a growing fame attaches to Vanessie's one-pound cheesecake servings. Open from 5:30 to 10:30 p.m. daily.

El Farol, 808 Canyon Rd. (tel. 983-9912), is an artists' bar and hangout with the casual friendliness of those legendary art cafés of New York and Paris in the 1920s and '30s, all on a more modest scale, of course. It is also a restaurant worth seeking out, serving the only authentic Spanish tapas—those great appetizers served in the wine bars of Spain—to be had in the area. On the tapas you'll find curried chicken, tortellini, tortilla española, shrimp and sun-dried tomatoes, ceviche of scallops, grilled cactus with romesco, and calamari rellenos. Regular dinners include such chef's selections as lamb brochettes or Cornish game hen. Prices go from as low as $5 for a modest selection of tapas to $16 for a chef's selection. Food is served Tuesday through Saturday from 6 to 11 p.m.; the bar opens daily at 4:30 p.m.

For pizza enthusiasts, the necessary address is the **Fresco**, 142 Lincoln St. (tel. 982-4583), at the corner of Marcy Street, a block from the Plaza, where the pizza can be calzone (ham and mushrooms), seafood (shrimp and squid), vegetarian (with sweet-and-sour red onions and goat cheese), Napoli (on a thin crust with basil), or with brie and walnuts. Open for lunch weekdays and for dinner seven nights a week, the Fresco also has specialties from its mesquite grill: chicken breast with pasilla chili sauce, or chicken mole, both $12.50. Hot tapas include fried brie with lingonberries or shallot vinaigrette, escargots in walnut sauce, or carcioffi Ripieni (artichoke stuffed with sausage dressing). An Italian garden salad or Caesar salad goes for $5.50. There is full bar service.

Moe's Ribs, 319 Guadalupe St. (tel. 983-9729), has plain tree-trunk posts separating wooden booths, a hint that the food is what's important—probably the best barbecue in the region. Moe claims: "We take no shortcuts, use no artificial smoke flavorings, nor do we use electric or gas barbecue pits to simulate true wood smoking. We start with the finest aged beef, meaty pork ribs, spicy hot links, boneless hams, and plump chickens. We season each with our own natural blends of spices and then cook them right here in our slow-smoking pits. We use only select hardwoods to create the exceptional flavor of our barbecue. Each meal is custom-sliced when ordered, and only then is it topped off with our own home-made scrumptious sauce." The taste of the resulting meat seems to bear out Moe's claims. Nothing here goes for over $10, and there is take-out service. Moe's is open for lunch and dinner daily except Sunday.

La Casa Sena, 125 E. Palace Ave. (tel. 988-9232), in the historic Sena Plaza, comes closest to being the perfectly imagined site for an old traditional southwestern restaurant hidden away in a quiet, pretty garden square. Inside it has the traditional vigas in the ceiling, beehive fireplace, regional furniture, and Indian weavings—and the food is good too. A century ago this was the home of Major

José Sena, his wife, and his 23 children, and it's easy to imagine that their spirit has left its mark on the place. A specialty is native trout stuffed with herbs, wrapped in vine leaves, and baked in clay; another is rack of lamb with Sandia chile jelly, perhaps accompanied by a red chile pasta salad with sun-dried tomatoes and prickly pear cactus. Evenings in the adjoining cantina, where another specialty, sopa en gieta con queso (black-bean soup), is served in a hollowed-out loaf of native bread, the waiters break into song (they like Broadway show tunes) between courses. Check the avocado-lime pie or chocolate natillas for dessert. Open daily for breakfast, lunch, and dinner. Entrees go for $10 to $17; the cantina menu runs $2 to $13.

BUDGET RESTAURANTS: The **Burrito Co.,** 111 Washington Ave. (tel. 98-CHILE), offers the pleasure of open-air sidewalk-café dining behind a pretty white picket fence, just a few steps from the Plaza, under awnings decorated with Perrier logos. Ristras (bright-red strings of red peppers) hanging from a second-floor balcony above add a festive note. Better than the pleasant surroundings, however, is the good, imaginative, regional-style, low-priced fast food. You place your order at a counter inside, where one of a platoon of eager employees scribbles your first name on a receipt so as to identify your tray when it appears within two minutes from the kitchen. Owner Rick Helmick claims in fact that his crew is so good they can have a burrito in a customer's hands within 40 seconds, outpacing McDonald's, for example. (Indeed Helmick has just opened a branch of his Burrito Co. at 3297 Cerrillos Rd. in the fast-food-store neighborhood.)

In spite of the fast pace, the restaurant starts from scratch on each order, beginning with a breakfast menu each day (opening 7:30 a.m.) that has a 95¢ breakfast taco (egg, chorizo, cheese, and salsa) and several breakfast burritos, at $1.50 to $3, involving bacon, eggs, potatoes, and cheese. Regular breakfasts and blueberry-and-banana-nut pancakes are also served, as well as huevos rancheros, with authentic Chimayo red and Hatch green chiles, at $3.50.

Later in the day, a treat might be a blue-corn chicken enchilada plate with red or green chiles, sour cream, refried beans, posole, and a flour tortilla ($5); or a couple of carne adovado tacos with fixings ($3.80); or a remarkable tortilla-chip pie, made of ground beef, beans, cheese, and onions on a bed of corn chips, topped with red chile (just $1.50). A popular combination plate of beef taco, enchilada, and tamale, with beans, posole, and tortillas, is $5; a green chile cheeseburger is $3.45. In addition to the sidewalk seating, indoors there are booths with wide, slatted wood benches. You can buy homemade chile by the gallon ($19), and salsa and posole to go, as well. Also sold are "Chile Addict" aprons, T-shirts, and bumper stickers.

Another good address for an inexpensive lunch or supper is **Souper Salads,** 2428 Cerrillos Rd. (tel. 473-1211), open seven days a week to 9 p.m. with good, fresh salads (no chemical additives) from a 60-item salad bar, numerous freshly made soups, and some calorie-conscious sandwiches. Soups include vegetable beef, seafood gumbo, green chile with cheese, cream of zucchini, clam chowder, broccoli cheese, mama mia chicken, chicken ole, and red bean with rice and sausage. One sandwich special, the "New Deal," involves avocado, mushrooms, Swiss cheese, sunflower seeds, and ranch dressing between slices of whole-wheat bread; other sandwiches are tuna salad, ham, or turkey, all with cheese slices. Hot homemade cornbread and gingerbread is served with all meals; salad, soup, and a sandwich will cost $6 to $7.50.

O. J. Sarah's, 106 N. Guadalupe St. (tel. 984-1675), sets a modern tone with white plastic chairs and tables under plain beams, with cheerfully bright mural paintings of vegetables on the walls. This is the place for a late breakfast (to 1 p.m. weekdays, all day on weekends), when hot, fresh cinnamon rolls are a favorite. Specialties are cottage cheese pancakes with raspberry sauce, and the fresh-fruit smoothie, a house creation. Sour-cream enchiladas are a lunchtime choice, as are the tuna cheese melt, the guacamole burrito, and a first-rate burger. Prices for breakfast and lunch range from $2 to $5. Open seven days from 7 a.m. for breakfast and lunch only.

4. SIGHTSEEING

If your goal in traveling and visiting various places is to absorb a sense of its past, of what makes it special, what identifies it, then Santa Fe is as important to you as anywhere in the Southwest. The city itself, with its mixture of peoples and its indigenous urban architecture derived from early Indian and Spanish forms and designs, gives a sense of the Southwest as well as the museums of the city do in their own more special ways. A city ordinance limits new building to a height of 35 feet. Since 1957 the city has enforced laws protecting its heritage of adobe architecture and prohibiting high-rise construction, a fact that now gives Santa Fe a serene and pleasing aspect not to be found in any other American city.

Everywhere one walks in central Santa Fe there are timeless dust-colored adobe façades with their beam ends—*vigas*—protruding, their flat roofs, their placid acceptance of the almost year-round sunlight that in the Southwest is like another element. Stroll along the narrow Santa Fe River and over a bridge to the new capitol; visit the old houses and churches. Watch the Indians selling their crafts and jewelry under the portal from a vantage point on a bench in the Plaza, center of all life in Santa Fe. There's a day to be given over to shopping or browsing in the galleries of Canyon Road and the shops of Guadalupe Street.

SPECIAL TERMS: Southwestern art often involves regional and traditional objects or materials. A **fetish** in this context is a sacred bird or animal made of wood or stone, used by Pueblo Indians in ritual ceremonies; some have a prayer bundle tied to them, and if there is an arrowhead it is a hunting fetish. **Kachina dolls** are wooden images of costumed dancers who represent certain spirits; they are mainly produced today by the Hopi. **Santos** are Christian religious figures carved by *santeros;* three-dimensional figures are called **bultos. Yeis** are stylized representations of Navajo gods seen in sand paintings and weavings. Besides the natural semiprecious item, there are two kinds of **turquoise**—stabilized (hardened artificially) and reconstituted, man-made, or artificially dyed, the latter not suitable for Indian jewelry.

MUSEUMS: There are more than half a dozen museums in and around Santa Fe that house collections of Indian art and cultural artifacts. Two-day passes to all four state-run museums cost $5.

The Palace of the Governors

One of four museum units of the state-run Museum of New Mexico, the Palace of the Governors takes up the north side of the Plaza, shading the walkway with the shelter of its portal, where the Indians of various pueblos sell their wares daily. Their daily market is in effect one of the programs of the Museum of New Mexico, which restricts selling space to Indians only. It is called the **Portal Program,** and there is even a Portal Committee to check up on the vendors and keep non-Indians out—for there is good tourist business to be had, especially at the summer visitor peak.

Indians, usually about 80 of them, set up early in order to get space. They come from the Santo Domingo, Santa Clara, Cochiti, Jemez, San Ildefonso, and certain other pueblos of northern New Mexico; a few Hopi and Navajo come from farther away. Gold, silver, and turquoise jewelry, pottery marked by the varying pueblo styles, beadwork, paintings, woven rugs and wall hangings, sand paintings, and Indian foods make up their stock in trade in a marketplace unique in the U.S.

Inside the Palace of Governors, built in 1610, the oldest public building in continuous use in the country, you get an idea of why you came to the Southwest: to absorb, perhaps, that special sense of an ancient way of life. Start with the theme of the "center space" in Pueblo Indian architecture seen in detailed models of pueblo apartment complexes or arrays of artifacts that came out of that civilization: "centeredness and unity, dominion of whole over parts, simplicity, balance, order, harmony, sacredness of all things."

All on the ground floor, the spacious rooms of the palace are devoted to various eras of the state's past, starting with the oldest, that of the Indians, and following on through that of the Spanish conquerors and settlers, then the later Mexican rule and eventual American annexation. The dioramas showing exquisitely made miniatures of the early Indian pit houses that date from the 1st century A.D., through other displays showing the early pueblos and later complex "classic" pueblos, make you want to visit the real ones—and of course this is the idea, for both ruins such as Chaco Canyon and the present-day lived-in pueblos are all within reach from this city.

Original pottery and basketry from prehistoric pueblos, even their ancient rough-made ladders, are displayed. There is a sandal 900 years old, and there are samples of every sort of jewelry and pottery. A major attraction is the full-scale model of Acoma, the Sky City—a pueblo isolated atop a mesa to the south of the town of Grants, N.M., lived in today, and claimed to be America's oldest community—that was constructed by William Henry Jackson, of the Bureau of Ethnology in Washington, in 1880. In the angles of its walls and roofs against the rays of the sun, both in summer and winter, the architecture shows early knowledge of passive solar heating. Here, too, is Jackson's model of the Taos pueblo, the original having changed surprisingly little in the passage of the years since the miniature was made.

The Hispanic side to the New Mexico story is illustrated by the emplacement of an entire early chapel typical of the middle of the last century, with a simple, bright-colored altarpiece made by a folk artist named José Rafael Aragon, who made it for a church up in Taos in 1830. Religious figures in three dimensions appear in the carved work: St. Francis, St. Michael, St. Anne.

Even the odds and ends that elsewhere seem to clutter up museums here find a right and necessary place, such as a great old door from a jail in the Santa Ana pueblo, called a pintle door for the grain visible in its wood, that was apparently used at one time as a testing board for a blacksmith who made branding irons—it has the signs of scores of ranches all over it. There is also a tiny New Mexico state flag, three by four inches, that was smuggled to the moon by one of the astronauts.

Portraits of many of the Spanish governors and bigwigs from the era of their dominance fill one of the great rooms, and there is another space devoted to the art of the Indians. Especially winning are paintings done by the modern children of the Taos pueblo, all of them aged 11 or 12. There is a bursting of color and of seemingly moving forms in the work of these Pueblo Indian children, especially up in the sky. In almost every picture you see action in the sky, a sky with patterns of storm, of cloud, of motion. Nearby are kitsch items showing how modern Commercial Man has taken Indian designs and symbols and wrenched them into forms suitable to his own aims: a liquor bottle in the form of an eagle dancer labeled Ezra Brooks Kentucky Bourbon, a neon motel sign in the form of the Zia symbol for the sun (with the horizontal beams sticking out from either side of the orb), a quilted toaster cover made to resemble a pueblo apartment complex. In spite of this apparent theft of Indian motifs as if no one was there to notice, there is still the strong sense, in New Mexico, that the Indians are alive and on the scene —and in fact regaining here and there traces of their ancient strengths. (See the description of Indian pueblos, below.)

The palace, which has been the site of residence for 100 governors over the centuries, in its earliest days had a tower serving as a chapel. During the Pueblo Revolt of 1680, when the Indians routed the Spanish from Santa Fe, they turned this chapel into a *kiva*—a ceremonial chamber—for their own rites. There was also another tower that stood over a prison dungeon, but all this was demolished by 1714. The building was occupied by Confederate soldiers for a month during 1862, the rooms still decorated with ears cut off the heads of captured or killed Apaches and Comanches who raided the town—the ears decorated the walls, and there were Indian scalps hanging on display in the office of the governor. A later governor of the Territory, Lew Wallace, also used the office here and completed his novel *Ben Hur* while in office.

Displays out of early New Mexico life include a stagecoach, an early working printing press, and a collection of *mestizajes,* portraits of early Spanish colonists detailing typical costumes of the time. Also on display are pieces from the silver service used aboard the battleship U.S.S. *New Mexico* from 1918 to 1939, and the mural-size Segesser hide paintings, on elk and buffalo hides, done in the early 1700s, showing Spanish Colonial events. One of the best shops for books on the Southwest is a part of the gift shop here, which also sells arts-and-crafts items in competition with the Indians just outside the front door.

The palace is open seven days a week from 10 a.m. to 5 p.m., except that from November through March it's closed on Monday. Admission is $2.

The Museum of Fine Arts

Also a part of the Museum of New Mexico, the Museum of Fine Arts is next door to the Palace of the Governors at the northwest corner of the Plaza, on West Palace, and also has a $2 admission, with the same hours as the palace, 10 a.m. to 5 p.m.; closed Monday from November through March. The most notable works here are those by Santa Fe and Taos artists of the early 20th century, the era when this area first became an artists' center. Typical of these works are aquatints by Doel Reed, a resident painter for a quarter century, originally from Indiana, whose feelings for nudes, jagged lines of rocky horizons, and the contrasting dark-and-light façades of southwestern buildings marks him an original; especially in his nudes there is a pleasingly familiar hint of Picasso or even of early impressionists. On another level a vast mural that for size at least could vie with the famous ones in Mexico shows an early scene out of some imagined Spanish Colonial history, a priest giving bread to a hungry Indian child; this bit of sweetness takes up a whole wall in the auditorium. Best of all for visitors searching out the soul of the region are the paintings done by Indians themselves, mostly showing Indians in costume doing ceremonial dances. They are the work of artists who were taught in the 1930s by the director of the Santa Fe Indian School, Dorothy Dunn. The stylized tempera paintings were done by Indians, often right on the reservation during the dances, mostly in small format of about 1½ by 2 feet, and it is worth seeing these colorful, spirited primitive works—some not looking primitive by any means—and comparing them with run-of-the-mill paintings of Indian subjects seen ad nauseum in the schlock-art stores here and elsewhere around the country. Indians were in fact first encouraged to draw and paint pictures of Indian subjects here in Santa Fe as early as 1910 by the director of the museum at that time, Dr. Edgar Lee Hewell, and it was Dorothy Dunn who continued his encouragement to a point where her Indian School, with its art studio, had a major influence in causing Indian artists to appreciate the values of their traditional designs and to use them in their paintings.

The museum was the first in the country to emphasize the art of a particular region, and the building itself, built in 1917, is one of the best examples in town of adobe architecture—it was extensively restored in 1982. A gift shop has prints and postcards of some of the works displayed as well as books on southwestern arts.

Shows and exhibitions in 1989 and 1990 will include "Alcove Show 7," with new work by contemporary New Mexico artists, from January through April 1989; "The 1930s: Photography in New Mexico," with work by Russell Lee, Arthur Rothstein, Dorothea Lang, John Collier, Jr., Edward Weston, Ansel Adams, and Paul Strand, to run from February to June 1989; and from July 14, 1989, "Supreme Instants: The Photographs of Edward Weston," running to September. From August to September 1989 is a retrospective exhibit titled "Will Shuster: A Santa Fe Legend"; and from October to February 1990 there will be a juried exhibition of southwestern artists entitled "Southwest '89: A Fine Arts Competition." From May through the summer of 1990 a selection of 19th and 20th century art will be shown, titled "Masterpieces of the American West: The Anschutz Collection"; and from September into 1991 some choice pieces from New Mexico painting over the past half century will be displayed under the title "Art in New Mexico: 1940 to the Present."

The Museum of International Folk Art

Still another property of the Museum of New Mexico, the Museum of International Folk Art was established in 1953 to promote "understanding among the various peoples of the world." Hours are the same as the other branches of the state museum, 10 a.m. to 5 p.m. daily (closed Monday November through March), and admission is $3 (or $5 for a two-day pass to all state-run museums). Located two miles south of the Plaza on Camino Lejo off Old Santa Fe Trail, the museum has since 1982 housed the 106,000 pieces of the collection of Alexander and Susan Girard, making it the largest folk-art collection in the world. A new wing was built to hold the vast assemblage of dolls and miniatures of figures, animals, and entire towns. Of the total collection, about 10,000 pieces, arranged in lifelike miniature settings, are on display.

A recent addition is a 100,000-piece miniature circus. There are video shows on various regional crafts too. Folk-art-influenced toys, as well as pictures and postcards showing items from the collections, are sold in the gift shop.

A present exhibit set to run through 1990 is "Behind the Mask in Mexico" *(Detras de la Mascara en México),* an environmental display focusing on five villages in Mexico where masked dances are performed on religious holidays. Also new, opening in July 1989, is the Hispanic Heritage Wing, site of permanent exhibits of traditional and contemporary Hispanic folk arts in the Southwest—it occupies a renovated wing of the museum.

The Museum of Indian Arts and Culture

This newest Santa Fe museum, which opened in 1987, at 710 Camino Lejo, next door to the folk-art museum, gives both an anthropological perspective of American Indians and their own perception of their lives today and in the past. The spacious new building has 10,000 square feet of exhibits based on the collections of the Laboratory of Anthropology that interpret Southwest Indian culture. Those collections include over 50,000 pieces of pottery, weaving, jewelry, carvings, and other Indian crafts, and more than three million archeological artifacts. There are daily artist's demonstrations as well as regular programs in a 70-seat multimedia theater. Visitors are invited to try their hand at such participatory activities as weaving and corn grinding, and there are regular performances of Indian music and dancing by Pueblo, Navajo, and Apache groups. Indian concession booths also purvey Native American foods. Hours are 10 a.m. to 5 p.m. daily; closed Monday November through March. Admission is $3.

Wheelwright Museum

Once called the Navajo House of Religion, this repository of Indian art with ritual significance is on Camino Lejo, off the Old Santa Fe Trail. It was founded by Mary Cabot Wheelwright half a century ago. She preserved the art of a Navajo medicine man, Hosteen Klah, who took the designs of sand paintings used in healing ceremonies and made them into the woven pictographs that are a major part of the museum's treasure. The museum is built in the form of a Navajo hogan in adobe, with its doorway facing east and a ceiling in interlocking "whirling log" style. Various shows of Indian crafts and designs are put on during the year, and at dusk in summer a storyteller gathers listeners around him outside a teepee. Case's Trading Post is decked out like an emporium on the reservation a century ago, with a good variety of crafts for sale as well as books on related subjects. The museum is open from 10 a.m. to 4:45 p.m. Monday through Saturday and 1 to 4:45 p.m. on Sunday; admission is free. For information on current exhibits, call 982-4636.

Institute of American Indian Arts

Indians from 70 tribes attend this institute at 1369 Cerrillos Rd., where a museum exhibits current work in various shows during the year. The aim of the school, operated by the U.S. Department of the Interior, is to encourage Indian artists to create works out of their own traditions or experiences, and most successful contemporary Indian painters in the region have attended at one time or another. Films on subjects relating to art or Indian life are shown, open to the public, on Thursday evenings. The museum is open from 9 a.m. to 5 p.m. weekdays and 1 to 5 p.m. weekends, admission free. For information on exhibitions or movies, call 988-6281.

A Nearby Village Museum

Your visit to an open-air village museum, **El Rancho de las Golondrinas,** occupying 200 acres in La Cienega, N.M., ten miles southwest of Santa Fe via I-25, begins at a monument in Juan Bautista de Anza Memorial Plaza. It is dedicated to a Spanish governor of New Mexico who stopped here in 1780. Privately owned by a Finn, Y. A. Paloheimo, who is a Wild West buff, and maintained by a foundation staffed by volunteers, the Rancho is open in summer and fall only and charges $2 admission for tours on Wednesday and Saturday. Reservations must be made ahead by telephone: 471-2261.

Artisans demonstrate their traditional crafts here during two festivals held off-season, one the first weekend of March, the second the first weekend of October. Craftspeople are also on hand on open-house Sundays, the first one of each month during the summer season. People dressed as villagers in colonial times become a miller of corn, a baker, a blacksmith, and other journeymen and women.

Buildings have been brought to the property to be preserved as examples of colonial and Territorial styles of architecture. An 1878 schoolhouse came from Raton, 150 miles north. A small, rather affectingly simple chapel is used for mass during the festival days; it is a spot where many northern New Mexicans still are married. A 200-year-old loom is used in a summertime weaving workshop. Local plants are grown for use in a herbal workshop. The restored 18th-century Baca House has an intriguing carved bedstead signed "este es de Guillermo" ("this is by William"), but this is followed by the words "como su lengua," a comment reading approximately, "in a pig's eye!" Farmhouses and sheds, another chapel, and a watermill are scattered around the hayfields, and the worn paths connecting them are a fine place to stroll under a western sun. Picnicking is encouraged, and there are tables.

CHURCHES: One block east of the Plaza, **St. Francis Cathedral** was begun in 1869 under the direction of Archbishop Lamy, the French clergyman who naturally favored the Romanesque style to recall the great cathedrals of France. Completed in 1886, it replaced an earlier parish church of adobe, Our Lady of the Assumption, that dated back to 1610 when the city was first built, though it, too, had been destroyed and rebuilt over the years. It later carried the name of St. Francis in honor of the founder of the Franciscan religious order (the saint became the patron of the city in 1823).

French architects designed the cathedral and Italian masons were brought here from Italy to build it. A Mexican wooden figure in the north chapel, called *La Conquistadora,* is the oldest representation of the madonna in the U.S., and has some special local history connected with it. In 1680 when the Indians ran the Spanish out of town, the losers rescued this statue and carried it with them on their escape to Mexico—they went as far as Juarez, just across the border. When the Spanish returned 12 years later to take Santa Fe again for the Spanish king, they brought the statue along with them for protection, and when they were successful named her "Our Lady of Conquest."

In the middle of the 18th century the people of Mexico had a gift in the form of two additional altars made for the people of Santa Fe, and they are visible in the cathedral too. The founder, Lamy, is honored by a bronze figure outside—his grave is under the main altar. He was responsible for a renaissance of church influence in the Southwest, and built 85 churches in the region.

The **Santuario de Nuestra Señora de Guadalupe,** 100 Guadalupe St., is a 1760 church serving as a museum that is operated by the Guadalupe Historic Foundation. It is the oldest shrine to the Virgin of Guadalupe, patroness of Mexico, in the U.S. The deep-red color of the altar wall was reproduced when the church was restored some years ago, by the original method of dyeing the plaster with oxblood. Religious art shows are held here, and there are chamber music concerts, flamenco dance programs, dramas, and lectures. The museum is open from 9 a.m. to 4 p.m. Tuesday through Friday and 10 a.m. to 3 p.m. on Saturday; closed Sunday and Monday. Admission is 50¢.

Another religious edifice no longer consecrated for worship is the **Chapel of Our Lady of Light,** on Old Santa Fe Trail, patterned after the Sainte-Chapelle in Paris and used in a religious girls' school on the grounds (now a hotel), of the Sisters of Loretto.

According to legend, when the choir loft was completed in 1878 the designers had neglected to include any access to it, and there was no space for an ordinary stairway because of the height of the balcony. Instead of installing a ladder, the sisters made a novena to St. Joseph hoping for a solution more esthetic, and, supposedly in reply, a carpenter on a donkey turned up and offered to build a stairway in a restricted space. He made curved pieces of wood by soaking them in tubs of water and is remembered as having worked only with a saw, T-square, and hammer. A fabulous spiral stairway is the result of his visit, although he did not stay on to collect his fee and disappeared as mysteriously as he arrived.

It has no center support and is held together entirely by wooden pegs, resting only on the floor and upon the balcony at the top. The wood is spliced in several places along the trajectory of a perfect spiraling curve. An engineer, Carl Albach, who climbed the stairway frequently while supervising electricity installation in the chapel, recalls, "Each time I went up or came down, I seemed to feel a small amount of vertical movement, as if the two 360° turns were taken out of a large coiled spring." Called the Miracle Staircase, the masterpiece, some will tell you in Santa Fe, was really the work of St. Joseph himself.

Open daily from 9 a.m. to 5 p.m. and maintained by the Historic Santa Fe Foundation, the chapel fund is supplied by a small admission fee.

Oldest mission church in the U.S. is the **San Miguel Mission,** Old Santa Fe Trail at East De Vargas, dating probably from the first year or two of the city's existence, which was 1610. The Indians tore out the interior during the Pueblo Revolt of 1680, but the church was rebuilt in 1710 and has been refurbished occasionally over the years since. Because of its design, with high windows and thick walls, the structure was occasionally used as a temporary fortress during times of attack by raiding Indians. Reredos—depictions of religious figures painted on wood, often used as partitions or screens near the altar—are among the examples of artworks in the church. One painting has holes that may or may not have been made by Indians' arrows—legend says that's where they came from.

Probably the most fascinating artworks in the church are instructional paintings done on buffalo hides and deerskins by missionaries to illustrate Bible stories to their Indian converts. The chapel is named for a boys' school that took it over for its use during the last century, a school run by the Christian Brothers, who still maintain the structure today.

A modern structure is **Cristo Rey Church** on Upper Canyon Road, probably the largest modern adobe building anywhere and a classic example of New Mexico mission architecture. It was built to be a home for some great stone Spanish Colonial altar screens, as a commemorative marking of the 400th anniversary of Coronado's explorations in the Southwest.

HISTORIC HOUSES: With the help of a map of central Santa Fe gotten free at the visitor center (corner of West Marcy and Sheridan), visitors can easily go to most of the houses of historic interest on foot. For those wanting more detail, a book is available, published by the Historic Santa Fe Foundation and sold in all bookshops, entitled *Old Santa Fe Today,* with map, photos, and descriptions of 50 sites around town within walking distance of the Plaza.

Many of the houses are private residences, not open for inspection inside, but they are well worth the visit for a feeling of Santa Fe life in the past. The 300 block of West San Francisco Street has an example of hacienda buildings dating from the 18th century, the **Ortiz Houses.**

The **Gregorio Crespin House,** 132 E. De Vargas, is recorded in early deeds as having been sold in 1747 for 50 pesos. Originally in pueblo-style design, Territorial embellishments were later added, involving trim of bricks along the roofline. At 352 E. De Vargas is the **Adolph Bandelier House,** home of the famous archeologist for whom the fabulous prehistoric ruins at Bandelier National Monument are named. The 1830-era **José Alarid House,** now an art gallery, stands at 338 E. De Vargas. The mid-18th-century **Boyle House,** built as a hacienda, is seen at 327 E. De Vargas.

Canyon Road is a quarter-hour walk from the Plaza, and also has some historic buildings as well as its many art galleries and restaurants, including the **Juan José Prada House** at no. 519, believed built around 1760; and a former hacienda called **El Zaguan** at no. 545, where there was once a special "chocolate room" for afternoon refreshments of the owner and family.

Sena Plaza, a block from the main Plaza on East Palace, site of La Casa Sena restaurant, is a lovely and tranquil patio surrounded by a few tiny, quiet shops where in the upper stories the territorial legislature met for a time in the 1890s;

originally the little square was part of a 31-room hacienda built in 1831. Adjoining it is **Prince Plaza,** 113 E. Palace, a patio and residence until 1900, now housing the Shed restaurant—a house in the Territorial style with great wooden gates that were put up to keep out Indian attacks. The 1857 **Padre de Gallegos House,** 227-237 Washington, was the residence of a local priest whose untrammeled deportment got him defrocked upon the arrival of Bishop Lamy in town in 1852— Gallegos later went on to represent the Territory in Congress and was later U.S. superintendent of Indian Affairs. This, too, is a good example of the style of the Territorial era.

The last of the poured-mud adobe houses can be seen at the **Oldest House,** on East De Vargas near its intersection with Old Santa Fe Trail, a venerable structure said to have been built by Pueblo Indians and thus the oldest house in the U.S. Among residents over the centuries, legend says there were a couple of witches during part of the 18th century. Just off the Plaza is the **Delgado House,** 124 W. Palace, a fine Victorian residence dating from 1890, now the property of the Historic Santa Fe Foundation. This organization has its own offices in another fine Territorial residence at 136 Grant, the **Tully House,** built in 1851. The 1870-era **Bergere House,** 135 Grant, was once the scene of an 1880 visit to Santa Fe of U.S. President Grant and his wife. Wisteria growing over adobe walls is a Santa Fe tradition, as exemplified at the pretty **Tudesqui House,** 129 E. De Vargas, built in the early 19th century.

OTHER SIGHTS: History buffs can explore the extensive collections of books and other materials on southwestern lore in libraries: the **New Mexico History Library** is at 110 Washington, the **Archives of New Mexico** is at 404 Montezuma, and there are reading rooms set up for those wanting southwestern subject matter at both the **Santa Fe Library,** 120 Washington, and the **New Mexico State Library,** 325 Don Gaspar.

Although only 25 years old the **Capitol Building,** called the "Roundhouse," is in the form of the timeless Pueblo Indian *kiva*—the circular ceremonial room —and also has historical displays installed in the rotunda by the Museum of New Mexico staff. It's across the Santa Fe River on the Old Santa Fe Trail a short walk from the Plaza. **Santa Fe River State Park** makes a pleasant place for a stroll on your way—a tree-lined walkway with picnic benches just perfect for a lunchtime break. The obelisk back at the Plaza, incidentally, is the only one in the U.S. put up to remember Union Army forces south of the Mason-Dixon Line.

5. THE ART SCENE

Although there are over 125 commercial art galleries in Santa Fe, many of them along the increasingly famous Canyon Road row of dealers, local artists also have access to other outlets for displaying their work. One of these is the nonprofit **Armory for the Arts,** 1050 Old Pecos Trail (tel. 988-1886), where group shows are held throughout the year. This follows a tradition of group shows by local artists that started with Los Cinco Pintores (the Five Painters), early Santa Fe resident artists: Walter Mruk, Jozef Bakos, Fremont Ellis, Will Shuster, and Willard Nash. They were called "the five nuts in the five mud huts" on Telephone Road, an unpaved street whose name was soon changed to the more artistic-sounding Camino del Monte Sol by another artist, William Henderson.

The **Center for Contemporary Arts,** 291 E. Barcelona Rd. (tel. 982-1338), is a second publicly supported art center, a multidisciplinary art facility aimed to serve "those who take risks," says its co-director Bob Gaylor: "The art that doesn't take risks doesn't need support." The center has a 143-seat theater and a rehearsal hall, as well as exhibit space for visual artists; a sculpture garden is under construction. The center tries to bring together musicians, sculptors, painters, dancers, film and video makers, actors, and performance artists in order "to forge connections between various art disciplines," according to Gaylor. Besides continuous visual art exhibits and work space for artists, the center has programs in poetry and literature, a concert series of new music, plays, dance performances, visual-and-sound installations, and showings of experimental films.

CANYON ROAD: Along this mile-long one-time burro trail within a quarter-hour walk from the Plaza are some 75 artists' and artisans' workshops and galleries. A study by the New Mexico Art Division has determined that the art business generates $1 billion annually for the state, and a good portion of that must come from Canyon Road. Here are a few of the many places worth a visit.

The **Munson Gallery,** at no. 225, established in 1860, has a conservative selection of southwestern landscape paintings in various media. **Economos,** at the same address (several shops share a little plaza here) has some American Indian art as well as pre-Columbian and Mexican colonial pieces.

Across the road at no. 223, **Carole LaRoche** displays her memorably bright-pastel abstract paintings in acrylic on paper. At no. 400 the **Linda Durham Gallery** displays modern and creatively innovative abstract paintings and sculptures by John Connell, Richard Hogan, and Holly Roberts. Another well-established gallery for Indian art, particularly pueblo ceramics, is the **Robert F. Nichols Gallery,** at no. 419.

The **Linda McAdoo Gallery,** no. 503, has representational and impressionistic works by Rod Goebel, Robert Daughters, and Joan Potter. Drawings from century-old Indian ledger books are among the treasures at the **Morning Star Gallery,** at no. 513. The **Ernesto Mayans Gallery,** at no. 601, has artworks from the 19th and 20th centuries, including work by such artists as Tommy Macaione, Bernard Plossu, and Whitman Johnson. This gallery's wintertime invitational shows attract Santa Fe artists who exhibit elsewhere because of the nonregional cast of their work.

Native folk art and expressionistic landscapes are shown at the **Waxlander Gallery,** no. 622. The **Running Ridge Gallery,** at no. 640, has contemporary paintings, sculpture, and ceramics. Oil paintings and watercolors by **Howard Bobbs** are seen at his gallery at no. 651, while at no. 702½ the **Nove Collection** has works by Ron Robles.

ELSEWHERE IN SANTA FE: The **Governor's Gallery,** on the fourth floor of the state capitol, has solo shows by New Mexico artists. It's open from 8 a.m. to 5 p.m. weekdays.

The **Jamison Galleries,** 111 E. San Francisco St., has a permanent exhibit of landscapes and portraits by the Nebraska artist Alton Larsen. The oldest of the major galleries, Jamison shows mostly art associated with the Southwest, although a Maine artist, Alfred Morang, is represented by a scene of a city in the snow. New Mexico scenes in watercolor are the work of a young local native, Gloria Roybal. Another landscape painter, using regional subjects in watercolor and oil, is Frank La Lumia.

As well known as any Santa Fe gallery is **Elaine Horwitch,** 129 W. Palace. Horwitch opened an Arizona gallery 25 years ago, added the Santa Fe store a decade ago, and now has three other locations beyond her Santa Fe premises (Sedona, Scottsdale, and Palm Springs). She has introduced artists in the contemporary southwestern field such as Fritz Scholder and Randy Lee White.

An annual New Mexico Emerging Artists show is held for two weeks every May at the **C. G. Rein Galleries,** 122 W. San Francisco.

6. ANNUAL FESTIVALS AND OTHER EVENTS

Summer is festival time in Santa Fe and the Plaza is the center of the good times. There are a couple of markets for artisans' wares that partake of fiesta moods—one for Indian products and one for Hispanic. There are music and arts festivals too, and various yearly sports events and special contests such as a balloon rally or a rodeo.

LA FIESTA DE SANTA FE: This celebration, bringing out the essence of the spirit of the city, was first staged in 1712 on this same Plaza to mark the reoccupation of Santa Fe by the Spanish, after they had been routed by the Pueblo Indians in the Pueblo Revolt of 1680. Don Diego de Vargas was the commander of the Spanish troops in 1692 who retook Santa Fe, and by the end of the following year he had repopulated the city with his countrymen, who brought with them the famous wooden statue, *La Conquistadora,* they had managed to salvage on their retreat 12 years before. It was this carved madonna, de Vargas said, that had helped him to victory over the Indians. Eight years after his death the Fiesta was established to honor *La Conquistadora* and celebrate that reentry of Spain into New Mexico. It was to be an annual affair with a mass and a sermon, giving a religious cast to the event that in spite of the high spirits associated with it still pervades it today.

Fiesta in Santa Fe today involves all the people of the city, Indians and Anglos (the southwestern term for anybody neither Hispanic nor Indian) as well as those descended from the early Spanish colonists who founded it. It is always held on the second or third weekend of September, whichever is nearer the middle of the month. Certain Fiesta-related events, such as a foot race called the Old Santa Fe Trail Run and certain arts-and-crafts shows, traditionally take place over the Labor Day weekend.

The Fiesta officially begins with a mass on Fort Marcy Hill overlooking the city just northeast of the Paseo de Peralta—this was the 1846 site of the first U.S. military post in the Southwest, now marked only by some mounds. The mass is offered at the Cross of the Martyrs up here, which stands in memory of Franciscans killed in the Pueblo Revolt those many years ago. There is also an impressive candlelight procession at dusk that evening, departing from the cathedral down below.

A varied schedule of parties, street dances, and musical entertainments goes on all weekend (details available at the visitor center). A high point is the burning of old Zozobra, Old Man Gloom, a giant figure made of wood, chicken-wire, and canvas painted to resemble a grouchy Spanish grandee. When Zozobra is set alight and burned on that Friday night, it's a signal for the good times to begin, for the dancing to start, the music to sound forth. Every year there is an election of a new Don Diego de Vargas to lead a procession into the Plaza to take control of the city again, symbolically reenacting the return of the Spanish in 1692, and there is of course also a Fiesta queen crowned as well as a subsequent knighting of Don Vargas in colorful ceremonies. Choral groups alternate with bands and mariachis, and there are booths purveying food specialties of all the various Santa Fe traditions, Indian fried bread to tacos, hot dogs to sopaipillas. A carnival at which citizens appear in costumes of the early days ends the festivities. For all Fiesta information directly, telephone the Fiesta Line, 988-7575.

INDIAN MARKET AND SPANISH MARKET: Santa Fe visitors are fortunate, if they happen to be in town on the right summer weekends, to be able to go to the unique two-day crafts markets, one exhibiting Indian-made wares from all over the country and the other showing Hispanic-tradition goods. Both markets are policed to ensure that everything sold is authentic artisan-made merchandise.

The **Spanish Market** displaces the Indians under the roof of the portal of the Palace of the Governors for two days over the last weekend of July. Sponsored by the Spanish Colonial Arts Society, it was first started in 1929, and then revived in the 1950s with a growing regional and national interest in folklore and traditional crafts. Carved wooden *santos,* religious figures out of a Mexican tradition; rugs and wall hangings from weavers out of a different culture from that of the famous Indian weavers, Spanish weavers from the New Mexico mountains who work at looms in such villages as Chimayo or Truchas; tiles with various traditions out of Spain, Mexico, and early New Mexico; wrought iron, ceramics, and religious painting on wood—all are sold here by the people who make them, mostly to dealers. Bargaining with the sellers is certainly possible, but they are aware of the value of their work, which indeed is in considerable demand. Typical of the artisans is Santa Fean Angelina Delgado Martinez, a tinsmith who learned the art of fashioning delicately embossed mirror frames in tin from her grandfather. She is married to another artisan, Efren Martinez, who is a *santero,* a carver of *santos,* those wooden figures of saints. In order to place work in the market, craftspeople must be accepted first by a screening committee who judge the esthetic quality and authenticity of the work.

The weekend occurring two weeks before Labor Day is set aside in Santa Fe for the **Indian Market,** similar to the Spanish Market in that it appeals to retailers who replenish their stocks during the event. Organized by the Southwestern Association on Indian Affairs which has run it annually since 1922, the market is the largest all-Indian market in the country.

According to director Don Owen, "A first-time applicant must be an enrolled member of a registered tribe and be at least one-fourth Indian. We have no restrictions on traditional or contemporary art, but we do have very high standards."

A Standards Committee every year gives its approval for 400 booths to be set up by some 800 artists and craftspeople, all Indians who must prove that what they display is all genuine handcrafted work done by the seller himself. No fewer than ten "evaluators" constantly patrol the Market to ensure that these high standards are kept up. With so much to display, the market gets under way early, and brisk sales are already going on in the Plaza, site of the market, by 7 a.m. on Saturday morning of the market weekend. Prize-winning pottery, blankets, rugs, woodcarvings, jewelry, sculpture, and paintings tempt the thousands of potential buyers, including, of course, many tourists. As in the Spanish Market a bit earlier in the summer, it is possible to try bargaining, but again the supply of authentic crafts seems well below the demand. The organizers of the market raise money from exhibitors' fees to fund crafts scholarships and grants in the amount of over $30,000 every year. During the afternoons of the sale there are some events associated with it, held in the patio of the Palace of the Governors: crafts demonstrations, and Indian dancers, and even the modeling of Indian costumes.

SANTA FE FESTIVAL OF THE ARTS: The Sweeney Convention Center near the visitor center, at West Marcy and Grant, is the scene of the annual arts festival, running for a weekend in late October. It draws most of its work from Santa Fe artists, who compete for prizes, sell their works, and get considerable exposure as well. The event originated in 1977. Among a variety of specially highlighted shows there is one for new talent and various ones for different media such as painting, sculpture, and photography. For information, call 988-3924.

OTHER EVENTS: A four-day **rodeo** goes on every year in early July, beginning with a western parade on a Thursday morning followed by evening performances starting at 8 p.m. that night and on Friday, Saturday, and Sunday. A covered grandstand provides seats for spectators to this traditional western entertainment, presenting the regulation competitions in bull riding, bronco busting, steer wrestling, calf roping, barrel racing, and so-called bullfighting, the latter a Santa Fe specialty in which neither bull nor cowboy is supposed to be hurt. A band cheers on brave riders and ropers and the usual rodeo clowns cavort to draw the attention of bulls after they have dumped their riders. Held at the rodeo grounds on Rodeo Road, off Cerrillos Road east of the airport turnoff, the event also presents trick-riding demonstrations, cowgirl contests, and animal acts. Local rodeo fans take along a warm jacket for the cooler hours of the evening, and a cushion or even a backrest—it's a long show, lasting nearly until midnight. Tickets and information about the rodeo are sold at La Fonda Inn on the southeast corner of the Plaza (tel. 982-5511). Daytime over rodeo weekend there is also a "Rodeo Wagon" ticket seller right in the Plaza. The Santa Fe rodeo has been held since 1848.

The Downs at Santa Fe (tel. 471-3311) has a closed-circuit television system to show instant replays of the final stretch run after every race, and live transmission of out-of-state races for legal betting. Highlight of the racing program is the Santa Fe Futurity for two-year-olds. It's the park's richest race, grossing over $300,000. Other high purses are attached to the Coquette for fillies, the Downs Quarter Horse Derby for state breds, and the Walter Goodwin Handicap. The Santa Fe Derby is restricted to horses three years old and up. A 48-day schedule starts in mid-June. General admission is $2; box seats, $2.50 and $3.50; admission to the Turf Club is $4, and to the Jockey Club, $7. Valet parking is available for $3.50. Seniors get free admission on Wednesday, and women are free on Friday. The track is 11 miles southwest of the city off U.S. 85 (Cerrillos Road) beyond the airport turnoff.

7. MUSIC AND OTHER PERFORMING ARTS

The Santa Fe Opera, founded in 1957, is a major American company that sets a high standard for other performing organizations in the city: the Santa Fe Desert Chorale, the Festival Theatre, the Orchestra of Santa Fe, and the Community Theatre, among others. Besides all this and frequent performances by touring companies in music, dance, and theater, Santa Fe provides a rich choice in music and entertainment in its restaurants and clubs, drawing from the two regional strains of Hispanic and country and western tradition, and adding various periods of jazz from Dixieland and ragtime to big bands and fusion. This nevertheless leaves plenty of room for a lively rock-and-roll scene in many locations in and around the city. Summertime is the high time, especially for opera and the classical concerts, but there is still plenty of sound in town all year, any night of the week.

CLASSICAL AND TRADITIONAL: The **Santa Fe Opera** occupies a sweeping, soaring almost bird-like structure out on U.S. 84 five miles northwest of the center of the city, a composition of adobe-like concrete and wood that seems to move in great curves in every direction—a setting of serenity that uses the open sky and the backdrop of a mountain range to the greatest advantage. During evening performances the lights of the distant town of Los Alamos provide a background to the stage. The company is known for staging American premières of little-known European works or brand-new opuses. An example was the première of Pier Francesco Cavalli's *L'Orione,* an early baroque Italian work rarely heard anywhere. It is a period about which opera buffs have a growing interest, shared by conductor Raymond Leppard, whose productions are usually sung in an English version. The annual opera season runs from late June through July and August, with seats priced at $10 to $45 Monday through Thursday and $15 to $50 on weekends; standing room goes for $3. Information on the program and ticket reservations is available by phoning 982-3855.

The **Santa Fe Desert Chorale** was organized in 1983 to bring to the city the old European tradition of the summer choral festival. Director Lawrence Bandfield says, "Our purpose is to prepare and present to the Southwest a seasonal, diversified choral repertoire performed by an ensemble of professionals." Programs involve various periods and styles of choral music: Renaissance, baroque, romantic, and contemporary. The composers range from Palestrina, Guerrero, Bach, Handel, Demantius, Brahms, and Mendelssohn, to Britten and Argenta. The schedule of programs, all in the lovely Santuario de Guadalupe (at the corner of Guadalupe and Agua Fria), begins in mid-June and continues to early August. The overall aim of director Bandfield is to put on four 90-minute programs during each summer season and to alternate them repeatedly. Admission is $12.50. For scheduling and tickets, call 988-2282.

Another local choral group, the **Chorus of Santa Fe,** also presents a few programs during the year, usually at the St. Francis Auditorium of the Fine Arts Museum. For information and tickets, call 471-3935.

The **Santa Fe Chamber Music Festival** originated in 1973 and provides summertime lectures, special concerts, and instrument demonstrations for youth, and popular "Sunday-Monday" programs dedicated to work of a given era or musical school; some of those featured in the 1988 program were Beethoven, music of the Americas, and a series devoted to Baroque music. Music begins at 6 p.m. on Sunday, and the same program is repeated on Monday beginning at 8 p.m. A composer-in-residence appears in lectures and Saturday discussion-rehearsal sessions, free of charge to spectators, who can preview the music planned for the next day's concert. The local musicians have issued records of their music and have also appeared in concerts on the West Coast. Tickets at $12.50 to $15 are available at the Festival box office in the lobby of the St. Francis Auditorium, on the Plaza. For reservations and information on programs, call 983-2075.

The **Orchestra of Santa Fe** presents concerts throughout the year at the Sweeney Center. For information and tickets, telephone 988-4640.

The **Armory for the Arts,** at 1050 Old Pecos Trail (tel. 988-1886), is a multi-use arts center occupying the old National Guard Armory which was converted into a home for the arts in 1974, with a 340-seat theater and an art gallery, studio, and workshop space. Open all year, the gallery and theater both welcome artists of local and national note. Recent dramatic productions have been an Anne Sexton play, *Transformations,* and a version of the Walt Whitman work *Song of Myself.* Gallery shows range from crafts and paintings to photography and ironwork, and there are classes in kathak, martial arts, belly dancing, and flamenco.

The **Santa Fe Community Theatre** also produces short-run productions of melodramas and straight plays at its premises at 142 E. De Vargas. Telephone 988-4262 for information and tickets.

For three weeks in the summer a revolving schedule of drama is presented to the public at the Greer Garson Theater at the College of Santa Fe by the **British American Theater Institute.** For information and tickets, call 983-6713.

MUSIC IN CLUBS AND LOUNGES: Many of the downtown hotels as well as cocktail lounges and dance-hall-size spaces book musical groups of various per-

suasions. Solo performers and rock groups on national tours give summertime concerts at the **Soleri Theatre** of the Santa Fe Indian School and at the Downs at Santa Fe, with such personalities as Joan Armatrading, B. B. King, or the Grateful Dead; country music stars also perform. But year round in the lounges and clubs there is music nightly.

Club West, at 213 W. Alameda (tel. 982-0099), has its front decorated with a great mural in the form of an imitation reflection, as if in a mirror, of the Santuario de Guadalupe. Inside, the joint is jumpin', however, with the likes of rockabilly Little Charlie and his cohorts, or others. Cover charge of around $5 varies with performers.

The **Bull Ring,** at 414 Old Santa Fe Trail (tel. 983-3328), has blues and jazz, no cover, with music Tuesday through Saturday.

The Forge (tel. 982-4333), at the Inn of the Governors, Alameda at Don Gaspar, has blues or jazz groups to 1:30 a.m. Tuesday through Saturday, with no cover.

At **Vanessie,** 434 W. San Francisco (tel. 982-9966), this well-established bar and lounge thrives along with a newer restaurant on the premises. Adding the dining room seems not to have affected the casual cheer in this bar, which is rapidly attaining the status of a landmark in Santa Fe. The action here begins at 8:30 p.m. when the pianist takes his place at the piano bar. A frequent standby is local musician Doug Montgomery. Music continues nightly to 2 a.m., except Sunday nights when midnight is the time limit. A private parking lot, reached from the 400 block of Water Street, adjoins the restaurant.

El Farol, a restaurant and bar at 808 Canyon Rd. (tel. 983-9912), is known for its jazz and folk-music sessions every night of the week, carrying on until 2 a.m. (except Sunday to midnight), presenting musicians with a range from Joan Baez to saxophonist Pharaoh Sanders. Also present sometimes are the Cuicana singers from Albuquerque, who do songs in the little-known Nahuatl language of Mexico. They accompany themselves on such rare musical instruments as the charengo, a gourd-shaped guitar with an armadillo-hide back.

Mr. R's Country Western Night Club, 2911 Cerrillos Rd. (tel. 473-4138), in the Ramada Inn, has live bands every night except Sunday. Just about the biggest dance floor in town accommodates square dancing and line dancing, alternating with free-style. Monday nights there are free dance lessons, and every day at 4 p.m. there's happy hour.

Jazz or folk musicians are presented weekend evenings at **La Fonda,** on the Plaza (tel. 982-5511).

Down in the so-called ghost town of Madrid, N.M., 30 miles south of Santa Fe right on the main highway (N.M. 14), is the **Mine Shaft Tavern,** with live music every day, even at lunchtime, and guitar players afternoon and evening.

8. SHOPPING IN SANTA FE

Because it is a nationally known center for arts and crafts, Santa Fe has attracted scores of shops and boutiques selling specialized foods, clothing, souvenirs, and of course, examples of every kind of artisan skill. There are registered Indian traders and purveyors of fossils and minerals, specialists in posters and prints and a place that deals in sheepskin products, hand-painted tiles and natural-fiber clothing, bookshops with hundreds of titles on southwestern subjects and importers of goods from Mexico. Antique dealers are not hard to discover, and there are jewelers specializing in regional designs and materials: gold, silver, turquoise. Santa Fe is laid out so that it's easy to find most of these shops, for they occupy the streets radiating out from the Plaza, except for Canyon Road, where many of the art galleries rub shoulders with crafts shops and other boutiques.

IN THE PLAZA AREA: At 200 Old Santa Fe Trail, **Santa Fe East** specializes in jewelry by Luis Mojica, David Dear, and Kim Rawdin—mostly modern pieces with a feeling for traditional silver patterns. The warm colors of 19th-century Oriental rugs are displayed at **Stephen A. Miller Oriental Rugs,** 212 Galisteo St. Stones from the desert are hard to sort out unless you're an expert, but the sorting and polishing is all done for you at **Mineral & Fossil Gallery,** 118 Don Gaspar Ave., which has geodes, petrified wood, unset gemstones, and polished pieces made into jewelry or bookends.

It's great fun to browse among the inventive crafts items, many brought in from lesser-known crafts areas of Mexico, at **Artesanos,** 222 Galisteo, where the street number is written out in garlands of ristras (dried red peppers). There are mirrors outlined in embossed tinwork, carved doors, leather chairs, and intricate wooden games and toys. Across the street at no. 217, the **Overland Sheepskin Co.** has the warmest, most comforting, most luxuriant-feeling parkas, coats, hats, and slippers you've ever laid eyes or hands on.

A fabric-arts gallery showing pillows, wall hangings, and quilts in both contemporary and traditional design carries the portentous name **Quilts to Cover Your Fantasy,** at 110 W. San Francisco. Fancy belts, buckles, and boots are the stock in trade of the long-established **Tom Taylor,** whose shop is in La Fonda Hotel, 110 E. San Francisco. Advertising "the world's finest Panama hats," the **Montecristi Custom Hat Works,** 118 Galisteo St., purveys models for both men and women. Dresses and shirts in western-style cuts of genuine leather are shown at **Salamander Leathers,** on the Plaza at 78 E. San Francisco.

Hand-woven dresses, sweaters, and shawls, along with jewelry with a modern southwestern spirit, are displayed at **Handwoven Originals,** in the Inn at Loretto, 221 Old Santa Fe Trail. **The Rainbow Man,** 107 E. Palace, has a hodgepodge of gift items from around the world, as well as the country's largest collection of Edward S. Curtis photographs. Also on display is furniture handcrafted by Ernest Thompson.

Ceramic ware from the Nambe pueblo and handmade furniture is shown at **Nambe Ware,** 112 W. San Francisco. Custom furniture and doors in southwestern and Spanish Colonial styles are at **Southwest Spanish Craftsmen,** 116 W. San Francisco. Traditional beadwork, pottery, Indian jewelry, rugs, and old western relics are viewed at **Koshare Trading Co.,** 312 Sandoval St. The place for chic secondhand clothes (called "vintage clothing" here) is **Act 2,** 520 Montezuma, in the Sanbusco Center.

CANYON ROAD: A shop named **The Streets of Taos,** 200 Canyon Rd., has Navajo rugs, and pueblo Indian jewelry, basketry, and pottery. **Spider Woman Designs,** 225 Canyon Rd., is a weaving and design studio with clothing, regional antique furniture, Indian artifacts, and decorative accessories. The **Native Market,** 555 Çanyon Rd., has serious and unserious curios and folk art, as well as weavings and other crafts. Fantastic Mexican dance masks from several areas of the republic are shown at **Folklorico,** 642 Canyon Rd., along with religious art and Mexican colonial furniture.

As much fun as a visit to a museum of surrealistic art is antique browsing at **Lestat,** 653 Canyon Rd., a complex of rooms full of surprisingly bizarre objects from all over the world; there are art deco chairs, brass birdcages, a Portuguese armoire, a wall hanging from Tibet, and an entire Chinese opium den (not open for business). Along with all this is some innovative contemporary jewelry—quite amazing to behold are its cactus-like pieces fashioned from pyrites and opals.

Across the road, at no. 656, are two unusual jewelers. **Tresa Vorenberg Goldsmiths** makes 14- and 18-karat gold jewelry, chains, and bracelets, as well as pieces in silver. Also within this small complex is **Silver Sun,** offering modern Indian designs in silver and Cerrillos turquoise jewelry.

Fabulously carved doors, wood screens, and chests in original designs are made and sold at **Volker de la Harpe,** 707 Canyon Rd. A newly made door with a solid Spanish Colonial feeling, carved in 21 squares containing bas-relief leaves, is priced at $2,000; an ornate buffet, at $3,000. Museum-quality Indian art, including early beadwork, pottery, and wrought silver, is offered at the unfortunately named **Toys for Big Boys,** 720 Canyon Rd.

Two excellent antique shops await you at the far end of the road: the **Frightened Owl,** at no. 1117, and **Architectural Antiques,** at no. 1125.

9. INDIAN PUEBLOS

Of the 19 pueblos in New Mexico, the **Eight Northern Pueblos,** which have formed an association for marketing their handcrafts, are all within range for easy day trips using Santa Fe as a base. They are the Tesuque, the Nambe, the Pojoaque, the San Ildefonso, the Santa Clara, the San Juan, the Picuris, and the Taos. (Taos Pueblo is described in Chapter IV, "Taos and Northern New Mexico.") Santa Fe itself was once an Indian pueblo—or the site of one, for by the time the Spanish arrived in the 16th century the inhabitants there had disappeared.

The pueblos where Indians live today are thought to have been founded some 800 years ago when communities to the west were abandoned because of a prolonged drought. There are theories that perhaps the early populations of Anasazi—the "old people" of whom we have no direct trace today—gave up their caveside apartments because they had simply chopped down all the trees in the areas they lived in, thus making way for erosion and the ruination of their farming soil, which was already precariously irrigated. In any case we have no proof that modern pueblo Indians are all descended from the earlier Anasazi—not yet, at any rate. But the similarities of the *kivas* (the circular ceremonial rooms) in the ruins and in a few of the modern pueblos, as well as the structure of the adobe apartment houses, both in some of the ruins and in the occupied pueblos, makes one think there must be a constant line through time that links the early people with the modern.

Pueblo Indians should not be called tribes, which means a political unit with a common authority. Their communities are each an individual organization with no direct political ties to the other pueblos, and each has its own dialect of one of three distinct languages: Keresan, Tanoan, and Zunian. They all, with the exception of Pojoaque, today continue to occupy traditional pueblo apartments built of adobe, one atop another, although many live in houses outside the actual pueblo complexes. Among all the eight northern pueblos photography is allowed, as well as sketching and painting, on payment of certain fees that vary with the pueblos, but photographs may not be taken of the ceremonial dances.

SAN JUAN PUEBLO: Just 36 miles north of Santa Fe via U.S. 84 and N.M. 68, the San Juan Pueblo (tel. 852-4400) makes a good place to begin visits to pueblos because it is the site of the **Eight Northern Pueblos Artisans' Guild Shop** where the work of craftspeople of the various communities is shown. It makes a good place to understand the varieties in such objects as pottery, ceramic figures, baskets, and drums—each pueblo generally follows a style that is refined by the particular talents of the individuals who make the designs and do the work. One circumstance that tends to hold these eight pueblos together is that they all speak languages of the Tanoan language group—either Tiwa or Tewa—so that they can usually converse without recourse to English or Spanish.

The black pottery of San Ildefonso and Santa Clara Pueblos is displayed along with Taos drums or bowls by the Picuris that sparkle with faint encrustations of mica. The Nambe send in beadwork earrings. Altogether throughout the eight pueblos about 250 artisans are contributing work to the outlet. It is open from 10 a.m. to 4 p.m. daily.

The first Spanish capital of New Spain was established at this pueblo by Don Juan de Oñate in 1598; they called it San Gabriel, and later moved the capital to Santa Fe. Today its population is 1,713. Besides the Guild shop, the eight pueblos also meet here regularly at the headquarters of the Eight Northern Pueblos Council to take concerted action on issues that concern all of them.

Pottery made here is traditionally red or brown, which is also sold in another crafts shop dealing only in San Juan Pueblo–made wares: the O'ke Oweenge. Another traditional San Juan product is hand-woven monkscloth spun on long spindles.

The largest of the eight pueblos, San Juan observes the **Feast of San Juan** about June 24 every year. There is a buffalo dance the day before, and during the feast day a Comanche dance is performed. Other ceremonies are held during the year, including a turtle dance on December 26.

TESUQUE PUEBLO: One of the smallest pueblos is Tesuque, eight miles north of Santa Fe just to the west of U.S. 84, with a population of 288. Jewelry and pottery are made by a few Tesuque women, and shown in their houses here. The sandstone formation called **Camel Rock,** unmistakable from a vantage point on the highway, is part of Tesuque land and marks an Indian-operated campground two miles north of the entrance to the pueblo, also off U.S. 84, where there are 40 sites for camping vehicles, many with full hookups. Another enterprise is Bingo, running from 5 p.m. Monday through Saturday.

A mission church and adobe houses, most dating to the 13th century, surround the plaza here. Photo fee is $3. November 12 is the day of the Harvest Dance for the annual **San Diego Feast Day,** with buffalo, deer, flag, or Comanche dances. For information, call 983-2667.

POJOAQUE PUEBLO: The smallest of the northern eight pueblos is Pojoaque, population 125, on a mesa 16 miles north of Santa Fe just to the east of U.S. 84. There are only ruins remaining of the old pueblo, around which the Indians now live in houses scattered up and down several dirt roads. This pueblo nearly became extinct a couple of generations back but is now coming to life again with a new pueblo organization in its tribal council. Craftspeople produce some pottery, embroidery, beadwork, and silver jewelry for sale to visitors who inquire at the governor's office (tel. 455-2278). December 12 is the day of the **Our Lady of Guadalupe Feast,** with a bow-and-arrow or buffalo dance.

NAMBE PUEBLO: Lying 30 miles north of Santa Fe, Nambe (tel. 455-7752) is reached via U.S. 84 to N.M. 4, then east five miles to the pueblo turnoff at a direction sign. Ranching and farming are the main occupations in this pueblo, where Spanish is spoken widely along with the native Tewa. Near the pueblo at the Nambe Falls recreation area every July 4 there is a **Waterfall Ceremonial** that over a 14-year period made the people money enough to build a new church—it was constructed entirely by Indian workers in 1975. A new pueblo-style headquarters is solar heated. Nambe mica-encrusted pottery and Nambe woven cotton belts are sold in the homes of artisans. The governor's office has information on the craftspeople and on fishing permits in the recreation area. Traditional feast day, **San Francisco Day,** October 4, has the elk dance ceremony.

SAN ILDEFONSO PUEBLO: The black-on-black pottery that is this pueblo's specialty was made famous by the late Maria Martinez, whose family carries on her tradition. An arts-and-crafts center has locally made pottery and jewelry available, and in addition there are several painters in residence here. A museum of Indian art and artifacts is open Monday through Friday from 8 a.m. to 4:30 p.m. With a population of 445, the pueblo is 20 miles northwest of Santa Fe via N.M. 502. The **San Antonio Feast Day** is June 4, the **Harvest Dance** is on September 8, and the pueblo feast day is January 23. Photo fee is $2. For information, call 455-2273.

SANTA CLARA PUEBLO: With a population of 1,217 this is the second largest of the Tewa-speaking pueblos. The people here claim as their own the cliff dwellings and ancient house ruins of the Puye Cliffs about five miles west of the pueblo, where traditionally they once lived. Although they migrated to the Rio Grande in the 13th century, in memory of their former home they return to it during the last week of every July and for two days perform ceremonial dances and offer their wares for sale to visitors. Doors marked with pottery signs mean that visitors are welcome to go in and watch artisans at work. The dances here are some of the few in any pueblos where photography is permitted—for a $5 fee. The pueblo is reached via N.M. 30 just south of Española, 30 miles from Santa Fe. The **Santa Clara Feast Day,** August 12, has corn and harvest dances. For information, call 753-7326.

PICURIS PUEBLO: Reached via N.M. 75 north of Española, this pueblo of 196 people lies about 50 miles north of Santa Fe in a high mountain valley where the Indians have stocked trout ponds and set up a museum for visitors. There is also a picnic area and campground. Mica-laden clay is the base for the Picuris pottery still made by a few women here. The annual **San Lorenzo Feast** goes on August 9 and 10, with traditional ceremonial dances and a footrace. For information, call 587-2519. A year-round fishing season in the pueblo reservoir is open to visitors for fees from $2.50 to $5 daily.

10. RUINS IN THE SANTA FE REGION

Many of the fabulous cliff dwellings, mysterious towers, and apartment complexes of the Anasazi people who disappeared from the Southwest in the 13th century are preserved, and in many places partially restored, as national monuments or state preserves, with a few of them under direct control of Indian reservations. At dozens of sites open to visitors there is the thrill of getting physically close to an ancient people, sometimes climbing up steep ladders to inspect their cave dwellings with their inscriptions and drawings and the soot from their fires still darkening the stone of the ceiling. You may marvel at the skillful stonework of masons who fashioned smooth, flat stone pieces into fine-patterned walls and walkways. Where bits of the wooden beam ends still protrude from over the windows, in the ancient architecture obvious still today in the living pueblos, we are brought back through time to the immediacy of those old lives who knew this same sun and heat and dust that we know here now. The ruins of those communities show us how they were designed to take advantage of the warmth of the sun in winter, yet to protect residents from the heat of the summer middays.

PECOS NATIONAL MONUMENT: When the Coronado expedition arrived at the site here in 1540 they found a pueblo with 2,000 Indians living in it, and Coronado reported back to Spain: "It is feared throughout the land. The people here pride themselves that no one has been able to reduce them." It wasn't until 1591 that the Spanish returned here, when Castaño de Sosa finally occupied the pueblo with mounted men equipped with cannon. His description of the pueblo in that year read: "The houses in this pueblo are in the manner of houseblocks. They have doors to the outside all around, and the houses are back to back. The houses are four and five stories. In the galleries there are no doors to the streets. They go up little ladders that can be pulled up by hand through the hatchways. Every house has three or four apartments so that from top to bottom each house has 15 or 16 rooms. The rooms are well whitewashed. The dress of the men—as it was the cold season—most of them wore a blanket of cotton and a buffalo hide over it. The women dress with a blanket drawn in a knot at the shoulder and a sash the width of a palm at the waist."

By 1620 Franciscan monks had established a mission at the Pecos pueblo and introduced Spanish farming methods. It was destroyed in the 1680 revolt but rebuilt upon the Spaniards' return 12 years after. Other disasters wreaked havoc on the community: a Comanche-led massacre in 1750 and an epidemic of smallpox in 1788.

The early pueblo had 660 rooms and many *kivas,* some of the inner rooms being used for food storage. Traditionally they raised corn, beans, and squash in irrigated fields along the Pecos River, and they also hunted game. By the end of the 18th century the pueblo was fast declining in population and no longer had a resident priest. In 1838 the 20 survivors of the pueblo finally abandoned Pecos and moved west across the Rio Grande to take up life with their relatives at Jemez. The pueblo has been empty since then.

Because the descendants of the Pecos people still live in the Jemez pueblo, their empty home has special significance for them. An official of the National Park Service, which administers the area, comments, "In this sense Pecos has not been abandoned at all. . . . the pueblo and its people have simply parted company."

After a stop at the visitor center for a map of the area, visitors see ruins of the convento where mission fathers lived, a series of cells built around a patio attached to the church. A *kiva* is restored here—you can descend into its dark interior on a ladder; it was built out of the bricks of the original church the Spaniards built, after the Indians took over from them and destroyed it in 1680. Two major mission churches were built here. There remain the foundations of a big 17th-century one and the standing walls of the 18th-century structure that supplanted it. Other partially restored Indian ruins including other *kivas* are to be seen along a half-mile walk that also leads past the north pueblo—vast unexcavated mounds that make you wonder what treasures and artifacts may still lie buried there. It was an even earlier pueblo than the Pecos pueblo, with five-story buildings housing 2,500 people.

Archeological surveys at Pecos still continue to find sites showing facets of the Indians' means of livelihood in prehistoric times. Evidence of terraces and dams and overnight houses at some distance from the community has been unearthed. There is evidence that the site was occupied by one people or another for several thousand years. Among recent digs are some 9th-century pit houses, the first ever found in the Upper Pecos River area—perhaps once used seasonally by their builders as a base for farming here.

Pecos National Monument, 25 miles southeast of Santa Fe, is reached via I-25, with an exit at the Glorieta-Pecos interchange, then via Alt. U.S. 84 to the town of Pecos, then south a mile on N.M. 63 to the park entrance.

BANDELIER NATIONAL MONUMENT: Bandelier is located 46 miles west of Santa Fe via U.S. 84 north of Pojoaque, then N.M. 4 west to the park. The ruins and trailheads are down at the bottom of Frijoles Canyon but **Ponderosa**

Campground is up at the top—it has tentsites, tables, fireplaces, and a dumping station.

The monument was named for the Swiss-American scholar Adolph F. A. Bandelier, who surveyed the ruins here and studied Pueblo Indians in the region in the 1880s. His so-called ethnohistorical novel, *The Delight Makers,* has as its locale Frijoles Canyon, where the author imagined the Indians' life as it was in prehistoric times.

This fabulous wild area of 46 square miles includes a canyon sharply cut through by the Rio de los Frijoles (Bean Creek) that creates an oasis all along its banks in this hot dry land. The canyon slashes through the Pajarito Plateau, which is of geological interest because it is part of a caldera—a saucer-shaped depression resulting from the collapsed summit of a volcano.

Although there are 60 miles of hiking trails in the area, a favorite for backpackers, the ruins are easily accessible on foot from the visitor center along a two-mile stretch of the canyon where they are built up into the walls of tufa—dense volcanic ash. (A fact given out to visitors: A million years ago the volcano spewed out 50 cubic miles of this tufa, enough for a road to the sun.)

The trail leads to groupings of terraced houses where visitors climb in and out of many of the rooms, which were occupied sometime after the Spanish first arrived in New Mexico, even though they did not discover this isolated canyon Shangri-la for years. Guided tours are organized by the National Park Service, although visitors are free to explore the ruins on their own. For information on scheduled programs, call 672-3861. Many visitors get the biggest thrill out of climbing up a series of shaky-looking (but solid) ladders hewn from twisted piñon trunks and branches to the interior of a cave dwelling 140 feet above the canyon floor in the side of the canyon. The trail along the canyon floor, passing as it does beneath bushy cottonwoods along the prettily flowing stream, makes a pleasant walk.

At night around a campfire the park rangers or local Indians talk to groups of visitors about the history, culture, and geology of the ruins, or about Indian legends. On a moonlit evening the guided night walks reveal a different, spooky aspect of the ruins and cave houses, outlined in the two-dimensional chiaroscuro of the thin cold light from the starry sky. Daytimes, there are also nature programs for adults and children in which the unusual variety of fauna and flora is explained. Because of the climatic differences between canyon rim and its stream-irrigated bottom, and the contrast between desert sereness above the lush growth below, many different kinds of life, plant and animal, can all survive within proximity. A small museum at the visitor center shows some artifacts found in the area.

More ruins exist in the backcountry attainable on foot, but backpackers are required to register before setting out to any of them. The gorges of **Alamo Canyon,** the pueblo ruins of **San Miguel and Yapashi,** and **White Rock Canyon** of the Rio Grande, the **Painted Cave** and beaver dams upstream along the Frijoles River are all destinations for hikers. Where the main ruins take only a 45-minute walk and the **ceremonial cave**—the one you climb into via ladders—a hike of two hours, a trip to the **Stone Lions Shrine** takes eight hours, and one to the Painted Cave and the Rio Grande takes two days. The required wilderness permits for backcountry hiking are free of charge.

Eleven miles north of Frijoles Canyon via N.M. 4 in the detached **Tsankawi** section of the park is a high mesa holding an unexcavated ruin of still another ancient pueblo. From here there are great views of the valley of the Rio Grande and the mountains to the east and west. A self-guiding two-mile trail makes a circular route through this ruin, taking about an hour and a half. It follows an ancient trail that has been worn 18 inches into the rock floor in some places over

..e many centuries since the place was first inhabited. Rock carvings from prehistoric times are to be seen along the way.

CHACO CULTURE NATIONAL HISTORIC PARK: These fabulous communities of ruins in isolated Chaco Canyon are reached via a scenic route, 200 miles west of Santa Fe via Bandelier National Monument, by continuing west of Bandelier on N.M. 4 and N.M. 126 to N.M. 44, then turning southwest at Nageez. From this Indian community there is a 26-mile stretch of graded dirt road fine in dry weather but dangerous in rainy weather, not only muddy and slippery but also flooded where arroyos cross it. Inquire at Nageez before leaving the paved highway.

The Park Grounds

Rivalling Mesa Verde National Park in grandeur, Chaco is visited by relatively few people because of its distance from the amenities of modern civilization. It does have a campground with tables, fireplaces, and a water supply, as well as a visitor center open all year. Even before you have had the opportunity to visit the ruins, Chaco Canyon seems to emit an aura of peace and a sort of silent welcome. Somehow you feel you have come to the right place at the right time, although the first impressions of sandy cliffsides in this wide, dry, flat-bottomed cut in the plateau have nothing of the lushness of, say, the riverbanks of cottonwoods back at Bandelier. There is not much growing that is green here— cactuses, yes—but the sense of entering a serene old kingdom is undeniable. Perhaps it is the contrast between a lowering sky permitting magisterially controlled rays of sunlight to beam down just on chosen spots of the dry earth, and the following brilliant fathomless blue of that sunlight-filled sky in all this openness, that makes the special impression. (Remember to bring in some firewood if you're camping—there is none to be had in the canyon.)

Up and down the canyon the various communities stand in their proud ruins, some of them nearly intact enough to make likely squatters' projects should the National Park Service lower its guard a bit. They are all within five or six miles of each other, just near enough to be neighborly, far enough to keep their own independence from one another. The strong sense of a living civilization comes through strangely here in Chaco Canyon even though the residents have been gone for at least 600 years.

A complex road system connecting Chaco with other Anasazi communities, including Mesa Verde 100 miles to the north, is still visible in vestiges in the desert plateau. The communications and irrigation systems were advanced, and held together a civilization that reached out as far as California to the west, Texas to the east, and Mexico to the south. The thousands of people who lived in this mile-wide canyon left behind structures as advanced in style and architecture as any of the Anasazi, and have been the subject of study for more than a century. Of 2,000 sites recorded over this time there are 11 full-size pueblos where hundreds or thousands of people once lived. Of smaller ruins uncovered there are now at least 400. It is as rich an archeological site as we know of in North America, representing the height of prehistoric Indian life.

The earliest inhabitants of the canyon are thought to have lived here 10,000 years ago, nomadic hunters whose spear points have turned up. Various other peoples are traced through their weapons or basket remnants down to the first who settled here, giving up the nomadic life, about A.D. 700. They built the first pueblos of simple one-story adobe houses.

It wasn't until the 11th century A.D. that the big apartment complexes, such as the great 800-room Pueblo Bonito, were built. Some of these ruins are accessible directly from an auto road running up and down the canyon—these include Pueblo Bonito, Chetro Ketl, Pueblo del Arroyo, Hungo Pavi, and Una Vida. None of these involves anything more than a short walk along paved pathways. Others of the ruins take half-day backcountry hiking to reach and return from, and permits, free of charge, must be taken out at the visitor center before departing on any of them. They include Peñasco Blanco, Casa Chiquita, Pueblo Alto, Tsin Kletsin, and Wijiji.

The Pueblo Ruins

Pueblo Bonito, which once rose four stories, has no fewer than 37 *kivas*— ceremonial rooms of the kind still used in the inhabited pueblos elsewhere in the Southwest. **Chetro Ketl** had 500 rooms and 16 *kivas*. The others each had several hundreds of rooms, all built of walls of the thickness of a single stone, held together with mud mortar, but done so skillfully that the heights of even four stories held fast for centuries. Working without metal tools or known mathematics, the masons later supported outside walls with thin veneers of facing stone, the walls tapering as they rose. Another style of masonry, called McElmo, appears in an 11th-century house in **Kin Kletso** ruin, where the walls were built with an inner core of rubble and thick outer veneers of sandstone. Half a dozen masonry styles used at various periods in the 10th to 12th centuries still draw the admiration of architects today.

But it is the sweeping magnificence of this lost and ruined city as seen from 200 feet above on the rim of the canyon that impresses visitors most, the great circular outline of Pueblo Bonito, its many *kivas* forming circles within the great half circle of the community, all of it in the glowing sandstone browns and tans of the land and stone around it. Eventually there were 75 such compact towns all connected with one another in this region of New Mexico. Aerial photos show 300 miles of roads connecting them and the Chaco Canyon pueblos, the longest running 42 miles straight north to Salmon Ruin and Aztec Ruin (also open to visitors, the first a state area, the second a national monument). Settlements were spaced along the roads at travel intervals of one day. They were not simple trails worn into the stone by foot travel, but rather engineered roadways 30 feet wide with a berm of rock to contain the fill; where the road went over flat rock, walls were built along the sides of it. It is this road network that makes scholars believe that Chaco was the center of a unified Anasazi society involving pueblos throughout northwestern New Mexico and beyond.

Chaco Canyon cuts through an expanse of the San Juan Basin that is larger than Massachusetts, a real desert land without trees except for a few planted by the CCC along the arroyo in the monument 50 years ago—cottonwoods that still survive here and there. It is still a puzzle as to why these early people chose this arid place to build some of the most impressive public architecture north of Mexico. Trails up into the cliffsides of the canyon toward the more distant pueblos are marked by cairns, and none is difficult, though the sun in summer gets fearfully hot even at this altitude of 6,200 feet. A quart of water for every two hours on the trail is recommended.

Along the **Pueblo Alto** trail, hikers may be able to discern the alignment of a part of one of those ancient Anasazi roads heading north. Also seen are the **Jackson Stairs,** the most impressive staircase of any of these hair-raising hand- and foothold indentations cut into the sides of the canyon in various places—visitors are *not* permitted to try going up or down it. At one point the trail passes through a great narrow cleft in a vast rock where a breeze constantly wafts through, a cooling spot in summer where—according to the evidence of grinding surfaces and grooves in natural shelves and on the walls—the people liked to grind their cornmeal and sharpen their stone tools.

On the **Peñasco Blanco** trail, a pictograph—a picture painted on a rock wall—of a star is dated by the National Park Service simply by circumstantial evidence as having been put there soon after July 5, 1054, because that was the date of a supernova, the sudden appearance of an especially bright star, being visible in the night sky here in conjunction with a crescent moon, also shown. But a Park Service writer admits, "We don't know for certain how old the rock art is, what it means, or even who did it."

At Pueblo Bonito not far from the roadway are great chunks of sandstone that are the broken remains of **Threatening Rock,** a piece of the cliff that hung over the Anasazi pueblo promising dire results to the apartments below it. The Anasazi tried to keep it from falling on them by propping it up with posts and masonry piles, and by building up its base securely with mud. When the Navajos, who came here long after the Anasazis had disappeared, were asked to explain the remains of these efforts, still visible today, they reported a legend that the older people had brought baskets of white shells and turquoise to the rock as offerings to the spirits to keep it from falling. The Navajos called it "the place where the cliff is propped up," until it did finally fall in, in 1941. There was no turquoise to be found in the rubble, but there were indeed some Anasazi prayer sticks.

Examples of Chaco-made pottery are to be seen in the visitor center. It is of white clay with black geometric design of a stylized sophistication; turquoise ornaments were also made in the canyon and in its dependent pueblos in large quantities from gemstone imported from far away. More than any other area in the Southwest, Chaco was a producer of necklaces, bracelets, and pendants of this coveted blue-green mineral. A stone frog, as a single example, has startling eyes and teeth of turquoise. Many seashell necklaces also attest to the fact that trading was done over great distances from Chaco. Remains of macaws and parrots suggest contact with Mexico.

Una Vida Pueblo, reached by a one-third-mile-long walk from the visitor center, is an unexcavated ruin with walls standing and visible. Some of the rooms were in fact dug out and cleared a quarter century ago, but then were filled in again in 1979. Why were the dozen rooms filled in? A National Park Service writer explains: "The answer involves conservation and preservation. Unexcavated sites remain static, or change very little. The surrounding dirt holds walls stable, preserved by nature. Once exposed, they are susceptible to damage by the weather: rain washes mortar away; wind dislodges mortar; and repeated freezing cracks the stone. Natural stability requires much less maintenance." In effect we do have many unexcavated pueblos as nationally owned property in this part of New Mexico, property safe in the bank, one might say, that will deteriorate hardly at all in the future if left buried. When you see some of these suspicious-looking hills in this flat country you may suspect there's a hidden pueblo underneath. The Park Service would like to keep many of them hidden just this way for whatever the future may hold. In any case there is no possible disappointment to any visitor in the ruins already uncovered at Chaco—one of our truly great American archeological treasures.

Camping is free of charge, and the **visitor center** is open from 8 a.m. to 5 p.m. in summer, to 4 p.m. in winter. Summertime there are free guided tours of Pueblo Bonito daily and of other ruins several times per week, and campfire talks nightly except Monday. For information on times, call 988-6716. The nearest motels are in Farmington, 50 miles north (see Chapter IV, "Taos and Northern New Mexico") and the nearest food shop and gas station at Nageez, 26 miles northeast.

11. OUTDOORS IN THE SANTA FE AREA

Santa Fe's surrounding country is great for outdoors action all year, with 1,000 miles of trails in a national forest starting at its city limits, a ski area overlooking the city, cross-country trails, trout-fishing streams and lakes, hunting areas, and white-water rafting in the wild springtime rapids. There are sailboard enthusiasts and rockhounds and bicyclists, the latter pampered by tours that haul them and their bikes to the tops of the mountains so their treks are all downhill. Since the city is in the middle of a year-round tourist area it is populated with all the necessary sporting-goods outlets for every specialty.

CAMPING: Campgrounds around Santa Fe run the gamut from the primitive mountain hideout to the portable-suburb recreation-vehicle parking-lot with a busy social life, but the tendency is to take advantage of the scenic delights of forest and mountain.

Apache Canyon (tel. 982-1419), 11 miles southeast of Santa Fe on I-25, is reached via exit 294 or 290. A cool aerie at 7,000 feet, it has showers, toilets, complete hookups, a store, playground, laundry, recreation room, picnic tables, and dump station.

Even cooler is the pastoral scene of **Aspen Basin** in Santa Fe National Forest, 15 miles northeast of the city on N.M. 75. Open from May to October, it has 15 units.

Also in the national forest, but in a $5-fee area, is **Black Canyon,** eight miles northeast of Santa Fe on N.M. 475, at 8,400 feet elevation, with 52 units suitable for trailers and a fishing stream. Open May to October.

Owned by the Tesuque Indian Pueblo is **Camel Rock Campground,** on the main highway to Taos (U.S. 84) eight miles north of Santa Fe, with pull-through full hookups for trailers, a laundry, showers, and store.

On the road up to the ski area is **Hyde State Park,** eight miles above the city on Hyde Park Road (N.M. 475) at a height of 8,000 feet. There are shelters, water pumps, tables, fireplaces, toilets, and firewood. It's open year round, at $3 per vehicle.

Ranchero de Santa Fe is one of the KOA chain, 12 miles southeast of Santa Fe on I-25, with a laundromat, recreation room, store, and supply of ice and propane.

Santa Cruz Lake, 40 miles northeast of Santa Fe via N.M. 76 and N.M. 4, has fishing and boating on a reservoir and free camping offered by the Bureau of Land Management, 42 sites, open April to October.

Santa Clara Canyon is 30 miles northwest of Santa Fe via N.M. 30 and N.M. 5. Owned by the Santa Clara Pueblo, it is open April to November for a fee, and there is lake fishing and firewood available.

Villanueva State Park, 40 miles east of Santa Fe off I-25 and south on N.M. 3, is open May to October, with tent and trailer sites, shelters, tables, toilets, hot showers, and a playground, at a fee of $3 per vehicle.

Further information on national forest campgrounds is available from the headquarters of Santa Fe National Forest, 1220 St. Francis Dr., Santa Fe, NM 87501 (tel. 505/988-6940). Information on state parks may be had by calling 827-2726.

HUNTING AND FISHING: Mule deer hunting is good in the Jemez mountains west of Santa Fe and in the Pecos Wilderness of the Santa Fe National Forest, east of the city, during the fall hunting season. State and public lands to the northeast including the Barker, Urraca, and Neblett Wildlife Areas, as well as Carson and Santa Fe National Forest lands in that region, afford public access to seasonal **elk hunting.** To the northwest of the city elk are taken around Mount Taylor and the Jemez Mountains. A few licenses are issued annually by the state for hunting **bighorn sheep,** which stay up in steep cliff country. **Wild turkey** is taken in the uplands, while the fly routes of **geese and ducks** take them near towns to the east of Santa Fe: Watrous, La Cueva, and Las Vegas. Hunters using bow and arrow have separate seasons from those using regular hunting rifles.

Fishermen get their best catches in the spring just as the high mountain ponds and lakes thaw enough for them to get in a cast, for at this time of year the fish are hungry. In late fall the San Juan River is considered a good fishing bet— there is a stretch of it below Navajo Dam two miles long restricted to fly fishing only. Navajo and El Vado Lakes have special seasons for the snagging of kokanee salmon. For most species, in most places, the fishing season begins April 1 and continues through to the end of the year.

For **information on licenses and seasons,** get in touch with the **New Mexico Game & Fish Dept.,** Villagra Bldg., Santa Fe, NM 87503 (tel. 505/827-7911).

HIKING: The **Santa Fe National Forest** has over a million and a half acres in two divisions that are crisscrossed by well-blazed hiking trails. The Pecos Division, east of the Rio Grande, takes in the southern Sangre de Cristo mountains where in the heights the **Pecos Wilderness** soar to over 13,000 feet at Truchas Peak. Great forests of aspen, pine, fir, and spruce cover these slopes and valleys. The Pecos Division is the part next door to Santa Fe, over which the Santa Fe Trail still passes. To the west of the Rio Grande, the **Jemez Mountains** rise to nearly 12,000 feet at Chicoma Peak. Within this area are Indian pueblos, **Bandelier National Monument,** the city of Los Alamos, and certain private lands, but most of the mountains are within the national forest. Among the variety of animals to be seen are hawks and eagles, black bear and elk, mule deer and a few rare Texas white-tailed deer, as well as a few bighorn sheep. There are martens, minks, muskrats, and beavers, as well as many raccoons. Game birds are geese, duck, grouse, quail, pigeon, and mourning dove. Wildlife share the forage in forest lands with cattle owned by about 400 stockmen who pay for permits to use this country as range.

Backpackers admire the beauty and quiet of the 167,000-acre Pecos Wilderness and the 41,000-acre **San Pedro Parks Wilderness,** where visitors are also welcome on horseback. Free permits are required for every hiking party in these areas in order to prevent overuse because, as the Forest Service points out, "Overuse is a matter of equal concern to wilderness travelers and the Forest Service." Rangers will sometimes recommend the more lightly used areas of these parts of the national forests and hikers are usually glad to have the advice.

One delight in hiking in the Santa Fe area is the great variety of flora and fauna due to the fact that five of seven existing biological zones exist within a 40-mile area between low and high points: the **Rio Grande Gorge** at 6,000 feet, and **Baldy Peak** at over 13,000 feet. At low elevations the climate is traditionally desert-like, hot and sandy with growths of yucca, cholla, and cactus. At the higher elevations—where even in summer there may be sleet coming down—pine, spruce, aspen, and firs make the thick, dark-green cover that looks so soft and upholstered from far off.

The **Santa Fe Sierra Club** organizes day hikes and overnight backpack trips. Information is available from their headquarters at 1709 Paseo de Peralta (tel. 983-2703).

An easy way to sample the delights of mountain hiking near the city is a 2½-hour walk on a trail that starts eight miles north of the city from a point on Hyde Park Road. The beginning of this trail—called the **Bear Wallow–Winsor–Borrego Triangle**—leaves the roadside at the point where a sign reads: "Enter Santa Fe National Forest/Leaving Hyde State Park." The Borrego Trail leads to the Bear Wallow Trail, all clearly marked, to take you alongside a trout stream under a thick cover of pine and fir. Farther on you encounter signs into the Winsor Trail, which you follow back to the Borrego Trail once again.

This area may be crowded in summer, but the wilderness areas are much less frequented. To really get away from it all, a drive across the Rio Grande Valley to the **San Pedro Wilderness** in the Jemez range is said to be the answer—many square miles of wild country and very few other people around. Hikes may be made out of **Bandelier National Monument** to archeological sites over well marked trails.

For maps showing **trails in the national forests,** apply to the headquarters at 1220 St. Francis Dr., Santa Fe, NM 87501 (tel. 505/988-6940).

SKIING: The **Santa Fe Ski Area,** opened in 1947, is up in the Sangre de Cristo range in the Santa Fe National Forest only 16 miles from the center of the city, and operates an average of 140 days a year, opening at Thanksgiving and continuing to around Eastertime, daily from 9 a.m. to 4 p.m. The best conditions, however, don't ordinarily develop until after the first of the year. Santa Fe is renowned for its good springtime skiing that brings out sports people dressed in shorts and bikinis. Unless this practice is carried out with gradually increasing exposure to the sun, however, there is a real danger of severe sunburn.

The base of the area lies at an altitude of 10,340 feet, rising 1,660 feet to the top. Equipment includes one triple- and three double-chair lifts, two Poma lifts, and a rope tow, all of which move as many as 6,400 skiers hourly on busy weekends. Two-thirds of the runs are intended for beginners and intermediates, with the rest reserved for the experts. Forty instructors are on the staff of a ski school providing daily lessons for adults and kids of various levels and ages. A ski shop rents boots, skis, and poles at $12 daily. Daily lift rates are $24 for adults, $15 for children.

A cafeteria at the base, La Casa, provides soups, sandwiches, and a daily lunch special. Halfway up the mountain a more elaborate hostelry called the **Sierra Lodge** has a full dinner menu and maintains the favorite after-ski meeting place, a full-service Red Chair Bar. A picnic room and sundeck are available for skiers who bring their own pack lunches.

You can get **information on skiing conditions** by calling 982-4429, or for a taped report, 24 hours daily, 983-9155.

Other Skiing Areas

Below the ski area, hiking trails leading into the national forest woodlands make ideal cross-country ski trails. The **Borrega Trail** loop, popular with hikers in warmer months, is one of these. It departs from a point on the Hyde Park Road, leading up to Santa Fe Ski Area, at the border between state park and national forest land. A mile below the ski area, at a picnic area, another excellent cross-country route, the **Aspen Vista Trail,** leads a somewhat tough six miles uphill to Tesuque Peak, but there is a marvelous view of the valley below you, and think of that free, easily sloping downhill ride all the way back to your starting point. Skiers also go into the **Pecos Wilderness** for overnight winter camping, but they must take out permits with the Forest Service.

Cross-country is also good over in the **Jemez Mountains,** to the west of the city, with trails generally covering more level terrain than up in the Sangre de Cristos. Roads in **Del Norte and Peralta Canyons** are popular with these ski-walkers, and **Graduation Flats,** near Los Alamos, is another good area.

For information on cross-country skiing, including groups planning overnight treks, get in touch with the **New Mexico Ski Touring Club** in Albuquerque (tel. 505/255-1954).

Another downhill ski area within easy reach of Santa Fe is **Pajarito,** five miles west of Los Alamos, with 26 runs and an hourly lift capacity of 4,000 skiers, on four chair lifts. It is open Wednesday and weekends from 9 a.m. to 4 p.m., with lift rates of $20 for adults, $14 for children. Equipment rental is $12. For information, call 662-5595.

WHITE-WATER RAFTING: A "wild and scenic river" is the designation of the Rio Grande in northern New Mexico, reaching south from the heights in Colorado, and one stretch of this, called the **Taos Box,** consists of 16 miles of beautiful, rollicking, terrifying rapids where white-water buffs love to test their mettle. In 1983 at a peak of high waters after a spring thaw, a whole new rapid was created at the junction of Taos Creek with the river; the creek poured in with such mighty force it pulled down the cliffsides into the flow. One six-mile stretch of the Rio Grande is called the "race course," and is the scene of annual raft races every spring. Protected by **Rio Grande Gorge State Park,** accessible via U.S. 84 and N.M. 68, 50 miles north of Santa Fe, the river is probably best approached by visitors on one of the commercially organized raft runs or float trips. Another stretch of the river is managed by the Bureau of Land Management of the federal government. Information on the state of the river may be had from its office in Taos (tel. 758-8851).

Among outfitters organizing white-water trips, notable is **Rio Bravo River Tours,** 1412 Cerrillos Rd., Santa Fe (tel. 988-1153, or toll free 800/451-0708), which has day trips through the Taos Box during the spring and early summer runoff. Rafters float from the launch site in the early morning as far as Manby Hot Springs for a lunch break and a bath in the springs. After lunch comes a 15-mile stretch through to the newly formed Sunset Rapid at Taos Junction. This trip costs $60 weekdays, $65 weekends, lunch included. A half-day trip puts in near the village of Pilar and runs through the "race course" noted above, at $25 per person, $30 on weekends.

Another white-water outfit in Santa Fe is the **Southwest Wilderness Center,** P.O. Box 2840, Santa Fe, NM 87501 (tel. 982-3126, or toll free 800/DE-TOURS). Its director says, "We believe participation adds to your trip and whether it be teaching you to paddle raft or introducing you to the natural and human history of the Southwest, our guides add that extra dimension." The one-day Rio Grande Gorge trip runs from April through October (but telephone ahead to assure yourself of any real white water running in mid and late summer). The eight-hour trip, departing at 8:30 a.m., costs $55, including lunch. A half-day trip through the "race course" costs $35.

BICYCLING: Weekend training rides are organized by the **Sangre de Cristo Cycling Club** at two locations of a bike shop called Pedal Power, one at 612 Agua Fria (tel. 983-8724) and the other at 1331 Cerrillos Rd. (tel. 982-0664).

ROCKHOUNDS: A dry arroyo may be a likely hunting ground for mineral lovers around Santa Fe or elsewhere in New Mexico, which has recorded finds of 440 different minerals, more than any other state except California. A destination of special interest to these buffs is an area now owned by the University of New Mexico about four miles west of Picuris pueblo north of Santa Fe, where there are two mineral mines open to visitors. These are the **Harding Pegmatite Mine** and the **Iceland Spar Mine.** A road heading south from N.M. 75 leads to a parking lot near the Harding mine, from which point visitors may take a self-guided tour of pits, dumps, and quarry. The Spar mine lies nearby.

The mines have been a source of lepidolite, a transparent mica with various commercial applications; and microlite, a radioactive mineral. Much beryl for the strengthening of copper was once taken from this source as well. Calcite from the other mine produced some of the largest crystals ever seen. Aquamarine, a form of beryl, is another mineral found here, and there is an abundance of rose muscovite, a blue-green fluorescent apatite, and the semiprecious feldspar and spodumene. Nearby in **Hondo Canyon** there is yellowish staurolite crystal available in streambed gravel, some in inch-thick chunks.

12. TRIPS OUT OF SANTA FE

Besides all the ruins and natural scenic attractions of mountain, forest, canyon, and lake throughout the northern New Mexico country, there are villages and towns within easy reach of Santa Fe that make likely destinations for the visitor. There is the atomic city of Los Alamos, with its impressive, perhaps daunting, museum of death-dealing weapons; there is the Old West atmosphere of Las Vegas (the New Mexico one, not the gamblers' one); there are the tiny ghost towns that are attracting enough permanent residents to lose their licenses as ghost towns—almost. Tiny mountain ridge villages still are home to weavers of the old traditional Hispanic-patterned woolen rugs and wall hangings made with an art apart from that of the Indians but somehow complementing it, on horizontal looms more familiar to non-Indians.

MOUNTAIN VILLAGES: From Santa Fe, drive north on U.S. 84 about 15 miles to the junction of N.M. 4 at Pojoaque, then take N.M. 4 northeast toward **Chimayo,** the first stop on the so-called Mountain Road, or King's Road, to Taos. Chimayo is a rustic village famous for its weavers and its sanctuary. The Ortega family, still active here, brought the weaving tradition from Spain when they settled in the valley in 1692, and today hand-loomed rugs, blankets, and garments of all kinds are in demand by lovers of high-quality woolens and strong original design.

Visitors are welcome to watch the weavers at work on half a dozen looms in **Ortega's Weaving Shop,** where blankets decorate the walls and, folded, fill shelves. Other similar establishments where the weavers work on the premises in Chimayo are the **Chimayo Trading Post** and **Trujillo's.**

A small-time Lourdes has become the vocation of the locally famed **Santuario de Chimayo,** dating from 1816. It contains miraculous mud that believers rub upon themselves to be cured of every kind of illness, and there are scores of discarded crutches displayed that supposedly show the powers of this mud. During Holy Week there is a pilgrimage of people flowing into Chimayo hoping for cures. Just left of the altar transept in a small separate room is a two-foot hole in the dirt floor from which the miraculous mud is scooped out. Originally a spring believed by the local Indians to have healing powers, when it dried up people kept hoping for good results by daubing a bit of the mud upon themselves, and the tradition continues.

The highways N.M. 4 and N.M. 76 join in Chimayo, and the High Road rises into the foothills of the Sangre de Cristos in a northeasterly direction to other villages that rival in their spectacular mountain sites the perched villages of southern France and Italy. **Truchas** is the highest of these, at 8,000 feet, an adobe village built like many of these isolated communities in a fortress design, houses joined around a square for protection from the outside, with grazing and cropland stretching off into the abrupt rise or fall of the mountain slopes. Sheep are a major product for the wool they provide the weavers along these crests, and there is a short growing season for hay and other crops. Toward the end of summer you see on nearly every housefront a string of bright-red chiles hung there as if in decoration. These are called *ristras,* and are outside to permit the peppers to dry out for preservation. Later in the year they darken to a rich maroon.

From these heights the highway descends through a forest to the next village, **Las Trampas** (The Traps), so named because this was originally famous beaver-trapping country. The church here, begun in 1760, is dedicated to the 12 Apostles, and the legend is that only 12 workmen were allowed to build it—it took them 20 years. Next up the road is **Peñasco,** still another alpine site of the kind that draws many artists to this string of villages, where they paint many of the pastoral scenes so frequently seen in the works sold in galleries down in Santa Fe or Taos. The highway gives a visitor the pleasure of finding a separate world not quite believable, with a horizon outlined in snowy peaks and rolling farmland below of a richness of green that makes you want to touch it, walk in it. There was a sign along the highway up here in Spanish that touched the feeling of the people here: *Donde hay fe, hay paz. Donde hay paz, hay amor. Donde hay amor, hay Díos. Donde hay Díos, no falta nada.* —"Where there is faith, there is peace. Where there is peace, there is love. Where there is love, there is God. Where there is God, nothing is lacking."

Travelers may continue north via routes N.M. 3 and 68 to Taos, or make a leisurely return trip with other stops on the way back to Santa Fe. One of these might be at **Cordova,** on a side road off the highway a couple of miles between Truchas and Chimayo, a tiny community made famous by its woodcarvers, particularly the **George Lopez** family. They produce both religious and popular or comic wooden figures. A likely topper to a mountain-village tour is dinner at the **Rancho de Chimayo** (tel. 351-4444), which has a dining room in an old adobe ranch house that serves some of the best New Mexico–style dishes in this part of the state. Warmed by a fire in winter, it is comfortably cool inside in summer. Specialties are corn tortillas of beef, chicken, or pork, called flautas, or the house-style carne asada (broiled steak strips with refried beans). Dinners run $8 to $13, and there is a bar and a small gift shop.

Lodging
The **Hacienda Rancho de Chimayo** (tel. 505/351-2222) is a recently re-stored historic adobe ranch house, the family home of Epifanio and Adelaida Jaramillo, who established the family still operating the adjoining restaurant and now the bed-and-breakfast inn. The Jaramillo family has been living here in Chimayo since the 1700s. Seven guest rooms open onto a courtyard. Each room is furnished with Victorian antiques and has both private bath and separate sitting area. Pastry, fresh fruit, juice, and coffee are served for breakfast. Rates are $72 double.

Nearer the main highway between Santa Fe and Taos (N.M. 68) is a remarkable bed-and-breakfast lodge called **Chinguague Compound,** P.O. Box 1118, San Juan Pueblo, NM 87566 (tel. 505/852-2194), situated at the outskirts of the pueblo two miles from the highway, on the bank of the Rio Grande. Looming to the east are the Sangre de Cristo mountains and to the west the Jemez range. Cottonwood trees shade a compound of old adobe houses, three of them available for guests. One has two bedrooms with private baths and a living room, dining room, and kitchen; another has a double bedroom, living room, and kitchen; a third, a bedroom and kitchen. A vineyard and an apple orchard grow outside the windows, and there is fishing and birdwatching along the river. Rates for doubles run $55 to $70, with a 10% increase in the winter season.

A bargain bed-and-breakfast accommodation in a ten-room adobe house can be had at **La Puebla House,** N.M. 3, Española, NM 87532 (tel. 505/753-3981), on a quiet side road a mile from the highway to Chimayo. Guests enjoy the living area with its heavy beamed ceiling, small library, tiled floor, and easy chairs. In the cool months there's a fire in the fireplace. The rate with breakfast is $35 for two, $20 single.

LOS ALAMOS: Perched high in the Jemez Mountains 35 miles northwest of Santa Fe, via U.S. 84 north and N.M. 4 west, Los Alamos is of course famous first of all as the site of **Los Alamos National Laboratory,** where in 1943 a group of scientists secretly began the development of the atomic bomb. The laboratory continues its atomic research, while the **Bradbury Science Museum** shows visitors replicas of those first atom bombs and much other material relating to the development of our atomic age. The laboratory is presently involved in research in nuclear medicine, fiber optics, lasers; the Bradbury Museum provides its show window to the public.

The **Puye Cliff Dwellings,** 25 miles north of Los Alamos, are reached via N.M. 4 and 30 north and then N.M. 5 west to the site, part of the Santa Clara Pueblo reservation (admission is $4). High on a nearly featureless plateau, the volcanic stone rises in a soft tan façade 200 feet high into which the Anasazi found niches to build their masonry houses that could be reached only by ladder. Down below are remains of a pueblo—walls three to four feet high where visitors may walk from room to room. Available year around on Tuesday and Thursday is a guided tour, pueblo feast, and dance performance package at $20 per person, starting at 9:45 a.m. at the Puye Cliffs Harvey House. After touring the ruins, visitors share a feast with Santa Clara pueblo senior citizens. There is a sale of arts and crafts, followed by a dance performance. The pueblo telephone is 753-7326. A couple of miles beyond the cliff dwellings, the pueblo has a sylvan setting for a picnic and recreation area under a stand of cottonwoods along a mountain stream, where visitors are welcome ($4 fee).

Back in Los Alamos, the focal point for cultural events is the old **Ranch School,** built in 1911, which somehow in this atomic environment seems a long time ago—it was built in the adobe style by the architect of the renowned La Fonda Inn back in Santa Fe. A **historical museum** has artifacts of the history of the area, including some archeological specimens; and the **Fuller Lodge Art Center** displays the work of area artists.

The **Valle Grande** is a fabulous sight for travelers visiting the Los Alamos area. Beyond the entrance to Bandelier National Monument driving west on N.M. 4 you approach the edge of the world's largest volcanic caldera, a vast, sunken green meadow of 175 square miles that covers what is left of a great volcano that erupted a million years in the past.

Also within easy reach of Los Alamos, via N.M. 4, 30, and 5 to U.S. 84 north to a point just beyond the village of Abiquiu, is the **Ghost Ranch Living Museum,** operated by the U.S. Dept. of Agriculture and open seven days a week, 8 a.m. to 6 p.m. from May to September, to 4:30 p.m. (closed Monday) from October to April. The wide-open area provides unique glimpses of animal life in natural habitat: colonies of prairie dogs, running red foxes, glowering owls, pumas, bobcats, badgers, raccoons, and even skunks occupy their separate compounds. Antelope and mule deer graze while dozens of species of birds dart around casually overhead. Dedicated to an appreciation in the public mind of environmental problems, the museum also has planted a "miniature national forest" to illustrate conservation techniques. For information on special programs, call 685-4312.

Food and Lodging

Pleasantest lodgings in Los Alamos are at the modern **Los Alamos Inn,** 2201 Trinity Dr., Los Alamos, NM 87544 (tel. 505/662-7211), offering spacious paneled bedrooms with comfortable sofas and leather-upholstered armchairs, and the warm colors of Indian-blanket wall hangings. The 105 rooms are priced from $46 to $54 for doubles, and there is an outdoor pool, a lounge, and a restaurant serving three meals daily.

Hilltop House, at Trinity and Central Streets, Los Alamos, NM 87544 (tel. 505/662-2441), offers mountain views from its quite spectacular three-story-ceilinged dining room decorated in stained-glass windows and lampshades in a grand and spacious room. Kitchenettes are available in some of the 85 rooms, and there is a gas station and convenience store within the complex. A flyer advertising the Loft Lounge suggests that you have a cocktail "while drinking in the beauty of the piñon and juniper-studded mesas and mountain ranges." Doubles rent at $52 to $56, and suites run $125.

GHOST TOWNS ON THE TURQUOISE TRAIL: Following the Turquoise Trail (N.M. 14), the "back way" between Santa Fe and Albuquerque, is an easy way to visit some authentic ghost towns. Even though the famous turquoise, gold, silver, and coal mines are closed, travelers in these dry, cactusy foothills can still sense the rip-roaring life of a century ago—and even the shades of those Spanish conquistadores who searched for fabled cities here.

To reach the three ghost towns of Cerrillos, Madrid, and Golden, all south of Santa Fe, take the La Cienega exit off I-25.

Cerrillos

Cerrillos is in a fabled turquoise-mining area dating back into mysterious prehistory. This semiprecious stone, known in the Old World since 4,000 B.C., got its name from the French for "Turkish." In Mexico it was sacred to the Aztec royal house and was forbidden to commoners; it was believed to have an affinity to its owner, to grow pale in prophecy of a coming misfortune, or to glow richly with its wearer's good health. A visitor might still find a bit of raw turquoise—called chalchuite by the Aztecs—in the tailings of an ancient pit mine.

The Spanish worked these mines, using local Indian slave labor, until 1680 when a rockfall killed 30 of the miners. When the Spanish tried to replace the dead with other slaves there resulted a famous Indian uprising in which the Spanish were driven out of the region, south to El Paso. The ghosts of those killed miners are thought still to be lurking around that vast rocky ore pit.

Although the miners have gone, a few shopkeepers, lovers of tranquility, and artists have moved in. But in spite of the general store and an old-style western tavern, Cerrillos does keep that untroubled serenity peculiar to a ghost town. In fact a continual subject of talk in the **Cerrillos Bar** is just that: When does a ghost town stop being a ghost town? How many—or how few—residents may it reasonably have? The ornate Victorian bar, incidentally, is part of the original Tiffany Saloon, founded by the New York jewelry family.

Bearded ranchers in ten-gallon hats will be glad to discuss the ghost-town question with you, or shoot a game of billiards. One of the cowboys buys cigarette papers to roll his own out of Edgeworth tobacco. The walls have amateur paintings of New Mexico barns and ranch houses, all for sale. Next door, the **general store** offers flea-market items, antiques, and—in case you missed the free stuff out there in the desert—some old turquoise.

Cerrillos once had eight daily newspapers, several hotels, and two dozen saloons, serving miners from 30 mines, but today only the Palace Hotel stands, in ruins, used only as a stable for llamas that go on backcountry pack trips. A venerable adobe house called **Casa Grande** shelters a trading post. During the last gold and silver boom here in 1879, when American settlers rediscovered old Spanish and Indian mines, a freshly established newspaper warned newcomers of the housing shortage: "Bring a tent. If this is not possible, then bring along wagon sheets, canvas, table covers, door mats, gunny sacks, umbrellas, with which to improvise a tent-shack or tepee in which to live until you can make a dugout or build a house. There are families here living in coke ovens. Others have nothing but a house lot."

Madrid

When the precious metals petered out, there was still coal: the Turquoise Trail towns survived by supplying fuel to locomotives of the Santa Fe Railroad until the 1950s, when the railroad converted to diesel fuel. Three miles down the road from Cerrillos is Madrid, which used to produce 100,000 tons of coal a year. Pronounced with the accent on the first syllable, Madrid was reborn a dozen years ago by an influx of artists and craftspeople who liked the idea of paying no rent—a situation, alas, since changed. A number of shops sell old clothes and old housewares.

The **Coal Mine Museum** invites visitors to go down into a real mine, saved from the abandoning of the town in 1956. The old mine offices, steam engines, machines, and tools are shown. It's called a "living" museum because blacksmiths, metalworkers, and leather workers ply their trades here in restoring parts and tools found in the mine.

In Madrid in 1919 a new, idealistic mine owner named Huber transformed a gloomy scene into a showcase village with a new recreation center, hotel, hospital, school, church, post office, department store, drugstore, auto showroom, beauty shop, fire station, dental office, tennis and basketball courts, golf course, shooting range, a brass band, and a Christmas light show that drew early transcontinental planes to detour over the town for a look. But the town emptied when the mine closed, and in 1976 the owner's son sold everything at auction: tipple, breaker, tavern, church, store, houses, roads—the lot. A handful of diehards bought property and stayed on.

Today the **Mine Shaft Tavern** continues its lively career under the ownership of Hank and Edie Salkeld, who provide good western food and western-style music. They have also added the **Madrid Opera House,** claimed the only such establishment on earth with a built-in steam locomotive on its stage (the structure was an engine repair shed; the balcony is made of railroad track).

Golden

Golden, the third of these towns, lies 11 miles south of Madrid. Its sagging houses with their missing boards, and the wind whistling through the broken eaves, make a purist's ghost town. There is a general store open though, as well as a bottle seller's "glass garden." Nearby are ruins of an Indian pueblo called **Paako,** abandoned around 1670. Such communities of mud huts were all the Spaniards ever found on their avid quests for the fabled Seven Golden Cities of Cibola—fictitious places the Indians told them about. At night it is said one may hear the clanking of Spanish armor as the ghosts of those luckless adventurers march toward their false dreams.

LAS VEGAS: Once known as the "gateway to New Mexico," this pleasant town of 16,000 people hit a period of great prosperity a century ago when the rail line came through to supplant the Santa Fe Trail. A booming frontier town busy shipping cattle from millions of acres of surrounding ranchland, Las Vegas put up scores of fancy Queen Anne and Victorian-style houses and hotels that remain today as a visual entry to that lavish era. The town's earlier history, going back to the first Spanish visits in the 16th century, is also seen in adobe architecture still standing alongside the ornate structures of the late 1800s. The town, 70 miles west of Santa Fe, has 87 registered historic sites that make it absolutely worth a trip from any direction. There are few places in the West with a better preserved collection of Territorial-style buildings. The **Las Vegas Chamber of Com-**

merce, at 727 Grand Ave. (tel. 425-8631), provides a map to follow on a self-guided tour of these historic points of interest.

Sights in Town

You can begin next door at the **Rough Riders Memorial and City Museum** (tel. 425-8726), which celebrates Teddy Roosevelt's Spanish-American War campaigners, 40% of whom came from Las Vegas. After passing some faint Santa Fe Trail ruts beloved of pioneer wagon buffs, you will (if you follow the map) arrive at the 1898 **Castaneda Hotel**, now being restored—the lounge is open. It was originally a railroad hotel. In the Plaza–Bridge Street historic district most of the notable structures can be found. The 1879 **Stern and Nahm Building** has cast-iron columns and pressed and folded sheet-metal ornaments above. Decorative brickwork adorns the 1895 **Winternitz Block.** The Italianate commercial style is exemplified in the fancy arched windows of the **Anicito Baca Building,** modeled after Italian palazzos. The **E. Romero Hose and Fire Company,** put up in brick in 1909, has banded piers capped by pressed-metal capitals with dentils in a strange neoclassical architecture.

The 1888 **Hedgcock Building** has arched window hoods like those of the Baca building, and has served both as police station and jail as well as for a shoe factory and a store. Presently it is the home of the Citizens' Committee for Historic Preservation. The **First National Bank** occupied one of the several mass-produced cast-iron-façade structures built in the city during the Territorial era, this one dating from 1880. Brick embellishes the façade only of the **Courtroom Building** of 1885, which has inner walls of cheaper local stone and arched windows that originated with the local mason who made them. Two **Veeder Buildings,** the first of 1880 and the one next to it added in 1895, show the love of the flamboyant Italianate architecture of the time. The brickwork decoration done with local inspiration has a Moorish flavor.

The **Plaza Hotel** gave the town the finest hotel in the New Mexico Territory back in 1881. Its three-story façade topped with a fancy broken pediment decoration was the town's pride and joy, and it has been happily restored recently (see below). The **Charles Ilfeld Building** began as a one-story adobe store in 1867, grew to two stories in 1882, and finally reached three stories with an Italianate façade in 1890. The **Louis Ilfeld Building,** nearby, shows the classic architecture coming into favor at the turn of the century in a storefront now serving as a bookstore. The only building on the Plaza earlier than the Mexican-American War of 1846, which made the territory a U.S. possession, is the **Dice Apartments,** with a one-story front that was originally of adobe but is now covered with concrete. The other adobe on the Plaza has also been stuccoed: it is **Our Lady of Sorrows Parish Hall,** which sports a curve-topped façade described by the Preservation people as "a piece of folk picturesqueness." The last new building on the Plaza is the **Romero Building** of 1919, in a red-tiled California Revival style.

Nearby Sights and Activities

Now serving as a college, the famed **Montezuma Hotel** is three miles out of the center of town on N.M. 65. Its site has been famous for its curative hot springs from early history, and there are legends that Aztecs journeyed here from Mexico in prehistoric times. Once a luxurious resort with 172 rooms, it still makes a fascinating visit. The springs are open to visitors—for information, call the Arts and Recreation Program (tel. 454-1401).

Annual events include **Cinco de Mayo,** Mexican independence day on May 5, with festivities in which everybody joins the local Hispanics, including local Indians; a **Fourth of July** parade, picnic, and night fireworks; a **rodeo** in mid-August, and **arts-and-crafts fairs** in mid-October and mid-December.

Three **ghost towns**—La Liendre, Loma Parda, and Watrous—lie about 25 miles from the town. La Liendre is southeast via N.M. 104 and 67; Loma Parda and Watrous are to the northwest via I-25 and N.M. 477 and 161. The **Las Vegas National Wildlife Refuge** has 8,000 acres for nesting waterfowl. It is open daily from 8 a.m. to 4:30 p.m., five miles east of town via N.M. 104 and 281.

Storrie Lake State Park is five miles north of town via N.M. 3, with campsites on the lake, a popular spot for boating and fishing. Thirty miles north is the beautiful and isolated **Morphy Lake State Park,** reached via N.M. 3 to Mora and a four-mile dirt road south to the park, where the gem-like setting of the pretty lake is formed by a basin of pine forest. There is primitive camping and trout fishing. Also out of Mora, via N.M. 38, 18 miles to the north, is another delight for lovers of out-of-the-way beauty, **Coyote Creek State Park,** with campsites beside a stream dotted with beaver ponds, where the fishing is good and well-marked hiking trails lead out for a day or a week's excursion.

Food and Lodging

Accommodations in Las Vegas include one you should stop in to see no matter where you are staying, the restored **Plaza Hotel,** on the Plaza, Las Vegas, NM 87701 (tel. 505/425-3591). The stately old hostelry has a fascinating history, a good lounge as well, with a restaurant, pool, tennis, and saunas also available to guests. The hotel's front windows look out on the center of Las Vegas life, the Plaza, where in 1846 a ceremony marked the takeover of New Mexico by the U.S.A. It was built in the days when western towns, newly connected with the East by railroad lines, vied with one another in constructing fancy "railroad hotels," as they were known. This one was erected by a group of businessmen under the leadership of Benigno Romero, styling themselves the Plaza Hotel Company, just over a century ago. The result was the finest hostelry in the New Mexico Territory. Then in 1983 another local group, called the Plaza Associates, completely restored the inn to its former grandeur.

Downstairs, the lobby and parlor are framed by stately walnut staircases, and the adjoining dining room has restored original stencilling on the walls. On the second and third floors are two-room suites, adjoining rooms, and octagon rooms that overlook the conservatory downstairs. The rooms open onto spacious hallways that have casual seating areas, all in the original century-past architectural style. Many rooms have a view of the Plaza. In the lounge and at the piano in the lobby there is often live music in the evenings. Rates for double rooms are $50 to $55; suites, $70.

You'll find good modern rooms at reasonable prices at the **Regal Motel,** 1809 N. Grand Ave., Las Vegas, NM 87701 (tel. 505/454-1456, or toll free 800/528-1234). Cable television is available in all 50 units; rates are $34 double.

Besides the fanciest place in town, the continental-style dining room of the Plaza Hotel, a good "home-style American" eating place is the **Hillcrest,** 1106 Grand Ave. (tel. 425-7211), which also offers some New Mexico specialties on its menu, as well as full bar service daily.

CHAPTER IV

TAOS AND NORTHERN NEW MEXICO

□ □ □

Taos is one of those gem-like little towns where the local regard for traditional architecture, combined with surrounding natural beauty, has drawn the eye of artists. For nearly a century painters, graphic artists, and sculptors have made Taos an art center, many of them settling here to form a sort of informal colony. It is one of the very oldest American towns—the Tiwa Indians living in the traditional apartment complexes in Taos Pueblo nearby have been in residence for 1,000 years at least. The village itself was settled by the Spanish in 1617.

Life in Taos moves in and out of the Plaza, around and around the Plaza, just like the life in old villages in Spain and Mexico. Although the population is only a little over 3,000, the summertime scene is one of crowded sidewalks, shops, and restaurants, with a never-ending traffic jam on the main road through town (Pueblo Road), for Taos has become a major tourist attraction in the Southwest.

Its 6,000-foot altitude and dry climate give Taos sharp clear air that is mild in summer and invigorating in winter—especially for skiers who for the past few years have been flocking to the Taos area in increasing numbers to take to the slopes at five local ski-lift and resort operations. The winter season in Taos is in fact becoming nearly as busy as the summertime.

Taos began as the northernmost outpost of the Spanish empire based in Mexico, and later became a trading center where the so-called Mountain Men who trapped for furs in the wilds came to trade their goods with dealers arriving from the east via the Santa Fe Trail. Plains Indians, even though they sometimes attacked the New Mexico Indians in their pueblos, also attended the market festivals—under a temporary truce set up during the fair.

Spanish and Mexican rule ended in 1846 when the U.S. took charge of the New Mexico Territory. During the Civil War, local Confederate sympathizers tore down the U.S. flag in Taos, but Union patriots, including resident army officer Kit Carson, nailed another to the tallest pine tree in town and guarded it night and day. In memory of this exploit the flag in Taos still officially flies over the town 24 hours a day.

The town's international renown as an art center had its start at the turn of the century when, as legend has it, two young artists on a sketching tour through the Rockies had a wheel break on their horse-drawn buggy just outside Taos. The two, Ernest Blumenschein and Bert Phillips, took the wheel in for repairs, and were captured by the beauty of the Sangre de Cristo mountains as a background to the adobe outlines of the Indian pueblo and the Spanish houses and churches, all blending with the earth around. Eventually they settled in Taos and with other newcomers, also artists, founded the Taos Society of Artists in 1912. Today there are some 80 galleries in Taos showing mostly the work of the several hundred artists and craftspeople residing here.

The art colony has also encouraged serious interest in oldtime Indian and Spanish crafts, examples of which are displayed in two notable museums, the **Harwood Foundation** and the **Millicent Rogers Memorial.** The paintings, ceramics, furniture, and other crafts of early natives and settlers carry the essence of the spirit of the Southwest; they should not be missed. There are summer schools, seminars, and workshops in arts and crafts too; one school occupies the former residence of Mabel Dodge Luhan, the grande dame of the Taos art colony who brought D. H. Lawrence to live here in the '20s.

Not surprisingly it is art that animates the festivals in Taos that draw the biggest crowds—a spring affair the last week of May and a somewhat more serious **Arts Festival Week** the first week of October. The Plaza and adjoining streets are lined with the stands of artists and craftspeople. Crafts are made and displayed for sale also, year around, at **Taos Pueblo,** where ceremonial dances, open to the public, are held several times a year. The most important is the Feast of San Geronimo in late September.

Taos has an annual balloon rally in late October, a Mexican-style rodeo and fiesta in July, and a county fair in August. Openings of art exhibits occur all year and make a favorite kind of party for Taoseños and visitors too. In summer there are chamber-music concerts and plays produced by a professional repertory company. Hotel lounges and clubs book local music groups of all persuasions as well as an occasional touring band or singer.

Outside Taos are vast expanses of national forest land reaching up into the mountains, having many miles of riding and hiking trails, numerous campgrounds, and streams and lakes for fishing—especially for trout. The Rio Grande, a fishermen's favorite in the region, has cut a sharp-sided canyon not far from Taos, accessible by road into a state park. White-water raft trips are made through the "box" of this gorge.

There are **ghost towns** in the area too, and some tiny villages with early Spanish churches in traditional adobe that hold treasures in altar paintings and murals within them. Spanish-American weavers, following a technique different from that of the Indians, still ply their trade in mountaintop workshops. The

Taos area has also preserved cooking traditions that originated in Spain and Mexico but have been modified over the centuries to become a unique cuisine of New Mexico. Many restaurants have *ristras* hanging on their walls—bunches of dried red peppers—and serve tostadas with fiery chile sauce and sopaipillas with honey: a deep-fried pastry.

Taos vies with Santa Fe as a center of restored historical structures that keep for us the sense of the changing centuries in New Mexico and the Southwest. There is Kit Carson's House, Governor Bent's House (the first U.S. Territorial governor, who was assassinated here), the hacienda of an early mayor named Antonio Martinez. In the nearby village of Ranchos de Taos stands a Franciscan church some 275 years old. Artists' homes—those of the founders of the present colony—are in several instances opened to the public as museums and galleries. Since the paintings and other graphic productions in Taos have traditionally been done on subjects peculiar to the Southwest—the Indian, the adobe building, the cowboy, the wagon trail—a visitor to these museums and galleries is soon imbued with a strong feeling for this regional mystique. Because of this, Taos makes an ideal gateway to the Southwest for any visitor from the worlds outside it.

1. ORIENTATION

Taos lies in the center of the extreme northern portion of New Mexico, 50 miles south of the Colorado line, at the feet of the Sangre de Cristo range of mountains to the east. Just a few miles west of town the Rio Grande sweeps down from Colorado through the spectacular Rio Grande Gorge on its way south to El Paso, where it becomes the U.S.–Mexican border all the way through Texas to the Gulf of Mexico. For travelers coming from the north or east Taos makes a good starting point for exploring the Southwest because of its proximity to regional marvels: vast expanses of wild fir-covered mountain slopes protected in national forests that offer campsites and trails; popular ski resorts; an Indian pueblo; traditional adobe architecture in many villages and towns.

Two other towns, **Raton** toward the east and **Farmington** to the west, also make good gateways for travelers arriving in northern New Mexico. They have all tourists' facilities as well as nearby attractions of their own, such as mountain lakes and state parks, or at the town of **Aztec** to the west, restored prehistoric ruins. The whole of northern New Mexico, particularly in the higher elevations, is good hunting and trout-fishing country. The highest point in the state, Wheeler Peak, just north of Taos, rises to a height of 13,161 feet. Spectacular, twisting mountain roads, nearly all paved and well-maintained, provide some of the best scenic auto trips in the U.S.

GETTING TO AND FROM TAOS: Taos is reached easily by highway from the north and east via I-25 (from such Colorado points as Denver, Pueblo, and Trinidad) south to Raton, N.M., then via U.S. 64 west through Cimarron and Eagle Nest to Taos (100 miles from Raton). From the northwest via Farmington, N.M., the route is also over U.S. 64, heading east almost exactly 200 miles to Taos. The drive from Santa Fe, 70 miles south of Taos, takes a superhighway (N.M. 84) north to Española, then N.M. 68 bordering the Rio Grande up to Taos. The so-called back road between Taos and Santa Fe, via N.M. 76 north to N.M. 3, traverses mountain ridges dotted here and there by tiny old villages of craftspeople, a delightfully scenic route.

Daily **bus** service from Albuquerque and Santa Fe is provided to Taos by Moreno Valley Transit, Inc., based in the newly incorporated city of Angel Fire (tel. 505/775-2292 in Taos, or toll free 800/422-0412). The rate from Taos to Albuquerque is $25. A dozen **airlines** provide service from every part of the country to Albuquerque. Direct transport to Taos is also provided by **Faust's Transportation** (tel. 758-3410, or toll free 800/345-3738). The charge for the 130-mile trip is $35 per person. These coaches also make runs to the community of Red River and to Taos Ski Valley and Angel Fire.

Avis is the only car-rental agency presently in Taos, with a desk at the Kachina Lodge (tel. 758-8676).

GETTING AROUND: The only way to see the main part of Taos is on foot, as all life is centered on the **Plaza,** from which it radiates into nearby side streets: Kit Carson Street, Bent Street, Ledoux Street, North Pueblo Road, and South Santa Fe Road. Unlike most western towns, where the blocks seem long and the destinations far apart, Taos has a European-style compactness that makes it ideal for exploring on foot.

Parking can be difficult during the summer rush, when the stream of tourists' cars moving north and south through town never ceases. Not everyone knows about all the free parking lots, however, especially about the municipal lot behind Taos Community Auditorium, just off Pueblo Road a block north of the Plaza traffic signal. Another lot just to the north of the Plaza has parking meters. Two commercial lots charge only $2 for all-day parking: one behind the main Plaza and another off Kit Carson Street. Two blocks north on Pueblo Road there is free parking until 5 p.m. daily at Kit Carson State Park.

Guided walking tours help you make the most of the long and varied history of Taos. Departing daily at 11 a.m. from the Taos Inn on North Pueblo Road, they take visitors into several historic houses and museums. The 1½-hour trips, operated by **Taos Historic Walking Tours,** cost $5 per person. Register at the desk of the Taos Inn or by telephone at 758-3861.

USEFUL INFORMATION: Emergency telephone numbers in Taos include Taos Country Sheriff (tel. 758-3361), New Mexico State Police (tel. 758-8878), and Taos Ambulance (tel. 758-1911). . . . The **tourist information desk** of the Taos Chamber of Commerce is two blocks south of the Plaza, on South Pueblo Road (tel. 758-3873, or toll free 800/732-8267). . . . The **post office** is five blocks north of the Plaza on North Pueblo Road; the ZIP Code is 87571.

2. WHERE TO STAY

Taos has half a dozen good motels or lodges with swimming pools, bars, and restaurants that keep good standards of moderate luxury at prices from $45 to $75 for a double, as well as a handful of more elaborate resorts outside the town. In Taos, too, are several acceptable budget motels, and there are even a few rooms available in historic houses.

Two private booking outfits can help visitors find accommodations during the busy winter skiing season: the **Taos Valley Resort Association** (tel. 505/776-2233, or toll free 800/992-SNOW), and **Taos Central Reservations** (tel. 505/758-9767, or toll free 800/821-2437).

IN TOWN: The **Hotel la Fonda de Taos,** on the Plaza, Taos, NM 87571 (tel. 505/758-2211), is a small, traditional southwestern inn in the center of the life of the town. Rates are $65 double, with three suites going at $85. Rooms give a fascinating view of the Plaza outside and each is decorated individually in regional antiques. The lobby, with its heavy leather-upholstered chairs and its heavy beams, makes an excellent site for a gallery of paintings on western sub-

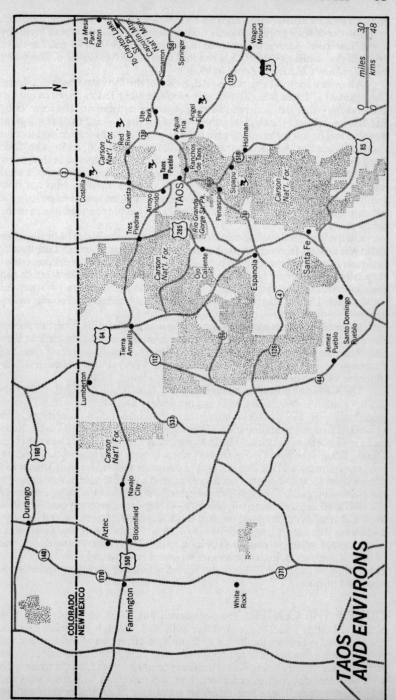

TAOS
AND ENVIRONS

jects, all by local artists. Saki Karavas, a New York City native who runs the hotel, is the owner of ten paintings, mostly nudes, painted toward the end of his life by D. H. Lawrence. Karavas shows them in a private gallery for a $1 fee. Lawrence brought the paintings to the U.S. when they were banned in England, along with his novel *Lady Chatterley's Lover,* in 1929.

A hangout for local artists is the Adobe Bar of the **Taos Inn,** Paseo del Norte, Taos, NM 87571 (tel. 505/758-2233, or toll free 800/TAOS-INN), an old historic hostelry that has undergone a million-dollar restoration. The busy lobby has as its centerpiece the original public well of the town—and there is still good water in it. The inn is the only one in town to provide room service, and there is even an oyster bar. A small double costs $50; twin beds, $70; and a suite, $95. Each of the 40 rooms is decorated in the regional style of exposed beams, white walls, and newly built working adobe fireplaces. These are the work of a local woman of Indian and Hispanic background, Carmen Velarde, who not only built them all but designed them as well—each one a bit special to go into the room it is meant to warm. She is also the maker of the big rounded hearth in the lobby.

Off the lobby is a small room that used to be called the Radio Room—when radio was new to Taos—now used to celebrate openings of art exhibits, usually one-man or one-woman, shown here. Besides the low prices on drinks at what they call their "happier" hour (4 to 7 p.m.) and those art shows, local artists and their followers are drawn to the inn to hear jazz piano or folk singers who perform most nights. The inn also hosts an annual Meet-the-Artist series of soirées in December.

Many of the rooms look out onto a patio with a swimming pool; in summer there are outdoor tables there for dining (see my recommendation for Doc Martin's Restaurant), and a Jacuzzi. Although the rooms somehow give off a sense of rusticity—part of the structure dates back to the 17th century—there is still cable color TV in every one. A private parking lot adjoins the inn.

The **Kachina Lodge** North Pueblo Road, Taos, NM 87571 (tel. 505/758-2275, or toll free 800/528-1234), is a big, cheery Best Western with 63 rooms priced at $55 to $70 double. It goes in big for pseudo-Indian decorations, with geometric designs on an imitation adobe façade facing busy North Pueblo Road half a mile north of the Plaza. The Indian motif is followed through in the Hopi Dining Room, the Kiva Coffee House (where guests face a huge totem pole behind the counter), and the Zuni Cocktail Lounge. Between May and October in a dinner show local Indians put on dances around a bonfire near diners' tables by the swimming pool. The high, heavy-beamed ceiling gives the lodge an aura of the 1940s, all in excellent repair, however—a step into the recent past. The Pow Wow Cabaret has country-and-western bands live on weekends. Several hallways and rooms downstairs where guests may meet and gather serve also as an extensive gallery of western art, again all by local artists. The Navajo Living Room, one of these display areas, has a marvelous fireplace at one end and a big and genuine Navajo rug on the floor. There is also a jewelry counter purveying Indian-style silver and turquoise.

OUT OF THE CENTER: The **Sagebrush Inn,** Santa Fe Road, Taos, NM 87571 (tel. 505/758-2254, or toll free 800/428-3626), is two miles south of the plaza and is famous locally for its Saturday-night rock-and-roll sessions and every night for live bands. It has 63 rooms, with rates at $60 to $95 double. An attractive Sagebrush Dining Room has heavy beams overhead, bright white walls with New Mexico–theme decorations, and Mexican chairs with straw seats and backs; and outside in summer, tables are set out for diners under great cotton-

wood trees that let through dappled sunlight. The impressive lobby has a n
fireplace, leather sofas, and a great Navajo rug, and there is a *portal*—a r
ground-level porch—across the end of the building. Public rooms display l
crafts: carved *santos* (wooden religious figures in brightly painted colors) a
conventional artworks. There are tennis courts on the premises, and a second
restaurant, open for dinners, called Los Vaqueros, specializes in western-style
steaks and prime rib.

Out on Morada Road about one mile east of Taos center is the historic house
of Mabel Dodge Luhan, the grande dame of the Taos art colony from the '20s,
now open for bed-and-breakfast for $55 double. Called **Las Palomas de Taos,**
Morada Road, Taos, NM 87571 (tel. 505/758-9456), it is a rambling adobe-
style structure used primarily as a study center on the culture of the Southwest, a
nonprofit institution that schedules summertime seminars and crafts workshops.

The **Quail Ridge Inn,** Taos Ski Valley Road (N.M. 150), Taos, NM 87571
(tel. 505/776-2211, or toll free 800/624-4448 outside New Mexico), is four
miles north of the Plaza. A full-time tennis pro teaches racquet swatters how to
improve their games year round on six outdoor and two indoor heated courts.
The 37-acre resort is 12 miles from Taos Ski Valley and thus draws many skiers
during the long winter sports season from Thanksgiving to April. Four indoor
racquetball courts also provide the sports-minded with space at any time of year.

Rates run from $59 double in the "low" season (June through December
and during early April) to $75 in the "high" season, which corresponds to the
skiing period. Among the 110 various accommodations available are one- and
two-bedroom suites, costing $69 to $220, according to season. The rooms,
some also with kitchenettes, are of a striking modern design, three or four built
within a separate structure so that in case a group of vacationers wants to use it
this way it can all be opened up to interconnect one room with another. Rooms
have queen-size beds, sleeper sofas, and color television, as well as full-length
baths, fireplaces, and telephones. Kitchenettes have all equipment, including
dishwasher and disposal system.

There are also ski packages of seven nights' stay, and during the summertime, tennis clinics. Besides all this there are indoor Jacuzzis, saunas, and a heated
pool. The handsome complex blends beautifully into the landscape with its towering backdrop of mountain peaks, and is the creation of New Mexico architect
Antoine Predock, who won a *Western Home* magazine award for excellence for
the project, completed in 1976.

3. WHERE TO EAT

IN TOWN: Although Taos is a small town, several of its restaurants aspire to an
international level of cuisine, and at least one of them has assembled a wine cellar
to equal any in the Southwest. This of course has happened because of the stream
of visitors from all over the country and from foreign countries, since the West is
very big among European travelers, particularly Italians and Germans. At the
same time there are the sorts of small eating places one associates with art centers,
where sandwiches, salads, soups, and quiches are served in modest premises.

More interesting perhaps to the newcomer to the region is the authentic
New Mexican cuisine that has its roots in Mexico but has become its own separate
branch of the taco and enchilada scene, both because recipes have been altered
over the years and because the New Mexico climate produces ingredients that are
not exactly like those south of the border.

Beyond these general categories is the western tradition of good steaks and
prime rib, upon which several restaurants base their popularity. There are fast-

...urse, as everywhere, and an occasional workday café where
...y to work stop for the special breakfast. Low-priced all-you-
...to be found.

...rants

...ck up the main thoroughfare, Pueblo Road, from the Plaza, in the
...n, is a somewhat grand establishment in classical Spanish décor, **Doc
...rtin's Restaurant** (tel. 758-2233), named for a country doctor who arrived
out here in the 1890s and had a house where the present inn stands today. Many
turn-of-the-century Taoseños were known as "Martin's babies," and the good
doc was often paid in farm produce. It was his widow who built the Taos Inn,
using that ancient water well as its focal point—the one now making a centerpiece in the inn lobby. The doctor's office stood where the dining room is today.
The restaurant is proud of its breakfast specialties: huevos rancheros (Mexican-
style eggs, scrambled with chiles) at $5, or crab Benedict for $7. Lunches at
around $7 may be a seafood chalupa or a sweet-and-sour stir-fry; the Taos Inn
club sandwich is also a crowd pleaser, at $5. Dinner entrees, at $10 to $17, may
include roast duck, pollo nativo (chicken breast with chicken sausage and blue-
corn polenta), a sizable shrimp burrito, or steak picante.

A historic street a block north of the Plaza is Bent Street, where the outdoor
patio garden of the **Apple Tree** restaurant (tel. 758-1900) makes a delightful setting for lunch or dinner in good weather. There are cozy small dining rooms inside as well, fitted out with adobe walls, board floors, and beamed ceilings. The
menu, written daily on a blackboard, provides such fare as softshell-crab tacos,
salads, soups, and hamburgers. At dinner a salmon steak with dill sauce, chicken
Lombardy, and scampi are offered; entrees run $10 to $14. Home-baked desserts
include hazelnut torte, blueberry crisp, and mud pie. There is a Sunday champagne brunch. Hours are 11:30 a.m. to 9:30 p.m. seven days.

Moderately Priced Restaurants

To begin at the center of town we must always start with the Plaza, perhaps
over an order of half a side of pork ribs on a balcony table at **Ogelvies** (tel. 758-
8866), on the northeast corner of the square. The Spanish décor, red-tile floor,
and wrought-iron railings make the terrace an ideal spot for sunning and watching the streams of people crisscrossing the Plaza below you—a great spot for an
evening cocktail too. Lunch specials at around $6 include a chalupa: a flour tortil-
la filled with guacamole, lettuce, chicken, melted cheese, sour cream, and a sauce
based on chiles that is a house creation. Open from 11 a.m. to 10 p.m., Ogelvies
provides a full menu of soups, quiches, steaks, seafood, and sandwiches. Its bar,
handsomely set off in Spanish tile, makes a likely meeting place around cocktail
time, and draws a certain coterie of sports enthusiasts who come in to watch baseball or football games on the tube, or shoot a few games of darts.

Not far off the Plaza, a block along Kit Carson Street hidden within a warren
of art galleries is a restaurant some locals consider the best in northern New Mexico for regional specialties: **Roberto's** (tel. 758-2434). When Bobby and Patsy
Garcia, both Taoseños, opened the place in 1966 their byword was "only native
dishes," and they keep mostly to that standard. There are three small, simple, and
charming dining rooms each with five tables, and a corner fireplace in one of
them. Every entree brings with it, first, an order of the famous New Mexico
sopaipillas. Garcia says he makes his from flour, baking powder, lard, and a bit of
water and salt rolled together, cut into quarter-inch-thick squares, and then deep-
fried in lard. They are served here in the regional tradition with honey and butter.

The Garcias are open six days (closed Tuesday) for lunch and dinner, only
between Memorial Day and Labor Day; during the rest of the year they are, in

principle, open on weekends, but a telephone call is advised as occasionally during the cold weather the two may disappear for some skiing.

Garcia says a difference between Mexican-style foods here and those served in Texas or California is that here the ingredients are preserved in a dried form, resulting in differing recipes, variants on standard Mexican-style dishes. Many of the recipes used have come from relatives on both sides of the family. Garcia serves homemade refried beans (frijoles refritos) with chicos—dried kernels of corn. Tostadas with hot sauce also are served as an appetizer to such popular local dishes as stuffed peppers (chiles rellenos), which comes with beans and Spanish rice. The chile relleno combination plate, which includes an enchilada and a taco as well, costs $8.50; other specialty plates are priced about the same. A rib steak and french fries is $10. California wines are $2 a glass; Mexican beers, $2 a bottle.

A pleasant, low-key atmosphere is set by the simplicity of the old building, dating to 1834, and carefully chosen local craft items are displayed in a small showcase at the exit, for sale to guests. Hours are noon to 2:30 p.m. for lunch and 5:30 to 9 p.m. for dinner.

A Special Breakfast

Up Pueblo Road to the north is **Michael's Kitchen** (tel. 758-4178), on the west side of the street, a coffeeshop and bakery open from 7 a.m. to 8:30 p.m. year round and a great place for fresh breads and pastries, to eat here or take with you. This is a lively meeting place for local craftspeople over "coffee and . . ." during the day, starting out with hefty breakfasts of pancakes, huevos rancheros, or the "poor man's eggs Benedict," both $5.

OUT OF TOWN: There are several additional choices on the outskirts worth considering.

The Stakeout, on Stakeout Drive off N.M. 68, two miles south of the Plaza (tel. 758-2042), is open seven days for dinner only, from 6 to 10 p.m. It specializes in beef but also serves seafood and teriyaki dishes. Another specialty is quail, $12 for a pair. The pride of the house is the 24-ounce rib-eye steak at $24. Entrees include rice, salad bar, and sourdough bread.

For romantic-style dining in a historic house, the **Brett House** (tel. 776-8545) provides the setting four miles north of Taos on Ski Valley Road. It is open six days for dinner, from 6:30 to 9:30 p.m.; closed Monday. There is a Sunday brunch from 11:30 a.m. to 2 p.m. Ask for the nightly special not on the menu. Entrees cost $14 to $22.

Barbecue lovers head for the hickory-fired pit of the **Casa de Valdez,** on Santa Fe Road (tel. 758-8777), a couple of miles south of the Plaza. Open seven days from 11 a.m. to 9 p.m., the house specializes in moderately priced *comidas norteñas* (northern Mexican-style meals).

4. THE ART COLONY

It is the artists and their work that have animated Taos for three-quarters of a century, commencing with the founding in 1912 of the Taos Society of Artists by a group of young painters, then unknown, whose names today in Taos carry the weight of the Founding Fathers in New England: J. H. Sharp, O. E. Berninghaus, E. Irving Couse, Buck Dunton, Victor Higgins, Walter Ufer, Martin Hennings, Kenneth Adams, Ernest L. Blumenschein, Bert Phillips.

Their numbers have grown into the hundreds, their creative spirit amplified by subsequent arrivals of crafts-oriented artisans from all over the U.S. and many other countries. Their work fills about 80 art galleries in Taos, as well as other shops selling weavings, ceramics, jewelry, and furniture. Although a good deal of the subject matter is clearly done in a realistic style, there is much else that is experimental or abstract or in some way avant-garde. The latter often bemuses visitors from other states who do not live, as Taoseños do, surrounded by all kinds of art on every side. It is a temptation for some artists to snub these people as if they were hopeless Philistines, while other artists like to explain their work but may sound just a bit condescending in the attempt. One of the best approaches to this welter of art—and much of it, everyone admits, will not go down in art history —comes from *Taos News* art writer Clyde Davis. He suggests that newcomers without much experience browsing in art galleries simply follow their own good instincts. "Ask questions if you like, keep quiet if you choose. Do what is comfortable. Beware the atmosphere that puts you off, the gallery person who puts you down. Taos is a friendly place, removed by more than just distance from the art cloisters of the east." He does recommend, however, keeping a wary eye on price tags: "Hype is as much a part of the art game as it is in other aspects of life in the '80s."

The few specialized museums showing the art and the crafts of Taos creative people are the very best way to get the flavor of the Taos art scene. Each has its own history and background, and its particular artistic aims. The commercial galleries, of course, are there to make money as well as to deliver the joys of art to the world, and sales are good. Thus buyers are clearly finding what they like. Visits to the museums first, however, will show you the best standards Taos artists have been setting for themselves over the years, and provide you works to judge other art by—when you are tempted to spend a few hundred, or thousand, dollars for a canvas to take home with you.

ARTS AND CRAFTS MUSEUMS AND EXHIBITS: The **Harwood Foundation,** 25 Ledoux St., a few minutes' walk from the Plaza, has been in the center of the life of the art colony since it opened in 1923 as a small library and art-exhibit room. Now it has an important collection of Taos-related art, as well as serving as the town's public library and as a cultural center with a number of programs under way. There are films, concerts, lectures, classes in various arts, crafts, and allied subjects, and children's programs. Occupying a two-story adobe building that dates back to the 1860s, its top floor has some of the best paintings on display done by those early members of the Taos Society of Artists: Walter Ufer, Ernest Blumenschein, Victor Higgins, Herbert Dunton, Bert Phillips, and Oscar Berninghaus. Artists who came a bit later are also represented here: Leon Gaspard, Andrew Dasburg, Emil Bisttram, and Dorothy Brett, and there are living artists whose recent work is also shown.

Retablos are religious paintings on wood done by Hispanic artists in an early churchly tradition continuing today; they decorate the altars of the old Spanish-style churches still to be found in the mountains of this part of New Mexico, as well as the walls of many Hispanic homes. They picture saints, usually, or illustrate Bible stories. The collection here was originally assembled by Taos art patron Mabel Dodge Luhan in the early years of the art colony here.

Also shown are the wood sculptures of a self-taught "primitive" named Patrocinio Barela, figures carved within a carapace of the same wood in a rounded simplicity that gives a feeling of strength and serenity. Other collections include watercolors by Frieda Lawrence, a wife of the English writer; and Rio Grande tinware and Spanish Colonial furniture.

The Harwood exhibits are open, free of charge, from 10 a.m. to 5 p.m. Monday through Friday, to 4 p.m. on Saturday; closed Sunday. For information on cultural programs, telephone 758-3063. The library, incidentally, stays open to 8 p.m. on Monday and Thursday evenings.

Nearby on Ledoux Street, the **Ernest L. Blumenschein House** is open daily from 9 a.m. to 5 p.m. for an admission fee of $2 (or admission to all three properties of the Kit Carson Foundation for $5). Blumenschein, originally from Pittsburgh, died here in 1960, one of the first Taos artists to make a commercial success of his work. His daughter, Helen, is still a resident of the town, having grown up in the Ledoux Street house, furnished and decorated largely as it was during the artist's lifetime. A painting on an easel is one that Blumenschein had added to by overpainting. During a melancholy period in his life he added to a portrait of the angel of death the figures of mourners as well as a casket. His wife, Mary, was also a painter, and there are some of her works here, as well as those of daughter Helen. One of Blumenschein's most famous works, *The Church at Ranchos de Taos,* is also displayed—the subject is a landmark a couple of miles south of town. The bedroom has the New England–style spool bed that Mary Blumenschein, a Rhode Islander, had made here to her specifications. The low-ceilinged old house itself is worth the visit (it dates from 1797) and the sala—the big room the artist used as a studio—was for years a notorious local dancehall. The low doors were a problem in moving the artist's oversize canvases out of the house. Daughter Helen recalls, "We just cut a hole up through the wall, took the murals through, then filled in the wall again."

Something of a curiosity is the collection of ten D. H. Lawrence nudes shown at the **Fonda de Taos Hotel** ($1 admission fee), sensuous works in warm colors with such titles as *The Kiss* or *The Rape of the Sabine Women.* Lawrence was brought to Taos by Mabel Dodge Luhan, the art patron of the area—she married an artist herself, Tony Luhan, a local Indian. Owned by the hotel's proprietor, Saki Karavas, the paintings are said to be worth $1.5 million. After a one-day exhibit in London in 1929 they were banned from the United Kingdom. In 1925 Lawrence made his last trip to Taos, and later contracted tuberculosis in Mexico. He was advised to return here for a cure but never made it until after his death— his ashes are buried in a mountainside cabin where he had once been Mrs. Luhan's guest.

Just four miles north of Taos, off N.M. 3, is the **Millicent Rogers Museum** (tel. 758-2462), open daily from 9 a.m. to 5 p.m. May 1 to October 31, and Wednesday through Sunday from 10 a.m. to 4 p.m. November 1 to April 30 (closed Monday and Tuesday during the winter period). Admission is $3 for adults, $1 for children under 17 and senior citizens. Millicent Rogers was a wealthy woman who moved to Taos in 1947 and began to assemble a collection of original jewelry, basketry, pottery, and paintings out of two New Mexico traditions, that of the Pueblo Indians and that of the Hispanics. The museum states that its purpose is nothing less than "the acquisition, preservation, research, display, and interpretation of the art and material culture of the Native American and Hispanic peoples of the Southwest, focusing on northern New Mexico."

Indian art displays are built around Millicent Rogers's collection of Navajo and Pueblo jewelry, textiles, pottery, kachina dolls from the Hopi and Zuñi tribes, paintings from the Rio Grande pueblos, and basketry. A famous family of Pueblo Indian potters at the San Ildefonso pueblo, that of Maria Martinez, has recently provided the museum with great examples of these unique ceramics: black pottery etched with brown and tan geometric forms. A watercolor of eagle dancers painted by an Indian artist half a century ago is remarkable for its color and vivacity; the intricacy and brightness of color in a Navajo blanket over a century old are amazing. Kachina dolls—ceremonial figures still made by the Hopi —are a subject all to themselves; the details of the early ones collected here from the last century could keep one absorbed for hours.

Hispanic traditions are illustrated in *santos,* wooden, painted religious images. *Our Lady of Talpa,* for example, is a standing figure of the saint in an ornately decorated gown, wearing a crown, and holding the kingly infant in one arm and a raised feather in her other hand. A Death Cart made in 1900 out of tiny miniature logs is carrying an evilly grinning skeleton draped in a black cloak. Bright primary colors are a standard mark of these "primitive" artists' work: a *Christ with Mourners* is painted with blood streaks so red as to appear to be bleeding from the wood.

The **Taos Fire Department,** on Placitas Road just to the west of the Plaza (tel. 758-2201), might not seem to be an art lover's destination, but nevertheless that is what it is. It has an irreplaceable and excellent collection of the work of early Taos artists on display, free of charge, Monday through Friday from 8 a.m. to 4:30 p.m. The collection was started in the 1950s when the Taos firemen, all volunteers, asked their artist friends to decorate their recreation room. Some artists loaned paintings, but many gave them to the fire station outright—and thus it has one of the finest art collections in town. Hostesses at the exhibit are wives of retired firemen. Curator is Clark Funk, also a retired fireman.

The **Stables Art Center,** next door to the Taos Inn on North Pueblo Road (tel. 758-2036), is a display and sales operation run by the nonprofit Taos Art Association, and is open free of charge daily all year from 10 a.m. to 5 p.m. Lectures on art-related subjects and classes in sketching and painting are held at the center. Teachers are all working artists of the town.

COMMERCIAL GALLERIES:
Almost all of the galleries and dealers' rooms in Taos are within walking distance of the Plaza. There are so many that in some streets you can practically go from door to door and look at nothing but art, art, and more art, with perhaps a bit of craft sandwiched in. Here are random samplings of the material you are likely to find in these places.

Several galleries are right on the Plaza. In the North Plaza Art Center, **Bryans Gallery** shows the paper embossings, drawings, oil, acrylic, and pastel paintings, and brass sculpture of some two dozen regional artists; the **Desurmont-Ellis Gallery** features the contemporary paintings of Richard Bergquist and Adeline de la Noe; **Burke Armstrong Fine Art** prese￼ ￼ orks of historic and present-day Taos artists; and the **New Directions Galle.** ￼ ntemporary work by regional people.

Magic Mountain Gallery, on the Plaza, represents a dozen regional artists, including James Roybal and Joseph Lonewolf. Off the northwest corner on Teresina Lane, the artist-owned **Western Art Gallery** specializes in J. D. Woods' realistic western bronzes, landscapes, and cowboy paintings. At the southwest corner of the Plaza, the **Whitaker Gallery** displays two floors of paintings by southwestern watercolorists and oil painters. The **Fennell Art Gallery,** on the south side of the Plaza, has contemporary works.

On Kit Carson Road, a block east of the Plaza, are more galleries. The **Jordan Company Gallery,** in the Adobe Wall Motel, represents traditional and contemporary artists of New Mexico and Texas; the **Rod Goebel Gallery** has impressionistic, expressionistic, and abstract works; and the **E. S. Lawrence Gallery** shows such award-winning Taos artists as Valerie Graves. Cowboy and Indian subjects predominate at **Stewart's Fine Art,** but paintings by abstract and expressionist artists are also shown. The **Total Arts Gallery** shows regional works, as does **El Taller Taos Gallery,** close by.

On East Kit Carson Road, look for "historically important" works at the **Mission Gallery.** No fewer than 55 regional artists' work are at **Gallery A.** What might be called semi-abstract landscapes in acrylics, the work of Cliff Harmon, are among the art seen at the **Torreon Gallery,** 116 E. Kit Carson.

On nearby North Pueblo Road, at no. 400 you will find traditional paintings and drawings by Francis Donald at the **Shriver Gallery.** At no. 609, **Philip Bareiss Fine Arts** has contemporary art by such spirited abstract artists as Ginger Mongiello, and folk art too. Contemporary Southwest oils and watercolors are displayed at the **Taos Art Gallery**. At no. 800, the **Spirit Runner Gallery** offers contemporary watercolors.

On Ledoux Street, the **Tally Richards Gallery** shows works by such artists as Earl Linderman and Fritz Scholder. Aficionados of Indian artist R. C. Gorman's work may see his paintings at the **Navajo Gallery,** 5 Ledoux St.

At 4 Bent St., the **Morgan Gallery** shows art and jewelry by Ed Morgan and other artists, and at 6 Bent St. there are contemporary paintings at the **Salobra Gallery.**

5. SIGHTSEEING

In and around Taos are several historic structures, two of them used as museums to re-create the Territorial era of the last century, the styles and furnishings of which have painted in our minds the idealized picture of the Old West we carry with us. But the artifacts displayed in Taos are the originals.

HISTORIC HOUSES: The **Kit Carson Home and Historical Museum,** a National Historic Landmark, on East Kit Carson Road, is open from 8 a.m. to 6 p.m. daily, except during winter months when closing time is 5 p.m. There is a $2 admission fee, or a $5 combination fee for this and the two other Kit Carson Foundation properties. The 1825 structure served as a home for Carson while he lived in Taos as an army officer. His office and headquarters were also on the premises, which has 12 rooms, all restored to the style of the era when Carson brought his bride to live here in 1843. An interesting kitchen fireplace in the regional adobe style, whitewashed outside, has two openings. It is bell shaped and is called a *fogon de campaña.* The Spanish who colonized the area were fond of adages and wrote them on little plaques to hang on the wall. One in the kitchen here reads: *Nadie sabe lo que tiene la olla mas que la cuchara que la menea* ("Nobody better knows what the pot holds than the spoon that stirs it").

Also near the town center is the **Governor Charles Bent House,** the home of the trader, agent, and first governor of the New Mexico Territory who established Fort Bent in Colorado. He was murdered in an uprising in 1847 in his own house as his wife and children escaped by digging through an adobe wall into the house next door; the hole is still visible. The house is a block north of the Plaza on Bent Street, and is open daily from 10 a.m. to 4 p.m., with an admission fee of $1.

About 2½ miles west of Taos Plaza on Lower Ranchitos Road (N.M. 240) is what is billed as the last original Spanish hacienda in the Southwest, the **Hacienda de Don Antonio Severino Martinez,** the owner of which was an early mayor of the town. It is one of the properties of the Kit Carson Foundation, and admission costs $2 or use of the $5 combination ticket to this, the Carson House, and the Blumenschein House. It is open daily from 9 a.m. to 5 p.m.

The 1804 ranch, built like a fortress, has been extensively renovated. The layout includes 21 rooms around two patios or placitas. The outside wall is of thick adobe without windows or doors, save for a single entrance, built this way for use as a refuge from Indian raids. These were the work of Comanches and Apaches from the plains, not the nearby Pueblo Indians, who themselves were often victims of these attacks.

A great low-ceilinged family room 32 feet long has a heavy table and period Spanish chairs. There are bedrooms, a granary, and a so-called Trade Room where Martinez showed merchandise he brought up from Mexico in the Chihuahua trade. (Before the Santa Fe Trail reached the area some years later, trade in these parts was mainly on a north-south axis with Mexico.) A kitchen has the old-style primitive cooking fireplace, with a separate pantry next door. A Registered National Historic Building, the hacienda retains 3½ acres of its original land grant.

OTHER POINTS OF INTEREST: Four blocks north of the Plaza is **Kit Carson State Park,** with an entrance on North Pueblo Road. The cemetery was established here in 1847 after the rebellion in which Governor Bent was killed. A death toll of 150 Indians was also recorded, in a massacre harking back to the much earlier Pueblo Revolt in 1680, when the Indians routed the Spanish from northern New Mexico for 12 years. Here you can see the grave of Kit Carson and his kin.

Built in the 1770s, the **Church of Saint Francis of Assisi,** in the village of Ranchos de Taos, two miles south of Taos, is probably the most photographed, sketched, and painted structure in the Southwest—one of the most beautiful of the simple churches and missions put up by the Spanish. Its painting of Christ by Henri Ault, done in 1896, is said to glow at certain times. The form of a cross is also said to appear occasionally in the painting.

COLORFUL EVENTS: Besides the traditional ceremonies at Taos Pueblo, listed separately, a number of annual events also draw visitors to Taos. The main events aimed at drawing visitors take place in summer, starting with the spring arts festival. There is also a two-day rodeo at the **Sheriff's Posse Rodeo Arena** off South Santa Fe Road, with the standard events: bull riding, bronco riding, barrel racing, steer roping, etc. An exhibition of glider soaring also takes place in June out at Taos Municipal Airport six miles west of town, the **Taos Soaring Fiesta.** Late July is the time for the **Fiestas de Taos,** starting out with a parade in the Plaza led by a Fiesta Queen. There are also a fashion show, pageant, and fiesta masses. Also in July is the two-day bicycle race, **Tour de Taos,** which includes the seven-mile, 1,500-foot ride up into Taos Ski Valley, a distance winners have covered in under half an hour.

July is also the time for a chamber-music festival, with concerts on four Saturday afternoons, by the **Taos School of Music,** held in the Taos Community Auditorium. The Armory is the scene in August of the **Taos County Fair,** which besides the usual exhibits of agricultural items and animals also displays locally made arts and crafts.

The first week in October is the time for the **Taos Art Festival,** the big event of the year. Also in October is the **Balloon Festival,** a three-day series of flights involving 50 balloons. The meet starts off with a Saturday parade of all the balloon baskets around and around the Plaza in their pickup trucks.

For information on all events in Taos, ask the **Taos Chamber of Commerce,** at its tourist information office on South Pueblo Road (tel. 505/758-3873, or toll free 800/732-8267).

MODERN ARCHITECTURE: Visitors will be rewarded if they keep their eyes open for examples of creative architecture from the hippie period of the '60s —some original layouts are indeed still being put up around Taos. The freedom of spirit that such an art center seems to radiate has attracted builders who might not experiment so freely elsewhere. An architectural writer on the Taos *News,* Lee Friver, comments: "All the conventional knowledge was suspect in their minds, so the structures are a wild assortment, from towers to pit houses, to domes to circles, to houses built right up against the mountain, with the mountain still in the living room."

POPULAR MUSIC: Three motels regularly schedule weekend entertainment in the form of jazz combos, country and western, or rock bands. The **Kachina Lodge,** North Pueblo Road (tel. 758-2275), has country-and-western groups. The **Sagebrush Inn,** South Santa Fe Road (tel. 758-2254), regularly books rock bands in its lounge. **Carl's French Quarter,** in the Quail Ridge Inn on Ski Valley Road (tel. 776-8319), has live dinner shows. The **Hacienda Inn** on South Santa Fe Road (tel. 758-8610) has dancing to live bands.

In town there's live music at **Ogelvie's,** on the Plaza (tel. 758-8866), and also at the **Adobe Bar** of the Taos Inn, on North Pueblo Road (tel. 758-2233).

6. TAOS PUEBLO

Taos Pueblo, with a population of 1,346 Tiwa Indians, is one of the oldest continuously inhabited communities in the U.S., vying with Acoma Pueblo, also in New Mexico, for this distinction—they have both been active population centers for probably 900 years or longer. The Taos community is just two miles north of the Plaza of the town of Taos but forms a world of its own, two strikingly ancient-looking apartment complexes of adobe houses built one upon another to form porches, balconies, and wonderful roof angles reached by ancient ladders. Between the two complexes runs a bright, fast-flowing stream, and a footbridge, recently rebuilt with stout beams, joins the two shores. To the north looms the 13,151-foot peak of Mount Wheeler, the state's highest, with the long green fir-covered slopes leading up there forming a timeless background to the old pueblo.

The Indians are proud of a new **visitor center** at the entrance to the pueblo. Here jewelry and locally made drums are sold, and there is a small **museum** of Pueblo Indian crafts and historical displays concerning the Indians.

The first Europeans to arrive at the pueblo were soldiers in one of Coronado's expeditions hunting for the Seven Cities of Cibola, legendary hiding places of fabulous treasures of gold. They were followed by missionaries who began the never-completed attempts at Christianizing the Indians. The Spanish were routed from northern New Mexico altogether during the Pueblo Revolt of 1680, in which the Taos Indians joined with other Pueblo Indians in ridding themselves of Spanish occupation for 12 years.

The Taos Pueblo is one of the most conservative of all Indian communities today, still eschewing such modern conveniences as electricity or plumbing, although the visitor center is equipped with them. Originally the wall all around the pueblo was much higher than it is today. It once made the community into a secure fortress. Adobe bricks are used to repair the buildings, and the surfaces are regularly refurbished by molding on new layers of mud and straw. Thus the tone of the buildings blends in with the land around, since the houses are made of the very earth itself. The bright-blue painted doors repeat the clear blue of the sky outlined by the brown outlines of the buildings.

The Taos, or Tiwa, Indians here speak the Tiwa language, one of a group of Pueblo languages called Tanoan shared by several others of the 19 pueblos in New Mexico. In these languages there is no direct word for "no," or any word for "never." The Taos Indians welcome visitors, who are free to walk around most parts of the pueblo for an entrance fee of $2, or $4 per carload.

There are half a dozen tiny **shops** selling pueblo-made crafts items— drums, silver and turquoise jewelry, beadwork—as well as some Hopi kachina dolls. Extra fees of $5 are charged for picture taking, and $15 to $35 for sketching or painting. Bread is baked in beehive-shaped outdoor ovens and is sold in most of the little shops. The nearby **Indian Horse Ranch** (tel. 758-3212) organizes horseback rides, including overnight trips on the 95,000-acre Taos reservation.

Public ceremonies go on at various times of the year and visitors are always welcome, but no photography is permitted. The annual schedule is January 1, turtle dance; January 6, deer or buffalo dance; Easter Sunday dances; May 3, corn dance and dawn footraces; June 13, San Antonio Day, corn dance; June 24, San

Juan Day, corn dance; July 25, Santiago Day, corn dance; July 26, Santa Ana Day, corn dance; September 29, San Geronimo Eve vespers and sundown dance; September 30, San Geronimo Day, trade fair, footraces, and pole climb; December 24, torchlight procession of the Virgin Mary; December 25, deer dance. Information on hours is available from the visitor center daily from 9 a.m. to 5 p.m. (tel. 758-9593).

7. OUTDOORS IN THE TAOS AREA

Besides skiing in five modern-equipped areas, listed separately, the area around Taos offers great hiking, camping, fishing, hunting, horseback riding, ghost town exploring, and white-water rafting.

HIKING AND CAMPING: Rio Grande Gorge State Park, accessible from N.M. 68, 16 miles south of Taos, has spectacular views of the steep-sided gorge from four campgrounds that have shelters, tables, fireplaces, and drinking water. Hiking trails lead into the "box" of the gorge where canyon walls are steepest and highest.

The tiny community of Pilar, along the state highway outside the park, is the site of a budget bed-and-breakfast hostel affiliated with American Youth Hostels, the **Plum Tree** (tel. 505/758-4696). A café provides simple low-cost food, while sleeping-bag accommodations go for $15, including breakfast. There are private rooms for couples and families. The hostel is a good headquarters for hikes, and free guided trips leave every Monday morning in summer (on cross-country skis in winter). Raft trips as well as canoe and kayak lessons are also organized here, and fine-arts and nature-study workshops are held in summer.

Carson National Forest has 1,392,253 acres in three vast, mountainous sections around Taos, the largest west of the town. East of Taos in the Sangre de Cristo range and north up to Wheeler Park other stretches of wilderness offer hundreds of miles of hiking and riding trails along with 37 camping and picnic areas. Detailed maps are available at the office of the superintendent of Carson National Forest on Cruz Alta Road in Taos. Note that Wheeler Peak is in a special wilderness area, accessible by trail, which because of its altitude and climate has flora and fauna unique in the Southwest.

Horseback riding is organized at **Lobo Ranch** (tel. 776-8526) year round, with day and overnight trips. Both western and English saddles are available. The ranch is ten miles north of Taos off the road between Arroyo Hondo and Arroyo Seco; telephone for directions.

The **Rio Grande Gorge Bridge** spans the deepest part of the canyon 650 feet above the river on U.S. 64, 15 miles northwest of Taos, and makes a good picnic place as well as starting point for hikes down into the dark depths of the gorge itself. A hairpin-turn road makes its way down to the state park along the riverbanks.

WHITE-WATER RAFTING: For information on white-water rafting, see Section 11, "Outdoors in the Santa Fe Area," in Chapter III.

FISHING: Sporting-goods stores sell New Mexico fishing licenses, required for fishing in all state waters except privately owned ponds. Brown, cut-throat, and rainbow trout are prize catches in the area. The Red River, the upper Rio Grande, Rio Hondo, Costilla Creek, Rio Pueblo, and the Santa Barbara River are popular with local anglers. Eagle Nest, Eagle Rock, and Cabresto Lakes are also fishermen's destinations. The streams and lakes are mostly stocked and have access by car. The season opens April 1 and runs through to the end of the year.

Trout limit is a daily catch of eight. You can get detailed information from the **New Mexico Game and Fish Dept.,** Villagra Bldg., Santa Fe, NM 87503 (tel. 505/827-7882).

HUNTING: The 100,000 acres of the Valle Vidal unit of the Carson National Forest is home to a herd of trophy elk—this lies east of the town of Costilla. Hunting permits are issued in a drawing.

National forest wilderness areas also attract hunters: the Latir and Wheeler Peak areas are accessible from the Questa Ranger District, and the Pecos Wilderness to the south, reached via the Jicarita Peak Trail. Detailed forest maps are obtained at the Forest Headquarters in Taos.

There are antelope in the high plains, and in the mountains are deer, bear, and cougar, and bighorns in the Sangre de Cristos, above Taos. Seasons are established for wild turkey, dove, quail, pheasant, prairie chicken, and waterfowl. Detailed information is available from the **New Mexico Game and Fish Dept.,** Villagra Bldg., Santa Fe, NM 87503 (tel. 505/827-7911).

HOT SPRINGS: The **Ojo Caliente Mineral Springs** spa, 35 miles southwest of Taos, is built around five hot springs giving mineral waters used for both drinking and bathing. You can get a mineral bath followed by sweat bath and massage all for $20. First you soak in a hot tub or steaming indoor pool, then lie limp in a great towel. Founded in the 1860s and open all year, the spa is a favored retreat for Nordic skiers after wintertime cross-country treks that may overstretch little-used muscles.

SPECIAL DESTINATIONS: **Eagle Nest** is a top-of-the-world village lying high in the Sangre de Cristo range 32 miles northeast of Taos. Mountain slopes with dark ramps of blackish pine reach down easily toward a wide, flat man-made lake often stirred by sharp breezes, and good for sailing.

Five miles farther north via N.M. 38 is the ghost town of **Elizabethtown,** where ruins of an old hotel are set off by the 12,500-foot mountain peak behind it. Once this was a real town—the first one incorporated in the Territory, in fact—and a county seat. Gold claims were staked out nearby in 1866 and soon the area caught gold fever. At one time in 1869 Elizabethtown had saloons, stores, dancehalls, and two hotels. When the gold rush ended, the population departed; a fire in 1903 razed most of the town, leaving a few ruins today.

Trampas, south of Taos, is an early Spanish Colonial village that still keeps its early adobe buildings as well as its famous San José de Gracia Church. The legend is that since the church was dedicated to the 12 Apostles, only 12 men were allowed to work on its construction—they took 20 years to build it. Villagers paid for the work by giving up a sixth of their crops every year. A silver bell, named Refugio, was rung for solemn occasions, while a golden bell named Gracia, with a lighter tone, was used for happy occasions such as weddings and festivals. The church is considered one of the best standing examples of Spanish Colonial building and is a Registered Historic Landmark.

Questa is a small community 24 miles north of Taos on N.M. 3, the site of a locally renowned molybdenum mine where most of the local people find employment.

Red River, the ski resort 12 miles east of Questa and the highest city in New Mexico (at 8750 feet), also has a lively summer season, beginning with a Memorial Day weekend old fiddlers' contest and buffalo-chip-throwing match. The weekend also draws visitors to square dances and contests in jalapeña pepper eating and in chug-a-lugging. A Chile-Challenge cooking contest is also held during the weekend. The town is also famous for its "aspencade," a September festival aimed at bringing foliage viewers into the spectacular foothills. A ski lift, it should be noted, operates for sightseeing during the summer, on Pioneer Road, where the lift house at the base provides a restaurant and bar.

8. SKI RESORTS

The Taos area has five ski resorts within easy traveling distance of town: Angel Fire, Red River, Sipapu, Rio Costilla, and Taos Ski Valley. They constitute a fast-growing ski area where the dry, sunny days make for powder snow conditions considered generally first-rate, with a long season too, stretching from Thanksgiving into April. Angel Fire has six chair lifts; Red River, four gondolas and two chair lifts; Sipapu, three T-bars; Rio Costilla, one triple-chair lift and a Poma lift; and Taos Ski Valley, six gondolas and one chair lift.

ANGEL FIRE: Angel Fire (tel. 505/377-2301, or toll free 800/633-7463) is 26 miles east of Taos via U.S. 64. The resort was host to the World Cup Freestyle finals competition in 1983, although two-thirds of its trails are rated for beginner or intermediate skiing. Cross-country trails over the golf course lead into 20 miles of marked trails in the foothills below the steeper slopes. In the downhill trails there is a vertical drop of 2,180 feet, and their lengths total 34 miles; the longest—"Heading Home"—is 3½ miles. The six lifts can carry 7,900 skiers up onto the slopes per hour, so there is hardly ever any waiting in line here.

The Angel Fire Ski School is staffed by teachers certified by the Professional Ski Instructors of America. Children aged 4 to 11 take part in a "Mountain Masters" program of instruction from 10 a.m. to 3 p.m. Ski rental, including poles and boots, is $14 daily. Three- or five-day packages, including lift tickets and lessons, cost $80 and $130. Straight lift tickets are $24 daily, $16 for a half day.

The **Plaza at Angel Fire,** on Angel Fire Road (tel. 505/883-6921, or toll free 800/835-6373), has a dozen shops around it, and inside, two swimming pools and a whirlpool, a lounge, and a restaurant. Rooms have radios and cable TVs, and many have fireplaces too. Skiers ski to the door; there is also an ice rink. Double rates are $75 to $135.

A special attraction in late January every year is the annual Bob Harney Memorial Shovel Race down a 1,400-foot course on "The Bump" in Angel Fire Village. The race originated when maintenance crews started riding their snow shovels down the slopes after work, and became official in 1974. Besides shovels and scoops, entrants rig up special vehicles such as a steel bedstead, complete with headboard and spiral box spring, mounted on skis for running the course.

In nearby Eagle Nest, the **Gold Pan Ski Lodge** (tel. 505/377-2286) has bunk facilities for 64 skiers, along with a full community kitchen, a dining room with fireplace, and a game room. Rates are $16 per person, and $10 extra for two meals daily. The Gold Pan also rents standard motel units at $35 to $38 double, $50 double with kitchenette.

RED RIVER SKI AREA: The Red River Ski Area (tel. 505/754-2223, or toll free 800/348-6444) has a vertical rise of 1,530 feet, 27 trails, and an average annual snowfall of 175 inches. The area starts its snowmaking operations on the first of November with one of the most complete systems in New Mexico; on several occasions Red River has been the first resort in the U.S. to open. About three-quarters of its 120 acres of trails are serviced by the machines. Lift-ticket fees are $23 for adults and $13 for juniors (but children traveling with their parents ski and stay in the lodges for free). Package programs including lodging at local motels reduce costs. A discount period after Christmas is also in force.

Lodging in Red River includes the **Alpine Lodge,** on the bank of the Red River (tel. 505/754-2952), with motel rooms and some with kitchenettes. Rates are $40 to $56 double.

The **Golden Eagle Lodge,** on Main Street (tel. 505/754-2227, or toll free 800/621-4046), has fireplaces, a free ski shuttle, and in summer, hiking tours. Rates are $30 to $36 double.

For nightlife, **Texas Red's Steakhouse & Saloon** (tel. 754-2964) has a big television screen for Monday-night football, while a $40 season pass will get you in every Wednesday, Friday, and Saturday night to hear the Great American Honky Tonk Band in the **Motherlode Saloon.**

For all details about lodging and restaurants in Red River, call the **Red River Chamber of Commerce** in City Hall (tel. 505/754-2366, or toll free 800/348-6444).

SIPAPU AND RIO COSTILLA:
A family-style ski area 25 miles southeast of Taos, near the village of Vadito, **Sipapu Lodge Ski Area** (tel. 505/587-2240) is in Carson National Forest. There is a triple-chair lift and two Poma lifts serving 18 trails; lift rates are $18. The lodge has bunkrooms, housekeeping units, and a trailer park as well as ski shop, grocery store, and service station.

Newest area in Taos County is **Rio Costilla** (tel. 505/586-0570), up near the Colorado state line, which has 14 trails served by a triple-chair lift (3,800 feet) and a Poma lift, with elevation at 9,500 feet at the base, 11,500 feet at the peak. The area, an hour's drive from Taos via N.M. 3, has lift rates of $20 daily. Easy trails have easy-sounding names (Bambino, Niño, Ladies' Knee), while the most difficult trails are named Geronimo or Tequila Plunge. The area is also planning to add seven more ski lifts, to increase the resort's capacity by 8,000 skiers daily.

For room reservations in the Costilla area, call toll free 800/722-5438.

TAOS SKI VALLEY:
The best-known resort around Taos is Taos Ski Valley (tel. 505/776-2295), with difficult runs from dizzying heights, and a continental air provided by 12 lodges and hotels mostly in alpine architectural style. You can get a Taos Ski Valley report 24 hours a day on tape, updated daily at 8:30 a.m., by calling 758-0088; road conditions as well as the snow on the slopes are reported. The season runs from a few days before Thanksgiving through the second week of April. Skier capacity is 7,000 per hour via six double-chair lifts, a triple-chair lift, and two surface lifts, serving no fewer than 73 different runs, half of them expert level, the rest intermediate or beginner slopes.

Full-day lift tickets are $27 (except novice lifts, at $15). Those over 65 years of age get a break: $5 a day for all lifts. For children, an all-day Kinderkafig program for those aged 3 to 6 includes ski school, lunch, and supervised skiing, at $32; a program for juniors aged 7 to 12 costs $38 a day. Rental of equipment is extra: $12 for adults, $7 for children.

Newcomers arriving at the base of the resort are confronted with what appears to be a nearly vertical snowy drop of slope riding into the clouds. Indeed a sign here reads: "Don't panic!" The fact is that only one-thirtieth of the slopes are visible from the base lodges; the easier runs are up out of sight.

Lodging
The Valley is 18 miles from Taos via N.M. 150. Developer Ernie Blake had the idea of a whole planned environment when he built the resort—perfect skiing until nightfall, then good food and camaraderie in the evening. For this three lodges are notable: the St. Bernard, the Edelweiss, and the Thunderbird. The St. Bernard is directed by its French chef, Jean Mayer, a European champion who

also supervises a ski school here. His brother, Dadou Mayer, runs the Edelweiss. The Thunderbird is famous for its weekly Saturday buffet with such adornments as whole salmon or a turkey set up as if about to take flight. Entertainment in the lounges may be the Taos Jazz Quintet or a belly dancer. A jazz festival is held in January.

The **Hotel Edelweiss** (tel. 505/776-2301) organizes packages in the Taos Ski Valley tradition of requiring ski lessons no matter how good a skier you are —the philosophy of developer Blake is that every skier will leave the valley more skilled than when he came. Daily rates, including two meals, are $125 to $150 per person double. Says Dadou Mayer, proprietor, "You never have to do anything—even the smallest decision. Everything is preplanned. You don't even have to choose the menu." Mayer is famous for his many-coursed breakfasts and lunches, served personally to his guests with loving care. Dinners are served at the St. Bernard, next door, by brother Jean Mayer.

The **Hotel St. Bernard** (tel. 505/776-2251) runs packages similar to those of the other hostelries. The hotel boasts a complete wine cellar and a cheerful rathskeller for drinks around a modern copper-chimneyed fireplace. The first-rate cuisine is served table d'hôte with only one sitting: at 8:15 a.m. for breakfast, 12:15 p.m. for lunch, and 6:15 p.m. for dinner. Rates are $160 and up, American Plan.

The **Thunderbird Lodge** (tel. 505/776-2280) provides rooms with three meals daily at $94 per person, double occupancy. A "Learn to Ski Week" package, similar to that of the other lodges here, costs $860 per person in a double room. These packages start on Saturday afternoons, ending at noon the following Saturday. The lodge also provides a sauna, whirlpool, and free entertainment in the bar. Swiss fondue is offered as an "after-ski" treat on one afternoon.

Furnished condominium apartments may also be rented. The **Kändähar** (tel. 505/776-2226), for example, has apartments beginning at $240 a day, with fireplace, bath, and kitchen, and arranges weekly ski packages. **Rio Hondo Condominiums** (tel. 505/776-2646) has two-, three-, and four-bedroom apartments renting for $900 to $1,775 weekly.

Lower in price are lodgings out of the resort area but nearby. **Austing Haus Hotel,** just 1½ miles down the road from the resort (tel. 505/776-2649), has rooms at $55 to $95, and there's a free hot tub on the premises. A bit farther down the mountain, nine miles away in the community of Arroyo Seco, is the **Abominable Snowmansion** (tel. 505/776-8298), a bunkhouse dormitory accommodating 55 people, which has a big lodge room with a circular fireplace and piano. Family-style breakfasts and dinners are served in the dining room. Rates are $15 to $28 per person per night.

For all information on lodging at Taos Ski Valley, call the **Taos Valley Resort Association** (tel. 505/776-2233, or toll free 800/992-7669).

Other Facilities

Taos Ski Valley has a sportswear store, a pro shop, a rental shop and repair facility, but no grocery store—food shopping has to be done down in Taos, 18 miles away.

A Faust's Transportation (tel. 505/758-3410) express skiers' bus departs for Taos Ski Valley from the Albuquerque airport and from the Taos Plaza seven days a week.

9. DESTINATIONS EAST OF TAOS

The northeast corner of New Mexico is a land of high flat plateaus reaching out from Texas and Oklahoma, moving gradually up into the foothills of the

Rocky Mountains. There are grasslands leading gently up into spectacular skylines of peaks and wooded ridges where outdoors lovers find streams, ponds, and lakes for fishing and shoreside camping. The gateway city in the extreme northern part of this part of the state is Raton. Other communities, smaller, keep an old-fashioned western plainness that is disappearing in places more widely visited by tourists.

RATON: At an elevation of 6,600 feet, this small city of 9,400 population enjoys a dry climate with mild winters. Located below Raton Pass seven miles from the Colorado border on I-25, Raton takes advantage of its gateway position with two dozen restaurants and 21 motels that provide all the standard services for travelers. Raton also welcomes train travelers to New Mexico as a station stop for regular Amtrak service between Denver and El Paso. Early coal mines that once fueled the steam trains have seen a resurgence of activity in recent years around Raton, which is just over a century old.

A recently renovated racetrack, **La Mesa Park,** is a big attraction, its combination betting and lounge area being a major innovation under bright skylights, with closed-circuit monitors set up in 75 locations. A new general-admission grandstand seats 1,000 for races running from May 1 to October 1, with post time at 12:30 p.m., on weekends only. Friday races, with free admission for women, starting at 3 p.m., are held also during the summer season. Race results are available from a "hot-line" telephone (tel. 445-2333).

Drama, comedy, and mystery are included in the fare provided in July and August by the **Shuler Theatre.** The **Raton Museum,** at 216 S. 1st St., across from the railroad depot, displays a wide variety of items from the early days of the town; it's open from 1 to 5 p.m. Tuesday through Sunday. The public is welcome at the 18-hole course of the **Raton Country Club** (tel. 445-9957). There are two movie theaters, a roller skating rink, and a municipal swimming pool.

Just eight miles north of town is the small, popular **Sugarite Ski Basin** (tel. 505/445-5000), on Walton's Mountain at a base elevation of 8,100 feet. From a warming lodge here a 1,300-foot Poma lift takes skiers up to 100 acres of gentle slopes called the Meadows. A double-chair lift rises from that area another 2,000 feet to the trailheads of more difficult runs. Open from Thanksgiving to Easter, Friday through Sunday, the area has a ski school and rental shop. Fees are $18 for all lifts, daily. Ski packages are set up with the **Melody Lane Motel** in Raton (tel. 505/445-3655, or toll free 800/421-5210 outside New Mexico) with such attractive deals as a four-day stay, with two meals daily and lift tickets, at under $350 for two people.

Among Raton motels near the racetrack is the **Holiday Inn,** on Clayton Road (U.S. 64), Raton, NM 87740 (tel. 505/445-5555, or toll free 800/255-8879), with double rates of $56 to $70.

Among restaurants, **Tinnie's Palace,** on 1st Street at Cook (tel. 445-3285), has a cocktail lounge and serves steaks and seafoods.

For detailed information on lodging and restaurants in Raton, call the **Raton Chamber of Commerce** (tel. 505/445-3689).

OUTDOOR AREAS EAST OF RATON: Some 85 miles east of Raton, near the Oklahoma and Texas borders on N.M. 370, north of the town of Clayton, is **Clayton Lake State Park.** The rolling grasslands here are part of an area where two great parcels have been set aside as national grasslands. The lake is stocked with trout, catfish, and bass, and there is a boat dock.

Lying 30 miles west of Raton via U.S. 64 west to the town of Capulin, then north on N.M. 325, is **Capulin Mountain National Monument.** It is one of the few places in the world where you can walk into a volcano. A two-mile road leads to the summit of the mountain, from which a short hiking trail leads right to the bottom of this crater to its vent, giving the rare chance of inspecting the inside of a volcanic mountain. The view to the west from up here is spectacular: the snow-capped peaks of the Sangre de Cristo mountains make the background to a vast flat plateau of rangeland. Visitors should first stop at the visitor center half a mile from the park entrance (open from 8 a.m. to 4:30 p.m. Labor Day to Memorial Day, from 7:30 a.m. to 6:30 p.m. in the summer season). Besides the volcano itself, the plant and animal life are of interest, particularly when the wildflowers are blooming in late spring and early summer. Spring brings a wide variety of birdlife to the monument as well.

At **Chicosa Lake State Park,** near the town of Roy, there are interpretive exhibits of historic ranchland in these parts, with a real herd of longhorn cattle, as well as a campground and showers.

CIMARRON: The quintessential western town of hundreds of cowboy movies, Cimarron seems to hold a special place in our imagination. It is 37 miles southwest of Raton via U.S. 64, which follows the old Santa Fe Trail.

In the 1840s Lucien Maxwell, an associate of Kit Carson, had a mansion in Cimarron which was the center of his landowning, cattle-ranching empire. Maxwell's lasting fame came from his ownership of the largest piece of land ever recorded in U.S. history: 1.7 million acres. This tract, covering northern New Mexico and part of southern Colorado, came into Maxwell's possession when he married Luz Beaubien, the 13-year-old daughter of an original grantee of the property. Maxwell ruled his domain like a feudal lord, collecting tribute in livestock, hay and grain, or gold dust.

You can still see the **Maxwell Ranch,** built in 1857, where the tycoon entertained his cronies in the salon and dining room, both furnished opulently with heavy draperies, gold-framed paintings, and two grand pianos hauled in from the East. In the gaming room the tables saw action at high stakes, as guests bet silver Mexican pesos or pokes of yellow gold dust. Gold was struck on Maxwell's land in 1867, near Baldy Mountain, bringing in a rush of prospectors. Maxwell sold out altogether three years later.

While in Cimarron Maxwell also operated the **Aztec grist mill**—it still stands in good condition—a stout, three-story stone structure with massive beams supporting the floors. The water wheel once activated by the Cimarron River is now gone, but the old wooden screws and gears that powered the grinding stones are still in place.

Today the old mill is a museum holding documents, photographs, and artifacts of Cimarron's life and history, overseen by oldtime Cimarron residents Buddy and Babe Morse, who like nothing better than to talk about the western lore of the town and the Santa Fe Trail that led to it. Among three floors of exhibits, there are a few items that visitors may purchase and take home with them: Santa Fe Railroad spikes at 50¢ each, or perhaps a buffalo skull, with impressively curving horns, at $195. A fully equipped chuck wagon displays aging cans and food cartons a century old.

In this old town on the Santa Fe Trail the era of Indian fighting and range wars seems very close. Among its notorious residents were such lawless characters as Billy the Kid, Clay Allison, Bob Ford, and Black Jack Ketchum. The recently restored gem of a Victorian inn, the **St. James Hotel,** is as good a reason as any to stop in Cimarron, but there are other reasons as well, notably the delight that comes from being at an altitude of 6,500 feet in the Sangre de Cristo mountains, part of the Rockies.

Oklahoma oilman Waite Phillips' **Philmont Ranch** can also be visited. This 22-room mansion, built in 1927, has arched windows painted with scenes of the Santa Fe Trail, and a private library with an intriguing porthole-like window framing the Sangre de Cristo mountains in the distance. Phillips donated the property to the Boy Scouts of America and here the Scouts keep 250 saddle horses and a herd of Hereford cattle on the ranch, which also serves as a training facility for Scoutmasters. During their treks the Scouts ride horses, pack burros, pan for gold, climb rocks, do rifle target shooting, study archeological sites, and fill in with old-fashioned hiking, camping, and cooking.

On the Scouts' property also is the **Seton Memorial Library,** holding books, art, and natural history collections of the late naturalist and writer Ernest Thompson Seton (1860–1946), the first chief scout of the Boy Scouts of America (he wrote the original *Boy Scout Handbook*).

A **Kit Carson Museum,** seven miles south of the Philmont Ranch in the community of Rayado, is constructed in the style of a 19th-century Mexican hacienda. Summer tours here are given by staffers in historic costume, and there are crafts demonstrations—a smithy, furniture making—as well as the practice of oldtime farming methods.

Other historic buildings standing in Cimarron today are the **Dahl Brothers Trading Post,** on the Plaza (1854); **Swink's Gambling Hall** (1854); the **National Hotel** (1854); the **Old Jail** (1872); the **Cimarron News and Press Building** (1872); and the **Colfax County Courthouse** (1872).

Where to Stay and Eat

The central attraction for tourists is the lovely old **St. James Hotel,** 17th and Collinson, Cimarron, NM 87714 (tel. 505/376-2664). It was built in 1872 by a Frenchman, Henry Lambert, a former chef for Napoleon and for Abraham Lincoln. His new hotel was a rare luxury on the Santa Fe Trail. Its two-foot-thick adobe walls enclosed a saloon, a dining room, gambling rooms, and lavish guest rooms fitted out with Victorian furniture. Most of it has been restored today, with loving care, by its present owners, Ed and Pat Sitzberger, who took over the place in 1983. Only the downstairs bar had been in use for the last 25 years, but the Sitzbergers managed to reopen the entire two-story hotel in 1985. Ed, a Cimarron native, grew up, he says, practically "in the backyard" of the hotel; restoring it had been a sort of lifelong ambition. His wife, Pat, an established watercolorist, now displays her works, most of them southwestern landscapes, in the dining room.

They have returned the lace and the cherrywood to the bedrooms, and have brought back fancy lamps and heavy silken curtains, the better to evoke the days when famous guests such as Zane Grey, who wrote *Fighting Caravans* at the hotel, were residents. Annie Oakley's bed is here, and a glass case holds a register with the signatures of the notorious Jesse James and Buffalo Bill Cody.

Overstuffed chairs and a round oak table grace the lounge. The hotel also keeps, it is said, three ghosts out of the past—plus one imp. One of the ghosts is that of Mary Lambert, wife of the original builder; she died here in the 1890s at the age of 33. The other shades are those of long-departed guests. An early legend tells of gunman Clay Allison dancing on the bar in the present dining room; in the corridor sits one of those original roulette wheels, where Allison played his favorite betting game.

The restaurant of the St. James is relatively ambitious: appetizers may include snails in mushroom caps, while entrees could be pollo Gismonda (breaded chicken breast in a spinach ring with mushrooms and rice) or tournedos in a pastry shell with romana sauce. A specialty is veal marsala. Fettuccine Alfredo or stuffed flounder Florentine is also usually on hand. Full dinners with wine run $16 to $19.

There are 15 rooms, some with bath, at $50 to $60 double.

Sights Outside Cimarron

Ten miles west of Cimarron is **Cimarron Canyon State Park,** part of a wildlife area where camping is free if you have a state hunting or fishing license. The Cimarron River offers trout fishing, and there are great backpacking trails in the park. Rock climbers attempt to scale crenellated formations of granite known as the Palisades.

South of Cimarron via Springer and I-25 south to Watrous, then north for eight miles on N.M. 477, is **Fort Union National Monument,** open during daylight hours only, and picnic tables are on hand. A visitor center provides information on the life of the fort before it was abandoned at the turn of the century. Today it's in ruins, much of it old adobe, and the National Park Service people here are working on experiments to find means of halting the deterioration of what remains, using chemical sprays, epoxies, and new applications of adobe mud.

The fort was set up to guard the Santa Fe Trail, for 60 years the main link between New Mexico and the states back east. Wagon ruts are still visible from those prairie schooners that came through by the thousand. For many years the fort was the headquarters of an open war between the army and the nomadic tribes of New Mexico.

Also in the area, on N.M. 38 north of Mora, is **Coyote Creek State Park,** hidden away in the Sangre de Cristo mountains. There is a stream with several beaver ponds, good fishing for trout, hiking trails, and a campground.

10. DESTINATIONS WEST OF TAOS

The main gateway from the northwest into New Mexico is the busy little city of Farmington, not far from the famous Four Corners area where four states meet at one point (New Mexico, Colorado, Utah, and Arizona)—the only such spot in the country. In this dry mountain land there are Indian reservations, more state parks, and important prehistoric ruins.

FARMINGTON: This coal-mining and oil- and gas-producing center, with an estimated population of 37,000, is a major center for tourists to the Four Corners. Through the year an enthusiastic chamber of commerce organizes a number of annual events: an Apple Blossom Festival in April, several rodeos through the year, the Connie Mack World Series and a county fair in August, a cultural heritage festival in October, and an arts-and-crafts fair in November, as well as opera productions by a local company and theatrical and concert series too.

For all information, contact the **Farmington Convention and Visitors Bureau,** 203 W. Main St., Farmington, NM 87401 (tel. 505/326-7602, or toll free 800/541-1398).

Lodging

The Inn, 700 Scott, Farmington, NM 87401 (tel. 505/327-5221, or toll free 800/528-1234), is a meeting place for Farmington people, with its attractive public areas: an enclosed tropical garden perfect for conversing over a drink during most months of the year, a busy bar and lounge, a heated indoor pool, and men's and women's saunas. The rooms have extra-large beds, refrigerators, and cable color TV with 24-hour movies. Rates are $53 to $63 double.

Quiet rooms with basic amenities—air conditioning, cable service and movies on the TV, a swimming pool, and free coffee in the morning—are available inexpensively at the **Redwood Lodge,** 652 E. Main St., Farmington, NM 87401 (tel. 505/326-2288), with rates of $21 double.

Dining

O'Henry's, 4601 E. Main St. (tel. 327-5221), is a popular meeting place for Farmingtonians after work, for drinks in the lounge. The restaurant starts the day with breakfast, then offers a daily luncheon buffet. Spanish specialties (New Mexico style) as well as continental dishes are offered at dinner, at moderate prices.

Transportation

There are a dozen car-rental agencies in town, including these three with offices at the Four Corners Regional Airport: **Avis** (tel. 327-9864), **Hertz** (tel. 327-6093), and **National** (tel. 327-0215).

Mesa Airlines (tel. 326-3338, or toll free 800/637-2247) connects the city with other New Mexico points and with Durango and Telluride, Colorado. **Texas, New Mexico, & Oklahoma (TNM&O) buses** (tel. 325-1009) run to Albuquerque and return. **Roadrunner Taxi** (tel. 327-1909) is on duty 24 hours daily.

TRIPS OUT OF FARMINGTON: The ruins of a fabulous 500-room Indian pueblo abandoned around 600 years ago make up **Aztec Ruins National Monument,** 14 miles northeast of Farmington via U.S. 550 in the town of Aztec (tel. 334-6174). The visitor center and park are open from 8 a.m. to 5 p.m. (except in summer when closing time is extended to nightfall). The country's only example of a completely restored *kiva*—a circular enclosed ceremonial room—is the highlight of a visit. Pioneers named both the ruins and the town after ancient Mexican Indians who never had any connection with this region. The people who lived here until they mysteriously disappeared around A.D. 1300 were called the Anasazi—a Navajo word for "the old people." Besides the highly impressive stone masonry visible in the old walls, there are examples of handcrafts of the Anasazi, baskets and pottery, in a small museum in the visitor center. There is an entrance fee of $2 per car.

Salmon Ruins, 11 miles east of Farmington on U.S. 64 (tel. 632-2013), was a planned community of over 700 rooms, a multistory pueblo overlooking the San Juan River. It is one of the most recently excavated ruins in the West. Archeologists found that the first residents lived here only two generations, then disappeared, to be replaced a century later (during the 13th century) by emigrants from the great Mesa Verde complex to the north in Colorado. But they, too, abandoned the site in the late 1200s. A small museum administered by the county archeological research center displays artifacts from the site.

A federally protected area of weird rock formations, petrified logs, and fossils is the **Bisti Badlands,** 32 miles south of Farmington on N.M. 371. A walk among the huge turrets, buttes, spires, and pinnacles makes you feel you're on an undiscovered planet.

Shiprock, 29 miles west of Farmington via U.S. 550, is named for the striking rock formation to the southwest of town, a landmark of the Navajo Indians who live here. Their reservation extends into a vast area of Arizona across the state line; they are the most populous tribe of American Indians, with over 150,000 members.

The town of Dulce, 80 miles east of Farmington on U.S. 64, is the headquarters of the **Jicarilla Apache Reservation,** which covers high plateau and mountain country comprising 750,000 acres along N.M. 537. A modern lodge run by the Indians at **Stone Lake** welcomes fishermen and hunters of elk, deer, bear, and fowl on the reservation. At Dulce and Mundo Lakes, where the trout fishing is good, the tribe operates public campgrounds. An all-night Indian celebration, with races, dancing, and a rodeo, goes on at Stone Lake every September 14 and 15. The Indians set up tents and tepees and make a lively encampment, and the visitor is welcome to join them. The town of Dulce has a crafts museum that has been reviving interest in traditional leatherwork, beadwork, and basketry.

A favorite trip for visitors to northern New Mexico departs from the town of Chama, about 100 miles west of Farmington; trips may also be taken from Antonito, Colorado. The **Cumbres & Toltec Scenic Railroad** (tel. 756-2151 in Chama), billed as "America's longest and highest steam railroad," is a historic project of the states of New Mexico and Colorado leased to an operating concession. The 64-mile route "represents the finest remaining example of what was once a vast network of narrow-gauge lines which laced together the commercial outposts of the Rocky Mountain region," according to the operators.

The line originally served mining camps in the San Juan Mountains of Colorado, and passes through forests of pine and aspen, past fantastic rock formations, and through the magnificent Toltec Gorge of the Los Piños River. It crests at the 10,015-foot Cumbres Pass, the highest in the U.S. used by scheduled passenger trains. When the old steam locomotive stops up here to take on water, passengers descend to the trackside to take pictures. Halfway through the route, at Osier, Colorado, the *New Mexico Express* from Chama and the *Colorado Limited* from Antonito meet, stop, and exchange engines. Round-trip day passengers return to their starting point after enjoying a picnic or catered lunch beside the old water tank and stock pens up here. Through train excursions in a round trip, with overnight accommodations at either end, cost $121, including meals. The regular day trip is $27, or a through trip for the full 64 miles with return by van the same day is $41.50. Reservation requests for trips running daily from June 4 through October 9 can be made by telephone or by writing C&TS RR, P.O. Box 789, Chama, NM 87520; or C&TS RR, P.O. Box 668, Antonito, CO 81120.

For information on lodgings around Chama, call the **Chama Valley Chamber of Commerce** (tel. 505/756-2306). Near the train station is a bed-and-breakfast inn called the **Jones House,** at Terrace and 3rd Streets, Chama, NM 87520 (tel. 505/756-2908), a 1912 structure giving great mountain views and providing fresh baked breads at breakfast and afternoon coffee and tea; rates are $42 double. On U.S. 84 a good bet is the **High Country Inn** (tel. 505/756-2384), with double rates of $46.

Chama eateries include the **High Country Restaurant,** adjoining the inn, with a bar and standard American-style fare emphasizing steaks; and **Vera's Mexican Kitchen,** on N.M. 17 (tel. 756-2557), a moderately priced spot for traditional New Mexico cooking, with beer and wine available.

Two reservoirs near Chama are the centerpieces of **El Vado Lake State Park** and **Heron Lake State Park.** A scenic trail between the two makes a delightful short hike. El Vado offers waterskiing, a boat dock, and a marina, and is a favorite of ice fishermen in winter. Heron is designated a "quiet lake" with motor crafts restricted to trolling speed. It also has good fishing as well as a visitor center with interpretive displays. Both parks have campgrounds.

About 50 miles west of Farmington, with access from N.M. 511, are two separate areas of **Navajo Lake State Park** around a 13,000-acre lake surrounded by sandstone mesas and forests of juniper and piñon. A visitor center with interpretive displays is near a boat ramp and campground at the Pine River site, and there is a marina with boat rentals and supplies. Another campground is set up on the east shore of the lake at Sims Mesa.

Other fishing spots around Farmington include the San Juan River, open for trout fishing for eight miles below Navajo Dam, a stretch called by local boosters "the hottest trout waters in the Rocky Mountain West." Farmington Lake, three miles east of Farmington, and Jackson Lake, nine miles north, also offer trout, bass, and catfish.

Visitors to the area are advised not to miss **Angel Peak,** 35 miles southeast of Farmington on N.M. 44, a National Park Service recreation site with a campground affording views of stone formations in red, yellow, lavender, and every shade of brown. The easy trails and overlooks make the spot great for a day's or an overnight's outing.

CHAPTER V

ALBUQUERQUE AND ENVIRONS

□ □ □

With a population of over half a million, Albuquerque is New Mexico's largest city, but keeps about it the bustling booster spirit of western towns of half a century ago when "progress" was a fashionable word and growing bigger was unquestionably synonymous with getting better. The city first jumped away from its origins around the Plaza in Old Town when the railroad came through in 1880 and caused a new Albuquerque to be planted around the passenger and freight depots. Now "downtown," so reminiscent of a hundred small plains cities in the '30s and '40s, is being supplanted by vast commercial and shopping complexes far away from the *Saturday Evening Post*-style center, within quick reach by car via the long, wide, straight, flat streets and avenues of the sprawling grid that reach nearly to the foot of the Sandia Mountains 20 miles east of the old center.

In spite of the leveling, gentrifying effect of the spread of chain restaurants and fern bars, interchangeable condos and placeless superhighways, Albuquerque retains strong elements of its original western spirit, still feeling somehow closer to the plains to the east, the directness of the Texan, than to the thin, chic optimism and faddishness of California. It is a young city: the people are young in years and in energy. The university plays a central role in life here, both by its geography just east of downtown and for the part it takes in the life of its city through its outstanding museums and cultural programs.

The city does have its awful sprawl of commercial strips along the main east-west highway. The notorious old Route 66 still goes straight through town, where modern-day pioneers heading west used to "get their kicks," even though most of its traffic has been diverted to the Interstate. But it is not all that long ago that Albuquerque had for a main drag a movie-set-like row of false-front hotels, bars, and stores lined in front with hitching posts and wooden sidewalks along a muddy, rutted roadway crowded with wagons and buggies and figures on horseback. From that shot-in-the-arm railroad connection in 1880 came the impetus to grow, to build, to move out in every direction without a thought for the future —without any plan at all. Albuquerque did in fact grow so big and so much before there was any thought to saving any of its land for public use that there was hardly much chance to plan anything when the time finally seemed right to try to control the place a bit. This action did not occur until 1975, but nevertheless it has provided the citizens (and visitors) with some green spaces, and there are more to come. Altogether, a visitor viewing the city for the first time from a vantage point within a car speeding in over the Interstate, which makes a huge cross in the middle of town with its east-west and north-south trajectories meeting and corkscrewing in and around one another, might suppose himself lost in a Los Angeles–style wasteland of urban sprawl. But parts of Albuquerque are very special indeed—you just have to make sure to find them.

One of these, of course, is the Plaza of Old Town, which rivals the Plazas of Santa Fe and Taos for historical interest, architectural beauty, and lively shopping and restaurant-going scenes. Another is an ultramodern, innovative complex of starkly designed, glistening glass-and-steel bank buildings clustered around a tiled open space containing a pool and a fountain, terraces and tables with parasols, the whole concealing a brightly lighted futuristic warren of underground shops, bars, and eating places that could make you imagine you'd come to Montréal on the Rio Grande—it's called First Plaza. That good familiar old western-style downtown is just outside in case you feel a dire need for a touch of reality after an hour or two under the glassed-in waterfall from that pool upstairs, visible from both outdoors and below ground as well.

The city was established in 1706 by Spanish colonists who had permission from King Philip of Spain to establish a new *villa*—a tightly knit community of houses clustered around a plaza—on the banks of the Rio Grande. The site in a curve of the river provided for irrigation and a wood supply from the cottonwoods, willows, and olive trees growing along the shore. The first structure to be built was the San Felipe de Neri Church, still in place although since enlarged and remodeled. Its original walls are intact, however, and it serves both as the heart of Old Town and as the meaningful starting point or center of the entire city, including its ancient and its modern parts as well. But the city nevertheless has never stayed quite put—when the course of the river shifted, so did parts of the city. Then the railroad brought its competing town center a mile and a half to the southeast of the Plaza—New Town was long its name.

The city was long a supply center for the series of forts that were built and manned throughout the Southwest to protect pioneers from Indian attack on their grueling treks to new homesteads out here. Today it has added to its original mercantile base by developing supply depots for military bases and building experimental scientific laboratories in a wide variety of specialized fields. Its warm, sunny climate and healthful altitude—varying from 4,200 to 6,000 feet—also bring in many vacationers and retirement residents.

The fairgrounds is the site for the annual State Fair and for a colorful and locally renowned annual arts-and-crafts show. Indian pueblos in the area welcome tourists, and along with other pueblos throughout New Mexico have worked together to create the remarkable Pueblo Cultural Center, a showplace of Indian crafts of both past and present. The country's longest aerial tramway takes visitors to the top of Sandia Peak, guarding the city from the east and site of a first-rate ski area in season.

The city boasts a wide-open cheerful nightlife based on a seemingly bottomless supply of country-and-western performers as well as numerous local and West Coast–import rock bands, bluegrass performers, and jazz musicians.

As the city grows apace, new luxury-level hotels rise to welcome the increasing flow of visitors on business and on vacation, and the variety and quality of available cuisine should satisfy anyone who makes the effort to track down just what he likes best. Traditionally known for their western steaks, many city restaurants also provide authentic regional dishes from the state's Hispanic tradition, which are not quite like those south of the border.

With its gleaming skyscrapers and international air flights in and out of town night and day, Albuquerque may appear headed for something like grand metropolis status, but in spite of those fancy hotels and tasseled menus written out in French there is a lot of down-home small-town plainness left in Albuquerque—a plainsman's spirit that doesn't like to put on airs for anybody, a spirit most visitors seem to take to easily indeed.

1. ORIENTATION

GETTING TO AND FROM ALBUQUERQUE: Albuquerque sprawls out on a high plateau just to the northwest of the geographical center of New Mexico at distances of 802 miles from Los Angeles, 1,460 miles from Seattle, 1,350 miles from Chicago, 2,029 miles from New York, 1,424 miles from Atlanta, and 670 miles from Dallas. Its center is at the junction of Interstate highways 25 and 40.

It is served by daily passenger service via **Amtrak** trains from and to Los Angeles and Chicago (tel. 242-7816 for passenger information).

Texas, New Mexico, and Oklahoma Coaches (tel. 242-4998) and Greyhound (tel. 243-4435) bus lines connect the city with other points throughout the U.S.

Airlines serving Albuquerque International Airport are American (tel. 242-9464), America West (tel. toll free 800/247-5692), Continental (tel. 842-8220), Delta (tel. toll free 800/221-1212), Eastern (tel. toll free 800/EASTERN), Southwest (tel. 831-1221), Trans World (tel. 842-4404), and United (tel. 242-1411).

GETTING AROUND ALBUQUERQUE: Shuttlejack (tel. 243-3244) runs frequent limo service between the airport and city hotels. Regularly scheduled city buses cover the city; for information call **Sun Tran** (tel. 843-9200). The **Albuquerque Trolley** (tel. 242-1407) runs hourly service downtown and to the Plaza.

Car-rental agencies include **Avis** (tel. 842-4080), **Budget** (tel. 884-2666), **Hertz** (tel. 842-4235), **National** (tel. 842-4222), and **Thrifty** (tel. 842-8733).

Taxis include **Checker** (tel. 243-7777) and **Yellow Cab** (tel. 842-5292). You can get touring and **highway-condition information** for the Albuquerque area by calling 841-8066.

Sightseeing tours are run locally and various distances through the state by a number of operators, including: **AAA Travel Agency** (tel. 291-6700), **Southwest Gray Line** (tel. 265-8311), **Jack Allen Tours** (tel. 266-9688), **Sun Tours** (tel. 881-5346), and **Tour New Mexico** (tel. 884-9115).

The **Sandia Peak Aerial Tramway** runs all year. For information, call the tram office (tel. 298-8518). Old Town is best visited on foot; for self-guiding maps to this historic area stop in at the **Old Town Visitor Information Booth,** 305 Romero NW.

USEFUL INFORMATION: You can report a police, fire, or rescue **emergency** in the Albuquerque area by phoning 911. The number for the **police** is 768-1986; and for the **fire department,** 243-6601. You can reach the headquarters for the **New Mexico State Police** in the city at 841-8066. For **road and weather conditions,** call 841-9256.

Albuquerque hospitals with emergency rooms include **Heights General Hospital** (tel. 888-7800), **Presbyterian Hospital** (tel. 841-1234), and **St. Joseph Hospital** (tel. 848-8000). The city **ambulance** service number is 765-1100.

AAA members can call **emergency road service** at 884-6611. Call 988-2211 for **time** of day and current outdoor **temperatures,** 243-1371 for a **weather report.** To get **ski reports** for Sandia Peak, call 242-9052.

For travel information, contact the **Albuquerque Convention and Visitors Bureau,** 625 Silver SW, Albuquerque, NM 87102 (tel. 505/243-3696, or toll free 800/284-ALVB).

2. WHERE TO STAY

From the scores of modest-to-flashy motels along old U.S. 66 (Central Avenue) to such elaborate and expensive resorts-within-inns as the Doubletree and the Sheraton Old Town or the Marriott, Albuquerque, a year-round city for visitors, usually has space to take care of them all. Since most of the city has grown horizontally instead of vertically, there has usually been enough space laid out for parking lots at both modest motels and fancy digs. With average daily high temperatures reaching 70° and above all the way from April to October, the multitudes of swimming pools—small and large, kidney-shaped or "Olympic" size—are happily used by guests during much of the year, and there are some indoor ones too, of course. The city, incidentally, gets only eight inches of rainfall all year.

There is a big demand for campgrounds for recreational vehicles in and around the city because of this salutary climate, and a good number of these have installed modern facilities of every kind within recent years.

OLD TOWN AND DOWNTOWN AREAS: Albuquerque's Old Town, around the original Plaza, and its current downtown harbor a number of hosteleries ranging from deluxe to budget. Here are my recommendations:

Luxury Choices

The **Sheraton Old Town,** 800 Rio Grande Blvd. NW, Albuquerque, NM 87104 (tel. 505/843-6300, or toll free 800/325-3535), is a high-rise structure of innovative and pleasing modernity built in 1975 next door to the Plaza in Old Town, the only major hostelry in this area. A subtle architectural relationship connects this high brown-and-tan façade and its sharply outlined white balconies with the traditional adobe of old-style pueblo buildings. The good effect is probably due to an artistically pleasing use of space, warm colors within high-ceilinged lobbies, and lavish use of traditional textures such as tile and stone. The idea was to recapture that elegant Territorial-style atmosphere once known in famous old hotels long since torn down, like the old Alvarado and the Franciscan. Yet modern materials and ideas are used everywhere—for once this is not a copy of anything out of the past. It was not the exact visual picture but that elusive southwestern-style spirit that the builders wanted to capture, and many locals believe they have succeeded.

Architect John Peter Varsa, who designed the inn, started with a stained-glass window with the letters "LOBBY" spelled out in colored glass; it once adorned another of the city's ghost hotels, the Savoy. Today it looms over the main entrance to the vast yet warm-feeling lobby of the Old Town. Copper is part of the secret in what makes the place feel western and authentic: copper telephones especially made for the hotel, copper sculptures sprouting their branches against adobe-like backgrounds, an old copper mail chute out of still another missing hotel. The lobby brings more comment, probably, from casual visitors who come in just to look around, than any other part of the 190-room inn.

Guests enjoy a view to the south from any of the ten floors from the glass-enclosed elevator lobbies. Originality and individuality do not stop within the guest rooms—each one is furnished uniquely down to an original oil painting on a regional theme. Movies or sports events are shown (for a $5 fee) on the television screens. Rooms have such furnishings as inlaid coffee tables, deep leather-upholstered sofas, and fresh greenery.

Two restaurants, the Customs House and the Café del Sol, provide American and Mexican food, while the Fireplace Piano Bar and the Taverna Entertainment Lounge enliven the city's nightlife. Attached to the premises is the Mercado Mall, with several shops, while the historic Plaza, with some 140 emporia of every sort, is only a block's walk away.

Room rates—including use of the pool, tennis courts, sun terrace, and Jacuzzis—are $84 to $92 double. Children under 17 share their parents' room free.

Another first-class hotel, this one right downtown next to the Convention Center, is the **Doubletree,** 201 Marquette Ave. NW, Albuquerque, NM 87102 (tel. 505/247-3344, or toll free 800/545-4444). Its lobby, too, makes an impression on the first-time visitor in a blending of color and pattern, mostly tans, browns, and blending maroons and yellows that suggest desert flowers or sand, in carpeting and wall decorations. A grand flight of stairs leads down from the lobby to the Promenade Café, brightly lighted through an atrium roof 30 feet overhead—just the spot to meet someone for a date and to make a dramatic entrance. Clusters of old-style streetlight globes on wrought-iron pillars give the big room a Gay '90s air. The Mayfair Restaurant makes its bid as the best continental-style eating place in the city. At night the Mayfair Lounge and Juliana's of London provide live entertainment and dancing; the latter, a private club, extends membership privileges free to guests. While in town, guests also have free membership at a country club, for golf and tennis, as well as at a health club, for swimming, racquetball, and the use of a Jacuzzi and Nautilus equipment.

Spacious rooms are decorated in a modernistic southwestern style with warm colors echoing those of the carpets and wall hangings of the lobby: browns, yellows, oranges in geometric patterns. Rates are $85 to $105 double, and children under 14 share their parents' room free.

The **Albuquerque Hilton,** 1901 University Blvd. NE, Albuquerque, NM 87102 (tel. 505/884-2500, or toll free 800/821-1901), has a 12-story coppery-brick façade of balconied picture windows looking out on a broad, sunny plaza. Guests in the 450 rooms, priced at $75 to $95 double, can use two heated swimming pools (one indoors and one outside), two tennis courts, saunas, a whirlpool, a shuffleboard court, a game room, and a putting green. A 24-hour coffeeshop supplements a dining room open for lunch and dinner. The Bolero Lounge has music and dancing nightly, and the Library Bar makes a subdued luxurious setting for an early-evening rendezvous. The Hilton is near the junction of the east-west and the north-south Interstates.

Moderately Priced Lodging

Also adjacent to this Interstate intersection is the **Holiday Inn,** 2020 Menaul Blvd. NE, Albuquerque, NM 87107 (tel. 505/884-2511, or toll free 800/HOLIDAY), with 297 rooms priced at $76 double, and a bar, lounge, pool, and restaurant.

Howard Johnson, 900 Medical Arts Square, 801 Encino Pl. NE, Albuquerque, NM 87102 (tel. 505/243-5693, or toll free 800/654-2000), has 120 rooms at $44 double, and offers a bar, lounge, pool, and restaurant.

The **Rio Grande Inn,** at 1015 Rio Grande Blvd. NW, Albuquerque, NM 87104 (tel. 505/843-9500, or toll free 800/528-1234), is near Old Town and the Plaza shops, and has a bar and lounge, pool, and restaurant, and 170 guest rooms priced at $38 double.

CENTRAL AVENUE (BUDGET LODGING): This is Route 66, the famous highway from east to west where you get your kicks, and it offers a gamut of motels in the lower price ranges. Some are a few miles from the center of the city, at the eastern approaches, while others are not far from downtown.

Typical of the Central Avenue accommodations is a standard chain, **Travelodge,** at 3711 Central Ave. NE, Albuquerque, NM 87108 (tel. 505/265-6961, or toll free 800/255-3050), located between the downtown and uptown parts of the city, near the fairgrounds and the University of New Mexico campus. With its gleaming white openwork concrete baffles shading the bright sunlight from the balconies here and there, and its cheerful yellow umbrellas over poolside tables, it makes an oasis among the straight highways and cross streets of the newer part of the city. Both radios and TV are provided in all rooms, and there is free coffee in the morning; rates are $26 double.

HOTELS AROUND TOWN (MEDIUM PRICED): The **Clarion Four Seasons,** 2500 Carlisle Blvd. NE (at the intersection of I-40 and Carlisle NE), Albuquerque, NM 87110 (tel. 505/888-3311), has 377 rooms at $79 double. Two restaurants, the Crystal Room for continental cuisine and Delfino's for steaks and Mexican food, are part of the premises, which also include a show lounge, Don Quixote's, and a 24-hour coffeeshop. An indoor garden patio has a pool, and there is another pool outside, along with a sauna, whirlpool baths, a game room, and a putting green.

The **Albuquerque Marriott,** 2101 Louisiana Blvd. NE (at the intersection of I-40), Albuquerque, NM 87110 (tel. 505/881-6800, or toll free 800/228-9290), occupies a modern 16-story structure with 414 rooms at $93 to $105 double. A solarium has the indoor part of an indoor-outdoor pool and a hydrotherapy pool. There is a health club with exercising gadgets and weights, men's and women's saunas, and an electronic game room. There are a couple of good bars, the dim Quiet Bar off the lobby, and Nicole's Lounge with music, board games, and a daily happy hour; dinners are served here and at the elegant Herbs & Roses restaurant.

3. WHERE TO EAT

Although food in Albuquerque used to be prepared mainly with a western plainness, with steaks the big dinnertime favorite, or consisted of the New Mexico specialties in Hispanic cuisine, now the continental style appears in many kitchens, particularly in the big new hotels and motels. More and more seafood and other fresh ingredients are being flown into town so that the inland location has a less narrowing effect on food sources than it used to. Walkers and shoppers

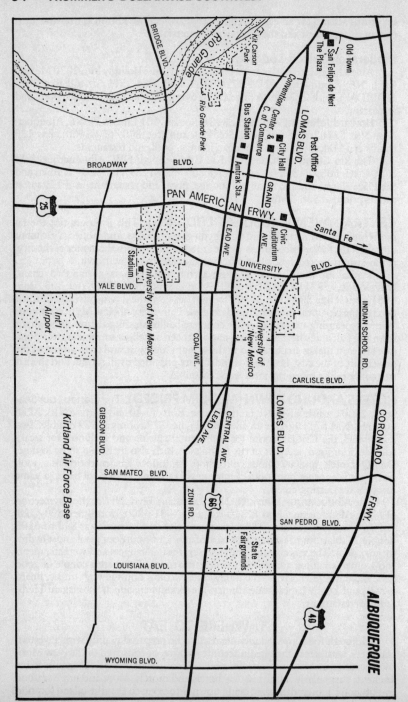

around the Old Town Plaza can find plenty to choose from in menu specialties and price range. The downtown area has many good lunch spots and a few luxury dinner options, while elsewhere the list of likely entries grows apace as the city expands; several good eateries combine first-rate entertainment with the good things from their kitchens.

THE OLD TOWN AREA: In addition to dining rooms in such Old Town hotels as the Sheraton, there are a number of good dining choices in and around Old Town, in all price ranges. Let's start with—

Luxury Choices

A quiet, intimate restaurant superbly furnished in Victorian antiques, with fresh white linen and sparkling glassware on the tables, **Antiquity,** 112 Romero St. (tel. 247-3545), is open for dinner Tuesday through Saturday to 10 p.m. Occupying a diminutive one-story adobe structure, the restaurant provides continental specialties worth seeking out. Appetizers might be smoked trout or onion soup, followed by an entree of salmon en papillote (baked in parchment with champagne and dill) for $14, or a cioppino, a sort of Italian-style bouillabaisse involving crabs, squid, clams, mussels, and various fish with a wine-and-tomato sauce, at $18. An ambitious preparation is the Henri V crown filet under artichoke heart and béarnaise sauce, served with crabs' legs and either lobster or scampi ($25). Another choice is a chateaubriand for two, at $40.

Maria Teresa, at 618 Rio Grande Blvd. NW (tel. 242-3900), established in the historic Armijo hacienda dating from 1840, was decorated and lavishly furnished in Victorian grandeur by local designer John Meigs to make it a regional showplace. The Salvador Armijo House itself has the traditional portal, or roofed ground-level porch covered with wisteria vines, along the front of the structure. Inside, the thick adobe walls have niches and spaces for period paintings in gilt frames, a so-called fainting couch for the ladies, brass chandeliers, panels in stylized designs of etched or stained glass, and beveled mirrors, among other antiques. Classical music underlines the intimacy of five small dining rooms. Prime aged beef, New Mexican specialties, and seafood entrees are priced at $10 to $22. Open for lunch and dinner to 10:30 p.m. seven days a week, the restaurant has full wine and liquor services.

Medium-Priced Restaurants

High Noon in Old Town, at the corner of San Felipe NW and Mountain Road (tel. 765-1455), serves lunch daily from 11 a.m. to 3 p.m. and sandwiches to dinnertime at 5 p.m., which continues to 10:30 p.m. A couple of trees are growing unperturbed in the dining room, their tops nudging the ceiling, and their green fronds go well in the background of brick floor, light-toned beams, and whitewashed walls Southwest style. A photo of the original building (of which the present structure is a restored version) informs us that it was built in 1785. Dinners are accompanied by live music on a classical guitar Thursday through Sunday.

Lunch might be a good hot sandwich like a Reuben, a barbecued beef, a hamburger, or a dish of liver in port wine with mushrooms. For dinner a house specialty is peppersteak or a five-bone rack of lamb with a unique sauce, at $21. Three dining rooms welcome guests into cheerful, brightly lighted areas with skylights and broad windows, and there is a traditional beehive baking oven, the *horno,* of white painted adobe, in the entranceway.

Right on the Plaza, **La Hacienda** (tel. 242-4866) is part crafts-and-jewelry emporium and part bustling restaurant, spreading in and out through half a dozen blue-tiled rooms furnished with sturdy Mexican chairs and tables. A portal shelters the sidewalk outside with its beamed roof that also protects a mural depicting the arrival of the first 12 families of settlers, Spaniards led by a friar to establish the Villa de Albuquerque in 1706. Inside, the costumes of the waitresses go back to that early era. If the atmosphere of the old Plaza lives on unchanged anywhere, it lives on here, and travelers ought not to miss visiting the shop or the dining rooms. The interior was originally a turn-of-the-century mansion. Mexican dishes are available at about $5 to $6, as well as sandwiches and steaks. Dinner is served to 9 p.m.

A block north of the Plaza at 800 Rio Grande Blvd. NW in the Sheraton Old Town is the **Customs House** (tel. 842-6765), open daily except Sunday for lunch (replaced by Sunday brunch) and seven days for dinner, with such entrees as Pacific broiled salmon at $12 or steak Scandia with asparagus and crabmeat at $16. With a rustic seafaring décor the restaurant is also a cheery pub where, before dinner, convivial happy-hour topers sample the fresh oysters or shrimp.

An American Indian Restaurant

Within easy walking distance—three blocks—of the Plaza is a special restaurant that might be missed because of its location in a museum, the restaurant of the **Indian Pueblo Cultural Center,** at 2401 12th St. NW (tel. 242-4943). Reasonably priced, authentic specialties of the Pueblo Indians of New Mexico are offered during the winter from 8:30 a.m. to 3:30 p.m. (an hour later in summer), seven days a week. Dishes include an Indian hot dog on Indian fry bread with red or green chile, a dish of posole (dried corn simmered in a beef stew, served with fry bread and chile), or a pueblo fried burrito. The dining room has modern polished pine tables with decorative Indian wheels and murals of deer on the walls. You can take along with you a loaf of Indian bread, Indian cookies, or a slice of Indian pie.

DOWNTOWN (LUXURY DINING): The downtown area has a number of relatively inexpensive lunch spots for both office workers and tourists, but I'll concentrate on two top choices.

With its modern tile mosaics in Indian geometric designs serving as murals and its tables covered with linen outlined in brown bands to tone with colors in paneling and carpet, the **Mayfair Restaurant,** in the Doubletree Hotel at 201 Marquette NW (tel. 247-3344), has an atmosphere of solid luxury that can equal any other eating establishment in the city. Details are just right: the yellow rose, fresh and fragrant, in its flute-like vase; the napkin newly creased in a convoluted fan shape; the gleaming coffee urn on a sideboard in hammered copper. Closed Sunday, and Saturday at lunchtime, the Mayfair serves lunch, and dinner to 11 p.m., the other days.

Also on the premises of the Doubletree is the **Promenade Café,** reached from the grand lobby down a sweeping staircase and lighted by a glassed roof. The Promenade is open Monday through Saturday for a buffet lunch, and on Sunday a brunch is offered. Saturday night is Steakout time: a 20-ounce T-bone dinner for $9.75, including salad, potato, and hot bread, served from 6 p.m. on. A steak and Maine lobster platter is $15.

RESTAURANTS ELSEWHERE IN ALBUQUERQUE: Around town are some top choices as well as moderately priced restaurants, some serving ethnic cuisines. I'll begin with—

Luxury and Showplace Restaurants

Among the prettiest spots in town is **Nicole's** in the Marriott, at the intersection of I-40 and Louisiana Boulevard (tel. 881-6800), with a light-green tone to the upholstery and carpet, French-style antiques, and a certain genteel air of delicacy, not a spot for gunslingers or cowpokes. Sconces hold discreetly glowing lamps and coppery mirrors seem to diffuse reflections gently. Starters for dinner include fresh oysters, shrimp bisque, and spinach salad, veal Caroline (sautéed veal and shrimp in sauce), rack of lamb provençal, and boneless breast of chicken marsala are among the entrees. Soufflés are a specialty. The room is open daily for lunch and dinner to 11 p.m.

The **Cooperage**, at 7220 Lomas NE (tel. 255-1657), is built to resemble a huge new wooden beer barrel from the outside. Inside, the conceit is continued and, being round, has upholstered benches following this curved inner wall all around a small stage set up for a jazz combo (music Wednesday through Saturday). A fancy bar has carved wooden pillars holding arches against a mirrored wall, and the mirrors in panels reflect the scene of music fans dressed with a certain elegant flair. Vast Halloween-like globes made of bits of glass somehow joined together, as in early leaded glass, illuminate the scene with a gentle glow. Modern and avant-garde levels of jazz are played here, sometimes on electrified instruments (an electrified keyboard instrument reminiscent of the piano, a guitar that can drill notes into your ears). Much fruit and vegetables are included in the price of drinks, which are therefore served in hefty glasses. A Tahitian Typhoon, for example, consists of rum, brandy, fruit juice, and bits of tropical fruit, at $4. These fruits also occupy space in the elaborate salad bar, which has a variety of homemade dressings to choose from. The house specialty is prime rib, and entrees cost $7 to $17.

The restaurant is open both for lunch and dinner, Monday through Saturday from 11 a.m. to 2:30 p.m. and 5 p.m. to midnight, on Sunday from 4 to 10 p.m.

Moderately Priced Restaurants

An attraction for nostalgic folk drawn to the post–World War II era, the **66 Diner**, 1405 Central Ave. (tel. 247-1421), is a typical highway diner of the time restored to its round-windowed, glass-bricked, steel-boothed glory. The Seeburg jukebox is also original and has jitterbug music of the '40s. Good cheeseburgers and meatloaf specials are accompanied by beer and wine. Open daily.

Fat Humphrey's, 3624 Central Ave. (tel. 266-1981), makes a bid for purveyor of the best submarine sandwiches in the city. There is a choice of some 40 subs, from hot pastrami, corned beef, or Italian sausage to the Fat Humphrey deluxe: ham, salami, cappicola, pepperoni with provolone and trimmings. All the pasta is made on the premises—manicotti, lasagne, spaghetti—and there are soups and chili. In summertime especially the chicken salad, tuna, shrimp, or chef's salad—the latter with turkey, ham, roast beef, and Swiss cheese—are in great demand. A follow-up might be a piece of fresh-baked cake or pie, and there is also a low-calorie imitation ice cream called "whispy." Entrees range from $3.59 to $5.50. Open Monday to Saturday from 10 a.m. to 10 p.m.

Ethnic Cuisine

The **Belgian Café**, 7400 Montgomery Blvd. NE (tel. 881-3323), has Belgian décor, Belgian cuisine, and a Belgian chef, all providing a somewhat rare eating experience in these parts. Soups are a specialty—Belgian carrot soup with puréed vegetables; Belgian beer stew with beef, onions, and spices; or Hungarian mushroom soup with green peppers—each served with a crusty roll. Other specials are the grilled ham with melted cheese and pineapple slice, and the cocorico salad: diced breast of chicken, mandarin orange slices, and sliced almonds in homemade brandy mayonnaise. The Belgian waffles are of course a big draw, served plain or with fruit and whipped cream, and there is a combination Belgian coffee and chocolate milk served with whipped cream. Belgian torte, puff pastry, or cheesecake complete the array of choices. Lunch here costs around $5 to $7. Open Tuesday through Friday from 8 a.m. to 4 p.m., Saturday and Sunday from 9 a.m. to 4 p.m. Closed Monday.

An Albuquerque tradition of over 30 years is the **Cocina de Carlos,** at 4901 Lomas NE (tel. 268-9231), founded by Carlos and Ophelia Montoya and now run by their son, Robert. Specializing in New Mexican cuisine and reasonable prices, the Cocina is open for lunch and dinner seven days, with all tacos, enchiladas, burritos, and sopaipillas made from scratch daily. Specials for lunch start at $4.25, and dinners are $8. There is a classical guitarist Thursday through Sunday evenings, and full bar service.

Open seven days is a cheery Italian-style restaurant, **Lo Stivale** (meaning "the boot"), at 1435 Eubank (tel. 294-0019), serving lunch Monday through Friday and dinner seven nights to 9 p.m. Fresh homemade gnocchi, ravioli, manicotti, lasagne, stuffed shells, and tortellini are served as dinners for around $8 with soup or salad. Special dinners for two are popular here, with such items as braciole at $16. Beer and wine are available.

The **New Orleans Café,** 7400 Montgomery NE (tel. 888-1362), specializes in such Créole dishes as seafood gumbo and blackened fish, served in a garden setting. A standby is red beans and rice with sausage. Dinners run $9 to $14. Lunch is served daily; dinner, Wednesday through Saturday. Beer and wines available.

At Sandia Peak

The **Firehouse** (tel. 292-3473) and **High Finance** (tel. 243-9742) are two unusual restaurants at Sandia Peak, where the world's longest tramway takes summertime rubberneckers and wintertime skiers to a height of 10,360 feet. The Firehouse, down below, has an old steam-powered fire engine serving as its bar, and windows on all sides—the views of the city and the Rio Grande Valley are great. Grilled steaks, lobsters, and standard menu items are offered at both restaurants, open from 11 a.m. to 2 p.m. and 5 to 11 p.m. daily. A High Finance Special offers a $5.25 tram ride to the restaurant at the top with a minimum of a $6 tab for food or drinks. The restaurants can be reached via Tramway Boulevard north off I-40, or via Tramway Road east off I-25.

4. SIGHTSEEING

Albuquerque was named in honor of the Spanish duke Don Francisco Cuervo y Valdez, the 13th Duke of Alburquerque—early spellers of the town left out the first "r." The original plaza of the first Spanish settlement here in 1706 remains where it has been from the first, set off by the old San Felipe de Neri Church and other early structures, some hiding their adobe interiors under modern façades. Later the Rio Grande shifted its course, causing a move in the commercial center of the town; and then in 1880 when the railroad was put through two miles from the Plaza, there was a whole new town built up there. But the Plaza remained the center of Old Town through all those years as it still does today, and it probably has never been busier. Some 40 shops, many appealing to tourists with their displays of arts, crafts, or souvenirs, crowd the areas in and around the Plaza, and there are several restaurants there as well that cater especially to visitors.

The town grew over the years from its site as a trade center, being a station on the old Chihuahua Trail into Mexico. It was trade with the Spanish colony to the south that first sustained New Mexico, but later when the Santa Fe Trail brought in more direct communications with the states back east, the emphasis changed to American commerce, given further impetus by the railroad. But its growth absorbed and held onto various parts of its ethnic heritage—Hispanic and Indian—still obvious today, giving the city its special flavor.

Within easy reach of the city are Indian pueblos, sites of prehistoric ruins from old Indian civilizations, national forest lands with trails and campgrounds, ghost towns, and wildlife areas. Within the city, its historic structures and museums afford a particular attraction for anyone drawn to the special character of our southwestern traditions.

OLD TOWN: The first people the Spanish encountered in the area along the Rio Grande where Old Town stands were Tiwa-speaking Indians, pueblo dwellers who farmed by irrigation with techniques as advanced as those used elsewhere in the world in the 16th century. (See Section 9, "Ruins in the Albuquerque Region.") Hernando de Alvarado is said to have explored the area in 1540—it was part of the claimed province of Tiguex. But permission to colonize along the riverbanks did not come until 1598, when a colonist down in Zacatecas, Mexico, Juan de Oñate, was allowed to establish settlers in farms and ranches in what became Old Town. El Paraje de Huertas—the place of the orchards—occupied what later became the Plaza, but the settlers were routed from their ranches during the Pueblo Revolt of 1680. Some of them did return under Spanish protection when Spain reconquered New Mexico 12 years later.

The villa, or cluster of farmhouses grouped together with a common wall for mutual protection, that was named for the Duke of Albuquerque, had no plaza or central meeting point except for its church; by 1780 the **Plaza** was taking form, however, as the heart of the little community. Mexico won independence from Spain in 1821 and increased trade with this outpost to the north that also became an important station on the Sante Fe Trail. The U.S. took possession after the Mexican War, in 1846. During the Civil War Confederate forces briefly occupied the village.

Up to just over a century ago the community around the Plaza numbered a population of under 2,000, with a few stores serving local farmers and ranchers. These left the Plaza to relocate along the railroad when it was built a mile and a half east, after which Old Town took on a quiet character of residential area for long-established Hispanic families and some early Anglo-European residents. At one edge of Old Town there arose a red-light district drawing its business from New Albuquerque over by the train station.

A few artists and craftspeople, discovering the attractive serenity of the Plaza in the 1930s and 1940s, moved in and set up studios and shops here. In the 1950s there was a widespread movement around Old Town to restore the early adobe look of the houses, bring back the flat roof, pull down old façades to reveal ancient adobe if it survived—this was the Pueblo Revival. Today these structures blend with Spanish Colonial houses, Territorial-style buildings, and Victorian mansions.

When the Confederate troops departed from the Old Town occupation they buried a couple of cannons behind the church—they are now in the Albuquerque Museum. Replicas of them adorn the Plaza, however. The neighborhood is one of the few remaining places to inspect the regional architectural style known as Pueblo-Spanish, or just adobe, a structural brick simply made of mud and straw, then sun-baked (but they are costly to build with today, authentically made ones selling for $2 apiece). The traditional features are the flat roof and the soft, rounded contours of building outline made possible by the final coverings of the adobe bricks with protective layers of mud.

The buildings that have been subject to the Pueblo Revival are usually made to resemble real adobe work by being plastered over original construction. Sometimes adobe bricks were covered over with cement stucco. The bricks are rectangular, usually 10 by 18 inches and three to four inches thick, built with simple mud for mortar and then covered. Architectural elements traditional in the early buildings may include a ground-floor porch, the *portal,* usually shading a brick floor set into the ground; *vigas,* long beams supporting the roof, their ends protruding through the façade in what may be the most characteristic visual specialty of this style; *latillas,* stripped branches layered between the vigas; *corbels,* carved wooden supports for the vertical posts and the vigas; and the plastered adobe-brick *banco* set right into an outside wall.

There are nearly a score of historic houses and other structures around the Plaza and in adjoining Romero and San Felipe Streets. According to old archives it was in the Plaza, where Governor Cuervo y Valdes founded the villa in 1706, that he and his officials marked the occasion by throwing stones to the four points of the compass and shouting *"Viva el Rey!"* ("Long Live the King!"). Originally surrounded by an adobe wall, the Plaza's present stone wall dates from 1937 and was a WPA project.

The cynosure on the Plaza is certainly the **Church of San Felipe de Neri,** at the northwest corner. Its original structure from 1706 was on the west side of the Plaza; it was replaced by the present church in 1793, and records show that it has been in continuous use since its original founding. The windows are some 20 feet from the ground and its walls are four feet thick—structural details needed to make the church also serviceable as a fortress against Indian attack. A spiral stairway leading to the choir loft is built around the trunk of an ancient spruce. A medieval mood in the church comes out of the hand-carved confessionals, altars, and images. Parish registers, the earliest in Old Spanish script, preserve a complete record of the history of the church. Gothic spires added a century ago give the church a European air from the outside, while inside the earlier years seem to survive in ancient woods and retablos.

Next door is the **Rectory,** built about 1793 and modified by having a second story and porch added in the late 1880s. The adobe building was at that time faced in brick, since which alteration the brick façade has been covered with stucco—to resemble, somewhat, the original construction. Also on the North Plaza is **Loyola Hall,** the Sister Blandina Convent, built originally of adobe in 1881 as a residence for the Sisters of Charity teaching locally. After a second story was nearly completed, all in adobe, it collapsed, so masons had to come in to make it more solid by building a stone foundation. (There was a good reason that adobe houses were not built to more than a single story.)

The Jesuit fathers built **Our Lady of the Angels School,** 320 Romero, in 1877, the only public school in town at that time. A charming single-story adobe, it had two classrooms, and was used also as a temporary town hall.

The **Antonio Vigil House,** 413 Romero, is a single-story adobe-style residence with the traditional viga ends sticking out over the entrance door. Built in 1879 of terrones (a sort of specialized adobe unit made out of dried sod), it was a small rooming house. Nearby at 309 Romero is the **Charles Mann Barn,** an adobe structure used for farm storage; it was erected in 1906 on the west side of the Plaza. Traditionally very young schoolchildren of Albuquerque believe that the barn belonged to Charlemagne, from "Charlie Mann."

At 301 Romero is the **Florencio Zamora Store,** built in the 1890s of soft "pugmill" brick, still another adobe variant, for Zamora, a butcher and grocer here. Later Charlie Mann bought it for use as a store. At 205 Romero is the **Jesus Romero House,** in a sturdy style known as combination "Prairie and Mediterranean," built in 1915 by another grocer—the most recent major residence to go up on the Plaza. The **Jesus Romero Store** at 121 Romero is on the site of an earlier structure housing the town's first bank. This store has a hipped roof and

Territorial and Queen Anne structural features, and dates from 1893. A saloon and barbershop once occupied **El Parrillan,** next door, a single-story adobe dating from 1898; a second story was added in modern times.

The **Manuel Springer House,** on the South Plaza, was originally the residence of still another grocer, and had a hipped roof and bay windows, still visible under its commercial façade today. Also on the South Plaza is the **Cristobal Armijo House,** a two-story adobe completed in 1886 in combined Italianate and Queen Anne architectural styles. The first-floor façade was plastered, carved, and painted to look like brick, the second story finished off in real brick; both surfaces are now stuccoed over. Its original owner was an early banker.

The **Charles A. Bottger House,** 110 San Felipe, is made of concrete, dates from 1910, and has painted ceilings and a red-tile roof. **Casa Armijo,** in the 200 block of San Felipe, dates from before 1840 and was a headquarters for both Union and Confederate armies. It has its own *placita*—a little plaza or patio of its own. The **Ambrosio Armijo House and Store** on San Felipe is an adobe structure of 1882, and once had the high false front of wooden boards so typical of western towns in movies. It has a fine staircase of carved wood supposedly brought in from St. Louis. The **Herman Blueher House,** at 302 San Felipe, was built by an early booster and successful businessman in 1898, a three-story Italianate mansion with fancy porches on two levels now obscured by storefronts. At 306 San Felipe is the **Fred Stueckel House,** a simple four-room adobe with some Queen Anne-style trim added; it dates from the turn of the century.

Note: The **Old Town Visitors Center** (with rest rooms) provides all visitor information from 10 a.m. to 5 p.m. Monday through Saturday, on Sunday from 11 a.m., with an information window at 305 Romero (tel. 243-3215). For suggestions on shopping around the Plaza, refer to Section 5.

MUSEUMS: Albuquerque has several museums of interest, both historical and technological.

The Indian Pueblo Cultural Center

At 2401 12th St. NW is the Indian Pueblo Cultural Center (tel. 843-7270), a facility that will cheer and encourage anyone who cares about the future of American Indians in general and the Pueblo Indians in particular. Organized with the support and participation of the 19 Indian pueblos of New Mexico, the organization has a first-rate historical, archeological, and ethnographic museum; an excellent arts-and-crafts market purveying authentic wares made by Indians; an arts program presenting crafts demonstrations and instruction, dances, and films on Indian subjects; an educational program that reaches many schools; and last but not least, a good authentic Indian restaurant. (See Section 3, "Where to Eat.")

The spacious U-shaped structure in the flat-roofed adobe style has two stories above ground and one below, and was designed after the 9th-century Pueblo Bonito, the ruins of which make a central attraction for archeologists and ordinary visitors up at Chaco Canyon, 150 miles to the northwest. Pueblo Indian history is followed from prehistoric times through to the present in the lower level of the museum, while the upper level has small sections set apart for displays of crafts and of historic interest concerning each of the modern 19 pueblos throughout New Mexico. Original paintings are displayed along with modern crafts offered for sale—these are of the highest quality, guaranteed by high standards set by the center in accepting goods for display.

Docents are available for guided tours of the museum, open Monday through Saturday from 9:30 a.m. to 5:30 p.m. Admission is $2.50 for adults, $1.50 for senior citizens, $1 for students. Wholly owned by the 19 pueblos, the museum is a nonprofit organization that has been open since 1976, surviving entirely on admission fees and contributions, along with income from its shops and restaurant—no government money is received.

Around the enclosed plaza within the confines of the building, the walls display murals that are the work of modern Indian artists from various pueblos. The permanent exhibit on the lower level is intended to take the visitor right through the history of the Southwest from prehistoric times to the present. Stone tools recall prehistoric cave dwellers. A bit farther on is a symbolic sipapu through which you are invited to step in order to enter the world of humans. A legend goes with this magic hole, source of life: the Indians began their life underground where the source of life resides but were encouraged to emerge out into the world by animals—the badger, the mole, the one-horn buffalo—who bored a hole for them as a passage. They were able to climb up through this hole thanks to a strong web woven for them by Spider Woman, who figures in the legends of all the Pueblo Indians, and in those of the Hopi in Arizona as well. Once through the hole, the museum visitor emerges in a "new world of the Southwest" at the time when the ancestors of the present Indians, the Anasazi ("old people"), first got here. Farther along is a scale model of the actual Taos Pueblo of today, or as it was at the turn of the century—there is hardly any difference now, because the pueblo leaders have not permitted electricity, plumbing, or other modern advances to modify the Taos Pueblo in any way. The big outdoor bread ovens called hornos are now used by all the Pueblo Indians, having adapted this form from the Spanish; they can be seen in the model here and in a painting near it.

Of particular interest to Indians from other parts of the U.S. are weapons from the Pueblo Revolt of 1680, an outbreak that effectively rid the Indians of the sight of any Spanish for 12 years, and is sometimes thought of (at least by the Indians) as the only time they ever won a war against the invading Europeans, Custer's Last Stand being a brief victory in a doomed cause, from the Indian viewpoint.

A reproduction on a small scale of one of the Catholic chapels the Indians were forced to build for the Spanish, many still standing today, recalls the era of Spanish proselytization of the natives. There is also a wall map of the Santa Fe Trail that first opened in 1821 and began bringing in traders and eventually settlers from the East, the "Anglo" contribution to the ethnic combinations of the Southwest (the appellation is still used today for anybody neither Hispanic nor Indian). The porch of an early railroad station marks the latter arrival of the Atchison, Topeka & Santa Fe Railroad in New Mexico.

As you leave the historical section, at the top of the stairs you'll see another mural, this one illustrating the ceremonial years of Pueblo Indians. In summer they perform the corn dance. Wintertime is the season for the buffalo dance, performed by a male buffalo dancer encircled by a water serpent. Next to this work, done by Indian artist Dennis Silva, is the way into the contemporary exhibits, one for each of the 19 pueblos. This, too, makes a capital way to get a sense of the varieties of life, art, and crafts among these various peoples. Note at the start of these displays the remarkable photographs of Indians from the Smithsonian Institution collection taken between 1880 and 1910. The 19 pueblos use three separate language groups. One of these, Zuñi, is spoken only by the Zuñi. A second, Keresan, is used by the Acoma, Laguna, Santa Ana, San Felipe, and Cochiti Pueblos. The rest use either the Tewa or the Tiwa tongues in various accents. The Indians have a tradition that the gods made them speak in these different tongues to force them to cut out all the quarreling among the pueblos.

The **gift shop** sells the work of the Indians of the 19 pueblos. A wool throw rug is priced at $15; kachina dolls, between $160 and $350; watercolors picturing Indian scenes or figures, around $350. The code of ethics of the Indian Arts and Crafts Association guarantees work here to be stylistically authentic, the creations of pueblo members only.

The Albuquerque Museum

The Albuquerque Museum, on Mountain Road NW at 19th Street (tel. 242-4600), aims "to preserve and exhibit art, history, and science of the middle Rio Grande region." It is open from 10 a.m. to 5 p.m. Tuesday through Friday and 1 to 5 p.m. on Saturday and Sunday; closed Monday. Admission is $2 for adults; seniors and children of school age, $1. Free guided walking tours of Old Town leave from the Walking Tour exhibit area at the end of the west corridor on Wednesday, Thursday, and Friday at 11 a.m., and on Saturday and Sunday at 1:30 p.m.

The museum shows temporary exhibits of special Southwest subjects. Also shown permanently is a heraldic wall hanging illustrating the coat-of-arms of the Spanish house of Alburquerque. It was given to the city in 1956 by the 18th Duke of Alburquerque to commemorate the 250th anniversary of the founding of the Spanish settlement here. Called a *repostero,* in silk with gold and silver thread, it was made in 1665, is 12 feet square, and displays a wonderful dragon.

An instructive exhibit among the numerous crafts shown concerns blanket design and style from the 1850s through the years. Saltillo design elements included bands and stripes with diamonds, chevrons, and leaves, for example. Weaving traditions among Hispanics and New Mexico Indians grew up separately, though both used wool yarn.

Among slide shows created by people hoping to show off their towns or cities to good advantage there are many that resort to clichés and tub-thumping boosterism, but the one on Albuquerque shown here is several cuts above almost anything you will likely have seen elsewhere in this genre: an excellent 40-minute tour of the history of the place shown in black-and-white and color, with movement provided by the interspersing of images from three projectors ingeniously programmed to show interlocking sights one moment, then an individual one-lens projection the next. The photography of the latter part of the 19th century and the early part of the 20th shows a rip-roaring Main Street scene aswarm with buggies, wagons, horses, draymen, cowboys, and cattle drivers, with the typical false-front stores, saloons, and hotels in the background. A first-rate unsentimental narration and apposite music help the sharp overall impression that you are getting something of a taste of the real life that was lived in this place.

As we progress through the years, the makers of the program do not omit the bad spots, the ugly commercial strips along the highways, the uncontrolled urban sprawl; yet there is, finally, now a plan in force in the city—only created in 1975—to provide new parks and other green strips for future citizens. A certain devil-may-care western atmosphere has always pervaded this city ever since it knew its first boom when the railroad came in. A contemporary commentator a century ago vowed that any law-abiding mayor from any small city or town in Vermont who got one look at the anything-goes scene of Albuquerque (back in 1880) would simply turn tail and run away to hide in the woods. *Anything,* it was said back then, was legal in Albuquerque.

The New Mexico Museum of Natural History

A new institution across the road from the Albuquerque Museum, this state-run center opened in 1986 on money drawn mostly from taxes on oil, gas, and coal produced in the state. It is an unusual museum in that it began nearly from scratch, without any major collections of artifacts or other materials. The museum celebrates the life of the region and the changing landscape over the eons through innovative use of video displays, polarizing lenses, and black lighting.

Visitors walk a rocky path through the Hall of Giants between fighting life-size dinosaurs while overhead winged reptiles fly. Guests then step right into a seemingly live volcano with lava pouring around their feet. Elsewhere, in a cold cave festooned with stalagmites, saber-toothed cats and woolly mammals are seen.

An atrium in the lobby immediately draws your attention to a 22-foot-wide relief map of the earth showing the surfaces of continents and seabeds; a network of 2,500 fiber-optic elements monitors the pulse of the planet, flashing wherever earthquakes or eruptions occur—about every three seconds.

The museum is at 1801 Mountain Rd. NW, and is open daily from 10 a.m. to 5 p.m. Admission is $2 for adults and $1 for children. For information on special exhibits, call 841-8836.

University of New Mexico Museums

University of New Mexico museums open to the public include the **Art Museum,** in the Fine Arts Center, Cornell and Redondo Streets (tel. 277-4001), open Tuesday through Friday from 10 a.m. to 5 p.m. and 7 to 10 p.m. and on Saturday and Sunday from 1 to 5 p.m. free of charge. The permanent collection, from which monthly exhibitions are drawn, emphasizes 20th-century paintings, prints, drawings, and photographs.

The **Maxwell Museum of Anthropology,** at University and Ash Streets (tel. 277-4404), has one exhibit of interest to visitors to the region: "People in the Southwest." Rare discoveries of artifacts from ruins of the region are displayed, and there is a gift shop selling southwestern crafts, jewelry, and books on the Indian and Hispanic cultures. The museum is open Monday through Friday from 9 a.m. to 4 p.m. and on Saturday from 10 a.m. to 4 p.m. Admission is free.

Also on the campus, in Northrup Hall, are the **Geology Museum** and the **Meteorite Museum** (tel. 277-4204), which between them display ancient dinosaur bones and recently delivered moon rocks. Hours for both museums are Monday through Friday from 8 a.m. to noon and 1 to 4 p.m.

The National Atomic Museum

Reached through the gate of Kirtland Air Force Base on Wyoming Boulevard SE, the National Atomic Museum (tel. 844-8443) is open free of charge seven days from 9 a.m. to 5 p.m. and displays historical materials on the atomic age, beginning with a letter from Albert Einstein to FDR written to encourage the development of the atomic bomb. The development of the whole Manhattan Project is traced here, and there is a film entitled *The Ten Seconds That Shook the World,* shown daily. Missiles in full-scale models are shown along with a F-105D fighter bomber that delivers them to targets.

OTHER PLACES TO SEE IN ALBUQUERQUE: The reptile house and the rain forest are, either one of them, worth the trip to the **Rio Grande Zoo** at 903 10th St. SW (tel. 843-7413), open daily from 9 a.m. to 5 p.m., with admission at $4 for adults, and $1.50 for senior citizens and children aged 3 to 11. The shady walks under huge cottonwoods make strolling around the grounds a pleasure, and there are all the standard animals in modern, cheerful, natural-habitat surroundings. The reptiles are mainly interesting in their amazing variety, while the rain forest is indoors and populated by scores of exotic species of birds, many of them in good voice. Great apes have a piece of jungle to themselves, and there are giraffes, elephants, and tigers which look at home under the warm skies of the region. There are polar bears and kangaroos, bald eagles and rattlesnakes, bears and seals, and of course the New Mexico state bird, the roadrunner. A café and snackbar has a pleasant outdoor terrace, and miniature animals in varying materials are sold in the gift shop. An innovation is the selling of "Zooparent" certificates to anyone wanting to adopt a zoo denizen simply by paying for its food for a year (you leave the animal here of course). Such certificates go for varying prices: $10 for a turtle, say, up to $3,800 for a polar bear.

Sandia Peak Tramway, at the end of Tramway Road off I-25 (tel. 298-8518), is open seven days all year, from 9 a.m. to 10 p.m., to provide a spectacular trip on the world's longest tramway. It is mainly the scene of avid skiers in the wintertime, but locals and visitors alike love the ride for the view and for the restaurant at the top any time of the year. The 15-minute trip covers 2.7 miles, ascending 4,000 feet to Sandia Park at 10,360 feet elevation. In the spring there are searchers for mountain wildflowers mixing it with intrepid hang-glider fliers who like to make it down on their own. At night the view of the lights of Albuquerque make it easy to take in the luxury of the bar or dining room of the High Finance restaurant, whose menus are printed up as banker's ledgers. As a ski area this is the nearest one to a big city of any in the U.S. (see Section 10, "Outdoors in the Albuquerque Area").

The top is a good destination on a hot summer day because temperatures are at least 20° cooler up here. Animals viewed on the wild slopes from the tram cabin occasionally include bears, bighorn sheep, deer, eagles, hawks, and a rare mountain lion. Round trip costs $9, $7 for students and children; or one way—and hike down—$7 and $6. Also available are chair-lift rides in combination with the tram tickets.

5. SHOPPING

For travelers who have spent a week or a month in the deserts, mountains, or small towns of the Southwest there might be a growing yen to do some serious shopping. Nowhere in the region could you get a better shopping "fix" than in Albuquerque, which, first of all, has the two largest shopping malls in the state within two blocks of one another, both on Louisiana Boulevard just north of I-40: the **Winrock Center,** named for Winthrop Rockefeller, who built it; and the **Coronado Center.** Winrock has 100 stores, including J. C. Penney, Montgomery Ward, and specialty shops; Coronado has no fewer than 147 merchants, including Broadway Southwest, Goldwater's, Mervyn's, and Sears.

Visitors are usually more interested in regional specialties, and here of course there are artists and art galleries, although not so thickly populated as in Santa Fe and Taos; and crafts and fancy-clothing emporia—the ones around the Plaza make a sort of shopping center of their own for the tourists, with over 40 merchants represented. Besides these shoppers' destinations the **First Plaza Galeria,** downtown at 3rd Street and Tijeras Avenue, also has craft shops as well as gourmet food stores, while the Sandia Pueblo Indians run their own crafts store on their reservation land at the edge of the city.

MOSTLY FOR ART: In such purlieus of traditional design and materials gleaned from Hispanic and Indian lore as Old Town, it's hard to draw a line between a work of art and a utilitarian pot or carved spoon or woven wall hanging. Some of the would-be art, as in those ever-repeated portraits of Indian children with the huge wet eyes, isn't art, while sometimes an ordinary-looking stone metate begins to appear anything but ordinary after you've looked at it a while and run your hands over its rough surface—it becomes quite artful in some mysterious way.

Work by Albuquerque watercolorist Dyanne Strongbow is shown at the **Adobe Gallery,** 413 Romero NW in Old Town. Her themes are Indian figures; one of her paintings was used as the official poster for the annual Santa Fe Indian Market; another was chosen as the official poster for the city of Albuquerque. She has studied Pueblo Indians for sources for her work; of Choctaw lineage herself, she says that that "really broadened my horizons." Legends and myths often make a background to her portrayals of Indian men involved in an ancient ritual, often with some symbolic eagle or buffalo in the background.

Well into its second decade is what its founders claim to be "the oldest cooperative gallery in the country"—the **Galeria de Artisanos,** at 206½ San Felipe NW in Old Town. Three local artists began it as an outlet for their own representational-style works on New Mexico subjects with the hope of discrediting the common idea that Taos and Santa Fe were the only places in the state producing saleable artworks. At present a dozen artists have joined the co-op, all local artists whose works make up the art on display.

MOSTLY FOR CRAFTS: Although there are crafts sold elsewhere in the city, Old Town is the acknowledged center for the biggest and most varied shops as well as for smaller ones specializing in original objects of art or furniture.

An old adobe is home to **Mariposa,** 113 Romero, which has several rooms displaying original crafts objects including ceramics and jewelry of modern design. **Peddler's Cart,** 7602 Menaul NE, has pottery and other crafts by southwestern designers, as well as some paintings. The **Piñon Tree Gallery,** 400 San Felipe, has many antiques in an upstairs room with a balcony overlooking the Plaza and church outside; modern crafts are also sold.

Around the Plaza you will discover the **Casa de Avila,** 324 San Felipe, displaying the miniature wooden New Mexico–style churches of woodcarver Caroline Johnson. An Indian-owned and -operated Indian arts shop is the **Bear Paw,** in the Poco a Poco mini-mall at 324 San Felipe NW.

You might like to try out a sturdy Santa Fe–style bench or table at **Schelu,** 306 San Felipe NW. On the South Plaza is the **Covered Wagon,** with a wide variety of traditional Indian jewelry made on the premises, and rugs, pots, and kachinas, as well as the world's largest turquoise nugget, mined in 1954, weighing 152 lbs.

Although these are only a few samples of the variety available on or near the Plaza, a couple of major galleries for crafts outside the area ought not be neglected: first, the **Weyrich Gallery,** 2935 Louisiana Blvd. NE, with both contemporary and traditional tapestries, jewelry, ceramics, glass, and woodcarvings; and the **Weems Gallery,** in the Eastdale Shopping Center, at Eubank and Candelaria NE, showing a great hoard of works by 100 area craftspeople, including potters, sculptors, and a few painters.

Also worth a shopping trip is the **Bien Mur Indian Market Center,** on the Sandia Indian Reservation seven miles from downtown Albuquerque, reached via I-25 north to Tramway Road. The name "Bien Mur" comes from Indian words for the "big mountain"—Sandia Peak—rising just to the east of this striking structure, a circular two-story stucco in the basic form of the ceremonial *kiva,* with six central pillars forming a circular center inside from which great wood ceiling beams reach out to the walls; a balcony area runs clear around at the second-story level, making for a wide area of selling space. The work of Indians of various pueblos is sold here, such as a Jemez pot with vivid black-and-red geometric designs, an overlay silver buckle of Hopi design, or a silver Navajo Naja necklace with turquoise nuggets on an 18-inch bead strand. Besides jewelry and pottery, the store has Indian-made clothing, blankets and rugs, and kachina dolls. Open seven days.

6. ANNUAL EVENTS

Spanish dances, Plaza gunfights, rodeos, a balloon meet, and arts-and-crafts fairs are a few among many events, each with its niche on the annual calendar in

Albuquerque. It is a rare week in the city when no celebration is taking place; usually there are at least a couple to go to. There are the Christmas luminary tours in winter, bicycle tours and raft races in the spring, arts fiestas in the summer, and the state fair and a balloon rally in the fall—among a lot of other annual occasions for merriment, competition of a sporting nature, or general edification and the absorbing of culture.

WINTER: At Christmas for 300 years the villages along the Rio Grande have been displaying lights called **luminarias,** at first simple bonfires of pine boughs. Lanterns replaced the fires a century ago when colored paper was first imported here from China. Soon after, when brown wrapping paper came with goods brought in by train from back East, this was used as the basis for the luminarias, and today they are simply made of a brown paper bag weighted with sand, with a candle in the bottom. One of these may not look like a whole lot of decoration for a holiday season, but wait until you see hundreds of thousands of them flickering their dim but persistent points of light from every part of the city. The lights are set out in nearly every possible position, whole families setting to work to dot them along rooftops, walls, the edges of gardens or driveways or sidewalks, and the tension builds toward sundown at Christmas eve, when they are lighted. Processions of cars with their lights dimmed parade through the city to see the spectacle. Visitors may see the best of the luminarias on a cheerful bus tour organized by the city, at a cost of $4 per passenger (tel. 766-7830 for information).

All winter, and on into the year, western-style gunfights are staged in the Old Town Plaza between 1:30 and 5:30 p.m. by amateur sheriff's deputies and bad guys who make their headquarters at the Old West Photography Studio on the Plaza. Warning shots five minutes before a show give the signal to all within earshot; further information is available from the studio (tel. 842-8838).

SPRING: An early sports event the third Sunday of March is called the **Sun Sports Spring Run,** a four-mile jogging race open to many categories that leaves at 9 a.m. from the intersection of Juan Tabo and Montgomery. Call 294-5760 for information.

The third weekend of April is the time for the annual **Rio Grande Bicycle Tour,** in which around 800 bikers race 100 miles through communities south of the city, starting off at 6:30 a.m. from the University of New Mexico. For information, contact New Mexico Wheelmen (tel. 299-6989).

The third weekend of May is the time for the **Great Rio Grande Raft Race,** sponsored by the City Parks and Recreation Department, and departing from the riverside at North Beach at 9 a.m. on Saturday, continuing to the finish line at the Corrales Bridge. Different categories are open to rafts transporting various numbers of crew, for homemade craft, and for canoes and kayaks. For information, call 766-4857.

Also over a May weekend is the **San Ysidro Fiesta** in the suburb of Corrales. Friday night there are food booths and arts-and-crafts displays, on Saturday a parade and dancing followed by vespers, and on Sunday a special mass. For information, call Corrales City Hall (tel. 897-0598).

SUMMER: The first weekend of June presents a busy schedule, starting with the **San Felipe Fiesta** in Old Town, with a carnival, food booths, and entertainment in the Plaza. Call the Old Town Visitor Center (tel. 243-3215) for information. The same weekend sees an **Old-fashioned Fair** in the so-called ghost town of Madrid, reached via I-40 east and N.M. 14 north: crafts studios hold open house, and there is an auction and street entertainment.

Another jogging run also goes on during the Sunday of the first weekend of

June. The **Leroy Bearman Memorial Run,** named after a local sportswriter, the contest benefits sports programs not otherwise funded and covers ten kilometers, starting at 8 a.m. from Kit Carson Park. It's open to anyone 11 years of age or older. Call 884-6787 for information.

The second June weekend sees **Our Lady of Guadalupe Parish Fiesta,** with games, food, a rummage sale, raffle, and entertainment, running all afternoon on Saturday and Sunday.

On the third weekend comes the state's largest crafts exhibition, the **New Mexico Arts and Crafts Fair,** where over 200 artisans set up their booths and stands to show their work in every kind of crafts skills. There are crafts demonstration and other entertainment. For information, call 884-9043.

An unusual event takes place in July on the night before the Fourth—the annual **New Mexico Track Club Midnight Run** of four miles over a course through the campus of the University of New Mexico, the whole length lined with lighted luminarias, those Christmasy paper bags with candles inside. The run starts at midnight at the Santa Ana Dormitory; for information call the New Mexico Athletic Congress at 268-9330. Earlier, fireworks are set off by the Old Town Optimist Club at the state fairgrounds; for information call 766-7474. University stadium also has fireworks at dusk on the eve of the Fourth, put on by American Legion Post No. 13. For information, call 243-1901.

On July 4 during the day there is an **Indian Market** at the Indian Pueblo Cultural Center, 2401 12th St. NW (tel. 843-7270), with ceremonial dances and crafts demonstrations. There are all-day fiestas in the outlying towns of Madrid to the northeast and Tome to the south.

During one weekend in mid-August the **Bernalillo County 4-H Fair and Rodeo** takes place at Tingley Coliseum, with rodeos two nights at 7:30 p.m. For information, call 243-1386. On the Saturday of the third weekend of August is the annual **La Luz Trail Run,** in which some 300 runners try racing up to the top of Sandia Peak via a roadway with a 12% grade. The run starts at 8 a.m. from the Juan Tabo Picnic Grounds. For information, call 268-9330. The last weekend is the time for the all-day **Fería Artesana** at Tiguex Park, with entertainment, an outdoor folk mass, and many crafts stands and booths. For information, call 766-7660.

FALL: Running through 12 days in mid-September is the **New Mexico State Fair,** with thoroughbred and quarterhorse racing, an RCA-sanctioned rodeo, national country-and-western stars, a midway, an Indian village, a Spanish village, livestock shows, and displays of foods, arts, and crafts. It's at the fairgrounds on Central Avenue (tel. 265-1791 for information).

The second week of October is set aside for the spectacular **Albuquerque International Balloon Fiesta,** held annually since 1972, when it was started with 16 balloons ascending from a shopping center. Today over 500 balloons from 15 countries take part in the week-long ascensions, events that over the seven days draw half a million visitors. A few passengers from among the visitors manage to book short rides by paying up to $125 for the privilege. All week, balloons are seen sailing past windows in the city's office buildings. The tradition is that when one lands by accident or design in somebody's backyard, the host welcomes his visitors from the sky with champagne.

The world's largest ballooning event goes on from launching grounds off Osuna Road, reached via I-25, the Cutter Balloonport, covering 400 acres. A hot-air balloon championship contest run during the fiesta involves many of the balloonists and their crews. Among events are several mass ascensions of all the balloons at once, along with races involving particular rules, airplane stunt flying, an armed forces parachute team demonstration, and even a balloon concert by the New Mexico Symphony. One race, the Roadrunner-Coyote competition, is like the hare-and-hound races elsewhere, in which one balloon, the roadrunner, takes off and tries to maneuver so the following coyote balloons cannot catch him; winner is the coyote who lands the closest to his target, the roadrunner. The tumbleweed drop involves the dropping of a tagged tumbleweed in the middle of the balloonport, the balloonist having arisen at least two miles away from this target, steering his way there by means of rising and falling to find the best wind currents for his intended route. In Blackjack, bags with streamers on them are dropped from balloons onto a huge grid marked on the field, with squares giving scores from 1 to 11, the purpose being to score as close a total up to 21 as possible. In a key grab, keys to a new car are tantalizingly displayed atop a pole for the lucky pilot who can maneuver his craft close enough to grab them—if he does, he wins the car.

Over the first weekend of November the annual **Southwest Arts and Crafts Festival** is held at the fairgrounds, an invitational juried show of regional works drawing 150 entrants from Friday morning through Saturday to Sunday at 6 p.m. For information, call 262-2448.

In December, on the Sunday before Christmas at the Rio Grande Zoo a sweet-natured **living nativity scene** is staged, with live animals and live people, from 2 to 4 p.m. For information, call 843-7413.

7. MUSIC AND OTHER PERFORMING ARTS

For opera, symphony, and touring-company productions, the main location is the 2,094-seat Popejoy Hall in the Fine Arts Center on the campus of the University of New Mexico, a modern facility dating from 1966. The theater is alive with one kind of performance or another nearly one night out of two throughout the year.

Popular music is purveyed in lounges in the major hotels and in a variety of clubs with particular styles usually played: jazz, rock, or country and western. A few of these operate as full restaurants as well as nightclubs. Hispanic-traditional, international rock from soft to punk, cowboy ballads, and Dixieland can all be sampled easily and happily by short hops, all within a few minutes' drive from one to another.

CLASSICAL: The **Albuquerque Civic Light Opera,** 4201 Ellison NE (tel. 345-6577), presents five Broadway musicals annually in Popejoy Hall. The **Albuquerque Little Theatre,** 224 San Pasquale SW (tel. 242-4750), presents Broadway plays with occasional celebrity guest stars in a season running from September to July.

The **New Mexico Symphony Orchestra** (tel. 842-8565) presents an annual season of 45 concerts at Popejoy Hall. Various touring companies and artists appear here during the year. The New Mexico Symphony provides musical background for the **Southwest Ballet Company,** 670 Juan Tabo NE (tel. 294-1423), which presents international stars during its regular season.

COUNTRY AND WESTERN: The **Caravan East,** 7605 Central NE (tel. 265-7877), has two bands nightly and Nashville stars every month, and there are free dance lessons on Saturday at 4:30 p.m.

Cowboys, 3301 Juan Tabo NE (tel. 296-1959), has live C&W music seven nights a week, with new touring bands every week.

Extra Point, 7605 Central NE (tel. 265-7601), is next door to Caravan East, but a bit smaller; it has live bands Thursday through Sunday.

The **Sandia Inn,** 4007 Menaul NE (tel. 883-9871), has local bands nightly except Sunday, with a weekend happy hour starting at noon and free appetizers.

Sundance Saloon, 12000 Candelaria NE (tel. 296-6761), has bands nightly and on Friday afternoons, along with a happy hour from 2 to 9 p.m.

Local bands play weekends at the **Wine Cellar,** Lomas and San Pedro NE (tel. 268-6706).

The **Silver Bullet,** 1400 University SE (tel. 242-5400), has live bands Wednesday through Saturday.

ROCK AND JAZZ: The Cooperage, 7220 Lomas NE (tel. 255-1657), has
live jazz Wednesday through Saturday.

The **Albuquerque Mining Co.,** 7209 Central NE (tel. 255-0925), is a gay bar presenting live progressive bands nightly.

Annex II, 4100 Central SE (tel. 265-7877), has live rhythm-and-blues bands playing Tuesday through Sunday.

The **Chelsea Street Pub,** in the Coronado Center (tel. 883-4605), has live rock bands from the Chelsea circuit playing most nights.

With music aimed at "metal and thrash maniacs," **Club R.E.C.,** on Arno SE just south of Gibson, serves no liquor and has no telephone, but showcases touring bands regularly.

Live rock six nights a week is offered at **Confetti,** 9800 Montgomery NE (tel. 298-2113), which also has New Mexico's largest television screen.

Jazz and rhythm-and-blues by such groups as the Rio Grande Red Hot Chili Jazz Preservation Society and others are at the **Cotton Club,** 6210 Fourth NW (tel. 344-9919), with music Monday through Saturday and some Sundays too.

Boogie, blues, and rhythm-and-blues groups hold forth at **El Madrid,** 423 First SW (tel. 242-0829), known as "a club with some funk" that hosts some touring bands. There is music every night.

Live rock bands play nightly except Sunday at **Señor Buckets,** 4100 San Mateo NE (tel. 881-3110), which offers a free buffet weekday afternoons from 3 to 8 p.m.

A large dance floor invites dancers to live bands at **Studio 66,** 10205 Central NW (tel. 836-2939), nightly Tuesday through Saturday.

Jazz and light rock groups hold forth at the **Taverna** of the Sheraton Old Town, 800 Rio Grande NW (tel. 843-6300), Tuesday through Saturday. Hors d'oeuvres are free from 4:30 to 6 p.m.

8. INDIAN PUEBLOS

Of the 19 pueblos in New Mexico, the so-called **Eight Northern Pueblos,** an association set up for the purpose of advancing the sales of crafts and securing other benefits for their members, includes the Tesuque, the Nambe, the Pojoaque, the San Ildefonso, the Santa Clara, the San Juan, the Picuris, and the Taos. The Taos Pueblo is described in Chapter IV, "Taos and Northern New Mexico," while the other seven members of the Northern Pueblos are described in Chapter III, "Santa Fe and Surrounding Country." The remaining 11 pueblos, described below, are within a day's drive or less from Albuquerque; one, the Sandia, borders the city limits.

Visitors are welcome at all the pueblos, but some charge for a visitor's permit and all make a charge where photography, sketching, or painting is allowed. In principle no photographing of the ceremonial dances and rites is permitted. The governor's office in each pueblo may be reached by telephone for information on picture-taking, or sketching and painting permits.

ACOMA PUEBLO: Acoma Pueblo (tel. 552-6604) occupies a spectacular site atop a mesa that rises 365 feet out of the desert. It is 50 miles west of Albuquerque, reached via I-40 west to N.M. 23 at Paraje, then 14 miles south to the mesa.

Also called **Sky City,** the pueblo is now accessible by a steep car road to the top. Entrance fees are $5. As in all the pueblos, photographs of Indians may not be taken without permission of the subject. There is a shuttle bus in operation.

The pueblo is said to be the oldest continuously occupied community in the U.S., and certainly it is one of the oldest, since the Indians moved to the area in A.D. 600 and have lived up here since A.D. 1075. The first Spanish who encountered it in 1540 called it "the greatest stronghold in the world."

The way to the mesa over N.M. 23 passes another flat-topped landmark called **Enchanted Mesa,** where the Acoma lived until they moved over to Sky City. The legend is that an earthquake destroyed the only passable trail up to the top of Enchanted Mesa, trapping some of the Acoma to die there. The ones who happened to be safe down below built the present pueblo three miles to the south. It is now considered a National Historic Landmark.

The adobe walls of Sky City blend into the sandstone of the mesa. The pueblo occupies 70 acres in an oval area, with four streets lined with some of America's oldest houses. Most are two stories high, and some have ladders for access to the upper rooms. Under the bright-blue sky there is a feeling of isolation and timelessness. A door opens and an old woman makes her way out, carrying a couple of decorated pots of her own manufacture.

A handful of Acoma still live here year around, but the pueblo is used mainly as a summer place for many Acoma whose permanent homes are in the plains below in the settlements of Acomita, McCartys, and Anzac. There is generally a refreshing breeze wafting over the broad plaza in front of the **Church of St. Stephen,** which dates from 1639. It is of warm-toned adobe, with Spanish belltowers, and inside, huge beams bracing its high ceiling, the wood for which was dragged from forests 30 miles away.

Dirt for a cemetery was hauled up here in shoulder baskets centuries before there was any roadway to the top—access was via a steep climbing trail where holes for fingers and feet were drilled into the soft stone. The headstones survive in the cemetery. Next to the church, in an adjoining structure, the old, austere cells of the long-ago-departed missionaries, with the small windows that catch a blaze of desert light, are also open to visitors.

The church itself is a silent, peaceful space with a clay floor. In the old Spanish tradition it has no benches or pews except in the choir loft. Its 17th-century doors are considered masterpieces of the carver's craft. An early monk has left a painting of St. Joseph on one wall, and there is an ornate altar. A statue of St. Stephen occupies a niche in the altar, except when it is taken out for a procession on the annual feast day, September 2. Visitors are welcome at these festivities, during which the statue is placed in a bower of cornstalks and aspen branches. Dances go on all day in the plaza.

Water is supplied by a shallow reservoir fed by rare rains. There is a tiny store in one of the adobe houses, where a woman bakes bread in a beehive oven and sells it to her neighbors or for a visitor's picnic. A few Acoma ceramic pots and postcards make up the stock; the outside world has intruded very little up here.

The Acoma also have **Mesa Hill Lake** on their reservation land. It has a picnic area and access to fishing boats. Fishing season is March 1 to December 15, with permits sold for $3 to $15 at the lake (in Acomita).

Information on all Acoma ceremonies is available at the tribal office in Acomita. There are deer, arrow, and buffalo dances in the **Governor's Feast** in February. **Village Feast Day** takes place in the village of McCartys in May. A rooster pull is a feature of **St. John's Day** on the mesa, June 24, and also of a June 29 festival honoring **Sts. Peter and Paul.** Acoma is the site of the **St. James Day Feast** and the **Feast of St. Ann,** on July 25 and 26. On August 10 there is a summer corn dance at Acomita during **Village Feast Day** in honor of St. Lawrence. A harvest dance is the highlight of **Old Acoma Feast Day** on the mesa top, September 2. **Christmas** festivities lasting several days begin with a midnight mass at the church in Old Acoma.

COCHITI PUEBLO: The Cochiti Pueblo (tel. 465-2244) is about 40 miles north of Albuquerque, halfway between this city and Santa Fe, the northernmost of the Keresan-speaking pueblos. It is reached via U.S. 85, then north on N.M. 22 and N.M. 16.

The pueblo territory runs along the bank of the Rio Grande, where fishing and hunting for doves and ducks is allowed on purchase of a permit from the pueblo governor for $2 to $7.

Cochiti women make noted pottery, especially the renowned storyteller figures. Beadwork and soft-leather moccasins are other specialties. The pueblo is famous for its double-headed drums widely used in ceremonies held here. They are made from sections of hollowed-out cottonwood or aspen logs and then covered with leather tightly laced with rawhide thongs, making for a sharp resonance that can be heard for considerable distances.

The big event of the year is the **San Buenaventura Feast Day,** July 14, when the corn dance and rain dance are performed. Other planned events among this community of 893 population, which is divided into two groups—the Turquoise people and the Squash people—begin with a turtle dance and corn dance on **New Year's Day,** January 1. On January 6 the celebration of **King's Day** and the installation of new tribal officials is marked by eagle, elk, buffalo, and deer dances. **Eastertime** is the occasion for the spring corn dance and the basket dance, and there are such dances also on May 3 for **Santa Cruz Day,** and for several days around **Christmas.**

ISLETA PUEBLO: The Isleta Pueblo (tel. 869-3111), with a population of 2,974, is 13 miles south of Albuquerque off U.S. 85, the largest of the Tiwa-speaking groups. The main pueblo, called Shiaw iba, is on the west side of the Rio Grande. The original pueblo was abandoned and destroyed in the Pueblo Revolt of 1680, but another was built on the same spot after the Spanish returned. Grasslands and wooded areas along the river make up the Indian land here, upon which the growing sprawl of Albuquerque is encroaching. Some governmental agencies and commercial interests are leasing property from the Isleta, many of whom work in the city.

Some of the women manufacture so-called tourist pottery—red ware with red and black designs on a white background. Although its lineage goes back not many years, making it keeps alive the old pottery skills.

Sunrise Lake is owned by the pueblo and affords fishing for fees from $2 to $7 daily, and there are picnicking and camping sites ($2 to $6).

The Isleta hold an **evergreen dance** in late February, and stage a **Spanish fiesta** with a carnival, food stands, and religious events on August 28. The big day of the year is the feast day honoring **St. Augustine,** September 4, when there is a harvest dance performed.

JEMEZ PUEBLO: The Jemez Pueblo (tel. 834-7359) is 46 miles northwest of Albuquerque via I-25 north to Bernalillo, then northwest on N.M. 44 to San Ysidro, then a final 2½ miles northeast on N.M. 4 to the reservation. The population of 2,148 includes the descendants of families from the Pecos Pueblo, east of Santa Fe, which was abandoned in 1838 and has now become a national monument where the ruins of the Pecos houses are still visible to visitors (see Chapter III, Section 10, "Ruins in the Santa Fe Region"). The Jemez are the only remaining people to speak the Towa language of the Tanoan group. Crafts made here include some baskets made of yucca leaves, some weaving, and a small amount of pottery.

Two rectangular *kivas* are central points for groups of dancers during ceremonial feast days that bring in Indians from other pueblos and turn the Jemez celebrations into Indian fairs. The Jemez people are famous for their excellent dancing. Occasions to view them are the **Feast of Our Lady of Angels** on August 12 and the **San Diego Feast** on November 12, when the Pecos bull dance is performed.

There is fishing and picnicking along the Jemez River on government forest lands, and permits are sold for use of the **Dragonfly Recreation Area,** where there are campsites. Pueblo stores sell fishing permits at $2 to $5 daily, and permits for game hunting may be bought from the pueblo governor's office.

LAGUNA PUEBLO: The Laguna Pueblo (tel. 552-6654) is located alongside I-40, 45 miles west of Albuquerque, the youngest and second largest of the pueblos (pop. 6,067). The land is good for grazing, with the result that over the years small settlements arose close to areas where flocks were looked after, but always closely tied to the mother pueblo of Laguna, at the site of the **San José de Laguna Mission.** A rich uranium deposit here has made this pueblo one of the most modern of Indian communities.

In spite of the building of modern housing projects, however, Laguna Indian traditions and dances continue to be followed and practiced. A great fair is held here on the big day of the year, the **Feast of St. Joseph,** March 19, with a carnival, sports events, and trading of crafts, and performances of the harvest dance and social dancing. Other dates when dances are held in Laguna are August 28 for the feast day of **St. Anthony** at Mesita village, September 8 for the celebration of the **Nativity of the Blessed Virgin Mary** in Encinal village, September 19 for the fiesta honoring **St. Elizabeth** in Paguate village, October 17 for **St. Margaret and St. Mary's Day** at Paraje village, and June 24 and July 26 in Laguna for the **Fiesta of St. John** and the **Fiesta of St. Anne.**

SANDIA PUEBLO: The small Sandia Pueblo (tel. 867-3317) is on U.S. 85, 14 miles north of Albuquerque, and is known by the Indian name Nafiat, meaning "sandy." The pueblo was abandoned during the Pueblo Revolt but finally restored when the Sandia people returned to it in 1742. It is a tradition here that the ancestors of the Sandia people once occupied a pueblo in what are now prehistoric ruins in Coronado State Monument (see Section 9, "Ruins in the Albuquerque Region"), which gives us another clue in the mystery of the disappearance of the Anasazi peoples from all over the Southwest in the 13th century.

Revenue for the tribe comes in part from rental of land for the Sandia Peak tramway. They also operate the **Bien Mur Indian Market Center** (see Section 5, "Shopping"), a modern emporium selling crafts by Indians from many pueblos and other tribes elsewhere in the U.S.

In spite of a small population—302 people—the pueblo keeps up its annual ceremonies, including an **Indian dance** in honor of newly elected governors in January and the big day of the year in honor of the patron saint of the pueblo, **St. Anthony,** a corn dance celebration, on June 13.

SAN FELIPE PUEBLO: San Felipe Pueblo (tel. 867-3381), with a population of 2,074, is 30 miles northeast of Albuquerque over I-25, on a mesa on the west bank of the Rio Grande. A traditional-style pueblo, it is known for its beautiful ritual ceremonies. The plaza has been worn into the shape of a bowl by the feet of the dancers over the centuries. In the biggest of these dances, hundreds of men, women, and children move through their rhythmic steps all day long in the spring corn dance on May 1, performed in honor of the pueblo's patron, **St. Philip** (San Felipe). The dancing is done to a great chorus of male singers intoning music that reaches back into prehistory and evokes strong emotions in participants and in visitors too. Other ceremonial events here are a January 6 **corn dance,** a February 2 buffalo dance for **Candeleria Day,** and many dances over several days around **Christmastime.**

SANTA ANA PUEBLO: Santa Ana Pueblo (tel. 867-3301), about 30 miles north of Albuquerque, reached via I-25 north to Bernahillo, then eight miles farther on N.M. 44 close to the point where the Jemez River flows into the Rio Grande, has a population of 498. Farming is productive in the watered riverbank land around this confluence of rivers, with the result that the people have built their houses out in this land mostly, leaving the pueblo looking somewhat deserted.

Ceremonial bands and red cloth belts are still woven by the male Santa Ana crafters. The art of making ceramic pottery had at one time dwindled to the point where there was but one Santa Ana woman still making any, but in the nick of time she realized the danger of losing the craft altogether, and before her death trained 20 young Indian women to follow in her footsteps in the pottery craft. Finally, as interest in crafts grew in the pueblo, a crafts co-op called the **Ta-Ma-Myia Co-operative Association** was set up as a sales outlet.

The Santa Ana Pueblo is not generally open to visitors (ask at the governor's office before attempting to go in), except for ceremonial days, when guests are welcomed. **New Year's dances** include the turtle dance and corn dance. January 6 is **King's Day,** time for performances of the eagle, elk, buffalo, and deer dances. The spring corn basket dance is done at **Eastertime,** and there are other dances performed for **St. Anthony's Day** on June 29, and for **St. Anne's Day** (the patron saint) on July 26. **Christmas** celebration dances, as in many pueblos, go on for several days in late December.

(*Note:* The prehistoric ruin of **Kuaua** in Coronado State Monument is nearby; see Section 9, "Ruins in the Albuquerque Region.")

SANTO DOMINGO PUEBLO: Santo Domingo Pueblo (tel. 465-2214), with a population of 3,361, is 50 miles northeast of Albuquerque on the east bank of the Rio Grande, reached via I-25 north to N.M. 22. A traditional farming community little changed since before the arrival of the Spanish, the pueblo is known for its handcrafts of pottery, jewelry, and weaving. They are renowned as astute traders and often will swap with visitors for the value of their crafts rather than selling it for mere money.

The most dramatic of all the pueblo ceremonials is the one here on the pueblo's **feast day,** August 4, when the corn dance is performed as it is done nowhere else, a lavish production involving clowns, scores of singers and drummers, and 500 tireless and skilled dancers in imaginative traditional costumes. Other festive occasions during the year include **King's Day,** January 6, with elk, eagle, buffalo, and deer dances; **Candelaria Day,** February 2, with the buffalo dance; the **Eastertime** spring corn dance and basket dance; the **St. Pedro's Day** corn dance, June 29; and many traditional dances in the **Christmas** season.

ZIA PUEBLO: Zia Pueblo (tel. 867-3304), with a population of 581, is located eight miles north of the Santa Ana Pueblo on N.M. 44. The pueblo blends in so perfectly with the soft tans of the stone and sand of the desert-like land all around it that it's very hard to see, like a chameleon on a tree trunk. The pueblo is known for its famous sun symbol, now become the official symbol of the state of New Mexico, and for its arts and crafts. When schoolchildren recite the salute to the state flag in this state, they say: "I salute the flag of the State of New Mexico, the Zia symbol of perfect friendship among united cultures." Watercolor paintings are a prized product of a few artists of this community and there is some first-rate pottery made here as well. **St. Lawrence,** the patron saint, is given a celebratory corn dance on his day, August 15.

ZUÑI PUEBLO: Farthest from Albuquerque is the Zuñi Pueblo (tel. 782-4481), and with a population of 6,602, also the largest of the pueblos and the only one speaking a unique language not of any other language group. It is 175 miles west of Albuquerque, reached via I-40 west to Grants and N.M. 53 to the pueblo, four miles beyond Black Rock.

The pueblo operates a **campground** for recreational vehicles (capacity, 45), with full hookups, toilets, showers, picnic tables, and grills.

The pueblo is world-famous for its jewelry of turquoise, silver, shell, and jet; there is also a revival of Zuñi basketmaking. The finest fetishes are made by the Zuñi—stones carved into animal forms. Main Zuñi events are the **Zuñi-McKinley County Fair and Rodeo** in late August and the annual **tribal fair** the same month.

OTHER INDIAN GROUPS: Three other groups of Indians of New Mexico are not considered pueblo Indians. They are the Jicarilla Apache, numbering 1,939; the Mescalera Apache, numbering 2,404; and the Navajo, most of whose total of over 120,000 members live in Arizona, but whose reservation extends into northwestern New Mexico.

The **Jicarilla Apaches** have a tourism office in northwestern New Mexico in Dulce (tel. 759-3255), on their land that extends south from the Colorado border for 65 miles, comprising 750,000 acres of sagebrush flats, mountain ranges, and deep-mesa canyons. Some of the best hunting lands in the West are within the reservation. There is a vast area called Horse Lake Mesa containing wild game that is fenced off to keep out predators: Rocky Mountain elk, mule deer, bobcats, and waterfowl inhabit the region. Yearly events include the Little Beaver Roundup during the second weekend of July, with a parade, rodeo, footraces, and dances. On September 14 and 15 is the Stone Lake Fiesta, with a rodeo, pow-wow, footraces, and dance—at Stone Lake.

The **Mescalero Apaches** have a 460,000-acre reservation between Ruidoso and Tularosa in southeastern New Mexico (see Chapter VI, "Southern New Mexico"). The **Navajo Nation** lives on a reservation of 14 million acres in northeastern Arizona, with part of it reaching into New Mexico (see the Arizona chapters).

9. RUINS IN THE ALBUQUERQUE REGION

Prehistoric Anasazi ruins within easy range of Albuquerque include the isolated, austere communities in three separate locations of Salinas National Monument, the delightful graffiti of El Morro, and the partially stabilized pueblo foundations of Kuaua—to the south, to the west, and to the north, respectively.

SALINAS NATIONAL MONUMENT: Most extensive of these ruins are within Salinas National Monument, which has a **visitor center** in the high, breezy hamlet of Mountainair in the old 1923 Shaffer Hotel that still has Indian-swastika bas-relief decorations on the walls and false beam ends poking out of the façade outdoors. Stained-glass inserts in the transoms and over the main windows add to a sense of stepping back to the time of the Model-T: layers of history on other layers, for the ruins here go back 1,000 years. Salinas was established in 1909 as Gran Quivira National Monument and still appears on many maps by that name. The original inhabitants themselves called it Cueloze. They occupied a point at the meeting place of two prehistoric civilizations, the Anasazi to the north and the Mogollon to the south.

Preserved within the monument are the ruins of three pueblos—Abo, Quarai, and Gran Quivira—and the remains of the Spanish mission ruins that were built there. The earliest sites discovered, from Anasazi and Mogollon cultures, date from A.D. 700 to 800. They interacted with the Apache, who arrived in the 16th century. In the following century the Spanish expanded their colonization into the region to bring government institutions, missions, and trade, but the pueblos continued their separate existence nonetheless until about 1670, when the Salinas area was abandoned. Two language groups, the Tompiro and the Tiwa, immigrated to different destinations, the first to the lower Rio Grande around El Paso, the latter joining other Tiwa-speaking pueblos still in existence today.

Abo

Abo, one of the three parts of the monument, is a mile north of U.S. 60, and nine miles west of the visitor center in Mountainair. This was a Tompiro pueblo and the site of the construction by the Spanish of the **Church of San Gregorio,** one of the most architecturally sophisticated of mission churches. A flowing spring shows why this spot was chosen for a pueblo site. Within easy range, the pueblo residents had access to salt from the lagoons east to the present town of Willard, as well as to good crops of piñon nuts from the surrounding forests. The heavy timbers for the beams of the mission church had to be dragged down from the Manzano Mountains, a tremendous effort, but it served for only 50 years before the community here was abandoned. The history of the relationship between Indians and Spanish at Abo is a complex and interesting one, starting off with Indian resistance—there was a week's battle in 1601—and ending with cooperation to the extent that the Indians were helping to build the church and mission structures.

Abo was excavated and the mission ruins restored to a level that stabilized them in the 1930s; turkey pens and grape seeds were also found, showing that Abo had vineyards a century before the California missions did. Turkeys had been domesticated before the arrival of the Spanish and were an important source of food for the early Indians—the only domesticated animal they had except the dog. The Spanish took the domesticated turkey home to Spain, from which it quickly spread to wide acceptance throughout Europe.

Gran Quivira

Gran Quivira sits alone on a barren plain 26 miles south of Mountainair, via N.M. 14, where there is no ready supply of spring water as at Abo. Still, it was the home of an estimated 2,000 Jumano Indians. The name Quivira comes from the quest for gold of the Spanish, which never met with any success here or elsewhere in New Mexico. The Jumanos are gone, their history and very existence determined only from what can be gleaned in the ruins of their pueblo here and in other ruins nearby. There are 17 mounds containing the remains of their houses as well as *kivas*. Most impressive are the ruins of the massive **San Buenaventura Mission,** the church structure reaching 126 feet from end to end to accommodate a numerous congregation. There is a legend of buried treasure in this infertile community that arose a century after it was abandoned. Historians have conjectured that the Indians made up the story long after they had left the vicinity simply in order to sell spurious treasure maps to greedy Spanish gold hunters.

Today a self-guided trail leads visitors through 300 rooms of the pueblo, past six *kivas,* and to ruins of a smaller church, **San Isidro,** dating from 1629, as well as those of the larger San Buenaventura (begun 1659). An on-site **visitor center** has archeological displays and an audio-visual program, and there is a windy picnic area.

Quarai

Quarai, eight miles north of Mountainair off N.M. 14, is the site of the massive walls of the **Church of the Immaculate Conception,** begun in 1728. Of it, southwestern writer Charles F. Lummis comments: "An edifice in ruins, it is true, but so tall, so solemn, so dominant of that strange, lonely landscape, so out of place in that land of adobe box huts as to be simply overpowering. On the Rhine it would be a superlative; in the wilderness of the Manzano it is a miracle."

The vast size of the church here, with an interior length of 100 feet and walls 40 feet high, contrasts with the modest size of Indian-designed pueblo rooms and *kivas.* Yet with Indian labor the Spanish built this church in only two years. It is reported from Spanish writings that the altar was richly decorated with objects brought from Europe: altar linens from Rouen, brass candlesticks, incense burners, chalices, paintings of saints. White gypsum was used to whitewash the inner walls. The essential conflict between the invading Spanish civilization as represented by its church and the Indian culture is exemplified in a puzzling emplacement of an Indian *kiva* within an open-air courtyard called the garth, where priests and monks meditated in private. A writer for the National Park Service comments: "To find such a structure in the middle of a Christian mission raises all kinds of questions. This is especially true since these first priests were highly dedicated, strongly motivated men. They believed in the holy purpose of their missionary program and many thought that the Indian religious dances were a form of devil worship. Why then is there a *kiva* in the middle of the *convento?* Did the priest build the church and *convento* over an old pueblo and *kiva?* Or did the Indians dig the *kiva* at a later date? The answers to these questions remain hidden." Although the structure of the *kiva* is simple—a circular room of stone— its functions were as complex as those of the Catholic churches built to replace them, serving as a location for private ceremonies of a single clan or as the point of origin for a wider all-pueblo ceremony eventually held in the open plaza.

A self-guiding trail leads from a small **museum** at Quarai. Besides the massive church there are remains of a three-story pueblo occupied by Tiwa-speaking people who moved here in the 12th century from Isleta and Sandia Pueblos to the north. They tilled fields in the Estancia Valley below the pueblo and traded salt for other goods with the Plains Indians. Although very little excavating has been done at Quarai, there is an estimate of the Indian population, before the arrival of the Spanish, at around 700 people. Archeologists believe earlier dwellings may exist under the ruins now visible, and plan eventual digs here.

Quarai was abandoned in the 1670s, when increasing attacks by Apaches added to miseries of drought and disease; the Indians found new homes with related tribes in other pueblos along the Rio Grande.

EL MORRO NATIONAL MONUMENT: Another destination that has a

fascination for anyone who likes to look history straight in the eye is El Morro National Monument, 120 miles west of Albuquerque via I-40 west to Grants and N.M. 53. Looming up out of the sand and sagebrush is a bluff 200 feet high holding some of the most fascinating old messages in the country. Its sandstone face displays a written record of nearly every explorer, conqueror, missionary, surveyor, sourdough, and pioneer—and tourist too—who has passed this way since the first Spaniards came by the Zuñi Mountains on the horizon here. In 1605 the explorer Don Juan de Oñate carved the first inscription of the hundreds of historic graffiti that make this the birthplace of wall-writing in America. Compare graffiti in the New York subway, for example, with Oñate's famous line here: *"Paso por aquí el adelantado Don Juan de Oñate del descubrimiento de la mar del sur a 16 de Abril de 1605"* ("passed by here the Governor Don Juan de Oñate from the discovery of the Sea of the South on the 16th of April 1605"). This is the first graffiti left to us by any white man in America, but El Morro also boasts earlier carvings by Indians, petroglyphs whose meanings remain hidden.

The graffiti, early examples in Spanish, and after 1849 in English, are easily recognizable. Somehow the actual words scratched out plainly for us to see bring these historical characters back with a strange force. From the medieval twists of Old Spanish script we eventually get into the more easily read sweeps and curls of 19th-century penmanship, or chiselmanship. The prettiest writing of all simply celebrates "E. Pen Long, Baltimore, Md." Capitals are made with loving care, spiraled ends tapering off delicately, and a National Park Service folder asks: "This man is entirely unknown—is your name Long? Perhaps you can give us a clue."

A paved walkway makes it easy to walk to the writings, and there is a stone stairway leading up to other treasures. One reads: "Year of 1716 on the 28th of August passed by here Don Feliz Martinez, Governor and Captain General of this realm to the reduction and conquest of the Moqui." Confident of success as he was, Martinez actually got nowhere with any "conquest of the Moqui," or Hopi, Indians. After a two-month battle they chased him back to Santa Fe. Another special group of visitors was the U.S. Camel Corps, trekking past between Texas and California in 1857. The camels worked out fine in mountains and deserts, outlasting horses and mules ten to one, but the Civil War ended the experiment. When Peachy Breckenridge, fresh out of the Virginia Military Academy, came by with 25 camels, he noted the fact on the stone here.

El Morro was at one time as famous as the Blarney Stone of Ireland—everybody had to stop by and make his mark. But when the Santa Fe Railroad was laid 25 miles to the north, El Morro was no longer on the main route to California and from the 1870s the tradition began dying out. Atop Inscription Rock via a short, steep trail are ruins of an Anasazi pueblo occupying an area 200 by 300 feet whose name, Atsinna, suggests that carving your name here is a very old custom indeed, for the word, in Zuñi, means "writing on rock."

CORONADO STATE PARK AND STATE MONUMENT: Twenty miles north of Albuquerque, via I-25 to Bernalillo and N.M. 4 west, is Coronado State Park and State Monument at the prehistoric Anasazi pueblo of **Kuaua.** An archeological museum displays artifacts discovered on the site, which has been stabilized. A score of rooms can be seen, and a *kiva* restored so that visitors may descend a ladder to the enclosed space and imagine the ceremonial atmosphere the site once knew when its clans were using it for their rites so long ago.

The state park has **campsites** with tables sheltered in permanent concrete structures that are welcome shelter from steady winds and fierce midday summer sun—and an occasional bit of rain. There are hot showers and hookups provided too.

10. OUTDOORS IN THE ALBUQUERQUE AREA

The ideal climate of the Albuquerque area makes it a likely spot for all kinds of sports and outdoors action all year long. Average daily high temperatures are an ideal 70°, with winter highs averaging 47° and summer under 90°, which, in an area of low relative humidity (43%) never becomes unpleasantly cold or swelteringly hot. Besides city sports such as golf and tennis, and wilderness fun in hiking and horseback riding and camping, the city has a ski area at its doorsteps.

GOLF: There are 11 public and private courses in Albuquerque, ranging from the public Ladera Golf Course with 27 holes to the 18-hole private Paradise Hills Country Club where motel guests are welcome on the greens and fairways. Tournaments include the PGA-rated **Charlie Pride Golf Fiesta** and the **William H. Tucker Invitational,** a collegiate meet. Although October and December are thought to be the most pleasant golfing months, public clubs are open from dawn to dusk all year long. They will make arrangements to find partners for visiting sportsmen and -women.

The **Albuquerque Country Club,** 601 Laguna SW (tel. 247-4111), has 18 holes over 6,204 yards, caddies, a snackbar, a halfway house, tennis courts, and a pool, open to members and guests only. **Four Hills Country Club,** also private, at 911 Four Hills Rd. SE (tel. 299-9555), has 18 holes over 6,722 yards, electric carts, a snackbar, tennis courts, and dining room and a pool. **Paradise Hills Country Club & Lodge,** at 10035 Country Club Lane NW (tel. 898-0960), is private but welcomes guests at the motel on the premises. It has 18 holes over 6,895 yards, carts, a driving range, a dining room and snackbar, tennis courts, and two pools. **Rio Rancho Golf Course,** at 500 Country Club Dr. in the suburb of Rio Rancho (tel. 892-8440), has 18 holes, carts, a clubhouse with a dining room and lounge, tennis courts, and a pool. **Tanoan Country Club,** at 10801 Academy NE (tel. 822-0433), has 18 holes over 6,807 yards, carts, a driving range, a dining room and snackbar, a pool, and tennis courts.

Public courses are the following: **Arroyo del Oso Golf Course,** at 7001 Osuna NE (tel. 884-7505), has 18 holes, a driving range, a putting green, a chipping area, a pro shop, and a snackbar. Three PGA pros are available. **Los Altos Golf Course,** 9717 Copper Ave. NE (tel. 298-1897), has an 18-hole course, a 9-hole executive course, a driving range, putting greens, a pro shop, and a restaurant. Three PGA pros are available.

Also public is **Puerto del Sol Golf Course,** 1600 Girard SE (tel. 265-5636), with nine holes, a driving range, chipping greens, a practice sand trap, and rental carts. The public **Ladera Golf Course,** 3401 Ladera Dr. NW (tel. 836-4449), has 27 holes including an executive 9-hole course, putting and chipping greens, a driving range, carts, a snackbar, and a pro shop. Two pros are on the scene.

Two **University of New Mexico courses** are also open to the public, the **South Course,** on George Street SE (tel. 277-4546), having 18 holes, three regulation practice holes, putting greens, a chipping area, a pro shop, dining room and snackbar; and the **North Course,** on the North Campus, two blocks off Lomas and north on Yale (tel. 277-4146), with nine holes, pitching and putting greens, a clubhouse, and a snackbar.

TENNIS: The good local weather also encourages tennis at the city's 140 public courts, where official and unofficial tournaments go on at various times through the year. Besides the public courts there are five private tennis clubs in the city. A tennis program is run by the Albuquerque Parks and Recreation Department on soft-surface courts equipped with night lighting, locker rooms, and showers, as well as reasonably priced private instruction. For information, call 291-6281.

SKIING: Sandia Peak (tel. 296-9585) has 19 ski runs, five graded easy, ten difficult, and four most difficult. It can be reached by car by driving 25 miles to the parking lot at the day lodge on the east side of the mountain, via I-40 east out of the city to N.M. 14 and N.M. 44 north. The world's longest aerial tramway also takes skiers to the top, from which point they have their choice of the trails. The tramway leaves from a base station on the west side of the mountain reachable ten miles from the downtown section via I-25 north to the Tramway Road exit. During ski season the operating hours, depending on day of the week, are from 8 or 9 a.m. to 9 or 10 p.m.

Three chair lifts and two Poma lifts carry skiers up the west slope to the peak. Rates for all lifts are $21 for all day, and $15 for all lifts for those aged 11 and under or 62 and older. Round-trip tram-ride prices are reduced for purchasers of ski-lift tickets. Group lessons cost $21 per person. Rentals of equipment are $11. Snowshoes are also rented at the lower tramway terminal. At the automobile access at the day lodge there is a parking charge.

HIKING AND CAMPING: The **Sandia Peak Tramway** (see "Skiing," above) runs all year for trips to the edge of **Cibola National Forest,** which reaches south 50 miles through the Sandia Mountains and Manzano Mountains in a vast area of wooded slopes and valleys crisscrossed with marked hiking and horseback trails. **Manzano Mountains State Park** is another starting point for hiking trails, reached via N.M. 14, branching south from I-40 west of Albuquerque at Tijeras, about 40 miles from the city in a beautiful land of isolated ranches and sweeping woodland. There are campsites emplaced along a loop road affording spectacular views.

Nearer the city, for day trips, is **Indian Petroglyph State Park,** in the West Mesa area, reached via I-40 west over the Rio Grande to the N.M. 448 north exit, then immediately bear left on Atrisco Drive for three miles to the park. Stone carvings showing human and animal figures and geometric designs take you into prehistory. **Belen Valley State Park,** 20 miles south of Albuquerque via I-25, occupies a delightful site under cottonwoods on the banks of the Rio Grande, rendezvous of many species of birds and a birdwatchers' destination. There is fishing along the shore, picnic tables, and trails to hike along the river.

Reached from I-40 west of Albuquerque 130 miles, **Red Rock State Park** is near the town of Gallup in a fantastic setting of ochre and crimson rock formations—buttes, towers, pinnacles. There are campsites with full hookups. The site is the scene of the annual Gallup Inter-Tribal Indian Ceremonial every August where visitors crowd an 8,000-seat arena to watch a rodeo, Indian ceremonies, and other events. A visitor center has interpretive displays that explain the geology of the area.

Back in Albuquerque there is a short hiking trail through cottonwoods in **San Gabriel State Park** along the Rio Grande near the Plaza in Old Town, open days only for picnics, walks, and sports. Also in the city, bordering the river, is **Rio Grande Nature Center State Park,** off Tingley Drive, a wildlife refuge and study center with trails along the river. **Rio Bravo State Park,** on the west bank of the Rio Grande, also in the city, off U.S. 85 (Isleta Boulevard) half a mile south of the junction with Rio Grande Boulevard, is designed to preserve a stretch of the cottonwood forest, the bosque, that originally covered the whole river valley. Hiking trails leave from a sports field and outdoor amphitheater.

Campgrounds

Among recreational-vehicle campgrounds in the city, two stand out, both in the KOA chain: the **KOA Albuquerque Central,** at 12400 Skyline Rd. NE (tel. 296-2729), and the **KOA Albuquerque West,** 5739 Ouray Rd. NW (tel. 831-1911). Both provide full hookups, convenience stores, a laundry, game rooms, and other campers' luxuries.

Two Indian-operated campgrounds within 60 miles of the city are the **Holy Ghost** and the **Dragonfly Campgrounds,** on land of the Jemez Pueblo, reached via the village of San Ysidro from Albuquerque over I-25 north to Bernalillo, then northwest on N.M. 44. Both campsites are off N.M. 44: Holy Ghost is 19 miles from San Ysidro, and Dragonfly, 25 miles. Permits for camping are at the Jemez Pueblo civic center, 2½ miles northeast of San Ysidro. Camping costs $6 per unit daily; Holy Ghost has spring water available. Sites are open year round.

FISHING: Kokanee salmon, and cutthroat, rainbow, brown, and brook trout are all taken in New Mexico waters, under licensing and limit regulations of the **New Mexico Department of Game and Fish**—get printed regulations from this agency at the Villagra Building, Santa Fe, NM 87503 (tel. 505/827-7911).

Fishing on the Indian reservations is not controlled by the agency and state licenses do not apply there. Legal possession of fish caught on Indian land should be accompanied by a document issued to the fisherman by reservation officials.

11. DESTINATIONS EAST AND WEST OF ALBUQUERQUE

Among other notable communities along the way to or from Albuquerque on the busy east-west highway I-40 are Tucumcari, the gateway on the east, and the small cities of Grants and Gallup to the west. There are attractions to keep travelers interested, as well as fed and lodged, in all three locations.

TUCUMCARI: This town of 8,500 people in a dry plain at an altitude of 4,000 feet is the main welcoming point to travelers coming into New Mexico from the east, a town all spread out along the old U.S. 66 highway. It has a dozen restaurants and over two dozen motels. You can get information from the **Tucumcari Chamber of Commerce**, 404 W. Tucumcari Blvd. (U.S. 66), Tucumcari, NM 88401 (tel. 505/461-1694).

The **Tucumcari Historical Museum**, 416 S. Adams, is open seven days in summer from 9 a.m. to 6 p.m., to 5 p.m. in winter but closed on Monday. An early sheriff's office, an authentic western schoolroom, a hospital room of the early West, a real chuck wagon, a historic windmill, and a barbed-wire collection are among the treasures.

The moon-like **Mesa Redondo,** rising 11 miles south of town via N.M. 18, gives visitors a sense of entering a strange unknown world. To the north, 27 miles distant over N.M. 104, is **Conchas Lake State Park,** with a reservoir 25 miles in length. Two modern marinas provide facilities for boating, fishing, and waterskiing here. Camping and picnic areas attract visitors to the south side of the lake—there are full hookups available as well as a nine-hole golf course. **Conchas Lake Lodge** (tel. 505/868-2988) here has 38 rooms for guests ($38 to $60 double) with air conditioning, a restaurant, lodge, and general store. The northern site offers rental cabins, a trailer park with hookups, a marina, a store, and a restaurant.

Ute Dam is 22 miles northeast on U.S. 54, near the town of Logan, and has docking facilities on a lake, campsites, and rental boats. Quay County around Tucumcari is noted for its blue quail hunting, said to be the best anywhere in the U.S.

Food and Lodging

Many of the two dozen motels in town are situated along Tucumcari Boulevard (old U.S. 66), easily accessible from I-40 just to the south of the town center. Among the more pleasant accommodations is the **Pow Wow,** a Best Western, at 801 W. Tucumcari Blvd., Tucumcari, NM 88401 (tel. 505/461-0500). There is a cool, minimally lighted lounge for that sigh of relief after a stretch of highway at 100°, as well as a restaurant; for energetic children, there's also a swimming pool. Free golfing nearby goes with room rates of $40 and up, double.

A budget accommodation, the **Blue Swallow,** 815 E. Tucumcari Blvd., Tucumcari, NM 88401 (tel. 505/461-9849), is a small establishment with modest-sized air-cooled rooms and the extra advantage for families of a playground for the kids. Double rooms go for $25.

Besides a very long commercial strip of fast-food eating places serving travelers emerging from the vast empty lands all around, interspersed with the motels all along Tucumcari Boulevard is the **Pow Wow restaurant** in the motel noted above, which offers a luncheon buffet as well as full dinners and a lounge. Otherwise the choice is a Mexican restaurant, **La Cita,** 812 S. 1st St. (tel. 461-9660), which offers good steaks as well as regional specialties.

GRANTS: This town of 12,000, 78 miles west of Albuquerque on I-40, was the center of a uranium boom now over.

Nearby Attractions

Nearby attractions are **El Morro National Monument** (see Section 9, "Ruins in the Albuquerque Region"), the **Bandera Crater Ice Caves,** 26 miles south via N.M. 53, and **El Malpais National Recreation Area,** old lava flows east of town. On a hot day the ice caves make an attractive visit, for the temperature inside never goes above freezing.

The **Chamber of Commerce Museum,** at 500 W. Santa Fe Ave., has a collection of the richest uranium ore–bearing samples in the U.S. There is a model uranium mill too. Excellent dioramas on loan from the Museum of New Mexico depict life among Indians and early settlers, and there are many relics and archeological specimens shown.

Among trips out of Grants, N.M. 547 takes you 11 miles northeast to **Mount Taylor,** 11,301 feet in elevation. The route passes by two attractive picnic areas, **Lobo Canyon** and **Coal Mine Canyon,** the latter also having campsites, a water supply, rest rooms—and a nature trail. Another destination from Grants is **Bluewater Lake State Park,** reached via I-40, 18 miles to exit 63, then seven miles south over N.M. 412. The high lake, at 7,400 feet elevation, is on the slope of the Zuñi Mountains and is stocked with trout; rental boats are available. All around the lake are stands of juniper and piñon. There are campsites, boat ramps, a café and store, and rest rooms.

Still another trip takes you to the lava flows of **El Malpais** via I-40 east seven miles to exit 89 at Quemado, then ten miles south over N.M. 117. Along the way you see the lava flow for miles, and finally arrive at **La Ventana,** or the **Rainbow Bridge,** which was blown by the wind out of the sandstone cliff. Many craters are visible in the flow, which follows the Continental Divide here. The area, protected by the Bureau of Land Management since 1974, has 84,000 acres of cinder cones, lava tubes, ice caves, sandstone formations, and pine forests. Malpais (Spanish for badlands) is considered one of the most outstanding examples of volcanic landscapes in the U.S. The most recent flows date back only 1,000 years —Indian legends tell of a river of fire over the fields of their ancestors.

At the Sandstone Bluffs overlook on N.M. 117, the largest **natural arch** in the state and other smaller arches can be seen among the cliffs, some 500 feet high. Volcanic cinder cones known as the Chain of Craters can be seen west of the lava field, reaching 20 miles from Bandera Crater to Cerro Brillante. The largest of all the cinder cones, **Bandera Crater,** is on private property, reached via N.M. 53 at a point 25 miles south of I-40. For a fee visitors may hike up Bandera Crater and see an ice cave; the operation is called Ice Caves Resort.

Perhaps the most fascinating phenomenon of El Malpais are the lava tubes, formed when the outer surface of a lava flow cooled and solidified over a flowing river of molten lava. When the lava river drained, tunnel-like caves were left. Ice caves within some of the tubes have delicate ice-crystal ceilings, ice stalagmites, and floors like ice rinks.

The **New Mexico Museum of Mining,** 100 Iron St., Grants (tel. 287-4802), is the world's only uranium-mining museum; retired miners lead visitors on tours of a realistic artificial mine. Admission is $2, and it's open from 10 a.m. to 4 p.m. Monday through Saturday and 1 to 4 p.m. on Sunday.

Food and Lodging

Grants has over two dozen restaurants, including fast-food establishments, as well as more than a dozen motels. For information, ask at the **Grants Chamber of Commerce,** 100 N. Iron, Grants, NM 87020 (tel. 505/287-4802).

The **Inn at Grants,** at the East Grants interchange of I-40, Grants, NM 87020 (tel. 505/287-7901, or toll free 800/545-6267), offers a touch of luxury in this semi-arid land, with an indoor pool surrounded by lush jungley plantlife, and a fruit bar with tempting tropical refreshers, for pretending you're in Hawaii. Rooms have longboy beds and refrigerators; there are two saunas; and a restaurant, lounge, and coffeeshop make this a spot for a one- or two-day break in a long trip. Rates are $51 to $57 double.

A good budget family accommodation can be had at the **Lariat Lodge,** 1000 E. Santa Fe Ave., Grants, NM 87020 (tel. 505/285-5333), which among its two dozen rooms has seven family units available, some with kitchenettes. Double rates are $20.

Known for its steaks, **La Ventana,** 110½ Geis St. (tel. 287-9393), also has rare prime rib and a salad bar lavish even among the elaborate ones common in the Southwest. There's a complete bar, and service daily except Sunday for both lunch and dinner.

Chinese dishes are served at budget prices at the **Canton Café,** 1212 E. Santa Fe Ave. (tel. 287-8314); call ahead for orders to go.

GALLUP: Gallup, which calls itself the Indian Capital, is 138 miles west of Albuquerque on I-40 at the western gateway to New Mexico, 20 miles from the Arizona state line. The big event of the year, in this town of 20,000 population, is the annual **Inter-Tribal Indian Ceremonial,** which celebrates its 68th running in 1989. Held over four days starting the second or third Thursday of August every year, the event provides a place for the performance of Indian ceremonial dances of many tribes throughout the U.S., as well as a marketplace for their arts and crafts. Dances are held on three evenings, beginning on a Thursday, and on the final day, Sunday afternoon, in an arena in Red Rock State Park, six miles east of Gallup.

During the four days there are All-Indian rodeo competitions with all the traditional events including roping, steer wrestling, bronco and bull riding, and women's barrel racing. An Indian game, the fruit scramble, is played by children, who also stage a tug-of-war. The display of handcrafts in an exhibit hall is called the largest by American Indians anywhere in the U.S. Artists and craftspeople give demonstrations. The hall opens before noon on Thursday and remains open to Sunday evening, with an admission charge of $2. Tickets to afternoon and evening events in the area are $5 for afternoon rodeo and sports competitions and $7 for the evening ceremonial dances, $3 for children to either. All seats are general admission, without reserved seating, but advance purchase may be made from the **Inter-Tribal Indian Ceremonial Association,** P.O. Box 1, Church Rock, NM 87311 (tel. 505/863-3896, or toll free 800/233-4528).

Another part of the weekend fun is the parades in downtown Gallup on Friday and Saturday mornings. A flyer from the association explains that "the Ceremonial began as a gathering of nearby Indian and non-Indian residents, mission and government entities, and reservation traders. Through the years it has expanded to include Indian tribes, artists, and specialty traders from all over North America, and visitors from all over the world, while retaining something of the reunion atmosphere of old."

Part of the vast Navajo lands lie only ten miles to the north of Gallup. Red Rock State Park is the site of nightly **Indian dancing** all summer, starting at 7:30 p.m.; admission is $3. Another **Arts and Crafts Fair** is held downtown in March every year, sponsored by the Gallup Area Arts Council. Mid-June is the time for the annual **Gallup Lions Amateur Rodeo,** with a parade and barbecue; admission is $5 for adults and $2 for children.

Indian Crafts Shops

Gallup has about 50 Indian craft shops, many selling machine-made jewelry that under New Mexico law must be labeled "machine manufactured." The Gallup–McKinley County Chamber of Commerce issues a list of reputable dealers of authentic Indian-made crafts made by hand. Some motels and restaurants also have showcases selling authentic Indian jewelry or crafts.

Among purveyors of Indian-made goods are **Thunderbird Supply,** 1907 W. 66th Ave.; **Thunderbird Jewelry Co.,** 1923 W. 66th Ave.; the **Nugget Gallery,** 3328 E. 66th Ave.; **The Trailblazer,** 210 West Hill; **Gilbert Ortega Indian Arts,** 3306 E. 66th Ave.; **Blackbird Trading Co.,** 2105 W. 66th Ave.; **Indian Jewelers Supply Co.,** 601 E. Coal Ave.; and **Tobe Turpen's Indian Trading Co.,** 1710 S. 2nd St.

Food and Lodging

Because of its situation on a major east-west traffic artery, Gallup has more than the normal complement of travel services, with 30 motels and 70 eating places including the fast-food emporia. Information on them can be obtained from the **Gallup Chamber of Commerce,** 103 W. 66th Ave., Gallup, NM 87301 (tel. 505/722-2228).

The **Inn at Gallup,** 3009 W. 66th Ave., Gallup, NM 87301 (tel. 505/722-2221, or toll free 800/545-6276), has a cheerful, bright lobby with an art deco chandelier over potted native plants—yucca and cactus—that add color to sofas and armchairs upholstered in Navajo designs. An enclosed pool has a thick jungle of greenery growing all around, and a garden terrace for cocktails is a favorite local early-evening destination. Rooms have king- or queen-size beds and refrigerators, and there is a lighted tennis court and a game room. Rates are $57 to $67 double.

The **Blue Spruce Lodge,** 1119 E. U.S. 66, Gallup, NM 87301 (tel. 505/863-5211), offers double rooms at $20 to $24.

Restaurants that have full bar service in Gallup include the **Prime Time,** at the Inn, 3009 W. 66th Ave. (tel. 722-2221), specializing in steaks and seafood; and **Pedro's,** 107 S. Burke (tel. 863-9755), providing Mexican specialties.

CHAPTER VI

SOUTHERN NEW MEXICO

□ □ □

Southern New Mexico is a young-feeling area even though the first European discoverers marched through 450 years ago. It's a land of flat ranchland, precipitous fir-covered mountains, sparkling ponds and reservoirs, canyons and deserts, and small towns with rows of pickup trucks angle-parked in front of the hardware store or the saloon. It has a desert so hot and bleak that it's called the Journey of Death, and a fabulous natural wonder, Carlsbad Caverns, that has drawn well over 17 million visitors. It has a luxury resort run by an Indian tribe and the world's richest horserace on a track in a mountain town. It has the isolated site of the first atomic explosion and ancient apartment houses built by prehistoric people within the shelter of overhanging cliffs. A historic army fort competes for visitors' attention with a modern facility for the study of astronomy by radio. There is a lovely old Spanish mission and the southernmost U.S. ski area. Summertime draws visitors to festivals, crafts shows, rodeos, and agricultural fairs, while mountain wilderness covering thousands of square miles draws hikers, campers, fishermen, and hunters.

1. ORIENTATION

It is 400 miles across southern New Mexico from east to west, the flat prairie of ranchland broken one-third of the distance across to the west by the first of several north-south mountain ranges, the jumble of peaks, valleys, and ridges known as the Jicarillas, the El Capitan Mountains, the Sacramento Mountains, and the Guadalupe Mountains. Desert valleys of pure sand, such as that occupied by White Sands National Monument, separate those chains from the San Andres Mountains. Farther west, across the Jornada del Muerto, are the Datil, the Gallinas, the San Mateo, and the Mimbres Mountains; the Black Range marks the Continental Divide, beyond which lies the Mogollon Range.

For such a vast area there is no one center, but rather several centers. The biggest town in the southern half of the state, and easiest of access by air, is **Las Cruces,** 225 miles south of Albuquerque and 45 miles north of El Paso, Texas. **Mesa Airlines** (tel. toll free 800/432-5267) makes connections between Albuquerque and Las Cruces; ten national airlines serve Albuquerque International Airport. Las Cruces is also at the junction of two major Interstate routes: I-25 from the north, which starts up at Buffalo, Wyoming, and serves Cheyenne, Denver, Santa Fe, and Albuquerque; and I-10, which connects Los Angeles with Jacksonville, Florida. Bus service by **Greyhound/Trailways** arrives and departs daily at Las Cruces, as well as at Deming, Lordsburg, Silver City, Socorro, and Truth or Consequences. There are **car-rental agencies** in Alamogordo, Carlsbad, Las Cruces, Roswell, Ruidoso, and Socorro (see listings under those towns for information). The towns of Lordsburg and Deming are served by **Amtrak** passenger trains plying the route between Los Angeles and El Paso, Texas.

Another major center for visitors to southern New Mexico is **Carlsbad,** also linked to Albuquerque by flights of Mesa Airlines. Carlsbad, in the Pecos Valley, lies on U.S. 285, along with Artesia and Roswell, other valley towns to the north. A busy tourist area in the central part of the southern half of the state includes **Alamogordo** and the mountains to the east and northeast where are located the Mescalero Apache Reservation, the Cloudcroft Ski Area, the town of Ruidoso and its famous racetrack, the restored Territory-style town of Lincoln, the village of Tularosa with its rose festival, and the spectacular lava beds of the Valley of Fires.

Silver City makes a likely touring center in the extreme southwestern part of the state in a spectacular copper-mining area where mountains to the north hold secrets of Anasazi ruins and hundreds of miles of wilderness trails for hiking and horseback riding. Besides all these tempting destinations, just 50 miles south of Las Cruces is the different world of Mexico via its border city of Juarez, and 60 miles south of Carlsbad, Guadalupe Wilderness National Park, in part of the chain of the Guadalupe Mountains that begins in Lincoln National Forest to the north.

2. LAS CRUCES

With a population of 51,500, Las Cruces is the largest town in southern New Mexico, an important farm center in the rich flood plain of the Rio Grande Valley where major crops are cotton, lettuce, sorghum, and corn, as well as pecans—the world's largest orchard is the 4,000-acre Stahmann Farms here. It is famous for its green chiles, and is home to the International Connoisseurs of Red and Green Chile. Calling itself "headquarters for sun country," the town, at an elevation of 3,896 feet, has a mild climate with hot summers.

A local slogan is: "Since 1535 a great place to visit!" Those first outside visitors were a group of Spanish explorers led by Alvar Nuñez Cabeza de Vaca; five years later on his search for the Seven Cities of Gold, Coronado marched through the valley with 300 soldiers. Later in the 16th century the Camino Real was traced up from Chihuahua through here to Santa Fe. A campsite along the route known as Estero Largo was named Las Cruces after an event in 1830, when Apaches attacked and killed a party of travelers camping here, on their way south by oxcart from Taos. They were buried with crosses marking their graves, after which time the site was called La Placita de Las Cruces—the place of the crosses, later shortened to Las Cruces.

WHERE TO STAY: The **Mesilla Valley Inn,** 901 Avenida de Mesilla, Las Cruces, NM 88005 (tel. 505/524-8603, or toll free 800/528-1234), a part of the Best Western chain, is a rambling complex of 170 rooms at the Mesilla exit of I-10. It is a cocktail-hour and evening meeting place for locals out on the town, who flock to its lounge and piano bar during "happy hour" and attend live entertainment after dinner. An oyster bar is a rare feature during that happy hour, incidentally; there is a popular Sunday brunch in the restaurant, where for dinner steaks and prime rib are the standard favorites.

Among the bigger first-rate motels, the Mesilla Valley is probably the best. Rates are $36 to $40 double.

A bed-and-breakfast establishment with considerable charm in Mesilla (a pretty village adjoining Las Cruces), the **Meson de Mesilla,** 1803 Avenida de Mesilla, Mesilla, NM 88046 (tel. 505/525-9212), has 13 rooms with private bath, all of course offering a full breakfast to guests. A courtyard invites sitting about for talk with a drink or a book, swimming in the pool, or admiring the native flora. Guests may use bicycles to ride a short distance to the old Mesilla Plaza, site of the venerable San Albino Mission and a number of antique, art, and souvenir shops. Rates are $45 to $75 double.

The **Royal Host,** 2146 W. Picacho Ave., Las Cruces, NM 88005 (tel. 505/524-8536, or toll free 800/541-9312), offers a picnic area, a restaurant, and swimming at modest rates of $24 to $39 double.

WHERE TO EAT: The **Double Eagle,** on the Old Mesilla Plaza (tel. 523-6700), is the most luxurious dining spot in the area. The recent restoration of the 150-year-old hacienda has put the imposing Territorial-style premises on the National Historic Sites register. Its 30-foot-long bar has Corinthian columns in gold leaf, and there are Gay '90s oil paintings of nudes, and 18-armed brass chandeliers hung with Baccarat crystals. A woman's ghost is said to frequent one of the several exquisite small dining rooms. The lush red of carpet and chair upholstery contrasts richly with the dark tones of polished wood in tables, sideboards, and paneling. Specialties include quail, prawns from the Bay of Bengal, mountain trout, and boneless chicken, and there is a lavish salad bar, international-style desserts and coffees, a good wine list, and a choice of over 100 beers from around the world. The restaurant is open every day for lunch, and for dinner to 10:30 p.m. Entrees go up to $25.

La Posta de Mesilla, just off the Old Mesilla Plaza (tel. 524-3524), also occupies a historic building 150 years old, originally an inn built along a travel route by the Spanish government. Such historic characters as Billy the Kid, Kit Carson, and Pancho Villa are said to have been sheltered here at one time or another. New Mexico–style Mexican combinations at $8 to $10 are the mainstay of a wide-reaching menu that includes top sirloin, New York-cut and T-bone steaks, guacamole salad, green enchiladas, red enchiladas, sour-cream enchiladas, meat enchiladas, sopaipillas served hot with honey—and even hamburgers for the kids.

Chinese food may be eaten on the premises or ordered to go from the **Chinese Phoenix,** 1202 Madrid (tel. 524-4241), open Tuesday through Sunday from 11 a.m. to 8:45 p.m.

Low-priced barbecue plates are offered at **Smokehouse Barbecue,** 3900 W. Picacho (tel. 524-7102).

SIGHTSEEING: Downtown Las Cruces is proud of its new $10-million mall landscaped with shrubs, trees, fountains, and domed displays concerning the history and culture of the area. The mall is the site of the **Community Theater** (tel.

523-1200), which puts on six productions every year. The **American Southwest Theater Company** (tel. 646-4515) also presents a season of plays. A gallery showing the work of local artists is within the **Branigan Cultural Center** (tel. 524-1422), which also houses a museum of local historical objects, open from 10 a.m. to noon and 2 to 5 p.m. Tuesday through Friday, 11 a.m. to 3 p.m. on Saturday, and 2 to 5 p.m. on Sunday.

County offices now occupy the famous old **Amador Hotel,** at Amador and Water Streets, open for visitors nevertheless from 9 a.m. to 3 p.m. Monday through Friday. Built in 1850 as a boardinghouse for teamsters, the building has also served as a post office, jail, courthouse, and theater. It is in the old adobe style with the beam ends of the *vigas* sticking out over the entranceways and balcony roof. It is said that while it was a hotel, at various times Benito Juarez, Pat Garrett, and Billy the Kid were guests.

A "bicentennial" **log cabin** dating from 1879 and brought in for the nation's big birthday a few years back, from the Black Range Mountains to the west, is open for visitors from 8 a.m. to 4 p.m. in summer at 671 N. Main St. It has original furnishings and artifacts from the late 1800s.

For local history buffs, the **grave of Pat Garrett** is of some interest, to be found in the Masonic Cemetery, on Brown and Compress Roads. Garrett was sheriff of Lincoln County during the famous Lincoln County War, and is best known as the man who shot Billy the Kid. Garrett also died from gunshot wounds, in a later gunfight.

The **mural water tower,** north of Lohman Avenue on the west side of I-25, is usually described by its size rather than for its esthetic impact, a panoramic picturing of the journey up the Rio Grande Valley here in 1598 by the Spanish company of Juan de Oñate. It covers 14,000 square feet of the side of the water tank. Also visible outside is an old **grinding wheel** from an 1853 flour mill, at Water and Lohman. At the same corner is **Our Lady of the Foot of the Cross Shrine,** which has a full-scale reproduction of Michelangelo's *Pietà*.

The Playhouse, 1201 N. 2nd St., is a major visitor attraction with a vast collection of dolls and dollhouses from Germany, France, the Orient, and the Americas. It is open from 1 to 5 p.m. Tuesday through Sunday for a $2 admission. The **New Mexico State University museum,** at University Avenue and Solano Drive (tel. 646-3739), has prehistoric artifacts, historic materials, and arts and crafts of the region. It is open free from 10 a.m. to 4 p.m. Tuesday through Saturday, and 1 to 4 p.m. on Sunday; closed Monday.

An old house of the Territorial era open to the public is the **Armijo House,** on Lohman Avenue near the Loretto Mall. Although it houses a savings-and-loan establishment, it is open to visitors from 9 a.m. to 4 p.m. weekdays free of charge.

Mesilla

Mesilla is a one-time Mexican village three miles from the downtown mall (take Avenida de Mesilla to the town) that keeps its colonial charm in a plaza fronted by an old church and various small shops purveying arts and crafts. The village was the crossing point of the north-south Camino Real and the east-west Butterfield Overland Stagecoach route linking Los Angeles with the east. The Gadsden Purchase, which brought Mesilla into U.S. territory, was signed here on the plaza in 1854. The village is the former capital of the Arizona Territory and its plaza today draws visitors to the **San Albino Mission** with its twin towers surmounted by crosses. The village is also remembered for having been western headquarters for the Confederate forces during the Civil War. A historic structure is **La Posta** (see "Where to Eat"), a block from the plaza in a flat-roofed adobe 150 years old; there are nine dining rooms and some crafts shops within the complex, where you are welcomed in an entryway by the flamboyant colors of tropical birds. It was here in Mesilla that Billy the Kid was sentenced to hang in 1881, but he escaped and had to be tracked down later.

Other Las Cruces Sights

Las Cruces, founded in 1849, began outstripping Mesilla in size when the Santa Fe Railroad opened a line and depot in the town in 1881. A land-grant college founded in 1888 has evolved into the modern **New Mexico State University** here, with a huge campus of 6,000 acres and 12,000 students.

A special occasion for visitors is the **Farmers' Market,** held under shading canopies on the downtown mall on Wednesday and Saturday mornings (except during the winter months), where sellers of fruits and vegetables mingle with craftspeople exhibiting their wares.

The Holiday Inn at University and Main has a **stagecoach collection** displayed free of charge.

OUTSIDE LAS CRUCES: Fort Selden (tel. 526-8911), 12 miles north of Las Cruces via I-25, is a state monument open Thursday to Monday from 9 a.m. to 5 p.m.; closed Tuesday and Wednesday. Built in 1865, it housed the famous Black Cavalry, the Buffalo soldiers who protected Mesilla from Indian raids. It was also the boyhood home of Gen. Douglas MacArthur. The original post was built of standard local-style one-story adobe buildings, the roofs laid with cottonwood *vigas* (beams) and covered with peeled willow saplings and dirt. The buildings formed a rectangle around a parade ground, with officers' quarters to the north, a single house and two doubles. West of these was the commander's quarters. Opposite the officers' quarters were the enlisted men's barracks, in two long dormitories each big enough for an entire company. There was also a complex of administration offices, storerooms, workshops, a guardhouse, a small hospital, and corrals for horses and mules. A bakery, a magazine, and a laundry also occupied their own structures. It was isolated duty, with the nearest railroad 549 miles north in Colorado, and the nearest telegraph 263 miles away in Santa Fe. Nevertheless troops here never got into any major Indian battles, only minor skirmishes with Mescalero and Mimbres Apaches. Scouting parties hardly ever went out of the fort after 1875, and by 1878 the post was closed, the need for protection having ended. But two years later it was reopened for a time to provide protection to the newly arriving railroad lines. But the railroad, permitting fast deployment of troops from a central location, was ringing the death knell for these small isolated forts in the West, and Selden was closed permanently in 1891, along with 27 other frontier forts—thus ending a special period of American military history.

Leasburg Dam State Park (tel. 524-4068), a mile north of Fort Selden on U.S. 85 on the banks of the Rio Grande, is built around a dam that channels water from the river to irrigate the whole upper Mesilla Valley. It also makes a good fishing spot, as well as a paddling course for canoes or kayaks. The park has campsites with shelters, electricity, showers, a dump station, and a playground.

Aguirre Springs National Recreation Area (tel. 525-8228), reached 22 miles northeast of Las Cruces via U.S. 70, is a spectacular site for mountain viewing and a departure point for trail hikes. There are picnic areas and campsites, but no water supply.

La Cueva is reached by following University Avenue out of Las Cruces past the golf course to the base of the Organ Mountains, a gravel road to a cave that still holds a legendary local ghost. The Hermit Monk, as he was called, Juan Maria Augastiniani, an Italian aristocrat, wandered through New Mexico as a youth in the last century, became a monk, and moved into this cave. It became the tradition for villagers in Mesilla to watch for his fires at night. Then the fires ceased, and a search party discovered the monk—murdered. The mystery remains complete, but his ghost is reputed still to be on the premises.

Highway N.M. 28 south of town takes you to **Stahmann Farms** (tel. 526-2453), the world's largest pecan grove, producing millions of pounds of nuts annually. Visitors are welcome, and there is a retail pecan store.

Tortugas is a tiny Indian community at the eastern edge of town inhabited by Tiwa-speaking Pueblo Indians who have lived here for two centuries, and have a tradition of staging a fiesta in honor of **Our Lady of Guadalupe** on December 10 to 12. Events include a four-mile pilgrimage to the top of nearby "A" Mountain, and a descent by torchlight, a mass, and traditional Indian dances and singing.

ANNUAL EVENTS: Visitors can look to have some fun at almost any season during the various annual festivals and fairs going on around Las Cruces. There is a **women's softball tournament** in March with vocally enthusiastic fans at Maag Park; for information, call 646-4048. The Singing Men of Las Cruces (tel. 524-9654) provide an **Easter sunrise concert.** There are **May Day** booths exhibiting crafts and food on the university campus; for information, call 646-3255. June brings a **horse show** (tel. 524-7758). Maag Park is the site of fireworks on the **Fourth of July.** A big show is the **Pan American Fiesta** (tel. 524-8521) in September, on the downtown mall, with a parade, folk dancing, mariachis, and a barbecue. Also in September is the famous **Chile Festival** up in Hatch, a small town 30 miles north on I-25, which besides eating involves a skeet shoot, a black-powder shoot, a horseshoe competition, a fiddlers' contest, an art show, and a dance; the recipe contest is the big event. For information, call 646-1939 in Las Cruces.

A big food festival in Las Cruces is the **Whole Enchilada Festival** in October, with entertainment on the downtown mall, street dancing, a chile cookoff, ethnic food booths, parades, games, and the world's largest enchilada. For information, call 524-1968. Also in October is the **Southern New Mexico State Fair and Rodeo** at the fairgrounds, 575 S. Alameda Blvd. (tel. 526-8179). Still in October there is an annual **Holy Cross Retreat House Fiesta** at the retreat house in Mesilla Park, reached over N.M. 478 south, where a barbecue, entertainment, dancing, games, and an auction are scheduled; for information, call 524-3688. In December there is an **arts-and-crafts fair** at the University-Community Arts Center, 207 Avenida de Mesilla (tel. 524-0014).

3. ALAMOGORDO–RUIDOSO AREA

Alamogordo, a town of 30,000, about 70 miles northeast of Las Cruces and about the same distance north of El Paso, Texas, is famous for nearby Trinity Site, still off-limits to civilians (there is a one-day tour in October), where the first atomic bomb was exploded on July 16, 1945. Because of the attractions of White Sands National Monument and other sites of a different sort of natural beauty in the Sacramento Mountains to the east, the town has become a base for tourists. It has the International Space Hall of Fame, a ski area and Indian-operated resort not far away in the mountains, and a number of state parks nearby.

Ruidoso is a resort town named for its site on a noisy stream, most famous for its racetrack where the world's richest race is run, with a $2.5-million purse. Outdoors lovers, hikers, horseback riders, fishermen, and hunters are drawn to the surrounding Lincoln National Forest. Not far away, the restored village of Lincoln is becoming a sort of western Williamsburg-in-the-mountains.

You can rent a car in Alamogordo from **Avis** at the Holiday Inn, 1403 White Sands Blvd. (tel. 437-3140); from **Hertz,** at the Municipal Airport (tel.

437-7760); and from **National,** also at the airport (tel. 437-4126). In Ruidoso, **Avis** is at Sierra Blanca Regional Airport (tel. 257-2389), and **Hertz** also (tel. 257-5722).

WHERE TO STAY: Both Alamogordo and Ruidoso offer motel accommodations, and there's a luxury resort nearby on the Apache reservation.

Alamogordo

The **Desert Aire,** 1021 White Sands Blvd., Alamogordo, NM 88310 (tel. 505/437-2110), has 96 rooms, all wired for cable television. There is a lounge and coffeeshop on the premises, as well as a separate dining room. Rates are $42 to $50 double.

The **Alamo Inn,** 1400 White Sands Blvd., Alamogordo, NM 88310 (tel. 505/437-1000), offers double rooms at $25.

Ruidoso

The **Village Lodge,** 101 Innsbrook Dr., Ruidoso, NM 88345 (tel. 505/258-5441), offers luxurious new suites in this resort area at a location on Alto Hwy. just across from the ranger station. Each suite accommodates a maximum of four guests, and consists of a living room with a wood-burning fireplace, a kitchenette with a wet bar, a bath, and a bedroom. The living room has a hide-a-bed, and there are separate television sets (with movies available) in the two rooms. All cooking equipment is provided. The facilities of the adjoining resort, Innsbrook Village, are available to guests, including swimming, tennis, golf, and trout-pond fishing.

The daily rate for two persons is $62 to $90. Besides a pool, there is a recreation room, shuffleboard court, and playground.

Carrizo Lodge, on Carrizo Canyon Road, Ruidoso, NM 88345 (tel. 505/257-9131), is a venerable spa recently accepted on the National Registry of Historic Places, where guests in individual rooms or in suites attend art classes in a school on the premises. Besides the esthetic endeavor, guests use a pool, sauna, and hot tubs, and enjoy an arcade room, a cocktail lounge, and a restaurant. Rates are $50 double. For information on art classes, write to Carrizo Lodge, P.O. Box 1371, Ruidoso, NM 88345.

In the Area

The **Wortley Hotel,** Lincoln, NM 88338 (tel. 505/653-4500), is the centerpiece of a historical restoration in the nearby town of Lincoln, where the courthouse, from which Billy the Kid made his famous escape, has been restored, along with several other structures and the hotel. Originally built to house men running the town's first general store in 1878, the hotel is owned by the state and leased to a managing partnership. There are eight rooms with ceiling fans, brass beds, and fireplaces, and breakfast goes with the room rate of $40. A Victorian dining room provides homemade green chili, homemade tortillas, roast beef, or baked chicken.

To stay in the mountains around Ruidoso for fishing, hiking, or skiing in winter, go to the **Dan Dee Cabins,** 310 Main Rd. (in the Upper Canyon), Ruidoso, NM 88345 (tel. 505/257-2165). The four-acre property is within a few steps of trout fishing in a stream. The pine-shaded cabins have fireplaces, televisions, queen-size beds, and outdoor barbecues, and rent for $39 to $54 double, depending on season.

The **High Country Lodge,** on N.M. 37 north of Ruidoso in Alto (P.O. Box 137), Alto, NM 88312 (tel. 505/336-4321), is a high-country family resort at an altitude of 7,300 feet, making it popular with summer vacationers as well as with winter sports enthusiasts. The reasonably priced apartments all have living room with fireplace, two bedrooms, a fully equipped kitchen, and bathroom, as well as color TVs and outdoor grills, all at $53 to $58 for two, with children under 13 staying free; there is a $6 daily maid service charge if needed. An enclosed heated pool, recreation area with fireplace, tennis court, playground, sauna, and hot tub, as well as Ping-Pong and horseshoes, are all provided. There is trout fishing nearby, and sleds are available in winter.

You'll have an especially pleasant bed-and-breakfast stay at **Sierra Mesa Lodge,** on Fort Stanton Road in Alto (P.O. Box 463), Alto, NM 88312 (tel. 505/336-4515). The inn, on a hillside overlooking the Capitan Mountains, has five rooms with private baths. The "Victorian" has a brass bed, antique oak furniture, and a brocade love seat; the "French Country" is in the French style; the "Oriental" has authentic Oriental pieces and a bed with canopied bonnet and mirrored headboard; the "Country Western" has a pineapple step-up bed and western pieces; and the "Queen Anne" has a high poster bed with canopy and window seat. Waffles, quiches, omelets, and fresh bread go for breakfast. There is no smoking, nor children under 14 allowed. Rates are $65 for two including breakfast.

A Luxury Resort

The **Inn of the Mountain Gods,** on the Mescalero Apache reservation (P.O. Box 269), Mescalero, NM 88340 (tel. 505/257-5141, or toll free 800/545-9011), is a vast resort with an 18-hole golf course and 250 luxury rooms. It is the successful dream of the tribal president, Wendell Chino, who wanted to help his people get into the recreation and tourism business. An impressive copper fireplace draws the eye as you enter the three-story lobby, decorated with trophies of wild animals from the mountains: bear, antelope, and elk. Outside from the deck is a fabulous view of the 12,000-foot-high Sierra Blanca and the pristine waters of Lake Mescalero.

The golf course was designed by Ted Robinson, whose work includes the famed course at the Princess in Acapulco. The tenth hole requires the tricky business of hitting to an island in the lake, then over water again to the green. Six outdoor and two indoor tennis courts, a swimming pool, whirlpool, saunas, a stable, and a trap-and-skeet range are also available here. Rowboats and canoes take to the waters of the lake, stocked with lake trout. There is hunting for mule deer and white-tailed deer on the 460,000-acre reservation in season; an elk herd, recently diminished, is growing apace. A package hunt deal is held during September, time of full rut and bugling season. In winter buses shuttle skiers to the nearby Ski Apache resort, also owned by the tribe (see "Outdoors," below).

There is a piano bar in the lobby and live entertainment seasonally in the Ina-Da Lounge; the establishment also has two gift shops, golf and tennis pro shops, valet and room services, and facilities for bicycling, badminton, volleyball, and horseshoe pitching. A number of the reservation Indian population of 2,500 have found employment with the resort, which is operated by the tribal council. Rates are $65 to $118 double. The resort is reached via U.S. 70 south of Ruidoso.

WHERE TO EAT: In Alamogordo, a good bet for breakfast, lunch, or dinner is the **Hourglass** dining room of the Holiday Inn, 1401 S. White Sands Blvd. (tel. 437-7100). There are full, hearty breakfasts served, and at lunch and at dinner there is a popular salad bar, all-you-can-eat style. Mexican specialties are made from scratch, of fresh ingredients, and the full menu also has steaks and seafood. There is full bar service.

The **Inn of the Mountain Gods** (noted under "Where to Stay"), up on the Mescalero Apache reservation, has two restaurants open to the public, both in scenic surroundings in this luxury resort. On the lower level of the main building there is the Dan Li Ka dining room (tel. 257-5141), offering American and continental cuisine. It is open for breakfast, lunch, and dinner seven days a week; a Sunday brunch is served until 2:30 p.m. A more casual atmosphere can be found in the Apache Tee Restaurant and Lounge, open only in the summer and fall season. Overlooking the wide expanses of golf course and lake, it also serves three meals daily.

The **Incredible Restaurant,** on N.M. 37 north of Ruidoso (tel. 336-4312), is a popular spot for lunch or dinner—prime rib, steaks, seafood, and specialty drinks in a lounge that has live music most nights.

For a sample of the kind of chuckwagon dinners so popular in the West, try the **Flying J Ranch,** a mile north of Alto on N.M. 37 (tel. 336-4330). A menu at $10 includes sliced beef in sauce, potatoes, beans, biscuits, cake, and applesauce. After dinner, served at one seating only at 7:30 p.m., there is a musical show by the Flying J Wranglers. The establishment is closed Sunday, as well as from Labor Day to Memorial Day.

SIGHTSEEING: In Alamogordo, the **International Space Hall of Fame,** at Scenic Drive and Indian Wells Road, has films and exhibits honoring the people who have pioneered space flight. Satellites, space capsules, lunar rocks and soil, and rockets are shown. The fantastic Omnimax film theater has a screen four stories high for the projection of realistic films taken in space. The structure housing the center, called the "Golden Cube," is of architectural interest. Visitors are invited to an annual ceremony to induct new members of the Hall of Fame on the first Saturday of October.

Part of the complex is the **Tombaugh Space Center,** with a planetarium projector, 20 special-effects projectors, and a laser light system that can show 2,354 stars, the Milky Way, all the visible planets, the sun, and the moon, and can duplicate the night sky anywhere on earth anytime of the year. Laser concerts with special effects and musical accompaniment are a regular feature here. For information, call 437-2840, or toll free 800/545-4021. The museum is open seven days a week from 9 a.m. to 6 p.m. Admission to both the theater and the Space Hall of Fame is $5, $3.50 for children and seniors.

Next to the Alamogordo Chamber of Commerce at 1301 White Sands Blvd. is the **Tularosa Basin Historical Society Museum,** open from 10 a.m. to 4 p.m. Monday through Saturday and 1 to 4 p.m. on Sunday. It displays artifacts and photographs out of the history of the surrounding Tularosa Basin.

La Luz is a small, historic village three miles north of Alamogordo that has attracted a number of resident artists and craftspeople who live and work here and display some of their products for sale. Worth seeing are the old adobe corral and the small Our Lady of Light Church.

White Sands National Monument

About 15 miles southwest of Alamogordo on U.S. 70/82, White Sands National Monument is probably the most memorable natural area in this part of the Southwest. An area of 230 square miles of pure-white gypsum sand in wave-like dunes reach out over the floor of the Tularosa Basin. Preserved here in the monument is the best part of the world's largest gypsum dune field, where plants and animals have evolved in special ways to adapt to the bright-white environment. The surrounding mountains, the Sacramentos to the east, with their forested slopes, and the sere San Andres to the west, are all made of this gypsum in massive layer upon layer. These have been slowly eroded over the past millions of years by rains and melting snows to be carried down into Lake Lucero. Here the hot sun and dry winds evaporate the water, leaving the pure-white gypsum in crystals, in the dry lake bed. Then the persistent winds blow these crystals, in the form of minuscule bits of sand, in a northerly direction, adding them to growing dunes. As each dune grows and moves farther from the lake, new ones form, rank after rank, in what seems an endless procession. Some creatures that have evolved here have a bleached coloration to match the whiteness all around them. Some plants have also evolved means for surviving against the smothering pressures of the blowing sands. The plants and animals together make up a special community here of living things adapted to a strange world. The plants and animals, dependent on each other, can thus survive this desert environment.

Open from 8:30 a.m. to 5:30 p.m. daily, a **loop drive** through the "heart of the sands" begins at the **visitor center** on U.S. 70 and winds through the dunes for 16 miles. Information available at the center will tell you what to look for on your driving trip, along which there are a number of pullouts at points of special interest. At one point visitors see dunes that are stabilized by vegetation. Farther on are examples of fourwing saltbush, with leaves that, though salty, make food for small animals living here. Another plant to note is the iodine bush, another force for stabilizing the dunes, named for the color of its sap. Farther on, a vast dune is noted, one that has to be plowed clear frequently, else it would obliterate the loop road. Sometimes, as the National Park Service admits, the wind wins and the road does have to be routed around a dune. The dunes are in fact all moving slowly to the northeast, pushed by prevailing southwest winds, some at the rate of as much as 20 feet a year.

Few plants can survive in the moving sands; among some that do are skunkbush sumac, soap tree, yucca, rubber rabbitbrush, and cottonwood. Gypsum pedestals stand clear because plants that once grew into the former dune here bound a column of sand grains tightly together with their roots; when the dunes moved on they left these columns standing free. In level depressions between dunes the water level, surprisingly, may be only three or four feet below the surface. Even though the water holds a lot of gypsum in solution, it is still useful to many plants, which explains the growth of vegetation in the apparent desert-like environment. Small cottonwood trees, for example, are able to exist here.

In the part of the monument called the "heart of the dunes" the road itself is made of hard-packed gypsum. Visitors are invited to get out of their cars and explore a bit, climb a dune for a better view of the endless sea of sand all around them. A couple of safety tips are emphasized by the Park Service: one, that tunneling in this sand can be dangerous, for it collapses easily and could suffocate a person; and two, that sand-surfing down the dune slopes, although permitted here, can also be hazardous, so it should be undertaken with care, and never near an auto road. Hikers are warned about the possibility of getting lost in a sudden sandstorm should they stray from marked trails or areas. But the reaction of a telephone lineman up in Albuquerque who once spent a day of his vacation down here comes closer to giving a sense of the place: "I just went out there in all that white sand and got me a dune and went up on it and looked and looked and just let it sink in, and I never saw anything like it, never felt anything like it. I think I could stay out there in that white sand for a real long time, and I don't know exactly why. There's just something fascinating about it, something that gets you."

In summer there are nature walks and evening programs at the visitor center. For information on these, call 437-1058, or when driving near or on the monument, tune a radio to 1610 AM for information on what's doing. Entrance fee to the drive is $1 per car.

More Area Sights

Off on U.S. 70 toward Ruidoso you soon come to the Gothic-style **St. Joseph's Mission,** built by local Indians between the two World Wars, with walls eight feet thick. The interior has the symbols of Apache mountain gods along with Roman Catholic saints in paintings and carvings.

Farther along on U.S. 70 in the Mescalero Apache reservation is the **Mescalero Cultural Center,** open from 9 a.m. to 4:30 p.m. weekdays. There are photos, artifacts, clothing, craftwork, and other exhibits showing the history and culture of the Mescalero Apache tribe. Besides the famous Inn of the Mountain Gods opened by the tribe in 1975, the Indians also engage in profitable lumbering and cattle ranching. Every summer at the beginning of July a four-day ceremony is reenacted in the tribal community of Mescalero, including the Apache maidens' puberty rites ceremony at dawn and a mountain spirits dance at night.

North from Alamogordo 38 miles via U.S. 54 and a side road east toward the Sierra Blanca is the fascinating **Three Rivers Petroglyphs,** a national recreation site where along a 1,400-yard trail there are over 5,000 petroglyphs, or rock inscriptions, carved by the Mogollon people who lived there between A.D. 900 and 1400. Ruins of an ancient village may be seen just south of the inscription trail. The area, open year round, is open free of charge and is run by the Federal Bureau of Land Management.

Ruidoso is the home of the richest horse race in the U.S., the $2.5-million All-American Futurity at **Ruidoso Downs,** on U.S. 70, 50 miles northeast of Alamogordo. The All-American is run every Labor Day. The racing season runs from May to Labor Day, Thursday through Sunday; post time is 1 p.m. Ruidoso itself is a pretty mountain resort town and base for outdoor activity; for information, contact the **Ruidoso Chamber of Commerce,** 720 Sudderth Dr., Ruidoso, NM 88345 (tel. 505/257-7395).

Out in the wilderness of the Sierra Oscura desert country, 30 miles due west of the town of Carrizozo, lies the mysterious never-never land of the **Trinity Site** where the first atom bomb was exploded in 1945. No visitors are permitted in the area, except once a year when a tour into this legendary country is set up, during the first week of October, by the Alamogordo Chamber of Commerce. To make a reservation for the trip, call 505/437-6120.

Twelve miles northeast of Carrizozo on N.M. 349, an interesting side trip takes you to the ghost town of **White Oaks,** founded in 1879 as a gold-mining town that once had a population of 4,000. When the new railroad bypassed the town in favor of Carrizozo, it fell into a decline and is but a shadow of its old self now.

An old town recently given a rebirth through the art of restoring of old buildings is tiny **Lincoln,** 30 miles east of Carrizozo on U.S. 380, which has regained its 19th-century splendor. Originally named La Placita del Río Bonito, its name was changed in honor of Abe Lincoln in 1869. The whole town is now a state monument, with a number of historic structures open to the public. The old courthouse has become a regional museum, which still keeps records of a bloody five-month period in the town's history in 1878 known as the Lincoln County War, fought over the issue of beef contracts for nearby Fort Stanton between various ranching and merchant interests. Among what locals considered the "good guys" in this little war was Billy the Kid, who nevertheless came to a bad end four years later. The courthouse still has a hole in it made by a bullet from the gun of the Kid. Also restored is the old **Wortley Hotel,** operating as lodging and restaurant open to the public (see "Where to Stay"). It has a veranda, great sideboards and tables in the dining room, and marble-topped tables and brass beds in the bedrooms. A **historical center** is open seven days a week in summer.

Twelve miles east of Lincoln on U.S. 380 at Capitan is **Smokey the Bear State Park,** with a museum dealing with the subject of fire prevention. Open from 8:30 a.m. to 5 p.m. daily, the park has the grave of the poster bear who was saved from further scorching during a forest fire by rangers and became the nation's symbol for forest-fire prevention.

ANNUAL EVENTS: Cloudcroft, the village on U.S. 82 about 20 miles east of Alamogordo, best known for its ski resort, is also the site of a juried arts-and-crafts show during the month of May, entitled aptly **Mayfair.** You can get information on the date and time from its sponsor, the Cloudcroft Chamber of Commerce (tel. 682-2733). Also in late April or early May in the village of Tularosa is the **Rose Festival,** with horse racing, a parade, a barbecue, parties, a carnival, and an art show, all sponsored by the Tularosa Chamber of Commerce (tel. 585-2855). **Armed Forces Day** in May is marked by ceremonies at Holloman Air Force Base and at the White Sands Missile Range, both near Alamogordo; for information on them, call the Alamogordo Chamber of Commerce (tel. 437-6120).

Fort Sumner stages **Old Fort Days** in June, with a Billy the Kid celebration, a parade, rodeo, bank robbery, staging of a melodrama, a barbecue, film festival, sports contests, and historic exhibits. Call the Fort Sumner Chamber of Commerce (tel. 355-7705) for information. Ruidoso has its **Summer Festival** in June, with concerts and entertainment; information may be obtained from the Ruidoso Chamber of Commerce (tel. 257-7395).

July is the time for the **July Jamboree** in Cloudcroft—Fourth of July celebrating with an arts-and-crafts fair, ethnic foods, and sports events at Zenith Park; for information, call 682-2733. Early July is the time also for the four-day series of ceremonies conducted by the **Mescalero Apache tribe** at Mescalero, involving the Apache maidens' puberty rites and the mountain spirits dance, among others. For information, call the tribal office at 671-4494.

Old Lincoln Days in Lincoln during August offer pageants, a parade, a fiddlers' contest, a Pony Express mail run, ghost town tours, food booths, and an art show. For information, call the Historic Center (tel. 653-4025).

In September Ruidoso is host to the world's largest **motorcycle convention,** with 4,000 cyclists participating in events over the last week of the month into early October. There is also a parade. For information, phone 257-7395.

OUTDOORS: Ten miles south of Alamogordo off U.S. 54 is the state's newest park, **Oliver Lee Memorial,** open from 7 a.m. to sunset daily, with a visitor center open daily from 9 a.m. to 4 p.m. Situated in Dog Canyon, one of the last strongholds of the Mescalero Apache, it was the site of some battles between the U.S. Cavalry and the Indians. The site has campgrounds, shelters, electricity, showers, and a dump station. The location, against the steep escarpment of the Sacramento Mountains at the mouth of the canyon, gives the area a visual appeal that has perhaps helped it draw human visitors since prehistoric times. Many springs and seeps support a variety of rare plant species, some on the endangered list. The site is named for a rancher who lived here and raised cattle at the turn of the century. Hiking trails into the foothills are well marked and provide delightful views of the canyon.

An unusual footpath fitted out with storyboards in Braille make **La Pasada Encantada**—the Enchanted Walk—a destination for the blind within the quiet stretches of Lincoln National Forest near the town of Cloudcroft. The loop departs from the Sleep Grass Campground, reached via a Forest Service road off N.M. 24 south of the town. The signs invite strollers to touch the various barks, leaves, and plants to be found along the way.

Valley of Fires State Park, west of Carrizozo on U.S. 380, takes in the Carrizozo Malpais, or badlands, involving a recent lava flow 44 miles long (that's recent, geologically speaking, for the eruption took place 1,500 years ago). The strangely folded, twisted formations draw you into them to explore, and you can do this thanks to a trail leading in and around. Everything is black and hard and weirdly formed here, yet there is considerable plant and animal life. There are campsites, shelters, a playground, drinking water, and rest rooms.

Lincoln National Forest has hundreds of miles of trails for hiking and horse-back riding as well as numerous primitive campsites, some accessible by car. For detailed information and maps, get in touch with the Forest Service headquarters in the Federal Building in Alamogordo (tel. 437-6030).

Skiing

Ski areas include **Cloudcroft,** 2½ miles east of Cloudcroft on U.S. 82 (tel. 505/682-2333, or toll free 800/824-9087), with 25 runs, of which 36% are for beginners, 44% for intermediates, and 20% for advanced skiers. Two ski tows and two T-bars have an overall capacity of 1,000 skiers per hour. It is open Friday through Monday in season from 9 a.m. to 4:30 p.m., with night skiing to 10 p.m. on Friday and Saturday. All-day lift rates are $20 for adults, $10 for children; ski rentals are $12 and $9. There is a snackbar at the site, and lodging in Cloudcroft and Ruidoso.

Ski Apache, 16 miles northwest of Ruidoso via N.M. 37 and then N.M. 532 (tel. 505/336-4356), has 40 runs, 25% of them for beginners, 35% for intermediates, and 40% for advanced skiers. One tow, seven chair lifts, and gondolas can handle 12,500 skiers per hour. The ski area is open daily from 8:45 a.m. to 4 p.m. Adult all-day rates are $27; children $18. Equipment rentals are $12 and $8.50. There is a snackbar, a restaurant, and bars on the site; ample food and lodging can be found in Ruidoso.

4. CARLSBAD

Carlsbad is a city of 28,980 on the Pecos River, 150 miles southeast of Alamogordo in the southeast corner of New Mexico. Founded in the late 1800s, the area it occupies was controlled by Apaches and Comanches until just a little over a century ago. Besides a good tourist business from nearby Carlsbad Caverns, the town thrives on farming, with irrigated crops of cotton, hay, and pecans. Pecans grow so well in Carlsbad that it is said that the nuts from just two trees in your yard will pay your property taxes. The area also has potash mines producing 85% of the U.S. total of this fertilizer. At 3,100 feet elevation, the town has hot summers and mild winters, with low humidity typical of a desert area where nights cool off quickly. The town has many parks, enough for an acre for every person living here, among them 100 softball fields. The town was named for the Czech spa of the same name, for spring waters nearby.

The Caverns are the big attraction, having had over 28 million visitors since opening in 1923, and a satellite community, White's City, has sprung up at the park entrance to serve visitors. Living Desert State Park and Guadalupe National Park, across the state line in Texas, also draw outdoor lovers and those interested in desert life.

Cars may be rented from **Hertz** at the Municipal Airport (tel. 887-1500) or from **National,** 1002 N. Canal St. (tel. 885-4161). There is daily service to El Paso, Texas, on buses of **Texas, New Mexico & Oklahoma Coaches, Inc.** (tel. 915/532-3404).

WHERE TO STAY: Since the total of visitors to Carlsbad Caverns is now running at just about three-quarters of a million per year, with half of this total coming during the summer months, accommodations should be booked ahead at the peak times. For information on room availability in over a dozen inns and motels in Carlsbad, get in touch with the **Carlsbad Chamber of Commerce,** Canal Street at Greene Street, Carlsbad, NM 88220 (tel. 505/887-6516).

A busy, popular hotel serving mostly Cavern visitors is the **Holiday Inn,** 3706 National Parks Hwy., Carlsbad, NM 88220 (tel. 505/887-2861, or toll free 800/465-4329), which has 123 units renting at $45 to $57 double. The inn also has a restaurant and a lounge.

Motel 6, at 3824 National Parks Hwy., Carlsbad, NM 88220 (tel. 505/885-8807), has well-maintained minimal motel rooms that include the use of a pool at low rates: $24 double.

Nearest to the national park entrance is the **Cavern Inn,** on U.S. 80, White's City, NM 88268 (tel. 505/785-2291, or toll free 800/CAVERNS), within walking distance of the visitor center. There is a restaurant and lounge on the premises, and double rooms go for $42 and up.

WHERE TO EAT: The **Velvet Garter Saloon & Restaurant,** 14 Carlsbad Caverns Hwy. in White's City (tel. 800/THE-CAVE), has a mural of the caverns in stained glass, and offers char-broiled steaks, Bev's chicken, catfish, shrimp, fajitas, and New Mexico specialties.

Tourists often add a memorable night to their adventures in cave country by having a dinner-with-musical-show at the **Flying X Ranch,** at 7505 Old Cavern Hwy., five miles south of the center of Carlsbad (tel. 885-6789). The air-cooled cow barn is open nightly except Sunday from early May to mid-September, offering one seating nightly at 7:30 p.m. for a $10 dinner of New Mexico beef simmered in the house barbecue sauce, served with potatoes, beans, biscuits, applesauce, ranch cake, lemonade, and coffee. Early arrivals enjoy free pony rides and hay rides, and after the chow there's a 1¼-hour western music show by the Flying X ranchhands.

CARLSBAD CAVERNS: **Carlsbad Caverns National Park** (tel. 885-8884), 25 miles south of Carlsbad, has an information and exhibit area in its visitor center open from 7:30 a.m. to 7 p.m. June through Labor Day, 8 a.m. to 5 p.m. Labor Day through May. Cavern trips leave continuously from 8 a.m. to 5 p.m. June through Labor Day, 8 a.m. to 3:30 p.m. September through May. Guided lantern trips through the undeveloped **New Cave,** 23 miles from the visitor center, can be made by reservation only. They are scheduled daily from May 28 through Labor Day and on weekends only during the rest of the year. A ranger talk at the cave entrance before the millions of resident bats fly out for the night is scheduled daily, May through September, just before sunset.

Near the main cave entrance is a half-mile self-guiding desert nature walk, and there is a 9½-mile one-way driving loop, **Walnut Canyon Loop Drive,** that starts half a mile from the visitor center, travels along a ridge to the edge of Rattlesnake Canyon, and returns through upper Walnut Canyon.

Backcountry hikers are asked to register at the visitor center before going out on any of the trails in the 46,755 acres of the park. Trails are poorly defined, but can be followed by the use of a topographic map available at the visitor center. Short day hikes or long trips are possible, but there is no water in the backcountry, and permits are required for overnight hiking. The **Rattlesnake Springs** picnic area is grassy and shaded with a water supply, picnic tables, grills, and toilets.

Carlsbad Caverns have as their setting the Guadalupe Mountains, which take the form of sharp cliffs at their southern tip, across the border in Texas. Around Carlsbad the range slopes downward to the level of the plains, 3,000 feet in elevation. The mountains were not explored until about a century ago. Among discoveries, the most famous was that of the caverns—even though Indians spoke of their existence long before. But it was Jim White, a guano miner, who is given credit for the first modern exploration in the early 1900s. By 1923 it had become a national monument, upgraded to national park in 1930. It is one of the largest and most spectacular cave systems in the world.

Altogether there are 70 caves in the park; of them, just two, **Carlsbad Cavern** and New Cave, are open to the public. The National Park Service has provided facilities to make it easy for everyone to visit the cavern, with elevators, a kennel for pets, and even a nursery for tots. Visitors in wheelchairs are common. There are two ways to approach a visit to the cavern: you can walk down into the cave through its natural entrance, or you can go down by elevator to a point 750 feet below the surface and begin your walk there. The paved walkway through the natural entrance winds into the depths of the cavern and leads through a series of underground rooms. This walk is 1¾ miles in length and takes about an hour and 45 minutes. Parts of it are steep. At its lowest point the trail reaches 830 feet below the surface, ending finally at an underground lunchroom whose existence seems to amaze many visitors.

It is at this point that those who have taken the easy way down, by elevator, join the hikers for the tour of the spectacular 14-story-high Big Room, with a ceiling looming 255 feet over the trail. The floor of this room covers 14 acres; a tour of it, over a level path, is 1¼ miles in length and takes about an hour. The Park Service has arranged it so that visitors may either join one of the frequent guided tours or simply wander through the cavern by themselves, but everyone is advised to wear flat shoes with rubber soles and heels because of the slippery and occasionally steep paths; a light sweater or jacket feels good in the constant temperature of 56° F, especially when it's 100° outside in the sun.

The cavern is well lighted and there are rangers stationed in the cave to answer questions. Many of the formations have names, such as the Hall of the Giants or the Temple of the Sun—or the Bottomless Pit. Attempts at meaningful descriptions of cave formations are probably doomed to failure, but one somewhat overwrought local writer commented that "the imagery of the cavescape resembles gemstones, favorite foods, delicate soda straws, frozen waterfalls, miniature castles, familiar and fairyland creatures—the only end to this fantasy is your imagination." The writer continued with a note about "silent chambers gracefully adorned with limestone draperies," and concluded, "Still pools of crystal dot the depths of this sculpturesque rockland. Even for someone not keen on caves, to leave unimpressed is an impossibility."

At sunset the crowd gathers at the cave entrance to watch the bats take off for the night, in season (they spend the winter down in Mexico). All day long they sleep in the cavern, then strike out on an insect hunt at night. (Pesticides have reduced their number from six million to a quarter million over the past 50 years.)

The other major attraction in the park is **New Cave,** not so new anymore, having been discovered in 1937 by a goatherd named Tom Tucker who was searching for some strays in the area. The cave was mined for bat guano commercially until the 1950s, and consists of a corridor 1,140 feet long with many side passageways. The lowest point is 250 feet below the surface, and the passage traversed by the tours is 1¾ miles long, but more strenuous than hiking through the main cavern; there is also a 500-foot rise in the trail from the parking lot to the cave mouth. No more than 25 people may take part in a tour, and everyone needs a flashlight, hiking boots or shoes, and a container of drinking water. New Cave is slightly warmer than the main cavern, at 62° F. Photography is permitted in the cave, but the use of tripods is not because of limited time for photo stops.

New Cave is reached by continuing south on U.S. 180 from the entrance to the park at White's City for five miles to a marked turnoff that leads 11 miles in to the parking lot. Although the cave tour lasts only an hour and a half, an extra 45 minutes is needed to make the hike to the cave entrance from the parking lot. In order not to miss the start of the tour, give yourself at least 1½ hours to reach New Cave from either the visitor center or the town of Carlsbad.

Fees for New Cave tours are $4 for adults, $2 for children under 16. For the Cavern, separate fees are $2 for adults, $1 for children.

OTHER CARLSBAD AREA SIGHTS: Presidents Park is a pleasant small amusement park on the bank of the Pecos in the town of Carlsbad, with a main attraction in a two-mile narrow-gauge steam locomotive train ride up and down the riverside, departing from an old-fashioned western train depot. A carousel dating from 1903 is another local favorite, and there are paddlewheel steamer rides in summer too.

Living Desert State Park, on U.S. 285 to the northwest of town, is a 45-acre piece of authentic Chihuahuan desert preserved with all its flora and fauna—there are 50 species of mammals, birds, and reptiles loose in the area, making it an ideal place for their study. A trail leads past extravagant cactuses and other desert plants, and a greenhouse shelters other delicate flora, including many exotics and succulents. There are 2,500 varieties of plants displayed. Animals arrive in the park through a rehabilitation program to care for sick or injured beasts, some saved in the nick of time, such as a robust porcupine taken from its mother just after she had been killed by a passing car on the highway. Golden eagles and great horned owls are among birds of prey reigning over the aviary. An exhibit of nocturnal animals shows badgers, spotted skunks, kit foxes, and ringtail cats in underground burrows. A prairie-dog town is a favorite with the kids. Larger mammals such as deer, antelope, elk, javelina, buffalo, and bobcat all share the little wilderness. Regional plants may be purchased at the gift shop. The park is open year round, from 8 a.m. to sunset in summer, 9 a.m. to 5 p.m. winter, for a $2.50 admission fee.

Lake Carlsbad has a three-mile-long beach in Carlsbad where there are boat docks, a playground, a picnic area with fireplaces, and of course good swimming. The Carlsbad Municipal Museum at the Carlsbad Chamber of Commerce, Canal and Greene Streets, exhibits potash, the locally famous deposit from which we get a lot of our fertilizer around the country, and minerals under ultraviolet lights. Admission is free and it is open from 10 a.m. to 6 p.m. daily except Sunday.

The Million Dollar Museum in White's City, south of Carlsbad, is a marvelous hodgepodge displaying 50 different collections, including a doll and dollhouse collection, an Indian mummy, old guns, and old vehicles.

Sitting Bull Falls cascades over the rim of a canyon in Lincoln National Forest on N.M. 137, 50 miles south of town, reached via U.S. 285 south.

The ruins of a stage stop on the Butterfield Overland Route between San Francisco and St. Louis is open at the Pinery, on U.S. 180, 55 miles southwest of town, from 8 a.m. to 4:30 p.m. daily.

Guadalupe Mountains National Park

Guadalupe Mountains National Park is 55 miles southwest of Carlsbad via U.S. 180. The Frijoles information station at this point is open from 8 a.m. to

4:30 p.m., and until sunset in summer. The **Pine Springs Campground,** a trailhead for backcountry hikers, has a water supply and toilets. **Dog Canyon Campground,** 70 miles from Carlsbad, reached through Lincoln National Forest to the north, also has a trailhead for hikers and campsites. There are daily ranger programs at Pine Springs Campground in summer, as well as guided walks and hikes; these continue only on weekends in winter.

Half a mile north of the visitor center is the **Frijole Historic Site,** the remains of an early ranch. Another old ranch is the **Williams Ranch Historic Site,** eight miles in from the visitor center, reachable on foot or by four-wheel-drive vehicle.

The park has desert land, canyons, and high forest for backcountry hikers, and 80 miles of trails. Water must be carried, permits are required, and camping must be in designated areas. Maps, permits, and information are obtained at the visitor center. The **McKittrick Canyon** day-use area for half-day hikes of two to four hours is open from 8 a.m. to 4:30 p.m., to 6 p.m. in summer. There is a 5½-mile round-trip hike to the **Pratt Lodge Historic Site,** or there is a nine-mile round-trip canyon hike. From Frijole Historic Site there is a two-mile hike to **Manzanita and Smith Springs** and return—a natural oasis overlooking the desert below. A five-mile hike starting at Pine Springs Campground goes to the narrows of **Pine Springs Canyon.** All-day hikes from Pine Springs Campground up to **Guadalupe Peak,** at 8,749 feet the highest point in Texas (the park is on the state line), take around eight hours. Another hike from Pine Springs Campground is up to **Hunter Peak,** then descending down **Bear Canyon,** a nine-mile loop trail through a forest of pine or Douglas fir.

The Guadalupe Mountains were once an immense reef poking up through a warm sea. Later fossilized as limestone and buried, they rose in the earthly forces of mountain building several million years ago. The southern end of these rough peaks makes up the park, while the northern part of the range lies within Lincoln National Forest. Deer, elk, mountain lion, and bear are found in the forests, which contrast strikingly against the desert around them. There is in these isolated basins and protected valleys a proliferation of vegetation rare elsewhere in the Southwest. **McKittrick Canyon** is one of the few spots in the park accessible by paved road—most of the 77,500 acres are reached only by foot trail. But McKittrick is one of the most beautiful spots, protected by its high sheer walls, with a green swatch of trees of many kinds growing along the banks of its spring-fed stream. It is a great spot for birdwatching and viewing other wildlife, and an especially lovely sight during fall foilage time, late October to mid-November. In spite of its southerly latitude, the mountains can experience rough, cold weather in winter, storms arriving fast and unannounced, so hikers are cautioned to carry adequate clothing as well as a gallon of water for every day on the trail. Call park information at 915/828-3251.

Further outdoor exploring, hiking, and other fun is offered in the mountain area to the north of the park in **Lincoln National Forest.** For information and maps relating to the 285,000 acres of the Guadalupe Ranger District, apply to the Forest Service office at the Federal Building in Carlsbad (tel. 885-4181).

ANNUAL EVENTS: Among annual events in Carlsbad, notable is the **Bat Flight Breakfast** at 5:30 a.m. at Carlsbad Cavern one day every August, where breakfasters wait to see the bats come back to their cave after a night out in the buggy skies. Organized by the Cavern Activities Association, the affair is backed by the Carlsbad Chamber of Commerce, whose office will give pertinent information at 887-6516. Also in August is the **TriState Arts and Crafts Show** at the Fine Arts Museum, also sponsored by the chamber, a juried competition with over 100 regional artists and craftspeople participating.

5. ROSWELL

Roswell (pop. 50,000) is one of those "sunstruck and windswept" western towns you go through on your way to some other destination in the West, and there is something about the place that makes you wonder how it would be to stay and look around the town for a while. Situated 75 miles north of Carlsbad in the Pecos River Valley, and 200 miles southeast of Albuquerque, the little city dominates a vast, little-populated prairie of ranchland, with the Capitan Mountains 50 miles to the west visible in that southerly outstretching of the great wall of the Rockies. From its founding in 1871 Roswell has been a cattle town; sheep and wool are also big locally. Its elevation of 3,500 feet gives it a hot climate in summer, mild in winter. In spite of its basic plainness it has some cultural aspirations, and a visit to its museums and nearby natural areas makes it well worth spending some time in Roswell.

Car rental for the area is **National,** at the Municipal Airport (tel. 347-2323).

WHERE TO STAY: The **Sally Port Inn,** 2000 N. Main St., Roswell, NM 88201 (tel. 505/622-6430, or toll free 800/545-6276), is another of those modern resort-like motels where the outdoors is brought inside—not that there's much bad weather to avoid in this part of the world, but it does get hot out there. Here an indoor pool is brightened by skylights and set off by looming green jungle plants, and by bright lawn tables and chairs in pastel colors. All the 124 rooms in this rambling motel have refrigerators, remote-control televisions, and extra-large beds. The location near the New Mexico Military Institute is reflected in the names of the dining areas: the Commandant's Room and the Reveille Room. Live music is offered nightly in the Orderly Room Lounge.

Rates here are $53 double, with weekend-special reductions offered. Guests are invited to use two lighted tennis courts or try their skills in the electronic game room.

Well-maintained modern accommodations at low prices are available at **Knights Inn,** 1505 W. 2nd St., Roswell, NM 88201 (tel. 505/623-6444), with double rooms at $28.

For all information on local accommodations, get in touch with the **Roswell Convention and Visitors Bureau,** 131 W. 2nd St., Roswell, NM 88201 (tel. 505/623-5695).

WHERE TO EAT: The **Cattleman's Steak House,** at 2010 S. Main St. (tel. 623-3500), has two rustic dining rooms where, as its name implies, broiled steaks are the specialty—the 1½-pound T-bone being listed No. 1. It comes with ranch-style beans, pineapple coleslaw, and iced tea by the carafe; a lesser delicacy here is the chicken-fried steak. Open seven days for dinner only.

The **Roswell Inn Restaurant,** 1813 N. Main St. (tel. 623-4920), has full bar service and a tempting buffet for all-you-can-eat enthusiasts; or you can order from a regular menu at breakfast, lunch, or dinnertime. There are lunch buffets and heartier dinner buffets, and the locally renowned prime rib or catfish on Thursday, shrimp on Friday, and a spectacular Mexican buffet on Saturday. Open daily from 6 a.m. to 10 p.m.

SIGHTSEEING: Calling itself "the bright spot of the Sunbelt," Roswell is a town where the people welcome visitors, and the **Roswell Convention and Visitors Bureau,** at 131 W. 2nd St. (tel. 623-5695), provides them with all needed information about what to see and do.

The **Roswell Museum and Art Center,** a local source of pride, at 100 W. 11th St. (tel. 662-4700), has 11 galleries of artworks, including representative paintings of the Taos school by Georgia O'Keeffe, John Sloan, Andrew Dasburg, John Marin, and Ernest Blumenschein. It also holds a treasure in the form of the largest collection of works anywhere by southwestern painter Peter Hurd, who was born in Roswell. The museum's **Goddard Wing,** named for rocket scientist Robert H. Goddard, who once did experiments in Roswell, has scientific displays. The **Rogers Aston Galleries** has a valuable collection of rare Indian artifacts. Hours are 9 a.m. to 5 p.m. Monday through Saturday and 1 to 5 p.m. on Sunday.

The **Roswell Symphony** (tel. 623-5882), in existence for a quarter century, gives an annual series of concerts; information can be obtained at its office at 103 W. 11th St. An annual three-day **Arts and Crafts Fair** goes on every spring at the fairgrounds.

The **Chaves County Historical Museum,** 200 N. Lea (tel. 622-8333), open Friday through Sunday from 1 to 4 p.m., is lodged in a restored Territorial house with 14 high-ceilinged rooms including a Victorian parlor, bedrooms with antique furnishings and clothing, and an early kitchen. The house, listed in the National Register of Historic Places, also contains a library and archives of the city.

Spring River Park, 1400 E. College, has a small zoo, a miniature train, a carousel, a prairie-dog village, and a picnic area with tables. A good destination for horse lovers is **Buena Suerte Quarterhorse Ranch,** 131 W. 2nd St. (tel. 623-5695), the home of some All-American Futurity winners at Ruidoso Downs and scores of other handsome steeds enjoying the 300 acres of pastureland here; visitors are welcome.

Reached via U.S. 70, nine miles northeast of town, **Bitter Lake National Wildlife Refuge** (tel. 622-6755) is a 24,000-acre area of river bottomland, marsh, stands of salt cedar, and open range. A variety of waterfowl find a winter refuge in and around seven lakes—cormorants, herons, pelicans, sandhill cranes, and geese. Gypsum sinkhole lakes covering an area of 700 acres are of a peculiar beauty. In the fall thousands of ducks show up to take shelter in the waterways here. Once threatened with extinction, the sandhill crane now appears in numbers of 10,000 to 50,000 every winter. Snow geese were unknown here 20 years back, but now turn up to the tune of some 60,000 every winter. All told, over 300 species of birds have been sighted. You can get information at the headquarters building at the entrance. It is open daily, dawn to dusk.

Bottomless Lakes State Park is 17 miles from Roswell via U.S. 380 east and N.M. 409 south to the entrance, and is open year round from 8 a.m. to 9 p.m. There are campsites for trailers or tents, and shelters, showers, a dump station, all water sports, and a snackbar. The center of recreation in this chain of lakes surrounded by rock bluffs is Lea Lake, the largest of the seven. The park got its name from a local legend that early cowboys tried to fathom the depth of the lakes by plumbing them with lariats all tied together to form long lines down into the limpid water, but no matter how many of them were spliced, bottom was never touched. (None is actually deeper than 100 feet.)

One lake is so shaded by surrounding bluffs that the sun rarely reaches it, so its name is Devil's Inkwell. Another, Mirror Lake, makes perfect reflections of the shoreline. Cottonwood Lake was named for a single tree standing at its edge. Two pools joined became Figure 8 Lake; another has always been called simply No Name Lake. Pasture Lake was so named because ducks were said to prefer this to the others. The clarity of the water of Lea Lake makes it a favorite with skindivers, and there is fishing for rainbow trout.

Among annual events in Roswell, note should be made of the **Eastern New Mexico State Fair** every September, with a rodeo, parade, rides, games, hot regional foods, agricultural exhibits, and arts-and-crafts displays. For information, call 623-6466.

6. TRUTH OR CONSEQUENCES–SOCORRO AREA

Nestled in the Rio Grande Valley between the San Andres chain to the east and the Black Range and San Mateo Mountains to the west, Truth or Consequences (pop. 5,500) and Socorro (pop. 8,000) are the main stops on I-25 between Las Cruces and Albuquerque; both offer restaurants, accommodations, and certain nearby outdoor attractions.

Truth or Consequences, sometimes called "T or C" for short, used to be Hot Springs until a fateful broadcast in 1950 when television producer Ralph Edwards began his weekly show "Truth or Consequences" with these words: "I wish that some town in the United States liked and respected our show so much that it would like to change its name to Truth or Consequences." The reward to any city willing to agree to this change was to become the site of the tenth anniversary broadcast of the program, which of course would put it on the national map in a big way. Since there were other American towns named Hot Springs, the locals were not terribly determined to keep that name. They had an election and voted to change it to Truth or Consequences. This name has since survived three protest elections over the years. The hot springs still supply bathhouses here, of course, sold individually in the public bathhouses or in series of as many as 21 treatments that may include sweatbaths as well as massage.

Socorro is known for its pretty San Miguel mission church and some good 19th-century houses. Nearby is a facility for the study of the stars by radio, while in a wildlife refuge the small population of whooping cranes has been slowly growing over the years—their arrival in the October migration brings out many crane-welcoming committees.

WHERE TO STAY: Among the accommodations available in these two towns, I recommend the following:

Truth or Consequences

The **Hot Springs Inn,** 2700 N. Date St., Truth or Consequences, NM 87901 (tel. 505/894-6665, or toll free 800/528-1234), has separate dressing rooms and king-size beds, a heated pool, free golf greens fees, and a complimentary breakfast, at $35 to $38 double.

For information on other nearby accommodations, get in touch with the **Truth or Consequences Chamber of Commerce** (tel. 505/894-3536).

Socorro

The **Golden Manor Motel,** 507 California Ave., Socorro, NM 87801 (tel. 505/838-0230, or toll free 800/528-1234), offers double rooms at $33 to $38. On the premises is a rooftop restaurant with a good view of the pool outside, a cool spot on a sizzling evening.

For a budget choice, try the **Sands Motel,** 205 California Ave., Socorro, NM 87801 (tel. 505/835-1130, or toll free 800/541-9312), with double rooms for $25.

For all information on accommodations, get in touch with the **Socorro Chamber of Commerce,** 103 Francisco de Avondo, Socorro, NM 87801 (tel. 505/835-0424).

WHERE TO EAT: The **Damsite Bar and Restaurant,** on N.M. 52 five miles east of the courthouse in Truth or Consequences (tel. 894-2073), inevitably has given itself the sobriquet "a damn site better." The lakeside restaurant and lounge do make a pretty place for a drink or dinner of seafood or steak. It's open seven days for lunch and dinner during summer, and closed on Tuesday from October to April.

A busy family restaurant in Socorro with low prices is **Jerry's,** 1006 California Ave. NE (tel. 835-2255), open 24 hours a day, seven days a week.

SIGHTSEEING AND SPECIAL EVENTS: There are attractions of interest to travelers in or near both Truth or Consequences and Socorro.

Truth or Consequences

Truth or Consequences is the site in May of the **Ralph Edwards Fiesta and Sheriff's Posse Race,** with a parade, fiddlers' contest, and stage show with Ralph Edwards. For information, call the T or C Chamber of Commerce (tel. 894-3536). The **Sierra County Fair** is held here in September at the fairgrounds; for information, call 894-2375. A **Pony Express Race** is also held later the same month, and in October an arts-and-crafts fair.

The **Geronimo Springs Museum,** at 3325 Main St. (tel. 894-6600), exhibits private collections of pottery from the Mimbres Indians dating from A.D. 950 to 1250; guns, photos, and memorabilia from the early days of the town in the last century; a farm and ranch exhibit; the Watson collection, which includes prehistoric artifacts and such pioneer items as branding irons and barbed wire; the Ballinger exhibit of burial paraphernalia; and a quail show.

Five miles from T or C is the largest lake in New Mexico, **Elephant Butte Lake,** covering 36,000 acres, where a state park has 5,000 acres of shoreside land. Fishing for black and white bass, catfish, pike, and crappie goes on all year long. Trout are stocked in the Rio Grande below Elephant Butte Dam. The park has sandy beaches for tanning and swimming, boating, sailing, waterskiing, and camping. There are frequent regattas. The lake was named for a huge rock formation that makes an island and looks faintly like the head of an elephant.

A couple of so-called **ghost towns**—abandoned mining centers that nevertheless do have a few live residents—are Winston and Chloride. **Winston,** 35 miles northwest of T or C on N.M. 52, was abandoned in the early 1900s when silver prices dropped and local mining became unprofitable. Some of the original structures are still standing from that era. A similar fate befell **Chloride,** five miles west of Winston on a side road off N.M. 52, where famed silver mines had such names as Nana, Wall Street, and Unknown. Chloride also figured in many battles in the turn-of-the-century war between cattle- and sheep-ranching interests.

Twenty miles south of T or C via I-25 is another recreation area, **Caballo Lake State Park,** which like Elephant Butte has year-round water sports, fishing, and campsites. The lake has the lofty ridge of the Caballo Mountains just to the east to make a handsome backdrop. There is a marina with full service and a shop for boaters, as well as full hookups for recreation vehicles. Reached from the same exit off I-25 is still another area, **Percha Dam State Park,** a lovely shaded spot under great cottonwood trees, part of the ancient bosque, or woods, the Spanish found bordering the Rio Grande when they first arrived in this area in the 1530s. The dam here diverts river water for irrigation. There are campsites, rest rooms and showers, hiking trails, and access to fishing here.

Thirty miles from T or C, via I-25 south to N.M. 90, then west, is **Hillsboro,** another ghost town fast losing its ghosts to a small invasion of artists and craftspeople. This town boomed after an 1877 gold strike nearby. Nine miles west of Hillsboro on N.M. 90 is **Kingston,** which was born with the rich silver strike at the Solitaire Mine a century ago, and is locally reputed to have been the wildest mining town of the region, with 22 saloons. It was once the residence of the infamous Albert Fall, one of the perpetrators of the Teapot Dome Scandal. Today, by contrast, life in Kingston is pretty quiet.

Socorro

Socorro, too, was a busy mining center in the last part of the 19th century. The spot was named for the place on the Rio Grande where exploring Spaniards, after having traversed the deadly desert they called the Jornada del Muerto, were given food (succor—*socorro*) by Pueblo Indians living here. A couple of priests stayed as missionaries to these Indians; one, Alfonso Benavides, became known as the Apostle of Socorro. In 1598 the priests, with the Indians' help, built a small church here, the **San Miguel Mission** (tel. 835-1620), which was replaced by a larger one, still standing, completed in 1628. It has massive walls typical of construction of the time, with huge carved *vigas* and supporting corbel arches. Lumber for these pieces had to be dragged in from mountainsides many miles off. Windows were placed high, as in other early mission churches, so the place could be used as a fort for protection against raiding Navajo or Plains Indians. The two priests taught the Indians the art of silvercraft to decorate the interior of the church. They made a solid-silver communion rail, a tabernacle, and vessels used in the mass. When the Pueblo Revolt forced the Spanish to abandon the church in 1680, they buried this communion rail and made a map so that its location could be found easily once the revolt was quelled. But over the 12 years the Spanish stayed out of New Mexico, finding refuge near El Paso, Texas, the map was lost, and on their return the silver rail could not be found, and never has been to this day. The church, though damaged, was still standing, and after repairs were completed in 1692, services were resumed and have continued to modern times.

The church was named in honor of San Miguel around 1800 when an Apache raider claimed he was frightened away from the church by a vision of a man with wings and a shining sword hovering over the door of the church. St. Michael, or San Miguel, is called the "angelic protector of the people." Four subbasements in the church contain the remains of priests who served in the church and of Gen. Manuel Armijo, last governor of New Mexico under the Mexican regime. The church occupies the center of a Spanish land grant of 17,000 acres given by the king of Spain; land surveys within this area measure distances from the church. Originally the church was built in plain pueblo style, but subsequent additions have added other architectural flourishes.

The **Mineral Museum** of the New Mexico Institute of Mining and Technology in Socorro (tel. 835-5420) is open from 8 a.m. to 5 p.m. Monday through Friday free of charge, and has the largest mineral collection in the state as well as an important fossil exhibit. Mineral specimens are for sale at low prices, and rockhounds can usually get tips from experts on the campus as to the best spots to hunt particular minerals nearby.

The town itself has many interesting **historic buildings** in the Gothic Revival and Territorial styles, including the old Opera House, the Golden Crown Flour Mill, the Illinois Brewery, the Eaton House, the Casa de Flecha. For information on historic buildings, call the Socorro Chamber of Commerce, 103 Francisco de Avondo (tel. 835-0424).

Thirty miles from Socorro, via I-25 north to the U.S. 60 exit, then east to N.M. 47, lies the little town of La Joya, and **La Joya State Game Refuge,** a special destination for birdwatchers. There is a small old Spanish church in the village. Continuing south, toward Socorro, through the village of San Acacia, you come to Lemitar, where there is still another old church.

South of Lemitar you arrive at **Escondida,** where motorists should ask directions to find a dirt road leading to **Indian pictographs** on the west side of the Rio Grande. They are the work of prehistoric Pueblo Indians and are on territory of the Federal Bureau of Land Management. For information, call the B.L.M. office in Socorro (tel. 835-0412). The bureau also occupies land where there are ruins of an Indian pueblo south of Socorro in the community of **Luís Lopez.**

The most famous of the region's wild areas is the **Bosque del Apache National Wildlife Area,** 18 miles south of Socorro off I-25 at the intersection of U.S. 380 at San Antonio. During migration periods, when whooping cranes and geese arrive—coming in October and departing in February and March—the area is a delight for birdwatchers, who may hike through the 57,191 acres to record some of the 295 bird species in their lifetime books; there are some 400 different sorts of mammals, reptiles, and amphibians in the watery area too. Whooping cranes are still rare, but a few score of them do winter here annually. Visitors are welcome daily all year from half an hour before sunrise to half an hour after sunset; for information, call 835-1828.

South Baldy Peak, 15 miles west of Socorro, is the site of a fascinating lab researching lightning, the **Langmuir Laboratory for Atmospheric Research** (tel. 835-5423). In summer it is open to visitors during daylight hours and is reached via U.S. 60 west and a forest road, the latter a twisting primitive track to the peak. Scientists from around the world interested in the study of lightning congregate here every summer. At the foot of the mountain, a campground at **Water Canyon** makes a shady spot for a night or a week—or just a picnic. Hiking trails maintained by the staff of Cibola National Forest make this a center for outdoors lovers.

Sixty miles from Socorro, also via U.S. 60 west, then turning north at Magdalena via N.M. 52, is a separate, isolated bit of the Navajo land called the **Alamo Band Reservation,** where there is a trading post with some Navajo crafts for sale.

The National Radio Astronomy Observatory has a **Very Large Array (VLA) radiotelescope** 39 miles west of Socorro on U.S. 60. The installation permits scientists to study cosmic objects, including the sun, planets, distant galaxies, and quasars at the edge of the universe. Instead of analyzing light, astronomers here study radio waves emitted by celestial objects. They can make images from these waves, received through 27 dish-shaped antennas that are interconnected to form a single telescope. The use of many antennas permits the making of detailed pictures of extremely faint objects, and makes the VLA the world's most powerful radiotelescope.

Radio astronomy sees the sky in a different way from optical astronomy: in the radio sky, the brightest objects are not nearby stars, but distant galaxies undergoing violent outbursts, ejecting great quantities of matter and energy far into space. A new class of small stars appears to our radio eyes, called quasars, so distant that the waves we receive from them started their trip toward earth billions of years ago. Thus we can look back in time as well as into space.

Federally funded, the VLA is used by astronomers from all over the world at no cost; proposals for using it are judged on their scientific merit. About 50 experiments are completed every month; observations go on 24 hours a day, seven days a week. Procedures may be viewed from windows outside; there is a visitor center open free of charge from 8 a.m. to sunset every day. A self-guided walking tour identifies the installations and structures. For information, call 835-2924.

7. DEMING, LORDSBURG, AND SILVER CITY AREA

Deming and Lordsburg, on the railroad, and Silver City, 50 miles to the north at the approaches to high mountain country, are in the wildest, least-populated part of the state, which includes that "bootheel" of the southwest corner of the state that pokes 40 miles down to the Mexican border. The two railroad towns, also being situated on the busy east-west artery I-10, see a good many travelers; Silver City is a base for outdoors lovers heading into the wild country of Gila National Forest stretching out 100 miles northward. It is an area favored by rockhounds, and even has a state park where visitors are encouraged to make off with souvenirs in the form of minerals of many types. The area is also the site of the last foreign incursion upon continental American soil, when followers of the Mexican bandit-revolutionary Pancho Villa staged a raid across the border into New Mexico in 1916—a state park is established on the site. Silver City is in the midst of operating open-face copper mines, the silver mining, and gold too, having been given up long ago—at least on a commercial basis. But gold panning thrives both among residents and visitors. The prehistoric houses of Gila Cliff Dwellings National Monument should be on the list of must-see places for anyone fascinated with the archeology of the Southwest.

WHERE TO STAY: All three towns have adequate accommodations, restaurants, and stores.

Deming

The **Holiday Budget Inn,** on Country Club Road (at the I-10 interchange east of town), Deming, NM 88030 (tel. 505/546-2661), besides the usual amenities in its 120 units, has kennels available for travelers' pets, a gift shop, and a tourist information desk. Rates are $34 to $36 double.

Deming has a dozen motels offering low rates year around. One of the best of these is a chain member, **Motel 6,** on Country Club Road (at the I-10 interchange), Deming, NM 88030 (tel. 505/546-9663), with a pool and double rooms at $24.

For all information on accommodations in Deming, get in touch with the **Deming–Luna County Chamber of Commerce,** U.S. 80 and Spruce Street, Deming, NM 88030 (tel. 505/546-2674).

Lordsburg

The **American Motor Inn,** 944 E. Motel Dr., Lordsburg, NM 88045 (tel. 505/542-3591, or toll free 800/528-1234), is a member of the Best Western chain. It offers 92 units all equipped with cable television, and there is a restaurant and lounge on the premises. Double rates are $38.

A likely family stopping place is the **Aloha Motel,** 816 E. Motel Dr., Lordsburg, NM 88045 (tel. 505/542-3567), which offers a playground as well as a pool, and cable television in its 42 rooms, which go for $25 double.

For information on accommodations in Lordsburg, get in touch with the **Lordsburg–Hidalgo County Chamber of Commerce,** 1000 S. Main St., Lordsburg, NM 88045 (tel. 505/542-9864).

Silver City

The **Holiday Motor Hotel,** on U.S. 180 East, Silver City, NM 88061 (tel. 505/538-3711, or toll free 800/528-1234), has a restaurant and bar to serve guests in its 80 rooms, opening with breakfast at 6 a.m. A soup-and-salad bar and Mexican specialties go along with standard menu items at noon and for dinner. There is live entertainment in the bar on weekends. Room rates are $39 to $51 double.

For information on accommodations, get in touch with the **Silver City–**

Grant County Chamber of Commerce, 1103 N. Hudson St., Silver City, NM 88061 (tel. 505/538-3785).

WHERE TO EAT: All of the following recommendations are moderately priced restaurants serving good food.

Deming offers the **Cactus Restaurant,** 218 W. Cedar St. (tel. 546-2458), with both Mexican and American dishes.

In Lordsburg, **El Charro,** 209 Southern Pacific Blvd. (tel. 542-3400), also serving Mexican and American cuisine, is open 24 hours and has a full bar.

Silver City has an excellent Mexican restaurant in **El Molino,** on U.S. 180 East (tel. 388-3232), with homemade tortillas and chimichangas; beer and wine are served.

Dinner with a Show

It's worth the short trip from Silver City on N.M. 15 seven miles north to the village of Pinos Altos for a dinner at the **Buckhorn Saloon and Opera House** (tel. 538-9111), open evenings only, from 6 p.m.; closed Sunday. There are four fireplaces and a pot-bellied stove to warm guests in wintertime, and various shows scheduled during the year on the oldtime stage. A wintertime warming drink is the house special, the Buckhorn, composed of hot chocolate and peppermint schnapps. Continental cuisine in appetizers and daily specials is augmented by western-style steaks, and the wine list is the best in the area.

SIGHTSEEING AND OUTDOORS ATTRACTIONS: Probably the single most famous attraction in southwestern New Mexico is the Gila Cliff Dwellings National Monument, but there are other sights to see in the towns of Silver City, Deming, and Lordsburg.

Gila Cliff Dwellings National Monument

At the end of a 44-mile roadway, N.M. 15, leading north from Silver City up into the Mogollon Mountains of Gila National Forest, a curving roadway that takes about two hours by car, is the Gila Cliff Dwellings National Monument (tel. 536-9461). The special emotional shock in store for newcomers to the Southwest when first they see cliff dwellings can be experienced here as well as at any of the other famous sites of the region. This comes in the immediacy of this stone-within-stone-on-stone relic of a disappeared civilization, its reality somehow exaggerated in the dazzling sunlight and contrasting shadow that from a distance make it look as two-dimensional as a stage set. The solid masonry houses here are still nearly intact, even though abandoned for 700 years.

Along the valley floor flows a stream, the water source of the Mogollon people who lived in this place for less than 100 years. They vanished, no one knows why, about A.D. 1350. Above, the vertical cliff is marked with mineral streaks of brown against the gray-white rhyolite tuff face that is called desert varnish. It is here, reached by a well-marked trail, that seven natural caves occur about 150 feet up on the cliffside. In these caves there is a complex of houses with 40 rooms.

A sense of the continuity of life from prehistory to the present is apparent in the soot from family cooking fires covering the ceilings of the caves. The original pine beams, the *vigas,* that supported the house roofs were destroyed by vandals around the year 1900 before the government took over the protection of the caves in 1907. The flat-stone masonry has survived the centuries in excellent condition, however, as it is bonded by a cement made of clay from the stream down below. Floors in the caves were made level by hard work with stone hammers. Basin-shaped depressions cut into the floor were lined with plaster and used for grain storage. One room was under construction when the Mogollon people made their mysterious departure. One theory is that a change in climate caused a drought and forced them to abandon raising corn.

The Mogollon people shared the Southwest with the Anasazi people to the north and the Hohokam to the south. Long before building the cliff houses, they lived in wide holes in the ground covered over with sod roofs, called pit houses. Corn, which had been cultivated in southern Mexico since 7000 B.C., began to be grown up here by the Mogollon around 300 B.C., a development that brought them to end their previous nomadic life. It was not until about A.D. 1000 that they built above-ground houses in the open, and some 200 years after that before their first cliff dwellings were put up.

The Mogollon raised pumpkins, squash, and beans by irrigation from the stream here. They grew cotton to make blankets and clothing, and learned to make pottery too, and turquoise ornaments—the turquoise, brought in from mines 50 miles to the south, was said to be the purest in the world. Bones were used to make needles, awls, and whistles, while various stones went into axes, grinders, arrow points, and knives. The characteristic Mogollon patterns are seen in geometric forms in black outline on white background on the pottery—there are samples in the visitor center here.

A hint of what eventually became of the Mogollon may lie in the fact that their yucca fiber sandals, examples of which were found in these caves in the early days of their discovery by American pioneers in the 1870s, look just like the sandals made and worn today by the Tarahumara Indians 500 miles to the south in the Mexican state of Chihuahua.

Mogollon characteristics, as compared with those of the Anasazi peoples once living in such areas as Mesa Verde, Canyon de Chelly, Chaco Canyon, and Hovenweep, to the north, included a rectangular *kiva,* or ceremonial room, for the former, where the latter's are circular. The Mogollon did not bind the heads of their infants as the Anasazi did, and they notched their axes in different ways. The black-on-white pottery of the Mogollon was another trademark. A half-mile trail leads to the caves. First it crosses a bridge over the West Fork of the Gila River, then follows the stream for a distance until it begins to climb to the level of the caves. The return path follows a different route, mostly in the shade of Ponderosa pines, alligator bark juniper, cottonwoods, or Douglas firs. Even in summer, at this 9,000-foot altitude it is rarely hot, but there is little snow in winter.

A century ago the canyon was a stronghold of the Apache guerrilla leader Geronimo—his Chiricahua Apache name was Goyathlay, meaning the Yawner. His fierce bands fought off American occupation of the traditional Indian land until 1886, when Geronimo was captured. There is a local legend of a lost tribe of Apache who escaped and hid out for years after they were all supposed to have surrendered. It happened that in 1883 the Indians killed a local judge and his wife in Silver City and kidnapped their young son, Johnnie McComas. The story goes that Johnnie became the red-haired, blue-eyed leader of that renegade exile Apache band.

The cliff dwellings are at the end of a road completed in 1963. Before that time the monument was the most isolated, least visited area of the national park system because of its inaccessibility, and it is still remembered that a regional director of the National Park Service got lost up here in 1942. Though only 533 acres in area, the monument is surrounded by three million acres of the **Gila National Forest;** the visitor center is unique in being a joint operation of the Department of the Interior and the Department of Agriculture. No roads of any sort lead into the fabled **Gila Wilderness,** adjoining the monument. Part of a 500-mile swatch of Ponderosa pine and other forest reaching all the way west to the Grand Canyon, the wilderness was established in 1924 and has 2,000 miles of trails for hikers and horseback riders. It is an area beloved of birdwatchers, lovers of views of untouched mountain and desert country, and those curious about desert and mountain wildlife.

The **visitor center** is open daily from 8 a.m. to 5 p.m. throughout the year. Visiting times for the ruins are 8 a.m. to 6 p.m. June 1 to September 1, and 9 a.m. to 4 p.m. during the rest of the year. The visitor center has information on activities in Gila National Forest and the Wilderness Area as well as material about the cliff dwellings. Improved campgrounds are available.

Silver City

The founders of the famous Naiad Queen silver mine near Silver City in 1873 were Henry B. Ailman and Hartford M. Meredith, who sold out their interest in 1880 and had identical Victorian mansions built next door to each other on Broadway in Silver City. The Ailman House today contains the **Silver City Museum,** 312 W. Broadway (tel. 505/538-5921), open, free of charge, from 9 a.m. to 4:30 p.m. Tuesday through Friday, 10 a.m. to 4 p.m. on Saturday, and 1 to 4 p.m. on Sunday; closed Monday. (The Meredith house was moved to a new site a few blocks away in 1905, where it eventually became part of a Spanish-style apartment complex.) The town used the Ailman House as its city hall for a decade, beginning in 1926, and then it became the volunteer fire station. The museum took it in 1967 and money grants in 1975 permitted restoration.

Collections include pioneer and Indian relics, objects from the early mining town of Tyrone, and the valuable John Harlan collection of 800 early photographs. There is also an impressive display of Casas Grandes pottery.

Because an early Silver City ordinance forbade frame construction, and because there is a good local supply of clay for brick making, many of the first houses of Silver City, built during the mining heydays a century ago, are of brick and have survived the years intact. Visitors may walk through the **Silver City Historic District** to view these buildings, which include mansard-roofed Victorian houses, Queen Anne and Italianate residences, and commercial buildings downtown in cast-iron architecture of the period. Some of these are still undergoing restoration. For information, get in touch with the Silver City Museum (tel. 538-5921). A flood in 1895 washed out Main Street and turned it into a gaping chasm, which was eventually bridged over; finally the "Ditch," as it's called, was made into a green park in the center of town.

Mine tours are arranged by some of the companies operating the copper pit mines in the area. Some 80 million tons of rock are taken out of the **Tyrone Mine,** owned by the Phelps-Dodge Corp., every year; the **Chino Mine** at Santa Rita is another big open-pit works. For information on seeing the mines, get in touch with Silver City–Grant County Chamber of Commerce, 1103 N. Hudson (tel. 538-3785).

Thirty miles from Silver City, south on U.S. 180 and then northeast on N.M. 61, **City of Rocks State Park** is an area of fantastically shaped volcanic rock formations formed from thick blankets of ash that hardened into a stone called tuff. This soft stone, sculpted by wind and water, forms the monolithic blocks that are reminiscent of Stonehege or the mysterious steles of Brittany. There are hiking trails, a cactus garden, modern rest rooms and showers, a playground, and campsites. Hot water is solar heated, while windmills pump it and make electricity; thus the park is self-sufficient.

Deming

Deming is the largest town in the area, with a population of 12,500. It was the meeting place of the second east-west railroad to connect the two coasts, and had a two-sided station, one for the Santa Fe from the east and one for the Southern Pacific from the west—with a Harvey House between the two.

Mesa Airlines serves this area from Albuquerque with flights daily to Grant County Airport. There is **Amtrak** service to Los Angeles and El Paso, and **Greyhound/Trailways** connections all over the U.S. Information on transportation, as well as on accommodations, lodging, and sightseeing, can be had at **Deming–Luna County Chamber of Commerce**, U.S. 80 and Spruce Street (tel. 505/546-2674).

The **Deming Luna Mimbres Museum**, 301 S. Silver (tel. 546-2382), in the basement of the old Deming Armory, is one of those charming everybody's-attic museums, with the left-hand oven built into a stove for an early left-handed cook, and an old wooden sign: "Warning, Fine of $2 to $10 for Leaving Your Team Untied." It shows some pioneer-era quilts and laces, a traveling kitchen from an early cattle ranch, a doll room with 500 dolls, and Indian pottery from the early Mimbres people who lived here around A.D. 1000. The museum is open free of charge Monday through Saturday from 9 a.m. to 4 p.m., on Sunday from 1:30 to 4 p.m.

Twelve miles southeast of Deming via N.M. 11 south and a connecting road running east, at **Rockhound State Park** visitors are encouraged to pick and take home with them as much as 15 pounds of minerals—jasper, agate, quartz crystal, flow-banded rhyolite, and other rocks—found here at the base of the wild Florida Mountains. Trails lead up toward this range across dry cactus-covered land and down into dry gullies and canyons. The campground here, which has shelters, rest rooms, showers, and a playground, gives a distant view of the untroubled mountain ranges all the way south to the Mexican border.

South 30 miles on N.M. 11 is the tiny border town of Columbus, looking across at Mexico, and here, too, is **Pancho Villa State Park**, which marks the last time there was a foreign invasion of American soil. A temporary fort where a tiny garrison was housed in tents was attacked by 600 Mexican revolutionaries who cut through the boundary fence at Columbus; casualties were 17 Americans dead. The Mexicans immediately retreated across their border. Soon an American punitive expedition was launched into Mexico, but got nowhere. Some ruins of that border fort, called Camp Furlong, are to be seen at the state park, which has a strikingly beautiful desert botanical garden worth the trip alone, as well as campsites with shelters, rest rooms, showers, a dump station, and a playground. Access to Mexico via the village of Palomas, Chihuahua, is three miles south.

Lordsburg

Over in Lordsburg, the western gateway to this part of New Mexico, visitors can also go **rockhounding** in an area rich in minerals of many kinds. Desert roses can be found near Summit, and agate is known to exist in many abandoned mines locally. Mine dumps southwest of Hachiti have lead, zinc, and gold in them. There is manganese in the Animas Mountains. Volcanic glass can be picked up in Coronado National Forest, and there is panning for gold in Gold Gulch. You can get information on rockhounding, sightseeing, accommodations, and eating places at the **Lordsburg–Hidalgo County Chamber of Commerce**, 1000 S. Main St. (tel. 505/542-9864). If you are approaching from the west on I-10, stop also at the tourist information center set up out on the highway by the State Travel Division.

Just south of Lordsburg is the ghost town of **Shakespeare**, once the home of 3,000 miners, promoters, and dealers of various kinds. The silver boom of 1870 was followed by a notorious diamond fraud two years later in which a mine was salted with diamonds in order to raise prices on mining stock; when the fraud became known it spelled the end of Shakespeare, which was soon abandoned. Today, 1½-hour tours are conducted on various weekends through the year for a $2 fee. For information, call 542-9034.

Other local attractions include the **Red Rock Big Game Refuge** for bighorn sheep viewing or photographing; it is 20 miles north of town on N.M. 464. One of the few places in the U.S. to have javelina hunting (wild pig) is Hidalgo County; there are also antelope hunts and good herds of Sonoran white-tailed deer in the Lordsburg area.

CHAPTER VII

INTRODUCING ARIZONA

□ □ □

Arizona is the home of Phoenix and the Valley of the Sun, where retirement meccas like Sun City are attracting a steady migration of Americans from colder climates to the north and east. It is dude ranch country where traditional working ranches are gradually turning into fancy resorts and going out of the cattle business altogether—with a few notable exceptions keeping to the simple old-style ways. It is Indian country, with most of the most populous Indian nation, the Navajo, within its borders, as well as the "center of the universe" home of the Hopi, and reservations of the White Mountain Apache, San Carlos Apache, Gila River Apache, Hualapai, Pima and Maricopa, Tohono O'Odham, Havasupai, and Quechan tribes.

Arizona has the high, clear mountain air of the White Mountains and the searing heat of the Sonoran Desert—the town of Yuma regularly sets summer heat records. It has ghost towns and burgeoning art colonies such as Jerome and Sedona, and recently made artists'-and-writers' communities such as Bisbee, where the closing of the copper mines made housing suddenly cheap and available. There are hokey attractions that are good fun, such as Tombstone with its macho O.K. Corral shootouts, and the magnificence of the Grand Canyon with sensual effects not much helped by verbal description. Arizona is recently populated by many, yet has an ancient history, with ruined cities dating back 1,000 years, the Pueblo communities of the Anasazi, Hohokam, Sinagua, and Mogollon populations, who disappeared mysteriously around 500 years ago.

Traces of early Hispanic colonization remain in the mission churches, a few still serving their faithful congregations. There is an overlay of Mexican influence in the southern part of the state, and considerable visiting back and forth across the border, especially at Nogales, a double town with a U.S.-version shopping mall and a loud, sprawling, colorful Mexican marketplace version.

About a third of the land of Arizona is wooded or forested, a quarter of it in grassland, and the rest desert, the latter not a lifeless region but an arid environment with its own special forms of life. The heights above 6,000 feet, of which there are considerable in the state, have great forests of Ponderosa pine and, in the highest parts, Douglas fir, spruce, and aspen. Below on the plateaus there are growths of piñon, evergreen oak, and chaparral. Grasslands are presently undergoing invasions of mesquite trees that, although their wood is prized for barbecue coals, eventually disrupt natural ecological cycles. Fabulous cactuses such as the saguaro and the organ pipe are preserved in national monuments and are seen in many hot areas of the south. Animal life is also varied according to climatic regions, which depend on altitude, and they are shown in one of the world's great zoological exhibits in Tucson.

Outstanding in the arts in the state is unquestionably the creative work of the Indians, whose crafts are not only displayed at trading posts on the reservations but also at art and anthropological museums in Phoenix, Flagstaff, and Tucson. There are symphonies in the two largest cities. Architecture is inspired in the state by the work of Frank Lloyd Wright, whose auditorium at the state university is the best-known modern structure, and by Paolo Soleri, who has two experimentally designed buildings open to the public around the Phoenix area.

HOW TO GET THERE: The two large cities of the state, Phoenix and Tucson, are both served by national airlines. Carriers serving Phoenix include Alaska Airlines, American, America West, Continental, Eastern, Northwest, Pacific Southwest, Southwest, Trans World, United, and US Air. Tucson is served by Aéro México, American, Eastern, Northwest, Pacific Southwest, Trans World, United, and US Air.

Phoenix and Tucson both have **Amtrak** service west to Los Angeles and east to Houston, New Orleans, and Chicago, and Flagstaff has service to Los Angeles and Chicago also. For information from anywhere within the state, the toll-free telephone is 800/421-8320.

Major **highways** through Arizona are I-8 from San Diego to I-10 between Phoenix and Tucson, I-10 from Los Angeles via Phoenix and Tucson east to Florida, I-40 from California through Kingman and Flagstaff east to North Carolina, and I-19 south from Tucson into Mexico. Most Arizona cities are served by bus by the Greyhound/Trailways system.

For general travel information on Arizona, get in touch with the **Arizona Office of Tourism,** 1100 W. Washington Ave., Phoenix, AZ 85007 (tel. 602/255-3618).

Note: The **telephone area code** for all telephones in Arizona is 602.

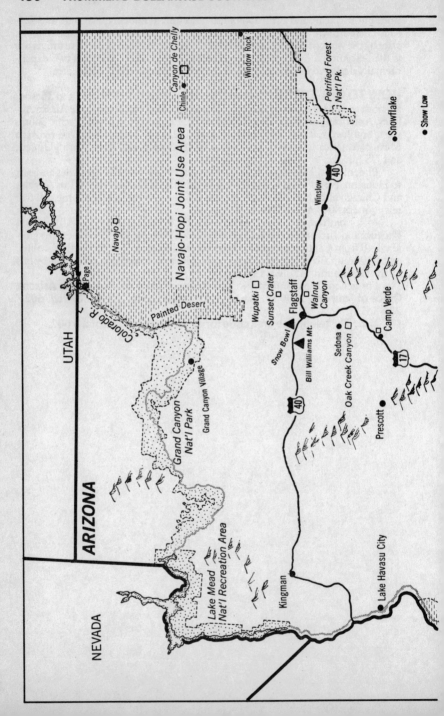

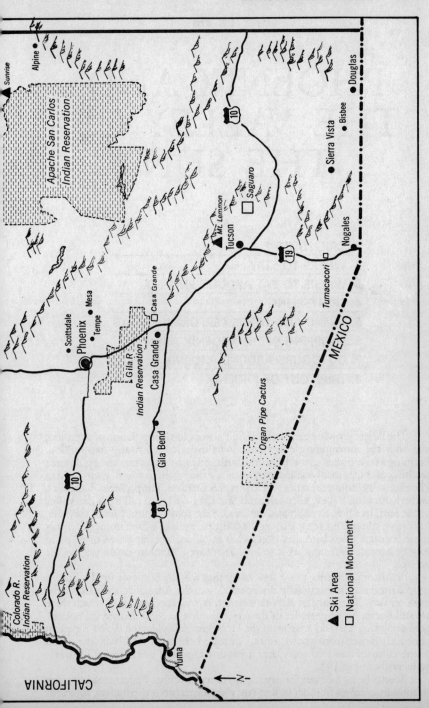

CHAPTER VIII

PHOENIX AND THE VALLEY OF THE SUN

□ □ □

The fastest growing city in the U.S., Phoenix has a population of a million, and with the surrounding cities and towns included it's nearly two million. Forming a continuous sprawl of north-south and east-west streets and boulevards reaching 60 miles east-west and nearly as far from north to south, metropolitan Phoenix—including the cities and towns of Scottsdale, Tempe, Mesa, Chandler, Gilbert, Paradise Valley, Glendale, and Sun City—likes to call itself the Valley of the Sun. In a hot, dry climate, the area, in the south-central part of the state, has drawn sun-seekers from all over the country, most of whom immediately become boosters who claim they don't even mind the scorching days of July and August because the humidity is so low. There are 300 sunny days a year on the average.

Prehistoric Phoenix was a sere valley that was the home of the Hohokam people until they mysteriously disappeared, like the Anasazi to the east, in the 14th century. They dug an elaborate system of irrigation canals of which there are still traces. An early settler of the city, founded in 1860, named it Phoenix, predicting that it would arise from the Hohokam ruins like the fabled Egyptian phoenix had risen from its own ashes. The town boomed in 1887 with the arrival of the railroad, and two years later it became capital of the Arizona Territory. Statehood came in 1912.

Besides being a center for day trips in every direction, Phoenix and its sister communities have a number of first-rate visitor attractions themselves, foremost among them several museums of particular regional interest. The Heard Museum of Anthropology and Primitive Art is practically a required stop for those about to visit ruins and Indian reservations, while a number of historically oriented museums cover all the ground between the prehistoric Hohokam and the recurrent waves of emigrant retirees. There are over 10,000 paintings in the Phoenix Art Museum, and the Scottsdale Center for the Arts also has a national reputation for exhibiting important artworks. Western art is the special purview of collections of Arizona State University.

Symphony Hall in Phoenix is the site of concerts by the Phoenix Symphony during a season extending from spring through the fall, while the Scottsdale Symphony performs at the Scottsdale Center for the Arts. Phoenix has a noted chamber music society, while literally hundreds of clubs and lounges throughout the sprawling metropolis present live music of every taste and vintage. There are a score of theaters in the valley too, including the oldest community theater in the U.S., the Phoenix Little Theater.

Obviously in such a climate outdoors action is a big draw, as may be seen in the fact that the area has over 1,000 tennis courts and no fewer than 68 golf courses. The metropolis has a dozen first-class resorts with luxurious amenities rarely seen so far from Palm Springs or Las Vegas—and most of them compete with one another in offering cut rates during the hot summer season: as much as 50% below winter rates. More modest motels also partake in the summer bargain pricing.

Phoenix has drawn newcomers not only from all over the U.S. but also from many foreign countries, some of whom have gone into the restaurant business to cook ethnic specialties. Thus Phoenix becomes unusual in the Southwest for its variety in cuisines, which add to the native varieties of Mexican-style, barbecue, western-steakhouse, and roadside-American cooking that have been in Phoenix somewhat longer.

Day trips easy to make let visitors see an experimental city called Arcosanti, a remote village somewhat out of western fiction called Tortilla Flat, the great Roosevelt Dam with its 25-mile lake, nearby prehistoric cliff dwellings in a national monument, the world's greatest collection of desert plant life in an arboretum, ghost towns, hiking and horseback trails in the mountains, a pioneer village, Indian reservations with crafts to be haggled over in a trading post, and a hayride into the hills for a steak cookout.

1. ORIENTATION

Phoenix lies 175 miles north of the Mexican border at Nogales in the south-central part of Arizona. Mileages to a few major cities are: Boston, 2,670; New York, 2,450; Jacksonville, 2,000; Chicago, 1,740; Dallas, 1,000; Seattle, 1,465; and Los Angeles, 390.

GETTING TO AND FROM PHOENIX: Air transport in and out of the Phoenix area is through **Sky Harbor International Airport,** only three miles from the center of the city at the Civic Center. National carriers serving Phoenix include **Alaska Airlines** (tel. 225-5058), **American** (tel. 258-6300), **America West** (tel. 894-0800), **Continental** (tel. 258-8911), **Eastern** (tel. 273-1096), **Northwest** (tel. 273-7325), **Pacific Southwest** (tel. 225-5134), **Southwest** (tel. 243-0653), **Trans World** (tel. 994-3994), **United** (tel. 273-3050), and **US Air** (tel. 943-3999).

Super Shuttle (tel. 253-5200) operates an airport shuttle for the metropolitan area making connections to all major hotels, motels, and resorts.

Taxi service is operated by **AAA Cab** (tel. 437-4000) and **Yellow Cab** (tel. 275-8501).

Amtrak service to Los Angeles and Chicago is provided at the passenger terminal in the railroad station, 401 W. Harrison St., Phoenix (tel. 253-0121).

Bus service by **Greyhound,** whose depot is at 525 E. Washington St. (tel. toll free 800/528-0447), includes direct routes to both Los Angeles and Dallas.

GETTING AROUND IN THE PHOENIX AREA: Buses cover the metropolitan area during daylight hours six days a week, with reduced service on Saturday and none on Sunday. Fares are 75¢. For schedules, call 253-5000. Cooperative Sunday transportation is available by calling **Dial-a-Ride** at 258-9977.

The **Molly Trolleys** run Monday through Saturday (fare $1, or $2 for an all-day pass) on four routes with stops at all Scottsdale resorts. For information, call 941-2957.

In central Phoenix there is a 25¢ **Central Shuttle** and **Capitol Shuttle** operating Monday through Friday, running at three- to four-minute intervals at peak periods of the day. Covering the main business and shopping areas downtown, they are also run by Phoenix Transit.

Car-Rental Agencies

Among many agencies in the highly competitive Phoenix market are the following: **Avis,** 1440 S. 23rd St. (tel. 273-3222); **Budget,** Sky Harbor Airport (tel. 267-4000); **Courtesy,** 101 N. 24th St. (tel. 273-7503); **Hertz,** 1215 S. 27th St. (tel. 267-8822); **National,** 1402 S. 22nd St. (tel. 275-4771); and **Phoenix,** 2247 E. Van Buren St. (tel. 231-0440).

Motor homes are rented for about $400 and up weekly at **RV Rentals,** 4618 Grand Ave., Glendale (tel. 275-9247).

Guided Tours

Phoenix is the home of nearly 50 different guided-tour operators, many of whom specialize in backcountry trips, white-water rafting, Indian reservations, or some other particular Arizona attraction. They take passengers by bus, van, or Jeep, usually picking them up at their hotels and returning them there at the end of the trip, which could be a day, overnight, or a week in duration.

Among a few of these are **Arizona Awareness,** 2422 N. 72nd Pl., Scottsdale (tel. 947-7852), giving desert trips led by a survival expert in an air-conditioned four-wheel-drive vehicle; and **Arizona Desert Mountain Jeep Tours,** 10110 E. Jenan Dr., Scottsdale (tel. 860-1777), offering desert trail hikes, target shooting, Verde River splash parties, and trips to abandoned gold mines.

Gray Line, 1350 N. 22nd Ave., Phoenix (tel. 254-4550), schedules many sightseeing tours within the metropolitan area and throughout the state as well.

Ninety-minute cruises on a sidewheeler steamboat are offered on Canyon Lake, northeast of Scottsdale, on **Dolly's Steamboat** (tel. 827-9144), at $8.50 per person. White-water trips by raft or tube through the Salt River Canyon are offered by **Salt River Recreation** (tel. 984-3305) in Mesa.

USEFUL INFORMATION: The **telephone area code** for all Arizona telephones is 602. . . . For **police, fire, or medical emergency,** call 911. . . . **Time and weather** reports are at 976-7600.

Area hospitals include Good Samaritan (tel. 239-2000), St. Joseph's (tel. 241-3030), St. Luke's (tel. 251-8100), Scottsdale Memorial (tel. 949-9616), and Maryvale Samaritan (tel. 848-5000).

GREATER PHOENIX

Metro Center →

BLACK CANYON FRWY.

State Capitol

19TH AVE.

MARICOPA FRWY.

7TH AVE.

City Hall

Civic Center

7TH ST.

State Coliseum & Fairgrounds

College

CENTRAL AVE.

Indian School

CAMELBACK RD.

17

BUCKEYE RD.

WASHINGTON ST.

MC DOWELL RD.

16TH ST.

24TH ST.

INDIAN SCHOOL RD.

Sky Harbor Int. Airport

Dog Track

VAN BUREN ST.

32ND ST.

THOMAS RD.

44TH ST.

HOHOKAM EXPWY.

Pueblo Grande Ruins

Stadium

Hall of Fame

Zoo

Desert Botanical Gardens

To Scottsdale

State University

← N →

For information on the **Phoenix Transit System** bus service in Phoenix, Glendale, Scottsdale, Tempe, and Mesa, call 257-8426. The number for paging at **Sky Harbor Airport** is 273-3377.

You can get tourist information for all area communities at the **Phoenix and Valley of the Sun Convention and Visitors Bureau,** 505 N. 2nd St. in Phoenix (tel. 254-6500), with desks in Terminals 2 and 3 of Sky Harbor Airport and a visitor center at the corner of Adams and 2nd Streets. To reach an **information hotline** with all current happenings of interest to visitors, call 252-5588.

The Visitors Bureau provides a free **reservation service** by toll-free telephone, permitting visitors to book hotel and motel rooms at any of scores of area establishments (tel. toll free 800/528-0483, or 800/221-5596 in Arizona).

For a statewide **driving conditions** report, call 262-8261. . . . You can reach the **Highway Patrol** at 262-8011. . . . For emergency **ambulance service,** call 263-8563.

2. WHERE TO STAY

The Phoenix area has a complete range of accommodations, with lavish resorts catering to rich winter residents that have been going for half a century, modern high-rise hotels overlooking the great sprawl of the city and into the distant desert, cheerful family-style motels with modest pools, restaurants, and cocktail lounges, and businesslike chain motels patronized by business people. There is the fabled Arizona Biltmore, where the stables were once sprayed daily with perfume, and there is also a 25-mile motel row along East and West Van Buren Street in Phoenix, and more motels on Main Street in Tempe and Mesa, that among them—and scores of other lodgings in the Salt River Valley—manage to put up over six million visitors to Maricopa County every year. A dozen major new hotels and resorts are abuilding too.

PHOENIX: If you want to be in the middle of everything, stay in Phoenix, which offers a wide range of accommodations choices. I'll begin at the top—

Luxury Resorts and Hotels

To begin with the best, the **Arizona Biltmore,** 2400 E. Missouri Ave. (24th Street), Phoenix, AZ 85016 (tel. 602/955-6600, or toll free 800/528-3696), which opened in 1929, did have stables in the old days that it sprayed, so the legend goes, with Chanel No. 5 so the horsy odors wouldn't trouble any sensitive noses among the guests. Today the horses are gone but most of the 1920s opulence remains, including the genteel tradition of a tea service free of charge to guests each afternoon. Designed by Frank Lloyd Wright, it's an internationally reknowned hostelry. Among noted guests, the Ronald Reagans honeymooned here; Clark Gable, and the Duke and Duchess of Windsor, were earlier lodgers. Originally owned by William Wrigley, Jr., of the chewing-gum fortune, the Biltmore was strictly a winter resort until 1973, when it first stayed open year round. Today it is part of the Westin Hotels chain.

The 37 acres of the resort are taken up partly with gardens impeccably manicured by no fewer than 26 gardeners; there are also two full 18-hole PGA-rated golf courses, with putting greens and driving ranges set apart for practice—and a pro shop of course. There is an exercise salon with massage available, beauty and barber shops, half a dozen boutiques—and within a few minutes' walk (or free limousine ride), the Biltmore Fashion Park, a shopping mall specializing in luxury goods, with 54 shops and some restaurants and cocktail lounges.

Among the organized social programs at the Biltmore are tennis clinics and tournaments on 18 courts, breakfast and barbecue lunch horseback rides (out of a nearby stable), Las Vegas nights, free cocktail parties, wine and cheese parties, bingo, bridge, and backgammon, a champagne tour of the nearby Wrigley mansion, and a separate slate of action for young people: roller skating, ice skating, treasure hunts, Ping-Pong, and surfing in "Big Surf," machine-made waves in a huge pool that's called "Arizona's own ocean," reached by van a short way off in the desert. There is jogging along the Arizona Canal and free croquet clinics.

Rooms have a western-style brightness in the colors of curtains and matching bedspreads, lots of oranges and greens that carry out the atmosphere of a tropical, luxurious hideaway you sense in the main rooms and outside. Recently the décor of the 120 rooms originally constructed in 1929 was refurbished according to the designs and architectural direction of Taliesin West architects at the Frank Lloyd Wright Foundation. Besides the poolside buffet, the hotel has three restaurants (see Section 3, "Where to Eat Around Phoenix"). Rates for rooms reflect the fact that Phoenix is booming and crowded in the winter season but still encouraging visitors in the hot season when noontime temperatures of 110° are known. Double rooms September to May are $160 to $240, reduced during the period June to September 10 to $70 to $105.

Another impressive resort is **The Pointe at Squaw Peak,** 7677 N. 16th St., Phoenix, AZ 85020 (tel. 602/997-2626, or toll free 800/528-0428), whose 580 suites occupy structures that ramble happily about a Spanish-looking community of adobe-like buildings with red-tile roofs separated by flagstoned patios, gardens, and arched passageways. Most of the elegant suites, some with two or four bedrooms, have private balconies; rooms are decorated in Spanish Colonial style, with tiled floors, handsome inlaid tables, bronze hanging lamps, and well-stocked wet bars with refrigerators. Guests use eight lighted tennis courts, indoor racquetball and squash courts, and play Ping-Pong, volleyball, and horseshoes. There are five heated pools, and exercise, sauna, and steam rooms; one of the pools has underwater music and a swim-up bar. Riding horses are available at the Hole in the Wall stables on the grounds. Rates start at $180 in winter, $58 in summer.

Closest to the business center of Phoenix is the first-class **Phoenix Hilton,** 111 N. Central Ave., at Civic Plaza, Phoenix, AZ 95004 (tel. 602/257-1525, or toll free 800/445-8677), with 534 rooms on 19 floors, each room sound-proofed. There are two restaurants and a bar serving a popular buffet. A recreation deck on the fifth floor takes up half an acre and provides swimming in a heated pool, sunbathing, jogging on a carpeted track, and relaxing in a whirlpool spa. Next to the deck is a health studio with a gym, exercycles, rollers, free-weights, and massages, as well as a sauna and a solarium. Double rates June to October are $59 to $109; October to May, $98 to $148.

Also next to the Phoenix Civic Plaza is the strikingly designed **Hyatt Regency,** 122 N. 2nd St., Phoenix, AZ 85004 (tel. 602/252-1234, or toll free 800/228-9000), with an eight-story-high atrium to welcome guests with an indoor garden and an air of things happening or about to happen. The sculptured brass sunburst dangling overhead sets the tone: ultramodern, a bit flashy. Fitting in with this mood is one of those revolving restaurants, the Compass, perched 24 stories atop the building, looking from a distance somewhat like a robot's head on a wide squarish body. The management suggests that while waiting to be served you "see how many golf courses you can count—Phoenix has more than 70!" The hotel has two bars and another restaurant besides the twirling one.

Rooms and suites are decorated in bright southwestern hues, much yellows, oranges, reds in carpeting, bedspreads, upholstery, and touches of brightness in lamp fixtures and geometric Indian-style decorative paintings and wall hangings that compete happily with bowls of fresh wildflowers. Rates are $115 to $135 double.

Moderately Priced Hotels

The **Fountains Suite Hotel,** 2577 W. Greenway Rd., Phoenix, AZ 85023 (tel. 602/375-1777), a new establishment in the hi-tech business corridor of northwest Phoenix, has 14 acres with tennis courts and a great circular pool. It's set in a desert landscape that provides a serene atmosphere for its two-room suites at modest cost. There are wet bars and refrigerators as well as two phones and two television sets in each suite. Room service is available, there is the Cabana bar, and you can work out in an exercise room, followed by a whirlpool or sauna bath. Rates are $57 to $96 double.

Near many downtown businesses, just off the Black Canyon Freeway, the **Hotel Westcourt,** 10220 N. Metro Pkwy. East, Phoenix, AZ 85051 (tel. 602/997-5900), has 300 rooms in a five-story structure including 22 suites, a large heated pool, a restaurant with dining indoors and out, a lounge, and a lobby bar. It is next to the Metrocenter shopping mall with 240 shops and 16 movie theaters. Guest rooms, in a southwestern modern-style décor, have original paintings, live green plants, white plantation fans, and shutters. By the pool are sunbathing pods, a putting green, and a lighted croquet court—and tennis courts too. Rates are $49 to $127 double.

Budget Choices

The **Kon Tiki Hotel,** 24th Street at Van Buren Street East, Phoenix, AZ 85008 (tel. 602/244-9361, or toll free 800/238-6161), might appeal to the kids, especially as a sort of Disneyland version of Waikiki, with Polynesian-style rooflines angling up into the sky and huge carved wooden masks looming out from posts on all sides. In fact the place advertises itself as "a little bit of Waikiki in the heart of Phoenix." There is indeed a lanai for lounging, and at night it is appropriately lighted, by torches. Greens and aquamarine appear the predominant color scheme in room décor; there are 110 rooms, including some with waterbeds. Free coffee and doughnuts and in-room movies are also offered, along with reasonable rates, ranging from $28 to $45 double. Hawaiian foods and drinks are served in the restaurant and lounge.

For those who like Arizona fun with less expense, the **Arizona Ranch House Inn,** 5600 N. Central Ave., Phoenix, AZ 85012 (tel. 602/279-3221), may be the right destination. In a quiet, secluded area, and offering many units with kitchenette, the inn occupies pleasant grounds where guests have simple good times around a modest pool or splashing in a whirlpool. The lounge has a billiards table, and the small coffeeshop offers a bright skylight, hanging plants, and a tiled Spanish fountain. All rooms are air-conditioned and have color television; Ping-Pong and shuffleboard are available diversions. Doubles are $34 to $54, and this price includes a continental breakfast. Kitchenettes raise the cost by $4 to $6, depending on the season, and children under 13 stay free in their parents' room.

SCOTTSDALE: While Scottsdale, as with the entire Phoenix area, has a number of medium-priced and budget hotels and motels, the following recommendations are all luxury resorts.

The **Registry Resort,** 7171 N. Scottsdale Rd., Scottsdale, AZ 85253 (tel. 602/991-3800, or toll free 800/528-3154), is a big sunny resort on 76 acres with 318 units for guests including rooms, villas, and suites. It has 21 lighted tennis courts, a health center, two 18-hole golf courses, and four swimming pools—plus four restaurants, one of them known for its French cuisine (see Section 3, "Where to Eat Around Phoenix"). Rates are $175 to $185 double.

A resort in the middle of a 3,000-acre so-called masterplanned community is the **Clarion Inn at McCormick Ranch,** 7401 N. Scottsdale Rd., Scottsdale, AZ

85253 (tel. 602/948-5050, or toll free 800/528-3130), on the shore of Camelback Lake, on which guests try their skills aboard Sailfish or take leisurely circuits in paddleboats. There are lighted tennis courts and the standard *two* 18-hole golf courses, a huge L-shaped pool, and a spa and saunas. Bedrooms are softly welcoming with mild-colored quilted bedspreads and matching draperies in blending grays and apricot tones. There are horseback rides and cookouts offered, and a dining room, the Four Peaks Restaurant, overlooking the water. Double rates run $65 to $165.

Another resort in this neighborhood is **Marriott's Camelback Inn,** 5402 E. Lincoln Dr., Scottsdale, AZ 85253 (tel. 602/948-1700, or toll free 800/228-9290), which has its own golf club with (of course) two 18-hole courses, the par-71 Padre and the par-72 Indian Bend. There is also a 447-yard pitch-and-putt course. There are ten tennis courts available, two pools, a shuffleboard court, and an exercise center. There are 120 acres of desert landscape with an exquisite garden and hiking trails. The 413 rooms, some with sundecks and patios, are decorated in breezy-bright southwestern yellows and oranges. There are two restaurants, a poolside buffet, and a lounge with nightly entertainment. Rates are $75 to $240 double, depending on summer or winter season.

The **Doubletree Hotel,** 7353 E. Indian School Rd., Scottsdale, AZ 85251 (tel. 602/994-9203, or toll free 800/528-0444, 800/352-6500 in Arizona), is close to the noted luxury shops of Scottsdale—Old Town Scottsdale and the Fifth Avenue shops. Rooms decorated with Mexican and southwestern artifacts offer a comfortable luxuriousness at rates of $49 to $115 double.

The **Sheraton Scottsdale Resort,** 7200 N. Scottsdale Rd., Scottsdale, AZ 85253 (tel. 602/948-5000, or toll free 800/325-3535), has 404 rooms and a free-form pool so long it has to be bridged in the middle, along with two others. Volleyball, shuffleboard, and tennis are indulged in by guests. For women there is what is called a body contour salon; men are referred to the health spa. Among accommodations are 36 private villas; there is a Garden Court restaurant near the pool and a pub dedicated to the spirit of Humphrey Bogart. The Sheraton keeps a casual air and notifies guests: "You can dress for dinner if you like, but don't feel obligated." Rates, depending on the season, start at $70 to $190 double.

Out toward Paradise Valley is **Marriott's Mountain Shadows,** 5641 E. Lincoln Dr., Scottsdale, AZ 85253 (tel. 602/948-7111, or toll free 800/228-9290), a resort on 70 acres at the foot of the local landmark, Camelback Mountain. The place is divided into three guest areas of one-story units, each with its own swimming pool and recreation facilities. Outdoing some of its neighbors, this resort has *three* 18-hole golf courses, as well as eight night-lighted tennis courts, therapy pools, table tennis, shuffleboard, and something new: an aerobic game field. Deep-napped light-colored carpets and orange and red tones in upholstery, spreads, and draperies characterize the décor in the bedrooms, each of which has its own private lanai. There are three dining areas and a lounge with nightly entertainment. Double rates vary between $65 and $205, depending on the season.

OTHER LOCATIONS NEAR PHOENIX:
In addition to Phoenix itself and neighboring Scottsdale, three other nearby towns—Carefree, Mesa, and Tempe—have accommodations convenient to Valley of the Sun sights and attractions.

Luxury Inns and Resorts

A small and elegant inn in the village of Carefree (famous for having the world's largest sundial, in the middle of town), 20 miles north of Scottsdale via Scottsdale Road, the **Adobe Inn,** 7415 E. Elbow Bend Rd., Carefree, AZ 85377 (tel. 602/488-4444, or toll free 800/872-2000), offers rooms with bars, refrigerators, views out on the desert and the mountains beyond, and wood-burning fireplaces. Complimentary breakfasts are provided, but children are not accepted as guests. There is a pool, a tennis court, a bar, and a French restaurant, La Marmite. Rates for doubles are $50 to $70 in summer, $100 to $130 in winter.

Also in Carefree is the **Carefree Inn Resort,** on Mule Train Road, Carefree, AZ 85377 (tel. 602/488-3551, or toll free 800/528-0294), with 197 rooms in a two-story structure fronting a garden patio and a swimming pool (there are two of these). There are two restaurants, tennis courts, and riding horses. Rooms have balconies or private lanais. Rates are $80 in summer, $182 in winter, double.

The **Saguaro Lake Ranch Resort,** 13020 Bush Hwy., Mesa, AZ 85205 (tel. 602/984-2194), 40 miles east of Phoenix, is open all year for vacationers looking for the old-fashioned dude-ranch experience up against the Goldfield Mountains, on the banks of the Salt River. There are riding horses of course, a main lodge with a big fireplace, and a swimming pool—plus Saguaro Lake nearby. American Plan rates of $150 per person double include three meals daily and horseback riding. In summer, river floating down the Salt River gives guests a thrill. Guests occupy pleasant, rustic, separate cottages called "ranchettes."

Also of special interest is a former resort built in 1918 for the use of executives of the Goodyear Tire & Rubber Co. on a 14,000-acre estate in the community of Litchfield Park, 15 miles west of downtown Phoenix. **The Wigwam,** on Litchfield and Indian School Roads, Litchfield Park, AZ 85340 (tel. 602/935-3811), has 224 units, closed in the summertime. Rooms are in Territorial-style structures set on beautiful grounds of desert gardens and tropical luxuriance; all the rooms and suites have private patios or terraces. There are three 18-hole golf courses, eight tennis courts, trap-shooting installations, and riding horses. The Terrace dining room is known for its quiet elegance (see Section 3, "Where to Eat Around Phoenix"). Operated on the American Plan, the resort charges $156 to $189 *per person,* double.

Moderately Priced Accommodations

In Mesa, just off the Superstition Freeway, is the **Dobson Ranch Inn,** 1666 S. Dobson Rd., Mesa, AZ 85202 (tel. 602/831-7000, or toll free 800/528-1356), with 212 rooms, a heated pool and adjoining spa, and design elements borrowed from colonial Spanish architecture. There is a restaurant offering optional outdoors dining and a lively lounge with dancing nightly. A member of the Best Western chain, the inn charges $59 to $79 double, depending on season.

In Tempe, a likely destination is the **Fiesta Inn,** 2100 S. Priest Dr., Tempe, AZ 85282 (tel. 602/967-1441, or toll free 800/528-6481), with 269 rooms, a health club, sauna, and spa, free airport transportation, and a restaurant open for three meals daily. There is also a cocktail lounge, free tennis, a big pool, and an exercise room. The Fiesta owns its own fleet of rental cars, which guests may take at unlimited free mileage at reasonable cost. Rooms are big on live greenery, patterned Indian-style carpets, and original southwestern-theme art on the walls. Double rates are $55 to $87.

Also in Tempe, at a location within easy freeway access of Phoenix, Scottsdale, and Mesa, is the **Sheraton Plaza Tempe,** 4400 S. Rural Rd., Tempe, AZ 85282 (tel. 602/897-7444, or toll free 800/325-3535), at the intersection of the Superstition Freeway. Palm trees surrounding a heated pool and whirlpool invite guests to lounge around in the quiet patio. Accommodations are all two-room suites, each with two television sets and two telephones, and most have refrigerators and wet bars too. Free cocktails in the evening and a free breakfast of juices, croissants, pastries, and coffee in the morning—and a newspaper at your door—add to a sense of welcome. Live bands play for dancing in the lounge in the evening, and there is a white-linen restaurant as well as poolside barbecues.

The hotel also has a sauna, exercise room, and gift shop, and offers free shuttle van service to the airport. Rates go from a summer low of $65 to winter highs of $140.

BED-AND-BREAKFAST: Bed-and-breakfast accommodations in the Phoenix area and elsewhere in Arizona are sought after by some travelers for the casual welcome and informality they find in staying in private homes. Facilities range from modest to luxurious, and prices are rated accordingly: modest is $35 to $40, deluxe is $45 to $60, and superior runs $65 to $110 for two people, including, of course, breakfast.

An enterprise that takes care of reservations for 200 of these establishments is **Bed and Breakfast in Arizona,** P.O. Box 8628, Scottsdale, AZ 85252 (tel. 602/995-2831), which will accept credit-card payment in advance for bookings, although the establishments individually require payment in cash or traveler's checks. A free listing will be sent on request.

Another bed-and-breakfast agency, **Mi Casa, Su Casa,** P.O. Box 950, Tempe, AZ 85282 (tel. 602/990-0682), has listings for doubles at $35 to $60, and will send a directory for $3.

3. WHERE TO EAT AROUND PHOENIX

Within the 60-mile sprawl of the area, diners find a special dimension in the lavish resorts, most with several different restaurants, where continental cuisine is the rule. Menus are ambitious and the food well served, for chefs with skill and experience have the key positions in the kitchens of these vacation centers. Resort dining thus seems to be in a category of its own, catering mostly to the so-called gourmet diner. The area has hundreds of other restaurants too—more than even its burgeoning population might indicate—because there are so many visitors (six million a year) and so many retired people who like to eat out.

LUXURY DINING: A good bet for the finest restaurant in the city is the **Orangerie** in the Arizona Biltmore, 24th Street and Missouri Avenue, Phoenix (tel. 954-2507), where diners relax in upholstered armchairs at tables set with fine linen and china, under sparkling modernistic chandeliers. Your choices for an appetizer might include a poached pear with cheese, pine nuts, and herbs; pheasant breast in a brandy sauce flavored with dates and chestnuts; or caviar (at $60 an ounce). There are radicchio-and-fruit combination salads, or spinach salad with crabmeat. Sparkling water fills your glass, and a fruit sorbet comes after your salad to freshen the palate. There are freshly made soups, both cold such as vichyssoise, and hot—cream of leek, for example. An entree might be sole stuffed with a Pernod-and-scallops mousse, wrapped in cabbage leaf, in a peppercorn sauce. Another choice might be venison with blueberries, or even wild boar. A beef choice is medallions glazed in Boursin cheese with garlic. Entrees are served with vegetable and potato as well as hot rolls, and for dessert there are such delicacies as soufflés or pastries made on the premises. There is an extensive wine list and a knowledgeable sommelier. Dinner for two runs up to $100. Open daily for lunch from 11:30 a.m. to 2:30 p.m. and for dinner from 6 to 11 p.m.

Young chef Christopher Gross is making a name for his French restaurant, **Vincent's,** 8711 E. Pinnacle Rd., Scottsdale (tel. 998-0921). He claims to "shop the world" for ingredients for his dishes, and he assembles an entire dinner—two appetizers, an entree, a salad, and dessert—to blend harmoniously into a dining experience that is a treat for the eyes as well as the taste buds. Such a sequence might begin with a plate of four kinds of fish from France served with two kinds of caviar (Norwegian and Russian), followed by ravioli stuffed with French mushrooms and Swiss morels, leading up to an entree of breast of squab with a red-wine sauce, served in a cabbage leaf stuffed with duck foie gras. The following salad would consist of goat-cheese medallions on Belgian and radicchio lettuces in a dressing of sherry vinegar, walnut oil, and Dijon mustard. Dessert might be a raspberry tart on an almond tuile iced with pastry cream and caramel sauce. Dinner, with wine, will cost up to $100 for two. Open nightly except Monday. A food critic on the *Arizona Republic,* Elin Jeffords, writes: "Pray the lobster with vanilla sauce is offered the night you attend."

La Champagne, the French restaurant at the Registry Resort, 7171 N. Scottsdale Rd., Scottsdale (tel. 991-3800), provides a roseate glow in its warm lighting, Wedgwood china, impeccably cylindrical napkins, and in a general air of opulence. King crab ravioli on spinach and snails baked in a crust with truffle sauce are two of the succulent appetizers, or there is a dreamy lobster bisque laced with cognac. Among salads, one of endives has a walnut-and-raspberry dressing; another is prepared at your table with a hot bacon dressing. A tenderloin of veal comes sautéed with crayfish—a rare, successful idea—and a champagne sauce comes with the filet of fresh salmon. A steamed sole entree comes with artichoke hearts, and there is breast of duckling in a wild-mushroom sauce. Potato amandine and fresh vegetables accompany all entrees. Desserts are chosen from an array of pastries and fruits with liqueurs displayed on a cart, or soufflés may be ordered. The wine list of over 200 selections is as extensive as any in town. Prices range from $8 to $10 for appetizers, $19 to $24 for entrees. There is piano music nightly. Open every night of the week from 6:30 p.m.

MODERATELY PRICED RESTAURANTS: In San Angelo Square, **Ernesto's Backstreet,** Indian School Road at 36th Street, Phoenix (tel. 957-0303), is a luxuriously appointed restaurant with prices well below most in this class. There is valet parking, and inside, the pillars and chandeliers set off classic Roman art. The long list of menu selections comes mainly from northern Italian recipes. Diners begin with a free appetizer of fried zucchini, and a cup of the soup of the day also accompanies each entree—often a freshly made minestrone. There are a dozen offerings of various salads and as many kinds of pasta dishes, a salad or pasta priced at $5 to $7. Among entrees, trout meunière at $6.75, veal marsala at $9.50, and scampi in a wine sauce at $12 are choices. There is an impressive wine list with some 200 choices. Desserts include crème caramel and cannoli Siciliana, or, concocted right at your table, cherries jubilee or crêpes Suzette. A topper might be a caffè Mephisto—coffee with cognac and Galliano in a lime-rimmed sugary glass, with cream and nutmeg. Ernesto's is open daily for lunch from 11 a.m. to 4 p.m. and for dinner from 4:30 p.m. until midnight.

White stucco makes the somewhat stark background for another reasonably priced eating place serving gourmet-level lunches and dinners, the accent in this case French. The **Petit Café,** 7340 E. Shoeman Lane, Scottsdale (tel. 947-5288), goes in for candlelight on white linens at dinnertime, for which an appetizer might be puff pastry with asparagus and hollandaise ($4.50) or fried Brie with apples and pears ($5). Dinner entrees, costing $13 to $17, include grilled fresh tuna with tomato and green pepper, grilled lamb with port wine and lingonberries, and roast duckling with raspberry-vinegar sauce. Luncheon entrees—fresh trout with hazelnut in lime sauce, or steak tartare, among other selections—go for $6 to $8.50. The house dessert specialty is soufflé au chocolat. Closed Sunday.

Caribbean and Créole cuisines are the specialties at the **Jamaican,** 7707 E. McDowell, Phoenix (tel. 949-7900), open for dinner nightly from 5 p.m. Live calypso music is provided by island musicians. The bar serves the Tropical Surprise—ginger beer with rum—as well as Blind Man's Punch, another rum concoction. The Yellow Bird drink is described as "mango with a pow." Appetizers at $7 are butter-fried crab or Créole-style crayfish (instruction is "eat by pulling the tail"). Main dishes, priced at $10 to $13, are accompanied by dirty rice, seasoned rice cooked with vegetables and herbs; or rice and peas, red beans and rice cooked in coconut milk. Pickapeppa is deboned chicken in tangy sauce. The jambalaya consists of seafoods, French garlic, sausages, vegetables, rice, and various herbs and spices. Peppered crab is simmered in pepper sauce. Chicken, shrimp, and crab curries may be ordered either medium or spicy. Other choices include blackened fish and blackened steak. For dessert there is fried banana à la mode, which has vanilla-bean sauce and rum; or chocolate mousse cake.

Fresh seafood in a desert town like Phoenix may seem a lot to ask for, but a California fishery has opened a local restaurant to supply the need: the **Fish Market,** 1720 E. Camelback Rd., Phoenix (tel. 277-3474). Four other restaurants in the small chain are all on the California coast. The owner says: "We cure and smoke the salmon, albacore, trout, and swordfish, as well as maintain a saltwater tank where the shellfish are kept alive and purge themselves of sand." The chain owns two Pacific coast fishing boats that bring in swordfish, albacore, wahoo, and thresher shark. Besides this the chain has part of an oyster farm in the San Juan Islands in Puget Sound, Washington, where Westcott Bay oysters, belon oysters, and Manila clams are harvested. An order of a dozen oysters at the oyster bar goes for $6; Dungeness crabmeat cocktail, $5.50; calamari vinaigrette, $3.50. Baked shellfish include oysters Rockefeller at $8 and clams Kilpatrick at $5.75. The smoked fish—salmon, lox, albacore—are around $7 the order. A favorite here is seafood sauté—shrimp, scallops, or calamari—with sliced onions, bell peppers, and mushrooms, cooked in wine, garlic butter, and pesto with Worcestershire, at $7 to $10.25. Among a score of entrees (each including potatoes or fishwife rice, cottage cheese, cherry tomatoes, sourdough bread and butter, and fresh lemon and tartar sauce), fresh Utah trout, red snapper, New Zealand orange roughy, or skewered Hawaiian shrimp with bacon go for $7.25 to $12.25. Two or three good California white wines are available at $11 to $16 the bottle, and there is Canadian beer at $2. To top off there's cheesecake or chocolate earthquake cake.

BUDGET RESTAURANTS: For an inexpensive kosher deli open daily except Saturday, try **Segal's New Place,** 4818 N. 7th St., Phoenix (tel. 285-1515). Matzoh-ball soup is $2, while sandwiches on rye, wheat, kaiser, white bread, or onion roll cost $4 to $5, with cole slaw or potato salad and a pickle: tongue, salami, chopped liver, corned beef, pastrami, turkey, roast beef, and egg salad among them. There are knishes at $1.20 and kishke at $1.75. I recommend the homemade stuffed cabbage at $4.75.

The **Pink Pepper,** 2003 N. Scottsdale Rd., Scottsdale (tel. 945-9300), offers a wide selection of Thai foods at reasonable prices. Soups include the zesty hot-and-sour shrimp-and-mushroom tom yum goong, or glass-noodle soup with chicken or pork. Specialties are Thai barbecued chicken marinated in coconut milk and served in hot-and-sour spices; and phra ram, boiled shrimp, chicken, beef, and pork on a bed of spinach with peanut sauce. There are curries too: a special pineapple-shrimp curry served in a fruit shell, or green curry with a choice of meat, based on green curry paste, coconut milk, and bamboo shoots. Seafood choices include seafood ginger (stir-fried shrimp, scallops, squid, and fish) or heavenly fish (a slightly fried pompano covered with ground pork, celery, mushrooms, onion, and ginger gravy). Entrees go for $5 to $8. Open daily for dinner.

Reasonably priced Arizona-Mexican dishes, along with a few Greek plates, are offered at the **Matador Restaurant,** 125 E. Adams, Phoenix (tel. 254-7563). Mexican dinners priced from $4.25 to $7.25 include Sonora enchiladas with sour cream, homemade tamales with red chile sauce, beef tongue chile verde with rice and beans, chimichangas, and beef or chicken fajitas with rice, beans, guacamole and tortillas. Also on order are quesadillas, flautas, tostadas, tacos, enchiladas, and burros. Greek gyros sandwiches of broiled lamb and beef with Greek spices come on pita bread, garnished with tomato, onion, and the house cucumber dressing. A specialty is mezethakia: baby lamb sweetbreads and livers sautéed in herbs and spices, at $6.75. (Wines are available at a liquor store located within the restaurant premises.) Among desserts are Boston cream pie, New York cheesecake, Veracruz flan, and deep-fried ice cream. Open seven days for lunches and dinners.

A dinner of baked or fried chicken, prime rib of beef, pork chops, or ground sirloin from between $5 and $6, including hot Roman bread, tossed green salad, and baked potato or spaghetti, is offered at **Monti's,** 1st Street at Mill Avenue, Tempe (tel. 967-7594), open seven days for lunches and dinners, to midnight on weekends.

At the **Pinnacle Peak Patio,** 10426 E. Jomax Rd., Scottsdale (tel. 967-8082), mesquite-fired grills outside broil up steaks by the hundreds that are served in half a dozen big rooms in the ranch-style restaurant, where long oilcloth-covered tables hold happy throngs of beer-drinking beefhounds in a noisy, bustling, happy eating event that goes on every night in the week (starting at noon on Sunday). In business for a quarter century, the "original cowboy steakhouse," as the place calls itself, is famous for its enforced casualness of dress —anybody who shows up wearing a necktie has it preemptorily cut off by a waiter or waitress wielding a pair of sharp scissors; the remains of this tie are then hung up in the rafters to join an estimated three-quarters of a million already there. Head chef Marv Dickson claims that nobody has ever got sore about having his tie cut off, either—probably due to the fact that whenever this traditional rite is carried out the victim has an audience of about a thousand fellow eaters to kid him out of whatever chagrin he might be feeling. Only steaks are served, a one-pound T-bone and a two-pound porterhouse, served with "cowboy beans," salad, and thick slices of fresh bread. A public notice reads: "ordering your steak well done will get you the boot!" The management is proud of the fact that their big steaks "hang over the edge of your plate." There is room for 2,400 diners inside and another 6,000 outside in the famous Patio itself, open April to October. Besides all the steaks, there are staged shootouts and country-and-western bands. Open Monday through Saturday from 4 p.m., on Sunday from noon.

You don't have to be a sports fanatic to eat at **Max's,** 6727 N. 47th Ave., in Glendale (tel. 937-1671), but it helps—it has what is claimed to be the world's largest collection of football helmets, trophies, jerseys, and pennants representing hundreds of American teams and individuals in football, baseball, basketball, tennis, bowling, soccer, golf, track, and wrestling. Owner Max Beyer has installed a six-foot-high wooden statue of a human figure with a great-beaked bird's head at the entrance to his restaurant, and he calls it the Jocko Bird—"just another old jock," says Max. There are over 400 football helmets to be inspected by anyone into such arcana—players give them to Max, who is still missing half a dozen from major colleges around the country. In spite of all the photos on the walls and the six-foot video screens showing replays of Joe Louis prize fights, the food is not neglected—choice Nebraska beef is the house specialty, in prime rib or steaks; barbecued beef and pork ribs are also excellent here. A range of fresh sandwiches—19 varieties—is served at lunchtime at $4.50 to $7, and there are no fewer than 75 original flavors of ice cream drinks available—as well as full bar service.

4. SIGHTSEEING

The sense of history is telescoped in Arizona to the point where an object as common and as recently manufactured as a radio can be considered an antique and displayed for its ancientness. This sense pervades the mentality behind turning the state capitol, a decent enough structure with a fine copper dome to celebrate the state's favorite industrial product, into a museum even though it wasn't built until 1901 and the state didn't get into the Union until 1912.

Similar questions invade the mind of an eastern visitor to Heritage Square, where a turn-of-the-century house is seen on a tour led by a guide who points out with respect the early electrical fixtures. By and large the delights for the tourist, beyond those of eating, drinking, dancing, and hearing music, lie mostly outside the city in the spectacular land of mountain, mesa, and canyon. But Phoenix and its sister communities do have one first-rate museum of Indian and other southwestern lore, the Heard; the art museum is a delight; and a botanical garden makes it clear why traveling in this part of the country can always be worthwhile if you keep your eyes open.

THE HEARD MUSEUM: The **Heard Museum of Anthropology and Primitive Art**, at 22 E. Monte Vista Rd., Phoenix (tel. 252-8848 for information on temporary exhibitions), should be the choice of any visitor who might be able to visit but one destination in the entire Phoenix area. Founded in 1929 by a world-traveled couple, Phoenix residents Maie and Dwight Heard, the institution aimed from the first to display and interpret materials from prehistoric and modern Indian life of the Southwest. Beginning with a collection assembled by the Heards, the museum has their catalogued assemblage of some 75,000 objects and many artifacts from American Indians outside the Southwest, the latter acquired more recently. Among famous treasures here is the collection of Sen. Barry M. Goldwater of 437 kachina dolls that date from 1870 to 1960.

Also of priceless value are the Read Mullan collection of Navajo rugs, the C. G. Wallace jewelry collection, and the Indian art collection of Fred Harvey, the famous tour operator and hotel builder of the '20s and '30s.

An outdoor sculpture court makes a peaceful spot for a quiet moment, where stout stone figures of Indians are neighbors to carefully tended and coiffed cactuses and other desert plants—a 12-foot-high crested saguaro practically upstages the artwork, and there are barrel cactuses, prickly pears, claret cups, hedgehogs, bunny ears, and Mexican old man, mixed with some pristine examples of ocotillo and agave.

Early magazine ads for tourists to take an "Indian detour" by leaving the Santa Fe trains and boarding a "Harvey car" touring bus at Albuquerque, to visit New Mexico Indian pueblos, makes that early adventure seem out of a distant world—even though the pueblos are all still right where they have always been for 800 or 900 years, and mostly unchanged too. A three-day tour to Taos and the Puye Cliffs cost $57.50 in the early '30s. Included in Harvey's Indian-art collection are twined basketry jars woven tightly enough to hold water, once they had been sealed with hot pitch from piñon branches.

There is a fascinating film loop showing a Zuñi potter at work, the skilled movements of fingers on clay somehow matched by strange, weaving flute notes in an accompanying taped musical composition that is original with the flutist, a Zuñi Indian himself, named Carlos Nakai (copies of this tape are for sale in the gift shop here).

New kachina dolls, made by the Hopi, may be purchased in the gift shop too—they cost between $200 and $400. Kachinas made a century ago were done somewhat differently from modern ones, and details of craftsmanship can be inspected, in both old and new dolls, with written explanations, in the Goldwater collection. One use of kachinas was, in the case of the ogre figure, to scare children into behaving themselves. The dolls were thought to have human qualities, and the ability to run races with men—and if the kachina won it was bad news for the humans. The winning kachina would mortify the human by cutting off his hair, smearing him with soot and grease, rubbing his face with dung, and whipping him with yucca branches.

The museum—open year round, Monday through Saturday from 10 a.m. to 4:45 p.m. and on Sunday from 1 to 4:45 p.m.—charges $3 adult admission, $2.50 for senior citizens, and $1 for students and children. Public tours, free with admission charge, are held on Saturday and Sunday at 1:30 and 3 p.m. and on Tuesday at 1:30 p.m.

A festive occasion here every February around the middle of the month is the two-day annual **Museum Guild Indian Fair,** where craftspeople exhibit and offer for sale authentic work. Each November there is a **Museum Guild Native American Arts Show** going on for a full week, with a similar purpose. Between mid-December and early January a ceramics show and sale is held in the museum, called, simply enough, CLAY.

HERITAGE SQUARE:
Although the structures are not very old in Heritage Square in downtown Phoenix, they are about all that has been saved of the past out of the center of the city in the tremendous building surge that accompanied boom times here. As the country seems to be shaken from the top so that northerners fall into the southwest corner, the hot, sunny Phoenix area, sprawling out across 60 miles of dry prairie and desert, has knocked down nearly everything in its path that showed the least signs of aging. The only remaining group of houses is right here in Heritage Square. The **Rosson House** was once a residence of the publisher of the New York *Herald-Tribune,* Whitelaw Reid. Wooden chairs have the bull's-eye design in their backs, and the bathtub has the thoughtful feature of oak rails that would not feel cold to the flesh when touched or sat on. Built in 1895 in the Victorian Eastlake architectural style, the house is open for guided tours Wednesday through Saturday from 10 a.m. to 4 p.m. and on Sunday from noon to 4 p.m. Three other turn-of-the-century houses are also open, all free of charge. And there's a crafts gallery, gift shop, and snackbar. You can get information on the square by calling 262-5071. It is just east of the Civic Center at 6th and Monroe Streets.

The Colonial Williamsburg style is shown in the **Burgess Carriage House,** also on the square, now used as a gift shop and starting point for the regular tours. **The Duplex,** built in 1923, has typical Arizona sleeping porches made of canvas and wood panels; it contains communications exhibits sponsored by newspapers, radio stations, and the phone company. The 1901 **Stevens House,** also on the three-block square, is a bungalow with a belled, hipped roof and has occasional exhibits put on by Arizona State University, its occupant. The **Stevens-Haustgen House,** also dating from the early 1900s, is a California-style bungalow; inside are changing exhibits on urban design and environmental subjects. The **Bouvier-Teeter House,** an 1899 bungalow, has historical displays arranged by the central Arizona Museum. The **Silva House** is a bungalow "with neoclassical revival references," according to Heritage Square architectural experts. There is an educational display shown inside on the history of the use of water in the valley. The Carriage House in the middle of the square has a three-stall horse stable where a buggy called a sidebar runabout is on display. The **Lath House Pavilion** is a meeting area near the center of the square combining elements of a botanical conservatory, a gazebo, a beer garden, and a shopping arcade; it is used for a variety of public events.

THE STATE CAPITOL:
It is something of a letdown to discover that the Arizona State Capitol is a museum, not because it lacks in handsomeness and historical interest, but for the missing buzz of political life that has moved a block to the

west into modern office buildings which serve as the actual House and Senate. The building, at 1700 W. Washington St., Phoenix (tel. 255-4675), is open for self-guided tours Monday through Friday from 8 a.m. to 5 p.m. free of charge; and there are tours led by knowledgeable guides daily at 10 a.m. and 2 p.m.

Arizona materials were used when possible in the building of the structure, completed in 1898—a copper roof left in a naturally tarnished state except for the dome, which is kept polished brightly. The outer walls are made of Arizona malapai, granite, and tuff. A figure of *Winged Victory* tops the dome; of zinc, she weighs 600 pounds. She holds a torch for liberty and a wreath for victory. She is also a weathervane.

Inside, on the floor of the rotunda is a huge mosaic of the state seal; and other mosaics illustrate three of the state's five famous **Cs**: copper, climate, and cotton (cattle and citrus are missing). On the second floor the governor's office is restored to its 1912 state, complete with a wax dummy of Gov. George P. Hunt at his desk. Portraits of Territorial governors adorn the hallway outside. Period furnishings and photographs are also of interest in the secretary of state's office in the south wing.

Most striking of all are the rooms that were the Senate chamber and the House of Representatives on the third floor. Old light fixtures, wall moldings, paints, and carpets were reproduced to restore the Senate and House. The Senate originally had only 19 members, so there are 19 desks in the room (there are 30 senators today). The House had 35 members at the time of statehood (there are 60 today). When these quarters became too small 25 years ago, the new House and Senate buildings were built.

THE PHOENIX ART MUSEUM: The Phoenix Art Museum, 1625 N. Central Ave. (tel. 257-1222), is open from 10 a.m. to 5 p.m. Tuesday through Saturday (to 9 p.m. on Wednesday) and 1 to 5 p.m. on Sunday. Admission is by voluntary contribution. It has important collections of Renaissance, 18th-century French, American, western, Mexican, and Chinese art, and a delightful experience in the 16 miniature rooms out of many periods and countries, each done with exquisitely detailed miniature furnishings and architectural detail. The rooms, only about a foot in height, are lighted from within and are seen through glass. They include an Italian dining room, a 1920s American penthouse, an American southern dining room, a Breton kitchen, a French Directoire salon, a Louis XVI bedroom, a Louis XV salon, an English lodge kitchen with a set of ninepins visible out in the garden through a tiny leaded window, a Georgian library from England, and an English Jacobean hall. The scale is one inch to one foot. The rooms were collected by one Mrs. James Ward Thorne, who left them to the museum on her death.

Temporary shows here regularly include regional works such as paintings of cowboys and Indians by members of the professional group calling itself the Cowboy Artists of America.

ARIZONA HISTORICAL SOCIETY MUSEUM: Rather charmingly corny in its eclectic approach to antiques and would-be historical value is the Arizona Historical Society Museum, 1242 N. Central Ave., Phoenix (tel. 255-4479), open from 10 a.m. to 4 p.m. Tuesday through Saturday free of charge. The tone is set by a rusting trolley car in the yard outside and by an early Admiral television set presented as an antique in the ground-floor exhibit area. There are also walls covered by the work of a local cartoonist of the county-fair-caricaturist school. A 1949 license plate is displayed.

Upstairs we learn that the Salt River Valley was once the ostrich capital of the U.S. In 1887 there was a feather boom for use on women's hats and many thousands of ostriches were raised in ostricheries around Phoenix. The birds had their heads covered with a paper bag before their feathers were plucked, which could be done only once every eight months—it took that long to grow new ones. But in 1914 the market dropped out of the ostrich feather market. The museum also has a nonfunctioning old-fashioned toy store, a dark but unconvincing "mine tunnel" leading from one room to another, and replicas of a drugstore and grocery.

The museum also owns one of the oldest adobe homes in town, the **Duppa-Montgomery Homestead,** at 116 W. Sherman, Phoenix (tel. 253-5557). Built in 1870, it is open Sunday through Tuesday from 2 to 5 p.m., and also has historical displays.

THE ARIZONA MUSEUM:

THE ARIZONA MUSEUM: Another historical museum based on the premise that one era's junk is a later one's treasure is the Arizona Museum, 1002 W. Van Buren St. (tel. 253-2734), open from 11 a.m. to 4 p.m. Wednesday through Sunday, with free admission. Among the tattered old newspapers and yellowing costumes out of the last century there is a fascinating calendar record carved into a wooden rod in the 1830s by a Pima Indian named Owl Ears; the marks and tiny figures recorded his tribe's wars with the neighboring Maricopas and Apaches. An aging Corona typewriter belonged to an early proponent of land reclamation, George H. Maxwell.

DESERT BOTANICAL GARDEN:

DESERT BOTANICAL GARDEN: After the constraint of indoor museums, there's nothing like some bright sunshine and desert flowers to reawaken the spirit, and there's no lovelier spot than the Desert Botanical Garden (tel. 941-1225) in Papago Park, with its entrance on Galvin Parkway (go south from the intersection of McDowell Road and 64th Street, or take the no. 3 "zoo" bus). The garden is open every day of the year from 9 a.m. to sunset (from 7 a.m. in July and August). Admission is $2.50 for adults; children aged 5 to 12 pay 50¢.

A self-guiding booklet leads visitors past 50 points along a winding path through the 140-acre compound, past prime examples of over 1,000 species of cactus and other desert plants. Almost all that grow here do so naturally; those that might be killed by the direct sun have slatted roofs overhead that soften the harshness of the sun's rays. Among oddities is the upside-down tree, the boojum, which looks like a huge parsnip and was named out of the Lewis Carroll work *Hunting of the Snark*. Some plants that live over 1,000 years are Joshua trees, the tallest American yucca, that bloom in early spring. Another tree, the ironwood, is so heavy—74 pounds per cubic foot—that it sinks in water. The garden has nearly all the 136 known species of century plants—agave—the most complete collection in the world. The garden's research botanist, Howard Scott Gentry, a few years ago concluded a lifetime work of 40 years' study of this plant.

A fascinating display shows cactus lookalikes in euphorbias from Africa, plants that started out millennia in the past with no resemblance to cactus at all, but over the eons evolved in similar directions so that it takes an expert to tell a real cactus from an imitator. One species smells like rotten meat while another looks like desert pebbles worn down by sand and wind; they can live two years without water. Another plant, the jojoba, produces an oil that can perfectly replace sperm whale oil as a cosmetics additive.

As the seasons change, so of course do the flowers, and visitors are advised when to look for what. Early spring is the time for desert poppies, goldfields, owl clover, mariposa lilies, evening primroses, wild larkspur; trees and shrubs blossoming from February to April include the blue palo verde, the Joshua tree, the soaptree yucca, the ocotillo, and the century plant. Summertime brings out thorn apple, telegraph plants, nightshades, buffalo gourds, desert marigolds, desert asters, and fleabane; trees in blossom will be the ironwoods, smoketrees, desert willows, mesquites, and the sotol bush. Wintertime, through the end of January, sees a few long-season native flowers in bloom: buckwheats, desert senna, brittlebushes, desert lavender, hummingbird bushes, and desert broom. March through April is the great time, of course, for wildflowers, such a special treat for flower-lovers in fact that the garden runs a **Wildflower Hotline** during those two months giving weekly recorded updates on Arizona wildflower locations (tel. 941-2867).

Other annual events at the garden are a January photo show, a February cactus show, spring plant sales in March, an arid-zone landscaping contest in April-May, Family Day on Labor Day, a botanical show in mid-October, fall plant sales also in October, a craft fair in mid-November, and in early December, luminaria night—the Hispanic tradition of candles in paper bags lighting pathways and walls in long sweeping rows.

A recent addition is a trail through a three-acre exhibit of plants of the Sonoran Desert: a saguaro forest, a mesquite thicket, a desert stream environment, and an upland chaparral habitat. Historic buildings along the way provide authentic settings.

The garden is the location also of the **Richter Library,** a nationally known source for botanists that specializes in desert plants. Lectures, classes, workshops, and field trips in the field of desert botany are all open to the public. The garden is supported by memberships, contributions, and admission fees, and has a first-rate bookshop where seeds for desert plants are also sold.

CHAMPLIN FIGHTER MUSEUM: Of a mystique a bit more metallic is the

Champlin Fighter Museum, 4636 E. Falcon Circle, Mesa (tel. 830-4540), which fêtes not boxers but hot war pilots and their planes—from two World Wars. Two hangars house craft from the U.S., England, France, and Germany: a Focke Wulf FW 190 D-12, the world's only Messerschmitt Bf. 109E-3 that still flies, the Red Baron's Fokker Triplane, the Flying Tigers' P-40 Warhawk. There is the world's largest collection of signed photos of fighter aces, oil paintings of planes in combat, and a gift shop with souvenirs, models, paintings, and books. All planes are in flying condition, with the exception of two or three in the process of restoration—the process is shown and explained to visitors.

The World War I craft include a Sopwith Pup and a Sopwith Camel, the latter named for its hump-shaped fairing over the forward machine guns. One of the few American-made planes in the war was a Thomas Morse S.4C designed by B. D. Thomas, shown here. The best Austrian fighter, also displayed, was the Aviatik D-I, of which only 700 were ever built and only two have survived. The world's first combat aircraft, the 1911 Rumpler Taube, was designed as a two-seater observation plane but modified to be used for dropping four-pound hand-held bombs. It was the first German plan to bomb Paris, both with explosives and with leaflets. But its name *taube* in German means "dove."

World War II planes include a Grumman Wildcat, the navy fighter thought not quite up to the capabilities of the Japanese Zero, so was replaced by the Hellcat, also shown, which had the highest kill-per-loss record of any fighter. The most powerful carrier-based fighter was the Vought Corsair shown, used through the war and after until 1965. Pappy Boyington and his famous "Black Sheep Squadron" flew this plane. The last of the Grumman planes was the Bearcat, which arrived too late to serve in the war. It set a world's record for climbing: from a standing start to 10,000 feet in 94 seconds. Largest and heaviest single-engine fighter was the P-47D Thunderbolt, used for ground attack and bomber escort. The plane with the reputation as the finest fighter of the war was the P-51D Mustang, serving mostly in Europe as a bomber escort; its liquid-cooled Rolls-Royce engine reached a top speed of 438 mph.

The museum is open seven days a week from 10 a.m. to 5 p.m., with an admission fee of $5 for adults and $2 for children under 15.

PIONEER ARIZONA: A "living history museum," the pretty western village of Pioneer Arizona, 12 miles north of Phoenix at the Pioneer Road exit of I-17 (tel. 993-0212), is open Wednesday through Sunday from 9 a.m. to 4 p.m. Admission is $4 for adults, $2 for ages 59 and older and for students. Several events enliven the village every November, when there are encampments of the Mountain Men and their families, and of Civil War troops, with battle demonstrations. Around Thanksgiving there is a harvest festival with church services, sing-alongs, dancing, and a turkey dinner. Throughout the year various crafts are regularly demonstrated at various points in the village.

The **carpenter shop** is the reconstruction of a shop from 1880 originally in the town of Prescott. The tools and furnishings, as well as the embossed tin ceiling, are original. There is some antique firefighting equipment outside.

Also from Prescott is the **opera house,** where melodramas are performed most weekends. The building, originally a store, was made into a place for stage shows shortly after its construction in 1877.

The **John Marion Sears House** of the 1880s is supposed to have been the first frame mansion in Phoenix; it has original Victorian-era furnishings. An 1880s gift shop has wall stenciling popular in the era of the shop's construction.

A **tin shop and weaving shop,** also with original tools and furniture, is the site of crafts demonstrations during the winter months. A reconstruction of Middleton & Pascoe's **blacksmith shop** in the town of Globe has all original items on display. Smithy John Cochran, who works here daily weekdays making wrought-iron pieces that are sold in the gift shop, explains his techniques as he goes about his work. The only modern amenity is an electric blower helping out the huge old hand-operated bellows in keeping the charcoal glowing hot. For some pieces he uses coal, and often lets groups of school kids pass around a piece, for ordinarily they will never have seen any coal before in their lives.

A bank has old ledgers, and a sheriff's office next door, reconstructed from an original in Globe, has volunteers dressed up as lawmen and bad guys on hand to regale visitors with a bit of mild histrionics on most weekends. A **miner's cabin** is rebuilt from one from the village of Clifton, dating from the 1880s. Nearby is a **stagecoach station** once located between Phoenix and Wickenburg on the Agua Fria River. A reconstruction of **St. Paul's M.E. Church** of Globe, originally erected in 1879, has a bell dubbed "God's alarm clock" because it was used for fire warnings as well as notice of church services. Weddings are held in the church frequently and there are religious services on holidays.

A charming **one-room school** has original students' desks and slates. In one of two **farmhouses** in the winter months you'll find someone cooking a typical pioneer-style dinner in the kitchen. Saguaro cactus ribs with mud between them are used in building the wattle walls of the **wagonmaker's shop,** which is roofed with mesquite poles, willow crosspieces, and then covered with burro brush and mud.

The museum has 550 acres. A nonprofit corporation, its stated purpose "grew out of a desire to preserve the pioneer values of faith, foresight, and fortitude." Items for sale in the gift shop include nail puzzles ($15) or pokers or shovels ($20) made in the blacksmith shop. There are also book ends, horseshoes, and door knockers.

A FOUNTAIN AND ZOO: The 560-foot-high stream of the **World's Highest Fountain,** in Fountain Hills, 14 miles east of Scottsdale Road on Shea Boulevard, can be seen every hour on the hour from 10 a.m. to 9 p.m. seven days a week.

Gold and silver spotlights play on the column of water at night. When going full force the stream of water moves at a rate of 7,000 gallons a minute—eight tons of water are in the air above the nozzle. The water is taken from a small lake in a park.

A Safari Train takes visitors to the **Phoenix Zoo** on a narrated ride through the main display areas in this 125-acre animal park at 5810 Van Buren St., off Galvin Parkway (tel. 273-7771). Hours are 9 a.m. to 5 p.m. September to June, and 8 a.m. to 5 p.m. June to August, open every day in the year. Admission is $5 for adults, $2 for children aged 4 to 12. Safari train rides cost $1 for adults, 75¢ for children.

There are five habitat zones: desert, grassland, woodland, mountain, and rain forest. The Arizona exhibit has mammals, birds, and reptiles of the Southwest. Many endangered species are represented also: gorillas, orangutans, gibbons, jaguars, ocelots, leopards, elephants, and the rare Arabian oryx among them.

FRANK LLOYD WRIGHT ARCHITECTURE: The **House of the Future** (tel. 957-0800), in the community of Ahwatukee, accessible in Phoenix from the Elliot Road exit of I-10, is a prism-shaped, partly copper structure designed by the Frank Lloyd Wright Foundation. Translucent panels let light inside but protect the interior from the glaring desert sun. A computer goes on duty as soon as you approach the entrance, as a keyless door opens to reveal an outdoorsy interior with fountains and a landscaping of lush greenery. A sunken conversation pit surrounds a fireplace that soars to the 32-foot-high ceiling. There are no walls, no exterior windows, no hallways, little furniture at all—no sense of boxing-in. Overhead, a children's loft does have sliding panels that close in for privacy, but the concept is mainly based on the idea of freedom of space.

It is built so as to respond to the environment, the system operated by a five-unit computer network that handles the climate control and can do the bookkeeping as well. A combined use of solar energy, passive energy, and traditional energy sources keep a constant interior climate. Sensors know when night falls or visitors come near and turn on the lights where needed. The computer also provides foolproof security, and is capable of telephoning the police or fire department when necessary.

A video show and display on some of the innovative features of the house conclude the tours, run Tuesday through Sunday from 9 a.m. to 5 p.m. with donations asked.

More Wright architecture is visible at **Taliesin West** (tel. 860-2700), off Via Linda, in Scottsdale (from Shea Boulevard, turn north on Via Linda/108th Street and follow the "Taliesin" signs). Set on the western slopes of the McDowell Mountains northeast of Scottsdale, the buildings, built by Frank Lloyd Wright and the Taliesin Fellowship starting in 1937, are the winter home, studio, workshop, and offices of some 70 architects, staff, and students of the Frank Lloyd Wright School of Architecture.

Public areas and buildings of Taliesin West are open for tours, including the theater, where a continuous slide presentation of Wright's work is shown, from mid-October through mid-May, except on rainy days. Because most of the tour is outdoors, Taliesin West is closed to visitors on rainy days. Otherwise tours are regularly given hourly from 10 a.m. to 4 p.m. at a fee of $5. Some tours are also scheduled during the summer; for information on summer hours, telephone.

OTHER MUSEUMS AND ATTRACTIONS: The prehistoric residents of the Salt River Valley, present site of Phoenix, were called the Hohokam, a people explained in the **Pueblo Grande Museum,** 4619 E. Washington St., Phoenix

(tel. 275-3452), an 81-acre archeological site where artifacts discovered in digs over the years are displayed along with educational information on the Hohokam culture. A prehistoric residential complex, the site was abandoned around A.D. 1450 for reasons that remain mysterious: the word Hohokam means "those who have gone" in a local Indian tongue. A National Landmark, the museum is operated by the City of Phoenix, and is open from 9 a.m. to 4:45 p.m. Monday through Saturday and 1 to 4:45 p.m. on Sunday. Admission is 50¢ (under 6, free).

Sponsored by the National Historical Fire Foundation, the **Hall of Flame,** 6101 E. Van Buren St., Phoenix (tel. 275-3473), is famous for its antique collection of firefighting equipment. Included are rare pieces from England, France, and Japan as well as nearer sources. The museum was founded by an industrialist, George Getz, after casually remarking to his wife as he happened to spot an old fire engine in a used-car lot: "It would be kind of fun to have one of those to drive kids around on." So for Christmas his wife bought him a 1924 American La France pumper and left it for him to find, tied up in a bright ribbon, out in the driveway. That was about 30 years ago. Today there are dozens of trucks, rigs, and all sorts of firefighting paraphernalia preserved in a nonprofit institution. A 1909 Brush fire chief's car is one prize; a horse-drawn ladder-company wagon from an early Phoenix company is another typical treasure. The museum is open at nominal admission charge, Monday through Saturday from 9 a.m. to 5 p.m.

There is $1 admission to the **Mesa Museum,** 53 N. MacDonald Rd., Mesa (tel. 834-2230), open from 10 a.m. to 4 p.m. Tuesday through Saturday and 1 to 5 p.m. on Sunday. Exhibits are mainly on southwestern history, but kids like to try out how it feels to be locked up for a minute or two in a territorial jail cell out of the 1890s, or to try to crack an early safe, pan for gold, or mill corn on an ancient millstone. Ancient Hohokam ruins are visible in Mesa in the **Park of the Canals,** at 1710 N. Horne.

Minerals from some of the most variegated deposits anywhere in the country are displayed free of charge at the **Arizona Mineral Museum,** 19th Avenue and West McDowell Road (tel. 255-3791), in the Mineral Building at the State Fairgrounds. There are also mineral samples, semiprecious jewels, and stones from various parts of the world, beyond the comprehensive Arizona collection. It is open from 8 a.m. to 5 p.m. Monday through Friday, and on Saturday from 1 to 5 p.m.

The garden of the **Mormon Temple,** 525 E. Main St., Mesa, is open to the public daily from 9 a.m. to 9 p.m. free of charge with guide service leading visitors to view many exotic plants and trees from all over the world; the temple itself is closed to visitors.

Rawhide, 23023 N. Scottsdale Rd., Scottsdale (tel. 563-5111), is a movie-style western village with a museum, steakhouse, and saloon, and craftspeople demonstrating their skills, open from 5 p.m. on weekdays, from noon on weekends.

South Mountain Park, 10919 Central Ave., Phoenix (tel. 276-2221), is the world's largest municipal park, containing 15,000 acres of desert land. There is a dance platform, and picnic areas, as well as 40 miles of hiking and riding trails. Highest point, at 2,330 feet, is Lookout Point. It's open from 6 a.m. to midnight.

Arizona State University, University Drive, Tempe, has museums open to the public: the **Anthropology Museum** (tel. 965-6213), in the Anthropology Building, shows field techniques and lab methods. It is open from 8 a.m. to 5 p.m. weekdays. The **Boulton Collection of Musical Instruments** is shown in the School of Music, Room 533 (tel. 965-7567), from 11 a.m. to 3 p.m. weekdays. The **Museum of Geology,** in the Physical Science Building (tel. 965-5081), open at varying hours weekdays, shows geologic specimens from space exploration and earthly sources; a special attraction is the demonstration of the earth's spin in the six-story Foucault Pendulum. Arts collections of various kinds and areas are shown in the **Matthews Center** (tel. 965-2874), open from 8 a.m. to 5 p.m. Monday through Friday.

The **Judaica Museum,** at Temple Beth Israel, 3310 N. 10th Ave., Phoenix (tel. 264-4428), is open from 9 a.m. to 2 p.m. Tuesday through Thursday and to noon on Sunday, with a permanent collection of life-cycle and holiday Judaica as well as three touring exhibits annually.

The **Salt River Project History Center,** 1521 Project Dr., Tempe (tel. 236-2208), has much material of interest to anyone fascinated by the vast irrigation projects of the valley that were predated by the canals of the prehistoric Hohokam. It is open from 9 a.m. to 4 p.m. weekdays, with prehistoric Indian artifacts and exhibits from the construction of Roosevelt Dam and on the history of electric power in the region.

The **Scottsdale Center for the Arts,** 7383 Scottsdale Mall (tel. 994-2315), is open free of charge from 10 a.m. to 8 p.m. Tuesday through Friday, from noon to 8 p.m. on Saturday and noon to 5 p.m. on Sunday. It has traveling exhibits and individual and group shows; there are also art classes, performances, and a film program.

5. MUSIC AND OTHER PERFORMING ARTS

The Phoenix Symphony, with its own chamber orchestra, vies with several other groups playing classical music around Phoenix. Theater comes in various levels, from the straight drama of the Actors Lab or the Phoenix Little Theater to melodrama and histrionic shootouts in the streets of such hokey western movieland towns as Rawhide. Music in the lounges and clubs offers a tremendous choice, from several dozen first-class resorts, all offering nightly entertainment, to more modest locations in every specialty of popular music in nearly every part of Phoenix and its neighboring communities.

CLASSICAL: The **Phoenix Symphony** is well into its fourth decade, now under the musical direction of Theo Alcantara, and has a season running from fall through spring. Concerts are held at Symphony Hall, 225 E. Adams St., Phoenix (tel. 262-6225). The **Chamber Music Society** of the symphony also plays at Symphony Hall.

Another attraction for music lovers is the **Scottsdale Symphony Orchestra** (tel. 945-8071), which appears at the Scottsdale Center for the Arts, Scottsdale Mall in Scottsdale. The **Gammage Center for the Performing Arts** of Arizona State University, University Drive, Tempe, also schedules regular classical music programs. For information, call 965-3434.

The **Arizona Opera** (tel. 840-0841) presents such works as *Lucia di Lammermoor* or *The Marriage of Figaro* at Symphony Hall in various appearances during fall, winter, and spring.

The **Performing Arts Theater,** 1202 N. 3rd St. (tel. 263-5770), presents a varied season of theatrical and dance programs: two musicals, two plays, ballet, and modern dance.

Programs of popular performing artists in a variety of styles are provided by the **Sundome Center for the Performing Arts,** 19403 R. H. Johnson Blvd., Sun City (tel. 584-3118), which seats over 7,000.

The **Louise Lincoln Kerr Cultural Center,** 6110 N. Scottsdale Rd., Scottsdale (tel. 948-6424), offers a season of performances of classical music and dance from September to May.

Other concerts as well as straight dramatic productions are the fare at the

Celebrity Theater, 440 N. 32nd St., Phoenix (tel. 267-0977), an intimate arena-style space. Drama, along with comedy and musicals, are the staples of the U.S.'s oldest community theater group, the **Phoenix Little Theater,** 25 E. Coronado, Phoenix (tel. 254-2151). The **Actors Theater** has a new stage at 320 N. Central Ave., Phoenix (tel. 991-9636).

    Arizona Metropolitan Ballet, 23 S. Morris, Mesa (tel. 273-7578), is the state's only professional regional ballet company, performing at various locations. From November to April the **Mesa Little Theater** produces a series of plays at the Gaslight Theater, 155 N. Center St., Mesa (tel. 834-2560). During every July, also in Mesa, the **Mesa Musical Theater** produces a musical on its stage at 53 N. MacDonald (tel. 834-2351).

MUSIC IN CLUBS AND LOUNGES: While country-and-western–style

bands can be heard in nearly every neighborhood any night of the week, there is plenty of competition from the rock groups (and sometimes they cross over infrastructurally within a single musical group). Here and there jazz is heard in the land as well.

Blues

    At **Char's,** 4631 N. Seventh Ave., Phoenix (tel. 230-0205), blues groups, including such bands as Big Pete Pearson and the Blues Sevilles, play nightly.

    Tony's New Yorker, 107 E. Broadway, Tempe (tel. 967-3073), has blues bands such as Chuck Hall and the Brick Wall, and the Stilletoes or Midnite Blues may be the draw at **Warsaw Wally's,** 2547 E. Indian School Rd., Phoenix (tel. 955-0881).

Jazz

    The **American Grill,** 1233 S. Alma School Rd., Mesa (tel. 844-1918), has combos Tuesday through Saturday night.

    Another Pointe in Tyme, at the Pointe at South Mountain Resort, 7777 S. Pointe Pkwy., South Mountain, Phoenix (tel. 438-9000), has groups every night, while at the **Camelback Inn,** 5402 E. Lincoln Dr., Scottsdale (tel. 948-1700), it's Tuesday through Saturday.

    Harvey's Neighborhood Bar and Grill, 2624 W. Dunlap Ave., Scottsdale (tel. 943-1010), features jazz groups on weekends.

    There's music nightly at **Timothy's,** 6335 N. 16th St., Phoenix (tel. 277-7634).

    At the **Scottsdale Café,** 7117 E. Third Ave., Scottsdale (tel. 945-6888), combos play Tuesday through Saturday.

    Dominick Occhiato performs regularly at **Sinatras' Lounge,** 4236 W. Dunlap Ave., Scottsdale (tel. 937-5760).

Rock

    Most nights, **Vinnie's,** 2110 E. Highland, Scottsdale (tel. 954-7838), has groups like Forward Motion.

    Anderson's Fifth Estate, 6820 E. Fifth Ave., Scottsdale (tel. 994-4168), presents the Groove Merchants or other groups.

    Bandersnatch Brew Pub, 125 E. 5th St., Tempe (tel. 966-4438), has one-night stands, and **Frankie's,** 9019 N. 19th Ave., Scottsdale (tel. 943-8567), has weekend gigs.

    Edcel's Attic, 414 S. Mill, Tempe (tel. 894-0015), presents entertainers for one- or two-night engagements.

    Chuy's, 310 S. Mill, Tempe (tel. 958-5568), is the venue of the Buddy Guy band and other groups, most nights.

Heydays Bar and Grill, 910 N. Hayden Rd., Tempe (tel. 966-1766), presents bands like Ground Zero on weekends.

The Mason Jar, 2303 E. Indian School Rd., Phoenix (tel. 956-6271), might be the host to Dirty Looks or to Wendy O. Williams.

Fonzie's Big Brother "Killer Joe" is a group sometimes heard at **Tang's,** 4431 W. Glendale Ave., Glendale (tel. 937-9329).

Country and Western

A favorite spot for nationally known bands, **Toolies Country,** 4231 W. Thomas Rd., Phoenix (tel. 272-3100), features live music seven nights a week.

The **Barn Steakhouse,** 6508 W. Bell Rd., Glendale (tel. 979-5811), presents groups nightly, and the **Hayloft,** 4346 W. Glendale Ave., Glendale (tel. 939-8481), is open nightly except Monday.

Bullock's, 2601 W. Bethany Home Rd., Phoenix (tel. 249-9852), has music most nights, and **Kangaroo Kountry,** 1707 W. Bell Rd., Glendale (tel. 375-1522) employs the Western Bred Band and other lively musicians.

Matt's Cocktail Lounge, 4015 N. 16th St., Phoenix (tel. 235-9909), has the Bustin' Loose Band on the premises some nights.

The Peso Dollar Band or the Border Wranglers may be on hand at **Rustler's Rooste,** at the Pointe at South Mountain Resort, 7777 S. Pointe Pkwy., Phoenix, (tel. 231-9111).

An emporium with two stages holding bands going strong at the same time is **Mr. Lucky's,** 3660 N.W. Grand Ave., Phoenix (tel. 246-0686).

6. SHOPPING IN THE PHOENIX AREA

What the visitor likes to buy around Phoenix usually goes into one of two general categories, one of them art, the other harder to summarize. "Western" might be the word to include the crafts of southwestern Hispanic and Indian traditions as well as cowboy garb and horsy paraphernalia. Of course the art offered in some galleries hardly makes that qualification, while sometimes an Indian blanket or a Mexican pot fills the bill quite well.

In any case art is well served by a variety of galleries showing the main strains of Arizona work: the western art of a traditional naturalistic nature taking the cowboy riding into the sunset as its subject matter, more innovative modern styles that take the same sun-bleached mesas and stark Indian visages and treat them in a hundred experimental ways, and other works not directly connected with Arizona or the West that get their spiritual impetus from the art currents from both coasts and elsewhere in the world.

As for shopping for crafts and other western items, souvenir shops of course are legion and there are myriad specialty boutiques and stores for both authentic Indian and Hispanic work, carrying a certain art value with it, and for such necessaries of the West as boots, cowboy hats, string ties with silver clasps, and genuine leather chaps.

But Phoenix with its burgeoning population, much of it from the northern midwestern states, in a score of fancy new shopping centers is appealing to a sense of chic that seems a far cry from the old western general store where the cowboy tied up his horse to a railing outside. One such collection of dainty shops, called Fifth Avenue, sets this new tone. But never fear, Pop, you can still buy a pretty good imitation bullwhip for the kids out at the tourist-trap souvenir store on the main highway into town.

MOSTLY FOR ART: To begin with a kind of art strongly identified with Arizona, the paintings of the 29 artists who make up the membership of the Cowboy

Artists of America can be considered a standard for the straightforward, realistic approach to regional material: bronze figures of mounted cowboys galloping in finely detailed stop-action naturalism, perhaps lassoing a dogie (with a fine metal strand representing the rope); paintings of horses, horses, and more horses with a wide-brimmed rider ever present somewhere within the frame; a painstakingly detailed still-life of boots, or a silver-buckled belt, or a saddle dumped down in carefully arranged casualness in front of a fire. Rustic was its inspiration from Frederic Remington and Charles M. Russell, and rustic this genre will remain.

For two decades the Cowboy Artists have held an annual fall benefit show of their works at the **Phoenix Art Museum,** 1625 N. Central Ave. (tel. 257-1222), where a number of typical western artworks are also on permanent display. Officially termed "Western American Realism" in the art-world jargon, the work of these artists—and other work in this style—is the most in demand by both local art buyers and visitors looking for something special to take home with them. This group, founded in the art-colony town of Sedona north of here in 1965, has already reached a certain pinnacle of success—a new museum exclusively for their work opened in 1983 in Kerrville, Texas.

The subject matter at the museum show is similar to that available in paintings and sculpture available to the public on sale in various local galleries. A reviewer in *Arizona Arts & Travel* magazine described it as "the Old West in the days of 18th- and 19th-century cowboys and Indians, sometimes glorified and romanticized, other times shown with careful documentation in realistic situations." A museum press release portrayed a few of the artists as coming "straight from the saddle to their studios"—these would include Bill Owen, Bud Helbig, and Frank Polk. But artists like Tom Ryan, Gary Carter, and Kenneth Riley spent years in art schools. A good many were originally advertising illustrators. Founders of the Cowboy Artists were Joe Beeler, Charlie Dye, George Phippen, and John Hampton. The sale of their works at the museum show brings in well over a million dollars.

The *Arizona Arts* critic attempted to account for the phenomenon of the huge current success of this genre of art: "Underlying the phenomenon was a yearning on the part of the American public to preserve that Old West heritage, to recapture and reexamine its values at a time when 20th-century American values seemed to many to be in danger of giving way to frighteningly complex, often unknown forces. Cowboy Artists of America art answered that yearning, in addition to providing art that could be lived with comfortably, like a member of a happy family."

Galleries

Works by such famous artists as Chagall, Matisse, Miró, and Picasso are shown at **Bishop's Gallery,** 4168 N. Marshall Way, Scottsdale. **Marilyn Butler Fine Art,** 4160 N. Craftsman Court, Scottsdale, shows such artists as Roy DeForest, Skyline Lowry, Susan Goldman, Jaune Quick-To-See Smith, Jesus Bautista Moroles, and Ben Goo. The paintings of R. C. Gorman and Leroy Neiman are on view at **J. R. Fine Arts,** 4225 N. Marshall Way, Scottsdale.

The **Bob Parks Gallery,** 7072 Fifth Ave., Scottsdale, specializes in his western bronze sculptures, and shows many paintings by western contemporary artists. Internationally known artists' work is displayed at the **Elaine Horwitch Gallery,** 4211 N. Marshall Way, Scottsdale.

An art display space, **Galeria Mesa,** at 155 N. Center, Mesa, operated by the city of Mesa, has exhibitions of contemporary art by regional artists throughout the year.

Helt Galleries, 1016 E. Camelback Rd., Phoenix, specializes in prints, limited editions, watercolors, photography, and sculpture with southwestern themes.

Such internationally known artists as Agam, Erte, and Vasarely show their works at **Circle Gallery,** 4224 N. Craftsman Court, Scottsdale. There are paintings, graphics, sculptures, animation art, and a unique "art to wear" jewelry collection.

Another specialist in southwestern art subjects, showing the work of regional artists such as Gerry Niskern, is the **Wilde-Meyer Gallery,** 4151 N. Marshall Way, Scottsdale.

Southwest Indian artists whose subject matter is often from Native American sources show work at the **Lovena Ohl Gallery,** 4251 N. Marshall Way, Scottsdale.

Contemporary southwestern-style art, including sculpture by Allan Houser and paintings and lithographs by Dan Namingha, is displayed at two locations of the **Gallery Wall,** 7122 N. 7th St., Phoenix; and 7051 Fifth Ave., Scottsdale.

MOSTLY FOR CRAFTS: For a breather from the western motifs, you might stop in at the **UNICEF Shop,** displaying one-of-a-kind pieces from around the world, 2109 E. Camelback Rd., Phoenix.

Wearable art and supplies for fabric artists, along with exhibits of handwoven goods for sale by Arizona textile artists, are seen at the **Textile Art Center of Scottsdale,** 4110 N. 70th St. at Fountain Square. Also offered here is instruction in fabric painting, printing, and dyeing.

American Indian arts and crafts and southwestern items are sold at **Godber's Gift Shops,** 9653A Metro Pkwy. West, in the Metrocenter, Phoenix.

A funny, hokey shop for stocking up on joke items, and perhaps a piece of junk jewelry or a cowboy hat for the kids, is the **Pinnacle Peak General Store,** 8711 E. Pinnacle Peak Rd., Scottsdale, which also sells antiques and brass- and copperware, and has a weather station, a wine cellar, and a soda fountain that serves breakfast and lunch.

A shop purveying nothing but items made in Santa Fe is appropriately called the **Santa Fe Connection,** 8240 N. Hayden Rd., Scottsdale. Among choices are quilts, pillows, wall hangings, and sweatshirts in southwestern and traditional designs.

Gallery 10, 7045 Third Ave., Scottsdale, prides itself on its displays of prehistoric, historic, and contemporary ceramics, textiles, artifacts, baskets, kachinas, and jewelry, claiming to be "one of the most important centers in the country for collector-quality American Indian art."

The French Provençal touch is seen at **Les Collines Provençales,** 4225 N. Marshall Way, Scottsdale, where Biot glassware, Moustier pottery, and authentic *santons*—traditional south-of-France figurines—are seen along with imported Provençal fabrics that seem to take well to the southwestern light and atmosphere.

Indian art, some old and some contemporary, along with a variety of Indian-made craftware, are seen at the **House of Six Directions,** 7051 E. Fifth Ave., Scottsdale.

MOSTLY FOR WESTERN DRESS: A few likely emporia for finding the right hat, boots, or western suit to parade back home in, include the following: the **Boot Barn,** 7005 N. 58th Ave., Glendale, has 6,000 pairs of western boots. **Frontier Boot Corral,** 403 E. Van Buren St., Phoenix, has boots, suits, and all the regional garb needed. **Porter's of Scottsdale,** 3944 N. Brown Ave., claims it's "the West's most western store." **Saba's Western Stores,** 7254 E. Main St.,

Scottsdale, with seven other local branches, has been the "interpreter of the western look" here since 1927. Largest Western store in the state is **Arizona Ranchman Co.,** in the Valley West Mall, 5719 W. Northern Ave., Glendale.

SHOPPING MALLS: The myriad shopping malls around Phoenix, particularly the conglomerations of luxury shops in Scottsdale, are of a tone different from the more utilitarian complexes in other parts of the country. They are newer and perhaps more imaginative in architecture, and they use the beauty of the southwestern outdoors to excellent advantage. Nearby resorts have made them a sort of extension of their panoply of recreation opportunities, and are connected to them by regular "trolley" routes (buses disguised as old-fashioned trolley cars).

More like fancy commercial-minded communities even more self-contained than the traditional shopping center elsewhere, the Arizona "outdoor malls," as they are sometimes called, have everything needed to sustain a luxurious life (as long as your money and credit cards holds out). There are more than a score of such havens for the acquisitive instinct in and around Phoenix, so well organized that they all have central offices with telephones where you can find out the latest news on your favorite shop, service, or restaurant. Here are the most important ones, with the addresses of their main entrances.

Biltmore Fashion Park, Camelback Road and 24th Street, Phoenix (tel. 955-8400), has 62 luxury shops, including I. Magnin, Saks Fifth Avenue, Gucci, and Polo/Ralph Lauren, as well as four restaurants. The **Borgata of Scottsdale,** 6166 N. Scottsdale Rd. (tel. 998-1822), is an Italian village fancifully re-created to contain 50 boutiques and several restaurants reached via narrow streets and courtyards through graceful stone archways and wide tiled terraces. **Camelview Plaza Mall,** at 70th Street and Camelback Road, Scottsdale (tel. 941-0216), has luxury businesses within an enclosed mall around Scottsdale's landmark building.

Chris-Town Shopping Center, Bethany Home Road between 15th and 19th Avenues, Phoenix (tel. 249-0670), has 150 stores, including Broadway Southwest, Dillards, J. C. Penney, and Montgomery Ward. In Chris-Town you can have snacks from McWilly's Ice Creme to Peter Piper Pizza, cash a check at a bank or have your income tax figured, have your car tuned up or buy an encyclopedia, or even sign up for service in the army, navy, air force, marines, or coast guard (their recruiters are all on the scene).

Fifth Avenue Shops, on Fifth Avenue in Scottsdale (tel. 945-1701), has 150 luxury shops in one-story structures on a palm-lined avenue where the rooflines and porches are outlined with tight rows of lightbulbs, a festive sight after dark. **Los Arcos Mall,** McDowell and Scottsdale Roads, Scottsdale (tel. 945-6376), has an arcade, 66 shops, 14 restaurants and food shops, and two movies. It calls itself a "unique blend of culture and commerce" because there are handpainted archways and handcrafted stained-glass and iron gazebos and fountains.

Metrocenter, on Black Canyon Hwy. between Dunlap and Peoria Avenues, Phoenix (tel. 997-2641), calls itself "one of the world's great shopping malls," and it certainly has a lot of shops. **Park Central Shopping Center,** on Central Avenue north of Thomas Road, Phoenix (tel. 264-5575), is the closest mall to downtown, with 70 stores, including Goldwaters, Hanny's, J. C. Penney, and Diamonds. There are ten restaurants as well. The entrance is graced by a 1,600-pound bronze figure, giant size, of an Indian sun worshiper.

Scottsdale Fashion Square, at Camelback and Scottsdale Roads, Scottsdale (tel. 990-7800), has Goldwaters and Diamonds department stores as well as 50 other shops and some restaurants. **Spanish Village,** with the hard-to-credit address of Ho and Hum Roads, Carefree (tel. 488-9644), has 22 specialty shops, all guarded at the entrance by the massive bronze sculpture of the "Conquistador." While in Carefree (north of Scottsdale via Scottsdale Road), note the world's largest sundial in the middle of the village. A bell pole has a three-century-old bell from Mexico on it.

A modern mall not far from downtown is **Tower Plaza,** 3905 E. Thomas Rd., Phoenix (tel. 267-8417). **Town & Country Mall,** at 20th Street and Camelback Road, Phoenix (tel. 955-6850), is the state's original open-air mall, with 55 specialty shops and restaurants. **Valley West Mall,** 59th Avenue at Northern, Glendale (tel. 937-2781), has the state's largest western store, Arizona Ranchman, among 75 shops and restaurants—and several department stores. **Westridge Mall,** 7611 W. Thomas Rd., Phoenix (tel. 245-1400), is a new mall with lush greenery, bright sun through skylights, a waterfall, and a sunken center court.

Note: Molly Trolleys circulate every 15 minutes between Old Town Scottsdale, Fifth Avenue Shops, Camelview Plaza Mall, and Scottsdale Fashion Square. A third trolley shuttles hourly between Scottsdale Road and the Lincoln Drive resorts, and the shopping malls. For schedules, call 945-8481.

7. OUTDOORS AROUND PHOENIX

Although there is no question that the sprawl across 60 miles of desert of seemingly endless suburbs that make up boom-town Phoenix and its neighboring communities is phenomenal, there is a western element to it always surprising to newcomers from elsewhere in the country: when it stops, it stops cold. At the cutting edge of the forces of urban development there may be a new condominium, a bit of watered sod, a wall, or a fence, and that's it—beyond is the pristine desert. Building almost always is contiguous—that is, spreading out from the center steadily rather than popping up here and there in scattered properties, the way it looks in the North and the East. So once you have finally gone beyond the city limits, you are very likely to find yourself in a wilderness area where the delights of discovering flora and fauna await you in a number of government-protected areas. Dams in the area have created lakes that have become recreation centers, and there are Indian reservations, ghost towns, a special desert garden, and hiking trails—or horseback riding trails—to explore, all on easy day trips out of Phoenix.

LAKES: The one catch among the pleasant attractions of the man-made lakes is the notice posted at all of them: "The level of this lake can vary significantly overnight." What this usually means is that the waterline might quickly recede below the normal shoreline, giving a somewhat bleak appearance, but docks and marinas are generally still usable at various water levels.

A series of lakes from dams on the Salt River leading downstream from **Roosevelt Dam,** 70 miles east of Phoenix, are popular destinations for Phoenicians and visitors to their area. Dedicated in 1911 by Pres. Theodore Roosevelt, it cost $10 million and rises 283 feet from streambed to its top. The base is 168 feet thick, of solid concrete that extends 30 feet down into the bedrock and as far into the canyon walls. **Roosevelt Lake,** impounded behind it, is 23 miles long and holds water enough for a three-year supply for the valley below it. Its 88-mile shoreline has many coves where there are camping and picnic sites maintained by rangers of **Tonto National Forest,** who also have charge of facilities at Apache Lake, Canyon Lake, Saguaro Lake, and Bartlett Lake, all within an hour or two from Phoenix by car. For information, call 261-3205.

Roosevelt Lake has three paved boat ramps, facilities for waterskiing, boat storage, boat rental, a courtesy dock, a fuel supply, grocery, bait and tackle shop, fishing licenses available, and swimming beaches. The lake is reached from Phoenix via U.S. 60/89 east to Apache Junction, then northeast 46 miles via the Apache Trail (Ariz. 88) to the dam, atop which a roadway is open to cars and trailer combinations under 30 feet in length.

Apache Lake, also along the Apache Trail, backs up behind Horse Mesa Dam and has two boat ramps, waterskiing, and facilities for boat supplies, fuel, bait, tackle, licenses, and groceries; there is a courtesy dock and boat storage, and rentals are available anytime. Picnic tables with grills and tent and trailer campsites are maintained by the National Forest Service. The lake is set off to the north by the Four Peaks of the Mazatzal Mountains, rising to a height of 7,645 feet. Nearby in the Three Bar game preserve are bighorn sheep, javelina, mountain lions, and eagles.

Besides the shoreside campsites reached from the highway there are others accessible only by boat. With its long main channel, the lake is popular with sailboat enthusiasts. On the lake is the **Apache Lake Resort** (tel. 602/467-2511) with air-conditioned rooms and a lakeside restaurant and lounge.

Below Apache Lake is **Canyon Lake,** formed by Mormon Flat Dam. It has three boat ramps and boat rental, as well as facilities for waterskiing, fuel, boat supplies, bait, tackle, and fishing licenses; there are picnic sites with ramadas, tables and grills, a swimming beach, and campsites for trailers and tents.

To the west of Canyon Lake is the last of the chain, **Saguaro Lake,** reached from Phoenix on U.S. 60/89 east to Mesa, then north on Country Club Drive to the Beeline Hwy. (Ariz. 87) to be followed 27 miles to Stewart Mountain Dam, behind which the lake is formed. Saguaro has two boat ramps, boat rental, facilities for waterskiing, fuel, licenses, and boat supplies and fishing gear. Picnickers have ramadas, tables, and grills, but there are campsites for tents only.

Reached also by another route is **Bartlett Lake,** 40 miles from Scottsdale, via Scottsdale Road north to Carefree, then a forest road 20 miles to the lake. Bartlett has a boat ramp, waterskiing, and swimming, but no other facilities or supplies except campsites for tents and trailers. An even more isolated campsite is open to boaters and fishermen 20 miles north at **Horseshoe Lake,** also accessible over forest roads.

Thirty miles north of Phoenix, via I-17 north to Ariz. 74, then 11 miles west, is a popular local water sports area called **Lake Pleasant,** formed by the Carl Pleasant Dam, and maintained by Maricopa County Parks and Recreation Department (tel. 262-3711). It has four boat ramps, boat rentals, fishing supplies and licenses, fuel; there is also a restaurant concession. Campsites here have full hookups, and there are showers and a dump station. Ramadas, tables, and grills welcome picnickers in separate areas of the lake, formed by damming the Agua Fria River.

RUINS: Another treat for visitors to the Roosevelt Lake area: **Tonto National Monument,** which has its entrance just three miles from Roosevelt Dam, to the east along the Apache Trail. To be visited are ruins of the Salado Indians, who built cliff dwellings and lived here between A.D. 1100 and 1400—another group of Pueblo Indians like those still living in New Mexico. Their houses were built along the Salt River, where the Indians farmed the shore lands. Archeologists find their heads slightly flattened in back, the result of the use of infants' cradle boards. Their teeth were damaged often, too, because, it is believed, of the grit in their stone-ground food.

Remains of their clothing show that women dressed in yucca-string skirts, fiber sandals of yucca or agave, cotton headbands, and had cotton carrying bags. In winter they wore blankets of cotton. Men's sandals were like the women's, and they wore breechclouts and occasionally elaborately woven cotton shirts. Ornaments in regular use were shell bracelets and pendants, stone beads, and turquoise pieces. Women wore their hair short, but men had long hair in fancy hairdos.

Salado archeology is known mainly from the Tonto site. Their culture seems to have been a blend of traits seen in those of the Anasazi, Hohokam, and Mogollon. It is believed that the Salado learned irrigation and the crafts of stone and shell working from the Hohokam peoples. The main original trademark of the Salado is the pottery style called Gila Polychrome; otherwise the artifacts resemble those of their contemporary neighbors. The last finds of Salado pottery were to the east and the south, suggesting that they eventually became absorbed into the Mogollon peoples in southern New Mexico. Most of the ruins and other archeological remains of the Salado were flooded by Roosevelt Lake in 1911, when the study of prehistoric Indians in the Southwest was just getting under way seriously. All we have left of the Salado civilization are three sites here at Tonto and another to the east near the town of Globe.

The three villages seen here are built in caves above the river: the Upper Ruin with 40 rooms, the Lower Ruin with 20, and the Lower Ruin Annex with 12. Some parts of the villages are two and three stories in height, like the pueblos still existing elsewhere today. They have been preserved by being within the caves. Walls were built of rough stones in courses two feet high kept in place with a mortar of mud; when each course dried another was added on top of it to a height of about six feet. Main beams and smaller crossbeams formed the ceilings, completed with layers of cactus leaves and reeds and a six-inch layer of mud left to dry.

Until the dam was built, the irrigation canals of these people were still visible here. They grew corn, pumpkin, squash, beans, and cotton. Half their food, it is estimated, came from wild sources in desert plants and animals: cactus fruit, mesquite and acacia beans, juniper berries, piñon nuts, jojoba nuts, acorns, hackberry fruits, flower buds of agave, yucca, and sotol. They got soap from yucca root, fiber for various articles including baskets from yucca, agave, and beargrass. Animal bones found here include those of deer, antelope, rabbit, and fox, as well as bobcats, cougars, badgers, prairie dogs, porcupines, and quail. Besides the bow and arrow the Salado hunters used clubs or netted or snared their prey. A bow and 26 arrows were found in the Lower Ruin.

The cotton material they used in clothing was dyed, and they had skills to produce materials that rivaled lace in delicate workmanship. A few whole bowls and jars have been retrieved; the design, black on white, is of a deceptively simple wide-strip geometric pattern, on a red fired-clay base. This so-called Gila Polychrome was a trade item and is found all over the Southwest.

Some of the artifacts the Salado people used are displayed at the visitor center, open every day in the year, free of charge, from 8 a.m. to 5 p.m. There are picnic tables and grills in the park. A self-guiding trail leads from the visitor center to the Lower Ruin; this trail is closed at 4 p.m. daily. A rough three-mile hike to the Upper Ruin requires that advance notice be given at the visitor center.

The other Salado site is the **Besh Ba Gowah Ruins,** a mile and a half from the town of Globe, 87 miles east of Phoenix via U.S. 60, or reached from Roosevelt Lake and Tonto National Monument by continuing southeast on the Apache Trail (Ariz. 88) for 30 miles to Globe. From town take South Broad to Ice House Canyon Road, leading to the site. This is a pueblo with 200 rooms built on a mesa near a tributary of the Salt called Pinal Creek. The houses were made of stones from the river, held together by adobe. Stores of grains and agricultural implements show that the people here too were farmers, like their relatives at the Tonto sites. Mexican copper bells and shells from the Gulf of California show that there was much trade carried on over considerable distances. Some artifacts from the site are shown in City Hall in Globe; the city administers the site, which is open to the public at all times.

Casa Grande Ruins National Monument, 50 miles south of Phoenix in the town of Coolidge, reached via Ariz. 87 south, consists of the most mysterious of remaining buildings left to us by prehistoric Indians in the area—in this case by the Hohokam people. Four stories in height, and built 650 years ago, the structure rises amid some 60 sites on the monument grounds. One puzzle is that the Casa Grande itself is built unlike other Hohokam buildings, but like those found in Mexico, of a desert soil with a lime content called caliche-earth. The thick walls are unreinforced and built of series of courses of this material. It appears to have been situated so as to dominate the village around it.

It was built to last for centuries. Inside are three parallel rooms with another room across each end. Trenches four feet deep hold the base of the foundation. Inside there was dirt to a height of five feet, making the floor begin at this level. Various theories have been developed as to the use of this structure. Wall openings in the upper stories could, it is suggested, have served for astronomical observation. Used for only a few generations, the Casa Grande was abandoned around 1450 when all the walled villages in the surrounding Gila Valley were given up, possibly because of drought. There are Pima Indians living nearby who share cultural traits with the disappeared Hohokam, and may be their descendants.

The place was given its present name by a Jesuit priest, Eusebio Kino, in 1694, who was led to it by Indians and found it in ruins at that time. Since that day it has remained a southwestern landmark for explorers and pioneers. Repairs were undertaken by the Smithsonian Institution in 1891, when the accumulated fill was cleared out of the inside and the walls stabilized. Several prehistoric villages within the monument boundaries have been excavated, and some have been covered with earth to preserve them.

Archeological evidence shows that the valley was farmed beginning around 1,500 years ago by the Hohokam, who learned the farming arts from Indians in Mexico. Characteristics of these people included the fact that they occupied small villages of separate, single-room houses made of mud and brush. They cremated their dead. They were good at carving shell and stone; their pottery was distinctive, with red designs on a buff-colored base. Their great achievement was the construction of some 600 miles of irrigation canals in the Salt River and Gila Valleys; these were as wide as six feet, and a yard deep. Influence from the higher cultures of Mexico is evident in ball courts, platform mounds, copper bells, and other artifacts of sophisticated manufacture.

Casa Grande, with its entrance on Ariz. 87, is open every day from 7 a.m. to 6 p.m. Hohokam artifacts are displayed at the visitor center, and there is a self-guiding trail through the ruins. Rangers give talks at various hours during the day, and guided interpretive tours are scheduled. A shaded picnic area has a water supply, but there is no overnight camping here.

HIKING: Five miles from the Apache Junction end of the Apache Trail is a good base for hikes into the beautiful Superstition Mountains, **Lost Dutchman State Park** (tel. 982-4485), which adjoins Tonto National Forest to the east. The mountains are named after Pima Indian legends and are the supposed site, somewhere, of the Lost Dutchman Mine. Even today an occasional searcher for Jacob Waltz's gold treasure can be found with a glint in his eye. Within the state park is a nature trail, and there are ramadas and tables for picnickers, as well as 35 campsites.

Sixty miles east of Phoenix on U.S. 60 near the town of Superior is a destination for hikers with a purpose, the **Boyce Thompson Southwestern Arboretum** (tel. 689-2811), with nature trails through 1,000 acres of fascinating desert plant life. Operated jointly by the nonprofit Arboretum Corp., the University of Arizona, and the State Park Board, the bit of Sonoran Desert preserved here has various trails for viewing the variety of plant life. Some of the giant saguaros are 200 years old, among every variety of cactus. Some European trees have been planted here: pomegranate, Chinese pistachio, and olive among them. A grove of eucalyptus offers a shady spot on a hot day.

Special event here is the annual April plant sale—usually some 20,000 plants change hands, many taken away by visitors from the north to nurture in home or office. Many drought-resistant trees and shrubs, as well as cacti and other succulents, go on sale at this time. Altogether there are 1,500 plant species identified within the property.

A couple of hours should be planned for walking the trails, the shortest and easiest being the Cactus Garden Trail; it's level, and takes only 20 minutes. The way into Queen Creek Canyon is via the Canyon Trail, a half-hour walk. An hour or longer should be allowed for the Picket Post Trail past Ayer Lake into an area of natural vegetation, returning to the visitor center by way of the canyon. The arboretum is open seven days a week from 8 a.m. to 5:30 p.m. Admission is $2 for adults (children under 17, free).

GHOST TOWNS:

Exploring ghost towns where the mines gave out a century ago or a decade ago is a special western pastime, where hiking in mountain or desert beauty gains another dimension, a philosophical question in the flimsy reminders of man's brief passage in these remote parts: What does it all mean? Of course there are rockhounds too who like to go through mine tailings left over from past operations. In any case, among the three dozen ghost towns in the state, three are within reach of Phoenix.

Cochran, in Pinal County, is about 70 miles from Phoenix, reached via U.S. 89 south to Florence, then 16 miles east over the Kelvin Hwy. and north on a dirt road to the Gila River. A high-clearance vehicle is recommended; ask in Florence. Cochran once had a railroad depot but now only a few ruins of frame structures remain; across the river, coke ovens can still be seen.

Goldfield, also in Pinal County, five miles from Apache Junction on Ariz. 88, was producing gold under a century ago. Still visible are four of the old mine shafts, stopes, and timbers, as well as some remains of early buildings. Goldfield, on the Apache Trail, is near the entrance to Lost Dutchman State Park.

Also within range of Phoenix is **McMillen,** in Gila County, about 85 miles distant, on U.S. 60 about 10 miles northeast of Globe; ask in Globe (ghost towns do not have identifying directional signs usually). The famous Stonewall Jackson Mine was discovered here in 1876, producing $3 million in gold; its ruins are visible.

HORSES:

Typical of riding stables in the Phoenix area is **Ponderosa Stables** (tel. 268-1261), where visitors may hire horses to go on their own or with guides, paying by the hour, half day, or day. Operating in South Mountain Park, the world's largest municipal park, with 15,000 acres, the stables are located at 10215 S. Central Ave., Phoenix. Free transportation to addresses in the Phoenix area is offered to all riders. Scheduled rides with small groups leave at various times all day, starting with a breakfast ride at 7:30 a.m., and ending with the dinner steak ride at 6:30 p.m. Dutch-oven potatoes, ranch beans, and garlic bread go with the steak, and if the moon is out, there's a moonlight ride back to base.

For those who prefer to watch professionals ride, **Turf Paradise** racecourse, at 19th Avenue and Bell Road (tel. 942-1101), has racing between October and

May. There are races every day but Tuesday and Thursday. Special buses ply between downtown Phoenix north along Central Avenue to the track on race days. Ladies get free admission on Wednesday, and senior citizens pay half price on Monday, Wednesday, and Friday.

GOLF: Among about 70 public golf courses in the Phoenix area, listed here are some of the most popular. **Ahwatukee Country Club,** 12432 S. 48th St., Phoenix (tel. 273-0544), is an 18-hole, 6,777-yard course. **Ahwatukee Lakes Country Club,** 13431 S. 44th St., Phoenix (tel. 275-8099), goes 4,038 yards, 18 holes, at par 60. **Arizona Biltmore,** 24th Street and Missouri Avenue, Phoenix (tel. 955-6600), is open to visitors with 36 holes of PGA-rated courses, a pro shop, and lessons. **Thunderbird Country Club,** 701 E. Thunderbird Trail, Phoenix (tel. 243-1262), has an 18-hole, par-71 course.

In Scottsdale, **Marriott's Cambelback Inn & Golf Club,** 7847 N. Mockingbird Lane (tel. 948-6770), has two championship 18-hole courses, open to visitors. Another Marriott golfing facility is **Mountain Shadows,** 5641 E. Lincoln Dr. (tel. 948-7111), with three 18-hole courses, two of championship caliber. The **McCormick Ranch Golf Club,** 7505 McCormick Pkwy. (tel. 948-0260), has two championship 18-hole, par-72 courses, each over 7,000 yards in length. Also in Scottsdale is the **Orange Tree Golf Club,** 10601 N. 56th St. (tel. 948-6100), with an 18-hole course and a golf shop.

8. TRIPS OUT OF PHOENIX

The spectacular mountain country of Tonto National Forest to the northeast and the hot desert country of the Gila River Valley to the south, as well as destinations such as Wickenburg to the northwest and Globe to the southeast, all have visitor attractions that sometimes take a bit of care in tracking down and finding. Sometimes a pickup truck or a four-wheel-drive vehicle is handy, but not for most of these destinations.

GLOBE: Ninety miles east of Phoenix via U.S. 60, Globe is a pleasant old mining town of 7,000 people nestling between the Apache Mountains to the north and the Pinal range to the south. It was the Old Dominion Mine that put the area on the map, finally ceasing its copper-mining operation here in 1931. Globe has adequate travel services.

Where to Stay

The Best Western **Copper Hills Inn** is off by itself in the foothills of the Mescal Mountains between the small cities of Miami and Globe, at the intersection of U.S. 60 and 70, Miami, AZ 85539 (tel. 602/425-7151, or toll free 800/528-1234). Set far back from the highway and walled off by motel units is an L-shaped pool with a pretty gazebo at one end; red-tile roofs strike a bright note. An ornate lounge has a mosaic mural in many colors behind the bar, while the dining room has visuals in a similar spirit—carved stonework over the fireplace and coppery flower-like sculptures. All this goes with bright modern rooms at $46 to $52 double.

A heated pool, telephones, and connecting rooms where required are available at modest cost at the **Ember Motel,** 1105 N. Broad St., Globe, AZ 85501 (tel. 602/425-5736, or toll free 800/453-4511). Rates are $25 to $30 double.

Where to Eat

The restaurant of the **Copper Hills Inn** (noted under "Where to Stay," above) has a standard American menu (with wine list) as well as a selection of Cantonese entrees, all at moderate prices.

A locally popular restaurant for steaks and prime rib is the **Crestline Steak House,** 1901 Ash St. (tel. 425-6269).

What to See

The **San Carlos Indian Reservation,** with its tribal office in the community of San Carlos, 20 miles east via U.S. 70 and Ariz. 170, has the world's largest cattle ranch—1.6 million acres. Coolidge Lake, 25 miles in length, offers some of the best bass fishing in the Southwest. Visitors are welcome to view the ranching operation or to enjoy camping, fishing, and hunting in areas specified. For information, inquire at the office of the San Carlos Apache Tribal Council in San Carlos (tel. 475-2361).

The **Besh-Ba-Gowah** ruins are located a mile and a half from downtown Globe, reached via South Broad Street and Ice House Canyon Road. The 200-room village was inhabited by Salado Indians, since disappeared without a trace, between about A.D. 1100 and 1400. Other villages have been traced along both sides of Pinal Creek here. A mystery here is the prevalence of slab-sided conical pits outside village walls that show no signs of ever being used for fires; perhaps they served a ceremonial purpose. Tools found in quantity on the site are shown in a display in City Hall.

The most spectacular attraction around Globe is the **Salt River Canyon,** accessible via U.S. 60, 30 miles north of town. The Salt River running through it divides two Indian reservations: the San Carlos Apache to the south and the Fort Apache Indians to the north. The tribes are cooperating in developing campgrounds and access to the canyon area, which locals dub a mini-Grand Canyon. The Fort Apache Reservation may be reached at the tribal office in Whiteriver (tel. 338-4346); call the San Carlos Reservation at 475-2361.

McMillanville, a mining camp just north of Globe, once had a population of 1,700 during the boom days of the 1880s. A few relics remain.

PAYSON: Ninety miles northeast of Phoenix, via Ariz. 87, is Payson, a town of 5,500 in the Tonto Basin, an area of spectacular mountain country, canyons, natural rock formations, ponds, and lakes.

Where to Stay

The **Swiss Village Lodge,** 801 N. Beeline Hwy., Payson, AZ 85547 (tel. 602/474-3241), has a long series of upstairs and downstairs motel units with balconies facing a wide grassy area, garden, and free-form swimming pool. Rooms have bright carpets in regional patterns of yellows and tans setting off fieldstone fireplaces and rich corner-to-corner window curtains. Outside, across the road, is a series of Swiss-style food and crafts shops. Rooms also have wet bars and refrigerators, and there is a restaurant, coffeeshop, and lounge. Rates are $55 double.

Practical kitchenette flats are rented at low rates at the **Charleston Motor Inn,** 302 S. Beeline Hwy., Payson, AZ 85547 (tel. 602/474-2201), with double rates at $30.

Where to Eat

Swiss-style specialties are offered at the **Swiss Village Lodge** (noted in "Where to Stay," above), 801 N. Beeline Hwy. (tel. 474-5800), while German dishes may be had, along with American-style steaks and other entrees, at the **Black Forest Inn,** 614 N. Beeline Hwy. (tel. 474-2307), both at moderate prices. Inexpensive New Mexican dishes are served at **La Casa Pequeño,** 911 S.

Beeline Hwy. (tel. 474-6329), and homemade Italian specialties are served at **Mario's Villa,** 1200 S. Beeline Hwy. (tel. 474-5429).

What to See

The town, occupying the geographic center of the state, is surrounded by the world's largest Ponderosa pine forest. At an altitude of 5,000 feet, its northern horizon is the majestic **Mogollon Rim** whose cliff edge runs for 500 miles to the eastward. There are many miles of trout streams, and seven lakes known to area fishermen for their good catches. Lands of three national forests are within easy reach of the town for use by hikers, backpackers, and horseback riders. A spectacular ride is along the unpaved rim road along the top of the Mogollon Rim for 42 miles, which is accessible 35 miles from Payson via either Ariz. 260 or Ariz. 87. These two highways fork just north of Payson and approach the rim in different directions, 260 to the east and 87 to the west. Both highways climb in switchbacks to the top, where drivers may turn off onto the rim road, which, besides views into the basin below, gives access to Willow Spring Lake, Woods Canyon Lake, Bear Canyon Lake, Knoll Lake, Blue Ridge Lake, and Chevlon Canyon Lake; a seventh, Black Canyon Lake, is reached by continuing east on Ariz. 260.

Zane Grey's Cabin, a shrine to the writer of western novels who published 80 books, notably *Riders of the Purple Sage,* is open to the public for a small donation. *Under the Tonto Rim* is another Grey title, and describes the cabin's location, reached from Payson by going 15 miles northeast to Kohl's Ranch, on Ariz. 260, and then making a left on a dirt road to the fish hatchery and the Grey cabin. Grey described the scene where he wrote many of his books: "I love wild canyons — dry, fragrant, stone-walled, with their green-choked niches and gold-tipped ramparts. I love to get high on a promontory and gaze for hours out over a vast open desert reach, lonely and grand, with its far-flung distances and its colors — I love the great pine and spruce forests, with their spicy tang and dreamy peace, murmuring streams and wild creatures."

Payson claims to be "the healthiest town in the West" because of its ozone belt. Members of the local economic development commission claim that there are only three ozone belts in the world (areas of pure air), the other two being in St. Tammany Parish, Louisiana, and in the Hartz Mountains of Germany. But the third, they say, is right here in Payson.

Payson also has the world's oldest rodeo, in mid-August, running for three days. There is an arts-and-crafts show in May, and an annual state championship loggers festival in late July. Also in August is an annual chili cookoff. In September there is music at a state championship old fiddlers' contest. For information, contact the **Payson Chamber of Commerce,** South Beeline Hwy. and Main Street (tel. 602/474-4515).

Two quiet villages at mile-high altitudes about 20 miles northwest of Payson, nestled under the Mogollon Rim, are named **Pine** and Strawberry, and make delightful spots for excursions or summertime getaways, well out of the searing heat of the desert country to the south. Five miles south of Pine, reached via an access road off Ariz. 87, is **Tonto Natural Bridge,** a massive, colorful rock formation well worth the short detour. It is the world's largest travertine arch, and has a five-acre farm on top of it.

Strawberry, three miles west of Pine, has the state's oldest schoolhouse, dating from 1885, a log building with fancy wainscoting on the inside walls. Its desks were proudly imported from back East along with a clock and a globe, and it served about 20 students a century ago. A scenic drive under the rim is named Control Road; it goes east from Ariz. 87 two miles south of Pine and continues across country to join Ariz. 260 near Tonto Village.

For information about the villages, contact the **Pine-Strawberry Chamber**

of Commerce, on the Beeline Hwy., Pine, AZ 85544 (tel. 602/476-3547). For September travelers, Pine has the added attraction of an oldtime county fair.

APACHE JUNCTION: This highway business-strip community 40 miles east of Phoenix on U.S. 60/89 at the junction of the Apache Trail (Ariz. 88) lacks tourist appeal from a scenic point of view, but can make a practical base for trips into the mountain, lake, and forest country to the east and north. It has excellent travelers' services, and prices generally considerably lower than those closer to the Phoenix metropolitan area. There are many travel-trailer or recreational-vehicle "resorts," as they are called locally.

For all information on travel services in the area, contact the **Apache Junction Chamber of Commerce,** at East Superstition Boulevard and Idaho Road, Apache Junction, AZ 85219 (tel. 602/982-3141).

Where to Stay

For trailer travelers or RV people, the following locations will welcome you. **Apache Trail KOA,** 1540 S. Tomahawk Rd., Apache Junction, AZ 85219 (tel. 602/982-4015), part of the national campground chain, welcomes both children and pets (which is often not the case in central Arizona). Facilities include 148 trailer spaces, showers, laundry, pool, playground, shuffleboard, planned activities, and rates by day, week, or month. There are two dozen other RV campgrounds or resorts in town that refuse children, although pets are accepted "on approval" in some of them.

Most motels accept children (but watch for "no children" signs in Apache Junction!). A pleasant one is the **Gold Canyon Resort,** 6210 S. Kings Ranch Rd., Apache Junction, AZ 85219 (tel. 602/982-9090), seven miles east of town, which has 60 furnished units at $56 double. Attractions in the foothills of Superstition Mountain include horseback riding, golf, tennis, and swimming in the pool, as well as wilderness hiking and birdwatching.

Where to Eat

For travelers determined to avoid the sameness of the fast-food chains, there are a number of likely choices in Apache Junction. For simple Italian home-cooking, good subs, and pizza, there is **Angel's Place,** 2885 W. Superstition Blvd. (tel. 982-5120), open from 11 a.m. to 9 p.m.; closed Sunday all year and also on Monday in summer.

For anybody starved after a long ride over the trail (or over the Interstate), the local advice is to head for the **Dirtwater Springs Restaurant,** 586 W. Apache Trail (tel. 983-DIRT), where gourmands are faced with the challenge of what is claimed as the state's largest steak, at 72 ounces. "Eat it all and the fixin's in one hour and it's on us" is the standing offer; take longer and you pay for it—$15 at last reckoning. Chimichangas and other Mexican foods are also served, and there is a saloon, a candy store, and an ice-cream bar.

Special Events

Apache Junction's annual event happens every January. Called **Lost Dutchman Days** (after the legendary lost mine in the nearby Superstition Range), it includes a parade, rodeo, art show, dances, talent show, and carnival.

PINAL COUNTY: A number of annual events take place south and west of the Phoenix metropolitan area in the small towns and Indian reservations of Pinal County, which is traversed by I-10 out of Phoenix going toward Tucson.

In February there are **Indian fairs,** the Mul-Chu-Tha in Sacaton, and O'Odham Tash in Casa Grande. In Maricopa, the festival of **Stagecoach Days** is held in March, and in April **Pioneer Days** are held in Kearny. Around September 10 Casa Grande is the scene of celebrations of **Mexican Independence Day.** The **Pinal County Fair** is held annually in Florence in mid-October, and auto racing at the fairgrounds over the Thanksgiving weekend.

State parks in the county include **Pichaco Peak** (tel. 466-3183), a 3,500-acre park with 34 campsites for tents or trailers; it is the site of the state's only Civil War battle. **McFarland Historical State Park,** at 5th and Main Streets, Florence, is the first Pinal County Courthouse, dating from 1882. Originally built of adobe, it was eventually plastered over and had wooden porches added, which deflected the summer sunlight and made the thick-walled, high-ceilinged rooms within a bit cooler. In 1890 the building became a hospital when a new courthouse was erected; it was made into a museum by the county historical society in 1963.

Rockhounds find much treasure in the hot, stony desert land of the county. Among common minerals and gemstones occurring in various areas are agate, amethyst, apache tears, bornite, calcite, chalcedony, chrysocolla, cuprite, galena, gold, gypsum, hematite, malachite, feldspar, peridots, petrified wood, rose quartz, desert rose, sulfur, thomsonite, and turquoise. Agate fields, reached over a county road (a high-clearance vehicle is recommended) 12 miles south of Arizona City, are one of many hunting grounds for rock collectors in the county. At **Apache Tears Mine,** three miles west of the town of Superior, just below Picketpost Mountain on U.S. 60, amateur miners can dig their own apache tears for a nominal fee; the gemstones were named for tears shed for victims of the Apache Leap Massacre.

A somewhat secret wilderness area is the beautiful **Aravaipa Canyon,** which has an access road off Ariz. 77 at a point 12 miles south of the community of Winkelman. This is federal land, managed by the Bureau of Land Management, which has a visitor station open daily from 8 a.m. to 5 p.m. to issue the required hiking permits for entering the canyon. Backcountry enthusiasts may like to visit the **Ashurst-Hayden Dam,** 12 miles east of Florence via graded county roads, where there is fishing for carp and catfish. From the dam a scenic wilderness trail leads three miles north to the narrow, towering-walled Box Canyon, passable by high-clearance vehicle.

For those interested in the way various parts of our economy work, there may be some interest in making a stop at **Cowtown U.S.A.,** outside the village of Maricopa, where many thousands of cattle are held for shipment to various parts of the land. Scientific methods of mixing cattle food and of getting it to the animals by remote control have a certain fascination; the operation was moved away from downtown Phoenix two decades ago so the aroma of steak-on-the-hoof wouldn't offend delicate noses.

A road easily passable that should, however, be taken somewhat slowly is the unpaved and spectacular desert route called the **Kelvin Highway,** which leads 40 miles from Florence east to the village of Kelvin. There are no services along the way, nothing but the desert and you.

The **Gila River Indian Crafts Center,** on Casa Blanca Road half a mile west of exit 175 of I-10 (tel. 963-3981), 30 miles south of Phoenix on the Gila River Indian Reservation, is an enterprise of the resident Pima and Maricopa Indians. A strikingly modern tower made of off-center cylindrical sections keeps an air of the Southwest about it as it dominates a courtyard. The crafts center sells authentic Indian-made jewelry of silver, turquoise, and beadwork—bracelets, earrings, rings, buckles, pendants, and necklaces. Pottery made by craftspeople of ten southwestern Indian tribes is sold here, as well as Navajo dolls, Seri woodcarvings, God's-eyes, and ceramic wind bells. There are silkscreen prints and paintings by noted Indian artists, as well as sand paintings, Hopi kachina dolls, and Navajo rugs. A coffeeshop has some Mexican and Indian specialties as well as standard sandwiches. A two-headed fetish pot is one of the standard items made on the reservation here by Maricopa artisans. Pima Indian baskets are famous for the beauty of their design; a few are for sale, and there are older ones displayed in a small museum.

Another scenic drive in the county is the **Pinal Pioneer Parkway,** a 45-mile desert route, part of U.S. 80/89, running between Florence and Oracle Junction. This is considered one of the most beautiful drives in Arizona and is all paved, with several rest areas along the way. About 32 miles along this route, heading southeast from Florence, is the junction with the **Park Link Drive** leading west 20 miles to Red Rock, still another scenic route that although not paved is easily passable by passenger cars.

The **Ak-Chin Reservation,** of the Maricopa Indians, 56 miles south of Phoenix near the town of Maricopa (tel. 568-2227), welcomes visitors to its St. Francis feast on October 4 and a tribal barbecue in association with an annual election the second Saturday of January. The tribe operates a large farming enterprise here.

Information on all tourist attractions in Pinal County, including the towns of Arizona City, Coolidge, Casa Grande, Eloy, Kearny, and Superior, may be had at the **Pinal County Visitor Center,** 270 Pinal St., Florence, AZ 85232 (tel. 602/868-4331).

WICKENBURG:
This pleasant little town of 4,000 people, 50 miles northwest of Phoenix via U.S. 60/89, modestly calls itself the Dude Ranch Capital, and has been regaling guests from the North and the East for so long that one of the guest ranches (as they are called nowadays) is an official National Historic Site.

Where to Stay
To begin with that historic property, the **Kay El Bar** guest ranch, off Rincon Road (north of town), Wickenburg, AZ 85358 (tel. 602/684-7593), accommodates guests in adobe houses that give the ranch a listing on the National Historic Register, and offers a pool and cookouts as well as plenty of horseback riding. Twenty guests are the limit here, and the ranch is open only from October 15 to May 15. Rates include all meals and use of ranch facilities: daily horseback riding, pool, and outdoor games. Lodge rooms, double, American Plan, are $165 daily. Children occupying premises with their parents are charged $25 daily for ages 2 to 6, $40 for ages 7 to 12. The ranch will arrange limo pickup at the Phoenix airport or will make pickups at the Wickenburg bus depot. There is a bar at the ranch.

Also offering American Plan accommodations in one-room, two-room, or four-room spaces in the lodge or in bungalows, is the **Rancho de los Caballeros,** five miles west of town on Vulture Mine Road, Wickenburg, AZ 85358 (tel. 602/684-5484), at the new Caballeros Golf Club, where guests have membership privileges on an 18-hole, 7,025-yard, par-72 course. Also offered is a swimming pool, tennis, a trap and skeet range, and horseback riding. Double rates are $168 to $216.

The **Wickenburg Inn,** off U.S. 89, Wickenburg, AZ 85358 (tel. 602/684-7811, or toll free 800/528-4227), is just north of town and styles itself a "tennis and guest ranch," having 11 acrylic courts in a valley protected from high winds. There is an instruction center with an acrylic hitting wall that gives a special rebound angle, and there are ball machines and stroke developers, clinics and private lessons. Half of the 4,700 acres of the inn property is set aside as a wildlife preserve, and there is a professional naturalist on the staff. There are riding and walking trails, and water holes with viewing blinds. Rooms are either in the lodge or in casitas of adobe brick construction with massive beams, hand-painted tiles, and fireplaces. Stables, horses, and wranglers of course go with the scene. Double rates are $130 to $260, American Plan, and tennis vacation special plans are offered.

Where to Eat

The delights of western-style barbecue are available every day but Monday at the **Frontier Inn,** 466 E. Center St. (tel. 684-2183), which is open daily for breakfast at 6 a.m., serving dinners to 9 p.m. Special Chinese ovens are used for the perfect barbecued meats cooked here.

A bit fancier is the newly appointed Rose Room, also in the western tradition (Territorial red-silk and brocade style), of the **Gold Nugget Restaurant,** 222 E. Center St. (tel. 684-2858). A few dishes in the continental manner compete with steaks and prime rib. Breakfast, lunch, and dinner are served from Monday through Saturday, Sunday dinner only. Breakfast runs $3 to $8; lunch, $3.50 to $11; and dinner tops out at about $15. Open from 7 a.m. to 10 p.m. daily.

What to See

Frontier Street downtown has been restored to a spanking-new version of the 1880s, with several stores and businesses in permanent old-style dress. The attraction down at no. 20 is the **Desert Caballeros Museum,** open Tuesday through Saturday from 10 a.m. to 4 p.m. and on Sunday from 1 to 4 p.m. In the adobe style with a portal along the street front, the museum has an artificially lighted imitation western town street *inside,* with such familiar landmarks as the old (but new-looking) Hassayampa Hotel, a post office, a church, and Ed & Stella's fancy house with a woman of ill-repute represented by a mannequin in a red dress. Possibly because of the dim lighting the effect isn't bad. A low-down saloon has a stuffed, lace-skirted young woman wantonly displayed atop an upright piano while the poker hand on the table nearby is a full house. The kind of strange objects you find only in small-town museums is Hazel Odle's Fairy Castle, a miniature palace difficult to describe involving a conch-shell pool and stars made of imitation pearls. An accompanying printed notice informs viewers that Hazel "used a wide variety of materials including tin cans and rattlesnake bones." Mrs. Odle, who made the castle in the 1930s, was one of the earliest teachers of art in Wickenburg. The museum asks visitors a donation of $1.50.

An old mining locomotive, No. 761, sits out in front of the tiny park at the center of town, near the **Jail Tree,** once used for tying up law-breakers when the town had no jail. Also nearby are the remains of the **Vulture Mine,** out of which Henry Wickenburg is said to have taken from $30 to $50 million worth of gold a century ago—the town was named for him. As for gold locally, the Wickenburg Chamber of Commerce reports in the standard optimistic way: "Some say the vein is still there." Outside town on Rich Hill are remains of 14 other mines, identifiable by V-shaped tailing dumps.

The second weekend of every February come **Gold Rush Days** with the crowning of Miss Gold Nugget, a parade and rodeo, and the state gold-panning championship contest. On the second weekend each November comes the **Four Corner States Bluegrass Festival** on Constellation Road, with prizes for such outstanding talent as best mandolin player, best flat-pick guitar player, and best oldtime fiddler. Opening Friday midday, events continue to about 8 p.m. on Friday, Saturday, and Sunday.

The **Hassayampa River Preserve** (tel. 684-2772), three miles east of town on the Phoenix highway at mile 114, is a piece of the natural environment owned and managed by the Arizona Nature Conservancy, a nonprofit organization aiming to protect endangered species and habitat. A shop selling books and a few gifts is set up in the historic ranch house at the visitor center, open to visitors free of charge Wednesday through Sunday from 8 a.m. to 5 p.m. A nature trail along the river bottom of the Hassayampa River winds through a forest of willows and cottonwoods. Waterfowl are often seen at Palm Lake, reached by a foot trail; there are 220 species of birds seen here. Guided walks are offered on Wednesday at 3 p.m. and on Saturday at 9 a.m.

For information on accommodations and other travel services or events around Wickenburg, call the **Wickenburg Chamber of Commerce** (tel. 602/684-5479).

CHAPTER IX

TUCSON AND SOUTHERN ARIZONA

□ □ □

A fast-growing city of 650,000 population in south-central Arizona, Tucson has a dry, sunny climate with under 12 inches of rain all year, and at its relatively low altitude of 2,400 feet, has hot summers and mild weather the rest of the year. There are 360 sunny days a year—over 90% of the time (compared to 75% for Los Angeles or 65% for Miami). Although a burgeoning center for light industry, it has traditionally been a place for winter visitors, and among some competing towns elsewhere in the Southwest, calls itself the dude ranch capital of the world. In spite of the fact that the number of these guest ranches has diminished over the past quarter century, there are still half a dozen excellent ranch resorts at the edges of the city that sustain the old tradition.

The earliest-known inhabitants of the site, Hohokam Indians, lived in a pit house that was discovered during building construction downtown in 1954. Reburied, the site may some day come to light again as a historical point of interest where early Tucsonans lived between A.D. 700 and 900. But the modern city had its beginning when the Spanish Presidio of San Agustin was laid out here in 1775, finally completed in 1783. The city came into the United States in the Gadsden Purchase in 1854, although it was another two years before American troops marched in to take official possession of the village. From this point on there was a slow, steady immigrant flow from the states back east. Some intermarried with the Mexican and Spanish families already established here. Many of these old Anglo-Hispanic families survive in Tucson today.

In 1867 Tucson was made capital of the Arizona Territory, a position it kept for ten years. As in many small towns in the Southwest, the arrival of the railroad brought boom times, starting in 1880. But the fastest growth has occurred since World War II. Today modern skyscrapers downtown are neighbors to some historic buildings of traditional adobe. Not far from the business center is the University of Arizona, which has several museums of interest to visitors. Within the university neighborhood are also the Arizona State Museum, containing archeological exhibits, and the museum of the Arizona Historical Society, with artifacts of city life over the past 100 years. An idealized, showbiz sort of history is seen at the edge of the city in an old movie set built in 1939, called Old Tucson, still used for television dramas—it is open to the public. A delight for any visitor to the Southwest is the beautiful Arizona Sonora Desert Museum, also just out of town, where displays of native plants vie with hundreds of animals, also native to the desert, in habitats of great naturalness. Also at the edges of Tucson in segments to the east and to the west is desert land of Saguaro National Monument, where lovers of desert life can follow hiking trails or marked motor routes in their explorations.

Besides the famous dude ranches, the city has many modern motels and hotels, and there is an international selection of restaurants of which at least one, the famous Tack Room, enjoys a national reputation for excellent cuisine. Cultural events at the university draw the public through the year, and the city also has a professional repertory theater and scores of places to enjoy live music of every kind.

SPECIAL EVENTS: Tucson and the surrounding parts of southern Arizona are hosts to a growing number of annual events of interest to visitors. **Arts-and-crafts fairs** are held nearly every week somewhere in the region. Notable among them are the Tubac Festival of Arts, in January; arts and crafts fairs in Fort Lowell Park, Tucson, in March and again in November; a Fourth Avenue street fair in April; crafts shows in the Bisbee Renaissance Festival in June; and displays at the Tumacacori Fiesta in December.

Among other events are the world's largest **gem and mineral show** in Tucson in February; the biggest **outdoor winter rodeo** in the U.S., also in February (it begins with the world's largest nonmechanized parade); **Territorial Days,** in the town of Tombstone in March; as well as a Tohono O'Odham **Indian pow-wow** in the village of San Xavier, also in March.

A six-week **Tucson Festival** begins each April—" a showcase of cultures"—while spring training of the Cleveland Indians baseball team continues at Hi Corbett Field in Reid Park. (The Tucson Toros start their regular baseball season the second week of April, same field.) A **Yaqui Easter ceremony** is held at Old Pasqua Village south of the city, and there is a ceremony marking the founding of the San Xavier Mission, and a mariachi concert, all in April.

The **Cinco de Mayo** Mexican victory over France is marked with a four-day fiesta in May, while in June and again in September there is **"Music under the Stars"** by the Tucson Pops Orchestra. In August the Arizona Historical Society holds **La Fiesta de San Agustin** to mark the city's founding, and in September comes the celebration of Mexican Independence Day.

1. ORIENTATION

Tucson is traversed by the east-west I-10 connecting to Los Angeles to the west and Jacksonville, Florida, to the east, with a junction near the downtown section with I-19 leading 63 miles south to the Mexican border at Nogales. It lies in a broad desert basin surrounded by four mountain ranges—the Santa Catalinas, the Rincons, the Tucson Mountains, and the Santa Ritas.

GETTING TO AND FROM TUCSON: The city is connected with the rest of the U.S. by interstate bus service provided by **Greyhound/Trailways,** with a station at 2 S. Fourth Ave. (tel. 792-0972). There is direct Amtrak service to Los Angeles and Chicago from the **Amtrak** depot, 400 E. Toole (tel. toll free 800/ 872-7245 for information and reservations).

Airlines serving **Tucson International Airport,** ten miles south of downtown via I-19 to Valencia Road, include Aeroméxico (tel. toll free 800/237-6639), Alaska Airlines (tel. toll free 800/426-0333), America West (tel. 623-8917), American (tel. 882-0331), Continental (tel. 623-3700), Eastern (tel. 622-1236), Northwest (tel. toll free 800/225-2525), Pacific Southwest (tel. 623-3428), Sunworld International (tel. toll free 800/722-4111), Trans Western Airways (tel. 624-2771), United Airlines (tel. 622-1214), and US Air (tel. toll free 800/428-4322).

GETTING AROUND TUCSON: Car-rental agencies at Tucson International Airport include **Avis** (tel. 746-3278), **Budget** (tel. 889-8800), and **Hertz** (tel. 294-7616).

There is regular **city bus service** from the airport downtown on the no. 8 line. **Sun Tran** operates bus service throughout the metropolitan area seven days a week from 6 a.m. to 10 p.m., for a 60¢ fare with free transfers, exact change only. Unlimited bus rides on a weekend pass, costing only $1, are good from 6:30 p.m. Friday to the last bus on Sunday. Deposit four quarters in the fare box and receive a pass from the driver. Senior citizens with a special ID card (available at City Hall Annex, 111 E. Pennington) ride for 20¢ anytime. Children under 6, with an adult, ride free. For schedule information, call 792-9222. Buses run every 15 to 20 minutes weekdays, every 30 to 50 minutes weekends.

Gray Line sightseeing tours to various attractions in and around the city depart from 180 W. Broadway Blvd.; for information, call 622-8811.

Taxi services include Allstate Cab (tel. 881-2227), Checker Cab (tel. 623-1133), and Yellow Cab (tel. 624-6611). **Handi-Car** (tel. 745-2244) has non-emergency service for the handicapped.

Airport transportation is also provided by Arizona Stagecoach (tel. 889-9681), Airport Limousine (tel. 889-9681), and Arizona Airport Express (tel. 741-1242).

USEFUL INFORMATION: The **area code** for all telephones in Arizona is 602. . . . **Police emergency** number is 911.

Tourist information is available from the **Metropolitan Tucson Convention & Visitors Bureau** at 130 S. Scott (tel. 602/624-1817). . . . The number for **time and temperature** is 791-7414, and for **weather information,** 623-4000. . . . For information on **road conditions,** call 294-3113.

Hospital emergency rooms in Tucson include those at the **University Medical Center,** 1501 N. Campbell Ave. (tel. 626-0111); **Tucson General Hospital,** 3838 N. Campbell Ave. (tel. 327-5431); **El Dorado Medical Center,** 1400 N. Wilmot Rd. (tel. 886-6361); **St. Joseph's Hospital,** 350 N. Wilmot Rd. (tel. 296-3211); **Tucson Medical Center,** East Grant and Beverly Boulevard (tel. 327-5461); **St. Mary's Hospital,** 1601 W. St. Mary's Rd. (tel. 622-5833); and **Kino Community Hospital,** 2800 E. Ajo Way (tel. 294-4471).

The "infoline" number for the public library system is 791-4010.

2. WHERE TO STAY

The Tucson area has over 100 guest ranches, hotels, and motels that make it a major tourist center of the Southwest. Among destinations of many Europeans and annual émigrés from the north and east are the guest ranches, some closed during the hot months of July and August.

GUEST RANCHES: The **Tanque Verde Ranch,** at the end of Tanque Verde Road, Tucson, AZ 85749 (tel. 602/296-6275), east of town, is an oldtime cattle and guest ranch with a history of cattle rustling and Indian fights. Founded in 1862 on a Spanish land grant, the ranch registered its R/C cattle brand in 1904. A broad brick-floored porch invites lounging in a hammock or on a padded bench with views of spacious, shady grounds. There are two heated pools, saunas, a whirlpool, an exercise room, and a health spa. Regular horseback trips include rides to breakfast, to picnics, and to dinner cookouts. Children are always welcome. There are usually after-dinner talks by one of the wranglers on some aspect of western lore, cowboy equipment, horse riding, or local flora and fauna. The property abuts the 1,385,000-acre Coronado National Forest to the east, and to the south is Saguaro National Monument, another area preserved in its natural desert state. There are also tennis courts for guests' use, as well as shuffleboard, horseshoes, and Ping-Pong.

Rooms and suites in the main ranch house and in cottages have warm-toned orange, yellow, and tan blends in carpets, and the warmth of brick walls and dark-wood beams. Some have southwestern-style fireplaces. Double rates, American Plan, are $149 to $200 May to December, and $189 to $260 January to April.

Hacienda del Sol, North Hacienda del Sol Road (off River Road), Tucson, AZ 85718 (tel. 602/299-1501), in the northern part of Tucson is a guest ranch originally built some 60 years ago as a girls' prep school catering to wealthy eastern families. It became a dude ranch in the early 1940s, with such guests as Clark Gable, Spencer Tracy, and baseball and golf stars. Its appeal today lies in its site overlooking the city, the patio gardens with cactuses and citrus trees, and a lingering 1930s atmosphere in the adobe houses with red-tile floors, brick fireplaces, and Indian-style rugs. A full-time social director makes sure there is plenty to do for those who want it: besides a heated pool, there's tennis, croquet, shuffleboard, a putting green, volleyball, badminton, Ping-Pong, horseshoes, and a full riding stable. There is a cocktail bar, and big-screen movies are shown every night. Regular events include mariachi concerts at dinner, a "cowboy steak ride," and bingo. Desert ecology is the subject of guided walking tours.

Many touches of elegance recall the era of the posh girls' school: the intricately carved Spanish-style ceiling beams, called *vigas,* in the library, where the shelves hold scores of signed first editions, works now more than half a century old. Stencilled designs in southwestern motifs still embellish the walls of the bathrooms in the former dormitory rooms. A two-room suite, once the domain of the headmistress, is now a favorite among habitués who return for a week or two every year—it has a picture-perfect view of the Santa Catalinas to the north. Outside that window hummingbirds hover and flit and other birds fly in and perch casually—the ranch uses 40 pounds of birdseed a week in its feeders.

Each of the 15 casitas has its own kitchen and dining room—a complete "little house"—and each has its own particular décor in the southwestern tradition. Many casitas were built, owned, and used by individual families during a period after the school closed in 1941.

Room rates go from $40 for small courtyard singles to $145 for large "west view" rooms with balconies or patios. Suites and casitas range from $180 to $275. For those staying five days or more, MAP rates at an additional $35 daily are offered. The dining room is open to the public (see "Where to Eat").

The **White Stallion Ranch,** 17 miles northwest of the city at 9251 W. Twin Peaks Rd., Tucson, AZ 85743 (tel. 602/297-0252), has a spread of 3,000 acres in cactus-and-sagebrush foothills where a homey ranch-like resort provides all

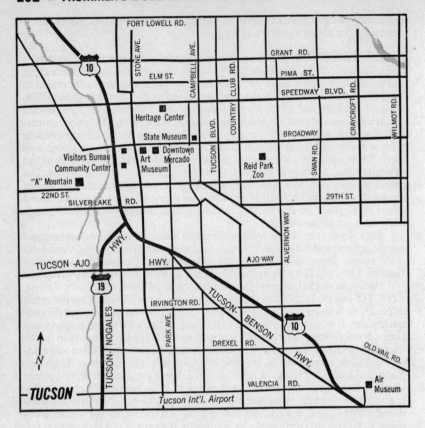

meals, horseback riding, tennis, swimming in a heated pool, hayrides, barbecues, and such sports as billiards and shuffleboard in the overall rates. The Allen True family, proprietors and hosts, raise their own quarter horses on the grounds, and to keep them in shape they run an amateur rodeo out here every week. In spite of the rustic background, Cynthia True's margaritas could be matched with the fanciest ones in town. Rooms all have bath or shower, guest capacity is 47, and rates are $82 to $87 (plus 15% service charge) *per person* in double rooms, $94 in suites. The ranch is closed summers.

For a real get-away-from-it-all weekend or week there's the delightful, remote, historic **Rancho de la Osa,** 70 miles southwest of Tucson via Ariz. 286, right on the Mexican border in Sasabe, AZ 85633 (tel. 602/823-4257). Restored to its original 200-year-old construction of handmade adobe blocks, rooms and suites have three-foot-thick walls, and most have fireplaces. A 250-year-old house now serves as the Cantina where cocktails are served before dinner; it was once a Spanish mission. The dining room welcomes guests to convivial meals of ranch-style recipes at long communal tables; the main hacienda was originally built in Territorial design and is one of the last of its kind still standing. There are plenty of good horses for riding into the wilderness—a national wildlife area bounds the property on the east—and cookouts, heated pool, and various daily activities are included in rates of $75 *per person* in double rooms. A weekend special brings guests Friday afternoon, with everything provided, including meals, to Sunday noon, for $200 *per person* in double rooms.

The **Middleton Ranch,** Amado Road, Amado, AZ 85640 (tel. 602/398-2883), 40 miles south of Tucson in the community of Amado, is reached via I-19 south to exit 48, then Amado Road east to the ranch. Open September to April, the ranch has just four double rooms, each with a bath and outside entrance. One of these, the master suite, has two bathrooms and a private patio overlooking the swimming pool. An oasis-like garden is surrounded by a wall, and there is a whirlpool. A corral of horses is just outside the ranch house, and escorted rides are included in the room prices, which run $150 double. The proprietors point out that with a small number of guests they are able to plan special outings such as overnight trail rides, hiking trips, or a picnic at a canyon waterfall.

HOTELS AND MOTELS: Tucson has accommodations in all price ranges in its hotels and motels. I'll begin with the best.

Luxury Accommodations

The one lodging place around Tucson that best exemplifies the gracious old spirit of the Southwest is the **Arizona Inn,** 2200 E. Elm St., Tucson, AZ 85719 (tel. 602/325-1541, or toll free 800/421-1093), in a quiet residential area, with a bright red-brick sidewalk along the front of a mild pink adobe. Besides Roosevelts and Rockefellers, more recent guests have included the likes of Frank Sinatra, Sammy Davis, Jr., and Burt Reynolds, among many show-business customers. Each room is furnished separately and differently from all the others, and a local writer noted that they "feel as though they are part of someone's home." The unhurried atmosphere extends to the 14-acre grounds, where there are gardens for strolling about as well as a pool and tennis courts. The inn opened in 1931 and draws regular wintering guests back year after year; some families have representatives of second-generation inn visitors among their members. Some rooms have sun parlors and fireplaces. Rates for double rooms range from $68 to $130, depending on time of year.

Also in the luxury class is **Loew's Ventana Canyon Resort,** 7000 N. Resort Dr., Tucson, AZ 85715 (tel. 602/299-2020), built on 94 acres in the northeast part of town in the foothills of the Santa Catalina Mountains. Besides 366 rooms, there are 26 suites with mini-bars, stocked refrigerators, and private terraces. Guests enjoy a 27-hole golf course, two heated pools, ten lighted tennis courts, and a mirrored aerobics rooms with ballet bar and available massage. Also on hand are weight equipment, a steamroom, a whirlpool, and a dry sauna, not to mention a jogging track and a croquet court. Public areas include the luxurious Ventana Restaurant serving food on Woodmere china and wines in Schottz Wiesel crystal. Hand-carved coyotes (in wood) welcome one to the Canyon Café; Bill's Grill takes care of loungers by the pool, and later at the Flying V Bar & Grill (décor: Hollywood meets the cowboy) there's a disco, in full swing beginning at 9 p.m. Free hors d'oeuvres may tempt croquet watchers after 5 p.m. in the Cascade Lounge. An innovation is a fancy high tea served daily at 3 p.m., at $10 per person. Daily rates for double rooms range from $95 to $145, depending on the time of year.

The **Tucson Hilton East,** 7600 E. Broadway, Tucson, AZ 85710 (tel. 602/721-5600, or toll-free 800/445-8677), is a brand-new (1987) seven-story luxury hotel with special appeal to business people, as well as vacationers and traveling families. Local architect Terry Lee designed a massive structure of glass panes and aluminum tubing reaching from ground to roof that lights the great inner atrium, a focal point filled with tall bamboo plants at the center of the sand-colored façade of recessed windows. Original works by local artists in the rooms and suites convey a southwestern feeling even in the abstract pieces. Artworks are also in the public areas: in the "champagne lounge" balcony overlooking the lobby, a watercolor gives a fine sense of desert foothills.

A terrace adjoining the restaurant (the Propre Place) on the second floor is a great place to watch the action around the pool, set in a sort of shallow amphitheater where there is a bandstand for evening shows. The terrace awnings are equipped with water sprays shooting a curtain of mist that lowers the summer temperature by an amazing 20° —an early success in air conditioning the outdoors, and most welcome in summertime Tucson, where it reaches over 100° regularly. (The innovative architect also designed massive blowers hidden in pedestals in the lobby to disperse smoke from a fire by shooting it out through vents in the roof high above, while sucking smoke out of all the corridors.)

Located east of the city center, the hotel has mountain views in three directions; guests may choose the view and the time of day of direct sunlight. On the seventh floor, the VIP Level, are semiprivate lounge, snack, and bar areas, and access to suites that have private terraces. Only guests staying at the VIP Level have slot cards that open the elevator doors at this floor. Free breakfasts, evening cocktails, and hors d'oeuvres go with the VIP rates.

Blue and rose are the dominant tones in the double and "king double" rooms, which are equipped with mini-bars (you can keep your own tab as you go). Bathrobes are provided, and certain bathrooms even have small television sets. Double rooms here cost $85 to $90, and suites run $137. Children of any age staying with their parents are always accommodated free of charge.

The **Viscount Suite Hotel,** 4855 E. Broadway, Tucson, AZ 85711 (tel. 602/745-6500, or toll free 800/255-3050), another recent addition to the Tucson skyline, opened in late 1986 with 216 suites as part of the English Forte Hotels International chain. The lancer's helmet on the bellman is about all that's obviously English about the place, although the management is proud of its "English service." The hotel was put up along with a huge coppery-glass bank building next door; the bank is supposed to glow in the daylight, and the more subdued pink hotel ("dusty rose" officially) to glow from within at night.

The centerpiece is the four-story atrium, complete with a sunken Atrium Café (open daily for breakfast and weekdays for lunch) furnished with antique green garden furniture. Also reached from the atrium is the more formal Oxford Club Restaurant, open daily for lunch and dinner (see "Where to Eat").

The hotel is popular with women whose concerns about personal safety are allayed by the glassed-in elevator, by the open balconies that give the only access to rooms, and by the two doors separating each bedroom from outside access. Each suite has a living room with desk and telephone, while the bedrooms have separate well-lighted vanity areas, with either one king-size bed or two double beds. There is a choice of two color schemes in the suites: plum, blue, and gray; or mauve and green.

The full breakfast that comes with the suite is just that: juices, bacon, sausage, eggs, rolls, toast, and coffee or tea. Hors d'oeuvres come free with evening cocktails, as does the airport transfer by hotel van.

The designer, Randy Creasman, let himself go to town with the lavish Presidential Suite on the top floor—it has two bedrooms and has become popular for two-couple getaway celebrations (it costs $350 a night). It may be the gold-plated fixtures on the bar and in the bathrooms that get them, or the emerald, peach, and light-green color scheme; there is a huge television, and one of the bedrooms has an Oriental décor, with black lacquered furniture.

Besides free newspapers and magazines, the hotel offers its guests a preregistration facility and fast checkout, some no-smoking suites, special women's suites, a ticket service, a paging system, and jogging maps. There is a heated pool, a sauna, a Jacuzzi, and an exercise room with weight-lifting equipment.

Winter rates are $89 single, $99 double; somewhat lower in spring and summer.

Sheraton Tucson El Conquistador, at 10,000 N. Oracle Rd., Tucson, AZ 85704 (tel. 602/742-7000, or toll free 800/325-3535), at the northwestern edge of the city, has 440 rooms, suites, and casitas looking out on gardens, pools, and a golf course. Modern furnishings and carpets, curtains, and bedspreads are in mild pastels that blend easily without drawing attention to themselves. Three restaurants include one serving continental cuisine in luxurious surroundings, one with western chuckwagon food indoors or out, and a coffeeshop open for breakfast, lunch, and dinner. Three bars also provide differing atmospheres. There are two golf courses and 16 lighted tennis courts, racquetball, and a health spa. Rooms are priced at $115 to $130 double, daily, depending on size of room and season; suites run $145.

The Medium-Priced Range

The **Mount Lemmon Alpine Inn,** 12925 N. Sabino Canyon Pkwy, in the isolated village of Summerhaven, Mount Lemmon, AZ 85619 (tel. 602/576-1500), at the end of the road up to the summit of Mount Lemmon, has become more of a special getaway scene since new owners Jackie and Jerry Groch took it over in late 1987. A great place to escape the summertime heat of the city down below, the lodge is the perfect starting place for mountain hikes and is also used by skiers from December into April.

At almost any time of year the cheery fireplace in the plain, simple barroom is a welcome center for exchanging talk of the trails, the skiing, the wildlife—even the look of the blue pine in the wall paneling. This wood, in a variety of browns and tans and blue-black striations, is cut from a Ponderosa pine. Just beyond the barroom is a tiny general store. There is a dining room and an outside terrace, as well, for lunches and dinners.

The mountaintop community of Summerhaven, for which the barroom serves as the main social center, is populated by some 75 people year around, many of them commuting daily over the twisting 25-mile-long Catalina Hwy. to Tucson. With its pullouts and scenic overlooks, it is one of the spectacular drives of southern Arizona. Besides a new fire station, the village supports a one-room school.

The altitude—around 8,000 feet at the inn—and the evergreen woodland looming in the heights all around combine to make a stay at the lodge memorable. The contrast between the snug warmth in the rooms and lounge and the bright starry cold night makes guests feel happy to have a warm place to stay. For a total escape from the everyday world of the city below, there's nothing like it.

Besides all the hikers and, in season, the skiers, many rockhounds and birdwatchers like to spend a night or two here. An information station, open year round, provides directions and maps for exploring the national forest lands. It is possible to hike up here from the northeastern outskirts of Tucson (or to hike down from the top) in a day. Visitors heading for the top should remember to bring warm clothing—even when the sun is hot down in the city.

The bar has that irreplaceable aura of being a port in a storm—it's the only one up here and offers such celebratory potions as the Snowshoe (hot chocolate with peppermint schnapps) and the Long Island View (Kahlúa with coffee and bay leaf).

Breakfast here can be Belgian waffles with whipped cream and strawberries, a three-egg omelet with cheese, ham, mushrooms, scallions, and cottage potatoes, or a breakfast pita with egg, ham, and salsa. There is available anytime a Swiss fondue for four people; other specialties are beef Stroganoff and an Alpine Bavarian grill (each at $7 to $8). Chicken and hamburgers are also available, along with cheesecake, apple cake, and pecan pie.

In addition to a dormitory room used mainly by skiers, the inn has six double rooms, each with two double beds. Including breakfast for two people, rooms are $65 to $75, $20 more for four to a room.

Lexington Hotel Suites, 7411 N. Oracle Rd., Tucson, AZ 85704 (tel. 602/575-9255, or toll-free 800/53-SUITE), is the only newly built property on the north side of the city. Although the hotel is in the foothills of the Catalina Mountains, a jog of a few miles over to Interstate 10 leads to a fast trip straight to the center of Tucson. Suites of various sizes have all the modern conveniences, including cooking facilities, at moderate prices, and the Lexington offers touches of luxury and an overall sense of good taste in the bargain. The slogan "a suite for the price of a room" applies to the one- and two-bedroom layouts as well as to the mini-suite. Off-white Formica-topped tables double as desk-like working spaces in the kitchen area; a pull-out sofa offers extra space. Windows open upon a patio that has a putting green, a whirlpool, and a pool (heated in winter). An atrium off the lobby houses a dining area where a copious continental breakfast is complimentary for all guests. Cooking utensils are supplied, and there is a thoughtful supply of soft drinks and ice in the refrigerator.

The hotel is near the new Foothills Shopping Mall and the Pueblo Museum. Just next door is Tohono Chul Park, a desert garden with tea room and gift shop, and the Haunted Bookshop, which has been called the best bookstore in the city.

Rates for mini-suites run $40 to $70, and for one-bedroom suites, $50 to $80 depending on season.

The **Ramada Inn Downtown,** 404 N. Freeway, Tucson, AZ 85745 (tel. 602/624-8341), glows in an orange-pink stucco that looks fine in the Tucson sunshine, set off by the orange trees in the patios (but beware—the fruit is bitter to the taste!). Right downtown, the inn nevertheless occupies a lush spread of 11 acres, with a big pool just right for lounging around outdoors and soaking up the sun (or a drink or two). A restaurant open from 6 a.m. to 11 p.m. combines Mexican dishes with its regular American-style fare, at reasonable prices. A lounge with a popular happy hour overlooks the semitropical courtyard. There's a putting green, and access to a nearby health club, with a racquetball court and a sauna, is free to guests. Rates are $89 to $99 double in winter, reduced to $49 to $52 in summer.

Budget Accommodations

The **Hotel Congress,** 311 E. Congress St., Tucson, AZ 85701 (tel. 602/622-8848), is one of those pleasantly businesslike hotels that set the tone of American downtown areas half a century ago—a kind of social focal point for local residents as well as a regular stop for business travelers. Built in 1919, it gained national notoriety in a fire in 1934 when firemen led to safety several male guests who turned out to be members of the John Dillinger gang out of Chicago. The restoration of the hotel is part of a $4.5-million downtown renovation project currently under way. The façade was renewed, the wiring completely replaced, and there are new lamps—but the rooms still keep their 1920s aspect, with original iron beds, venetian blinds, and steam radiators. There are the old wood dressers and writing desks—all polished up—and new carpets too, but it's still a step back in time.

The Congress continues its role as a downtown social center with the Club Congress, a 1930s-style barroom with booths along one wall and period neon; there are performances by singers or musicians on Thursday nights, and dancing on weekends. It's worth at least a quick stop at the Congress Club to see the original Pete Martinez rodeo and corral drawings. Latest addition to the commercial spaces in the hotel is a new restaurant with a sidewalk terrace: Bowen & Bailey.

Its downtown location, within walking distance of the Community Center and several museums, as well as the historic Presidio district, makes the hotel a good choice for bargain hunters. Its 42 rooms rent for just $23 double, with bath; and there are discounts for seniors and even a couple of small youth-hostel spaces.

Ghost Ranch Lodge, 801 W. Miracle Mile, Tucson, AZ 85705 (tel. 602/791-7565), is just three miles north of the city center and appeals to visitors with a liking for the simplicity and spaciousness of early tile-roofed ranch-style motel structures of the '30s and '40s. It's composed of long, low buildings with brick or wood-paneled interiors surrounding a great rectangular garden dotted with orange trees. There is a putting green and a shuffleboard court within this grassy expanse, while beyond a series of suites in its own cactus garden is a spacious swimming pool.

A cocktail lounge with heavy beams in the ceiling and red leather booths is a popular gathering spot for happy hour from 4 to 6 p.m. weekdays. The restaurant offers specials for breakfast (steak and eggs, pancake sandwich), lunch (steak sandwich Philly style, taco salad), and dinner (filet mignon, prime rib) among many entrees. It is open daily from 6:30 a.m. to 9 p.m.

Rates for double rooms run $48 to $58 in the winter season, $35 to $43 in summer; kitchenettes and two-bedroom suites are also available.

Days Inn, 88 E. Broadway, Tucson, AZ 85701 (tel. 602/791-7581, or toll free 800/325-2525), is another landmark hotel taking on a new life in the downtown area. Built in 1904 and long known as the Santa Rita, the hotel has recently undergone a million-dollar refurbishment, reopening under its new name in 1987 with 150 rooms and 16 suites in a downtown location near art, theater, and shopping attractions. A modern, pastel-hued environment in the lobby, with southwestern-style floor tiles and verdigris carpeting in the patios, has not completely lost the comfortable, homey solidity of the old Santa Rita. A barber and beauty shop and a travel agency occupy ground-floor space along with a new restaurant, El Jardin, open from 7 a.m. to 9 p.m. daily. In warm weather diners can sit on a terrace at tables with bright-orange umbrellas—a new bright note for downtown Tucson.

Rooms enjoy the quiet of old-style solid construction while being completely modernized and refurnished in pastel desert tans and browns. Good swing-out lamps make reading in bed or over a desk-bureau easy. Also on the premises are a pool, whirlpool, and sauna; no-smoking rooms are available, and all the king-size bedrooms come with refrigerators and sinks. Rates range from $42 to $50 for double rooms in the winter season, about 20% lower in summer.

El Presidio Bed & Breakfast, 297 N. Main Ave., Tucson, AZ 85701 (tel. 602/623-6151), is yet another example of a refurbished old treasure—the 1896 Julius Kruttschnitt home, in the American Territorial architectural style, now has three kitchen-parlor-bedroom suites offered along with breakfast. They all give upon a delightful garden patio tended with loving care by the house owners Gerald and Patti Toci, who have been restoring the place for a number of years. A soapstone fountain carved in Mexico is the focal center among year-round blossomings of flowers and plants—irises in early spring, followed by petunias, snapdragons, sweet alyssum, nasturtiums, roses, sorrel, geraniums, and year around some native cactuses. A carriage house in disguise houses the guest units, which are equipped with stove, sink, and refrigerator, a living room with a pull-out sofa (kids over 10 are welcome), pots and bowls of flowers, windows shaded by slatted-wood blinds, and such three-dimensional decorative items out of the Tocis' collections as coveys of wooden duck decoys, fleets of pressing irons from the last century, and a Victorian wagon full of early wooden toys. Details like bright ceiling lighting, comfortable beds with many frilly pillows, and an invitingly warm comforter (and electric blanket too) add home-like touches. Among the Tocis' collecting manias is one for old quilts.

Breakfast of juice, a bowl of fresh fruit, sweet rolls and muffins, and an omelet stuffed with mushrooms, along with fresh ham, is served in a sort of Victorian solarium just off the veranda that runs along three sides of the building. The interior of the house has hand-hewn pine *vigas* from the Santa Rita Mountains. A 12-foot-wide hallway or *zaguan* leads out into the garden, where shading the flowers are palm, pine, and mesquite trees.

The three suites, available only to nonsmokers for a two-night minimum, including breakfast for two persons, cost $55 to $70 daily, lower by the week.

A BED AND BREAKFAST AGENCY: Old Pueblo Homestays, P.O. Box 13603, Tucson, AZ 85732 (tel. 602/790-2399), makes reservations for 22 bed-and-breakfast establishments in and around Tucson, mostly with one or two units available, at rates from $25 to $75 double.

3. WHERE TO EAT

Beer in pitchers and home-fried potatoes, cowboy beans, fresh-baked biscuits, mesquite-grilled steaks make up the hearty fare of ranch life that the dudes expect when they come out here for a vacation of trail riding—with breakfast rides and barbecues a regular treat. While this approach to cooking is a specialty of the ranch resorts, it is also available in a few regular restaurants as well, especially ones specializing in thick-cut steaks. Tucson also has solid representation in the world of more luxurious continental cuisine. An Arizona style of Mexican cooking can be sampled in the numerous restaurants in the Hispanic tradition that range up and down the scale from fancy to plain and simple. Besides these, there are some eating places representing other ethnic persuasions such as Italian or Oriental.

LUXURY DINING: The **Tack Room,** 2800 N. Sabino Canyon Rd. (tel. 722-2800), open nightly for dinner from 5:30 p.m., is Tucson's most elegant restaurant, and its food is as good as any in the state. Diners sense a warm ease within the adobe walls and overhead *vigas* of this old hacienda. Serving plates of crystal and copper point up the quiet opulence of the atmosphere, enhanced perhaps by a cocktail before dinner by a wide fireplace, built of stones taken from the first territorial courthouse of Tucson. A seven-course gourmet dinner can be set up on special order a day ahead, with a wide variety of menu selections available. Rack of lamb bouquetière and beef Wellington are two specialties of the house. All bread, pastry, and desserts are made fresh daily on the premises, and there is an extensive wine list. Dinner for two with wine is usually priced near $100.

Ristorante Capriccio, 4825 N. First Ave. (tel. 887-2333), is noted for its imaginative, delicate sauces—cream-based sauces on pasta and various special sauces for other dishes, such as a green-peppercorn sauce laced with Grand Marnier for the roast duckling. Another treat here is I tre gemelli, a combination of three medallions of lamb, veal, and beef, each in its own sauce—lamb with mustard and peppercorn, veal with wild mushroom, and filet mignon with a garlicky, winy demi-glacé. Another choice is fresh veal in a zingarella sauce with shallots, garlic, and wine. For starters a rare treat is a spicy pasta called penne alla vodka—quill pasta with tomato, vodka, and cayenne in cream. A seafood pasta called fettuccine Giacomo is set off by a sherry-cream sauce. Desserts are lavishly prepared here; an example is a poached pear with chocolate leaf in raspberry and custard sauces, served with ice cream and almonds. Appetizers go for $3 to $7; pasta dishes, from $5 to $7; salads are $6; and entrees run $15 to $17. A dress code requires men to wear jackets. Open nightly from 6 p.m. except Sunday.

An addition to the handful of top-notch restaurants where the chefs care a great deal about the quality of the food served is the **White Dove,** in the Sheraton Tucson El Conquistador, 10,000 N. Oracle Rd. (tel. 742-7000), well worth the brief ride out of town to savor a long, slow, and delicious dinner. There are two seatings, by reservation, one at 6:30 p.m. and the second at 8:30 p.m. Specialties include a combination of medallions of veal, lamb, and venison in sauces; roast duckling in peppercorns and white wine; venison in a red wine sauce; filet of capon with olives and snails in garlic sauce; and rack of lamb with champagne, mustard, and rosemary. Starters might be a mock turtle soup with sherry, or ceviche; the dessert tray tempts with such pastry as a hazelnut mousse wafer or a filbert cream roll. Hot sourdough rolls go with the dinners. There is a good wine list, with a number of entries at around $20. Closed Sunday.

Trout in a lemon-butter sauce or a delicate veal casserole might be the choice in the dining room of the lovely **Arizona Inn,** 2200 E. Elm St. (tel. 327-7646), where diners step into a world of half a century past, genteel surroundings of gardens, potted plants, clear sunlight through skylights, and the scent of oranges alive on trees just outside the door. It is open seven days a week for three meals, and has a complete wine list. Lunches are about $16; dinners, $22 to $28.

MODERATELY PRICED RESTAURANTS: The **Bistro Med,** 7117 N. Oracle Rd. in Casas Adobes Plaza (tel. 297-0492), is a welcome addition to the growing number of eating places offering Mediterranean fare—Spanish, French, Italian, and Greek. The blue-and-coral décor seems to make the modest-sized dining room, with its wide windows, more spacious than it is. Soups, priced at around $2 the bowl, are a special treat here, among them minestrone, gazpacho, black bean, and vichyssoise. A specialty, bamya, a lamb stew with tomato and okra, is served with rice, at $9.50. The classic arroz con pollo at $8.50, made of breast meat, has saffron rice, with onion, red chiles, peas, and ham bits all baked together. Among as many as a dozen entrees is also a first-rate shish kebab at $12.75. Dessert might be mousse au chocolat. Tapas are served later in the evening for an after-the-show treat, and in warm months there is outside patio dining. Open daily except Sunday for lunch and dinner.

A good, solid lounge-restaurant for steaks and barbecue is **Gus & Andy's Steakhouse,** 1000 Oracle Rd. (tel. 624-2801), where a top sirloin goes for $12 and prime rib or half a slab of barbecued pork ribs for $10. There are $9 specials of beer-batter cod, ground steak, and chicken Kiev. Carafes of house wine go for $7.50; desserts might be cheesecake, baklava, or a good hot apple pie à la mode. Open daily.

Keaton's Restaurant, 7401 N. La Cholla, (tel. 297-1999), a bright new eatery on the north end of the city, is decorated with lightwood paneling and green-and-white tile. Thanks to its hickory smoker at the oyster bar, for $5 to $6 you can order smoked silver salmon, smoked freshwater trout, or smoked shrimp and scallops with fresh pasta. There is mesquite-broiled seafood as well: Alaskan king salmon, fresh Atlantic swordfish, or Hawaiian mahimahi with pineapple. Mesquite-broiled steaks and chops are also served—a filet mignon with sautéed mushrooms and a béarnaise sauce at $12.50, or lamb chops at $11.50. A specialty, veal Oscar, involving veal, Alaskan crabmeat, and white asparagus, is $12.50. There are good California wines at $3 the glass, or by the bottle. Open daily for lunch and dinner.

The **Oxford Club,** in the Viscount Suite Hotel, 4855 E. Broadway (tel. 745-6500), occupies a great sunny atrium at the heart of the new facility. Breakfast, lunch, and dinner are served daily. You can start the day with morning frittatas of tomato, mushrooms, and olive, or ham, onion, and bell peppers. Huevos rancheros—a tortilla with two eggs on it—and refried beans in a picante sauce are $5.25. True to the English origins of its owners, the establishment also provides authentic British fare, such as shepherd's pie (made of onions, beef, Worcestershire sauce, and beef stock, topped with creamed potatoes, and served with green vegetables) at $6, or beefsteak and oyster pie at $7. At $6.50 a traditional 18th-century veal-and-ham pie offers gammon, chicken, and eggs wrapped in flaky pastry and served with glazed potatoes. Dinners include a steak-and-kidney pie at $6, or several steaks at $12 to $15. The house specialty is bouillabaisse à la Marseillaise, at $15.

The **Propre Place,** in the Tucson Hilton East, 7600 E. Broadway (tel. 721-5600), specializes in new American cuisine and fresh baked goods served in a bright room with a terrace looking out on the swimming pool. Guests watch the cooks at work in a spanking-clean galley arrayed with copper pots; fresh fruits are decoratively displayed on beds of ice. A showcase holds an impressive wine rack where diners might browse for a moment before choosing something to go with lunch or dinner; nearly all wines are available by the glass as well as full bottle.

It's rare in Tucson to find a place worth going to especially for breakfast, but consider some of these morning specialties: Grand Marnier French toast, fresh cheese blintzes with sour cream and blueberry sauce, smoked salmon Jasmine (salmon with scrambled eggs, sour cream, pâté de foie gras with truffles, and hollandaise on a muffin). And there are bagels and lox too.

Among dinner choices are dishes prepared on the mesquite grill: lamb chops with rosemary-lemon sauce, filet mignon, New York strip, or mixed grill. Other specialties include roast duckling Ramona, boneless duck finished on the grill and served with a pink pepper-cream sauce; escalope of veal Broadway, sautéed veal with Alaskan crab, spinach, hollandaise, and bordelaise sauce; or seafood strudel Nantua, baked filo dough filled with crab, shrimp, scallops, salmon, vegetables, and spices, all with a lobster sauce. These entrees run about $15. Dining hours are 6 a.m. to 10 p.m. daily.

A noted traditional restaurant in the center of town, **El Charro,** 311 N. Court Ave. (tel. 622-5465), has been serving Tucson-style Mexican dishes since 1922 as proof of its owners' claim that the city is "Mexican food capital of the world" even if it isn't actually in Mexico. Carne seca (dried meat) is dried in the sun on the roof, and tamales are made with the house's own sauce and masa (dough). Daily specials draw their local supporters: stuffed avocado on Monday, seafood enchilada on Wednesday. There is a pleasant terrace ideal for dining outside nearly any time of the year in this warm climate. Open from 11 a.m. to 9 p.m. seven days, the house has beer and wine available.

RANCH-STYLE FOOD:

The **Last Territory,** 10,000 N. Oracle Rd. (tel. 742-7000), in the Sheraton Tucson El Conquistador, is open Tuesday through Saturday to midnight, to steak eaters seated at long tables with checked tablecloths and bentwood chairs, where at one end of the room a western band keeps up a cheerful din. A sunset trail ride is offered in a dinner package; riders make their way up to Pusch Ridge above the resort for a view of the sunset; other diners in an old buckboard take a route through the desert to the restaurant, which also has an open-air ramada for servings of big steaks, barbecued ribs, and chicken. Along with the music are some brief staged shoot-outs on Wednesday and Friday evenings. For the package rides with dinner, reservations should be made the previous day.

Steaks from $9.50 to $12 up to two pounds in weight are the specialty of the resolutely informal **Pinnacle Peak,** 6541 E. Tanque Verde Rd. (tel. 296-0911), where anybody showing up at the long, oilcloth-covered family-style tables for dinner wearing a tie has it snipped off forthwith by a waiter or waitress, to join the thousands already festooning the ceiling in the hall. Prime rib and barbecued pork ribs are also available, served with salad, bread, and pinto beans. Open seven nights a week.

INEXPENSIVE RESTAURANTS:

The **Cajun Kitchen,** 5004 E. Broadway (tel. 722-5990), purveys authentic Louisiana dishes by a native Cajun who serves up the food in Styrofoam packs. But don't be put off by that, nor by the modest prices of $4 to $6 for such dishes as fried catfish, fried oysters and shrimp, or a seafood platter, all with an "astonishing" potato salad, because the fare is excellent. Jambalaya, red beans with rice, and gumbo are served every day in large and extra-large portions, priced at $2.75 and $3.75—enough as a meal in itself. Open seven days a week to 9 p.m.

A good spot for breakfast, lunch, or a sandwich while touring downtown is **Leeann's Coffee Shop,** 178 N. Church St. (tel. 791-3818). A $2 breakfast includes bacon and egg; a three-egg green chile and cheese omelet with home-fries and toast or pancakes is $3. Tacos, burros, tostadas, and chimichangas are ready all day at around $2.50 to $3, and there are good hot pork tenderloin or chicken breast sandwiches at $2.75, or a turkey or ham grinder at $3. There is also an appetizing chef's salad at $3.50. Take-out service is fast.

The **New Sai Gon,** 6211 E. Speedway (tel. 885-2747), open seven days, serves authentic Vietnamese dishes at reasonable prices. As in traditional Chinese restaurants, the New Sai Gon has large tables with built-in lazy Susans for serving a wide variety of dishes to a large gathering. A specialty is the Vietnamese rice roll, thin rice pancakes wrapped around ground pork, bean sprouts, and Romaine lettuce, served in a vinegar sauce, at $2. One entree, chicken with lemon grass, combines green onions and a bit of hot red peppers for its unique taste; it costs just $3.50, as does stripped pork with broken rice. The shrimp with garlic and onions is $1 more. Lunches cost even less, and there are Monday-night television-sports-watching specials, with 50¢ beer and cut-rate spring rolls. Vegetarian dishes are guaranteed to contain no MSG. A number of Chinese dishes are also offered. A special treat is the Chinese breakfast served every Sunday at 9 a.m.

Mi Nidito, 1813 S. Fourth Ave. in South Tucson (tel. 622-5081), specializes in giant-size flautas, a specialty made of tortillas and stuffings, in a bustling and

cheerful atmosphere. Cactus shoots called nopalitos might vie with fresh asparagus as a delicacy; chicken topopo is a mixture of vegetables, chiles, avocados, and
lemony chicken. Owner-chef Ernesto Lopez has been experimenting with New
Mexican recipes here for 30 years; his red or white menudo (a tripe soup) and
green-chile enchiladas are first rate. A rice-based, sweetish drink called horchata is
a nonalcoholic choice (but beer and wine are also served). Spiced shredded beef
called birria goes for $5, and other choices are similarly low priced. A great des-
sert is a mango chimichanga with cream on top. Open daily except Monday and
Tuesday from 11:30 a.m. to 11:30 p.m. (later on weekends).

4. SIGHTSEEING

Tucson has some delightful outdoor attractions, notably the best desert museum in the country as well as federally protected areas in a national monument
of a particular southwestern beauty. There is an old Spanish mission that has become world famous for its serene outline of belltowers against a flawless sky, and
there are a score of museums for a wide variety of interests: fine arts, aircraft, Old
West, territorial history, archeology, geology, military, photography—and even
a museum of rodeo parade equipment. Annual events involving the artists and
craftspeople, and others that bring out the various cultures of local Indians or
Hispanics, are held all through the year. Historic structures saved from the bull-
dozer in downtown reconstruction can be inspected on a walking tour of a doz-
en locations. The state's largest university, with over 30,000 students, the
University of Arizona, has a number of places of interest to visitors among
its specialized museums. For a nearby escape from summer heat, an easy destination is 9,000-foot Mount Lemmon, reached by paved roadway just out of town.

THE ARIZONA SONORA DESERT MUSEUM: Reached via Anklam
Road over Gates Pass, 14 miles from downtown, "the museum," as it's called
around Tucson, is competing with the Grand Canyon as the prime tourist attraction in Arizona, and doing so in a natural piece of desert, just sand and cactus,
that might be thought incapable of generating anybody's interest—until you
look closer. All the animals of the desert live here, and all the plants too, in habitats so carefully nurtured that the place succeeds in doing what zoos always hope
to do: take you right into the lives of the animals as if you were an invisible ob-
server. A piece of the **Sonoran Desert,** which stretches from central Arizona
down into Sonora and Baja California in Mexico, is preserved here as the normal,
living background for the animals, and the job has been done so well that the
museum has rapidly attained an international reputation for general excellence.

One of four deserts on the North American continent, which also includes
the Great Basin, the Mojave, and the Chihuahuan, the Sonoran Desert is low and
hot, its lowest spot holding summer temperatures on the surface as high as
200° F. Solar radiation can become so intense that it can take all the water from a
plant. Annual rainfall in the whole desert averages under three inches, and there
are stretches of as long as two years when it never rains at all. But even in the most
desolate parts, plants survive by adapting. A classic example here is the creosote
bush, with leaves so small they check the loss of water in intense heat. The trick
makes it the most prevalent plant in the whole Sonoran Desert. To reduce water
loss it will drop its leaves or even die back to the ground. Then when the rain
finally comes again, the plant revives.

In spite of the minimal rainfall the Sonoran Desert is lush compared to certain other deserts in the world, and it has some 1,500 species of plants. It is this
variety, and the diversity of animal life that exists along with the plant life, that
makes the Sonoran Desert both difficult and fascinating to study. There are arid

areas typical of deserts where nothing seems to survive at all, and there are other places where high mountain slopes have pine and fir forests.

Some species of animals are unique to the Sonoran desert. One of these is the **Gila monster,** one of the world's two poisonous lizards, though it will attack only if provoked. (The legend that it won't give up on its bite until the sun goes down is a false one.)

The habitat missing in this particular part of the desert was limestone caves, so to remedy this lacuna the museum built its own, with a true-to-life authenticity so painstakingly done that many visitors refuse to believe the caves are man-made, right down (or up) to their stalagmites and stalactites.

A fascinating resident of the museum is the **packrat,** a nocturnal rodent which is either eating or nestbuilding, making its home in a prickly pear or cholla cactus, although sometimes it will move into a tree or a cave—the nests get as big as six feet wide and three feet high, and are built of anything a packrat can get its little paws on. Small household items, even watches and rings, sometimes turn up in their nests. A packrat will even use an old packrat nest instead of building its own, and in fact scientists here have found artifacts in these nests dating back as far as 14,000 years, and the evidence is that the nests were occupied the whole time. The animal binds its junkpile with a substance called urine cement, and picking apart an ancient packrat midden is like looking back in time. One midden had seeds and bones from prehistoric mammals and birds long since extinct, dating back 12,000 years.

Other residents turn up in these nests. The blood-sucking conenose, or kissing bug, for example, lives in these nests, feeding off the rodent and going out only infrequently for the blood of some other luckless beast. The black widow and brown recluse spiders also sometimes move into the nests, as do lizards and scorpions, all indebted to the packrat for their home.

The richest, densest animal and plant life in the Sonoran Desert is in the **Arizona Upland,** where there are mountain ranges; legume trees and cacti are the more prolific plants here. The green-barked palo verde is the most common of these trees, which can engage in photosynthesis through that bark even when all the leaves are missing. Ironwood and velvet mesquite are also common, and produce copious quantities of seeds, and the museum scientists have been on a long-term project looking into the possible use of desert plants as commercial crops. It is known, for example, that the prehistoric people who lived here used some 450 species of desert plants as food sources, some of them serving as major staples. New commercial crops most likely in this background would be the common trees mentioned. Although widely used now for broiling steaks, mesquite was traditionally also used in tools, weapons, fibers, and medicines. Its pods ripen all at once, making for easy harvesting, and when fully ripe they fall to the ground. Mesquite-pod flour is edible without cooking. Seeds from ironwood and palo verde have equal food value.

The symbol of the Sonoran Desert is the **saguaro,** a massive cactus that sometimes grows straight and sometimes twists in fanciful forms, having spectacular white and yellow blossoms. It grows as tall as 50 feet and seems to embrace other plants in a sort of family relationship. It takes 15 years for the saguaro to grow its first foot in height. Its blossom is the official state flower. Certain saguaros fan out at their top ends and are called crested, or cristate forms. Museum scientist Christopher Helms says: "Cristates are abnormal but not diseased; they are simply the weirdest form taken by a very weird plant." Saguaros survive with little rainfall with shallow root systems that absorb much water even from a light rainfall, then store it for future use. The plant also secretes a surface wax to prevent water evaporation.

Its spines grow to protect the plant from being gnawed on by thirsty animals; the spines also shade it from searing sun and prevent it from freezing in the cold weather. It grows interior wood ribs to support the tremendous weight of all the water it absorbs and holds; the ribs have traditionally served as building material for early inhabitants of the Sonoran Desert.

Many birds make their homes in saguaros, which retain warmth in the cool of the night. Gila woodpeckers and gilded flickers peck cavities in a saguaro arm for nest sites, which are often moved in on by such squatters as screech owls, elf owls, purple martins, and crested flycatchers. Often a hawk will make its nest in the fork of saguaro branches. White-winged doves feed on the saguaro blossom nectar. Lately intrusive, nonnative starlings have begun displacing native birds.

Saguaro fruit has been a staple of the neighboring Tohono O'Odham Indians for centuries. It is a greenish fruit the size of a duck's egg, holding inside a sweet red pulp full of little black seeds; the Indians make syrup, jam, and even wine out of it. In harvest season the Indians demonstrate their food-preserving techniques at the museum. Many desert rodents and other animals also devour the fruit, which serves the resident hawk as a sort of bait, even though the hawk doesn't eat the fruit himself.

The **kangaroo rat**—neither kangaroo nor rat—is an amazing example of an adaptation to an environment: it survives its entire lifetime without having to drink water. It does this by the use of kidneys much more highly developed than those of humans. Its vital fluids come from a metabolic breakdown of the plants it eats, and it loses no moisture from sweating, as it lacks sweat glands. Its long hind legs reduce the area of the body and the time the body is exposed to the hot ground surface. Another adaptation of this strange beast is its hearing, four times sharper than that of human beings. It can hear the faint scraping sound a snake makes in the sand or the flapping of an owl's wings in time to seek the shelter of its burrow.

Among common residents of the museum are spiders such as the **tarantula,** which may be seen ambling across a path. A young woman ranger on duty may stoop down to it to say hello and give it a little pat. If it raises its tail end in warning, she backs off, but the bite of this big spider is not deadly. The tarantula suffers from an undeserved reputation perpetrated by horror movies; it will bite only to protect itself, and has no venom. The smaller black widow, with the tiny red hourglass figure on the abdomen, is the dangerous one.

Passive defense is the art of the hundreds of species of **moths and butterflies** in the desert, camouflaging themselves from predators' eyes. Others resemble species that taste bad to birds, so predators leave them alone, as well as the originals that really do taste bad. Others have eye spots that appear on their wings resembling the eyes of a fierce owl.

There is a first-rate exhibit of **scorpions** here, some of which merit their reputations as dangerous to man, the bark scorpion especially. **Centipedes** have only 42 legs, not 100, and contrary to another legend can bite only with the mouth, not the feet. Desert snakes such as the **rattler** have a pit in the side of the head that serves them as a heat sensor to detect the presence of prey.

Among the most beautiful animals displayed are the **desert cats:** mountain lion, bobcat, and jaguarundi, occasionally still seen in the wild in the U.S. part of the Sonoran Desert, and the rarer jaguar, margay, and ocelot, which live in remote areas of the Mexican state of Sonora. Extremely rare, because of hunting for its beautiful fur, the **ocelot** has been on the endangered list for more than a decade. Now a few are being imported into the U.S. for breeding. Its relative, the margay, is an acrobat with rotating hind feet that let it hang from branches or move along upside-down like a sloth; it can leap off a tree and catch itself on a branch down below or run down a tree trunk head-first. The bobcat never occupies terrain without cover of some sort. The jaguarundi has short legs like a weasel and short fur. The habitat settings where these cats are displayed are among the best and most successful in the world both from the point of view of the visiting animal watcher and from that of the beasts themselves.

The museum was founded in 1952 by conservationist Arthur Pack, editor of *Nature* magazine, and William H. Carr of the American Museum of Natural History in New York. Carr saw the long-term aim of the museum "as a means of helping man to recognize and assume his responsibilities toward nature in order to gain some hope of assuring his future." A private, nonprofit institution, the museum shows over 300 species of plants and 200 species of animals, all in natural backgrounds just like that of the desert beyond the museum boundaries. It is one of the rare displays of living animals in the world where the viewer does not feel sorry for the animals because of their captivity. A mountain habitat covering an acre opened recently for mountain lions, black bears, wolves, and deer.

You can also see through underground windows a tunnel for burrowing animals; areas for Mexican wolves, black bears, and prairie dogs; a small mountain for bighorn sheep and antelope; and the geologically oriented Earth Sciences Center. That man-made cave, incidentally, is real enough to be the home for live bats.

Among stops visitors make on a tour of the museum, which ought to be given half a day, are the insect and reptile houses; the various breeds of cats in natural surroundings; the areas for javelina, coati, deer, kit fox, and coyote; a small cat grotto; otter and beaver pools visible from both top and below through glass; a walk-in aviary; an area for amphibians, fishes, and scorpions; demonstration gardens and cactus gardens; and a chuckawalla and tortoise house—among other separate sections, all connected by paved pathways. Demonstrations and talks are given at the ocotillo ramada near the orientation center at the entrance as well as at the palm ramada.

The Arizona Sonora Desert Museum (tel. 883-1380) is open every day of the year: from June 1 to Labor Day hours are 7 a.m. to sundown; other months, 8:30 a.m. to sundown. The admission charge is $6 for adults, $1 for ages 6 to 12; under 6, free. One charge covers all exhibits. Although the most direct route from downtown Tucson is via Gates Pass, drivers with trailers or motor homes are advised to take a somewhat longer route via Ajo Way and Kinney Road.

Talks and program listings are posted in the patio at the entrance. In Tucson Mountain Park, next door, there are picnic areas and campgrounds. The museum has a snackbar with dining areas indoors and out. Indoor exhibits are all in airconditioned buildings, and there are shade ramadas and water fountains around the grounds.

MUSEUMS IN TUCSON: The **Tucson Museum of Art,** 140 N. Main Ave. (tel. 624-2333), is open for adults, Tuesday through Saturday from 10 a.m. to 5 p.m. and on Sunday from 1 to 5 p.m. Admission is $2 for adults, $1 for seniors and students; free on Tuesday.

In a modern structure with ramps descending to lower levels at a gentle angle, the museum emphasizes western and Hispanic art as well as contemporary southwestern crafts, and pre-Columbian arts and archeology. There are western paintings by Albert Bierstadt, Frederic Remington, Charles M. Russell, and Newell Convers Wyeth. In its 20,000 square feet of display space the museum has a number of temporary shows, each held for five to six weeks, besides permanent exhibits. A quote from Joshua Taylor, late director of the National Gallery of Art, gives a sense of the importance western art takes here: "To build a collection of western art is a tribute to a concept—or corner of the mind—that has been a vital spark in our thinking over a long period of time. The works of art are not only a record of what happened, but perpetuate that happening—or would-be happening—to keep alive the image of wonder and the possible that we have long symbolically called 'the West.' The West has always been looked upon as a place where one finds those values that give emotional meaning to daily life."

Guided tours in English and Spanish are available daily from 10 a.m. to 5 p.m., and there are docent tours on Friday at 1:30 p.m. Crafts made by Tucson artisans are among items in a sales shop.

The **University of Arizona Museum of Art,** Speedway Boulevard at Park Avenue (tel. 621-7567), has permanent collections dating from the Middle Ages to modern times, and in addition mounts a dozen special exhibitions each year. It is open free of charge Monday through Saturday from 9 a.m. to 5 p.m. and noon to 5 p.m. on Sunday. There are works by such European artists as Picasso, Joan Miró, and Aristide Maillol, and others by Americans of various eras, including Frederic Remington, Stuart Davis, Edward Hopper, and Robert Rauschenberg.

The **Arizona Historical Society Museum,** 949 E. 2nd St. (tel. 628-5774), also next to the university campus, has a series of rooms on various parts of the state's history. It is open free of charge Monday through Saturday from 10 a.m. to 4 p.m. and on Sunday from noon to 4 p.m. It is also the headquarters of the Arizona Historical Society.

A display of brands used on cattle, burned into leather hide, sets the western tone. The samples were used for the purpose of filing the design of each brand with the Territorial Livestock Sanitary Board, before the advent of statehood in 1912. Hand-held radio receivers provide a talking description of a copper-mining shaft with an elevator cage, a drill, and mining figures. A postal history museum shows the first airmail delivery made in the city, when one Katherine Stinson flew a bag of mail in a single-engine airplane from the local fairgrounds to the main post office and dropped out a bag of mail; the date was November 5, 1915. An admired vehicle here is an imposing 1923 Studebaker Big Six, called "The Sheriff" because a dozen sheriffs around the state owned them. A Hispanic folkloric tradition is the *dicho* box, where old Spanish adages, many copied and donated by museumgoers, can be read. An example is *Al decir las verdades se pierdan las amistades* ("Telling the truth means losing friends").

The **Arizona State Museum,** Park Avenue at University (tel. 621-6302), also on campus, goes from artifacts and historic information to prehistoric Arizona Indians and their relationship to the environment. Topics ranging outside the Southwest are also considered in temporary exhibitions of various kinds having an anthropological interest. A game the early Indians played was trying to shoot an arrow through a small round hole in a large disc-like stone; the question that comes to mind was whether they ever thought to use this stone as a wheel, and if not, why not. A fence for trapping rabbits, also devised from prehistoric-relic research, looks like a modern fish weir of the kind used for trapping herring in the Bay of Fundy, except that when the rabbits were caught within the maze-like enclosure they were simply bopped by stone clubs. The world's oldest corn-cob is shown here, found in an excavation—it is 3,000 years old. The museum is open free of charge Monday through Saturday from 9 a.m. to 5 p.m. and on Sunday from 2 to 5 p.m.

Still another art center on the campus is the **Center for Creative Photography,** 843 E. University (tel. 621-7968), which has exhibitions of photographs out of historic archives as well as work by contemporary artists in the medium. Open to the public free of charge, the center is open Monday through Friday from 9 a.m. to 5 p.m. and on Sunday from noon to 5 p.m. Its photographic library with print collections is one of the major U.S. facilities anywhere.

Fort Lowell Museum, Craycroft and Fort Lowell Roads (tel. 885-3832), has parts of a reconstructed frontier military post open to visitors free of charge. Hours are Wednesday through Saturday from 10 a.m. to 4 p.m. (in summer, 9 a.m. to 1 p.m.). Fort Lowell was made a permanent base in 1866 and became the major depot for troops fighting the Apaches. Its location east of the city was moved in 1875 when new buildings (the present ones restored here) were built. Besides guarding supplies and escorting wagon trains, the garrison made many expeditions as far as the Mexican border chasing Apaches. Fort Lowell troops took part in the famous Geronimo campaigns in the 1880s; at capacity it had 18 officers and 239 enlisted men. By 1886, with the surrender of Geronimo, the main Indian wars in the region were at an end and the contingent was reduced in size. The post was at last abandoned in 1891.

The museum building is a reconstruction of the commanding officer's quarters, in front of which runs Cottonwood Lane, with trees now replanted as they grew originally along officers' row. The room arrangement is that of the 1880s, and the building is furnished as it would have been in 1886 when lived in by the post commander, Col. August V. Kautz of the Eighth U.S. Infantry, and his wife, Fanny, and their children. There is a parlor, dining room, bedroom, and the commander's office. Display cases in the halls show uniforms and equipment of the soldiers of the time, and there are maps, documents, and photographs from the days when there was an active military scene here. Nearby are ruins of the post hospital. Ruins of enlisted men's barracks are also still visible across the parade ground, and may also be restored in the future by the Arizona Historical Society, which serves as custodian.

The **Pima Air Museum,** 6000 E. Valencia Rd., off exit 269 of I-10 (tel. 574-0462), is open seven days a week from 9 a.m. to 5 p.m. (but no new admissions after 4 p.m.), charging adults $4; senior citizens, $3; children 10 to 17, $2; under 10, free. It displays 140 aircraft of various provenances and vintages, smaller craft in a display building with 20,000 square feet of space that also has engines, flight simulators, uniforms, and aviation memorabilia. Open to the public when guides are available is a DC-6 used by both Presidents Kennedy and Johnson. A Lockheed "Constellation" used as an Air Corps cargo carrier in World War II returned to civilian life as a TWA passenger liner after the war. A Consolidated "Liberator" bomber served in greater numbers than any other bomber in World War II; the museum's exemplar served in the Air Force of India until 1969. A war trainer is a Fairchild "Cornell." There is a Boeing Stratoliner, a B-17 Fortress, a C-124 Globemaster, and a P-63E Bell King Cobra, among many others. A B-52 Stratofortress is the plane that transported the fast X-15s that zoomed to the edges of outer space.

HISTORIC TUCSON: The downtown area called **El Presidio** still has remnants of walls that protected the presidio, or fort, that was built here in 1775. Bricks from these walls were used in the Edward Nye Fish House and in the Hiram Stevens House next door. A park extant today takes up what was the southern half of the presidio. On the west is City Hall, at the northwest corner of which is the **Kino Memorial,** a monument to Fr. Eusebio Francisco Kino (1645–1711). The dark stone of this monument was named by the Pima Indian words *schook* and *son,* meaning "dark" and "foot of," or, together, the dark stone from the foot of the mountain. In the Spanish pronunciation it came out Tucson.

The original fort here was some 750 feet square, bounded by the present Main, Pennington, Church, and Washington Streets, and its adobe walls were 12 feet high. Signs proclaiming original street names have been placed here by the Historical Commission that has restored some of the structures: Calle de la Guardia and Calle Real.

On Main Street at no. 119, the **Edward Nye Fish House,** dating from 1868, was built on the site of an old barracks, and has high ceilings of *vigas* (wood beams) with lacings of saguaro ribs. This and the **Hiram Stevens House,** next door (now the site of the Janos Restaurant), were the social center of Tucson a century ago. They are both examples of Sonoran-style architecture popular in the merging of the cultures—Anglo-American from the east, Hispanic from the south. Each house is of adobe, with recessed doorways and a center hall called a zaguan. A common courtyard linked the houses. The owner of the Stevens House, a Territorial representative to Congress, tried to shoot his wife here, but the legend is that a silver comb in her hair deflected the bullet and saved her, after which Hiram Stevens shot himself dead. This house and the Fish House are both the property of the Tucson Museum of Art, which uses Fish as a library and Stevens for an office and restaurant.

In the northwest courtyard of the park, a dark stone from Sentinel Peak marks the site of a Bicentennial **time capsule** buried in 1976, to be opened in the year 2026. One of the oldest buildings in the city is also part of the museum complex—**La Casa Cordova,** used as a display area for materials of the Hispanic history and culture of Tucson. Also of adobe and brick, the **Leonardo Romero House,** dating from 1868, is part of the museum art school.

Across Washington Street is the **Sam Hughes House,** dating from 1864. It was gradually enlarged after Hughes moved in with his bride, Atanacia Santa Cruz, and they began having to put up an eventual total of 15 children. North of this house on the west side of Main is the 1900 **Albert Steinfeld House,** in Spanish Mission-style brick stucco, of a local department-store family. At Main and Franklin, the 1877 **Rosalia Verdugo House** has old-style drain pipes for taking water from a flat roof. East on Franklin is the **McCleary House,** another Anglo-Mexican family homestead, originally a flat-roofed adobe with Victorian fanciwork added later.

The **Hoff House,** at Franklin and Church, dates from 1880. A French stonemason built the original structure housing the restaurant **El Charro** in 1900, a traditional eating place serving what it calls "true Sonoran cuisine." It is at 311 N. Court (tel. 622-5465). Nearby, at the northeast corner of the old presidio wall, is the pit house site where in 1954 archeologists found the remains of an Indian hut occupied between A.D. 700 and 900 and part of a Hohokam village of the same period. The discovery could only be mapped and photographed before it was asphalted over for a parking lot.

An original adobe house built between 1862 and 1875 has saguaro-rib ceilings and a corner fireplace, and is called the **Soledad Jacome House,** at 182 N. Court. Paintings showing scenes of 1,000 years of life in the "Old Pueblo," as Tucson is nicknamed, are shown at **Governor's Corner** in the Valley National Bank. It occupies the site of the former home of an early Territorial governor. The paintings are by Sheridan Oman, and visitors are welcome to view them during banking hours.

South across Alameda, the **Pima County Courthouse** combines various regional architectures in columns, arches, a decorated façade, a tiled dome, and an interior court. A part of the original presidio wall is preserved on the second floor of the building.

South along Church Street you can see the five flags that over the centuries have flown over the city: the Royal Crest of Spain (to 1821), the flag of the Republic of Mexico (to 1854), the Stars and Stripes, the Confederate Stars and Bars (briefly in 1862), and the state flag.

The **Charles O. Brown House** on Broadway has now become the Old Adobe Patio, a small complex of shops. **St. Augustine Cathedral,** dating from 1896, is modeled on the Mexican cathedral of Querétaro. Above the entrance is a bronze statue of St. Augustine and sculpted likenesses of Arizona saguaro and yucca, and a horned toad.

The **Tucson Community Center,** completed in 1971 on 18 acres, has a sports arena, a convention hall, a concert hall, a theater, gardens, pavilions, and parking areas. Within the complex is the **John C. Fremont House,** at 151 S. Granada, called the Casa del Gobernador, built in the 1850s by the family of José Maria Soza. It became the residence of a territorial governor in the 1880s and has been restored to architectural styles of that time. It is used as a branch display of the Arizona Historical Society and is open Wednesday through Saturday from 10 a.m. to 4 p.m. La Placita is a Spanish-style shopping complex around the Plaza de la Mesilla, with patios named for various Mexican cities. Here is the **Samaniego House,** a typical town house of the late 1800s.

South of the Community Center on Cushing Street is the **Montijo House,** dating from the Civil War and later remodeled into an elegant Victorian residence. Nearby on Stone Street is **El Frontizero,** the site of a Spanish-language newspaper founded by Carlos Velasco in 1878. During restoration of the building hand-set type was found under the boards of the floor.

Also on Cushing is the **Cushing St. Bar,** which combines an early country store and the Joseph Ferrin home, built over a century ago. Furnished in 1880s style, the walls of the restaurant are embellished with photographs dating back to that era showing how the neighborhood looked when the place was new. There is a collection of Mexican millstones in the patio.

Also in this barrio historic district south of the center is the renowned Wishing Shrine, **El Tiradito,** which celebrates the legend of a shepherd named Juan Oliveras who was murdered in a lovers' triangle. His body was buried in unconsecrated ground, where townspeople lit candles for him and prayed for him—and today candles are still burned here by those hoping wishes will be answered.

Walking tours are held every Saturday from November to March at 10 a.m. starting from the Fremont House, for a fee of $2 per person. For information, call 622-0956.

OLD TUCSON: Old Tucson, 201 S. Kinney Rd. (tel. 883-6457), is 12 miles west of downtown Tucson via Anklam Road and Gates Pass (trailers and motor homes should take the route via Ajo Way). This is a movie set originally built for the film *Arizona* in 1939. It gives another sort of history apart from that of the historic districts—a history of fictitious heroes and bad guys, showdowns, barroom brawls. It is the glorification of the macho gunslinger, and for nearly half a century it has drawn steady crowds. The place is open daily from 9 a.m. to 5 p.m., for a $6 admission charge (which includes several rides—a carousel, a Stutz-Bearcat replica, a ride into a mine, a stagecoach ride, and a narrow-guage train trip).

Over the years scores of movies have used the backgrounds here for their action, and more recently television series and commercials have also taken advantage of the authentic-looking saloon, sheriff's office, doctor's office, general store, and operable 1872 Reno steam locomotive. There is a restaurant and oldtime soda fountain on the premises.

SAGUARO NATIONAL MONUMENT: Saguaro National Monument preserves fascinating desert country in two units, one to the east and one to the west of Tucson, where the huge, dominating saguaro cactus looms everywhere on the horizon, their strangely angled arms seeming to semaphore some mysterious desert message. West of Tucson 15 miles, with its visitor center on Kinney Road a couple of miles beyond the Arizona Sonora Desert Museum, is the 21,254-acre **Tucson Mountains Unit,** containing a dense, vigorous cactus forest.

There are good dirt roads to nature trailheads, scenic overlooks, and other points of interest, and picnic sites with tables and shelters. To the east of the city 16 miles is the visitor center of the 62,322-acre **Rincon Mountains Unit,** occupying a saguaro forest spreading up against the slopes of the Rincon range. Each visitor center has displays of flora and fauna in the surrounding cactus land and information on roads and trails.

A nine-mile **Cactus Forest Drive** within the Rincon Unit lets visitors examine the desert scrub life closely. A paved one-way road runs through the saguaro forest. At the Javelina picnic area, a one-mile nature trail leads past a variety of cactuses and other desert plants, and affords easy photography opportunities. Except in summer, naturalist walks are conducted, with times posted in the visitor centers. Hiking into the Rincon Mountains, although a strenuous activity, is also possible, but overnight backpacking requires that a free permit be taken out with a ranger at the visitor center beforehand. From the lower levels of the desert to the peaks of the Rincons you pass through six different plant communities: desert scrub, grassland transition, oak woodland, oak-pine woodland, Ponderosa pine forest, and finally on the north slope of Mica Mountain, a Douglas-fir and white-fir forest.

It is at the lower levels, in the desert scrub community, that the giant saguaro grows. As visitors reach higher elevations and encounter different plant communities, they also find a differing variety of animals associated with each climatic tier. Among birds, there are some 200 species, some living here year round. There are 50 species of reptiles, but fewer mammals, mostly bats and nocturnal hunters, the rodents. Each group has some species in every different level of the park—desert, foothills, and mountaintops.

Down below at the level of the visitor center, the nature trails, and the picnic areas, what to look for includes desert tortoise, gophers, coachwhip snakes, ground squirrels, peccaries, coyotes, and mule deer. Common birds are Gambel's quail, the Gila woodpecker, the curve-billed thrasher, and at higher levels, the Mexican junco, Mexican jay, Steller's jay, and rufous-sided towhee. Also there are many cliff chipmunks and white-tailed deer at the higher elevations. Bird sounds are special in the desert, and might be the whistle of the curve-billed thrasher, the churring of the cactus wren, or the woodpecker's tap-tap; beyond those sounds may come the yips of coyotes in the distance.

But it is the saguaro, for which the park is named, that is the star in catching the imagination of visitors. By the time it has reached 20 feet in height and has developed a first branch, a saguaro will already be 75 years old. It may top out at 200 feet and live to be 200 years old. A mature plant, weighing several tons, can absorb much water after a heavy summer rain. During the long dry periods it uses its own stored water, shrinking as it does so.

Saguaros provide food for many desert animals. Birds eat the fruit and seeds while they are still on the branches. Coyotes, mule deer, and peccaries eat the fruit after it has ripened and fallen to the ground. Saguaros make sites for nests for a variety of bird species. The Gila woodpecker and the gilded flicker drill holes for their nests in the fleshy stems. Sap from the interior of the saguaro dries and forms a hard lining on the wall of the pocket. When the woodpeckers and flickers have raised their young and have moved out, other birds—screech owls, elf owls the size of sparrows, purple martins, sparrow hawks, and flycatchers—take over the property for their own families. The intersection of the trunk and an arm is a favorite site for a hawk's nest.

Desert temperatures reach 100° during the summer. There are sporadic, violent summer thunderstorms all summer, and sparser winter rainfall from December to mid-March, but the total accumulation is only 11 inches. The riotous displays of desert wildflowers reach their peak in April, with blooms appearing irregularly between February and May. Some years are much better than others for wildflower displays, depending on how nearly ideal the combinations of rain, sunlight, and temperatures may be. Another short blooming season, that for certain other annual wildflowers, usually hits its peak in August.

OTHER DESTINATIONS: The **Reid Park Zoo,** 900 S. Randolph Way (tel. 791-4022), is open daily from 9:30 a.m. to 4:30 p.m. Admission is $1 for adults, 50¢ for children under 15 and seniors. The zoo has natural habitat exhibits for animals from all parts of the world, including polar bears, rhinoceroses, and elephants. There is a gift shop and snackbar. From Africa, residents include zebras, addaxes, ostriches, and storks. From Asia come blackbuck, nilgal, muntjac, and the sarus crane. The Wallaby and emu are from Australia. There are familiars like lions, tigers, and monkeys, and rarer species such as the binturong and the kookaburra.

An open-air ride on the **Sabino Canyon Shuttle** (tel. 749-2861), departing from the Sabino Canyon visitor center off Sabino Canyon Road, east of downtown, reached via Speedway Boulevard and Tanque Verde Road, permits riders to stop at any of the scenic sites along the way and pick up the ride on the next bus that comes along. It runs from 9 a.m. to 4 p.m. daily, for a fare of $4. A desert oasis in the foothills of the Catalina Mountains, the canyon is watered by Sabino Creek and has shady stands of cottonwood, sycamore, ash, and willow trees. The shuttle bus is the only vehicle allowed on the seven-mile loop, although bicycles and horseback riders are also permitted here. A two-mile hike to Seven Falls, a series of breaks and rapids in the creek ending in a deep pool, is a favorite outing for locals. Monthly moonlight rides are usually booked up some days ahead, and take visitors through the canyon with the lights doused on the shuttle to give the natural splendor full play. The visitor center is administered by the U.S. Forest Service.

Star and planet shows are among the programs at **Flandreau Planetarium,** Cherry Avenue at East 3rd Street (tel. 621-4556), which has exhibits on the solar system, optical sciences, the Milky Way, meteorites, and astronomical art. It is open daily except Monday from 1 to 5:30 p.m. and 7 to 10 p.m. Admission is $3. From dusk on, visitors may use a 16-inch telescope to explore the skies. Time and space trips are simulated by a star projector in the 50-foot-high Star Theater. For a taped report of current shows, call 621-4706.

Mission San Xavier del Bac, on San Xavier Road off I-19 nine miles south of town (tel. 294-2624), known as the "White Dove of the Desert," is open every day from 6 a.m. to sunset free of charge, with masses daily at 8 a.m. plus two more on Sunday at 10:30 a.m. and 12:30 p.m. Often pictured as a sort of trademark of this part of Arizona, the mission is considered to be the finest example of mission architecture in the U.S., with its two white towers flanking an ornately carved central façade of tan stone. Completed in 1797, the mission occupies a site known traditionally as the *bac*—the place where water appears, because the Santa Cruz River appears nearby out of an underground passage. Foundations of an earlier church here were laid in 1700 by Fr. Eusebio Francisco Kino who named it San Xavier in honor of his patron, St. Francis Xavier.

Of the two towers, only the left one is complete with a dome; why the other was never finished has never been discovered. The name of its architect and details of its building are also unknown. It has a blending of various architectural styles that somehow result in near-perfect harmony: Moorish, Byzantine, and Mexican Renaissance. The structure consists of a series of domes and arches, with wood used only in window and door frames. All the surfaces are decorated, and there are many paintings of religious figures. Goal of many pilgrimages to the mission is the reclining statue of St. Francis Xavier seen to the left side of the chapel as you face the main altar. On either side of the communion rail, the images of lions represent the Lions of Castille on the coat-of-arms of the Spanish king in the late 18th century.

The ornate façade in its tan-reddish tint was left untouched in the most recent restoration of the mission in 1906, and traces of original paintwork still remain. Carved surfaces show curved arabesques, statue-like figures in niches, and looped draperies fashioned in brick and mortar. A rounded gable made of a double S-curve crowns the façade, below which the Franciscan coat-of-arms stands out in bold relief, an escutcheon displaying a cord, part of the Franciscan habit, above a cross, upon which are nailed the bare right arm of Christ and the clothed left arm of St. Francis. The whole is enclosed by a grapevine referring to the biblical line "I am the vine, you are the branches," from the Book of John. Monograms of Jesus and Mary are woven into the intricate vine design. In the far corners there are lions rampant—a salute to the Spanish sovereign. Of four figures in niches, the fourth is thought to represent St. Lucy. It is blackened by smoke and covered with candle wax because of a tradition the local Indians have always honored in invoking her aid against sore eyes and giving her thanks by burning candles to her.

To the left, inside the church, is a low doorway leading to the baptistry, a vaulted chamber with a brick pedestal holding a copper basin for baptisms. Farther along the inside wall of the church on the left is a door leading outside, and opposite this door, on the right-hand wall, is a false, painted door put there for visual balance. If you take the time to look closely at the lions on the altar, you note that they have ears set strangely on their foreheads, and that one of them has human hands instead of paws. Directly above the altar table, a statue of St. Francis Xavier occupies a place of honor.

Outside, to the left of the church is a small mortuary chapel with three bells in a pierced gable atop its roof. Beyond, the old cemetery has no markers, but within the chapel a marble slab marks the burial place of two early padres of the mission. Translated, the Latin inscription reads: "Here rest from their labors two renowned missionaries who departed this life in the midst of an arduous and very successful career in this region."

The first Friday after Easter is the day of the annual San Xavier Pageant and Festival that celebrates the founding of the mission. Mounted Conquistadors appear, as well as Indian dancers from nearby Tohono O'Odham communities and Yaqui groups south of the border. Bonfires and fireworks add to the excitement, which begins in the morning with the opening of booths purveying handcrafts and various local foods. On October 3 and 4 the church is lighted and there are fireworks also to mark the feast day of St. Francis of Assisi. Indians arrive in a procession for prayer at sunset. A similar ceremonial takes place on December 3 for the feast day of St. Francis Xavier.

5. MUSIC AND OTHER PERFORMING ARTS

Several theatrical and dance companies add to the cultural life of Tucson, where the musical arts are solidly represented by the Tucson Symphony and the Arizona Opera Company. Besides these sources, the University of Arizona has its own theatrical and musical events, and there is a citywide festival of the arts involving musical concerts of various kinds. As for nightlife, there is a wealth of country and western and rock music in town, and some jazz of various vintages too.

MOSTLY CLASSICAL: The **Tucson Symphony,** 443 S. Stone Ave. (tel. 792-9155), in its 61st season in 1989–1990, is the oldest symphony in the Southwest, and schedules a dozen concerts between September and April, including pop concerts and special events, in the music hall of the Tucson Community Center. The musical director and conductor is William McGlaughlin. Special concert buses depart from Park Mall, El Con Mall, and Casas Adobe Shopping Center; for information on them, call 625-8989. All concerts start at 8 p.m.

Free concerts of the **Tucson Pops Orchestra** are given on four Sundays in June and July in the Reid Park Bandshell. Audiences bring supper picnics and blankets and spread out on the grounds to hear the music. For exact times, call 791-4873.

The **Arizona Opera Company,** 3501 N. Mountain Ave. (tel. 293-4336), in 1989–1990 in its 19th season, produces four operas between October and May that are presented in the music hall of the Tucson Community Center and also in Symphony Hall in Phoenix. Tickets are $8 to $32, and may be reserved one month ahead.

Ballet Arizona, 186 E. Broadway (tel. 628-7446), gives three performances each year, one of them always the *Nutcracker* at Christmastime, with the Tucson Symphony. The state's only resident ballet company, it performs in the music hall of the Tucson Community Center.

The **Southern Arizona Light Opera Company,** Tucson Community Center (tel. 323-7888), produces light opera under its founder and director Hal Hundley using local talent and a full orchestra. Such shows as *West Side Story* have been presented.

The **Arizona Theater Company,** 56 W. Congress (tel. 622-2823), presents plays in the Tucson Community Center and in the Little Theater. The only professional resident theater in the Southwest, the theater stages its productions in Phoenix as well as in its hometown of Tucson. In 20 years it has presented over 100 plays, ranging from such classics as *Hamlet, Tartuffe,* and *My Fair Lady,* to contemporary plays like *Equus* and *The Elephant Man.*

The **Gaslight Theatre,** 7000 E. Tanque Verde Rd. (tel. 886-9428), has melodramas suitable for hissing and cheering Wednesday through Sunday, with an 8 p.m. curtain on Wednesday and Thursday, at 7 and 9:30 p.m. on Friday and Saturday, and at 7 p.m. on Sunday. Audiences sit at tables where throughout the proceedings they may eat free popcorn or order pizza, nachos, and hot dogs with soda, beer, or wine. This is a favorite destination of parents taking the kids out on the town.

Half a dozen new productions every year are staged by the **Invisible Theater,** 1400 N. First Ave. (tel. 882-9721), including a musical, classics, and off-Broadway plays. The small theater has space for only 78 in the audience. Starting its 19th season in 1989, the company, according to artistic director Susan Claassen, "takes its name from the invisible energy that flows between performer and audience."

The University of Arizona has theaters with differing aims. One is the **Studio** (tel. 621-1162), an experimental theater group of Department of Drama students. The **Mainstage University Theater** (tel. 621-1162) celebrates its 65th season in 1989, providing professional-level theater by the Department of Drama. Five plays are scheduled from fall to spring.

A month-long celebration of the city's ethnic variety is called the **Tucson Festival,** and goes on during the Easter season. A number of music and dance concerts are presented during these weeks. For information, call the Tucson Festival Society (tel. 622-6911).

MOSTLY POPULAR: Tucson is the southern Arizona center for occasional stage concerts by rock bands and groups into reggae, blues rock, ska, new wave, heavy metal, and blends of these and other styles (including blues, jazz, and bluegrass). The **Arizona Ballroom** of the Student Union of the University of Arizo-

na, the **Soundstage** at Old Tucson (the movie-set Wild West attraction west of the city), the **Unitarian-Universalist Church** and the **D.A.V. Hall** at 1730 N. First Ave. are all scenes of musical celebrations drawing large crowds of enthusiasts.

Rock and Blues

Berky's Bar, 5769 E. Speedway (tel. 296-1981), is the venue of such rhythm-and-blues groups as the Blue Lizards, playing Thursday through Saturday. Two blocks east at the **Chicago Bar,** 5954 E. Speedway (tel. 748-8169), there is live music every night but Monday with such groups as Sam Taylor and the Statesboro Blues Band or a "techno reggae rock" outfit dubbed Neon Prophet. A group playing what is mysteriously described as "psychedelic garage-styled space pop" occasionally holds forth at the 1940s-style **Club Congress,** 311 E. Congress (tel. 622-8848), in the restored old Congress Hotel downtown.

Reggae is offered along with blues and rock groups at **Gentle Ben's,** 841 N. Tyndall Ave. (tel. 622-7983). Rock music out of the 1950s is often served up by the Cadillacs at **Little Anthony's,** 7000 E. Tanque Verde (tel. 886-9428). Live music with a view is the scene at the Westward Look Resort north of town, in the **Lookout Lounge,** 245 E. Ina Rd. (tel. 297-1151), where a group called Jamtrak often provides the sound, nightly Tuesday through Saturday.

For fans of video rock the scene is **Loews Ventana Canyon Resort,** 7000 N. Resort Dr. (tel. 299-2020), in the Flying V Bar and Grill, where an electric Hollywood vs. Wild West décor is turned on nightly at 9 p.m. as a video disco with two huge screens on the dance floor's walls and smaller monitors at each table.

Top-40 rock is played nightly by such groups as Necromancer or Dave Pratt and the Sex Machine at **Mudbuggs,** 136 N. Park Ave. (tel. 882-9844). Blues-based rock is the specialty of musicians styling themselves the Boogie Animals, at **Jeff's Pub,** 112 S. Camino Seco Rd. (tel. 886-1001), playing Wednesday through Saturday.

Tucson's longest-running blues jam goes on every Sunday starting at 7 p.m. at **Poco Loco,** 3840 E. Speedway (tel. 326-7637), presenting groups like the Blue Tigers or Dave Prez and Friends. There is occasional "rowdy blues" Wednesday through Saturday at **Sneak Joint,** 1120 S. Wilmot Rd. (tel. 790-8316).

Jazz

A jazz trio called the Connection sometimes entertains at **Café Sweetwater,** 340 E. 6th St. (tel. 622-6464), offering live music Thursday through Saturday. A percussion, keyboard, and vibes group led by Homer Ceron may be on tap, among other local groups, at the **Cushing Street Bar and Restaurant,** 343 S. Meyer Ave. (tel. 622-7984), open nightly except Monday.

A mainstream jazz group called Hackensack is among choices at **Coffee Etc.,** 2744 N. Campbell Ave. (tel. 881-8070), from Wednesday through the weekend.

Sunday jam sessions, often starring the Puku Puku Jazz All-Stars, go on at the **Puku Puku Lounge,** 931 E. Speedway (tel. 791-2295). The **Westward Look Resort,** 245 E. Ina Rd. (tel. 297-1151), also has a weekly jazz showcase on Sunday afternoons from 4 to 7 p.m. A weekly jazz night goes on each Wednesday thanks to the music of the Glen Olson Trio at **Gentle Ben's,** 841 N. Tyndall Ave. (tel. 622-7983).

Country and Western

Wednesday through Sunday there is C&W or bluegrass live at the **Bar M Cattle Company,** 5861 N. Oracle Rd. (tel. 888-9480). Music styled as "folk blues" is offered at **Bentley's,** 810 E. University (tel. 795-0338).

Thursday is traditional western music night at the pleasant hilltop **Hacienda del Sol,** 5601 N. Hacienda del Sol Rd. (tel. 299-1501). Mike Gainey, a singer-guitarist, is the attraction at the **Solarium,** 6444 E. Tanque Verde Rd. (tel. 886-8186), Wednesday through Saturday.

Dancing outside on a patio to lively C&W is the attraction at **Li'l Abner's** on Friday and Saturday nights. The site is 2½ miles north of Ina Road on Silverbell Road (tel. 744-2800). Wednesday through Saturday nights and Sunday afternoons are the times for country dance music by the Jacks at **Ireland's Post Time Pub and Steak House,** Craycroft and Golf Links Road (tel. 748-1656).

Live music for country-style dancing is also offered at **Gadsden's Lounge** in the Doubletree Hotel, 445 S. Alvernon (tel. 881-4200), Tuesday through Saturday.

6. SHOPPING IN THE TUCSON AREA

Southwestern arts and crafts, Mexican imports, and light garb for warm weather are all available in the widest possible choices around Tucson, though it should be noted that Nogales, on the Mexican side of the border, is only a bit over an hour away by car, a town full of Mexican-made bargains. (See Section 8, "Trips Out of Tucson.")

MOSTLY FOR ART: Specializing in paintings of the West are the **El Presidio Galleries,** at 182 and 201 N. Court Ave., in the Old Town Artisans Complex—open seven days.

Western Americana makes up much of the subject matter of paintings and other art works shown at **Rosequist Galleries,** 1615 E. Fort Lowell Rd., open Tuesday to Saturday.

The **Beth O'Donnell Gallery Ltd.,** 4340 N. Campbell Ave., has contemporary oils, watercolors, and sculpture by regional artists. Open Tuesday through Saturday.

The **Etherton,** at 424 E. 6th St., is a gallery specializing in photography and showing early works as well as recent contemporary pictures.

The gallery of Ted De Grazia, a Tucson primitive-style painter who died in 1982, shows his somewhat sentimalized pictures of Indians and bullfights; there are reproductions available. Called the **Gallery in the Sun,** it's at 6300 N. Swan Rd.

The **Sanders Galleries,** 6420 N. Campbell, has traditional bronze sculptures of cowboys and Indians. There is a branch in the Westin La Paloma, 3800 E. Sunrise Dr.

MOSTLY FOR CRAFTS: Craftwork is well represented in the Tucson area.

Old Town Artisans Complex

A warren of scores of little shops displaying and selling the work of 150 local craftspeople is the pleasant, rustic Old Town Artisans complex, behind some 19th-century row houses whose façades remain, at 186 N. Meyer Ave., downtown. Taking up a whole block in the Presidio neighborhood, the complex has a quiet unhurried atmosphere not usually found in shopping centers, with a sunny patio just right for taking a lunch break or an afternoon coffee at a table of the **Courtyard Café,** or a delicacy from the **Old Town Bake Shop:** fresh-made cheesecake, strudel, or quiches.

Two jewelers working here are **Beth Friedman,** making gold, silver, and gemstone designs; and **Joe Begay,** who makes Navajo pieces of turquoise. There is **El Presidio** art gallery previously noted. Every spring, Indian craftspeople show their wares in 30 stands during an annual spring fiesta organized for the benefit of the Tucson Indian Arts and Crafts Fund.

Some of the early life of these buildings remains. For example, in the rooms to the east, along Telles Street, there was in the last century the bottling operation of Julius Goldbaum, who built his ceiling of packing crates and used a dug basement for storage. During restoration, hand-blown bottles with the Goldbaum label were discovered, along with pre-Columbian pottery. These are currently displayed in the hallway dividing the east wing from the rest of the building. The structure is also interesting in the various treatments of wall surfaces. If you walk north along Meyer Street you see several different ways of covering adobe. In the zaguan, a covered entrance to the courtyard, the adobe bricks and hand-hewn mesquite lintels are exposed. Next to this is a room where the walls were plastered with mud from the courtyard in the traditional way. Along Washington Street the influence of Goldbaum is seen again in rooms believed to have been his residence, with redwood wall panels (imported from California) and a ceiling made of whisky barrel staves. Parts of the building date back to the 1850s; restoration began in 1978.

North Fourth Avenue Shopping District

Near the city center, this burgeoning shopping area is noted not only for arts and crafts but also for funky clothing and jewelry out of the '30s and '40s, for kitsch decorative items and furniture from the same eras, and for food specialties, including naturally grown products and exotic coffees and teas. There are coffee shops and specialized bookstores too.

Antigone Books, 403 E. 5th St., specializes in books by and about women, as well as nonsexist and "culturally diverse" children's books.

The **Cabat Studio,** at 627 N. Fourth Ave., offers crafts made here by the Cabat family: ceramics, jewelry, and paintings. Also on hand are limited-edition prints and books on cactus, flowers, missions, and saints. **El Gato Resale & Costume,** 350 N. Fourth Ave., calls itself "the cat's meow of contemporary, tropical, and vintage styles" in custom costumes, including flappers' dresses, tuxedos, and custom-made poodle skirts.

The **Folk Shop,** 425 N. Fourth Ave., sells vintage guitars, mandolins, banjos, harps, autoharps, psalteries, books, and instrument kits. A wide variety of imported food specialties is stocked at the **Food Conspiracy Co-op,** 412 N. Fourth Ave.—dairy products, fresh produce, vitamins, cheeses, coffees, and bulk foods among them.

Navajo sand paintings, Indian jewelry, and Brazilian agate, as well as burlwood clocks and polished sandstone items, are seen at **Creations Unlimited,** 500 N. Fourth Ave. Antique jewelry is the specialty of **Friske Jewelers,** 543 N. Fourth Ave.

Specializing in books on the Southwest and books published by the University of Arizona Press, **Goodbooks,** 431 N. Fourth Ave., buys, sells, and trades new and used books, and will search out rare books on request.

Nostalgia in clothing items is the theme of **How Sweet It Was,** at 636 N. Fourth Ave., a shop full of garments dating back as far as the early 1900s. The **Latin American Bookstore,** 537 N. Fourth Ave., stocks bilingual dictionaries and encyclopedias as well as classical works and books by modern writers in English and Spanish.

Another vintage clothing mart, where you may not only buy but also trade old clothes for others, is **Loose Change,** 545 N. Fourth Ave. Some antique items turn up among the more modern used items at **Lost & Found Furniture,** 340 N. Fourth Ave. A craftsman specializing in the building of guitars, banjos, and mandolins is **Michael the Luthier,** 224 N. Fourth Ave.

Handcrafted wind chimes and metal sculptures are to be seen in the workshop of their creators at **The Metal Man,** 621 N. Fourth Ave. Funky clothes as well as more practical modern outfits can be had at the **Salvation Army,** 411 N. Fourth, which also sells used books and small appliances.

Calling itself "an indoor craft fair" **Westward Junction Gifts,** 630 N. Fourth Ave., is a consignment shop. A must stop for birdlovers is the **Audubon Nature Shop** at 300 E. University Blvd. (Its rare bird alert telephone is 798-1005.)

MALLS: Shopping malls housing major department stores and scores of other shops are **El Con Mall,** 3601 E. Broadway, with Goldwaters and J. C. Penney among 120 other merchants; **Park Mall,** Broadway at Wilmot, with Diamonds and Sears among 110 stores; the **Tucson Mall,** 4500 N. Oracle Rd., with J. C. Penney, Sears, and 175 other merchants; and the **Foothills Mall,** West Ina Road at North La Cholla Boulevard, with Goldwaters and 90 others stores. Also notable are the upscale **St. Philip's Plaza,** North Campbell at River Road; and **Plaza Palomino,** 2920 N. Swan.

7. OUTDOORS AROUND TUCSON

Because of its relatively low altitude (2,400 feet) and its southern location, Tucson enjoys a mild year-round climate, hot in summer, which permits all kinds of outdoor sports and activities without a break from one end of the year to the other, although the hot hours of summer middays are usually best spent in the shade. Maximum temperatures average 64° and minimum 38° in January, while in July the range is 74° to 98°. The city has 150 tennis courts, 15 golf courses, and tracks for auto racing and greyhound racing. Tucsonans escape summer heat by visiting the heights of nearby mountains, where higher altitudes provide cooler air: Picacho Peak and Mount Lemmon among the destinations. Twelve divisions of Coronado National Forest provide 50 recreational sites within easy reach of the city. Birdwatchers visit Madera Canyon to view species of Mexican birds not seen elsewhere in the U.S. There is skiing, incidentally, in wintertime just outside Tucson, despite its southern latitude.

GOLF: Besides nine private courses, some of which offer guest privileges, Tucson has the following public courses. The three municipal courses are **El Rio,** 1400 W. Speedway (tel. 721-4229), with 18 holes over 6,464 yards, par 70; **Randolph,** 602 S. Alvernon Way (tel. 791-4161), with 18 holes over 6,893 yards, par 70; and **Silverbell,** 3600 N. Silverbell (tel. 791-5235), with 18 holes over 6,109 yards, par 72. Greens fees are $12.50; electric-cart rental, $12. Reservations ($2 fee) may be made seven days ahead by telephone at any of the municipal courses.

Other public courses are the **Arthur Pack Golf Course,** 9109 N. Thornydale Rd. (tel. 744-3322), with 18 holes over 6,800 yards, par 72; **Cliff Valley,** 5910 N. Oracle Rd. (tel. 887-6161), with 18 holes over 2,223 yards, par 54; **Desert Hills** (tel. 625-5090), in Green Valley, with 18 holes over 6,183 yards, par 72; **Dorado,** 6601 E. Speedway (tel. 885-6751), with 18 holes over 3,680 yards, par 62; **Haven** (tel. 625-4281), in Green Valley, with 18 holes over 6,868 yards, par 72; **Santa Rita,** 22,000 S. Houghton Rd. (tel. 629-9817), with 18 holes over 6,109 yards, par 72; **Sheraton Tucson El Conquistador Resort,** 10,000 N. Oracle Rd. (tel. 297-0404), with 9 holes over 3,029 yards, par 35; and **Tubac Valley Country Club** (tel. 398-2021), in Tubac, with 18 holes over 7,151 yards, par 72.

TENNIS: Tucson's widespread tennis facilities include 15 private clubs with various numbers of courts, a score of high schools with several courts each, and another score of hotels and guest ranches that offer tennis to their guests.

Besides these, public courts, many lighted for night play, invite visitors. They include **Fort Lowell Park,** 2900 N. Craycroft Rd. (tel. 791-2584), with eight lighted courts; **Himmel Park,** 1000 N. Tucson Blvd. (tel. 791-3276), with eight lighted courts; **Jacobs Park,** 3300 N. Fairview, with two lighted courts; **James Thomas Park,** 3200 S. Forgeus Ave., with two courts; **Jesse Owens Park,** 400 S. Sarnoff Dr., with one court; **Kennedy Park,** Ajo Way at Mission Road, with two courts; **Manzanita Park,** 5300 W. Nebraska, with two lighted courts; **Marana Park** at Marana High School with four lighted courts; **Mission Park,** 5900 S. 12th Ave., with two courts; **Palo Verde Park,** 300 S. Mann, with two courts; **Randolph Tennis Center,** 100 S. Randolph Way (tel. 791-4896), with 24 courts, all but three lighted; **Stefan Gollob Park,** 401 S. Prudence, with four lighted courts; **Thomas Park,** 2945 S. Forgeus, with two lighted courts; and **Wildwood Park,** 6201 N. Parsly, with one lighted court.

SKIING: Mount Lemmon Ski Valley (tel. 576-1400), 35 miles from Tucson at an altitude of 8,250 feet, has skiing usually from Christmas through the end of March, offering a double-chair lift half a mile in length and two beginners' lifts, which are in operation in season from 9 a.m. to 4 p.m. daily. The fee for lifts is $15, or $12 for a half day. A special, including lift, ski rental, and lesson, is $25. There is a restaurant and a bar with occasional live entertainment. Of the 15 slopes here, three are expert and the others are all intermediate level, except for a beginners' slope. The rise between base and top is 900 feet.

WILD AREAS: Catalina State Park (tel. 628-5798), 12 miles north of Tucson via U.S. 89, is an area of 5,500 acres of desert land in the approaches to the Catalina Mountains to the east, with a varied array of flora and fauna in canyons and slopes and streams. The park is adjacent to the vast Coronado National Forest with its hundreds of miles of hiking and riding trails, and the resident bird list of the park—over 100 species—brings in birdwatchers. Picnic and camping areas have tables, grills, and water supply, and there is an equestrian center for riders who bring horses in by trailer. Nature trails make pleasant strolls of half an hour to an hour, while the park is also used as a base for backcountry exploring in the mountains beyond.

Mount Lemmon (see "Skiing"), site of the southernmost ski area in the U.S., draws summer visitors and locals escaping the heat of the city. The change from 2,400 feet down below to 9,000 up top means temperatures some 20° cooler. Visitors can drive to the base of the ski lift, which is kept operating in the summer, and picnic along the way or at the summit, especially beautiful in springtime wildflower season (April-May). Reached from Tucson east via Catalina Hwy., the Mount Lemmon area has several campsites along the way up, all administered by the Forest Service. One of these, at Rose Canyon Lake, has fishing for trout as an added attraction. Birdwatchers favor the Bear Wallow picnic ground, at an altitude of 7,600 feet.

Another birdwatching scene is **Madera Canyon,** 35 miles south of Tucson, reached via I-19 south to exit 39 at Continental, then Madera Canyon Road another 12 miles to the southeast. Hiking trails lead 70 miles in these foothills; one takes hikers to the peak of Mount Wrightson at an altitude of 9,445 feet. Operated by the Forest Service, Big Springs is the site of a campground with tables, grills, and water supply.

Among 39 campsites within a day's drive of Tucson, several are near the city, including **Crazy Horse Campgrounds,** seven miles east, off I-10 at the Craycroft Road exit, a commercial enterprise with 200 sites and full RV facilities; the **Tucson KOA,** nine miles north of Tucson via I-10 at the Cortaro exit, another commercial campground, with 150 sites and full RV facilities; and **Tucson Mount Park,** 14 miles west of downtown via Gates Pass, a municipal campground near three major area visitor attractions (Arizona Sonora Desert Museum, Old Tucson, and one section of Saguaro National Monument). It has 118 sites and full facilities for RVs.

8. TRIPS OUT OF TUCSON

The ranch country of greenbelt Arizona around Patagonia, the lavish shopping choices across the border in Nogales, huge open-pit copper mines, a western legend come to life in Tombstone, spectacular mountain roads, and an aura of surrealist cactus are among delights for visitors to destinations to the south, east, and west of Tucson.

WEST OF TUCSON: Kitt Peak National Observatory (tel. 620-5250), 56

miles from Tucson via Ariz. 86, then Ariz. 386 to the mountain, is open free of charge daily from 10 a.m. to 4 p.m., with 1½-hour guided tours on Saturday and Sunday at 10:30 a.m. and 1:30 p.m. The futuristic-looking telescopes include the McMath, the world's largest solar telescope, among a dozen huge instruments, some with facilities for viewers to visit. The observatory is funded by the National Science Foundation and managed by the Association of Universities for Research in Astronomy. A visitor center provides information for a self-guided walking tour of what amounts to the largest collection of astronomical instruments in the world. Programs in stellar, solar, and planetary studies are carried on here by scientists from all over the world. The visitor center has models of telescopes, and films produced here from pictures taken through the telescopes are shown on weekends. (There is also a gift shop with some Tohono O'Odham Indian-made crafts sold; the mountain is on the reservation.)

A solar vacuum telescope has a 41-inch mirror that sends the image of the sun down through vacuum tanks in a 75-foot-high tower, the purpose being to diminish distortion. Maps of the solar magnetic field are made daily to help scientists understand the processes going on within the sun. The huge McMath telescope brings in light through a shaft inclined at an angle of 32° to the horizontal for perfect alignment with the celestial north pole. This telescope captures the light of the sun in a mirror atop a 110-foot tower, and then the light is reflected down into other mirrors that focus a picture of the sun in to an observing room 300 feet away, where it is studied by computerized instruments. The building, made of copper, has coolants running through pipes in its surface in order to keep the temperature of the telescope constant. A light shaft 500 feet long has 300 feet buried underground.

A big infrared-research telescope permits vision in wavelengths outside spectrums normally invisible to human eyes. Visible from this height of 6,880 feet, 18 miles to the southwest in the plain below is the Indian town of Sells, and due south can be seen the home of the Indian god named I-I'toy, Baboquivari Peak. Views most days reach 100 miles distant, and the visitors' gallery has the advantage of being equipped with nonglare glass for easy photography of distance scenes, including mountains across the border in Mexico.

At **Sells,** 18 miles from the junction of the entrance road to the observatory, on Ariz. 86, the Tohono O'Odham Trading Post has some Indian-made baskets for sale, newly made ones as well as antiques. Nearby, in the tribal arts-and-crafts shop, other locally made pots and rugs are displayed and sold.

Organ Pipe National Monument (tel. 387-6849), 142 miles west of Tucson via Ariz. 86 and 85, has a visitor center 24 miles from the entrance to monument land outside the village of Why (where Ariz. 86 and 85 fork). Here, in the winter months, illustrated talks and other programs on the huge cactuses that grow in this part of the desert, and on other natural phenomena and the history of the area, are presented free for visitors. For those interested in having a taste of real desert country, Organ Pipe should be satisfactory indeed. A weather record shows winter days warm and sunny; by May temperatures are reaching 100°. In a typical year there were 84 days out of 100 in the summer when the 100° mark was broken—and these are always recorded in the shade. Measured in the sun at ground level, the mark goes up to 162°.

Therefore summertime hiking can obviously be uncomfortable and even dangerous, although wintertime, on the other hand, is a perfect time for it. Motorists have two loop drives into remote parts of the park, mostly restricted to one-way traffic, one of them 21 miles long and the other 51 miles long. The roads are twisty and unpaved but offer no difficulty for passenger cars. Growing in huge clumps everywhere within the 516 square miles of this huge park, the namesake organpipe cactus rises in many joined branches from a common base, thus differing from the saguaro common elsewhere in the Sonoran Desert. At night the organpipe has pale lavender flowers that open up to attract night-flying insects for pollination. Some other plants also have this facility for blooming at night in order to withstand the high heat of the desert. The fruit of the organpipe becomes mature in July; it splits open and exposes the seeds, which are eaten by birds.

The 21-mile **Ajo Mountain Drive** gives rare views of this remote desert country, at points moving close to canyon walls. The longer **Puerto Blanco Drive** follows historic routes of early travelers, paralleling the Mexican border. Points of interest include a man-made oasis at Quitobaquito and a display of senita cactus in Senita Basin. **Quitobaquito** is the site of an early irrigated farm area of the Tohono O'Odham who took water from the spring. Eventually a pond developed from it and there was a tiny community here, of which few traces remain today. The Puerto Blanco route takes about half a day.

From the visitor center there is a short nature trail leading to various cactus varieties: saguaro, ocotillo, prickly pear, barrel cactus, and of course organpipe. A one-mile trail encircles the campground, ideal for after-dinner strolls. There is also the 1½-mile **Palo Verde Trail** between the visitor center and the campground.

The **Victoria Mine Trail** starts at the campground and leads 4½ miles to the site of the Victoria Mine, the largest and earliest silver, lead, and gold mine in the area. An area rich in plant and animal life is reached via the **Estes Canyon–Bull Pasture Trail** (3½ miles round trip) into the Ajo Mountains. Permits must be taken out at the visitor center for backcountry hikes. Many of these follow old truck roads remaining unused since the park was made a wilderness area in 1978. One such trail leads north from the Victoria Mine 1½ miles to the Martinez Mine. Another trail, leading from the Puerto Blanco Drive at its junction with the Senita Basin Road, leads to a stone cabin of an early prospector at the Lost Cabin Mine. Other remains of mines in this area are the Milton Mine, where copper ore is still found in tailings; and the Baker Mine, near the thickest stand of organpipe cactus in the park. Other hiking destinations are Alamo Canyon and Williams Spring.

Climbs to various peaks—Mount Ajo, Diaz Peak, Diaz Spire, Kino Peak, Montezuma's Head, Pinkley Peak, Tillotson Peak, and Twin Peaks—are made by hikers even though there are no trails marked to the tops, which consist of crumbling stones and can be hard going. The highest of these, Mount Ajo, at 4,800 feet, is approached along a knife-edge ridge. Backcountry camping is permitted where campers are at least half a mile from maintained roads. Permits for hiking and overnight camping are free. The main limit on time spent camping is the amount of water a person is able to carry. Cookstoves must be used for any cooking as fires are not allowed.

The campground near the headquarters has 208 sites for trailers and tents, with tables, grills, rest rooms, and water supply. There are six species of rattlesnake in the park, and rangers ask visitors: "Please report rattlesnakes that pose a threat." Five miles south of the visitor center is the international border, giving access, two miles beyond, to the small town of Sonoita, Sonora, which has a couple of crafts stores and several small restaurants.

SOUTH OF TUCSON: Forty miles south of Tucson via I-19, at exit 21, is the burgeoning art center of **Tubac,** the oldest European settlement in Arizona. Adobe buildings cluster around St. Ann's Church, many of them housing shops where crafts in clay, wood, fabric, stone, and metal are practiced daily. There are displays of paintings and sculpture. The **Tubac Center for the Arts** is a creation of the Santa Cruz Valley Art Association, and exhibits and sells the work of its members; it is open Tuesday through Saturday from 10 a.m. to 4:30 p.m., on Sunday from 1:30 to 4:30 p.m. An annual event here is a nine-day arts festival every February, during which arts and crafts are displayed along several streets in the village, along with many food stands of various ethnic derivations. But anytime of year except at the height of summer, there are at least two dozen arts-and-crafts shops open for browsing and buying. Tubac had Arizona's first newspaper, and some of the equipment from it is displayed in the museum of the **Tubac Presidio State History Park** here.

Tumacacori National Monument, at exit 14 of I-19, is 47 miles south of Tucson and consists of the ruins of a typical frontier Spanish mission church, no longer consecrated, as a memorial to the introduction of European civilization in these parts. The Spanish set up such missions among the settled or Pueblo Indians, while in dealing with other, hostile Indians they set up forts they called presidios, like the one they built in Tucson. The mission here was built in the late 1700s by missionaries who named it San José de Tumacacori. The first contact with Pima Indians in this community came when Father Kino said mass here in 1691. A few years later the community had an adobe house, wheat fields, and herds of animals, and the missionaries continued holding services in the Indians' village, called Tumacacori. But there was a Pima Revolt in 1751, and the village was then moved to the present site and called San José.

Construction of the present church began around the end of the 18th century and was in use by 1822. The complete façade remains today, its adobe bricks exposed in a wide archway. A cross survives atop the rounded apex but a neighboring belltower is missing its roof and bell. In 1921 preservation work was undertaken to forestall further eroding of the old walls. Some original colors of the interior decorations of this baroque church can still be seen. A visitor center has dioramas illustrating early mission life here, and there are regular crafts demonstrations by local experts in such skills as tortilla making or basket weaving.

The monument is open for an admission charge of $1 per car, daily from 8 a.m. to 5 p.m. A local fiesta to which visitors are welcome takes place here every year on the first Sunday of December, lasting all day.

Nogales, Sonora, 60 miles south of Tucson, across the border from Nogales, Arizona, is a lively town for shopping and restaurant going, with a score of curio shops crammed with every kind of *artesanía* (crafts). The best-known restaurant is **El Cid,** Avenida Obregon no. 124 (tel. 2-64-00), serving steaks, fish, and Mexican dishes. Another good restaurant for Mexican specialties is **La Roca,** Calle Elias no. 91 (tel. 2-07-60). Both are open seven days a week for lunch and dinner.

The best lodgings in Nogales on the Mexican side are at the **Hotel Fray Marcos de Niza,** Campillo no. 91 (tel. 2-16-51), with 94 rooms, 15 suites, air conditioning, a restaurant and lounge, and its own parking lot.

Nogales, Arizona, motels include the **Americana,** at 850 Grand Ave., Nogales, AZ 85621 (tel. 602/287-7211), with a dining room, lounge, pool, and evening entertainment. Rates for the 101 units range from $42 to $50 double. Budget-priced rooms are available at $22 double at **Motel 6,** 2210 Tucson Hwy., Nogales, AZ 85621 (tel. 602/281-0703). You can get information on all tourist services on both sides of the border at the **Nogales Chamber of Commerce** in Kino Park, Nogales, AZ 85621 (tel. 602/287-3685).

A quiet, out-of-the-way stop for travelers is the village of **Patagonia,** 20 miles northeast of Nogales on Ariz. 82, where the attraction is the **Museum of the Horse** (tel. 394-2264). There are 45 carriages, coaches, wagons, and sleighs, and even a 400-year-old Mexican oxcart. Saddles, harnesses, bits, and spurs represent not only the western horse but horses from countries all over the world. There are paintings, all with horses in them, by such western specialists as Frederic Remington, Charles M. Russell, and Frank Tenney Johnson. Outside, the old Southern Pacific depot has been made into a senior citizens center whose picnic tables take up the old right-of-way. With a traditional balcony along its façade fronting this quiet thoroughfare, the **Stage Stop Inn,** Ariz. 82, Patagonia, AZ 85624 (tel. 602/394-2211), makes a likely place to break one's journey, offering a heated pool, a restaurant, and saloon. Rates are $35 double, $40 with kitchenette.

Some of the most appealing country in Arizona lies in the wooded hills and slopes of the Patagonia Mountains to the east of the village, where Forest Service roads lead to several ghost towns: Harshaw, Mowry, Washington Camp, and Duquesne. Adobe ruins and a cemetery can be seen at Mowry, once a center of an area of 100 working mines. Mowry grew up around a mine producing silver, lead, and zinc. The owner of the mine, one Sylvester Mowry, was jailed for selling lead for bullets to the Confederate Army during the Civil War, and his mine was confiscated. In 1905 Washington Camp had a population of 5,000; today it is empty. A driving tour of these old locations ought to include a map of Coronado National Forest. There is a great trip to be made from Patagonia east through this forest, past some of the ghost towns via the hamlet of Lochiel, to Coronado National Memorial at the eastern edge of the forest area. For those traveling with their own recreational vehicles, there's a lovely campsite at Parker Canyon Lake in the national forest.

Coronado National Memorial, accessible over the unpaved Forest Service road from the west or from a spur off Ariz. 92 from the north, lies 50 miles east of Nogales and has within its boundaries the spectacular heights of Coronado Peak, at 6,880 feet, rising more than half a mile above the rolling land around it. Below a shelter along the road, where a hiking trail takes visitors a short distance to the top, there is a visitor center that has displays tracing the Coronado Expedition of 1540–1542, when Europeans first set foot in this land. The memorial is near the point where Coronado entered the U.S. A three-mile trail from the peak, Joe's Canyon Trail, ends at the visitor center. Even though Coronado's travels were thought failures because he found no treasure, they paved the way for all future Spanish settlement and colonization in the Southwest. His expedition departed in 1840 from Compostela, Mexico, with 300 soldiers, four priests, and 800 Mexican Indians, and after attacking a pueblo and moving in for some months, was lured as far east as Kansas by tales of silver and gold that proved false.

SOUTHEAST AND EAST: The towns of Sierra Vista, Tombstone, Bisbee, and Douglas are the main centers for travelers in this area of dry mountainside and flat ranchland near the Mexican border. To the east of Tucson are Willcox and Safford.

Sierra Vista

About 70 miles southeast of Tucson via I-10 east to Ariz. 90 (junction at Benson), Sierra Vista is at an altitude of 4,700 feet on the eastern slopes of the Huachuca Mountains overlooking the San Pedro Valley. Nearby in **Ramsey Canyon Preserve** there is a great home ground for hummingbirds, where 13 species are known to proliferate. Near town is the **Fort Huachuca Historical Museum,** open Wednesday through Friday from 9 a.m. to 4 p.m. and weekends from 1 to 4 p.m., a historic frontier military post with several original buildings from the 1890s. Period artifacts and dress are displayed in an indoor facility.

The largest town in the area, Sierra Vista (pop. 29,000) has the **Thunder Mountain Inn** at 1631 S. Ariz. 92, Sierra Vista, AZ 85635 (tel. 602/458-7900, or toll free 800/528-1234); in the sharp clear air at this atmosphere it makes a fine place for a break in traveling or a short vacation. The mountains viewed out over the swimming pool are spectacular, and rooms open directly onto the enclosed lawn. A softly lighted lounge becomes the scene for nightly live entertainment, and a restaurant is open for breakfast, lunch and dinner. Rooms are $44 double.

Dining elsewhere in the area might lead you to the **Apache Pointe Ranch** off Ramsey Canyon Road (tel. 378-6800), where the specialty is buffalo steak. Regular beefsteaks are also first rate. It is open for dinner nightly.

Ghost towns in the area include **Charleston,** renowned for being "tougher than Tombstone," where the U.S. Army conducted training in house-to-house combat during World War II. Only ruins remain today.

There are many opportunities to enjoy the outdoors during a stay at the **Mile Hi,** R.R. 1, Hereford, AZ 85615 (tel. 602/378-2785), in a furnished cabin in the 280-acre Ramsey Canyon Preserve ten miles south of Sierra Vista. Rates are $55 double. Owned by the nonprofit Nature Conservancy, the preserve includes Ramsey Canyon, a National Natural Landmark, and has a great variety of birds, mammals, reptiles, amphibians, butterflies, and plants. Some 14 species of hummingbirds have been photographed here, more than in any other place in the U.S. Each of the six cabins is heated and has living and bedroom areas and a kitchen fully supplied; towels and linen are provided, and there is a barbecue grill. The preserve manager schedules guided hikes. There is a nature reference library open to guests as well as a bookstore and gift shop. The Huachuca Audubon Society welcomes guests to join its monthly meetings and field trips. There is a three-night minimum for reservations from April through August, the busiest visitor season. (Daytime visitors are welcome to hike in the canyon but must make reservations for admission on weekends because of increased visitation.)

Tombstone

A major tourist attraction, Tombstone, "the town too tough to die," is 70 miles from Tucson via I-10 east to Benson and U.S. 80 south. The silver-mining town was founded when a prospector named Ed Schiefflin discovered a ledge of silver ore in 1877. On his way to Tucson to file his claim, Schiefflin recalled a remark of a friend: "The only stone you will find in those Indian-infested hills will be your tombstone." So he named the place Tombstone. By 1881 there were 10,000 silver prospectors, miners, and hangers-on in town, making it bigger than both Tucson, the county seat, and Prescott, the Territorial capital. When a fire burned the new town, it was quickly rebuilt. There was legitimate theater in Schiefflin Hall and a new meeting hall for the Masons. The boom went on for another five years, with an estimated $37-million worth of silver mined, until water seeped into the mine shafts and ended the operations in spite of efforts to pump out the water. By 1886 the boom was over and the town appeared to be doomed, like hundreds of others that became ghost towns in the West. But because of its location in the heart of some of the state's best ranching country, cattle raising kept a few people occupied, and although most of the miners abandoned the place, it has never given up the ghost altogether. Today a population of 1,000 includes many who find employment in the variety of museums, souvenir shops, bars, and restaurants that attract nearly as many tourists as the Grand Canyon.

The old **Tombstone Courthouse,** now a state historic park, was built in 1882 and is open to the public as a museum. A clipping from the Tombstone *Nugget* in 1881 has a report of the shootout at the O.K. Corral here: "A day when blood flowed as water and human life was held as a shuttlecock." According to the report, the fight did not take place in the corral but outside on Fremont Street. But every Sunday there is a reenactment of the shootout in the corral, which has been restored to serve as a backdrop for the violence, viewed by crowds of tourists who take it as comedy. (Everywhere in the West there is this strain of buffoonery connected with such Wild West shootout scenes, as if the thud of a body falling to the ground was really the height of comic invention.) Another headline framed in the courthouse reads "Three Men Hurled into Eternity in the Duration of a Moment."

Deputy Sheriff Wyatt Earp and his brothers, Morgan and Virgil, came upon some suspected stagecoach bandits one morning; there was already bad blood between the Earps and the outlaws, Frank and Tom McLaury and Ike Clanton. When the Earps demanded that the others throw down their guns, the shooting started, and it was over within a few seconds. Frank McLaury was killed by a shot to the stomach fired point-blank. An aide of the Earps, Doc Holliday, picked off Tom McLaury as he reached for a rifle on his saddle. Clanton was also hit by a bullet and died a few minutes later. Morgan and Virgil Earp were both hit by bullets but not killed. The Earps were tried for murder and acquitted. The fight is reenacted on Sunday at 2 p.m. by a group of amateur lawmen and bandits calling themselves the Wild Bunch. Since the climactic shootout is over so fast, they stage half a dozen other skits—each based on gunplay—beforehand.

A display in the courthouse recalls a lesser-known incident in Tombstone, which occurred when 1,200 local copper miners went on strike here in 1917 and were arrested by state troopers, marched to a railhead, and forced to board boxcars, in which they were shipped across the state line into New Mexico. The workers, members of the International Workers of the World—the I.W.W., or Wobblies—later sued the sheriff and his deputies on a charge of kidnapping, but they were acquitted.

At the **Wells-Fargo Museum** on Allen Street the famous gunfight is further recalled in a display of the let's-pretend corpses, in their coffins and dressed to the nines, of the bandit victims. Old photographs of hangings in the town add a grisly dimension to our picture of life in the Old West. A somewhat terrifying collection of dolls fashioned to resemble the U.S. presidents and their wives is also shown—they have the kind of awful expressions you fear to meet in your nightmares, although Eisenhower simply comes out as a harmless clown.

The **Rose Tree Inn Museum,** at 4th and Toughnut Streets, has the world's largest rose bush in its courtyard, covering 8,000 square feet, and a souvenir counter purveying such objects as bits of barbed wire, local rocks, and old bottles at $1 each.

Tours of the **Good Enough Silver Mine,** at 5th and Toughnut Streets, lead underground by narrow stairway and are led by a guide through about 750 feet of tunnels. Visitors may pick out a bit of ore along the way to take along as a souvenir of the trip, before climbing the 85 steps up into the warm sunlight—it's 53° down below.

As cheery an atmosphere as anywhere in town is found in the **Crystal Palace,** a working saloon restored to its early grandeur, at 5th and Allen Streets. Built in 1879 as the Golden Eagle Brewery, it soon changed into a fancy saloon and became the center of action of the booming town—the finest among as many as 100 saloons in Tombstone. In spite of the end of the boom a few years later, the Crystal Palace remained in business until Prohibition, and it reopened upon Repeal. By 1963, when it was purchased by a local preservation organization, the bar had lost its Victorian finery. But the long bar with its fine mirror and carved, arched-back shelving, and its ornate hanging lamps, along with other furnishings and fixtures, are restored today; even the wooden sidewalks are back in place up and down Allen Street. Of a Sunday noontime, when cars are banned from Allen Street so tourists can take pictures of the old main drag without modern anachronisms, there will be ladies in fancy dress and men in black frock coats in the Crystal Palace—members of the Wild Bunch loosening up before the afternoon shootout performance. A couple goes out into the sunlight to try a few waltzing steps together as the lenses of a hundred cameras are riveted on them.

Access to **Boot Hill,** the local cemetery containing the remains of Clanton, the McLaurys, and various others shot or hanged in the town, is through a souvenir shop on U.S. 80 three blocks northwest of the center of town.

Back on Allen Street again, the **Bird Cage Theater** has relics of the old operahouse and vaudeville days but is no longer putting on any performances.

Reprints of contemporary accounts of the Earp shootout that appeared in the Tombstone *Epitaph* can be purchased at the office of the newspaper, still published weekly by journalism students of the University of Arizona, and also, in a separate monthly edition, as a historical journal. The office has artifacts of early days of printing the paper as well as a working press.

The big event of the year is the three-day **Helldorado Days** over the third weekend of October, during which there are numerous lynchings and shootouts and other festivities, including a carnival, fashion show, parade, and even special church services. The fashion show brings out costumes dating between 1878 and 1915. The festival started in 1929 to celebrate the town's 50th anniversary and has been held ever since.

WHERE TO STAY. Just out of the busy center of town, on a rise with a great view of the surrounding mountains, is the **Lookout Lodge,** half a mile west of town on U.S. 80, Tombstone, AZ 85638 (tel. 602/457-2223, or toll free 800/528-1234). The motel has a swimming pool and offers a free breakfast included in room rates of $48 double.

WHERE TO EAT. On Allen Street, the main drag lined with old-style western stores and other businesses with the wooden sidewalks out front, there is the **Longhorn Restaurant,** at the corner of 5th Street (tel. 457-3405), serving Italian, Mexican, and American dishes, and open for breakfast, lunch, and dinner seven days.

An original 1879 boarding house has become **Nellie Cashman's,** at Toughnut and 5th Streets (tel. 457-9933), a restaurant and pie salon open for lunch and dinner daily.

Bisbee

Bisbee, 95 miles from Tucson via I-10 east and U.S. 80, was a copper-mining center until 15 years ago, when the mines closed down and threatened to make a new ghost town of the place. But for certain folk on the lookout for a combination of good atmosphere and climate along with a certain peacefulness, the isolation of Bisbee is just right.

Among those taken by its steep, curving streets that cling to a mountainside still holding a lot of copper ore are artists, craftspeople, and even a handful of writers. When the miners lost their jobs they had to leave town to find work elsewhere, so their houses, all put on the market at once, either went begging or were sold cheaply. The news of these bargains spread slowly, but eventually did get to certain impecunious creative folk who wanted cheap studio space and liked the warm weather too. Thus Bisbee has taken a new lease on life. So far its growth has been slow, which may save it from the eventual tackiness other former ghost towns have suffered.

The **Lavendar Pit** is a fantastically huge gouge in the earth that was worked for copper until 1974 and can be toured by bus. In a quarter of a century of mining operations the staggering total of 350 million tons of ore was dug out of this hole. A tour of an underground mine, the **Copper Queen,** also out of production, is provided at the Queen Mine building in the center of Bisbee. The pit tour costs $3, the underground mine tour is $4, and there is a historic bus tour of the whole town available too, at $3.

George Warren remains a famous figure in Bisbee history as the original owner of the claim to what became the Copper Queen, eventually producing $40 million worth of copper. On a certain Fourth of July a century ago he had a few drinks and offered to bet his mining claim that he could outrun a man on a horse. The horse won and George lost the mine.

Railroads brought greater prosperity to Bisbee in 1899, and by 1900 it was the territory's largest town, with a population of 20,000. It was during this boom era that many Victorian mansions, and the **Copper Queen Hotel,** 11 Howell Ave., Bisbee, AZ 85603 (tel. 602/432-2216), were built. Erected by the mining company when the town was the largest mining community in the world, the hotel has survived through the years and has recently been restored, with a pleasant sidewalk café, complete with an awning over the tables on the terrace. The old plumbing fixtures are originals and what may be remarkable is that they work. The Copper Queen has 43 high-ceilinged rooms, a pool, restaurant, saloon, and gift shop. Rates are $36 to $65 double.

A short walk from the Copper Queen is a street leading into a canyon, the neighborhood being called **Brewery Gulch,** presently lined with storefronts and other structures that will soon house artists and craftspeople and their works, among other new enterprises gradually discovering Bisbee's recent incarnation as a budding art colony. The Gulch was once a famous hotspot for dancehalls and houses of ill-repute, and the dancehall girls remain known in local legend: Crazy Horse Lil, Red Jean who could lick any man, Black Jack who dressed like a man to hold up stagecoaches, Anita Romero ("men killed over her," says a historical note).

Worth making an effort to see in the **Mining and Historical Museum** at 5 Copper Queen Plaza (open Monday through Saturday from 10 a.m. to 4 p.m., on Sunday from 1 to 4 p.m.) is the Bisbee centennial quilt, a joint effort of a score of quilters that has fetching scenes out of the town's history illustrated within frame-like rectangles to make up the whole work. Serving as the headquarters offices of the copper-mining firm of Phelps Dodge until 1961, the building has paneled walls, oak desks, and polished narrow-board floors. Displayed are fascinating photos of pioneers who settled the town a century ago—miners and their families. Another display shows photos of descendants of those settlers, including Mexican-Americans now in various positions in town: bar proprietor, chief of police, beauty parlor owner, among them. Admission is free; donations welcome.

Also open to visitors is the **Muheim Heritage House,** at 207 Youngblood Hill (tel. 432-7071). Dating from 1902, the pioneer home stands out for its cupola with a flag flying from a mast above. A National Historic Site, the house contains period furniture. Donations in support of this restoration project are solicited in a unique way, according to a folder: "Concrete personalized stepping stones molded in the shape of the State of Arizona may be purchased by interested persons. They are being permanently placed in the grounds of the Muheim House as a tribute to their donors." The house is open Friday through Monday from 1 to 4 p.m.; admission is $1.

WHERE TO STAY. Other than the first-choice Copper Queen, the historic hotel noted above, Bisbee offers several additional choices.

An early 1900s hostelry, the **Inn at Castle Rock,** 112 Tombstone Canyon Rd., Bisbee, AZ 85603 (tel. 602/432-7195), is a broad, three-story structure with full porches running along the second and third levels, facing the street, where a stream flows between the inn and the roadway. Originally a miners' boarding house, today Victorian or art deco furnishings make each room different from all the others. Ten of the 12 rooms have private baths, and there is a pleasant guest lounge with a fireplace and a downstairs parlor with another fireplace, a piano, a small library, and a stereo. Rates are $38 double.

The **Bisbee Inn,** at 45 OK St., Bisbee, AZ 85603 (tel. 602/432-5131), is a restored version of the LaMore Hotel, which opened in 1917 overlooking Brewery Gulch, once a boomtown street lined with saloons and brothels. Oak antiques furnish the 18 rooms, which have washbowls with running water; showers and toilets are reached via the hallway. A hearty breakfast—fruit salad, juice, pancakes, waffles, bacon, ham, eggs, potatoes, French toast, cereals, and quiche without limit, along with coffee and tea—is included in the room rate: double rooms are $34 to $39. For nonsmokers only.

The recently restored **Oliver House,** 26 Sowle Ave., Bisbee, AZ 85603 (tel. 602/432-4286), built in 1908, has the homey spaciousness of a turn-of-the-century boarding house. Guests share a sunny common room and a kitchen, as well as bathrooms on each floor. Reached by a footbridge over one of the many canyon-like streets of the town, the hotel provides great views of the rooftops of many historic buildings. During the rainy season water flows over two small waterfalls at the front of the house. Breakfast is offered with the rooms, priced at $37 double.

WHERE TO EAT. The **Shepherd's Inn,** 67 Main St. (tel. 432-2996), in the 1910 former Elks Lodge building, continues the turn-of-the-century interior restoration everywhere in Bisbee, making a pleasant setting for good dining. Menu selections might be trout amandine at $8, stuffed sole Monterey with crabs, shrimp, cheese, and pilaf, at $8, or grilled salmon steak at $8.75. For lighter repasts or lunch there are soups, salads, and a good selection of sandwiches at around $3.50, and there are Inglenook wines by the carafe. Open daily for breakfast, lunch, and dinner.

The **Copper Queen Hotel** keeps up its impeccable standards in its warm restaurant where touches of Victorian luxury make guests feel somewhat special. There is a full bar and a good wine list, and entrees, such as a beef burgundy or a veal mornay, run around $9. It is open daily for lunch and dinner.

Douglas

The town of Douglas is 23 miles from Bisbee, right on the Mexican border, and at an elevation of 4,000 feet, it is 1,500 feet lower than Bisbee's somewhat rarified climate, so it gets hot in the summer. Its center lies just three blocks from the Mexican entry point, at Agua Prieta, a plain, neat community of one-story concrete shops in pastel colors lined up along three parallel streets—there are several crafts and curio shops, and liquor stores.

The attraction that might take a traveler out of his way a bit to Douglas is the **Gadsden Hotel,** 1046 G Ave., Douglas, AZ 85607 (tel. 602/364-4481), with 174 rooms in a five-story building that takes you back to the 1920s era of plain, solid architecture. The two-story lobby, keeping its art deco style in original Tiffany glass, lamps, light stands, marblework, and copper decorative wall fixtures, makes the place special indeed. There is a restaurant and lounge with Spanish tile murals. Rooms have private baths and many have balconies. Rates are $27 to $35 double.

Cochise County Information

For information about all travel services in Cochise County—including Tombstone, Douglas, and Bisbee—see the Bisbee visitors' bureau, 78 Main St. (tel. 432-2141). Bisbee has bus connection via Greyhound, and air connections to Tucson via Copper State Airlines and Sierra Vista Aviation flying to Bisbee-Douglas International Airport off U.S. 80, 17 miles east of Bisbee.

Chiricahua National Monument

Chiricahua National Monument, 125 miles east of Tucson via I-10 to Willcox and Ariz. 186 (tel. 824-3560), offers spectacular scenes of the Chiricahua Mountains for both motorists and hikers. A paved mountain road six miles long, the **Massai Point Drive,** gives a view of the entire park, whose outstanding features are weird stone formations in the shape of beasts and men, pinnacles and domes, surrealistic sculptures in endless creative variety.

Among 17 miles of **foot trails** are the 3½-mile Echo Canyon Loop, perhaps the most beautiful of walking trips, taking three hours; the seven-mile Heart of Rocks trail, taking five hours; the mile-long Sugarloaf Peak trail to one of the highest points in the park, a round trip of 80 minutes; the Rhyolite Canyon trail, a short nature path; the Nature Bridge trail, a five-mile round trip to the bridge, taking 2½ hours; and the Meadow trail, a short trail into Silver Spur Meadow.

Detailed information on these trails and on backpacking into the adjoining wilderness of **Coronado National Forest,** is available at the visitor center. Half a mile from the center, at **Bonita Canyon,** is a campground with 26 sites equipped with tables, fireplaces, and water supply; there are rest rooms nearby. (There is a limit of 20 feet on trailer length.)

The Chiricahuas are called a forested island in a sea of desert. In the different climatic levels live a fascinating variety of species of plants and animals—elevations go from 5,160 to 7,398 feet. The shaded bottoms of the canyons have dense vegetation that comes as a relief from the dryness of the desert down below, though there are desert spots up here too. Among trees, there are manzanitas with their bright-red stems, and madrones with their shedding bark, mingling with white sycamores and Arizona cypress. Slopes facing north have growths of oak, pine, and juniper, while the southerly facing slopes at the same altitude have desert-type plants: yucca, century plants, cactuses. It is a fabulous place to see wildflowers in the springtime. Deer, being protected from hunting, are fairly tame in the park, and there is an increase in the numbers of coatis and peccaries. Each vegetative belt spawns its species of birds and other animals.

The Chiricahuas are most famous, of course, as the stronghold of Cochise and Geronimo, the Chiricahua Apache warriors, who held off the inevitable onslaught of Western civilization upon their civilization for a quarter century. Some tribes of Apaches had moved up into these mountains to escape the Spaniards, from which hideout they would descend to the plains to plunder the invaders' horses, cattle, and grain. The conflict became crucial after the U.S. purchased this part of the world from Mexico in the Gadsden Purchase in 1853, which was the signal for wholesale settlement of the region by Americans. Skirmishes with the

Apache became open warfare after the 1861 Bascom Affair, when the army tried to capture Cochise for a crime that another band of Indians had committed. The act started a 12-year war with the Apache. Fort Bowie (see below) became the focal point of army action against the Apache. In 1872 the Chiricahua Apaches were placed on a reservation, but it was disbanded four years later. But when Geronimo surrendered, Indian resistance was virtually finished. Nevertheless in later years there were some one-man escapades by "Big Foot" Massai and the Apache Kid. Massai Point and Massai Canyon recall this intrepid warrior; Cochise Head commemorates another Apache leader—all within the park boundaries.

The entrance fee is $1 per car; campsites cost $5.

Fort Bowie National Historic Site

Fort Bowie National Historic Site, 25 miles north of Chiricahua National Monument, can be reached via Ariz. 186 and an unpaved road to the north at a point ten miles south of the ghost town of Dos Cabezas. There is no road into the ruins of the fort itself, but they are reached by a 1½-mile foot trail that begins midway in Apache Pass. The trail parallels the military wagon road and passes historic points of interest such as the Butterfield Stage Station ruins, the post cemetery, Apache Spring, and the earlier Fort Bowie. There is a small museum where trail-guide booklets are available. The point at which the trail into the ruins is taken, **Apache Pass,** separates the Chiricahua Mountains to the south from the Dos Cabezas range to the north, the latter named for two summits—the two heads, or *"dos cabezas."*

Fort Bowie is the story of how Tom Jeffords and one-armed Gen. O. O. Howard rode into Cochise's stronghold to negotiate a peace. It is the story of Lt. John Rucker trying to rescue a fellow officer from drowning in a flooded canyon and dying in the attempt. It is determined Gen. George Crook, struggling to cover a vast territory with a handful of men and an embittered Geronimo fighting against hopeless odds. Fort Bowie is the story of a band of Indians who tried to stop the U.S. Army, vanguard of an alien civilization.

The Spanish called it Puerto del Dado, the Pass of Chance, but it might have been called the Pass of Death. Apache Pass was the focal point of military operations against the Apaches for control of the entire region, to determine the pattern of frontier development throughout the Southwest. It was not until Geronimo's defeat that American settlement could proceed.

The Apache had probably first come here to live in the 16th century, a people who combined hunting and gathering wild foods with raiding their neighbors. Using the horses they got from the Spaniards, they soon organized a mobile guerrilla warfare as the means of protecting their homeland from outside invasion. But by the 1850s the wagon-trail links between East and West Coasts had to be protected from Indian attack. The overland mail, contracted to John Butterfield over his Butterfield Trail, had to cut through Apache Pass—the most crucial spot from the point of view of Indian danger. It ran from St. Louis through the Southwest to San Francisco. So the Apache Pass station was built here in 1858. The stage went through in peace for 2½ years, but the Bascom Affair, in which Cochise was wrongfully accused of raiding the ranch of John Ward and of kidnapping the son of a Mexican woman who lived with him, ended the truce when army troops tried to capture Cochise. He escaped but his companions did not; all of them were hanged—19 dead.

From this point on for 12 years there was open warfare between pioneer and Indian in these mountains, and conditions were worsened for the settlers when the Civil War caused the closing of many forts in the region. But the Union forces needed to defend the pass from passage by the Confederate Army hoping to reach the California goldfields, and to this end Fort Bowie was built in 1862. Peace eventually returned to the area when Cochise agreed to a settlement in 1872, accepting a reservation of 3,000 square miles in southeastern Arizona. At the same time a former army scout who had won the Indians' confidence, Tom Jeffords, became Indian agent. Yet two years later Cochise died, and in 1876 Jeffords was removed as agent with the tribe.

Discontented Indians kept leaving the reservation. The government then abolished the Chiricahuas' reservation, moving the Indians to the San Carlos reservation. Nevertheless Indian bands led by Geronimo and some other war leaders began terrorizing the settlers again. Gen. George Crook was put in charge of punitive expeditions out of Fort Bowie to hunt down the renegades, but Geronimo and his band eluded the army for ten years. They gave up only when their own Apache scouts were mobilized against them. Then both scouts and hostiles were shipped to forts in Oklahoma and Florida, and were finally settled at Fort Sill, Okla. By 1894 Bowie had outlived its purpose and was abandoned.

Willcox

Willcox, a small town (pop. 3,500) 80 miles east of Tucson on I-10, is a likely headquarters for touring this wild area of mountainous country, ghost towns, and hot desert valleys.

WHERE TO STAY. The **Plaza Inn,** 1100 W. Rex Allen Dr., Willcox, AZ 85643 (tel. 602/384-3556, or toll free 800/528-1234), has a pool and 59 rooms with refrigerators; waterbeds and wet bars are available. There is a restaurant and lounge. Double rates are $55 and up.

For a real getaway to the 1890s, take a room at the **Cochise Hotel** in the quiet farm village of Cochise, AZ 85606 (tel. 602/384-3156), 15 miles southwest of Willcox via I-10 and U.S. 666. Breakfast is available for guests, as are other meals on advance request. Artifacts including old ironware and bottles decorate the yard outside, surrounded by a pristine New Englandy white picket fence. Telephone reservations are necessary in advance for the five rooms in this quiet retreat, which has a small gift shop. Rates are $18.50 to $24 double.

WHERE TO EAT. Barbecue beef is the specialty at the **Regal,** 301 N. Haskell Ave. (tel. 384-9959), which also has daily specials and Mexican foods at moderate prices, and a cocktail lounge. It is open for breakfast, lunch, and dinner seven days a week.

SIGHTS. Information on the Willcox area is available at the **Cochise Visitor Center,** 1500 N. Circle 1 Rd. (tel. 602/384-2272). On the premises is a small Museum of the Southwest where a bust of Cochise has neighboring copies of printed wisdom from the Indian's stock of famous quotes. Another display makes a tribute to a local favorite son, Rex Allen, a western actor and singer. A small gift shop has some books on the lore of the area as well as representative southwestern crafts: pottery, blankets, beadwork, and paintings among them.

The visitor center can also give directions on reaching viewing points over **Willcox Playa,** a winter home for some 8,000 sandhill cranes, great waterbirds standing four feet tall with wingspreads of five to seven feet. The birds have been arriving in their annual October migration in greater and greater numbers since the 1950s, when the advent of irrigation increased cropland where the birds can feed. They stay in the area until mid-March. Best viewing time is at sunrise when the birds fly off from their roosts in the Playa to cropland around this swampy area. There is a Mexican duck-nesting area maintained by the Arizona Game and Fish Department on Kansas Settlement Road that makes one of the best vantage points for viewing these birds. During the day they are usually not visible, being hidden by grasses where they feed, but again at the end of the day they are seen in flight over the playa.

Cochise Stronghold, 30 miles southwest of Willcox via U.S. 666 and an unpaved access road, still holds the remains of the Apache leader somewhere within its fastness. In the heart of the Dragon Mountains, the Stronghold rises secretly above the anvil floor of Sulphur Springs Valley to a mile's height. The chief and his warriors used this natural fortress in their battles with the U.S. Army over a 15-year period. The area has two dozen campsites with tables and fireplaces, administered by the U.S. Forest Service. Clearly marked are an old Indian trail five miles long and a short nature trail.

Ghost towns in these parts include Dos Cabezas (where some nonghosts are in residence), on Ariz. 186, 15 miles southeast of Willcox, once a supply center for a number of mines in the area. Empty adobe buildings and a stage station can be seen here. Pearce, 29 miles south of Willcox and one mile off U.S. 666, is an old gold camp that once had a population of 2,000, all living from the wealth of the Commonwealth Mine. There is a store and post office open here, and many empty adobe houses, the store dating from the turn of the century and containing many antiques, including an early six-drawer cash register—one for each of six clerks. Ladders move on iron tracks for use in reaching merchandise on high shelves. A great bookkeepers' cage, which held four workers in the town's heyday, is still on the site. Although historic in interest, the store also still operates on a commercial basis, supplying staples to a few local residents. Remains of the famous Pearce mine are nearby.

The Amerind Foundation

The Amerind Foundation (tel. 586-3666), near the village of Dragoon, 65 miles east of Tucson, reached via I-10 at exit 318, has a fine museum of archeological artifacts relating to American Indian life in the region. Founded in 1937 by William S. Fulton, a Connecticut archeologist who spent many summers exploring archeological digs in the Southwest, the collection includes early examples of such Indian arts as Hopi prayer rugs, Navajo blankets, kachina dolls, and silver concho belts, as well as more recently made pottery, jewelry, basketry, hunting gear, cooking equipment, musical instruments, and tribal clothing. Especially prized by students of Indian crafts is the collection of baskets by the White Mountain Apaches. Hispanic tradition is represented in a collection of *bultos*, religious carvings introduced by Spanish missionaries. Currently being excavated is an area of ruins in the Mexican state of Chihuahua at Casas Grandes, from which artifacts found are being displayed here. Admission is $2, and hours are 10 a.m. to 4 p.m. daily. There is a shaded picnic area with tables overlooking the Dragoon Mountains.

Safford

Safford and Graham County are in delightful mountain country remote from big cities—Safford is 130 miles northeast of Tucson, via I-10 east and U.S. 666 north. Within easy reach are Roper State Park, with a 30-acre lake; Aravaipa Canyon, seven miles long and comprising a beautiful primitive area for hiking or riding; Black Hills Rockhound Park, dubbed the "fire agate capital of the world"; Bonita Creek Cliff Dwellings, prehistoric Hohokam ruins; hot mineral baths; the world's second-largest open-pit copper mine; the Coronado Trail, marked through the national forests; a motor road to the top of Mount Graham (10,720 feet); and a welter of weekly booster events in the town such as the youth fair and the annual benefit mud bog.

Probably the greatest treat in the area is the drive of 36 miles on the **Swift**

Trail to the summit of Mount Graham, in Coronado National Forest southwest of town; total mileage, including access via U.S. 666 nine miles south of town, round trip, is 84 miles, a 4½-hour drive not counting side excursions. It makes a fine day's outing. The Swift Trail, as it leaves the Bowie Hwy. (U.S. 666), continues paved for 22 miles, then becomes a curving gravel road. Along the way there is mesquite, creosote bush, and burro weed. At mile 11.2 there is a rough road to the right leading into Marijilda Canyon, not suited for passenger cars. The lane continues through Jacobson Canyon; at mile 14.8 Noon Creek is crossed, named for the time of day horse-and-wagon trips usually got here when they started from down below. At mile 17.2 the West Canyon picnic ground has cold water from a tap at this 6,000-foot elevation. Black alder, walnut, velvet ash, and sycamore grow here along with a few Chihuahua pines.

At mile 24.6 the road crosses Ladybug Saddle to the south slope of Mount Graham. Ladybugs swarm here at certain times of summer. A lovely secluded picnic spot needs a 20-minute walk along an old road to the left, at mile 28.5, leading to Snow Flat, a meadow by a small fishing pond that reflects the woods along the far shore. At mile 29.1 a steep road, passable by car, leads up to the Heliograph fire lookout tower two miles in, at an elevation of 10,028 feet. The tower has a lookout on duty during the season of high forest fire danger, May to July. From this point the highest point in these mountains, Graham Peak, is 3½ miles away as the crow flies. Back on Swift Trail, at the point where the fire tower road joins Swift Trail is another road going down into the canyon two-tenths of a mile to **Shannon Campground,** a spectacular camping site for ten campers, including RVs or tents, with tables, fireplaces, toilets, and a water supply.

At mile 29.5 the High Peak road goes off to the right up to Graham Peak, maintained for passenger cars for the first three miles and unimproved the remainder of the way up. Treasure hunters might like to stop at mile 30.3 and take the road to the left to Treasure Park, where 19 pack loads of stolen gold are said to have been buried by Mexican bandits shortly before the Gadsden Purchase in 1853. At mile 30.5 **Hospital Flat** has picnic and camping sites. The area was used as the site of a summer hospital for soldiers of old Fort Grant. At this height the trees are Douglas fir, Ponderosa pine, white fir, aspen, Englemann spruce, limber pine, and corkbark fir, a community continuing on up to the highest elevations (it's about 9,000 feet here).

At 34.8 miles, stop at **Fort Grant Vista Point** to look down from this height of 9,356 feet to Fort Grant at the foot of the mountain. Now a prison, it was established in 1872 as an Indian-fighting post. At mile 36.6 a road to the right goes to the Webb Peak lookout tower, 1.7 miles in, providing views for 100 miles around. Results of a 1956 forest fire are visible here. At mile 36.7 the road left follows a meadow to **Soldier Creek Campground,** two-tenths of a mile in, at 9,300 feet elevation, with 11 campsites, water, and rest rooms.

At mile 40 the road left goes to **Riggs Flat Lake** and recreation area, an 11-acre dammed lake providing good trout fishing. There are 46 campsites for RV or tents, water, and rest rooms, and access for power boats. At mile 42 there is a turnaround at the end of Swift Trail and a path leading up four miles to **West Peak Lookout,** a half-day hike.

Note: Mileage starts at Safford post office; the junction of U.S. 666 and the entrance to Swift Trail is at mile 7.5. Although motorists will not find the same sense of isolation and freedom so dear to hikers and backpackers, the Swift Trail comes close to giving them the same experience hikers get in wilderness areas.

Roper Lake State Park, six miles south of Safford reached via U.S. 666 and Roper Lake Road (tel. 428-6760), has two small lakes stocked with catfish, bass, bluegill, and crappie. Only electric trolling motors are allowed on fishing boats.

On the shore of the larger of the two lakes, Lake Roper, are 24 campsites; and on a peninsula there is a beach and picnic area with tables and ramadas.

Near the state park out on U.S. 666 is the **Collins Health Spa,** which provides mineral-water baths, sweats, reflexology, and massage. Baths are taken in tiled Roman-style tubs through which water is running at a natural temperature of 108°. After bathing, one is wrapped in sheets, plastic, and blankets for what spa personnel call "a good natural sweat." Any old aches and pains are then attacked by masseurs and masseuses. The art of reflexology as practiced here involves a compression massage of the feet, based on the theory that there are nerve reflexes in the feet connected to every part of the body. A naturopathic physician is on the premises all day on Wednesday, Thursday, and Friday to perform physical manipulation, electrotherapy, and make ionization tests of urine and saliva. For further information, call 428-2711.

WHERE TO STAY. Motels in Safford include the **Sandia,** 520 E. U.S. 70, Safford, AZ 85546 (tel. 602/428-1621, or toll free 800/528-1234), with 32 rooms, a pool, cable TV, and a restaurant adjacent, and double rates of $32 to $35; and the **Town House,** 225 E. U.S. 70, Safford, AZ 85546 (tel. 602/428-3474), with 34 rooms, a pool, and a coffeeshop, and double rates of $22 to $26. (This is also the best spot for breakfast; see below).

WHERE TO EAT. The **Town House,** 225 E. U.S. 70 (tel. 428-3474), is open daily for three meals and specializes in hearty breakfasts such as the "Hardy complete"— two eggs, sizzlin' bacon and grilled sausage, homemade biscuits and gravy. Huevos rancheros, a cattleman's special involving steak, eggs, and hash browns, and fresh cinnamon rolls are also among "all orders cooked to perfection."

INFORMATION. For all travel-service information in the area, get in touch with the **Safford-Graham County Chamber of Commerce,** 1111 Thatcher Blvd., Safford, AZ 85546 (tel. 602/428-2511).

CHAPTER X

FLAGSTAFF AND NORTHERN ARIZONA

□ □ □

A small, neat city of 40,000 on a 7,000-foot-high plateau in the center of northern Arizona, Flagstaff still keeps a plain western openness about it last seen in many other towns in the 1940s. There's the daily passenger train honking through on the way to the coast, the huge Little America truckstop restaurant at the edge of town, the half-century-old Monte Vista Hotel still the pride of downtown. A cheerful Indian outside a bar on Santa Fe Street will stop a visitor to pass the time of day. A Chicano waitress in a restaurant will happily take five minutes to explain how the pork in the carne adovado is prepared by marinating it in hot green chiles. The bright Arizona sunlight lacks the burning quality at this altitude that it has down in the desert country around Phoenix and Tucson, but it is as bright, or probably brighter in the clear atmosphere —so clear it has been the site of a famous astronomical observatory for nearly a century.

The country around Flagstaff has a variety of temptations for tourists, beginning with the Grand Canyon of course (covered in Chapter XI), 80 miles north. Prehistoric ruins are preserved at fascinating sites in three national monuments, and a chair lift takes visitors to a spectacular elevation, 11,600 feet, except in winter when skiers take over. There is a deer farm where visitors feed animals out of their hands. South, at somewhat lower altitudes, is the burgeoning art colony of Sedona in the fabulous red rock terrain of Oak Creek Canyon, and beyond that the Verde Valley with a number of pretty small towns, a famous ghost town rapidly repopulating itself, and as everywhere in the region, wilderness areas for hiking, hunting, and fishing. The town of Prescott is famous as a center for rockhounds as well as for being the site of the only Indian dances in the West performed exclusively by non-Indians (the Smokis).

1. FLAGSTAFF

Flagstaff was named for a pine tree that was stripped of its branches to serve as a pole for flying the flag here on the 100th anniversary of Independence Day on July 4, 1876. Originally a camping area for pioneers heading to California, the town grew up around a spring at the site. Today it is known for its lavish seven-week Festival of Native American Arts running from late June into August. At various times there are exhibits, sales, and demonstrations by groups of artisans from the Hopi Reservation and from the Navajo Reservation who set up stands at the Coconino Center for the Arts or at the Museum of Northern Arizona.

ORIENTATION: Flagstaff, at the center of northern Arizona 150 miles north of Phoenix, is on I-40, which links Barstow, California, to the west with Raleigh, North Carolina, to the east. It is served by **Amtrak** at the station at 1 E. Santa Fe Ave. (tel. 774-8679) by the *Southwest Limited* between Los Angeles and Chicago. Bus transportation is provided by **Greyhound/Trailways,** 3995 Malpais Lane (tel. 774-4573).

Car-rental agencies include **Budget,** 100 N. Humphreys (tel. 779-5632), and **Ugly Duckling,** 23 N. Leroux (tel. 526-2323).

Sightseeing tours of the area, including the Grand Canyon and the Navajo and Hopi reservations, are run daily by **Nava-Hopi/Gray Line,** 401 Malpais Lane (tel. 774-5003).

For visitor information, the **Flagstaff Chamber of Commerce** is at 101 W. Santa Fe Ave., Flagstaff, AZ 86001 (tel. 602/774-4505).

THE MUSEUM OF NORTHERN ARIZONA: This excellent museum (tel. 774-5211), three miles north of the center of town on North Fort Valley Road (U.S. 180), is open daily from 9 a.m. to 5 p.m. Admission is $2 for adults, $1 for students and children. Its purpose is to preserve, exhibit, and research materials from the natural and cultural history of the Colorado Plateau, an area encompassing all of northern Arizona, including the Grand Canyon and Bryce and Zion National Parks to the north in Utah. Current research includes a biotic survey of the Grand Canyon, the recovery of dinosaur remains, and the excavation of ancient pueblo sites. There is an extensive research library.

Visitors here are invited to try using for themselves a simple but ingenious pump drill made of wood of a design perfected by prehistoric Indians in the region. The drill is held vertically with a T-shaped piece wound clockwise so that its tip bores into the stone being worked on. Another exhibit that sets visitors to thinking long thoughts of the future is one displaying a plant called the San Francisco Peaks groundsel, which grows in the heights over town but only within a two-square-mile area and thus is on the endangered list. "Extinction is forever" is one of the central messages the museum puts over. The main threat to this delicate plant, it appears, is simple trampling. The Red Zion desert trumpet is another endangered plant shown, though there are some of these well protected within Grand Canyon National Park. Collectors of pretty plants are the culprits in causing the scarcity of the tiny Navajo Plains cactus, while a primitive buttercup called the Arizona bugbane has been almost completely eradicated by cattle grazing on them. Off-road vehicles are blamed for the paucity of the bear claw poppy. And so it goes—plants with various needs and temperaments falling afoul of the wantonness of man or animal, or at least to the spread of man's presence.

A good quiz to take, fun for everybody, is a display of various species of plants and organisms of the Southwest with multiple-choice identifications to be made. Prove you know your way around the desert or the mountainside. The excellent displays rarely fail to get visitors thinking about various aspects of ecological questions, and they illustrate the aim of the museum that is inscribed on a plaque at the entrance: "This museum displays ideas, not things."

The museum was founded in 1928 by Harold S. Colton, a University of Pennsylvania zoologist who explored Arizona during the summertime in a Model T Ford, eventually doing some archeological surveys of early sites. In the early 1900s there arose a huge wave of interest in Arizona archeology that resulted in shipping artifacts back to eastern museums by the carload. Colton and some Flagstaff residents wanted to find a way to keep some of these treasures here in Arizona where they were found. When Colton moved here permanently in 1926 he set about building a museum for this purpose, which first occupied part of the local Women's Club and made use of local residents' collections of artifacts donated for display. But by 1929 the museum was already operating its own explorations and digs, the first one in Medicine Valley. The present complex was started in 1934 and added to at various times since, built of native volcanic rock and roofed with rounded Spanish tiles, with some windows and doorways designed with the pointed Moorish arches. *Vigas* (beams) spanning the roof underside, visible in the lobby, are copied from ancient ones found in a Hopi village. Today the museum and research center occupy 30 buildings on 110 acres of land.

The aims of the museum include the study of both ancient peoples—the Anasazi to the northeast, the Mogollon to the southeast, the Patayan to the west, and here in the vicinity of Flagstaff, the Sinagua—and modern tribes. Neighboring reservations are those of the Navajo and the Hopi to the northeast and the Havasupai, Hualapai, and Apache in other parts of the state. Some recent finds of early artifacts are split-twig figurines, thought to have been charms for good luck in hunting, dating back (by radiocarbon method) to 3000 B.C.—they turned up in caves in the Grand Canyon. But the more advanced societies in prehistoric times based their economies on farming and food gathering rather than on hunting. The story of a nomadic group that eventually settled down to farming is graphically displayed in the Archeology Room.

An early culture, identified by the baskets and sandals that were typical of its craftspeople, is called the Basketmaker II (there may or may not have been a previous, similar culture that would be called Basketmaker I), dating back to 200 B.C. The dry climate has preserved their artifacts perfectly over the millennia. Part hunter and part farmer, the Basketmaker had tools by which he planted corn. The Basketmakers lived in caves in cliffsides near land that could be cultivated, which bordered rivers and streams. There are blankets these people made of strips of rabbit fur wrapped around yucca fibers, cordage made of human hair, aprons made from juniper bark, and baskets and sandals woven of plant materials. Pottery was molded in baskets first and then sun-dried. Mummified bodies permit us a close inspection of their physical appearance.

A more advanced culture, dating from A.D. 500, by which time the climate had improved from the point of view of crop growing, is designated Basketmaker III, which survived two centuries or so. They grew beans, squash, and cotton besides corn, and lived in pithouses—square holes roofed with beams filled in with grass and mud. As the years went on the communities tended to grow in size, with more and more pit houses grouped together. Pottery was now fired in baking ovens and given black designs on a gray background, or red on buff. They had also by now invented the bow and arrow, as opposed to the simple spear of their ancestors. It was these people who eventually evolved over many generations into the Pueblo Indian civilization still existing today.

The Pueblo periods are also divided into I, II, and III according to era and particularities of tools, weapons, and houses. The first ceremonial rooms, the *kivas,* came from the Pueblo I people (A.D. 700 to 900); Pueblo II builders (to A.D. 1100) began designing elaborate apartment buildings with hundreds of rooms; the final, or classic, period was the Pueblo III period (to A.D. 1300), during which great communities such as the five-story, 800-room Pueblo Bonito, in Chaco Canyon, was completed, housing some 12,000 people—the largest the world had ever known until a bigger one went up in New York City in 1882.

A rare opportunity to inspect the inside of a Hopi *kiva*—a circular underground ceremonial room—is afforded by the full-scale reproduction of one in the ethnology wing. Kachina dances are held here, and it is also a sort of club-like space for men's activities including the instruction of boys in ceremonial lore. Murals on the *kiva* wall were peeled with considerable difficulty from a real *kiva* in the ruins of an ancient pueblo called Awatovi, near Keams Canyon, discovered in 1936. Sophisticated, sprightly, angular dancing figures make up some of these illustrations, one of which has been named *Squash Blossom Girl.*

As fascinating as any subject in the Southwest is the process of weaving Navajo rugs, illustrated here by a working loom in the Navajo Rug Room. Where Hopi men do the kachina carving and the weaving, it is the Navajo women who produce their famous rugs, blankets, and wall hangings. Before the Spanish brought in sheep, the ancient Indians used cotton for their clothing, but since that time wool has been the preferred textile. Navajos began weaving only after 1700 or so, when they learned the art from Pueblo Indians of New Mexico. The earliest example here dates from around 1800, a patchwork cloak, as it is called, that was found in a grave in the Canyon de Chelly on the Navajo Reservation. Part of it is made of a red baize cloth called bayeta that was manufactured in England and used by the Spanish for trading with the Indians. The Indians had to unravel the cloth and twist it into yarn so they could weave it in their own fashion. In the 1920s there was a revival of traditional Navajo weaving, using old patterns that have certain design characteristics depending on the community involved in making them: Two Gray Hills, Chinle, Kayenta, and Crystal, for example, are all rug-making design styles.

Besides the main rug loom there is a smaller one for belts and sashes. The Indian looms differ from those originating in Europe in being vertical instead of horizontal and in having the entire pattern visible at all times, without any of it being rolled away out of sight. The Indians believe this arrangement gives them better artistic control of the whole design. But the Indian loom is capable of considerable variety in its product nevertheless; eight distinct weaves each need a different loom setup: a plain weave, two kinds of diagonal weaves, and five kinds of diamond twill. Rugs may have entirely different weaves on the two sides—this is called a two-faced rug. A display of native dyes shows where various colors originate in local plants and minerals, although most Navajo weaving today uses chemical dyes.

Silverwork is another special area of craftsmanship of both Hopis and Navajos. Mexican silversmiths first taught the Navajos the craft about 1860, and many Navajo jewelry designs come from Spanish-Mexican costumes and horse rigging. The squash blossom, actually a pomegranate blossom, is an example of this, originally a *naja,* a crescent-shaped ornament for the forehead of a horse rather than the breasts of a woman. Silverwork is made by heating the metal and incising the design with a die and a hammer, or by casting it, pouring molten silver into a sandstone mold.

Also shown here are Navajo sandpaintings that originated as part of a ceremony done to treat injury or disease. Relatives of a patient hire a singer to perform this ceremony during which a layer of fine sand on the floor of a house has a design drawn on it in tracings of finely ground colored minerals. This material is sifted on the sand base by the singer, or medicine man, between fingers and thumb, can take all day to complete, and is destroyed at sunset.

The museum also displays paintings from its three permanent collections. One is artwork by Indian schoolchildren—a series by a class of 12-year-olds of Taos Pueblo shows a great emphasis on skies, blue skies with human and bird-like figures moving and interacting. Another is a collection of paintings by established Indian artists, while the third collection is of American art of the West, including works by James Swinnerton, Maynard Dixon, Gray Bartlett, and several others.

Besides the exhibition and sale of work in the **Hopi Craftsman exhibit** on the July 4th weekend, and the **Navajo Craftsman exhibit** the last week in July, both held here, the museum holds an annual **Junior Indian Art Show** every spring with work by young Indians aged 6 to 18 in either reservation or public schools. But Indian crafts are shown and sold here all year in the first-rate gift shop set up as a source of income to the Indians. All winter, when tourists are few on the reservation, Hopis bring in their kachina dolls, pottery, and woven baskets for sale. There is also a selection of Navajo rugs and silverwork, Hopi silver jewelry, Zuñi silverwork, crafts from the Rio Grande pueblos of New Mexico, and baskets from the Tohono O'Odham and Pima of southern Arizona. Besides this there are a few historic collector's items.

OTHER FLAGSTAFF AREA ATTRACTIONS: The **Lowell Observatory,** one mile east of downtown via Santa Fe Avenue, on Mars Hill, was founded in 1894, and among its various accomplishments over the years was the discovery of the planet Pluto. The preponderance of cloudless nights all year and the steadiness of the atmosphere drew astronomers, including founder Percival Lowell (of the Massachusetts Lowells), to choose this mesa some 300 feet above the city as the base of their observations. A more recent discovery was of rings around Uranus, in 1977. Guided tours free to visitors begin at 1:30 p.m. weekdays only, with tickets given out at the Flagstaff Chamber of Commerce, 101 W. Santa Fe (tel. 774-4505).

The **Arizona Historical Society Pioneer Museum,** 1848 N. Fort Valley Rd. (tel. 774-6272), has the Kolb brothers' collection of old movie cameras and photos of the first trip on the Colorado River, and there are historic items out of the Rough Riders era, and military, furniture, farm, and lumbering items. Field trips and demonstrations are occasionally presented. The museum is open free of charge Monday through Saturday from 9 a.m. to 5 p.m. and on Sunday from 1:30 to 5 p.m.

Walnut Canyon National Monument, ten miles east of town, reached via I-40 east and an access road, offers a steep descent into a cave-lined canyon where ruins of some 125 rooms of a prehistoric pueblo have been uncovered. A trail leads to two dozen of these, and the others are visible from it. The round-trip hike, although only three-quarters of a mile in length, can be tiring because of the 7,000-foot altitude here and the 185-foot depth of the canyon floor. The people who lived here 500 years ago, the Sinagua, used present-day plants and animals for many of their needs: plants for food, fiber, dye, medicine, fuel, construction, implements, weapons, and ceremonial purposes, such as Ponderosa pine, piñon pine, juniper, Douglas fir, locust, aspen, willow, box elder, hop tree, holly grape, serviceberry, elderberry, snowberry, lemonade sumac, mountain mahogany, cliff rose, currant, saltbush, wild tobacco, Mormon tea, grape, agave, yucca, and of course the black walnut for which the canyon was named.

The Sinagua people moved into the canyon 900 years ago when a nearby volcano spread a porous layer of cinders over a wide area. The layer retained moisture and transformed a desert into an oasis, bringing emigrants from all directions to move in on the Sinaguas' home territory. Because of this incursion, it is believed, the Sinagua sought a refuge in the canyon, where they could also manage some marginal agriculture. Within the limestone recesses of the canyon walls they built over 300 rooms, using the cave locations both for shelter and for protection from attack. Within the canyon they had a water supply in the form of a stream, and considerable fertile land. Up on the mesa there was a forest to provide wood, while many plants grew in the canyon bottom. There was ample game as well.

The Sinagua people left behind them pottery, pendants, and masonry walls that show their skills and their appreciation of beauty. Somehow before their relatively recent arrival in the canyon, it appears that it had never been occupied, except transiently, by humans. Their houses were constructed with double walls of limestone slabs, the inner space filled with mud, which also served as mortar and plaster. Packed and dried, mud, too, is used for a floor. A hole above the door lets out some of the smoke from a cooking fire in the room. The Sinagua lived in the canyon only for 150 years and then, like the other prehistoric peoples of the Southwest, disappeared, abandoning their homes. The first modern knowledge of the existence of these ruins did not come until their discovery by pioneers in 1883.

The monument is open May 30 to Labor Day from 7 a.m. to 7 p.m. and the rest of the year from 8 a.m. to 5 p.m., at $1 per car. A visitor center supplies information, and there is a picnic area nearby at the top.

WHERE TO STAY: Offering striking southwestern-style appointments, such as a modernistic high-ceilinged, eight-sided lobby with heavy truss beams and a Territorial-style chandelier overhead, and a brick fireplace and adjoining beehive oven to warm guests who meet here, the **Ramada Inn East,** 2610 E. Santa Fe, Flagstaff, AZ 86001 (tel. 602/526-1399, or toll free 800/228-2828), has spacious lawns across which the San Francisco Mountains are outlined on the horizon. The combination of modern and Victorian styles works also in the dining room, in leaded-glass partitions between tables and fancy white-glass lampshades on fixtures suspended from ceilings. Rooms have rich paneling and textile patterns in bedspreads and curtains in geometric designs of colorful intricacy. There is an outdoor pool and playground, and besides the Mason Jar Restaurant, there is a coffeeshop. Rates are $52 to $65 double.

The restored **Hotel Monte Vista,** 100 N. San Francisco, Flagstaff, AZ 86001 (tel. 602/779-6971), will take many travelers back to the scene of a busy small-city hotel of half a century ago. This city landmark is a center of business life in Flagstaff, in its coffeeshop and its bar; it is also the place where Zane Grey wrote some of his western fiction in the earlier part of the century. Double rates here are $75.

Accommodations for two for as low as $32 are offered at the **Flagstaff Regal 8 Inn,** 2440 E. Lucky Lane, Flagstaff, AZ 86001 (tel. 602/774-8756, or toll-free 800/851-8888), in some of the 104 modern rooms. There is also an outdoor swimming pool.

Bed-and-Breakfast

Just outside town in a wooded setting is the **Arizona Mountain Inn,** Lake Mary Road, Flagstaff, AZ 86001 (tel. 602/774-8959), which makes an ideal base for forest hiking or, in winter, cross-country skiing; there is also a baseball diamond, a volleyball court, a basketball court, a horseshoe pitch, and a playground. The inn also offers rustic-style cottages, fully equipped, with bathrooms, fireplaces, and central heating. Rates vary according to size of accommodation and also with the season: cabins for two go from $50 to $80 daily, with higher-priced cabins for up to ten people also available.

WHERE TO EAT: Open daily except Monday for lunch and dinner is the **Christmas Tree,** 1903 N. 2nd St. (tel. 779-5888), known for steaks, prime rib, and homemade rolls and pies.

Restaurants specializing in Mexican foods include **Ramona's,** 1312 S. Plaza Way (tel. 774-3397), open seven days for lunch and dinner, with live entertainment on Friday and Saturday evenings; and **Las Primas,** 5200 E. Cortland Blvd. (tel. 526-2085).

For steak, try **Sizzler Steak,** 2080 S. Milton Rd. (tel. 779-3267).

2. SEDONA AND OAK CREEK CANYON

The town of Sedona lies below the Mogollon Rim at the mouth of Oak Creek Canyon at a distance of 28 miles south of Flagstaff and 120 miles north of Phoenix, and has become the most active art colony in Arizona. It was here that the regionally influential Cowboy Artists of America, now numbering 29 members, began their organization in a café back in 1965. Now new arrivals from all over the country are coming into the canyon to build their dream houses in the red-rock land of weird formations—turrets, bluffs, buttes, and spires—that rises up on either side of Oak Creek. The bright colorings of cliffsides, shaded with the green woodland, survive the impact of the builders somehow; the new houses are swallowed up in the general background. Oak Creek itself is a good trout stream bordered with cottonwoods that leads north from Sedona 16 miles up through its canyon to the Mogollon Rim. A highway, U.S. 89A, follows the stream and makes a switchback, twisting climb up the steep face of the rim on its route north to Flagstaff, providing spectacular views of the canyon below and the Verde Valley beyond it to the south.

Sedona was discovered by a few artists after the war and was put on the art map by the Cowboy Artists so that today there are an estimated 200 artists in town and another 200 craftspeople of various talents and interests. The plague of urban sprawl has so far been avoided, however, by the fact that the new building has been done spottily, with houses scattered in hideaways in all parts of the hills and woods around the town. A commercial strip is indeed abuilding to the west of town, but so far its half dozen blocks of shops and small shopping malls have not managed to spoil the overall scene of rustic countryside and indeed, up in the surrounding heights, scenic splendor. The official downtown area of town, in fact, remains only a block in length.

SIGHTS AND SHOPS: A favorite area with visitors is a shopping area made to look like an imitation Mexican village of a perfection never seen south of the border, with tiled patios, gardens, adobe walls, wrought-iron lamp fixtures, stone stairways out of a distant past—a wholehearted leap into a Spanish Colonial past nobody ever really experienced until now. It is called **Tlaquepaque,** after the suburb of the Mexican city of Guadalajara that is the legendary home of the strolling musicians called mariachis—and indeed there are live mariachis on the scene who come up here from Nogales and other border towns to ply their trade. As they move among the browsers ogling outdoor art shows or judging the wares in the 40 specialty and crafts shops, they make a pretty picture against a background of a chapel (built for its looks) or a fountain in the middle of the plaza.

A few of the shops house dealers of art, including one called **Sculptured Art,** specializing in contemporary and western-style sculptures in bronze, wood, ceramic, and stone. The **Casa de Artes** has paintings and lithographs by regional artists. **El Prado Gallery** shows contemporary paintings in the southwestern style. These and the other Tlaquepaque shops are all open year round: from 10 a.m. to 5 p.m. Monday through Saturday and noon to 5 p.m. on Sunday.

The outdoors delight in this red-rock country lies up along the sides of the canyon where foot trails or Jeep routes take visitors into a country that seems a secret hideaway. It was this backdrop of red rock formations that drew early moviemakers to Sedona in the 1920s. Such films as *Broken Arrow, 3:10 to Yuma,* and *The Cowboy and the Redhead* were made here, and the area is now a favorite for television films and commercials. One western-style artist, Bob Bradshaw, spans both the art world and the movie scene; when he's not painting scenes of bucking broncos he hires out as an extra.

One of the most beautiful areas around Sedona is reachable only on foot on a 14-mile (one-way) trail along the **West Fork** of Oak Creek Canyon. The trailhead is reached from a point along U.S. 89A, the highway that follows Oak Creek in the bottom of the canyon, just 7½ miles north of the Sedona–Oak Creek Canyon Chamber of Commerce in the center of Sedona (at the junction of Ariz. 179 and U.S. 89A). Just beyond the second bridge, a mile past Hoel's tourist cabins, there is a graveled pullout from which the trail departs. The stream has to be forded, since the footbridge over it was washed out some time ago.

The cultural center of life here is the **Sedona Arts Center,** at U.S. 89A and Art Barn Road. You can get information on current shows and programs by calling 282-3809. Local painters whose works are displayed here, Cowboy Artists of America founders who originally got together in the Oak Creek Tavern downtown, include Joe Beeler, Charlie Dye, John Hampton, George Phippen, Fred Harmon, and Bob McLeod. The barn is also the scene of musical attractions and various shows and meetings.

Other Sedona galleries show the work of local artists, particularly the **Red Rock Art 'n' Craft Co-op,** on Memory Arch Lane off U.S. 89A (tel. 282-2215), displaying paintings and sculptures of a dozen of its members.

A fairly young gallery is the **Creekside,** in the Artesania Center (tel. 282-1465), near the chamber of commerce. Oak-paneled swinging doors embellished with antique engraved glass give entry to an octagonal room showing western paintings by artist Roy Kerswill. Other regional artists shown in the Creekside include sculptor Doug Hyde, who works in Utah alabaster; and Bill Girard, who fashions bronze statuary with a southwestern flavor.

Other Sedona galleries, among many, are **Elaine Horwitch,** Schnebly Hill Road at Ariz. 179 (tel. 282-6290), representing nationally known painters; the **Son-Silver-West Gallery,** on Ariz. 179 (tel. 282-3580), showing traditional western paintings; the **Treasure Art Gallery,** three miles south of town on Ariz. 179 (tel. 282-3122), showing paintings in both impressionistic and realistic styles on regional historic themes; and the **Windrush Gallery,** on Ariz. 179 (tel. 282-7676), showing paintings and bronzes of the Cowboy Artists of America.

Among founders of the art colony here are the Egyptian-American sculptor Nassan Gobran, the English watercolorist Jeffrey Lunge, the bird painter Charles Murphy, the oldtime cartoonist Dan Bloodgood, and the Hungarian neorealist Stephen Juharos. Young artists, too, have taken up residence, forming what they call the "art underground" to produce works selling at comparatively moderate prices—a good opportunity for visiting art buffs sometimes to make happy discoveries.

Still active is another kingpin, or queenpin, of the art colony, now in her 80s, the painter famous in the '20s and '30s for her nude magazine-cover girls, Zoe Mozert. Today she says, "I was Sedona's first famous professional artist, but all they want now is girls pinched into blue jeans." More recently arrived in the colony is Del Yoakum, a one-time student of Thomas Hart Benton, who has spent two decades working at the Disney Studios and loves to paint pictures of birds, especially of the roadrunner, of which species he says: "They have a marvelous searching eye and don't miss a thing—and they can really stand off my big black cat!" Younger artists include people like Curt Walters, in his early 30s, who moved into town with his wife and two kids back in 1979 because he just likes canyons. He says, "Sedona's vivid light, dramatic sunsets, dense cloud shadows crawling over hills and houses, and dark moody skies after a storm inspire me to paint!"

Oak Creek Canyon is Zane Grey country—when his heroine first set eyes on it (in *Call of the Canyon*) she felt "at once a chill and a shudder." The most dazzling scene is from the edge of the Mogollon Rim, reached via U.S. 89A between Sedona and Flagstaff, looking down 1,500 feet into the canyon bottom, its steep sides upholstered in bigtooth maples, oaks, Arizona cypress, and willows, all contributing their special colors. It is an especially bright scene in the fall when the leaves turn to yellows, oranges, and tans, the colorful patches framed by the fairyland of buttes and skyscraper rock formations beyond them.

A botanist's heyday in the diversity of flowers and trees along the reach of the canyon and up to the lip of the Rim is due to the differences in altitude from north to south—6,400 feet down to 4,300 feet near Sedona. The difference in heights makes for a variety equal to that between areas normally 600 miles apart. At higher levels are Douglas fir, aspen, and spruce, and below in the warmer and drier climate grow manzanita, piñon, juniper, and oak. Alders border the stream up high, cottonwoods down below. Water ouzels—locally called dippers—dive-bomb the stream in their search for underwater insects that cling to the undersides of stones. Fluffy-eared, bushy-tailed squirrels and tree frogs are familiar to campers in the woods (the surrounding areas are part of Coconino National Forest and have many public campsites). Raccoons, an occasional coyote, or a rattlesnake may appear. There are deer, and in the distant heights, elk.

Slide Rock is great fun—a stretch of Oak Creek accessible from the highway where smooth stone is lubricated by algae to make a zippy, sliding ride for swimmers. The **West Fork** reaches into a canyon so narrow at one point that hikers have to go through it by sloshing through the streambed. The sheer walls at that point are striated and pitted as if by mysterious hieroglyphs. By 4 in the afternoon the sun has passed over the narrow opening of sky above the main canyon and it begins to get dark.

Various back-road trips into the red-rock country are offered by **Pink Jeep Tour** (tel. 282-5000). All-day van tours to Jerome and to Anasazi ruins are run by **Overland Stage** (tel. 634-0108). Seven miles up the canyon on U.S. 89A there is the **Encinoso picnic ground,** a good spot for sightseeing and a base for strolls along the stream. Information on camping and free permits are available at the **Coconino National Forest** ranger station on Brewer Road (tel. 282-4119). The 18-hole golf course of the **Oak Creek Country Club,** six miles south of town on Ariz. 179 (tel. 284-1660), is open to the public. You can take scenic plane rides from the airstrip of the **Sedona Air Center** (tel. 282-7935).

For all travel-service information, see the **Sedona–Oak Creek Canyon Chamber of Commerce,** at the junction of Ariz. 179 and U.S. 89A, Sedona, AZ 86336 (tel. 602/282-7722).

WHERE TO STAY: There are two dozen motels and guest ranches in and around Sedona. Fanciest is **Poco Diablo Resort,** south of town on Ariz. 79, P.O. Box 1709, Sedona, AZ 86336 (tel. 602/282-7333, or toll free 800/528-4275, 800/352-5710 in Arizona), with 143 rooms, villas, and suites with wet bars and refrigerators, a nine-hole golf course, tennis courts, swimming pools, and a restaurant and lounge with live entertainment. Rates are $75 to $105 double, depending on size of accommodation and time of week (weekends have a higher rate); children under 12 stay free of charge.

The **Arroyo Roble,** at 400 N. U.S. 89A, Sedona, AZ 86336 (tel. 602/282-4001, or toll free 800/528-1234), also has rooms with wide windows and balconies looking out on red-rock country. Decorative styles run to blends of burnt orange, sand, and royal blue, and there are oak dressers and cabinets, marble vanities, Spanish-tile bathroom floors, and solid-core ash doors. King-size or double queen-size beds are custom-made with extra-thick padding. There are free local telephone calls and cable television. A guest laundry and a rooftop observation deck are additional features. The spacious lobby has a modern fieldstone fireplace with a blazing fire on cool days. There is a pool for swimming; Oak Creek runs near the motel, also available for swims. Double rates are $60 to $70.

The **King's Ransom,** on Ariz. 179 (half a mile south of the center of town), Sedona, AZ 86336 (tel. 602/282-7151, or toll free 800/228-5151), is situated in the foothills of the red-rock bluffs, with spectacular views of the rusty-orange cliffs from the picture windows; the colors glow with an unlikely fire-like brilliance at sunrise and sunset. Lush pink roses grow around the outdoor L-shaped pool and there's a desert garden for strolling or cliff watching. Rooms all have balconies or private patios and are done in southwestern decor of tan-and-orange matching carpet and draperies, with geometric-patterned bedspreads. A dining room is open daily for three meals; patio dining is available, and there's a bar and lounge. Rates are $45 to $69 double, the lower rates applying in the winter months.

Economy-priced rooms at any time of year are offered in pleasant surroundings at the **Canyon Portal Motel,** 280 N. U.S. 89A, Sedona, AZ 86336 (tel. 602/282-7125). Double rates are $29 to $39, depending on season, and there are housekeeping units or refrigerators available. There are patios with canyon views, and complimentary coffee and hot chocolate is available.

Bed-and-Breakfast in Oak Creek

Graham's Bed & Breakfast Inn, 150 Canyon Circle Dr., in the nearby village of Oak Creek, AZ 86336 (tel. 602/284-1425), is a new structure built both as the innkeepers' home and as accommodations for guests. A central concern in choosing the site was assuring a view of the striking buttes and mesas of the red-rock country from every room in the house. Each of the guest rooms is furnished differently. The Heritage Suite, for example, is done in red, white, and blue in honor of the father of Marni Graham: "Memorabilia from his lifetime in the service is gathered in an antique pine hutch." This suite also has a marble shower for two. The Southern Suite was designed as a tribute to the mother of Bill Graham: "Soft blues, leaf greens, and gentle rose colors reflect southern grandeur and hospitality." Four-poster beds, a marble-topped washstand, a bureau, and a love seat are also included. Grandest of the suites is the San Francisco, with a California king-size bed and a double Jacuzzi. Breakfasts include home-baked breads, Swedish pancakes, or eggs rancheros. Rates are $80 to $115 double.

WHERE TO EAT: Two of the best restaurants in Sedona are to be found in the Tlaquepaque shopping complex. One of these is a French restaurant called **René** (tel. 282-9225), in a French provincial setting, open daily except Tuesday for lunch and dinner. For lunch you might order steamed mussels in white wine, ham shank with buttered potatoes and braised red cabbage, Swiss spaghetti, vol-au-vent toulousaine, or Madame Oak Creek veal and scallops madeira. Dinner selections may include chicken Bombay or Colorado rack of lamb for two ($40), starting off with such hors d'oeuvres as escargots au vin de Chambertin.

Also in Tlaquepaque is **El Rincon** (tel. 282-4648), open Tuesday through

Saturday from 11 a.m. to 8 p.m. and on Sunday from noon to 5 p.m., a great place to eat outside on the terrace in warm weather, or inside in warm southwestern décor—a white stucco beehive fireplace, copper plates on the walls, painted Spanish-style tiles. A margarita made with fresh pressed limes and freshly whipped eggwhites is a good starter, to be followed by any of a variety of Arizona-style Mexican dishes—enchiladas, tacos, tostadas, quesadillas, chiles rellenos—all served with the traditional sopaipillas (fried bread with honey). The house specialty is the chimichanga, a sopaipilla folded around the delicacy of your choice: shrimp, refried beans, beef, chicken, or red and green chiles. All ingredients are fresh—no preservatives or lard are used. The chef, a Californian, learned his cooking skills in Mexico. Dinners run $12 to $15.

The **Sedona Yacht Club,** on Ariz. 179 in the nearby village of Oak Creek (tel. 284-1510), offers luxurious continental-style dining in a room overlooking the golf course. The club is also popular on weekends for snacks and drinks outdoors at umbrella tables overlooking the 15th tee.

Equally known for its seafood and its wok dishes is **Shugrue's,** 2250 W. U.S. 89A (tel. 282-2943), open daily from 8 a.m. to 9 p.m.

3. THE VERDE VALLEY

Some 20 miles south of Sedona, the Verde River meanders across its broad valley past the towns of Clarkdale, Cottonwood, and Camp Verde, while in the heights to the west, clinging to its mountainside at a hair-raising angle, is the former ghost town of Jerome, now so populated with artists, craftspeople of various ilk, and shopkeepers that it has forfeited its claim to the title. Fort Verde is a historic military post that has been restored in the town of Camp Verde, and there are more prehistoric ruins, the majestic apartments of Montezuma Castle and the glowing pinkish stone of the houses of Tuzigoot, both protected in national monuments.

CAMP VERDE: This small town three miles east of I-17 lies 56 miles south of Flagstaff and 93 miles north of Phoenix, and is noted for **Fort Verde,** an army post built here in 1871. Now a state park, it has a museum (tel. 567-3275), open daily from 8 a.m. to 5:30 p.m. all year, with photographs taken at the fort between 1872 and 1890, military hardware from the period, and Indian artifacts. Officers' quarters and adjutants' offices have been restored—one a rambling house with a mansard roof and shake shingles. The post figured in the campaign of Gen. George Crook against the northern bands of Apaches a century ago. Nearby is a doctor's office from the 1880s equipped with medical instruments and supplies of the time. There is an admission charge of $1. For travel-service information inquire at the **Camp Verde Chamber of Commerce** on Main Street (tel. 602/567-9294).

MONTEZUMA CASTLE NATIONAL MONUMENT: Five miles north of Camp Verde via I-17, the so-called castle was misnamed by pioneers who somehow had the idea that Aztecs had once lived in the area, which was not the case. The best-preserved prehistoric ruin in the U.S., the five-story, 20-room pueblo high in a cliff wall overlooking the Verde River can be viewed only from below—visitors are not allowed within its walls. The monument is open daily from 8 a.m. to 5 p.m., except in the summer when it stays open to 7 p.m. A **visitor center** (tel. 567-3322) has displays of artifacts of the Sinaguan people who lived here until about A.D. 1450 when the place was deserted, for reasons never determined. Admission is $1 per car.

The earliest permanent settlers of the Verde Valley were Hohokam Indians from the Phoenix area who moved up here in the 7th century A.D., farming the bottom lands near the river and building villages on high ground in the foothills of the surrounding mountains. Excavations show that these early residents lived in single-family houses of wooden poles covered with brush and mud and furnished with a few basic utensils, such as a plain sort of pottery to hold food and water, and grinding stones for corn, nuts, and berries. There were arrowheads, scrapers for hides, and skinning knives as well. They also had an oval court for ball games very much like those found in early Mexico. Another trait that made them different from other peoples in the region was that they cremated their dead. The Sinaguan Indians, who lived in the high forest country to the north, differed from the Hohokam in that they made a polished brown kind of pottery with decorative markings and buried their dead; they also depended on hunting more than the Hohokam. In about 1125 some of the Sinaguan people moved down into the Verde Valley, taking from the Hohokam of the area the invention of irrigation canals that diverted water to otherwise arid cropland. They also built houses of rock and mud, copying those of Pueblo Indians farther north. It is these people who built the stone pueblos such as Montezuma's Castle, the construction of which is believed to date to the 12th century.

They also built a small pueblo nearby on the edge of a tiny lake still there today, and part of a separate section of the national monument called Montezuma's Well. The rim of the so-called well had limestone to be used for building rocks, and mud and clay for mortar came from a streambed close by. Along the course of the main irrigation ditch from the well they built one- and two-room farm structures. The mile-long ditch irrigated some 60 acres of farmland.

About the middle of the 13th century there occurred a kind of real estate boom in the valley during which the buildings were enlarged to serve as forts, being given high walls, parapets, peepholes, and sealed doorways. The population increased too, from additional immigration of Sinagua people out of the high country to the north, probably caused by a century-long drought that was at its worst during the final quarter of the 13th century. The spring-fed streams near the present castle provided a saving water source for these people. But there are signs that various elements of the population were in conflict, probably because of overcrowding and fighting over water rights. There was a time when the population was concentrated in a pueblo at the well, but then it was abandoned. Not very long after, sometime after 1400, the castle, too, and the entire river valley were abandoned by the Sinagua, who disappeared without a trace.

When the Spanish arrived in the 16th century they found Yavapai Indians here—possibly descendants of those early Hohokam who lived here even before the Sinagua came down from the mountains to join them in the valley. The Yavapai cremated their dead, like the early Hohokam, and they built similar houses out of poles and brush and mud, and they farmed the same plots of land along the river bottom land. It is conjectured that those Yavapai—or earlier generations of those people—could have fought the Sinagua and forced them out of the valley, but we have no record of what really happened. It may be that the Sinagua moved to the northeast to become ancestors of the modern Hopi. Oral traditions, according to scholars, make this a distinct possibility. The modern Hopi have a legend about a people who came up to join them from the south, a people without priests or ceremonies. They could well have been the mysteriously disappeared Sinagua.

Besides a good water supply for farming and good hunting in the valley, the Sinagua people had the rare good fortune of a nearby source of salt, which they mined from a deposit two miles south of the town of Camp Verde, visible today ne Road. There collapsed tunnels occasionally turn up the handle of one of their stone salt-picking tools. Matting and bits of unburned torches of the kind they used for light in the tunnels have also been recovered. In 1928 some preserved Sinagua bodies were also found, in the tunnel that had collapsed on them and sealed their doom. As for jewelry, they satisfied the decorative urge from a nearby deposit of a red stone called argillite, from which they made beads, pendants, and earrings. They also traded with other, traveling Indians for inlay ornaments made of shell from the Gulf of California. Turquoise was something else they got by bartering, and since their own pottery was utilitarian and without decoration, they imported a lot of fancy ceramics from other peoples who specialized in that art. Located strategically between the Hohokam to the south and the Pueblo peoples to the north, the Sinagua lived along trade routes and had salt, cotton, and argillite in quantity as trading materials.

Montezuma Castle sheltered about 50 people in the 17 rooms that are neatly fitted into the natural cave that shelters it and has kept it so well preserved. There were two trails to it, one up from the river bottom and another leading down from the top of the ledge. The Indians probably used ladders for coming and going, and also to get from one floor to another. Such ladders were either a single pole with notches or two poles with rungs lashed in place. The limestone walls are a foot thick, and have remained solid because of the excellent clay mortar holding the building stones together. The individual stones are fairly small, less than a foot across, because they had to be carried up here from the streambed.

The rooms range in size from 37 to 240 square feet, most of them averaging about 100 square feet. The pueblo was built without the use of any metal tools whatever, only picks and axes of stone, about six inches long. A groove was made in these axe heads so that a handle could be bent around it and lashed in place. Some roof timbers still show chopping marks. Cutting a big tree with such tools must have been a major project. Poles were laid at right angles to the roof beams, the whole finished off with a covering of grass, willow branches, or brush, and topped with a coating of mud as thick as four inches. T-shaped doorways are like those seen in pueblos as far away as Casas Grandes, 500 miles to the south in the Mexican state of Chihuahua—the wider breadth at the top is thought to have been made in order to permit entrance by people carrying bulky loads. The doors are low for two reasons: to keep out the cold and also to force any attacker to poke his head through first. Cooking fires were built right on the floors in cold weather, as the smoke-blackened walls and ceilings show; the only exit for the smoke was the doorway. In one room bats have worn off the accumulation of soot on the ceiling. It is thought that these flying mammals have occupied the castle for many years because when pioneers first found the place there was four feet of bat dung covering the floor.

Montezuma Well, three miles northeast of the castle, is reached via I-17 northeast with an exit at the McGuireville interchange. Its appeal is that of an oasis in an arid prairie, actually a limestone sinkhole into which a large spring flows, a rare geological formation. It was here that the early Hohokam and later Sinagua built their irrigation ditches. The rim is 70 feet from the surface of the water, which stretches 400 feet from wall to wall, and is 55 feet deep at the center. In spite of the placid appearance of the surface, the well flows at its outlet spring at the rate of 1½ million gallons a day. But the water reflects the blue sky like an immense mirror and is a favorite target for picture taking.

There are two rarities at the well. One consists of examples of undercut rectangular burial pits in which the Sinagua buried their dead at full length. The pits were dug down through limestone to a depth of three feet and then inward to form an undercut chamber about three by six feet in size. Into this the corpse was put, along with funeral offerings in the form of pottery and other artifacts. Then the tomb was sealed up with slabs of limestone and covered over with mud. Finally the pit itself was filled in, the only such burials known anywhere.

The most outstanding attraction at the well is the permanently preserved, almost fossilized irrigation ditches the Sinaguas are noted for. Because of the limestone content in the water of the well, particles would accumulate in the canals. As water evaporated, more and more would accumulate. When the fields had been watered, the stream was turned off into Beaver Creek to avoid flooding, permitting occasional drying of the channels, which left more lime particles in them each time. The result is that over the years they became cemented and thus preserved for the future. A National Park Service historian comments that they are "monuments to the first farmers of the Verde Valley."

TUZIGOOT NATIONAL MONUMENT: Reached from I-17 via Ariz. 279
to Clarkdale and an access road two miles to the east, Tuzigoot is 27 miles from Montezuma Castle and was also occupied by Sinagua people, who arrived here around A.D. 1125 and departed at the end of the 14th century. About 50 people lived in the pueblo on a promontory here overlooking the Verde River. Originally there were 77 rooms, many used for food storage, on the ground floor, with other rooms in a second story, and they covered an area of about 50,000 square feet. The rooms were about 12 by 18 feet in size, and were entered through rooftop hatchways by ladder. Today all that remain are walls three or four feet high, but the pinkish stone they are built of gives them a particularly warm appeal visually, especially when the light comes in at a low angle at dawn or at dusk. The name Tuzigoot is an Apache word meaning "crooked water."

The monument has a **visitor center** (tel. 634-5564), open from 8 a.m. to 5 p.m. (in summer, 7 a.m. to 7 p.m.). The admission fee is $1 per car. A museum in the visitor center displays grave offerings, turquoise mosaics of the Sinagua, and shell jewelry from trade with coastal Indians.

Nearby is another site, the **Hatalacva Ruins,** with 13th-century Sinagua trash mounds.

JEROME: This fascinating old gold-, silver-, and copper-mining town, 55 miles
southwest of Flagstaff via U.S. 89A, clings to a steep slope of Cleopatra Hill overlooking the Verde Valley, the San Francisco peaks 50 miles north, and a jumble of red-rock formations and canyons. When the last copper mine closed in 1953 it left a nearly empty town with only a handful of diehard residents, but a rediscovery by artists and craftspeople, not to mention merchants, has brought the population up to 450—too many, it is generally admitted, to call itself a "ghost town" anymore.

The 30° angle of the ground under Jerome's buildings gives them a hodgepodge aspect as if they might tumble into one another or break loose and bounce down the mountainside the 2,000-foot drop to the valley floor. In fact the town does have a solid blockhouse of a concrete jail that is famous for having slid clear across the road to come to rest on the other side. Strolling around Jerome is like mountain climbing, with the helpful difference that some of the sidewalks are fitted out with stairs. Between houses at the top of the town and those at the lower level, in the Gulch, there is a difference of 1,500 feet in elevation.

The history of Jerome starts with the United Verde Copper Co. in 1876, which opened a mine and a camp named in honor of Eugene Jerome, the main backer of the enterprise. When it folded two years later because of high costs of transportation out of the remote area, a new owner named William A. Clark came in and built a narrow-gauge railroad. By the turn of the century Jerome had the biggest copper mine in Arizona. Other mines opened too, and there were boom times until the stock market disaster of 1929. Phelps Dodge took over the

United Verde mine in 1935, ran it until 1953, and then closed it for good, ending the mining days. At its peak Jerome had a population of 15,000 but by 1955 it had dwindled to 100.

Today the **Jerome Historical Society** has a museum at 200 Main St. that recalls the boisterous life of what was once the most notorious mining camp in the country—"the billion-dollar copper camp," as it was called. The museum includes a gift shop and occupies what was once the Fashion Saloon, built in 1899. Just out of the center of town at the end of UVX Road is the **State Historic Park** (tel. 634-5381), with another museum related to the town's mining history; admission is 50¢. It occupies the mansion of "Rawhide Jimmy" Douglas, one-time owner of the Little Daisy copper mine here. The mansion was built originally to be a hotel for visiting investors and mining officials, and had a wine cellar, billard room, marble-walled bathrooms, and a very early central vacuuming system. It was made of adobe bricks. The shell of another of his properties, the Little Daisy Hotel, is still visible in Jerome.

Besides a number of shops purveying southwestern arts and crafts and regional minerals, the town has a local-hangout bar and restaurant, the **Miner's Roost Hotel,** at 309 Main St. (tel. 634-5094), and up the hill at 308 Clark St. a good restaurant with a fabulous view of the Verde Valley, especially at night, the **Jerome Palace** (tel. 634-9844), open daily for lunch and dinner. There is also a well-stocked, pleasant bar on the premises.

4. PRESCOTT

Prescott calls itself the "climate capital" for its dry, sunny mile-high situation in a pine valley between the desert to the south and the forested mountains to the north. Located 100 miles north of Phoenix via I-17 and Ariz. 69, and 90 miles southwest of Flagstaff via U.S. 89A, this bright, airy town of 25,000 is a center of mineral deposits in surrounding hill country where rockhounds find as wide a variety of treasure as anywhere in the Southwest.

SIGHTS AND ACTIVITIES: Settled in 1863 when gold was discovered in those hills, the town was the Territorial capital for three years—Arizona's first— and had the first school and the first sawmill in the territory. A famous landmark here is **Thumb Butte,** preferably viewed from town at sunset when a few stray clouds might reflect the pink and crimson of those western skies that are a bit much to believe even when you see them. Another landmark is the statue of Rough Rider organizer Buckey O'Neill on horseback in front of the courthouse —rated generally one of the best equestrian statues in the country.

Montezuma Street is the site of old **Whiskey Row** that once had 20 saloons but now has fancy stores as well. But the old Palace, rebuilt after a 1900 fire, is still going strong, with its fine long bar and high ceiling. That bar was saved from the fire despite its unwieldy weight and length when cowboys and miners hauled it away from the burning buildings—much of the town had caught fire during a drought when there was not enough water to quench it—and set it up on the courthouse lawn to save it. Legend is that the bar stayed open as usual, 24 hours a day, throughout the fire emergency.

Not only climate capital but also softball capital, with 15 softball fields usually occupied in season every day, and the sometimes capital of the western art world, Prescott claims the latter by reason of its annual **George Phippen Memorial Western Art Show** in May on the courthouse plaza. It is followed by a combined dinner and art auction that the local boosters insist is "one of the major recurring events in western art." Musical arts are not neglected: **Hendrix Auditorium** schedules various musical groups and soloists during the year, as well as four appearances by the Phoenix Symphony.

A group of early buildings that escaped the 1900 fire has been preserved and restored in what is dubbed the **Territorial Buildings Multiple Resource Area,** one of the best grouped examples of early southwestern American architecture. Besides the courthouse itself and the Palace Bar noted above, visitors are welcome at the **Sharlot Hall Museum,** 415 W. Gurley, named for a poet and state historian. The museum has displays of pioneer furnishings as well as artifacts and crafts items made by the nearby Yavapai Apache Indians. An early iron windmill behind the building is still working. A two-story log house dating to 1864, the territorial governor's lodgings, is also part of the museum complex, which has several structures open to visitors, including the 1877 **Bashford House,** an ornate Victorian structure with period furnishings, which also houses a gallery for the Mountain Artists Guild. A two-room log cabin called **Old Fort Misery** belonged to an early attorney, while the **Fremont House** was another governor's residence, that of John C. Fremont. On the grounds is an unusual garden containing 350 varieties of roses, one planted especially in memory of each of 350 outstanding women of the territory and the state of Arizona. The museum buildings are open free of charge (with donations asked) Tuesday through Saturday from 9 a.m. to 5 p.m. and on Sunday from 1 to 5 p.m. For information, call 445-3122. There is a gift shop.

Frontier Days

Prescott claims its rodeo to be the oldest in the U.S., having started with modest cowboy contests in 1888, and it is at any rate involved in one of the liveliest western festivals in this part of the world, six days of sports contests, art shows, parades, and concerts, climaxing in a finals rodeo on the last day, though there are rodeos every other day as well, approved by the Professional Rodeo Cowboys Association, with the standard events: saddle and bareback bronco riding, bull riding, calf roping, steer wrestling, team roping, barrel racing for women, wild horse racing, and steer roping. The days are scheduled so that July 4th is always one of the busiest, with fireworks at dusk on that day, all events held either at the courthouse plaza or the fairgrounds. For Frontier Days information, call 445-3103.

The Smoki People

Ceremonies of the Smoki People are staged by a group of local non-Indians who do not make their names known in public, but can be spotted around town by a telltale tattoo each sports on the left hand. Organized in 1921 to generate some enthusiasm for a flagging July 4th celebration, the Smoki dances have become a fixture in the summertime entertainment schedule of this part of the state. Though their costumes bear some resemblance to Hopi, Navajo, and Plains Indians ceremonial dress, there is no attempt to reproduce the actual designs or rites of real Indians. Nevertheless they claim to be re-creating "age-old Indian ceremonials."

Appearing only once every year in August, "during the dark of the moon" as their spokesperson describes it, the Smokis put on five dances that change from year to year as new choreography is added; only their favorite snake dance is always repeated. New costumes, such as long rows of arm feathers for the eagle dance, are also added regularly from year to year. Authenticity in re-creating ceremonies of prehistoric Indians no longer identifiable in the Southwest is claimed on the basis of research of reports of the Bureau of Ethnology. There are no professionals involved, however, either in the field of anthropology or in choreography or costume design.

A Smoki describes the scene, held at the Smoki museum for an audience of 5,000, this way: "The setting is an impressive pueblo, where a busy village scene greets the eye; many squaws are preparing food for hungry braves and papooses, who move about among the evergreen trees and lean-tos, joined from time to time by others coming from inside the pueblo building. People in costumes of many tribes are seen mingling in friendly companionship. Tantalizing fragrances combine with the pulsating rhythm of tomtoms to create an unforgettable atmosphere. . . . Sand painters place upon the ground their mystic symbols which tell the story of the ceremonials to follow."

Real prehistoric Indian artifacts are in fact displayed in the **Smoki Museum,** on North Arizona Avenue, which is also proud of its collection of western paintings by Kate Cory. It is open daily, June 1 to September 1. For information on ceremonials, held either the first or second Saturday of August, call the Prescott Chamber of Commerce (tel. 445-2000).

Recreation
Antelope Hills is a municipally owned golf course with 18 holes over 6,827 yards, a PGA pro, and a bar and restaurant, seven miles north of town on U.S. 89. The **Prescott Country Club,** 15 miles east of town on Ariz. 69, has an 18-hole, 6,763-yard course open to the public, and a pro shop and restaurant.

Hiking trails in **Prescott National Forest** draw day-trip or overnight explorers. For information, see the National Forest Service office, 344 S. Cortez St., where maps are available. One popular forest area is **Granite Basin Lake** recreation area, reached via Iron Springs Road to an access road to the site. Here and at various other scenic spots in the mountains are a number of Forest Service campgrounds.

TRAVEL SERVICES: Prescott is served by **Arizona Central** buses with connections to Phoenix and Flagstaff. **Prescott Municipal Airport,** seven miles north on U.S. 89 (tel. 778-6060), has commuter service to Phoenix via Golden Pacific, which also serves Sedona and Kingman. The toll-free telephone within Arizona is 800/352-3281.

For further travel service information, including choices of hotels and restaurants, see the **Prescott Chamber of Commerce** at 117 W. Goodwin, Prescott, AZ 86301 (tel. 445-2000 in Prescott, or 253-5988 in Phoenix).

WHERE TO STAY: The **Prescottian Motel,** 1317 E. Gurley, Prescott, AZ 86301 (tel. 602/445-3096), as the largest hostelry in town, with its busy Coach House Restaurant, is a local meeting place. All rooms have cable television. Rates are $42 double.

Motel 6, at 1111 E. Sheldon St., Prescott, AZ 86301 (tel. 602/778-0200), offers low-cost modern rooms and a swimming pool, at $22 double.

Housekeeping cottages in the national forest are available at **Loba Lodge** (tel. 602/445-1987), 4½ miles from town on the Groom Creek road (open only from March through December). Rates vary by cottage.

WHERE TO EAT: The oldest restaurant in Arizona, by its claim, is the **Pine Cone Inn,** 1245 White Spar Rd., 1½ miles south of town (tel. 445-2970), open for lunch and dinner daily, serving a traditional American menu of steaks, chops, and seafood; there is entertainment in the lounge nightly to 1 a.m.

Truss beams, captain's chairs, and barnside paneling give a solid rustic atmosphere to the **Prescott Mining Co.,** 155 Plaza Dr. (tel. 445-1991), a pleasant steakhouse also serving seafood. For dining in Victorian splendor it's the **Carriage House,** 2516 Willow Creek Rd. (tel. 445-0090), in a structure dating from 1877 that today specializes in continental cuisine.

5. SUNSET CRATER AND WUPATK

Two national monuments, Sunset Crater, about 15 miles, and V.
miles north of Flagstaff, both reached via U.S. 89 north, are sites of a voi.
changed the history of migrations in the region, and of more ruins of t.
dents who lived here a millennium in the past.

SUNSET CRATER: The main attraction here is a dead volcanic cone in a color-ful array of mineral formations formed in a series of eruptions over as long as two centuries, that began in A.D. 1064. The cone rises 1,000 feet from the surrounding arid land, dotted with sagebrush. It was responsible for sending out volcanic ash over hundreds of square miles in all directions, greatly improving the farming potential in the area. The new surface could hold moisture and pro-duce crops where previously the land was barren. People moved into the area to take advantage of the comparatively fertile land, living in cliff houses such as in Walnut Canyon or at Wupatki to the north in one of the largest pueblos known in the region.

Two miles from the access road off U.S. 89 is a **visitor center** (tel. 526-0586), which, at an altitude of 7,000 feet, is occasionally closed briefly until the snow is plowed out; in principle it is open year round: from 7 a.m. to 7 p.m. in summer and 8 a.m. to 5 p.m. in winter. Hand tools and domestic items from the Sinagua people who farmed these lands are shown in the visitor center museum, open free of charge; there is a good display also of geological samples from the area that help to explain the volcanic action that built the crater. Across from the center is a campground with tables, fireplaces, and water and toilet facilities.

WUPATKI NATIONAL MONUMENT: The special interest in this area of prehistoric ruins is that it was a cultural melting pot because of the influx of vari-ous peoples from different directions who came to take advantage of the im-proved farming conditions brought about by the volcano and the spread of ash on the surface of the earth. There were Anasazi farmers who had learned to farm in the arid country to the northeast, while Coconino people moved in from the west to join with the Sinagua people already living here at Wupatki. From central and south Arizona there also came incursions of Hohokam and Mogollon peo-ples. From all these influences there were many villages established within a rela-tively short period of time all over the lands around Sunset Crater. One of those lived in the longest was Wupatki, the Hopi word for "tall house." One of the rare springs in the area probably accounts for its location. It became the largest pueblo in the area by the 12th century, three stories high with over 100 rooms.

A great place to go and sit and ponder the fate of these long-gone peoples is a silent, stony amphitheater in which one can let the imagination create all kinds of early ceremonies that must have taken place here. One of two masonry ball courts discovered in northern Arizona is also in place here.

Overuse and high winds eventually stripped the land of the beneficent cover of volcanic ash, so the people had to give up and leave. After 1225 there were no longer any farmers in the area at all, and the place was abandoned.

The **visitor center** (tel. 527-7040) is 14 miles in, to the east, on an access road off U.S. 89; there is also an 18-mile paved road connecting Wupatki with Sunset Crater that goes through interesting communities of plants and animals in Coconino National Forest. The surrounding hills are still covered with cinders from the volcano and can be rough on the tires of any vehicle that tries to negoti-ate that surface. "Stay on the roads" is the advice of the rangers. Spatter cones and other lava formations look as if they have just cooled, and except for the sparse ants visible, the place must look as it did just after the last eruption of the volcano.

The Wupatki boundaries contain no fewer than 2,600 prehistoric ruins within them; besides Wupatki Ruin itself, one of the most impressive in the Southwest, there is **Citadel Ruin,** with 100 sites within a square mile, from small earth lodges to pueblos of considerable size. The Citadel has not yet been excavated. It was a fortified apartment structure with about 50 rooms. Below it is another ruin called **Nalakihu,** the Hopi word for "house standing alone." Other sites are **Lomaki** and **Wukoki.** Self-guiding trails lead visitors to both the Wupatki and the Nalakihu-Citadel ruins. The monument is open daily: from 7 a.m. to 7 p.m. in summer, 8 a.m. to 5 p.m. winter.

6. SCENIC DRIVES FROM FLAGSTAFF

Several drives through the national forest lands around Flagstaff are among the most spectacular for scenery in the state. Mostly on unpaved roads, these are all passable by passenger cars, except in wet weather.

ASPEN RIDES: What are called foliage tours in the East are "aspen rides" in the West. Two likely routes from Flagstaff are the following, one of them through **Hart Prairie,** an open space on the slopes of the San Francisco Mountains for which visitors follow U.S. 180 north out of Flagstaff on Humphrey Street for ten miles to Forest Hwy. 151, turn right, and follow this dirt road for another ten miles until it rejoins U.S. 180, a 40-mile trip.

Another foliage trip starting in Flagstaff is a steeper drive through **Lockett Meadow,** giving views of the inner basin of the San Francisco peaks. For it, follow U.S. 66 east through town to U.S. 89 and follow that 17 miles north past the Sunset Crater turnoff road to the first dirt road beyond it, leaving the highway to the left. Follow this a mile to Forest Hwy. 552, where an indicator is marked "to Lockett Meadow." This narrow, rough, steep dirt road is passable by passenger cars taking it slowly. From the meadow the return to town is by reversing the route. Distance is 45 miles.

HART PRAIRIE: This ride, giving a scenic view of the Coconino National Forest and the San Francisco peaks, begins ten miles north of Flagstaff off U.S. 180 on Hart Prairie Road (Forest Hwy. 151), which leads in one mile to a junction with Forest Hwy. 514 in an area called Kendrick Park. Turn right, go 2½ miles to Forest Hwy. 550, then take this two miles to Saddle Mountain, where cars can drive to the lookout station. Return to Forest Hwy. 550 and turn left, then go two miles to Forest Hwy. 523, turn right, go five miles to Forest Hwy. 514, turn right, and drive four miles to Forest Hwy. 417, then turn right on this road and follow it to its junction with U.S. 89. Go 5½ miles south on U.S. 89 to Schultz Pass Road (FH 420) and turn right, continuing for ten miles to a junction with U.S. 180, to return to Flagstaff. Total distance: 59 miles.

SCENIC LAKES DRIVE: This ride gives a good view of most of the beautiful lakes and fishing holes south and southwest of town, and closeup views of the two-million-acre Coconino National Forest. South of town from the Lake Mary exit of I-17, follow Lake Mary Road to Lower Lake Mary and Upper Lake Mary. Follow Lake Mary Road to the Ashurst Lake turnoff sign. After visiting Ashurst Lake, return to Lake Mary Road and continue south on it to Mormon Lake, alongside the roadway. Continue farther south to the Kinnickinick Lake turnoff, follow it to the lake, then return again to Lake Mary Road, turn left, and go south to the Stoneman Lake turnoff and turn right on it. After visiting Stoneman Lake, return to Lake Mary Road, turn right and continue to the Happy Jack lumber camp. Continue south to Ariz. 87 at Clint's Well, then turn left and go three miles to Forest Hwy. 751 to Blue Ridge Reservoir. After visiting the reservoir, return to Ariz. 87, turn right, continue to Winslow, then take a left on I-40 back to Flagstaff. The round trip is 185 miles.

ARIZONA SNOW BOWL: Take U.S. 180 (Humphrey Street) north for seven miles to the Snow Bowl turnoff, then another seven miles to the lodge at the base of the double-chair lift, open for skiers from Thanksgiving to Easter, and for sightseers the rest of the year (round trip is $5 for adults, $3 for children). For ski information, call 779-4577. The lift goes up to a height of 11,600 feet in the San Francisco peaks, from which the town is spread out below in one direction and Mount Humphreys rises nearby in another. Lunches or snacks are served at the base lodge for sightseers. The lift is a local favorite for those out to see the fall colors in the changing leaves.

METEOR CRATER: This moon-like commercially owned crater, made 22,000 years ago by a hunk of rock weighing millions of tons hitting the ground at 45,000 mph with the impact of 15 million tons of TNT, is 35 miles from Flagstaff via I-40 east and an access road to the south of the Interstate. The pit, 570 feet deep, could accommodate 20 football fields if the surface were smoothed out a bit. It is open from 6 a.m. to 6 p.m. in summer and 7:30 a.m. to 4:30 p.m. in winter, for a $4 admission. For information, call 774-8350. The crater was a training site for astronauts and has an astronaut hall of fame with photographs of space travelers. A museum of astrogeology provides background information on the nickel-iron meteor and the hole it made so long ago.

CHAPTER XI

THE GRAND CANYON AND THE COLORADO RIVER

□ □ □

1. GRAND CANYON NATIONAL PARK
2. PAGE AND LAKE POWELL
3. WESTERN ARIZONA

Entering Arizona at about the midway point of its northern border with Utah, the Colorado River is here trapped behind Glen Canyon Dam to form the waters of Lake Powell, making the centerpiece of the Glen Canyon National Recreation Area, most of which lies to the north of the state line in Utah. Below the dam, at the town of Page, Arizona, the Colorado enters Marble Canyon and continues its spectacular voyage through the most fabulous of our national parks, Grand Canyon. Hundreds of miles to the west, beyond the western end of the canyon, the river is again captured to form a vast reservoir, Lake Mead, behind Hoover Dam, which spans the river as it forms the Arizona-Nevada boundary. Below, the river sweeps through the hot desert country. California appears on the western shore of the river near Needles, and at Lake Havasu City, on the Arizona side, the London Bridge, lugged over here from England, looms improbably out of a hot desert background. Still another dam impounds water for Lake Havasu: Parker Dam, above the desert outpost of Parker. On through the desert the river flows south, finally passing Yuma and escaping into Mexico and the Gulf of California.

The Colorado River, within the Grand Canyon, has made the most complex series of canyons and gorges in the world. The central cut is almost exactly one mile deep from the south rim; the north rim is 1,200 feet higher. Some 4 to 18 miles wide, it is 217 miles long from its eastern beginning at the head of Marble Canyon to its western end at Grand Wash Cliffs. Within the national park, containing the most spectacular stretches of the canyon, the distance is 56 miles, with the meandering river at its bottom moving in a 105-mile course. The overall color impression of the canyon is of red, red of various hues, dark reds, brownish reds, combined with rock strata in many other distinct colors: tan, gray, green, pink, brown, slate, purple.

The canyon was discovered first by Europeans in 1540 by one of the Coronado expeditions, whose members saw little to keep them in the remote, forbidding area nor to bring them back again. Over two centuries passed before it was rediscovered by a couple of Spanish priests. It was not until the early 1800s that government mappers recorded the lay of the land here. Much exploration of the canyon is credited to the scientist John Wesley Powell, whose first expedition here was in 1869, a date marking the beginning of mineral exploration of the area. Today the park, containing 673,575 acres, and dating from its official creation in 1919, draws over two million visitors every year.

The strata of rock exposed on the walls of the canyon give us a view into history from a geological viewpoint, a wealth of evidence unmatched at any other site in the world. Earth processes shown here include all the various materials of the earth's crust, the erosion that cut the canyon into the plateau, and the uplifting, faulting, and volcanic action that are part of the building-up of the earth. There is one tremendous stretch of rock over four miles in width that traces the earth's history in an unbroken sequence. Nevertheless there are gaps—millions of years are unaccounted for in places where erosion wiped away the record. The rock of the inner gorge is around four billion years of age, consisting of the roots of mountains whose tops are long gone, eroded away. On top of this base are buttes that may be only 200 million years old, or younger, and there are newer rocks of comparatively recent date: 1,000 years ago in volcanic action.

Geologists call the cutting of this mile-deep canyon by the river one of the great events in the geological history of the earth. The water managed the job by using speed combined with such cutting tools as sand and gravel. The river today carries half a million tons of sediment a day. But there is a strange twist to the story: in cutting the canyon, the river stayed in place as the land moved upward against it. This reverse process explains the east-west course of the canyon across a slope facing south. The reason the canyon survives at all is its dry climate. In a rainy one the walls would long ago have washed away.

Life in the canyon through the ages is shown by the variety of fossils: seashells, dinosaurs, camels, horses, elephants. Between bottom and top of the canyon the climate varies so much as to have produced different life forms in both plants and animals. The bottom has plants requiring much water, for example, growing near the river, such as willows and cottonwoods; drought-resistant desert plants, at the other end of the scale, are perennials, mostly cactuses. Certain plants with deep root penetration take so much water that they diminish the flow of desert streams, such as mesquite, acacia, and tamarisk. Ponderosa pines are typical of the South Rim, along with piñon, juniper, scrub oak, mountain mahogany, and sagebrush; the moist soil of the North Rim provides living quarters for Douglas fir and aspen. Animal life, extremely varied, is often restricted to narrow areas, by species, because of the difficulty in negotiating the tumbled terrain.

A noted Grand Canyon resident is the black raven, which soars endlessly on updrafts, searching for dead animals among the cliffsides; another, returning each spring, is the turkey vulture. Insect-eating swallows and swifts are among the birds with the fastest flight of any in the canyon. Jays give their raucous calls.

Even in the much frequented areas of the park, squirrels hobnob with visitors and try to cadge food, though feeding them and other animals is against park rules. Deer show up sometimes, and elk, and coyotes. Gray foxes can be identified by a dark stripe on their backs, and there are rare sightings of bobcat and mountain lion.

1. GRAND CANYON NATIONAL PARK

Visits to the park are made in two areas, widely separated by road access, the South Rim and the North Rim, the latter closed in winter. Main headquarters for visits is **Grand Canyon Village,** 82 miles northwest of Flagstaff via U.S. 180. Desert View, the eastern entrance to the South Rim, is 32 miles west of Cameron on the Navajo Reservation. **Grand Canyon Airport,** nine miles south of Grand Canyon Village, is served by Republic Airlines and Scenic Airlines. Regular bus service from Flagstaff to Grand Canyon Village is provided by **Navi-Hopi Tours** (tel. 774-5003).

THE SOUTH RIM: Roads and visitor facilities are open year round, with the different seasons offering various advantages—or the contrary. Springtime can bring snow up until the middle of May, as well as crowds of students during school vacations. Hiking trails may be snowpacked and icy. Temperatures range between 32° and 60°. In summer, vacation time brings the biggest crowds and longest lines for all facilities. Campgrounds are full by 8 a.m. and motels by noon. There are frequent afternoon thundershowers. Temperatures range between 51° and 82°. Fall is considered the best time for a visit, with good weather and a lack of crowds, although some facilities are closed, and those remaining open are usually booked solid over holiday periods. Snow can arrive as early as late October. Temperatures range from 36° to 64°. Winter brings a special beauty with snow on the heights. Although the park has relatively fewer visitors at this time of year, most of the facilities are also closed; those remaining open may be booked ahead.

The **visitor center** in Grand Canyon Village, 3½ miles north of the South Entrance Station, is open every day and provides trail guides, maps, and publications about the canyon. There are exhibits here depicting the natural history of the canyon, and half a mile away, at **Yavapai Museum,** on the canyon rim, the geology of the area is explained, and superbly demonstrated too, by a picture window looking out on the vast canyon itself, with a view a mile down to the bottom. Elsewhere, on the East Rim Drive, the **Tusayan Museum,** next to the Tusayan Ruins three miles west of Desert Rim, describes the life of the prehistoric Indians living in the canyon 800 years ago.

The viewpoints over the rim of the canyon are reached along a rim road and access points, turnouts with picnic areas, or scenic viewing sites. From Grand Canyon Village the **West Rim Drive** follows the rim to **Hermits Rest,** 7½ miles away, giving access to several overlooks with parking areas, but this drive is closed to private vehicles in the summer and can be reached by a shuttle bus (or by bike or on foot). The 25-mile **East Rim Drive** to Desert View, 25 miles long, passes the Tusayan Museum and the best viewpoint of all, according to the rangers, **Lipan Point.** From various points, all well marked, self-guiding nature trails and other paths connect Mather Point and Hermits Rest, a stretch of nine miles along the rim. Canyon overlooks on both drives have other trails leading out from here for viewing the canyon from different angles and at different times of day.

Grand Canyon from the Air is seen from sightseeing planes running 50- to 55-minute tours for **Grand Canyon Airlines** (tel. 638-2407) at Grand Canyon National Park Airport, which has been flying these trips since 1927. An early sightseer commented after a flight: "The Grand Canyon, when seen from the air, becomes infinitely more majestic in its fantastic splendor, for the atmosphere acts as a huge magnifying glass, unfolding hidden and unsuspected beauty to the aerial voyager—charming minarets, stately temples, and sweeping vistas, all under the brilliant glow of changing, delicate colors that fascinate and challenge artist and poet alike. There is no point or promontory from which a view may be had,

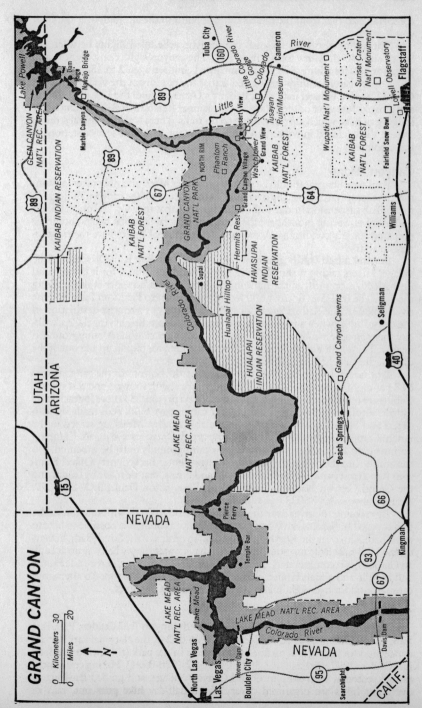

comparable to that from the eagle's vantage point in the air, high over the Canyon."

The airline also runs seasonal transcanyon scheduled flights between the South and North Rims, for a fare of $50. The canyon sightseeing flight is also priced at $50 for adults, $25 for accompanied children aged 2 to 15.

Other visitor facilities are located across the road from the visitor center in Grand Canyon Village, including Babbitt's General Store, the U.S. Post Office, and a bank. Just west of the village is a pet kennel (tel. 638-2631) for temporary lodging of pets, which are not permitted on trails. There is also a general store in Desert View (closed in winter) and one in Tusayan, as well as service stations at these points.

Canyon Hiking

Foul-weather gear should be packed on winter hikes, and note taken of summertime temperatures usually over 100° at the bottom of the canyon. Builders of the Kaibab suspension bridge found it so hot here that they worked only at night under lights. Spring months are the most unpredictable, when hikers should be prepared for any conditions. A special rule here is that mules have the right-of-way on all trails.

South Kaibab Trail begins near Yaki Point on the East Rim Drive east of the village. Hikers taking it should be in top physical condition, for it is steep and unshaded. As on most of the trails in the park, there is no water available along the way. The trail goes down 4,600 feet in seven miles to Phantom Ranch on the riverbank near the Kaibab Suspension Bridge. This was a tourist destination in the early 1900s, when a trail down to it was built along Bright Angel Creek. Today there are guest cabins, dormitories, and a ranger station. A campground is nearby. The South Kaibab Trail is not recommended for hiking up and out of the canyon; for this the Bright Angel Trail should be taken.

Dormitory lodging at **Phantom Ranch** at the bottom of the canyon costs $18 per night in bunk beds in buildings equipped with showers and rest rooms. Cabins are rented at $50 per night for one or two persons, $8 more for each extra lodger. Equipped with sink and toilet, the cabins have bunk beds made up with sheets and blankets; a showerhouse is available nearby. Meals are served in the ranch. Campers at the **Bright Angel Campground** may reserve meals. Camping permits here and for other Inner Canyon campgrounds must be procured. On the South Rim they are available at the Visitor Center Backcountry Office. Phantom Ranch reservations, for both lodging and meals, may be made by contacting the Grand Canyon National Park Lodges, Reservation Dept., P.O. Box 699, Grand Canyon, AZ 86023 (tel. 602/638-2401).

By crossing the river over the suspension bridge, built with one-ton cables that took 40 Indians to carry down here when it was built, it is possible to hike to the North Rim over the **North Kaibab Trail.** To return to the South Rim, however, the 10.3-mile **Bright Angel Trail,** which has a water supply halfway up at Indian Gardens, is recommended. There is also water seasonally at Three-Mile House and at Mile-and-a-Half House, distances measured from the top. An alternative campground for overnight hikers is located at **Indian Gardens.**

Trail Guides

Various hiker services are offered by **Grand Canyon Trail Guides,** P.O. Box 735, Grand Canyon, AZ 86023 (tel. 602/526-0924), the National Park Service concession for hiking and backpacking services in the park (their winter address is P.O. Box 2997, Flagstaff, AZ 86003; tel. 602/526-0924). Hiking equipment can be rented at their shop in Grand Canyon Village, and guided day-long or overnight hikes are organized. Every day a half-day hike goes out, rain or shine—a poncho is provided in case of rain. The route descends to 1,500 feet below the rim during a three-mile overall trip. Cost for this hike, $20, includes transportation, breakfast below the rim, and a water bottle. Departure is at 7 a.m., return by noon. There is a limit of eight hikers.

Once a week a full-day hike is offered, using only wilderness trails. Though the overall trip is only seven miles, hikers should be in fit condition in order to make it easily. Cost of $35 includes transportation, trail snacks, lunch, the use of a daypack, and two two-quart water bottles. Departure from the shop is at 7:30 a.m., return about 4:30 p.m.

Overnight hikes, depending on staff availability, are also subject to availability of campsites; information can be had at the shop, open from 7 a.m. to dusk, April through November.

Canyon Mule Rides

A one-day muleback trip down to **Plateau Point,** 1,400 feet above the Colorado River, departs at 8 a.m. in summer, 9 a.m. in winter, from the Bright Angel Lodge on the West Rim Drive. The ride returns in the afternoon via the Bright Angel Trail, arriving back at the corral between 3 and 4 p.m., depending on season. A two-day overnight trip to Phantom Ranch departs at 8:30 a.m. in summer and 9:30 a.m. in winter from the same point, descending the Bright Angel Trail to arrive at the ranch between 2 and 3 p.m. Riders have dinner at the ranch and are accommodated in a cabin for the night. After breakfast at the ranch, the return trip is via the South Kaibab Trail, which reaches the South Rim at Yaki Point. From here riders are transferred to the point of departure, Bright Angel Lodge, by bus. Price of this trip, including food and lodging, is $193 for one person, $336 for two. Reservations are made through Grand Canyon National Park Lodges, Reservation Dept., P.O. Box 699, Grand Canyon, AZ 86023 (tel. 602/638-2401).

Not everyone is allowed on the mule trips, which are considered strenuous. No one weighing over 200 pounds is allowed on the trips, and persons close to that weight are weighed to check their qualification. Riders must also be at least four feet seven inches tall and fluent in English. Pregnant women are not taken on the trip, nor are people who are afraid of heights. A printed notice informs riders that "the mules will not submit to any strapping on of crutches." Other requirements are a knowledge of riding in a western saddle, and the strength to stop a mule on cue and also to stay in the saddle for seven hours. The notice concludes: "Please consider carefully the exhausting nature of this trip before purchasing a ticket." Shoulder bags, backpacks, or purses are not allowed, although one camera may be carried by neck straps. On the two-day trip a small plastic bag is supplied, to contain overnight essentials and a bathing suit for wading in Bright Angel Creek. Long pants and solid shoes, and in summer a hat, are required.

The trips run right through the winter, when departure-time temperatures can be well below zero, so layers of warm clothes are recommended at that time of year. For would-be riders dubious about making the ride there is a home movie offered for sale by mail order, described thus: "Views photographed from mules descending steep switchbacks let viewers experience how it feels to be in the saddle." Priced at $16, the 150-foot super-8 color film is available from Fred Harvey Movies, P.O. Box 709, Grand Canyon, AZ 86203.

Guided Canyon Bus Tours

The **Fred Harvey Transportation Co.** runs guided bus tours of the South Rim, with stops at scenic viewing points, that offer commentary of guides knowledgeable in the lore of the canyon and its history, geology, and plants and animals. A daily **Hermits Rest Tour** departs at 9:30 a.m. and 2:30 p.m. in summer (in winter, in the morning only) on a two-hour 16-mile trip. At Hermits Rest there is a stop at a gift shop and snackbar. Fee is $12 for adults, $6 for children aged 2 to 12.

The **Desert View Tour** of three hours and 45 minutes covers the East Rim, 52 miles total. A stop at the Yavapai Museum is included, and the high point is a visit to the Desert View Watchtower, designed by Fred Harvey Company architect Mary Jane Colter after the prehistoric towers to the northeast in the Four Corners region; it was built at the turn of the century and has a gift shop in the form of a *kiva*, the Anasazi people's circular ceremonial room. Murals on the second floor are the work of a Hopi artist.

A **combination ticket** for both the Hermits Rest and Desert View Tours may be had at $20 for adults, $10 for children. For additional information on these tours, call 638-2361.

A **Sunset Tour** also departs daily depending on the time of sunset. Running an hour and a half, it is scheduled so as to arrive at Yaki Point for a spectacular view of the canyon as the sun disappears in the jumbled shadows to the west. Cost is $7 for adults, $3.50 for children.

THE NORTH RIM: The North Rim is a natural attraction to outdoor lovers put off by the crowds and the traffic along the rim drives on the South Rim. Access to the visitor station at the North Rim by car is some 200 miles from Grand Canyon Village via Ariz. 64 east to Cameron, north on U.S. 89 to Bitter Springs, then west on U.S. 89A to Jacob Lake, and finally south through Kaibab National Forest via Ariz. 67 to the center. At **Jacob Lake,** 45 miles north of the center, the National Park Service runs an information station jointly with national forest rangers. Another information station is located 13 miles beyond the North Rim entrance in Grand Canyon Lodge at **Bright Angel Point.**

Areas of the North Rim that can be visited by private car include a 26-mile paved road from Grand Canyon Lodge to **Cape Royal,** offering an eastward view out to the Painted Desert. There's another spectacular view across the canyon to the desert from **Point Imperial,** reached by road three miles off the Cape Royal Road. A primitive road needing high-clearance vehicles leaves the entrance road at a point three-quarters of a mile south of the North Rim Entrance Station— this is the Point Sublime Road, and goes to an overlook on the North Rim 17 miles distant: **Point Sublime.** In summer there are daily bus trips to Cape Royal departing from the Grand Canyon Lodge; at the destination there are talks on the geology of the canyon given. In summer there are evening programs every night in the campground amphitheater and in the Grand Lodge, presented by park rangers. During the day rangers also lead scheduled nature walks and wilderness hikes.

Lodging on the North Rim is available only at the **Grand Canyon Lodge,** open May to mid-October, with advance reservations advised. They can be had from T.W. Services, P.O. Box 400, Cedar City, UT 84720 (tel. 801/586-7686). Campers are advised to spend the night previous to arrival somewhere to the north outside the park, such as Jacob Lake, so as to be able to arrive early enough in the morning to get a campsite at the **North Rim Campground,** operated on a first-come, first-served basis and always full in the summertime. Nearby Forest Service camping is at **De Motte Campground,** five miles north of the park boundary, with water and rest rooms; and **Jacob Lake Campground,** at the junction of U.S. 89A and Ariz. 67, 32 miles from the park entrance, also with water and rest rooms. Reservations are not accepted at these campgrounds.

The North Rim is closed by snow from mid-October to mid-May in a climate considerably colder than that at Grand Canyon Village, so near as the crow flies across the canyon, yet so far. Accumulations of ten feet of snow are common here in the wintertime. Warm air rising from the Inner Canyon brings out the wildflowers in May even before all the snow has melted at Cape Royal. The drive to Cape Royal is probably at its most delightful in the summer, when the road goes past locust trees blooming with sweet fragrance and great green fields of mountain flowers. Elevations of 7,800 to 8,800 feet make for crisp summer days with no hint of the desert heat down in the distance; often the afternoon will bring a thunderstorm. Summertime averages range from 43° to 75°. More pleasant days follow in September until the North Rim closes, with great displays of color in the turning leaves of the aspens on the hillsides; temperatures range from 32° to 59° in the fall.

Though there is only a ten-mile hop from the North Rim to the South Rim, it's a challenge to hike from one to another, and not considered advisable to attempt in a single day's trip. Two miles from Grand Canyon Lodge is the trailhead of the **Kaibab Trail,** leading down the face of the North Rim to Phantom Ranch. From here by crossing the suspension footbridge, hikers can then start up the face of the South Rim via the **Bright Angel Trail,** a total of 23 rough hiking miles from rim to rim. There are campsites and indoor lodging at Phantom Ranch (see "South Rim," above).

. There are other trails going into the Grand Canyon wilderness open to backpackers, but hikers are advised to get some experience first on the Kaibab and Bright Angel Trails. Overnight permits are required for backpacking hikes, and reservations are usually necessary in advance for camping in four campgrounds within the Inner Canyon: Indian Gardens, Bright Angel Campground, and Cottonwood and Roaring Springs Campgrounds, the last two both on the North Kaibab Trail between the river and the North Rim.

SPECIAL INFORMATION: Hikers can make reservations for backcountry campsites in advance by writing to the **Backcountry Reservation Office,** P.O. Box 129, Grand Canyon, AZ 86023 (tel. 602/638-2474 for information only, from 11 a.m. to 5 p.m. M.S.T. daily). A 10¢ **park newspaper,** the Grand Canyon *Guide,* is available at entrance stations and other locations throughout the park, and contains information about all park activities. The **Grand Canyon Natural History Association,** a nonprofit organization, sells authoritative publications about the canyon and other subjects associated with the Southwest at information stations and visitor centers.

A number for all **emergencies** is 638-2477. On the South Rim there is a doctor, pharmacist, and dentist at the **Grand Canyon Clinic** (tel. 638-2551), on Center Road between the South Entrance Station and the village. On the North Rim there is a first-aid room with a registered nurse on duty at the information desk of the North Rim Lodge.

Park visitor activities are reported in a taped telephone message heard by calling 638-9304. Information on **weather and road conditions** in the park is available at 638-2245.

WHERE TO STAY: There are lodgings and accommodations within the park at Grand Canyon Village and outside, nearby at Tusayan, and 60 miles south in the town of Williams. There is also a lodge at the North Rim, and outside the park, accommodations at Kaibab Lodge, Jacob Lake, and in the town of Page, 125 miles to the northeast.

The South Rim

Over 750 rooms are available in seven lodges on the South Rim, all operated by a single concessionnaire, **Grand Canyon National Park Lodges,** P.O. Box

699, Grand Canyon, AZ 86023 (tel. 602/638-2401). Most rooms have private bath and telephone, and some have a fireplace. Pets are not accepted, but may be placed in a kennel. Restaurants in all the lodges are open to guests in all of them.

Most interesting of the lodges is the historic **El Tovar Hotel,** set back from the canyon rim but providing views out over the canyon from many of its windows. Of an early-1900s rustic design of local fieldstone and pine logs, the hotel has green roofs with many dormers, some with balconies. Massive fireplaces make the public lounges cheerful, and there is a lounge and dining room. Rates, the same whether single or double, are $86 to $110, from standard to deluxe, with suites at $135 to $200; additional persons in the room are charged $7.

Right on the rim is the newer complex of the **Thunderbird** and the **Kachina Lodges,** in a sort of contemporary pueblo architecture in pastel tans, with a flat roof. Picture windows give many of the rooms straight views right down into the depths of the canyon. Rates for both lodges, single or double, are $79 to $85.

Near the El Tovar is the **Bright Angel Lodge,** with cabins as well as the lodge built of logs, with a big fireplace, yet on a more modest scale than El Tovar. Many rooms here too have views of the canyon. There is a dining room with southwestern dishes on the menu, a beauty and barber shop, newsstand, coffeeshop, gift shop, snackbar, and coin laundry. Standard rooms in the lodge, single or double, are $34; cabins, also single or double, are $45 to $65; extra persons in rooms are charged $7.

Inland from the rim the **Maswik Lodge,** with a cafeteria, newsstand, and gift shop, offers either modern rooms at $50 to $77, single or double, or rustic cabins at $32, $7 for extra persons.

The two **Yavapai Lodges** at the eastern end of the village are distinguished as the East Yavapai and West Yavapai, two-story structures with standard-style motel rooms with windows looking out on the woods. There is a cafeteria, lounge, gift shop, and snackbar. Rates are $67, single or double, in East Yavapai and $57 in West Yavapai; extra persons pay $7. There is no charge for children 12 years of age or younger.

The **Trailer Village,** also run by the concession, has full hookups for RVs with bath facilities, and rates of $10 daily for two, 50¢ for additional persons.

Outside the Park

The concession also runs the **Moqui Lodge** (tel. 602/638-2401), just outside the south boundary of the park in the Kaibab National Forest, open March 1 to December 31, with a dining room, lounge, tennis court, and horseback rides available. Double rates are $53, with a $6 charge for additional persons; a lower rate of $44 double applies from March to mid-May and Labor Day through December, except on holidays.

The **Grand Canyon Squire Inn,** a mile south of the South Rim entrance, on U.S. 180 (P.O. Box 130), Grand Canyon, AZ 86023 (tel. 602/638-2681), has a dining room, coffeeshop, gift shop, pool, tennis courts, a bowling alley, a billiards room, a health spa, and a game room, as well as a hot tub and sauna. There are 150 rooms at $49 to $73 double.

Red Feather Lodge, on U.S. 180 south of the park entrance (P.O. Box 520), Grand Canyon, AZ 86023 (tel. 602/638-2673), has 185 units, a coffeeshop, steakhouse, pool, Jacuzzi, cable television, and a gift shop, plus rates of $40 to $70 double.

The North Rim

The **Grand Canyon Lodge,** Grand Canyon North Rim (P.O. Box 400), Cedar City, UT 84720 (tel. 801/586-7686), has a patio with "the world's best view," as the undisputed claim has it, and 200 rooms for guests, including rustic cabins that in spite of their western-style décor are equipped with bathrooms, carpets, and fireplaces. The lodge building itself is built of local stone and timber of a rough-hewn rustic beauty. There is a restaurant serving breakfast, lunch, and dinner, and a cocktail lounge and gift shop. Double rates are $39 to $59; the lodge is open late May to mid-October.

EATING PLACES NEAR GRAND CANYON: The in-park concession, Grand Canyon National Park Lodges, runs several snackbars and restaurants. The finest is the dining room of **El Tovar Hotel,** open for breakfast, lunch, and dinner, with a cocktail lounge next to the dining room and a full wine list available. Both American and Mexican foods are served in the dining room of **Moqui Lodge,** which has a cocktail lounge attached, and is open from breakfast through dinner. Three meals daily are also available in the **Bright Angel Coffee Shop.** Next door is the **Bright Angel Cocktail Lounge,** offering folk entertainment evenings. Steaks and barbecued beef, pork, and chicken are the specialties of the **Arizona Room,** which also serves cocktails and wines, open for dinner only, from 5 to 10 p.m. Opening at 6:30 a.m. and serving all day are cafeterias in the **Motor Lodge** and at the **Yavapai Lodges.** The latter also has a fast-food counter for hamburgers, fried chicken, french fries, and other such favorites. Only the Arizona Room, El Tovar Dining Room, and Bright Angel Coffee Shop are open all year.

WILLIAMS: Although it's 60 miles from the park entrance, the town of Williams, on I-40 30 miles west of Flagstaff, calls itself the "Gateway to the Grand Canyon" and is in effect the nearest town to the South Rim visitor center. With a population under 2,500 it nevertheless has 23 motels, sitting as it does astride a major tourist route through which most visitors from Nevada and southern California make their way to the park. The town is served by **Greyhound/Trailways** and has the **Williams Stage Lines** taxi service (tel. 635-9352).

Two **TraveLodge** (tel. toll free 800/255-3050) chain establishments offer good modern rooms and all facilities in town and just outside. The in-town location of TraveLodge, 430 E. Bill Williams Ave., Williams, AZ 86046 (tel. 602/635-2651), is just 59 miles from the entrance to Grand Canyon, and has 39 units among which are several family suites. Doubles go for $28 to $58, depending on season. The other TraveLodge, on I-40 (eight miles east of town), Williams, AZ 86046 (tel. 602/635-4491), is also within a short drive of Grand Canyon and offers a forested scene of foothills wilderness on a 40-acre property that gives many of the advantages of a small resort at motel rates. Outdoor barbecues and cowboy steak dinners in the restaurant are popular features. Room rates are $32 to $60 double, depending on season.

Modestly priced double rooms at $24 to $35 are available at the **Belaire Motel,** 620 W. Bill Williams Ave., Williams, AZ 86046 (tel. 602/635-4415, or toll free 800/453-4511).

Restaurants in Williams include **Rod's Steak House,** 301 E. Bill Williams Ave. (tel. 635-2671), open daily for lunches and dinner, serving prime rib and steaks, and cocktails too; and the **Coffee Pot Café,** 117 E. Bill Williams Ave. (tel. 635-4574), open every day from 6 a.m. to 9 p.m. serving family-style barbecue, beef stew, meatloaf, spaghetti, biscuits and gravy, hamburgers, and T-bone steaks.

Near Williams is the **Bill Williams Mountain Ski Area.** Nearby **Sycamore Canyon** offers woodland scenery somewhat more subdued than that of the Grand Canyon to the north, preserved in a wilderness area of Kaibab National Forest.

Annual events here are **Rendezvous Days** over the Memorial Day weekend, the **Arizona Cowpunchers Reunion and Old Timers Rodeo** on July 4th, and the **Bill Williams Mountain Men Rodeo and Parade** over the Labor Day weekend. State rodeo finals for high schoolers are held in mid-June.

For details on events and other information, stop at the **Williams Chamber of Commerce,** 820 W. Bill Williams Ave., Williams, AZ 86046 (tel. 602/635-2041).

2. PAGE AND LAKE POWELL

Near the point where the Colorado River once flowed over the Utah-Arizona border at about the midway point between east and west in Arizona, the **Glen Canyon Dam,** completed in 1964, now controls the flow of the river down into **Marble Canyon** and the Grand Canyon beyond it, changing its color, for one thing, by removing much of the silt it used to carry out to the Gulf of California. It was this reddish silt that gave the river its name in the first place—"colored," or "red" river. But now the water is nearly clear, except when roiled by flood surges of the Little Colorado at the point where it joins the Colorado some 50 miles below the dam.

A visitor center on the rim of Glen Canyon above the dam is the starting point for a self-guided tour of this huge hydroelectric project built by the Bureau of Reclamation to harness the waters of the river, now captured in Lake Powell, which fills the canyon to a distance of 180 miles behind the dam. The lake and the slopes of the canyon are now part of **Glen Canyon National Recreation Area,** most of which reaches in a northeasterly direction up into Utah, although the dam and the only town near the area, Page, are both in Arizona.

The turbines of the dam produce a million kilowatts at full capacity, enough to supply a metropolitan area the size of Phoenix and its surrounding Valley of the Sun. The dam is made of five million cubic yards of concrete built to a height of 710 feet above bedrock. The top of the dam is well over a quarter mile in length.

Lake Powell, following the twisting course of the canyon, though still as it reflects the sunlight, meanders in a narrow path like a river. Its canyon bed was first noted in the historical record by a Spanish Franciscan missionary whose exploring party found a crossing place over the Colorado here at a spot since known as the Crossing of the Fathers. The present name was given the canyon by John Wesley Powell, also an early explorer of the Grand Canyon, who named it for the wooded glens along the banks of the river. Not only did he name many places along the river, but he was also a champion of water reclamation, so it is his name that tags the newly made Lake Powell. Navajo Indians, whose reservation extends off to the south, are comparative newcomers to the area, arriving here only in 1860. The neighboring Hopis, whose reservation is surrounded by Navajo land, have been here many hundreds of years, however.

Although the huge rocky façades and cliffsides may seem barren at first glance, the area supports considerable plant and animal life. Streaks of color on the walls of the canyon may be lichen, and cactuses and the bayonet-tipped yucca plants are widely distributed. The mesa tops are bright with swatches of wildflowers in the springtime, and they pop up on the surface of dunes too, and along the banks of streams. If there is a heavy summer rainfall it will bring about a second blossoming of the wildflowers. Near streams are borders of cottonwoods, willows, and tamarisks. Higher up are Utah piñons and juniper.

Desert animals suddenly scurrying away from car headlights are usually busy at their nighttime hunting. Their tracks are often seen in sand in the morning: the dog-like footprints of coyotes and foxes; the tiny marks of rats, mice, and lizards; and the sharp hoof prints of deer. Isolated side canyons are often home to many of these animals. The largest of the lizards, the chuckwalla, lives entirely on plants; other lizards eat insects and other small animals. There is an occasional rattlesnake. Since the lake was filled the area has become a visiting place for increasing numbers of birds, including many species of waterfowl.

Lake Powell has facilities for various kinds of boating, swimming, waterskiing, and fishing. There are both powerboats and man-impelled rowboats, canoes, and kayaks, as well as numerous sailboats, which latter craft find space to tack in such wide places as Wahweap, Padre, and Bullfrog Bays. Small craft such as canoes are advantageous in exploring narrow side canyons. In summer and early fall the cool water is welcome to swimmers baked in the hot sun; there are beaches and coves throughout the lake frontage. Fishermen catch species that have been planted here: largemouth bass, rainbow trout, striped bass, and crappie. Below the dam at **Lees Ferry,** the clear, cold water of the Colorado is famous for trout fishing. State fishing licenses are available locally. Lees Ferry, incidentally, reached via an access road to the north off U.S. 89A, is also the site of a pioneer fort and trading post that can be visited; there are relics of old mines here too.

A world wonder reachable by boat on the lakeshore is **Rainbow Bridge National Monument,** accessible by a foot trail a mile from a marina where craft may be docked. Over the state line in Utah, it is one of the few National Park Service properties not reachable by car. Its lovely arching form is perfect enough to suggest the work of some artistic bridge builder who worked in the fabulous colors of red and orange Navajo sandstone. Varied browns and crimsons streak a salmon-pink background over much of the arch, colors brought out sharply in a late-afternoon sun that may make it easy to believe the Indian legend that the span is a rainbow turned to stone. Maidenhair fern and wild orchids near protected pools nearby add to the beauty of the scene. In April the redbuds blossom along the streams, and up higher are lupines, daisies, painted cups, asters, evening primroses, sego lilies, and yuccas. The natural bridge, incidentally, is the world's largest.

Although campers with vehicles are restricted to official campgrounds, those with boats are free to pick any likely piece of shore to be claimed as home for up to two weeks at a time. Such water campers are urged to pack out trash and not to camp under cliffs where rocks may crush their tents.

Besides the town of Page, which calls itself "the only municipality on Lake Powell's 1,900 miles of shoreline," there are half a dozen shoreside facilities of interest to visitors. The **Wahweap** area has a ranger station and information office, campgrounds, picnic shelters, a launching ramp, and a swimming beach, and there are boats for rent here. The campground, on the lakeshore reached via a loop road from U.S. 89, about five miles northwest of Page, has 178 campsites for tents or trailers, with grills, tables, toilets, and water supply. **Lees Ferry,** reached from the village of Marble Canyon on U.S. 89A, southwest of Page, has a campground and launching ramp. Other campgrounds, reached by road by circuitous routes through southern Utah or by boat up the lake, are **Bullfrog, Halls Crossing,** and **Hite.**

PAGE: This is a new town built in 1957 to house the families of the workers building Glen Canyon Dam, later incorporated in 1975 as it became the center for visitors to the huge new recreation area. The town, at 4,300 feet in elevation, has an average rainfall of six inches. Winter temperatures run from 24° to 45°; in summer, from 71° to 97°.

There are daily **Sky West** flights to Phoenix, Salt Lake City, and Las Vegas (tel. 645-9200). **Avis** car rental (tel. 645-2494) has an office at Page airport. Medical services are available at the **Lake Powell Medical Center,** 467 Vista Ave. (tel. 645-3808).

Page has half a dozen motels, including the **Holiday Inn,** 287 N. Lake Powell Blvd., Page, AZ 86040 (tel. 602/645-8851, or toll free 800/465-4329), with 129 units, a pool, gift shop, a coffeeshop, and a cocktail lounge, with rates varying seasonally, from $35 to $65 double.

LAKE POWELL RESORTS: Lake Powell Resorts is an organization operating half a dozen lodges and resorts at various points around Lake Powell. Reservations for any of them can be made by calling 602/278-8888 within Arizona, or toll free 800/528-6154 from out of state. They include the Wahweap Lodge and the Lake Powell Motel, both near Page, as well as resorts and marinas at Bullfrog, Hall's Crossing, and Hite, in Utah.

Wahweap Lodge, overlooking the bay of that name, has 272 rooms opening on either a garden or on Lake Powell. There are two dining rooms, the glasswalled Rainbow Room and the Cookie Jar Restaurant. In summer there is entertainment and music for dancing in the Driftwood Lounge. Rates apply to the lodge and to the other three resorts on the lake: from $53 to $75.75 double, depending on size of bed (king-size available) and lakeside or gardenside situation. The 24-room **Lake Powell Motel,** also operated by the Resorts company, is on U.S. 89 five miles northeast of Page, with double rates of $35.75 to $47.75.

Three of the resorts (Wahweap, Bullfrog, and Hall's Crossing) have **camper and trailer parks** with full hookups, rest rooms, laundry, showers, playgrounds, and stores, at $15 daily, $2.50 extra for running air conditioners. Housekeeping units are also available, at $49.75 to $66.25 double, at Bullfrog, Hite, and Hall's Crossing resorts.

The resorts also have **houseboats** for rent. A 36-footer sleeping six goes for $606 for three nights, $957 for a full week. Powerboats range from a 14-foot Whaler at $47 daily to an 18-foot Runabout at $145.

The Wahweap lodge also offers boat tours up to Rainbow Bridge National Monument (see above). An all-day, 100-mile round trip departs at 9 a.m. and explores some side canyons along the way, returning at 4:30 p.m. It is priced at $50.50 for adults, $25.25 for children. A half-day, 7:30 a.m. to 1 p.m. cruise to the natural bridge costs $39.50 for adults, $19.75 for children. One-hour cruises aboard Wahweap Bay paddlewheelers depart at 11 a.m. and 1:30 p.m. daily and cost $6.35 for adults, $4.40 for children. A two-hour cruise through Wahweap Bay to Glen Canyon Dam and Bridge, then into Antelope Canyon, where the red walls are streaked with so-called desert varnish, costs $16 for adults, $11 for children. Several other trips, including sunset and moonlight dinner cruises with champagne and a buffet, all for $33.50 are also offered. Other facilities include Jeep tours, and boat docking and servicing.

3. WESTERN ARIZONA

PIPE SPRING NATIONAL MONUMENT: A memorial to the American cowboy is an old fort and Mormon ranch at Pipe Spring, on the Kaibab Indian Reservation, in a remote prairie of northern Arizona 125 miles west of Page, reached via U.S. 89A to Fredonia and Ariz. 389 to the monument. One of the rare moist spots in the arid Arizona Strip, Pipe Spring attracted settlers for many centuries. Over 1,000 years ago Pueblo Indians lived here, and later the spot was an annual camping grounds of the nomadic Plains Indians, the Paiutes. The first Europeans to come by were Spanish missionaries exploring the area in 1776, and the spring was discovered again in 1858 by Mormon missionaries. By 1863 there was a Mormon ranch in the lush grassland established by a Texas cattleman named James Whitmore, who built a shelter and put in ponds, grapevines, and fences. A few years later he and his shepherd were killed by Navajo raiders intent on driving settlers out of the area. In 1868 the Utah Militia moved into Pipe Spring to keep the Indians south of the Colorado River.

A treaty with the Navajo in 1870, signed for the Mormons by Jacob Hamblin and the Grand Canyon explorer John Wesley Powell, brought peace to Pipe Spring and the surrounding prairie. Brigham Young wanted to use Pipe Spring as grazing land for the so-called tithing herd of the Mormon church, cattle contributed by Mormon families as representing a tenth of their incomes. Young also had a fort built to protect the spring and the herd, and the church members required to serve in it as cattlemen. The fort, begun in 1870 under the direction of Anson Perry Winsor, was called Winsor Castle, and had two rectangular two-story houses with walls connecting their ends to form a courtyard. Red sandstone for building was quarried from cliffs nearby and lumber brought in from a local sawmill. Mormons contributing their labor to build it thus paid off their tithes to the church. Besides the fort, two smaller structures were also put up to house the Winsor family and construction workers.

Winsor built up a big herd here, producing cheese, butter, and beef. By 1879 the ranch had 2,269 head of cattle and 162 horses. The trail by the fort became known as the Honeymoon Trail because of the many couples using it on their way home after marriage ceremonies in St. George Temple, 60 miles to the west. In the late 1880s there was a national turmoil over polygamous marriages among the Mormons during which the church decided to sell the ranch, out of a fear of government confiscation of their property. In the early 1920s the owners of the ranch interested Stephen Mather, the first director of the National Park Service, in making "a memorial of western pioneer life" of Pipe Spring, and it was made a national monument in 1923.

Historic tools that belonged to Joe Hopkins, one of the builders of the ranch, are displayed in the blacksmith shop. A bed in Winsor Castle has springs made of rawhide. The gardens and trees surrounding the houses were planted in 1868, irrigated by two ponds here since 1880. A collection of harnesses and farm equipment is shown in the former barracks, built in 1868. During spring round-up today cattle are still branded in the old-style juniper log corral. The courtyard and various rooms of the houses are open to visitors. Pictures of the early pioneers decorate the walls, and much of the furniture was made of Ponderosa pine a century ago. In the telegraph room a telegraph operator once lived and worked; there is a picture of the first one, Luella Stewart, over an original telegraph stand. A big table for hearty meals in the kitchen is set in Mormon fashion: the plates turned over and the chairs turned backward for kneeling to pray before morning and evening meals. The stove was brought in in 1895. The parlor was used for relaxation, the residents entertaining themselves by playing musical instruments, singing together, or reading. Families gathered here to read the Book of Mormon and the Bible.

Beyond the back wall of the parlor is the source of water for Pipe Spring, which comes out of the hillside. The fort was built right over the spring in order to protect it. Water was once piped across the courtyard to the spring room, but it now runs underground. Some water does still run into the spring room, but most of it has been diverted outside the fort. The spring gives 30 gallons of water per minute, always at a temperature of 56°. This cool water was used to help make the cream rise in fresh milk and to cure cheese.

The cheese room has a vat into which milk was heated to 89°. Rennet from the stomach of a calf was added to the milk to make it curdle, and the curd was heated to 102°. It was then cut, salted, and kneaded to remove some of the whey. The curd was packed in a cheesecloth, placed in a round, and pressed to remove more whey, resulting in a solid cheese. After pressing, the cheese was weighed on the stillyards. Production was 60 to 80 pounds of cheese daily.

The cattle that were the staple of life here were Texas longhorns, whose ancestors were brought to this country from Spain. Some had escaped from Texas ranges to become wild in the open prairie. As they learned to survive and protect themselves they became dangerous, especially to a person on foot. It took the developing American breed of cowboy to handle this beast, using his horse as a tool of his special trade. The wide-brimmed hat was equally practical for keeping the sun out of his face, and the neckerchief kept his nose and lungs protected from dust. The many pockets of his vest held various valuables. The boots were made for riding, not walking, the heels fashioned so as not to catch in the stirrup if the rider should fall or be thrown off.

Spring and fall roundups were the main events of the year around Pipe Spring and ranches throughout the West. In the spring, after having spent the winter on the range, cattle were gathered so that each calf could be given the brand of its mother; every addition meant more profit for the ranch owner. The fall roundup had another purpose—to pick out cattle ready for market. Weeks or even months on a cattle drive were the toughest part of the cowboy's life. Moving cattle was hard enough, the task made more difficult by Indian attacks or thunderstorms. After an early breakfast, the drive moved out each day as the chuckwagon went ahead to prepare lunch; after the noon break the wagon went on ahead once more to the campsite for that night where dinner would be prepared. At night a watch had to be kept over the nervous cattle. The routine went on changelessly day after day until the railhead was reached.

You can get further information on Pipe Spring, including times of roundups and branding of cattle at the ranch, from the superintendent (tel. 643-5505).

HOOVER DAM AND LAKE MEAD NATIONAL RECREATION AREA:
The extreme northwesterly point of Arizona is marked by **Hoover Dam,** confining the waters of the Colorado behind it in 110-mile-long Lake Mead, which stores a two-years' flow at any given time. The water produces four billion kilowatts of electricity, enough for half a million homes, and provides irrigation for three-quarters of a million acres in the U.S. and half a million acres in Mexico. The water also serves towns and industries in seven states.

The dam, 83 miles northwest of I-40 at Kingman, reached via U.S. 93 through the Detrital Valley, has tours led by Bureau of Reclamation guides daily from 7:30 a.m. to 7:15 p.m. Memorial Day to Labor Day, and 8:30 a.m. to 4:15 p.m. the rest of the year. There is a topographic model of the entire Colorado River Basin and a model of a generating unit, both on view in an exhibit building. Since it opened in 1937, over 21 million people have visited the dam.

Lake Mead National Recreation Area attracts five million visitors a year for swimming, boating, fishing, and waterskiing. There is no closed season on fishing in the lake, which has black and striped bass, bluegill, crappie, and catfish. The area also includes **Lake Mohave** below the dam, formed by Davis Dam, 67 miles downstream, and extends out from both shores in Arizona and in Nevada. Lake Mohave is stocked with trout from Willow Beach National Fish Hatchery. The lakes attract several species of waterfowl.

Both lakes have full facilities for boaters, fishermen, and campers: launching ramps, courtesy docks, facilities for boat storage and rental, fuel and oil supplies, stores selling groceries, bait and tackle, restaurants, picnic ramadas, swimming beaches, and dump stations. Lake Mead has 826 campsites; Lake Mohave has 322.

KINGMAN:
Nearest town to the Lake Mead National Recreation Area is Kingman, 143 miles west of Flagstaff on I-40, in a hot, dry basin between the

Cerbat Mountains to the north and the Hualapai Mountains to the south. Calling itself the "crossroads of the West," the town lies on the main routes between Phoenix and Las Vegas and between southern California and Albuquerque.

Sights and Activities

An attraction for visitors is the **Mohave Museum of History and Arts,** 400 W. Beale St. (tel. 753-3195), run by the Mohave County Historical Society. It is open free of charge weekdays from 10 a.m. to 5 p.m. and weekends from 1 to 5 p.m. A mural shows the history of the county from prehistoric times to the present. Carvings of turquoise in the form of fantastic animals, all made from locally mined minerals, make up the Colbaugh collection. The Andy Devine Room displays memorabilia from the local boy who made good in the movies. Displays of artifacts of early Indian life take up a couple of rooms, while another is used for exhibitions of paintings, sculpture, and crafts by the Mohave Artists and Craftsmen's Guild. Outdoors, there is a mining display with wagons, a head frame, a blacksmith shop, and an arrastra.

Also open to visitors in Kingman is the **Little Red Schoolhouse,** now the city library, a one-room structure built in 1896. **Locomotive Park** is named for a Santa Fe steam locomotive that ran between Los Angeles and Kansas City until 1957 and is now on permanent display. The **Bonelli House,** downtown, is a stately Territorial-style residence with a sedate white picket fence across its front yard, furnished in period style and also open to visitors.

Near town in the Hualapai Mountains there are campsites and cabins for rent in **Hualapai Mountain Park,** operated by the county. Thirty miles southwest, in the Black Mountains, is the famous ghost town of **Oatman,** with many original buildings still standing and wild burros occasionally loose on the streets. Founded in 1906, Oatman was a commercial center for mining camps with such evocative names as Goldroad, Gold Dust, Happy Valley, Old Trails, Snowball, Camp 49, Blue Ridge, Times, Tent City, Fairview, Rice, and Ryan. By 1931 the Oatman area had produced $36 million worth of gold. Movies made here include *How the West Was Won, Foxfire,* and *The Edge of Eternity.* Several shops are open along Main Street. Another ghost town, this one 20 miles northwest of Kingman off U.S. 93, is the old mining center of **Chloride,** where old mining shafts are sunk into the foothills of the Cerbat Mountains.

A time to remember in Kingman is the weekend in late September called **Andy Devine Days,** when there is an arts-and-crafts show at the county fairgrounds.

Food, Lodging, and Travel Services

Lodgings in Kingman include a dozen motels, all with rates pegged lower in winter than in summer. Moderately priced rooms can be found, for example, at the biggest of the motels, the **Holiday Inn,** 3100 E. Andy Devine, Kingman, AZ 86401 (tel. 602/753-6262, or toll free 800/465-4329), which is a meeting place for townfolk, in its restaurant and in its lounge. It has 116 units priced at $44 to $52 double, depending on season. There is cable television in all rooms, and an outdoor pool.

Budget-priced rooms are available at the **Imperial Motel,** 1911 E. Andy Devine, Kingman, AZ 86401 (tel. 602/753-2176), which has a pool and cable television, and double rooms at $20 to $25, depending on season.

Kingman has a score of restaurants including half a dozen offering full bar service and full-course dinners. The **House of Chan,** 960 W. Beale St. (tel. 753-3232), has a full menu of Chinese food, and a lounge. For steaks, the address is the **Dam Bar & Steakhouse,** 1960 E. Andy Devine (tel. 753-3523).

Further travel service information is available at the **Kingman Chamber of Commerce,** 333 W. Andy Devine, Kingman, AZ 86401 (tel. 602/753-6106).

BULLHEAD CITY: The recently established U.S. weather station here is threatening the title of the town of Gila Bend down toward Phoenix as the fanbelt capital of the country, what with setting new record highs in daily temperatures. It is also threatening boom-town records, having grown 300% between 1970 and 1980—and still booming. Much of the growth is due to the fact that the town, on the bank of the Colorado River, had free ferry service across to Nevada, where a dozen gambling casinos are alive night and day in the community of Laughlin. Now a new bridge connects the two towns. Since the gambling resort is hemmed in by government land and cannot expand—at least not until land-use policies of the government are modified, which may be about to occur —the 3,500-odd employees of the casinos commute from Bullhead City, which has also benefited hugely from the visitor influx the gambling facilities have caused. Motels and restaurants have sprung up in Bullhead City to take care of all the gamblers' needs as they cross and recross the Colorado River.

Although Laughlin itself has only a few hundred permanent residents, most of them living in a modest condo and a mobile-home cluster, it is far from a sleepy little village because of the sweeping invasions of gamblers, who pour in from California and Arizona mostly. On weekends there may be 50,000 people swarming in and out of the casinos. So called "red-eye" bus trips bring in citizens from Phoenix and Tucson, and there are retirees living in campers from the North and Midwest who make the area their winter headquarters mainly for their love of the sound of coins dropping into a slot machine.

Gaming and hotel operations total over $100 million annually. Owner of the largest casino and five hotels in the town bearing his name is Don Laughlin, who was 57 in 1989 and founded the village in 1966. It is expected that Laughlin, the town, will increase its population faster as condos, houses, and homes are built on the minimal land presently available. One casino executive says, "We can't rush things. We have to go through 23 state and federal agencies every time we make a move."

Bullhead City, on the Arizona side, is 35 miles west of Kingman, reached from I-40 via Ariz. 68 west and Ariz. 95 south. A mile up the Colorado River from town is **Davis Dam,** completed in 1953, which impounds Lake Mohave to the north. It was the recreational area around the lake that originally brought permanent residents to the otherwise desert scene, including many retired people.

Three miles north of Davis Dam, on the Mohave Lake, is **Lake Mohave Resort,** Katherine Landing, Bullhead City, AZ 86430 (tel. 602/754-3245), with a 50-unit motel on the lake, a park for RVs, a family-style restaurant, a cocktail lounge, a coffeeshop, and a store for groceries, bait, and tackle. There is a marina with full services for boats, including rentals of powerboats and houseboats. Similar services are offered by the same management in accommodations in three other area resorts on Lake Mead: **Lake Mead Resort,** 322 Lakeshore Rd., Boulder City, NV 89005 (tel. 702/293-2074); **Echo Bay Resort,** Overton, NV 89040 (tel. 702/394-4000); and **Temple Bar Resort,** Temple Bar Marina, AZ 86443 (tel. 602/767-3400), on the Arizona south shore of the lake.

Laughlin Resorts

Huge neon signs beckon Arizonans to cross the magic Colorado River to gambling-land aboard one of several small ferries continually shuttling between the shores carrying passengers back and forth. The original operation, Don Laughlin's **Riverside Resort and Casino,** 1650 Casino Way (P.O. Box 500A), Laughlin, NV 89029 (tel. 702/298-2535, or toll free 800/227-3849), has a 13-

story addition. Gaming areas have tables for 21, craps, poker, big six, roulette, bingo, and $50,000 keno, plus there are 1,000 slot machines. Laughlin avers that they are "the loosest slot machines in the Silver State." The resort has 661 rooms renting for $40 to $48 (depending on the view) Sunday through Thursday, and $52 to $60 on Friday and Saturday, as well as a waterfront restaurant specializing in steaks and other beef dishes from cattle raised on the company's 61,000-acre Laughlin Land & Cattle Co. ranch in the nearby Hualapai Mountains. The resort also has 300 spaces in an RV park with full hookups. Rooms have riverside balconies and there are two swimming pools.

The **Edgewater Casino Hotel,** 12020 S. Casino Dr., Laughlin, NV 89029 (tel. 702/298-2453, or toll free 800/257-0300), is a five-story structure within which are offered, it is advertised, "friendly games of chance." It is also claimed here that "even the slot machines are friendlier." Besides the usual gambling areas there are also a pool and a kids' game room, and a free shuttle van to other casinos in Laughlin. A bowling alley was the most recent attraction added. Good meals from breakfast through lunch and dinner cost under $4.

The **Nevada Club,** 2300 S. Casino Dr. (tel. 702/298-2512), offers Dixieland nightly as well as slot machines taking coins from a nickel up, and craps, 21, roulette, keno, and poker. It claims the "largest jackpot on the river" with $100,000 winnable on a machine called the $1 progressive video slots carousel. Some $1 slots also have light and sound effects.

Note: For casino jumping with ease, free van service among them is provided by the Nevada Club, the Riverside Resort, and the Edgewater Hotel. Visitors simply wait at the entrance to casinos for the next van. There is, however, taxi service in Laughlin, operating 24 hours with radio-dispatched cars (tel. 702/298-2299 in Nevada, 602/758-6900 in Arizona). The free ferries operate between the Arizona shore and the casinos from the parking lot across from the Bullhead City Post Office to the Nevada Club, from the parking lot at the foot of 2nd Street to the Edgewater Hotel, and from two lots to the Riverside Resort, one across from Bullhead City Airport and the other at the River Queen Motel. There is access to the Nevada side easily enough by driving across Davis Dam and then following the west-bank road three miles south to the casinos, all having parking space including room for RVs. The Riverside Resort has camper and trailer space with full hookups for 300 units.

Travel Services in Bullhead City

Bullhead City and Laughlin are 300 miles from Los Angeles and 230 miles from Phoenix, and the casinos serve a more casual crowd than does Las Vegas 90 miles to the north. The founder of Laughlin, Don Laughlin, says, "Eighty percent of our business is what Las Vegas has run off," by which he means people there are not treated with the courtesy and fairness he thinks they should be. At any rate, the casinos here have good odds on low minimum bets, cheap food, and friendly service that draw the camper-family and the retired folk, many of the women in pincurls rather than Saks Fifth Avenue garb, the men in T-shirts, and battalions of children invading the nongambling game rooms set up for them.

Bullhead City, which got a jump on its gambling neighbor across the river as a housing center for workers building the Davis Dam, completed in 1953, has ample motel accommodations and eating places.

Havasu Airlines (tel. 602/754-3922, or toll free 800/528-8047) serves Bullhead City Airport daily with flights to Las Vegas and Phoenix. Cities served by **Laughlin Aire** are Orange County, San Diego, and Palm Springs in California, and Scottsdale, Arizona.

Bullhead City **bus depot** (tel. 754-4655) offers service to California points, Phoenix, and Las Vegas.

Information about Lake Mead National Recreation Area, which includes Davis Dam and Lake Mohave, is available from the National Park Service (tel. 754-3272).

You can rent a car from **Avis,** on Ariz. 95 at Hancock Road, at Dunton Motors (tel. 758-5082).

Where to Stay

Besides rooms in the casino resorts on the Nevada side and in over a dozen motels in Bullhead City on the Arizona side, there are pleasant lakeside rooms at the above-mentioned **Lake Mohave Resort** on Katherine Landing, Bullhead City, AZ 86430 (tel. 602/754-3245). Situated just above Davis Dam on the Arizona side of the lake, the resort has a marina with boat rentals, and courtesy shuttle buses to and from the Laughlin casinos. A restaurant and lounge are appropriately furnished in captain's chairs and ships' wheels, pulley blocks, and nautical lanterns. The 51 motel units all have wide windows on the lake, and 14 of them have a kitchenette. Rental boats include patio and ski boats as well as fishing craft, and even houseboats for waterbound vacations or cruises up and down the lake. An excursion boat, the *Lady Katherine,* also makes daily voyages along part of the 230-mile lake shorelines. Double rooms here are $49 to $72, depending on season.

The **Super 8 Motel,** at 4th and Lee Streets, Bullhead City, AZ 86430 (tel. 602/754-4651, or toll free 800/843-1991), offers good value, with courtesy-car trips to Nevada casinos, a pool, and cable television. Rooms are $28 to $36 double, and there are a few kitchenette units available. Children stay free in their parents' room.

Note: For all information on resorts in Laughlin, including accommodations, call toll free 800/227-0629 from within Arizona, or 800/227-5245 from other states.

Where to Eat

Restaurants include the **Rib Ranch,** 135 Ariz. 95 (tel. 754-3349), open daily for breakfast, lunch, and dinner, specializing in barbecued ribs, barbecued prime ribs, barbecued pork ribs, as well as steaks, other beef dishes, and seafood.

The **Captain's Table,** at 7th and Long Streets in the River Queen Motel (tel. 754-3214), serves three meals daily from 6:30 a.m. and offers such choices as lobster, steak, king crab, trout, oysters on the half shell, shrimp, and prime rib.

LAKE HAVASU CITY: Twenty miles south of I-40 on the east bank of the Colorado River is Lake Havasu City, and arriving here by car is something of an experience. As you drive on the twisting highway through the gravelly desert slopes and flatlands of the Chemehuavi Valley, the barren peaks of the Mohave Mountains appear to be moving along with the car. The feeling of isolation, remoteness, is strong until clusters of glinting mobile homes appear on the horizon. Beyond are low, western-style ranch houses that seem to blend with the surrounding sand. The desert light makes all vistas bright but somehow two-dimensional, giving an additional sense of unreality to what now comes into view at the far edge of a stretch of stony ground. Impossibly, it is **London Bridge!**

Of course the word has long been out about the new location of the bridge, but one's first reaction no matter what one has been told is to deny it—there must be some big mistake here. But it remains in view, its flags flapping bravely against the western blue sky, its gentle arches outlined in reflections in the blue water below it. When the sun begins to set here the bridge gleams photogenically, the weave of the cloth in the flags catching the sunlight in changing patterns. After your hair calms a bit from its on-end position on your head, you may notice something else: a London bus, bright red and double-decked; a high-topped London taxi; and a pub along a roadway below the bridge.

At night the way of strollers over the bridge is lit by gas lamps, and there are English-looking shops under it on a terraced embankment, including, of course, one selling fish and chips. Once a visitor gets used to the bridge's presence, it's not surprising to find out that one of the two innovators who brought the thing over lock, stock, and barrel from England was the same man who designed Disneyland. Its purpose was to put this new real-estate-development community on the map, and indeed the hot desert has sprouted thousands of new residences as well as some lakeside resorts on Lake Havasu, formed of the waters of the Colorado River as they are impounded by the Parker Dam for a distance of 45 miles upriver; the dam is 20 miles down the lake from Lake Havasu City.

The bridge has also become a regional tourist attraction, lying as it does near the much-traveled east-west I-40 and only 75 miles north of another major east-west highway, I-10. The dam was built in 1938 but it wasn't until 1964 that the late Robert McCulloch, the chain-saw manufacturer, bought a 26-square-mile tract by the lake as the site of a planned town where he wanted to build new factories. Boat manufacturing is another McCulloch enterprise, and the lake provided a likely testing place. In spite of the July mean high temperature of 108°, McCulloch was quoted at the time he began building his town: "This beautiful land is the best place to live and work I have ever seen."

By 1968 the town was abuilding as planned, but there seemed an element lacking, in spite of the presence of shopping centers and facilities for golf, tennis, fishing, and water sports. The place needed a centerpiece, something with a little pizzazz. Then, like a gift, the solution came to McCulloch and his town planner, the Disney man C. V. Wood, when they saw a televised news item that London Bridge was indeed about to fall down—it was sinking into the Thames and would have to be replaced. Bids were asked for the materials in the bridge, and with a flourish worthy of Diamond Jim Brady, McCulloch made an offer of a cool £1 million Sterling, in those days worth $2.4 million. Then as a goodwill gesture he added another $1,000 for each of his 60 years, for a total bid of $2,460,000. It was enough to beat out other entrepreneurs who merely wanted to crack up London Bridge and sell the pieces for souvenirs.

The job of moving the bridge to Arizona began with numbering the 10,276 blocks of granite forming the surface of the bridge, after which they were each drilled out and lowered by crane into lighters that delivered them to docks for reloading into freighters. These ships then sailed for Long Beach, California, via the Panama Canal. The last lap to Arizona was covered by truck. Work on the Lake Havasu site was held up for a time when none of the "W" series of numbered stones could be found anywhere. It was finally discovered that one of the stone annotators back in London had been a Spaniard for whom the letter W does not exist in his alphabet.

Sculptured humps of Arizona sand duplicating the original arches made the core of the new bridge, which was then covered with concrete. When it dried the sand was removed. Then the stones from the real bridge in London were put on, each with a steel loop to hold it in place by fitting into a recess in the concrete. Rods secured the loops and mortar sealed the job. Thus the new version weighs but a third of the original and is 53 feet shorter. The leftover blocks were chopped up for souvenirs by a businessman who now boasts the world's first desk made of a slab of the London Bridge.

The original work of designer John Rennie, London Bridge replaced a predecessor that had been in use for 625 years. It took 800 workers 7½ years to build it, finishing in 1831. Here in Arizona 40 men built it in two years at a cost, beyond that for the materials from England, of $5.6 million. At the first dedication, King William IV and Queen Adelaide attended a lobster and beef banquet in a striped circus tent set up on the bridge. At the Arizona ceremony a century and a half later, in October 1971, the Lord Mayor of London was guest of honor at a similar banquet for 8,000 people under a tent much like the one used for the first party. Also as in the first event, a great balloon decorated with Union Jack stripes rose into the air before the eyes of 40,000 spectators, who also watched rockets, skydivers, and skywriting airplanes. Some Indians put "tribal tokens" in a time capsule that was buried in an abutment of the bridge and the taped bonging of Big Ben was heard over the land, as it still is today. One thing about the bridge may be hard to explain to future historians: how those shrapnel holes from German bombs in World War II got into a bridge way out here in Arizona.

Cruises aboard an excursion boat, the *River Queen,* depart from the **English Village,** under the bridge, on Wednesday, Saturday, and Sunday at 9:30 a.m., the two-hour trip costing $18. Dinner cruises on Thursday, Friday, and Saturday include hors d'oeuvres, dinner, and live entertainment at a lakeside restaurant as part of an overall four-hour trip for $24. Further cruise information is available by calling 855-2405.

Other attractions of the English Village include the British Pub and the City of London Arms Restaurant, a Picadilly Ice Cream bus, a London gift shoppe, the Thirsty Pretzel, the Bridgewater Station gift shop, the Shirt Shoppe, the Shooting Gallery, the London Bridge Rock & Jewelry Shoppe, the World's Largest Candle Shop, the Copper Shoppe, the Gallerie of Glasses glass-blowing establishment, the Incredible Machine (engraved portraits on acrylic), the Allison Manor Candy Shoppe, Native Creations Ltd., Pudding Lane Print Sellers, London Bridge Souvenir on a Penny, and paddleboats, canoes, and wet bikes.

Another shopping area is in a medieval village fashioned very roughly on the English city of York, called the **Shambles,** at 2126 McCulloch Blvd., a mile inland from the bridge. Upper half-timbered stories lean over the street below in Shambles Lane, and it is said that a person could shake hands from one house with a person in another across the lane. Concerts and art displays go on at the heart of the complex, called King's Square.

London Bridge Golf Club has two 18-hole courses, both off Acoma Boulevard, the Stonebridge course rated at par 70 and the London Bridge course at par 72. There are rental cars and clubs and a pro shop, as well as the Clubhouse Restaurant, open for breakfast, lunch, and dinner, with bar service for 19th-holers. For information and reservations, call 885-2719.

Where to Stay and Eat

The **Holiday Motel,** 245 London Bridge Rd., Lake Havasu City, AZ 86403 (tel. 602/855-4071), has 161 units, a pool, restaurant, cocktail lounge, and game room, plus entertainment six nights a week in the Living Room lounge. Buffet lunches and dinners are served in the dining room. Children under 18 stay free in motel rooms with their parents. Rates are $38 to $65 double.

Travel-trailer resorts include **Lake Havasu Travel Trailer Park,** 601 Beachcomber Blvd., Lake Havasu City, AZ 86403 (tel. 602/855-2322), with 167 RV spaces (at $18 for two people, plus $3 for every additional person) and a free launching ramp; and the **KOA London Bridge Campgrounds,** 3405 London Bridge Rd., Lake Havasu City, AZ 86403 (tel. 602/764-3500). Their daily rate is $15, with full hookup.

The only lakeside resort with hotel accommodations is the **Nautical Inn,** 1000 McCulloch, Lake Havasu City, AZ 86403 (tel. 602/855-2141, or toll free 800/892-2141), with its own 18-hole golf course, tennis courts, and heated pool. The Captain's Table restaurant serves breakfast, lunch, and dinner, and the Tiki Terrace offers dancing and nightly entertainment. Double rates are $65 to $160.

Travel Services

Lake Havasu City has direct air service to Las Vegas and Phoenix via **Havasu Airlines** (tel. 602/855-5011, or toll free 800/528-8047). **Alpha Airlines** (tel. toll free 800/824-2610) flies to Los Angeles.

For all travel information, get in touch with the **Lake Havasu Area Visitor Center,** London Bridge, Lake Havasu City, AZ 86403 (tel. 602/855-5655).

PARKER: This town on the Colorado River 160 miles west of Phoenix has a population of 2,500, and at an elevation of 450 feet shares with other places in the desert on both sides of the river some of the hottest summertime temperatures in the country, which means of course a bright, dry, mild winter climate as well. It is 12 miles southwest of **Parker Dam,** the world's deepest dam, which has 73% of its 320-foot height below the riverbed. Completed in 1938, it feeds a billion gallons of water daily into the Colorado River Aqueduct that takes it to southern California cities. Its impounded waters form Lake Havasu, 45 miles long.

The dam also produces hydroelectric power in the transmission system of the Western Area Power Administration, interconnecting power plants of Parker, Davis, and Hoover Dams. The transmission lines extend as far as Henderson, Nevada, to the north; Blythe, California, to the west; Yuma, Arizona, to the south; and as far as Phoenix and Tucson to the east. The combined capacity is enough to supply the needs of 4.5 million people. The plant is open to the public daily from 8 a.m. to 5 p.m.

Buckskin Mountain State Park (tel. 667-3231), just north of the dam, has 26 campsites with full hookups and riverfront cabañas with picnic tables and grills. There is a small historical museum at the visitor center, open daily from 8 a.m. to 4 p.m., and a small store with groceries, fishing supplies, and gasoline open February to November.

Where to Stay

Nearby on the lake is **Havasu Springs Resort,** Rte. 2, Box 624, Parker, AZ 85344 (tel. 602/667-3361), just around the bend from the dam, with a specialty of trailer floaters called Camp-A-Float: "Your RV on our boat." For $90 a day you move your whole camper or trailer aboard, which is supplied with 100 gallons of water and a 100-gallon sewage capacity. The shoreside RV park has full-hookup spaces. The resort also has two motel units, one overlooking the harbor and the other built around a swimming pool. They all have two queen-size beds, and the poolside motel has kitchenettes. Double rates are $45 to $80, with a 50% reduction November to March. Deluxe apartments are also available, sleeping six to eight persons, at $80 and up daily. Houseboats are another option—they are big enough to sleep ten people. Fishing boats with motors are also rented by the hour or day. The Marina Room Restaurant and Lounge (tel. 667-4593) are on the harbor, and there is also a game room and billiards tables.

For reasonably priced rooms in town, try the **Kofa Inn,** 1700 California Ave., Parker, AZ 85344 (tel. 602/669-2101), which has a large pool and a 24-hour coffeeshop; rates are $32 to $36 double.

For all travel service information, get in touch with the **Parker Area Chamber of Commerce,** 1217 California Ave., Parker, AZ 85344 (tel. 602/669-2174).

Where to Eat

The **Cattleman's on the River,** eight miles north of town on Ariz. 95 (tel. 667-3323), offers such entrees as steak Dijon, chicken Oscar, clams fettuccine, and scallops mornay. The house specialty is prime rib of beef Dallas style ("seared on the broiler and smothered with mushrooms, bell peppers, onions sautéed in butter and red wine," according to the menu); another special, running just under $25, is the baked lobster Chesapeake. There is dancing nightly in the lounge.

Parker eating places include a Mexican-style restaurant, **Los Arcos,** 1200 California Ave. (tel. 669-9904), with a full bar, open daily except Monday for lunch and dinner.

YUMA: Hot is the word for Yuma, a city with a population of 50,000 in the extreme southwestern tip of Arizona, 25 miles from the Mexican border at San Luís. Besides a prison become a state historic park, the city has numerous other points of interest. The city is on the **Amtrak** line to Los Angeles to the west and Houston and New Orleans to the east (for information in Arizona, call toll free 800/421-8320). The city is also on I-8 connecting with San Diego to the west and I-10 and the Phoenix and Tucson areas to the east, and is served by **Continental Trailways. Yuma International Airport** is served by America West and Sky West.

At only 130 feet elevation, the city has a hot summer season, and boasts a 93% sunshine rate of possible sunlight hours over the year. The area is a thriving irrigation-farm center and cattle-pen operating point, with many military and other government installations also at the base of the economy. Winter visitors down here for the sun increase the population temporarily by about half from November to March.

For information on all travel services, get in touch with the **Yuma County Chamber of Commerce,** 377 S. Main St., Yuma, AZ 85364 (tel. 602/782-2567).

Sightseeing

Yuma Territorial Prison State Historic Park, at Giss Parkway and Prison Hill Road (tel. 783-4771), is open daily from 8 a.m. to 5 p.m., for an admission of $1 for adults; under 17, free. Built by prisoners themselves in 1876, the builders were the first to be locked into the cells of this jail, which was operated for 33 years, up to 1909, when prisoners were moved to a larger facility. Among the 3,069 prisoners over the years, 112 died, most from tuberculosis. Of those who tried to escape, 26 made it and 8 were shot dead in the attempt. There is a pitch-dark cell for extra punishment, and the ball and chain that was used for recaptured escapees. After its jail days ended the structure was used as the Yuma high school. There is a prison cemetery and a small museum.

The oldest American-built structure in town is the **Custom House** (tel. 343-2500), on Second Avenue behind City Hall. On a river bluff, it was used as office and residence for the Customs Service until 1955. It is open, free of charge, from 10 a.m. to 4 p.m. Tuesday through Saturday.

The **Century House Museum,** 240 S. Madison Ave. (tel. 742-1841), is a regional effort of the Arizona Historical Society, one of the town's earliest houses, the home of a pioneer merchant named E.F. Sanguinetti. Exhibits are of artifacts from the Territorial era, and there is a garden and aviary with talking birds maintained here as they were a century ago. Admission is free, and the house is open from 10 a.m. to 4 p.m. Tuesday through Saturday and noon to 4 p.m. on Sunday.

Near the Territorial Prison across the Colorado River on Indian Hill Road is **Fort Yuma** and the **Quechan Indian Museum** (tel. 572-0661). One of the earliest forts in the Arizona Territory, it protected settlers at the Yuma Crossing of the Colorado River. It is today headquarters of the Quechan Indian Tribe and has a museum of tribal relics. It is open from 8 a.m. to 5 p.m. weekdays for an admission of 50¢.

The restored, spacious Southern Pacific Railroad Depot is today the home of the **Yuma Art Center** at 281 Gila St. (tel. 783-2314), open free of charge Tuesday through Saturday from 10 a.m. to 5 p.m. and on Sunday from 1 to 5 p.m. Contemporary art by regional artists is shown and a gift shop has original artwork for sale.

A recently added attraction of interest to railroad buffs is the weekend steamtrain runs on the **Yuma Valley Railroad** throughout the year. The *City of Gadsden* leaves at 10 a.m., and on some days a second run at 6 p.m., from the Yuma Valley Depot, 8th Street at the Colorado River. Operated by the nonprofit Yuma County Live Steamers Association, the 2½-hour-round-trip out into the desert country goes along the Colorado River and return, making a stop at the Cocopah Indian Reservation, where an arts-and-crafts stand welcomes browsers and buyers of reservation-made artifacts and works of art. There are special steak runs, serving dinner in the lounge car, on Friday nights during the winter months, costing $10 including train fare. Train trips cost $8, $7 for seniors, $5 for children. For information, call 783-7288.

Outdoors

The Yuma area has a couple of lakes with recreational facilities in waters impounded by dams on the Colorado River. There is **Laguna Dam,** 13 miles north, and **Imperial Dam,** 18 miles north. Twenty miles north, the **Senator Wash Dam** offers the waters of **Squaw Lake** for boating, fishing, camping, swimming, and waterskiing. **Martinez Lake,** 35 miles north, is reputed to be excellent fishing for bass, catfish, crappie, carp, and bluegill. Eighteen miles north on U.S. 95 is an oddity called the "swinging bridge to nowhere," the **McPhaul Bridge** that once spanned the Gila River but now has only sand underneath. Built in 1929, it is similar in style to the Golden Gate Bridge over San Francisco Bay.

Sports facilities include four golf courses: **Desert Hills Municipal,** with 18 holes at 6,700 yards, a PGA pro, carts, a pro shop, and a coffeeshop; **Mesa del Sol,** with 18 holes, carts, a pro shop, a clubhouse, bar, and coffeeshop; **Arroyo Dunes,** with 18 holes and a driving range, a dining room, and bar; and **Yuma Golf and Country Club,** with carts, a PGA pro and shop, a dining room, bar, and clubhouse. There are 15 municipal tennis courts, all lighted.

Where to Stay

A popular meeting place for townspeople is the lounge of the **Chilton Inn,** 300 E. 32nd St., Yuma, AZ 85364 (tel. 602/344-1050), one of the largest hostelries in the city, with 123 rooms. There is usually live entertainment in the lounge in the evening, and the restaurant is open daily for three meals. Rooms have in-room movies, there is room service, and guests enjoy a heated pool, a therapy pool, tennis, and racquetball. Rates are $45 to $70, depending on season.

Reasonably priced lodging in modern rooms with telephones and, in some, kitchenettes, is offered at the **Yuma Cabaña,** 2151 S. Fourth Ave., Yuma, AZ 85364 (tel. 602/783-8311), which includes use of a swimming pool in rates of $22 to $42, depending on season.

Where to Eat

Beto's, 812 E. 21st St. (tel. 782-6551), offers both Mexican and American dishes, as well as steaks and buffet service, with full bar service.

Chretin's Mexican Food, 485 15th Ave. (tel. 782-1291), also specializes in Mexican dishes and has full bar service.

Gene's, 771 Fourth Ave. (tel. 783-0080), has steaks, American and Chinese dishes, as well as full bar service, and is also open for breakfast.

For steaks, the **Sizzler,** 1360 Fourth Ave. (tel. 782-4491), is a setting for family dining.

CHAPTER XII

EASTERN ARIZONA AND THE FOUR CORNERS AREA

□ □ □

1. NAVAJO RESERVATION
2. HOPI RESERVATION
3. EASTERN ARIZONA

Eastern Arizona and the four corners area, where four states—Arizona, Utah, Colorado, and New Mexico—join at a single point, is the site of the vast Navajo Reservation that completely surrounds the homeland of the Hopi Indians, the two nations still living according to their separate old traditions, sharing a high arid tableland skirted by most pioneer and immigrant incursions into the West. Among the Navajo treasures is the Canyon de Chelly, a national monument with cliff dwellers' ruins along the sides of the canyons that in principle may be visited only with Navajo guides as escorts. Both Navajo and Hopi are encouraging the spread of the teaching of their own crafts, the Navajo of course famed for their weaving, and the Hopi now for their silverwork. The Hopi have a cultural center where craftspeople may be watched at work. The Navajo operate Monument Valley Tribal Park in the northern part of their reservation, an area of scenic wonders now provided with a campground and other accommodations. Nearby in Navajo National Monument are Anasazi cliff dwellings, some limited as to the number of visitors allowed each day because of their extreme fragility.

Along the Interstate south of the Indian lands are a couple of towns offering travel services, Winslow and Holbrook, and east and south from there is the wild, high, piny White Mountain region with great stretches of wooded wilderness, much protected within national forests. Also in eastern Arizona is the unique Petrified Forest National Park.

1. NAVAJO RESERVATION

The Navajo, with over 100,000 population on a reservation of 24,000 square miles, is the most populous of American Indian nations and along with the Apache were the most aggressive of the southwestern Indians. They are believed to be descended from bands of hunters and gatherers related to the Apache who did not develop a settled way of life until the 17th century. They learned farming methods from the already-established Pueblo Indians living in present-day New Mexico. They also preyed on the Hopi for horses, sheep, and cattle, in conflicts today ended in a tenuous peace that sees Navajos completely surrounding the Hopi homeland.

The extended family is the basis of the Navajo social system, made up of several married women with their immediate families, the women sisters or cousins to begin with, whose husbands, daughters, and sons, and eventual grandchildren are all members of this central unit. The individual wives, husbands, and children would occupy a separate dwelling called a hogan—they are five-sided or circular and were originally earth-covered—but the extended family works together in farming, sheepherding, and ceremonial life. A larger grouping of several of these extended families make a clan, of which the Navajo traditionally have around 60. Marriage must be outside the clan.

Like the Apache, the Navajo speak an Athabascan language. Unlike the Pueblo Indians from whom they learned so much when they settled the area, they do not generally congregate in tight villages but rather live in dwellings scattered throughout the countryside. Among arts the Navajos developed from contacts with the Pueblo Indians are pottery and sand painting, and their famous weaving. Their silversmithing arts they learned from 19th-century Mexicans.

The bleak period of modern history for the Navajo came during the years 1864–1868 when Kit Carson was ordered to stop their raids on settlers by destroying their crops and their herds and jailing 8,000 of them at Bosque Redondo, 180 miles south of Santa Fe, New Mexico. Some bitterness from this experience remains with the Navajo well over a century later.

Their woven blankets and rugs, made on a horizontal loom, are considered the best in color and design made by any North American Indians today. They learned from the Hopi how to build these looms, but unlike their teachers, among whom weavers are men, the Navajo weavers are women only. The Navajo widened the scope of textile design by the addition of a variety of geometric designs, such as diamonds and zigzags. Before 1800 they were made of the naturally colored wools, black, white, or a mixture making gray, with dyeing limited to a few dark browns. But after 1800 imported red cloth from Spain was unraveled and incorporated into woven patterns of rugs and blankets. Bright designs, some gaudy, came into favor with the introduction of aniline dyes toward the end of the last century and into the 20th—with geometric picturing of locomotives, automobiles, vegetable cans, and airplanes. There was a slump in the demand for such wares until a return to traditional designs after World War II reestablished a solid market throughout the U.S. and the world.

In principle designs may not depict living things, man or beast. A non-Indian woman who spent eight years with the Navajo learning their weaving art discovered this taboo when she wove the likeness of a snake into a weaving. Reticent to criticize her, her teachers finally informed her the snake would bring bad luck. She asked if she should burn it, but the reply was that the ashes would remain and the snake, and the bad luck, within them. The only way to do away with the snake would be to unravel the weaving. Loath to destroy her work, she continued to complete it, inserting a couple of ravens to guard the snake so that if it makes a move to foist bad luck on her they will nab it and kill it. The ruse seems to be working. There is, however, an exception to the Navajo rule about weaving likenesses of living things: when the weaving depicts a sand painting originally done by a man. In effect, a male Navajo may make a pictographic likeness of a person or animal and avoid any curse for it.

MONUMENT VALLEY: This 30,000-acre tribal park 170 miles northeast of Flagstaff, via U.S. 89, U.S. 160, and U.S. 163, is an area of fantastic rock formations lying partly in Arizona and partly across the state line in southeastern Utah. It is the first of nine tribal parks established by the Navajo within their nation, managed by their Recreational Resources Department, which has headquarters at the Navajo capital, Window Rock, Arizona (tel. 602/871-6647). For information on the Monument Valley Park, in Monument Valley, Utah, call the supervisor (tel. 801/727-3287).

Research teams in the valley have found over 100 ruins dating from before A.D. 1300, the signs that a population found ways to survive the arid land by marginal farming based on a system of scattered plantations where scarce rainfall was somehow caught and used for irrigation. Apparently, however, even this minimal waterfall failed during the 14th century, when the Anasazi, as the inhabitants are now called (from the Navajo for "old ones"), disappeared.

The rock formations in the valley are at least 25 million years old, the work of erosive forces upon an earlier volcanic uplift in the land surface that formed huge cracks and canyons. Valleys are still becoming wider today. Orange-red cliffs aged 230 million years are capped by younger rock 160 million years old. The wide flat valleys dotted with strange pillars, points, towers, and buttes have long been a favorite background for moviemakers, beginning in 1938 with John Ford's *Stagecoach.* Also remembered here are *How the West Was Won, The Eiger Sanction,* and *The Return of the Lone Ranger.*

Since the Navajo have a certain autonomy in their lands, their laws should be known. A Navajo bulletin on the valley asks visitors to "respect the privacy and customs of the Navajo people living in the valley. Closeup photographs of Navajo residents and their homes is allowed only with permission. Enter home areas only on invitation."

The **visitor center** has an arts-and-crafts shop, and is open daily from 8 a.m. to 7 p.m. May to September, to 5 p.m. October to April. It is four miles in from U.S. 163 on an access road. Open during daylight hours, departing from the visitor center, is a 17-mile dirt loop road winding through the valley of monuments, with stops at the following special-interest points: The Mittens and Merrick Butte, Elephant Butte, Three Sisters, John Ford's Point, Camel Butte, The Hub, Totem Pole and Yei-bi-chei, Sand Springs, Artist Point, North Window, and The Thumb. Also at the visitor center site is **Mitten View Campground,** with a camping fee of $7 per campsite equipped with table, grill, and ramada. There is a water supply, toilets, hot showers, and a dump station. Firewood should be carried in. Nearest store is at Gouldings, Utah, six miles west.

Accommodations can be found 28 miles south at the **Monument Valley Holiday Inn** on U.S. 163, Kayenta, AZ 86033 (tel. 602/697-3221, or toll free 800/465-4329), decorated in Indian style, with the tables in the dining room nestling under tepees and booths resembling somewhat the ancient cliff dwellings. A chile taco and Indian fry bread supply a taste of Navajo food. The location is the junction of U.S. 160 and 163 just south of town. Rates are $40 and up, double.

NAVAJO NATIONAL MONUMENT: Reached 140 miles northeast of Flagstaff via U.S. 80, U.S. 160, and Ariz. 564, the **visitor center** here has exhibits and a slide program to introduce the area attractions of cliff dwellings built by the Anasazi seven centuries ago. There is a picnic area and a campground with water supply and toilets; tables and grills are supplied too, but only camp stoves or charcoal are permitted. In summer, rangers put on nightly campfire programs concerning the archeology, history, and natural history of the monument.

cestors of many of the modern Indians of the Southwest lived in this plateau for a period of 1,300 years until they disappeared mysteriously in the 14th century. Ruins of these Anasazi people to be seen here were the homes of people who lived by hunting, trapping, gathering nuts and seeds, and growing a few vegetables such as corn and squash. By A.D. 400 permanent houses went up as farming became more solidly established on the plateau. Three cultural centers evolved: Mesa Verde, in southwestern Colorado; Chaco Canyon, to the southeast over in New Mexico, and here in the Kayenta area. The Mesa Verde and Chaco people migrated to the Rio Grande, but the local Kayenta people moved south into the Hopi lands. It is the modern Hopi, carrying on some of the ancient traditions of the Kayenta, who offer a view into the past pueblo life of those Anasazi. Today the area is occupied by Navajo who migrated here more recently.

Two areas of ruins are open to visitors under certain circumstances here. One, **Betatakin,** or "ledge house" in Navajo, is the most accessible. Resting on a steeply sloping floor of a large natural alcove with a roof nearly 500 feet high, Betatakin was built, lived in, and abandoned all within two generations between A.D. 1250 and 1300. Its 135 rooms include living quarters, granaries, and a *kiva,* or ceremonial room. Other *kivas* are thought to have existed here and have been destroyed by rockfall. The towering red sandstone walls of Betatakin Canyon have a pocket of aspen, Douglas fir, scrub oak, and box elder. Through this little grove leads a trail to the ruin from the canyon bottom—it is a shady spot rare in this arid country.

This ruin was discovered in 1909 by Byron Cummings, an archeologist, and John Wetherill, a rancher and trader who with his brother, Richard, discovered many of the major Anasazi cliff dwellings in the San Juan region. There is a viewpoint at the end of the **Sandal Trail,** a one-mile round-trip walk from the visitor center, from which the ruin may be viewed (you can see better with binoculars). Visiting within the ruin is permitted only in the company of a park ranger. In spring, summer, and fall there are regularly scheduled tours limited to 25 persons, involving a round-trip hike of four hours and some tough climbing on the return trip. The canyon is 700 feet deep—equal to the height of a 70-story building—and at the local altitude of 7,000 feet the hike can be fatiguing.

The other ruin, **Keet Seel,** was discovered in 1895 by Richard Wetherill, and is the largest cliff dwelling in Arizona, with 160 rooms: living quarters, storage rooms, courtyards, and five or six *kivas.* The name means "broken pottery" in Navajo, and gives an odd impression of having been lived in until fairly recently, although it has been empty for 700 years. Visits here are permitted between May and September depending on availability of park personnel to escort groups, limited to a total of 20 per day and 1,500 per year because of the extreme fragility of these stone remains. Advance reservations are recommended, to be made by mail (Superintendent, Navajo National Monument, Tonalea, AZ 86044) or by phone (tel. 602/672-2366). The primitive trail, eight miles in length, crosses the canyon stream several times en route. Horseback trips are a pleasant way to make the visit; horses are available from Navajo Indians near the visitor center. A full day is required for the Keet Seel hike.

Still another ruin, **Inscription House,** at the base of a cliff in an arm of Nitsin Canyon, has 74 rooms and a *kiva,* and there is a tree-ring date of 1274 that shows it was built about the same time as the other ruins. It is named for an inscription on a wall of one of the rooms reading: "C H O S 1661 A d n." The figure may in fact be 1881, not 1661. In any case this ruin is closed to the public.

CANYON DE CHELLY NATIONAL MONUMENT: Situated on the Navajo Reservation at Chinle, Arizona, two miles to the east of U.S. 191 at a distance

of 62 miles south of Mexican Water, and 75 miles north of I-40 at Chambers, the Canyon de Chelly is an approachable, more easily grasped version of the Grand Canyon to the west and is famous for cliff dwellings in its walls. They seem like miniature houses when seen from the mesa tops that rise anywhere from 400 to 1,000 feet above the canyon floor.

Reaching eastward from the **headquarters and visitor center** in the village of Chinle, the canyon forks at a point a few miles along to form the Canyon del Muerto reaching northward. The main canyon reaches 27 miles through the Defiance Plateau to its head near Washington Pass, and is still lived in by some 400 Navajos. They plant crops of corn and squash in the spring and harvest them at the end of summer, living in their traditional five-sided hogans, many still with the old-style turf roofs, that have always provided shelter as well as spiritual dimensions.

Even in the mesa-top communities where hogans may today have modern-style windows, shingled roofs, and television antennas, the exact placing of the door is of utmost importance: the kitchen must be built to the left, and when the owner dies, the entire house must be abandoned and its materials destroyed.

Rim Drive along the south rim is paved and always open to cars, which may pull up at any of four overlooks, each one higher than the last, until the pride of the canyon, **Spider Rock,** is reached. This is an 800-foot red sandstone monolith standing in lone grandeur on the canyon floor.

The only trail down into the canyon accessible without a guide is the **White House** trail, a mile down to the usually dry riverbed where the cliff dwellings perch on ledges not far above your head.

Other ruins can be viewed from up top, but the most satisfying trip is to take an **open-truck tour,** half day or all day, run by Thunderbird Lodge in Chinle in old six-by-six army trucks. On this trip pictographs can be examined and photographed closeup. A famous example of these is called **Spanish Mural,** and shows a procession of Spanish conquistadores with a priest along, carrying a cross.

More ruins are to be seen from auto turnouts along the north rim of the branching Canyon del Muerto. Since there is 40 feet of sand in the bottom of the canyon and flash floods occur without warning—not to mention quicksand—hiking in the riverbed is dangerous. Therefore no one is allowed to go in, either on foot or in a vehicle, without a Navajo guide.

Thunderbird Lodge, P.O. Box 548, Chinle, AZ 86503 (tel. 602/674-5842), was the original home of an Indian trader and has rooms made of stone and adobe built half a century ago, as well as a restaurant open May to October. There is also a grocery and general store. Rooms here are available all year, at rates of $42 to $64 double.

Half-day canyon tours are $26 for adults, $18 for children under 12; full-day trips with lunch are $40 for all. For reservations, call Thunderbird Lodge.

The Canyon de Chelly was a stronghold for the Navajo, who took refuge here around 1700 against incursions by the Spanish, the Mexicans, and the Americans. **Massacre Cave** here was named for 115 Indians killed by a punitive Spanish foray in 1805. One of Kit Carson's cavalry detachments marched into the canyon, capturing Navajo to be deported to New Mexico in 1864.

Cottonwood Campground, near monument headquarters, offers fireplaces, tables, and rest rooms.

HUBBELL TRADING POST NATIONAL HISTORIC SITE: Also on the

Navajo Reservation is one of the few remaining authentic Indian trading posts still in operation, thanks to National Park Service management: Hubbell Trading Post, a mile west of Ganado, Arizona, and 55 miles northwest of Gallup, New Mexico, reached via Navajo Rte. 3 from the east and west or Ariz. 63 from the north and south. The store today serves two functions, in its primary role as supplier of staples to its neighbors, and also as a historic reminder of an earlier era when trading posts were practically the sole contact between native and non-native people in the region. Much of the changes in the lifestyle of the Indians came about through the agency traders, and the same trade was also responsible for the first national awareness of the dignity and wealth of native arts, crafts, and culture.

Among the Navajo, the dean of traders was John Lorenzo Hubbell, known during half a century on the reservation for his honesty and hospitality and for his counsel to the Indians. The son of a Connecticut Yankee, born in New Mexico, he was self-educated and early became familiar with the language and the ways of the Navajo while traveling around the Southwest in a job as Spanish interpreter and clerk—he had learned Spanish from his Hispanic mother. He was known as Don Lorenzo to the settlers and as Double Glasses or Old Mexican to the Navajo, and he started his trading post here in Ganado in 1878. His position with the Indians was based on his interpreting for them the ways of the incoming American settlers, explaining government policy to them, writing letters for them. He also became such a trusted friend that he settled their family fights. He used his own home as a hospital for the Navajo during a smallpox epidemic in 1886, and though immune from a boyhood attack of the disease, the Indians credited him with supernatural power in escaping it.

By encouraging excellence in craftsmanship among the Indians, especially in rug weaving and silverwork, he had an enduring influence on the successful acceptance of Indian products on the American market, which he also influenced in establishing stage and freight lines and a chain of trading posts, as many as two dozen at one time, run by him and his two sons. He was also into ranching and politics, the latter on the liberal side, supporting women's right to vote and opposing the English literacy requirements for Hispanics wanting to vote. He was sheriff during part of the wars between cattlemen and sheep ranchers, backing the sheepmen during a time he recalled later: "I'd been shot at from ambush no less than a dozen times, and my home had been converted into a veritable fort. For one solid year not a member of my family went to bed except behind doors and windows barricaded with mattresses or sand bags."

Hubbell expressed his business philosophy: "The first duty of an Indian trader, in my belief, is to look after the material welfare of his neighbors; to advise them to produce that which their natural inclinations and talent best adapts them; to treat them honestly and insist upon getting the same treatment from them; . . . to find a market for their products and vigilantly watch that they keep improving in the production of same, and advise them which commands the best price. This does not mean that the trader should forget that he is to see that he makes a fair profit for himself, for whatever would injure him would naturally injure those with whom he comes in contact."

The Hubbell Trading Post today looks much as it did when Hubbell ran it, a place of social life for the Navajos as well as a store and a business center. They came to the post over long distances, covering dusty or muddy trails on foot or by horse and wagon, bringing with them their wares: hand-woven rugs, turquoise and silver jewelry. Today as in the old days the iron stove is fired up on cold days with fragrant-smelling piñon and juniper logs. Shelves are stocked with staples of rural western life as needed today as ever in the past: coffee, flour, sugar, candy, Pendleton blankets, tobacco, calico, pocketknives, and canned goods. Harnesses and other hardware hang from the ceiling.

Today in the trading post the Hubbell rug room has stacks of Navajo rugs and blankets that show the skill of the weavers. There are also baskets that were made by Indians of several southwestern tribes, saddles and saddle bags, bridles and Indian water jugs. There are some small framed paintings of Navajo rugs done by E. A. Burbank and other western artists, designs originally made as examples for the Navajo weavers at the behest of Hubbell.

Everybody stopped at the Hubbell trading post on his way through this country in the old days: Theodore Roosevelt, Nelson A. Miles, Lew Wallace, and Mary Roberts Rinehart among them. In the Hubbell house you can see a collection of western Americana assembled over the years by the Hubbell family. Since World War II the Navajo have replaced their horses and wagons with pickup trucks and they drive considerable distances to supermarkets and department stores that have competed with the old-style trading posts, many of which no longer exist. But the Hubbell post continues in operation as the oldest continuously operated post on the reservation, serving not only its primary Indian customers but also a growing stream of interested visitors from all over the U.S. and elsewhere.

The post is open daily in summer from 8 a.m. to 6 p.m., to 5 p.m. the rest of the year.

WINDOW ROCK: The capital of the Navajo nation has its administrative offices in Window Rock, Arizona, at the junction of Ariz. 264 and Navajo Rte. 7 at the extreme eastern limit of the state, a mile from the New Mexico line; the reservation land extends into New Mexico. The reservation, established in 1868, was administered from Fort Defiance, five miles to the north of Window Rock, until 1936 when the capital was moved here. The tribe is governed by a tribal council of 87 elected members and presided over by a chairman and vice-chairman, serving for four-year terms. Local governments in the form of chapter houses also have elected officials.

The town is named for a rock formation visible at **Window Rock Tribal Park,** a great window-like hole in a sandstone formation that has long had a central position in Navajo myths and ceremonies. Picnic tables, water, and toilet facilities are offered here to visitors.

Other facilities for travelers in Window Rock include two campgrounds: **Tse Bonito Tribal Park,** the site of a stopping place for the Indians on their "Long Walk" to New Mexico in 1864, with a small zoo; and **Summit Campground** (tel. 871-6646), nine miles west on Ariz. 264, a scenic site at an elevation of 7,000 feet in a stand of Ponderosa pine.

At the fairgrounds in Window Rock is the **Tribal Museum** (tel. 871-4941), open from 9 a.m. to 5 p.m. Monday through Friday free of charge, with exhibits on the archeology, geology, history, and culture of the reservation, not to mention a fossil dinosaur. Services are still held in the **Franciscan mission** here, established in 1898. The biggest North American Indian fair is held here in early September, the **Navajo Nation Fair,** with parades rodeos, livestock and agricultural competitions, crafts exhibits, a carnival, horse races, and western and traditional Indian dancing nightly, to which visitors are welcome. The site is the fairgrounds. The **Navajo Nation Zoological Park and Botanical Garden** is open daily free of charge from 8 a.m. to 5 p.m.

Other events during the year include a **Navajo science and culture fair** in April and the **All-Indian Days** in early July. For information on exact times, telephone 871-4941 in Window Rock.

2. HOPI RESERVATION

The Hopi homeland occupies dry, inhospitable country entirely surrounded by the Navajo Reservation, a strange land of sandy sagebrush mesa and brilliantly colored rock surfaces of the Painted Desert covering 631,000 acres. They are the westernmost of the Pueblo Indians, with a population of 6,000 in terraced stone and adobe houses built in a number of separate communities, most atop mesas. Mystery surrounds the origins of the Hopi. According to their own myths, their ancestors came onto the earth by climbing up through four successive *kivas,* or underground ceremonial rooms. Farming and sheepherding are the local means of sustenance, but many Hopi are forced to make a livelihood off the reservation.

The villages are reached from the south via Ariz. 87 a distance of 67 miles from Winslow, Arizona, to the village of Second Mesa; or from the east, 110 miles from Gallup, New Mexico, via Window Rock and Ganado, Arizona, over Ariz. 264 to Second Mesa.

Steep footpaths originally afforded the only access to the Hopi pueblos, but today roads cut into the mesas give visitors easier approaches by car to within a few hundred yards. Early outside visitors here approached from the east and named the biggest mesas First, Second, and Third Mesas. **First Mesa** has the villages of Walpi, Sichimovi, and Hano; Walpi occupies a scenic spot at the far tip of the mesa. On Middle Mesa, or **Second Mesa,** are villages called Mishongnovi, Shipolovi, and Shongopovi. **Third Mesa** has the village of Oraibi and the modern communities called Bacobi and Hotevila. Off the mesa 50 miles northwest is the village of Moencopi, while Kiakochomovi, or New Oraibi, lies at the foot of the mesa.

At the foot of First Mesa are the famous ruins of **Sikyatki,** where some of the richest finds in western archeology have been made. Designs found here went into a reintroduction of traditional Hopi pottery-making a generation ago. One of the villages is not Hopi at all, but populated by Tano people descended from refugees from the Pueblo Revolt in 1680. It is called **Hano,** named for the habit of the people to cry "Ha!" frequently as they speak.

Best known of the Hopi villages is **Walpi,** where there are ruins of early pueblo dwellings at the foot of the mesa. The community is famous for enacting the snake ceremony on alternate years. Most isolated of the villages, **Shongopovi,** means "place where the reeds grow." Above a spring here are the ruins of a 17th-century Spanish mission from which beams were taken into the constructions of some nearby Indian houses after the Pueblo Revolt.

The tiny village of **Shipolovi,** meaning "mosquitoes," was named for people who came here to live when driven off from the Little Colorado River by hordes of mosquitoes. South of this village is **Mishongnovi,** where at the tip of the mesa at Corn Rock are ceremonial shrines. Founded by a chief called Mishong, the settlers were permitted here by the people of Shongopovi on condition they protect those shrines at Corn Rock. There is a view to the south of the **Giant's Chair,** a rock formation that has some ruins at its base.

Along with Acoma, in New Mexico, the village of **Oraibi** claims title to the oldest continuously inhabited town in the U.S. It is proved that the houses have been lived in at least since A.D. 1150. At one time the largest Hopi village, it has declined in recent years. A church built by Mennonite missionaries here just outside Oraibi without the permission of the Indians in 1901 was a source of conflict among groups of Hopis with differing religious beliefs, but the traditionalists won out and the church was abandoned and finally, in 1942, struck by lightning and gutted. The missionary, H. R. Voth, did put together a valuable collection of Hopi artifacts, however, now displayed in the Museum of Natural History of Chicago.

The tradition of peaceful settlement of conflict that is a central part of Hopi lore is illustrated in a fight between two groups in Oraibi in the early part of this century between groups led by Tewaquaptewa, who accepted social change and the incursion of an Indian school, and by Yokeoma, a hide-bound traditionalist. Hostility grew between the two groups, and at snake dance time there were crowds ready to fight on both sides. When Tewaquaptewa tried to find a peaceful solution, he was greeted by abuse from his opponents; when he asked them to leave peacefully on four different occasions, they refused to reply. Yokeoma said he and his followers would have to be thrown out of Oraibi by force. Tewaquaptewa's men then grabbed Yokeoma and dragged him outside, and soon there were two lines of hostile Indians facing each other, brandishing knives, guns, and bows and arrows. But then some of the older Hopis ordered all the weapons put down so that a line could be drawn in the sand between the two factions. It was agreed that if Tewaquaptewa could push Yokeoma across this line, the loser would voluntarily leave Oraibi with his force. The pushers, Tewaquaptewa and his men, numbered about 100, while their immovable opponents were double that number. The pushing and shoving began and went on for two hours. A few government officials were on hand to act as umpires. From time to time the battle stopped while everybody took a short rest. Pushers occasionally abandoned the fight altogether, but the two principals were hard at it when finally Yokeoma cried out: "It is done! I have been pushed over the line!" The ceasefire was an effective end to the civil war, marked today by an inscription near that famous line, made in halting English by one of the Indians on the scene, and reading thus: "Well, it have to be done this way now, that when you pass me over the LINE it will be DONE, Sept. 8, 1906." The losers promptly founded the village of **Hotevila,** eight miles away.

The **Hopi Cultural Center,** "at the center of the universe," according to the Hopi people, is owned and operated by the tribe and offers a motel, restaurant, and complex of shops specializing in native crafts. There is also a museum, like the shops open daily from 9 a.m. to 6 p.m. The layout is built to resemble, in modern style, the traditional Pueblo village.

The Hopi villages specialize to some extent in various crafts, all displayed for sale in the shops here. First Mesa villages produce hand-coiled pottery, which may also be purchased from the potters themselves in their houses wherever a "pottery for sale" sign appears. Second Mesa villages are known for Hopi coiled baskets of yucca, the product of an intricate art form. Several silversmiths who ply their trade in the Cultural Center are residents of the community of Shongopovi here. Third Mesa villages and Moencopi make wicker plaques and baskets that combine kachina and geometric designs.

Kachina dolls, silvercraft, and garment weaving are all done by males. Photography in these villages is not permitted by the Hopi tribal authorities. During the summer months kachina dances are held—for information, call the Cultural Center (tel. 734-2401).

The **Hopi Cultural Center Motel,** P.O. Box 67, Second Mesa, AZ 86043 (tel. 602/734-2401), has double rooms at $36 to $44, some with television. A dining room offers standard menu items as well as some Hopi dishes such as game or corn stew. Weekend reservations several weeks ahead are advised from April to October.

Hopiland guided tours to many of the mesa localities depart from the Cultural Center daily. For information, call 734-6623.

3. EASTERN ARIZONA

The fascinating fossilized tree trunks of the Petrified Forest just south of the Navajo Reservation are the gateway south to the high mountain country of Apache and Greenlee Counties, the White Mountains full of little-traveled forest roads, and travelers' private discoveries of isolated trout streams and ponds—plus some great faraway skiing.

PETRIFIED FOREST NATIONAL PARK: This fabulous area is a north-south expanse with a wide acreage of the **Painted Desert** at its northern end, the park stretching between I-40 on the north and U.S. 180 on the south. A practical way to visit the park by car is to enter the park from I-40, when approaching from the east, then drive south through the park to exit at U.S. 180 and continue west from there. The opposite route is suitable for travelers coming from the west, entering at the South Entrance. Park headquarters is at the **Painted Desert Visitor Center** at the north end. Here a 17-minute film on how wood is petrified is shown. At the south end the **Rainbow Forest Museum** has exhibits of petrified wood and material showing the history and geology of the area. The scenic drive from one end of the park to the other, 27 miles long, has numerous pullouts at points where especially impressive displays of petrified wood are seen. There is also ample space here for cross-country hiking and overnight backpacking, with free permits to be taken out at headquarters. A general warning is that no water is available away from the developed areas.

At the northern part of the park there are overlooks giving views of the Painted Desert from eight different points. At **Kachina Point** is the **Painted Desert Inn Museum,** open in summer with exhibits on cultural history. There is a picnic area. The road winds six miles over the high desert, then crosses south over I-40 and the railroad tracks and the Puerco River to arrive at **Puerco Indian Ruins,** where Anasazi lived until about A.D. 1400 and left behind their houses, now visible as low walls. Here, well worth the steep descent down a 120-step stairway, is **Newspaper Rock,** a sandstone block covered with petroglyphs. A side road three miles long leads to **Blue Mesa,** where there are so-called pedestal logs that act as capstones to clays beneath. When the pedestal erodes, the log falls into the clay.

At the **Jasper Forest Overlook** the whole topography of the Petrified Forest can be surveyed, with countless petrified logs strewn down below. Logs with root systems show that some of the trees originally grew nearby. Destruction of fossils a century ago by gem collectors had citizens of the Arizona Territory petitioning the Congress to preserve these sites. Cracks and hollows of logs once held crystals of quartz and amethyst.

The flattops are remnants of a continuous layer of sandstone overlaying the earth's surface here. Campers hiking into the **Flattops Wilderness** may park at this turnout; campers must hike at least half a mile from traveled roadways before setting up camp. **Rainbow Forest** can be explored by hiking the **Long Logs** and **Agate House Trails,** where the bright colors of the petrified wood come from deposits of iron, manganese, carbon, and other minerals. Beyond the Rainbow Forest Museum the road leads another two miles to join U.S. 180.

The explanation of the formation of petrified wood—no samples of which may be taken from the park, incidentally—is that this plain was once crossed by main streams that nourished great stands of pines, or trees much like pines. Giant reptiles, amphibians, and dinosaurs lived in a jungle of ferns and other plants we know about today only by their fossil remains. When tall trees fell, the streams washed them into the floodplain here, where eventually they were covered over by a blanket of silt, mud, and volcanic ash that cut off oxygen and slowed the decay of the wood. Gradually ground water carrying silica seeped through the logs, bit by bit replacing the original tissues with silica deposits. When the silicas hardened, the logs, or exact replicas in silica, became our present petrified wood. The logs then lay under a sea for some 200 million years, but when the land beneath was uplifted it cracked these logs into pieces, and wind and water eroded them. There is much still buried in the area, where fossil-bearing earth goes down as deep as 90 feet. Protected as a national monument beginning in 1906, the Petrified Forest has been a national park since 1962.

Wood from outside the park is still collected and is sold in souvenir shops in the Southwest. It comes from the same geological deposits, and of the same quality of wood, as that found within the park. It can be bought rough or polished, and craftspeople make it into decorative objects such as jewelry, clocks, or bookends.

Although wilderness camping is permitted within the park, there is no campground accessible to vehicles. At the Painted Desert headquarters there is a restaurant and gift shop; at the Rainbow Forest end, a gift shop and fountain.

The park is open from 6 a.m. to 7 p.m. in summer, from 8 a.m. to 5 p.m. in winter. The admission fee is $1 per car.

HOLBROOK:
Nearest town for travel services from the Petrified Forest National Park is Holbrook, 20 miles west of the south entrance over U.S. 180, and 90 miles east of Flagstaff on I-40. It is also a gateway town for trips north into the Navajo and Hopi Reservations. Besides an ample range of motels and restaurants, the town has shops selling petrified wood in various forms.

Holbrook also has a **historical museum** in its handsome county courthouse, built in 1898, that is open summers only.

For further travel service information, get in touch with the **Holbrook Petrified Forest Chamber of Commerce**, 100 E. Arizona St., Holbrook, AZ 86025 (tel. 602/524-6558).

Where to Stay
Travelhost Motel, 109 W. Hopi Dr., Holbrook, AZ 86025 (tel. 602/524-6147), makes a pleasant headquarters for visiting the Petrified Forest and other sites in the region. It has 48 units, all equipped with cable television; some have kitchenettes, and there is a swimming pool. Rates are $45 double.

Whiting Brothers Motor Hotel, 2380 E. Navajo Blvd., Holbrook, AZ 86025 (tel. 602/524-6298, or toll free 800/453-4511), has 39 units, also equipped with cable television, at rates of $25 to $30 double.

Where to Eat
A local steakhouse is the **Plainsman**, 1001 W. Hopi Dr. (tel. 524-3345).

The **Cholla Restaurant**, 1102 W. Hopi Dr. (tel. 524-3329), has daily menu specials as well as full bar service.

Special Event
The town is home of the **Hashknife Sheriff's Posse** pony express ride between Holbrook and Scottsdale every January, commemorating the days a century ago when the pony express carried the mail from St. Joseph, Missouri, to Sacramento in as little as ten days. The Holbrook leg of the route is rerun yearly, with mail officially delivered for the U.S. Post Office, which marks all the mail carried with a special postmark. Those interested in receiving a postmarked envelope may send stamped, self-addressed mail to the Holbrook Post Office (Holbrook, AZ 86025) marked "via pony express" to arrive in Holbrook before the last week of January.

WHITE MOUNTAINS:
The White Mountains, spreading over large areas of Navajo, Apache, and Greenlee Counties and the Fort Apache Reservation in eastern Arizona, is an area attracting outdoorspeople of all tastes to a high country of sharp air and thick forests. Scores of primitive campgrounds are provided by the

Forest Service, which also maintains forest roads and trails to remote ponds and fishing streams. A number of small towns provide travel services, and there is a major ski resort operated by the Apache Nation.

Pinetop and Lakeside

These small towns, 50 miles south of I-40 at Holbrook, via Ariz. 77 and Ariz. 73, sit high in these mountains amid the world's largest stand of Ponderosa pine, with 57 fishing lakes within easy reach. The wilds contain frequently sighted bear, deer, elk, gazelle, and even a rare mountain lion. The towns grew along the highway until they met, and are considered today almost a single community.

Among nearly two dozen motels and resorts, several have private cabins with kitchens and some have fireplaces; unlike accommodations in the Phoenix area, for example, here not only children but pets, too, are welcome everywhere in a family-style vacation area that draws escapees from summer heat as well as winter sports enthusiasts, and hunters and hikers too. The **Double B Lodge** in the center of Pinetop (P.O. Box 747), Pinetop, AZ 86935 (tel. 602/367-2747), has 11 units (to $49 double) with kitchenettes, cabins or motel units, and some with fireplaces. The largest resort in the White Mountains is **Whispering Pines Resort** (P.O. Box 1043), Pinetop, AZ 86935 (tel. 602/367-4386, or toll free 800/521-0695), with its own restaurant and individual housekeeping cabins that have kitchens, fireplaces, and cable television. Doubles run $64 to $93.

Restaurants in Pinetop and Lakeside include the **Christmas Tree** at the Broken Arrow Lodge, on Woodland Road in Lakeside (tel. 367-3107), specializing in barbecued ribs, beef Stroganoff, and chicken and dumplings. For a special sandwich it's the **Blue Ridge Drive In** (tel. 368-6595) in Lakeside (closed Monday), where the specialty is the "best hamburger on the mountain—this ain't no downstream hamburger."

For fresh trout you can hardly beat Fred's Lake, where the **Trout House Restaurant** (tel. 367-4041), open for dinner every night from 5 p.m., prepares trout caught fresh daily. Fishermen may catch their own here from the private lake (no license, permit, or limit imposed, and tackle, bait, and cleaning available), and have them prepared in the restaurant. Ribs, chicken, New York strip steak, king crab, and spaghetti are also on a menu that offers beer and wine too.

The Whispering Pines resort has an Italian-style restaurant, **Campagna's** (tel. 367-5348), offering fresh veal, pasta, and seafoods. Prime rib and the "famous baseball steak" are specialties of the **Roundhouse Steakhouse** (tel. 368-4848), which has live entertainment Thursday through Saturday nights.

Emergency medical care is available through the **Navapache Hospital** emergency department (tel. 537-4375), four miles south of Show Low on Ariz. 260, offering 24-hour service. For local **highway conditions,** call 537-ROAD.

For all travel service information, get in touch with the **Pinetop-Lakeside Chamber of Commerce** in Pinetop, AZ 86935 (tel. 602/367-4290).

Apache Sunrise

The best skiing in Arizona is at this ski resort owned and operated by the White Mountain Apache Indians at McNary, Arizona, in the 1,664,000-acre Fort Apache Reservation, 30 miles south of Pinetop (reached by shuttle bus). For ski information, call 735-SNOW locally, or toll free 800/772-SNOW from elsewhere in Arizona, 800/882-SNOW from other states. The area has 45 ski runs, of which 15 are easy, 18 are difficult, and the rest "most difficult," departing from Apache Peak at 11,000 feet altitude. Some trails are over four miles in length. Eleven lifts give the area an uphill capacity of 13,000 skiers per hour. Skiing goes on between November and April with a 250-inch winter snowfall as well as the product of snowmaking machines when required. Friday and Saturday there is night skiing, and on weekends NASTAR races. A ski school includes a special branch for kids called Funland.

Nearby **Sunrise Lodge,** P.O. Box 217, McNary, AZ 85930 (tel. 602/735-7676), has 100 units, an indoor pool, fireplaces in public areas, a sauna, and a whirlpool spa. Rates are $62 double.

Outdoors in Apache Country

The **White Mountain Apache Indian Reservation** offers over a million and a half acres for such year-round sports as backpacking, fishing, and hunting. A limited number of hunters assures that game remains plentiful, and there are annual seasons on elk, mountain lion, black bear, and javelina. There are more than 3,000 in the elk herd, and no bull may be taken with fewer than six points; just 32 elk permits are issued each year, so that the hunters who get them are sure of an opportunity of taking a trophy bull. Two hunts are held yearly, with 16 hunters to each. The first one goes on during the last week of September, and the second follows over the first week of October. Hunts include five nights' lodging in cabins on Paradise Creek and at Maverick. Ranch-style meals are shared by hunters and guides. Each hunter has his own guide and a separate vehicle for elk, mountain lion, and bear hunts; guides are not required for the javelina hunts. Dogs are available for bear and mountain lion hunting.

Trophy caping of game animals is also provided, and for an extra charge game will be processed, wrapped, and frozen. The so-called kill ratio for elk hunters over the past ten years runs at 95%.

Camping in this great woodland is also permitted by the Apache, who have built campsites in canyons, beside streams, on mountaintops, and beside lakes. Most of the campgrounds are supplied with running water. The Apache Game and Fish Department, which administers the wilderness, wants to keep it as wild as possible, and thus requires permits for backcountry travel, as well as permits for camping at the designated sites. Fishing is open to purchasers of permits from the tribal office. Trails used in warmer months by hikers are also open to cross-country skiers during the winter, and there is a special area set aside for snowmobilers.

For all information and permits for activities on the White Mountain Apache Reservation, get in touch with the reservation **Apache Game and Fish Department** in Whiteriver (tel. 338-4385).

White Mountain Apache Motel-Restaurant, on Ariz. 73, Whiteriver, AZ 85941 (tel. 602/338-4927), is another tribal enterprise, with modern rooms and a bright café and dining room. A gift shop sells Indian crafts by various southwestern craftspeople. Doubles are $35.

Greer

Another woodland mountain village, Greer is 100 miles south of I-40 at Sanders, via U.S. 666 and Ariz. 260 and Ariz. 373, and makes an excellent base for hikes or cross-country treks through trails of **Apache Sitgreaves National Forest.** Nestled in the valley of the Little Colorado River, the town has such traveler services as lodges, cabins, motels, and restaurants.

Arizona's oldest lodge, the **Molly Butler,** P.O. Box 134, Greer, AZ 85927 (tel. 602/735-7226), has a saloon and dining room, a rooming house, and secluded cabins (rates from $22 to $35 for rooms, $45 for cabins).

Springerville

Another resort community in the White Mountains, this one 83 miles south of I-40 at Sanders via U.S. 666, Springerville has half a dozen motels and some restaurants as well as a couple of modest resorts. One of these is **Canyon Cove,** P.O. Box 1351, Eager, AZ 85925 (tel. 602/333-4602), open year round, with cabins in the woods fitted out with stoves and kitchens near Big Lake and Crescent Lake, ten miles from town on Ariz. 260. Cabins rent for $28 daily with one double bed, $42 with two beds.

In town, the **Springerville Inn,** Main Street, Springerville, AZ 85938 (tel. 602/333-4365), has a restaurant, cocktail lounge, 60 rooms with cable telelvision, and rates of $32 double.

South-of-the-border regional dishes are offered at the **Spanish Inn,** on U.S. 60 west (tel. 333-4416), with full bar service. Food may be ordered for take-out, and the place has been noted for 35 years for its charcoal-broiled steaks.

North of Springerville, **Lyman State Park,** with an entrance off U.S. 666, has a good swimming beach on a 1,500-acre lake, a launching ramp, and a campground with showers and full RV hookups. There is a store with a snackbar and boat rentals as well as fishing gear. Large-mouth bass, walleye pike, northern pike, and channel and blue catfish are caught here. A small herd of buffalo ranges near the park entrance.

Alpine

At an elevation of 8,000 feet, Alpine is still another wilderness exploration base with ice fishing and cross-country skiing popular in the winter season. Situated on U.S. 666 at a distance of 110 miles south of I-40 at Sanders, Alpine is on the eastern edge of the White Mountains in what locals like to call the "Alps of Arizona." Three miles from the small village, **Luna Lake** is a destination of trout fishermen. A slope called the **Golden Bowl** nearby is a draw for lovers of foliage in the autumn.

Motels include the **Tal-Wi-Wi Lodge,** on U.S. 666, Alpine, AZ 85920 (tel. 602/339-4319), three miles north of the village, with 20 units, a coffeeshop, cocktail lounge, and dining room with salad bar open for three meals daily. Rates are $38 double.

The **Alpine Country Club** (tel. 339-4944) has an 18-hole golf course, rental carts and clubs, and pro lessons, and is open to the public. You can find horses for riding at **Judd's Ranch** (tel. 339-4326).

Trailer parks with space for transient RVs include the **Alpine Village** (tel. 339-4476), with full hookups, bathhouse, and laundry.

Forest Service campgrounds at Luna Lake and Alpine Divide have tables, grills, rest rooms, and water supply; for information, call the Forest Service (tel. 339-4384).

GREENLEE COUNTY: More wild mountain country is to be discovered by continuing south on U.S. 666 another 125 miles from Alpine through remote woodland and a few high-altitude villages with such names as Beaverhead, Hannagan Meadow, and Stargo, down to the towns of Clifton, Morenci, and finally Duncan. The route, also known as the Coronado Trail, passes through **Apache-Sitgreaves National Forest** lands. At one point the road twists down the sharp face of the Mogollon Rim and elsewhere passes a number of towering mountain peaks. As the route comes near the town of Clifton it passes along Chase Creek and the gold-mining ghost town of **Metcalf.** Visitor attractions in this remote copper-mining area, other than those in the wilderness of forest and mountain, are few, but Clifton does have the **Greenlee County Historical Society Museum,** open Tuesday and Thursday from 2 to 4:30 p.m., occupying the 1874 house of one Henry Lesinsky, who built it—the oldest house in town. There are slag molds from the mine shown outside. Also in town is Clifton's first jail and an old narrow-gauge ore-hauling engine.

At Morenci there is a weekday 9 a.m. tour of the **Phelps Dodge smelter operation,** as well as the impressive sight of the world's second-largest open-pit mine. Northeast of Clifton, at **Limestone Canyon,** there is a famous mineral deposit of agate, blood-red jasper, and steel-gray rhyolite. Around Morenci are deposits of malachite, azurite, and chrysocolla, while south of Duncan there is fire agate and chalcedony. Agate digs are notable in the area elsewhere, such as at **Mulligan Peak,** reached via the San Francisco River route four miles northeast of Clifton, where, on the east side of the peak, a great boulder seems to stand guard over a field of agates and geodes, in banded colors ranging from purple to lavender and gray. According to local rockhounds, "You dig them like potatoes." Other rockhounding areas are reached by traveling southeast out of Duncan on U.S. 70 for 12 miles, then taking a road to the right to the Lazy B Ranch; along this road a sign indicates **Round Mountain,** the rock hunters' area. Another rockhounds' hunting ground is reached by traveling west on U.S. 70 out of Duncan toward Safford, and then taking a road to the left at milepost 318 where a sign indicates **Hackberry Ranch;** an agate site lies past the ranch house.

Accommodations include the **Rode Inn Motel,** 186 S. Coronado Blvd., Clifton, AZ 85533 (tel. 602/865-3313), with 30 units at $26 to $32 double; and the **Chapparal Motor Lodge,** on High Street, Duncan, AZ 85534 (tel. 602/359-2771), with rates of $35 double.

Eating places include the **Morenci Copper Room,** Main Street, Morenci (tel. 865-4111); and **Bailey's Steak House,** 236 North Ave., Duncan (tel. 359-2643).

The **Greenlee County Fair** is held in Clifton the first weekend of October, and there is team roping every Friday night in the summertime.

For information on all travel services in the county, get in touch with the **Greenlee County Chamber of Commerce,** 251 Chase Creek Rd., Clifton, AZ 85533 (tel. 602/865-3313).

CHAPTER XIII

INTRODUCING COLORADO

□ □ □

In its prairie, wheat and corn fields and ranchlands in the eastern part of the state, Colorado partakes of the spirit of the Middle West, and then as we move west into the wall of the Frontal Range of the Rockies that looms so suddenly before the view of easterners on their first trips out here, we are definitely in the Old West of cowboys and Indians, sourdough prospectors and railroad tycoons, false-front saloons and wooden sidewalks (there are still wooden sidewalks in the town of Grand Lake just west of the Continental Divide). It is the western tradition that attracts the visitors—along with those magnificent heights and heavy snowfall that draw eight million skiers to the state every winter—and it is thus the western scene in Colorado that this section emphasizes.

The first residents here were a people called Folsom Man 20,000 years ago. More recent cliff dwellers and pueblo builders, the Anasazi and Chace peoples, lived in Colorado a thousand years ago, then disappeared a century before the first Spanish explorers arrived on the scene. Where they went no one has proved, but ruins of their houses are sometimes found in such undamaged condition it may feel as if they had left only yesterday. The state has the greatest archeological treasure of any in the U.S. at Mesa Verde.

The Lewis and Clark expedition and mapping trips of Zebulon Pike opened up Colorado's modern history in the early 1800s, and then gold was discovered near Denver in 1858 and the "Pike's Peak or Bust" gold rush was on, bringing with it the building of a fabulous network of railroads, remnants of which still operate today to regale tourists rather than to haul gold and silver ore out of the hills. Colorado got its nickname, the Centennial State, when it gained statehood in 1876, a full generation before its neighbors to the south, New Mexico and Arizona.

The state's 104,000 square miles of territory would be considerably enlarged if it were ironed flat, for there are 1,143 mountains that rise to a height of over 10,000 feet above sea level. There are no fewer than 53 peaks rising to over 14,000 feet, with six times the mountain area of Switzerland. Eleven national forests comprise 15 million acres of land, and there are eight million acres controlled by the Bureau of Land Management also open to public recreational uses. Another half million acres are within national parks, monuments, and recreation areas under the administration of the National Park Service. Besides all this the state operates 30 state parks and recreation areas, and among many recreational services, stocks hundreds of lakes and streams with game fish.

The vast mountain land of Colorado is probably the greatest area in the U.S. for backpacking and hiking, and two-thirds of all this territory is within national forests, where the administration maintains over 400 public campgrounds. Wilderness areas of Rocky Mountain National Park also provide mountain hiking adventure, as do areas around Pikes Peak, Mount Evans, in the San Juan range in southwestern Colorado, in the country north of Glenwood Springs, in the Flattops and the Rabbit Ears Pass area near Steamboat Springs, and in the Ten Mile Range south of Vail.

Balloon instruction around Denver is available from **Life Cycle Balloon School,** 2540 S. Steele St., Denver, CO 80210 (tel. 759-3907).

Bicycling is popular everywhere, especially around Denver and Boulder. Maps and information on bike routes are available from the Colorado Department of Highways, 4201 E. Arkansas Ave., Room 235, Denver, CO 80222 (tel. 303/757-9313).

The state offers boating enthusiasts ponds, lakes, and rivers in various parts, from the world's highest anchorage at Grand Lake to waterskiing on Bonny Reservoir on the high plains. Large craft also take to Shadow Mountain, Granby, Blue Mesa, and Dillon Reservoirs. Navajo State Recreation Area in the south gives access to a 35-mile-long reservoir.

Rockhounding is carried on in various areas for recovery of semiprecious gemstones and petrified woods that take a high polish. Chalcedony varieties of quartz are widespread throughout the state. Agatized fossil bones that can be cut and polished are also found. Gemstones include beryl, topaz, phenacite, and aquamarine. Gold is found in every major mining area, and there is also silver, lead, copper, zinc, molybdenum, and uranium. Gold panning is a popular pastime. Information is available from the **Colorado School of Mines,** 1500 Illinois, Golden, CO 80401 (tel. 303/273-3000).

The most popular sport is skiing, covered completely in a separate chapter to follow. You can get telephone ski conditions throughout Colorado by calling 831-7669, and for cross-country trails, 879-3849. A telephone report on snowmobile-trail conditions is available at 422-1911.

Among thrills to be had merely by driving a car in Colorado is a trip to the top of Mount Evans on the highest paved auto road in North America, departing from Idaho Springs, 35 miles west of Denver, open June to September only; its summit is at 14,264 feet. There is also the world's highest tunnel, the Eisenhower Tunnel, at 11,000 feet, part of the east-west I-70. The state has a total of 36 mountain passes reached by cars. The highest, Independence Pass, has an altitude of 12,095 feet and is the main route between Denver and Aspen, except when closed by snow in the winter months. The highest continuous highway in the world is also in Colorado: Trail Ridge Road in Rocky Mountain National Park, crossing the Continental Divide at 12,183 feet.

The state's borders are rectangular, and its territory extends 387 miles east-west and 276 miles north-south. Cutting through the state in an irregular north-south line is the ridge of the Continental Divide. Major rivers are the Arkansas, Platte, Rio Grande, and Colorado. There are 1,000 miles of Interstate highways, including I-70 east and west from Denver, I-76 linking Denver with I-80 in Nebraska, and I-25 running north-south along the eastern slope of the Rockies. There are 9,000 miles of state highways and 67,000 miles of county roads.

The population of Colorado (1987) is 2,889,735 with an increase over the previous ten years of 630,000, most of this going to cities along the Front Range of the Rockies, including Denver, so that 80% of the people live in Denver and its area, Boulder, Colorado Springs, Pueblo, Fort Collins, and Greeley.

INFORMATION SOURCES: Information on recreation in public lands is available from a variety of sources, including the following:

U.S. Forest Service, Rocky Mountain Region, 11177 W. Eighth Ave., Lakewood, CO 80225 (tel. 303/236-9435).

Colorado Campgrounds Association (private campgrounds), 5101 Penn-

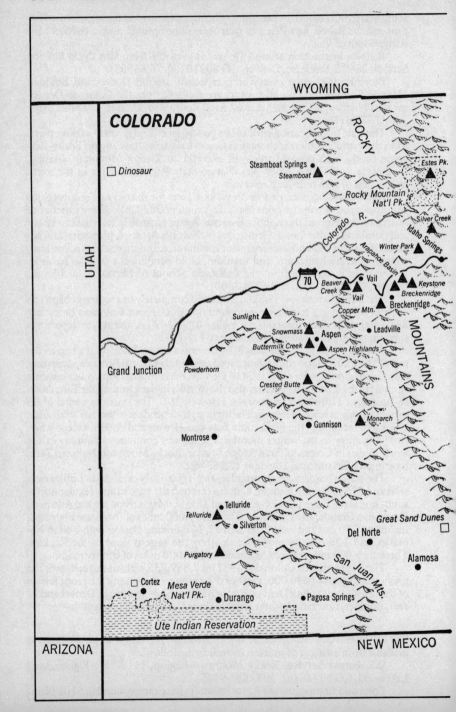

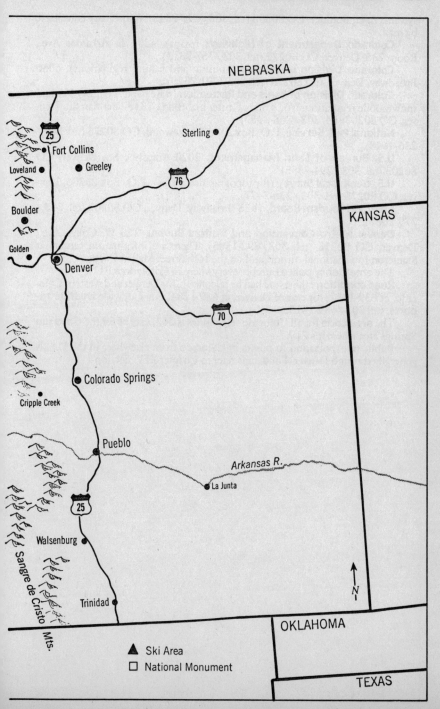

sylvania Ave., Boulder, CO 80303 (tel. 303/499-9343). A directory is available by mail.

Colorado Department of Highways (maps), 4201 E. Arkansas Ave., Room 235, Denver, CO 80222 (tel. 303/757-9313).

Colorado Division of Wildlife (hunting and fishing regulations), 6060 Broadway, Denver, CO 80216 (tel. 303/291-7529).

Colorado Division of Parks and Recreation (state parks, boating, RV, and snowmobile regulations), 618 State Centennial Bldg., 1313 Sherman St., Denver, CO 80203 (tel. 303/866-3437).

National Park Service, P.O. Box 25287, Lakewood, CO 80255 (tel. 303/236-4648).

U.S. Bureau of Land Management, 2020 Arapahoe St., Denver, CO 80205 (tel. 303/294-7555).

U.S. Geological Survey (for topographical maps), P.O. Box 25286, Denver, CO 80225 (tel. 303/236-7477).

Colorado Tourism Board, 1625 Broadway, Denver, CO 80202 (tel. 303/779-1067).

Denver Metro Convention and Visitors Bureau, 225 W. Colfax Ave., Denver, CO 80215 (tel. 303/892-1505). There are information centers at Stapleton International Airport and on the 16th Street Mall at Curtis.

The **emergency police** number everywhere in Colorado is 911.

Road condition reports are had by telephone, for Denver and western Colorado, at 639-1111; for east of Denver, at 639-1234. For statewide **weather reports,** call 303/639-1515.

The **area code** for all Colorado telephones is 303, except for the Colorado Springs area where it's 719.

Public transportation to points in Colorado from elsewhere in the U.S. is generally through Denver. For details refer to Chapter XIV, Section 1.

CHAPTER XIV

DENVER AND ENVIRONS

□ □ □

With a population of 550,000, Denver is at the center of a five-county metropolitan area with a population of 1.8 million. Called the Queen City of the Plains, Denver sits at the feet of the Rockies at the western extremity of the plains reaching east for a thousand miles. The architecture of the city reflects three boom eras in Colorado. The first, Victorian, occurred when silver was discovered in Leadville. Another, at the turn of the century, came when gold was discovered in Cripple Creek. The modern expansion has come about to some extent from mining and oil exploration in shale fields.

In 1865 Denver appeared to be doomed when the Union Pacific Railroad bypassed the city and took a route through Wyoming, but within a few years Denver businessmen raised the money to build their own railroad. Today Amtrak's east-west route goes through Denver instead of Wyoming. In 1983 Denver doubled its office space as part of a five-year building boom that added 16 skyscrapers, a $76-million pedestrian mall, and an $80-million performing arts center. Although construction abated in the late 1980s, the city is now building the world's largest airport, a new convention center, and half a dozen new shopping malls.

At a height of about one mile, Denver has a dry climate with only about 12 inches of rainfall annually. Spring-like weather in the winter is sometimes caused by the chinook, a wind bringing in warmth from the mountains to the west. The city is proud of its museums, including the modern Denver Art Museum in a six-story structure and the comprehensive Museum of Natural History. Models of scenes out of Colorado history are seen at the Colorado Heritage Center, and an innovative steel-and-glass world houses the Botanic Gardens. A special tourists' favorite is the tour of the U.S. Mint, which stamps out five billion coins a year.

One of the country's most elaborate centers of its kind is the Denver Performing Arts Center, larger than those in New York or Washington, with the country's first in-the-round symphony hall as well as three theaters. The city has some 2,000 restaurants, 30 theaters, 70 movie houses, and countless nightspots.

Denver's history begins as a mining camp when gold was found at the confluence of the Platte River and Cherry Creek in 1858. The strike was soon overshadowed by a bigger one 35 miles west in Central City, and Denver languished and eventually began growing as a trading center supplying various mining camps in the mountains. During the Civil War the Confederate army marched up from Texas hoping to seize the goldfields, but a volunteer army raised in and around Denver defeated the Rebels at the Battle of Glorita Pass, and saved Colorado for the Union. Two disasters at the time nearly finished Denver, however—a great fire in 1863 and a flash flood the following year. But the city was rebuilt out of its ruins.

Boom times came with silver strikes in the mountains in the 1870s. There was a time of lawlessness and gunplay of the style so often reenacted in the old western films, but soon the city developed a civic pride and restored order as lavish new buildings began to put it on the national map. Another economic boom accompanied the Cripple Creek gold strike. Thousands of trees were planted along wide boulevards in the town, parks were created with fountains and statues, and there was the acquisition of a 20,000-acre mountain park that became the famous Denver Mountain Park System. Today the city has more parks than any other city in the country.

A block of Denver's oldest buildings, Larimer Square, has been restored today, with courtyards, arcades, cafés, restaurants, and shops in Victorian structures, the sidewalks lighted at night by gaslight. Downtown today is divided into three districts. At the heart is the Civic Center, an expanse of three blocks with lawns and statues as a centerpiece to museums, office buildings, and the State Capitol.

The second downtown district is made up of most of the new steel-and-glass skyscrapers, in the middle of which a 12-block stretch has been closed off as a mall with gardens, open-air terrace cafés, and a system of electric shuttle buses (free of charge). A block away from the mall is 17th Street, known as the Wall Street of the West. Northwest from here, the third downtown district is a cultural and historic section. Besides Larimer Street, there is the recently renovated St. Charles district, with many restaurants, art galleries, and antique shops. Nearby is a Japanese cultural center, a block of international foods, and crafts shops.

On the 16th Street Mall is the Tabor Center, said to be the second-largest building project ever undertaken in the U.S. Occupying two entire blocks, it encompasses a 430-room Westin Hotel and a shopping plaza called the Shops at Tabor, where 70 stores are built on three levels.

Another downtown shopping center five blocks away from the mall is the Tivoli, which has 50 shops, a dozen movie theaters, and several restaurants. It occupies the premises of a vast old brewery still showing its tiled archways and copper brewing kettles from an earlier time.

1. ORIENTATION

Denver lies somewhat to the northeast of the center of Colorado at the junction of two major cross-country highways, I-70 between Utah and Baltimore, and I-25 between Wyoming and southern New Mexico. Denver is just 2,000 miles from Boston, 1,020 from Chicago, 1,030 from Los Angeles, and 1,280

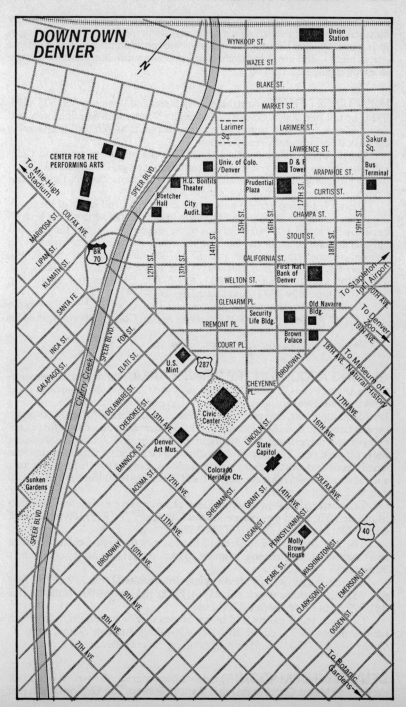

DOWNTOWN DENVER

N

WYNKOOP ST.

Union Station

WAZEE ST.

BLAKE ST.

MARKET ST.

Larimer Sq.

LARIMER ST.

LAWRENCE ST.

Sakura Sq.

CENTER FOR THE PERFORMING ARTS

To Mile High Stadium

SPEER BLVD.

Univ. of Colo. /Denver

D & F Tower

ARAPAHOE ST.

Bus Terminal

H.G. Bonfils Theater

Prudential Plaza

CURTIS ST.

Boetcher Hall

City Audit.

CHAMPA ST.

MARIPOSA ST.

LIPAN ST.

COLFAX AVE.

14TH ST.

15TH ST.

16TH ST.

17TH ST.

STOUT ST.

18TH ST.

19TH ST.

BR 70

12TH ST.

13TH ST.

CALIFORNIA ST.

KLAMATH ST.

WELTON ST.

First Nat'l Bank of Denver

To Stapleton Int'l Airport

20TH AVE.

SANTA FE

GLENARM PL.

Old Navarre Bldg.

To Denver Zoo

INCA ST.

Security Life Bldg.

TREMONT PL.

19TH AVE.

GALAPAGO ST.

Cherry Creek

SPEER BLVD.

FOX ST.

COURT PL.

Brown Palace

BROADWAY

18TH AVE.

To Museum of Natural History

ELATI ST.

U.S. Mint

287

CHEYENNE PL.

17TH AVE.

DELAWARE ST.

CHEROKEE ST.

13TH AVE.

Civic Center

LINCOLN ST.

16TH AVE.

Denver Art Mus.

BANNOCK ST.

ACOMA ST.

Colorado Heritage Ctr.

State Capitol

COLFAX AVE.

Sunken Gardens

12TH AVE.

SHERMAN ST.

GRANT ST.

LOGAN ST.

14TH AVE.

SPEER BLVD.

11TH AVE.

PENNSYLVANIA ST.

Molly Brown House

WASHINGTON ST.

40

BROADWAY

10TH AVE.

PEARL ST.

CLARKSON ST.

EMERSON ST.

9TH AVE.

OGDEN ST.

8TH AVE.

7TH AVE.

To Botanic Gardens

from New Orleans. It lies on a mile-high plain at the entrance to the Rocky Mountains just to the west, and temperatures call for medium-weight clothing in spring and fall, light clothing in summer—with provisions for a sweater or light coat at night—and medium-weight clothing with a warm outer coat for changeable winter ranges (20° to 60°).

HOW TO GET THERE: Amtrak, at 17th Street and Wyncoop (tel. 303/893-3911, or toll free 800/USA-RAIL), connects Denver with San Francisco, and serves eastern Colorado from Denver to such points as Winter Park, Granby, Glenwood Springs, and Grand Junction.

    Greyhound/Trailways (tel. 292-6111) is the major bus service in Colorado, serving ski areas at Winter Park, Steamboat Springs, Durango, and Vail, as well as providing runs to Colorado Springs, Fort Collins, Pueblo, Denver, and Colorado Springs. The bus depot is at 1055 19th St.

    Denver is a transportation hub for the entire West, and much of the traveling, when not by car, is by air to **Stapleton International Airport,** the seventh busiest in the world, just 340 miles west of the geographic center of the U.S., and only 15 minutes by car or city bus from downtown. The major airlines serving Denver include America West (tel. 571-0738), American (tel. 595-9304), Continental/Eastern (tel. 784-4800), Delta (tel. 696-1322), Mexicana (tel. 398-2270), Midway (tel. toll free 800/621-5700), Piedmont (tel. 251-5720), Trans World (tel. 629-7878), and United (tel. 398-4141).

    Regional and commuter airlines connect Denver with other points in the state. **Aspen Airways** (tel. 398-2150) serves Aspen, Colorado Springs, and Durango.

    Buses downtown cost 75¢; airport limos, $6.

GETTING AROUND IN THE DENVER AREA: The **Regional Transportation District** (tel. 778-6000), which calls itself "The Ride," provides good service within Denver and to the suburbs and outlying communities including Boulder, Longmont, Evergreen, and Conifer. Local fares are 75¢ (50¢ off-peak); express fares, $1.05; and regional fares, $1.75. There are reduced fares for passengers over 65 years of age. Peak hours are 6 to 9 a.m. and 3 to 6 p.m. weekdays only; off-peak fares apply at all other times. The various routes have different schedules of frequency including time of the last bus, varying from 9 p.m. to 1 a.m. Maps of all routes are available at the RTD office, 1600 Blake St., from 8:30 a.m. to 5:30 p.m. weekdays.

    Taxis have to be called by telephone or picked up at one of the few cab stands in the city. The main services are **Yellow Cab** (tel. 777-7777), **Zone Cab** (tel. 861-2323), and **Metro Taxi** (tel. 333-3333).

    The 16th Street Mall, running 12 blocks from the Civic Center northwest to Market Street, has free buses running up and down at a frequency of one every 90 seconds.

    Car-rental agencies include **American International** (tel. 399-5020), **Avis** (tel. 839-1280), **Budget** (tel. 861-4125), **Hertz** (tel. 297-9400), **National** (tel. 321-7990), and **Tropical** (tel. 320-1244).

    Campers, travel trailers, and motor homes may be rented from **American Land Cruisers,** 8950 Federal Blvd. (tel. 426-6699). **Apache Village,** 8630 W. Colfax (tel. 237-7701), rents folding camping trailers and other RVs.

DENVER INFORMATION: The downtown tourist information office is at the **Denver Metro Conventions and Visitors Bureau,** 225 W. Colfax Ave. (tel.

892-1505). Another information office, at Stapleton International Airport, is located between C and D concourses, and still another is on the 16th Street Mall at Curtis. The offices are open seven days a week in summer.

Emergency number for Denver is 911. . . . The area code for all Colorado telephones is 303 (except the Colorado Springs area where it's 719). . . . **Weather reports** for Denver are at 639-1515. . . . **Road conditions** are reported on a tape updated daily. For Denver and west, call 639-1111; for Denver and east, 639-1234.

Taped **ski reports** for all Colorado areas are available during the winter by calling 837-9907. . . . **Travelers Aid** has an office at 1245 E. Colfax Ave. (tel. 832-8194) and an office at Stapleton International Airport (tel. 398-3873).

2. WHERE TO STAY

Downtown on or near the new mile-long 16th Street Mall are numerous major hotels, including the historic Brown Palace, the new Marriott City Center, the Fairmont, the Executive Tower Inn, the Holiday Inn Downtown, the Comfort Inn, the Embassy Suites, the Radisson, and the Westin. Not far from the mall is the Governor's Court.

Seven hotels are clustered around Stapleton International Airport, including the Stapleton Plaza, Stouffer's Denver Inn, the Holiday Inn Holidome, the Hilton Airport, and the Sheraton Denver Airport. Nine hotels along the Interstate cutoff of I-225 and along I-25 include the Marriott Hotel Southeast, the Ramada Renaissance, the Sheraton Denver Tech Center, the Writers' Manor, the Hilton Inn South, and the Landmark Inn. The Merchandise Mart area is served by other hostelries, including the Regency Hotel.

DOWNTOWN: As noted, many of the big luxury hotels are located in the downtown area, as well as a number of smaller, less expensive hotels and motels. I'll begin at the top of the heap with—

Luxury Hotels

The **Brown Palace Hotel,** 321 17th St., Denver, CO 80202 (tel. 303/297-3111, or toll free 800/321-2599), is a historic, luxurious old hotel in the financial district occupying a V-shaped structure (viewed from above) that reminds one of the famous Flatiron Building in New York. Its impressive lobby is filled with sunlight during the day that pours through a glass roof ten stories overhead, making the details of wood paneling and onyx glow. The lobby counters are of marble and polished woods, but the details of check-in are all computerized nevertheless. The rooms are presented in a wide variety of furnishing styles and décors, from sedate silk Oriental wall hangings and antique settees in one, to warm reds in apple-design curtains and blending carpeting in another. A coffeehouse is open for breakfast and lunch, and the Palace Arms is open for formal dinners. Afternoon tea from 2 to 4:30 p.m. has become a growing tradition (with live harp music). The warmth of the glowing woods of the Ship Tavern has made it a Denver meeting place for generations (the hotel opened in 1892). The 231 rooms rent for $129 to $144 double.

The **Westin Hotel at Tabor Center,** 1672 Lawrence St., Denver, CO 80202 (tel. 303/572-9100, or toll free 800/228-3000), is a bright, light, and airy complex of private rooms and suites, public spaces, and restaurants in the heart of the best new downtown shopping areas (connected directly to the Tabor Center shopping malls). The lobby has spacious three-dimensional murals and modernistic fountains against a sand-tone background. The restaurant has pink linens and fresh tiger lilies on the tables. Rooms have refrigerators and wet bars, and guests have access to a pool, a sauna, and a lounge. Rates are $140 double.

Moderately Priced Accommodations

The **Queen Anne Inn,** 2147 Tremont Pl., Denver CO 80205 (tel. 303/296-6666), is an unusually pleasant bed-and-breakfast inn with ten rooms in an 1879 Victorian house across from a small park in downtown Denver. Besides the good continental breakfasts, there are wine tastings, high teas, refrigerators stocked with soft drinks and sparkling water, bowls of fresh fruit and carafes of apéritif wines—all provided free to guests. The architect of the pretty old house was Frank Edbrooke, designer of the famous Brown Palace Hotel not far away.

The inn offers special amenities such as piped-in classical music in each room, herb-scented soaps, writing desks stocked with a few volumes of fiction, and original works of art by regional artists. The original master bedroom, now called the Fountain Room, has a four-poster bed and five great windows overlooking the park, along with a luxurious sunken bathtub. In the Aspen Room, occupying a turret at the top of the house, the walls are painted in a continuous mural-surround of aspens at their colorful autumn peak. At the rear of the house the Columbine Room has a tester bed and a stained-glass window with a view of the fountain in the garden. All the rooms have private baths. No smoking is allowed; private parking is offered. Rates are $69 to $99 double.

The **Comfort Inn,** 401 17th St., Denver, CO 80202 (tel. 303/296-0400, or toll free 800/228-5150), formerly the Denver Inn, is probably the city's best buy in modern, comfortable accommodations with all the needed amenities, including an especially good free breakfast and a hot-hors-d'oeuvre-and-cocktail-party scene from 5 to 7:30 p.m., also complimentary, that never seems to run out of any of the fixings, and makes a cheerful contrast to many a lonely hotel lobby populated by traveling strangers. Here everyone is chatting within minutes of the first beer, wine, or gin and tonic.

Fresh croissants and danish, as well as cereals of various kinds, are on hand at breakfast, along with fresh fruit and juices and free copies of morning newspapers. There are great views of the new downtown skyscrapers from the higher rooms—the hotel is 22 stories tall—but on hot summer days some of those upper rooms tend to overheat in spite of the air conditioning system; a lower-level space is preferable. An advantage the Comfort can offer is a private overstreet walkway to the mezzanine of the Brown Palace Hotel (the Comfort Inn premises were once owned as an annex of the Brown). Rates are $51 to $59 double.

The **Oxford Alexis,** 1600 17th St., Denver, CO 80202 (tel. 303/628-5400), is, along with the Brown Palace, one of the few old-style traditional hotels to have survived the sweeping land-clearing projects that sprouted so many new skyscrapers downtown in the early 1980s. Both the Brown Palace and the Oxford were designed by architect Frank E. Edbrooke a century ago. The Oxford dates from 1891. Behind a simple brick façade the interior boasts marble walls, carpeted floors, stained-glass windows, frescoes, and silver chandeliers—all of which has been restored. A special attraction is the bar, called the Cruise Room, modeled after one of the bars on the liner *Queen Mary.*

During the restoration early architect's drawings were discovered that permitted craftspeople to reproduce features of ceilings, alcoves, and closets exactly as they had been originally. The chandeliers, stripped of thick enamel, were returned to their silver gleam. Some 1,300 antique pieces were imported from England and France—armoires, Oriental carpets, light fixtures, art deco chairs and tables, and bedsteads—to furnish the 81 larger rooms, fashioned during the restoration from the 200 original small rooms. Guests enjoy such amenities as afternoon sherry, the use of a health club, and limo service in a 1937 Hudson. Rates are $78 to $92 double.

Budget Choices

The **Colburn Hotel,** 980 Grant St., Denver, CO 80203 (tel. 303/837-1261), in the Capitol Hill district, has 150 recently renovated rooms and a restaurant and lounge, at $38 double.

The **Central YMCA,** 25 E. 16th Ave., Denver, CO 80202 (tel. 303/861-8300), has good inexpensive rooms for single people or couples from $24. Guests may use the pool, ball courts, and workout rooms.

OUT OF DOWNTOWN: Other than the hotel chains, represented largely along the Interstate accesses to the southwest of downtown, there are many scores of hotels and motels in a variety of categories as well as the western specialty of the full-service studio with kitchen rentable daily or weekly.

Near the Airport

Among a cluster of hotels within a few minutes' shuttle ride of the airport is the **Airport Hilton,** 4411 Peoria, Denver, CO 80239 (tel. 303/373-5730, or toll free 800/445-8667), with full amenities; children stay free with their parents, and double rates run $66 to $102. There is the Copper Dome restaurant and a lounge and coffeeshop, and, outside, a heated pool.

Also nearby is the **Sheraton Denver–Airport,** 3535 Quebec St., Denver, CO 80207 (tel. 303/333-7711, or toll free 800/325-3535), with 200 rooms and an indoor pool within a bright solarium, which also shelters a broad patio and hot tub. Just outside is a grassy stretch for volleyball, barbecues, or tanning. Movies and cable channels are free on the in-room television sets. Wild game and seafood are specialties of a restaurant named Whispers, while Rudyard's, the lounge, is the scene of nightly live entertaining. Rates for a double are $75 to $105.

Southeast

Loews Giorgio Hotel, 4150 E. Mississippi Ave., Denver, CO 80222 (tel. 303/782-9300), is a 200-room structure, stark in black steel and reflecting glass on the outside but all warmly Italianate on the inside, that was inaugurated in 1987 by the cutting of a ribbon fashioned from a 20-foot length of fettuccine. Murals and paintings in the Renaissance style, done for the hotel by artists Ted Schmidt and Richard Haas, re-create the atmosphere of an Italian villa. Columns are finished in faux marble and pillars are worked in faux wood grain. Hotel owner Jack Naiman wants guests "to feel as if they are staying in a fine hotel in Florence or Rome," and to this end traveled to Italy to select antiques for the rooms. Murals of frolicking nudes set the classic tone in the bar, where, says the manager, "as soon as you see the paintings, you'll know that we want our guests to have fun here."

A library with current newspaper and magazines, as well as a television and a carafe of complimentary Italian wine, is always open to guests; trays of Italian cookies are also on hand. Just beyond at the end of the hallway is a striking trompe-l'oeil mural by Richard Haas of a Renaissance terrace with columns on either side that appear to lead the viewer into the depths of a formal garden.

All the west-facing rooms have superb views of the Rocky Mountains rising abruptly just beyond the city. Baskets of fruits, soft drinks, and Italian sparkling water are supplied, and cable channels and pay movies are available on the television. A special attraction is free access to the Cherry Creek Sporting Club half a mile away, with free shuttle-bus service available. Here guests may use any of 16 racquetball courts, a Ping-Pong room, a basketball court, two squash courts, a spacious indoor pool for doing measured laps, and a casual outdoor pool in the sun with chaises lounges and a snackbar. There are scores of up-to-date exercise machines and weight equipment, a hydra spa, and an indoor restaurant.

Guests are offered a complimentary light Italian breakfast of toast with candied fruit and continental coffee; more copious breakfasts are readily available on the menu. Lunches and dinners are served in the Tuscany Restaurant (see "Where to Eat"). Free airport shuttle service is also offered. Rates are $105 to $120 double.

3. WHERE TO EAT

With a predominantly youthful population (median age 28) in a fast-growing metropolitan area, going out to eat is perhaps more of a pastime than in many cities. Denver's western tradition of barbecue and steak is being widely enlarged by the influx of newcomers from all over the U.S. and from foreign lands as well. There is a strong Hispanic tradition, of course, producing Mexican-style cooking with southwestern U.S. modifications, and the international, or "continental" cuisine fostered by the numerous chain hotels of the upper category as well as by some smaller, more experimental establishments.

LUXURY CHOICES: The **Café Giovanni,** 1515 Market St. (tel. 825-6555), was called "the best restaurant in Denver" by the *Post,* and it's open for lunch weekdays and for dinner Monday through Saturday; closed Sunday. Its motto is "a few things prepared perfectly," although the full menu has a score of entrees, including snails, salmon, various veal dishes, pork, beef, and pasta in Italian or French styles. There are three dining areas, a garden-level luncheon space traversed by an overhead entrance walkway. A grand stairway sweeps up into an elegant dining room. Among the specialties is a lobster-and-crabmeat soufflé; another is linguine fruits de mer, with scallops, shrimp, clams, mussels, and crabmeat. Also special are the house soufflés of owner-chef Giovanni Leone: a cold caramel praline soufflé or a hot mocha soufflé with French custard sauce.

The **Normandy French Restaurant,** 1515 Madison St. (tel. 321-3311), looks inside like an old French country inn. It is open for lunch Tuesday through Saturday and for dinner Tuesday through Sunday. Occupying a former residence built in the early 1900s, the restaurant has been in operation here for well over 30 years. Specialties include escalope de veau Marie Antoinette (a Normandy dish in a sauce of butter, mushrooms, and cheese), and mignons de boeuf sautés "diable" aux artichauts—beef served with artichokes, peppercorns, and madeira. A dinner goes for up to $25.

Another good French restaurant is **Pierre's Quorum,** 233 E. Colfax Ave. (tel. 861-8686), whose chef, Pierre Wolfe, offers an evening's pleasure he calls the "five-course mystery dinner," made up of dishes according to his various inspirations, at $25. Frogs' legs, sweetbreads, and game hen poire Zinfandel are among his specialties, and there are first-rate dishes such as chateaubriand bouquetière or rack of lamb. It is open for lunch Monday through Friday and for dinner Monday through Saturday. Just across from the Capitol, the Quorum is generally considered the best French restaurant in Colorado.

The **Buckhorn Exchange,** 1000 Osage St. (tel. 534-9505), is the state's oldest restaurant and saloon, with an embossed tin ceiling and checked tablecloths covering century-old poker tables adding to the Old West atmosphere. Some 500 stuffed animals and 100 old guns help the décor. A lunch choice could be a bratwurst plate or a pot roast sandwich. At dinner there are steaks running up to

$25 for the 24-ounce T-bone, as well as buffalo steak and elk steak. There is lunch weekdays and dinner seven nights a week. The bean soup is highly recommended. The bar itself is worth a look, fashioned 130 years ago in Germany of white oak, with ornate mirrors and elaborate carving.

The **Tuscany,** in Loews Giorgio Hotel, 4150 E. Mississippi Ave. (tel. 782-9300), is a luxurious re-creation of an idealized Italian country inn's dining room, decorated with modern versions of Renaissance murals that set off the fresh table linens and exquisite glassware and silverware under appropriately ornate chandeliers. Appetizers, priced in the $5 to $8 range, may include poached seafood marinated in oil, sliced salmon with olive oil, pizza with clams and mussels, or grilled raddiccio, zucchini, eggplant, and mushrooms. Pasta dishes, at $10 to $12, include taglierine, seafood in sauce, and risotto alla toscana. Ambitious entrees are regularly offered, as well: deviled squab at $13.50, scallopine di vitello at $17, or sautéed lamb chops with artichokes at $19, among other choices. Desserts at $3 to $5 include cassata, zuppa inglese, and Monte Bianco (cream of brandied chestnuts in whipped cream with grated chocolate). Coffees, including espresso and capitano, are also served.

MODERATELY PRICED RESTAURANTS: Some 18 miles west of downtown Denver, **The Fort,** 19192 Col. 8 off West Hampden (tel. 697-4771), is worth the trip to sample rare game and fixings and to enjoy the atmosphere of the re-created version of Bent's Old Fort. Hearty starters, priced from $4 to $7.50, include Rocky Mountain oysters Rockefeller, buffalo eggs, and buffalo boudies sausage. There is also buffalo tongue on hand and, for $12, the "historians' platter" consisting of roast buffalo marrow bones with sea biscuits, boudies, and tongue in Sam's sauce. All entrees come with "punkin and blue cornberry muskins," tossed green "sallat," potatoes or rice with quinoa, and a fresh vegetable. A salmon steak in dill sauce costs $15, or for $10 you may try "The bowl of the wife of Kit Carson—a spicy, pepper-hot meal-in-a-bowl, named by Sam Arnold: chicken breast meat in broth with rice, garbanzos, jack cheese, chipotle chiles, and avocado." Buffalo steaks are priced according to changing market conditions and is said to be "like beef wishes it tasted." A brace of broiled quail is $16, a Gonzales steak (stuffed with green chile) is also $16, and General Armijo's giant lamb chop (quadruple thick) is $22.

Back downtown again, **McCormick's Fish House and Bar,** 1659 Wazee (tel. 825-1107), occupying part of the historic site of the Oxford Hotel, has a pleasant turn-of-the-century restaurant with oak booths as well as a fine polished-wood bar adjoining. Seafood from all over North America is flown in daily and there is little in the seafood line that is lacking here: Dungeness crab from Alaska, Goose Point oysters from Washington state, mussels from Maine, fresh yellowfin tuna from Hawaii, swordfish from California, rockfish from Oregon, trout from Idaho. There are Apalachicola oysters, fried calamari, and fresh halibut served half a dozen ways. Lunches or light entrees are priced from $5 to $8; dinner entrees, $13 to $18.

A somewhat plainer-than-usual French restaurant with menu entrees listed on a blackboard is **Le Central Affordable French Restaurant,** 112 E. Eighth Ave. (tel. 863-8094), open weekdays for lunch and daily for dinner. Choices include chicken, duck, lamb, veal, tenderloin steak, and always-fresh fish.

Mattie Silks', in the Marriott Hotel City Center, 1701 California St. (tel. 297-1300), has a modern southwestern décor that makes it a popular luncheon spot ($6 to $10) and dinner-date rendezvous (to $20 per person). Chicken-cashew salad or fettuccine carbonara are lunch specials, while dinner might be a daily special of beef or fish. Also at the Marriott is **Marjolaine's** (tel. 297-1300), open seven days for lunch and dinner in a Victorian background. There is a breakfast buffet as well, and a Sunday brunch. Lunch prices are $4 to $9; dinner, $5 to $16. Shrimp, fresh fish, and steaks are specialties.

Spaghetti (in five various sauces) is offered in the cheerful, rambling **Old Spaghetti Factory,** 1215 18th St. (tel. 295-1864). Open for lunch five days, for dinner seven evenings, in an atmosphere of Victorian relics including a period bedstead and an entire trolley car. Dinners are $8 top.

Mataam Fez, 4609 E. Colfax Ave. (tel. 399-9282), is a rarity—a Moroccan restaurant out West—in an authentic décor of low round tables, brass trays, and intricately designed wall tiles. Overhead there is a bright-colored silk tent, and courses are served in running relays by waiters in caftans. A traditional five-course dinner begins with lamb lentil soup and has three kinds of salad and b'stella, flaky filo dough containing a mixture of eggs and game hen with a sauce spiced with 32 various herbs, and topped with crushed almonds, sugar, and cinnamon. Couscous is among other menu items. Lamb is prepared with honey, almonds, eggplant, or onions, and there are various chicken specialties, too, to regale the adventurous eater. Lunch is served weekdays, dinner every night.

BUDGET CHOICES: A really good, traditional Irish-style bar and restaurant with fast, cheerful service, **Duffy's Shamrock,** 1635 Court Pl. (tel. 534-4935), has the special advantage of serving everything on its menu daily until 1:15 a.m. In operation for over 30 years, the place has been thriving at its present location since 1974, specializing in imported Irish beers and Irish coffees as well as a dozen beers on draft: Guinness stout, Watney's, Labatt's, Bass Ale, and Harp, as well as domestic brews. Daily specials may include prime rib at $6, barbecued beef at $3.75, or a stuffed bell pepper in Créole sauce at $3.50. Fried prawns go for $6 and a hot roast beef sandwich for $3.60. Sandwiches on every kind of bread are also offered at modest prices: a hamburger for $2.70, a Reuben for $3.15, a Braunschweiger for $2.85. Great homemade chili is $2.55, and spaghetti with meat sauce only $2.85. If you're still hungry after the sandwich, order the Duffy's Special: hot raisin and custard pudding with blueberries, rice, and cream.

The question of whether a local enterprise could do as well as the fast-food chains in serving appetizing food quickly at moderate prices is settled by the cheerful young folk running the **Brick Oven Beanery,** 1007 E. Colfax Ave. (tel. 860-0077), with branches at 10890 E. Dartmouth and at 8715 N. Sheridan. The proprietors list their good points like this: "Native foods—the freshest, selected locally, prepared daily; crusty bread—hand-kneaded, baked in our brick-lined ovens; slow-roasted meats—hot from the rotisserie, hand-carved; side dishes—unique, superb, made here; salads—crispy fresh, abundant, unusual; desserts—wicked good; bottled beer—icy cold; domestic wines—by the tumbler; malts and sodas—thick and old-fashioned, 1950s style; fast-food style—quick, self-serve, convenient, fun; great prices." These perhaps hyperbolic claims stand up well to a visit to the Beanery, where a copious hot turkey sandwich goes for $3, a leg of lamb dinner for $3.25, or a wild-rice meatloaf for $5. A half chicken, marinated in lemon juice and herbs, served with mashed potato and sage-nut dressing with creamed-corn gravy, salad, and fresh bread, is just $5.50.

A great choice for down-home Mexican food at low prices is **Las Delicias,** 439 E. 19th St. (tel. 839-5675), where the premises have been growing apace over the past years until today the establishment occupies half a dozen interconnected rooms, all faced in plain red brick. The food is prepared with care and complete knowledge of the Mexican cooking traditions, with spicy salsa served automatically of course. Copious dinners of carne asada with all the broiled, tangy taste intact, cost just $6, or a carne de puerco adovado is offered for $5, all served with plenty of fresh hot tortillas.

Another pleasant spot for an inexpensive meal, **Tandoor,** 1514 Blake St.

(tel. 572-9071), near the 16th Street Mall bus line, has free Indian-style hors d'oeuvres served in the Elephanta Bar daily from 5 to 7 p.m. Entrees priced from $5.50 to $6 include marinated chicken served with yogurt and herbs, grilled over charcoal, enveloped in a pita, with lettuce and tomato; sliced meatball in curry sauce, also in a pita, with lettuce and tomato; or shrimp salad with celery, almonds, and poppy seed dressing. The "vegetable nirvana" involves bean sprouts, cheeses, carrots, celery, tomatoes, fruit, cucumbers, and nuts with yogurt. Chicken or shrimp biryani with rice, saffron sauce, and nuts is also served. Evenings there is sitar music and belly dancing; an Indian spice shop occupies the basement room. Open for lunch, Monday through Friday, from 11 a.m. to 2 p.m.; Sunday brunch from 10:30 a.m. to 5:30 p.m. Dinner is served Monday through Saturday from 5:30 to 10 p.m., on Sunday until 9 p.m.

4. SIGHTSEEING

Downtown walkers might begin exploring the restored Larimer Street between 14th and 15th Streets, or strolling along the mile of the 16th Street Mall. Larimer Street has the turn-of-the-century atmosphere recaptured in shops and restaurants; the mall gives access, too, to businesses, shops, and eating places, and is a prime people-watching part of the city.

The city's parks are also fine walking places during most of the year, and Denver has more space devoted to green than any other American city. They include City Park to the east of downtown off Colfax, Cheesman Park on Capitol Hill, and Washington Park south of the center. The Platte River Greenway is a recent addition to these areas, a path for bicycling or running alongside the Platte River that widens into a greensward at the edge of the central city.

Capitol Hill and Swallow Hill are the sites of many turn-of-the-century mansions built by mining and merchant interests in the boom days of the city, which came to an abrupt close upon the silver crash of 1893. More recent boom-time building comes from the energy business, of which Denver calls itself the modern capital. After the turn of the century, when Victorian houses such as the Molly Brown House and the Pearce-McAllister House (both now open to the public) were built, construction was restricted to brick only because of the danger of fire with wood buildings. The boxy Denver standby called the "Denver Square" is a form of housing of which numerous examples still stand—always of brick, and plain on the outside. The theory was that because of the silver crash nobody wanted to look rich even if he was, so these squarish residences kept all the luxury hidden from sight—inside.

STATE CAPITOL: Free tours of the Colorado State Capitol are given year round, more frequently in summer. Visitors not on tours are also welcome, and they are permitted to climb into the dome between 9 a.m. and 4 p.m. on weekdays. The building, made of granite from a quarry in Gunnison, Colorado, by stonemasons from several states, is supposed to be built to last 1,000 years. Its most salient feature is its gold dome, rising 272 feet above the ground, commemorating the beginnings of the state when gold was struck in the nearby mountains. At first sheathed in copper, the dome's surface was immediately replaced with gold after a public outcry, since copper is not a Colorado product. The gold leaf was produced out of only 200 ounces of gold, the gift of miners to the new building in 1886, the year construction began. It became worn out by the late 1940s, and new gifts of gold replaced the gold surface in 1950. Workers were plagued by hordes of gnats immersing themselves in the adhesive used to keep the gold leaf in place.

Murals dating from 1940 adorn the walls of the first-floor rotunda, picturing the history of the state with an emphasis on the value of water in every facet of life here. Brass balusters flank the marble steps of the grand staircase leading from the first floor to the upper stories. From this point on the first floor, also, one has a fine view upward to the underside of the dome, a vertical distance of 180 feet. The rotunda, at the heart of the building, echoes the layout of the national Capitol in Washington. South of the rotunda is the governor's office, paneled in walnut and lighted by a massive chandelier. The room is used for administration work and for staff meetings and press conferences; there are memorabilia of earlier governors.

Visitor galleries to both the House and Senate have access from the third floor, reached by stairs or by elevators with bronze panels that illustrate Colorado history: a buffalo, a tepee, a covered wagon, a pick and shovel, a train, a herd of cattle, and a cog wheel all play a part. Wainscoting throughout the building is of rare Colorado rose onyx, of a coloration known only at a single site near Beulah. Linear designs in the stone are often taken for depictions of people, animals, or objects; on the outside west walls of the first-floor rotunda are designs supposedly resembling George Washington, Molly Brown, and Franklin Roosevelt. The town of Marble, Colorado, supplied the marble in the floors and stairs. Tunnels below the building connect it to other state structures nearby, some still with trackage for the coal cars that used to supply heating furnaces, since replaced by area steam heat.

The **Colorado Hall of Fame** occupies space near the top of the dome, involving stained-glass portraits of Colorado pioneers, including early governors, the founder of the *Rocky Mountain News,* Kit Carson, and the Ute leader Ouray. Who was to have a stained-glass window and who was not caused terrible rows in Denver in 1900—the only unanimous choice was Ouray the Indian. Doorknobs throughout the building are embellished with brass bas-reliefs of the state seal.

A granite step on the west side of the building has an engraved marker reading "Elevation 5,280 One Mile High 5-12-89." Though it is a favorite of tourists' snapshots, in 1969 zealous Colorado State University students found out that the step was slightly in error, and now a geodetic survey plug is embedded three steps above the original marker, giving Denver two "mile high" marks on its Capitol. Views from the dome on clear days are spectacular, with the face of the Rockies to the west, and below them the stately City and County Building in the near distance. The east lawn has a statue of an Indian over a dying buffalo entitled *The Closing Era,* dating from 1893, when it was exhibited at the Chicago World's Fair before being installed here. The Indian holds a bow that has no string. For many years a wire, representing the bow string, was regularly replaced whenever it disappeared, but today the bow is left stringless permanently. A cavalryman in bronze at the west portico marks soldiers from the Colorado Territory who served with Union forces in the Civil War. Two black walnut trees flanking this memorial came from the home of President Lincoln.

Various levels of the interior of the Capitol may interest visitors. The basement has hearing rooms open to the public. On the first floor, the west lobby has a case showing moon rocks and another displaying dolls in miniature ball gowns as worn by various governors' wives. To the right of the main lobby, the governor's reception room is open to the public. The second floor has a hearing room, as well as main entrances to the House and Senate, while the third floor, besides giving access to the legislative galleries, has more hearing rooms open to visitors. Says Gov. Roy Romer: "Colorado's state capitol is a particularly beautiful building that all can enjoy."

MOLLY BROWN HOUSE MUSEUM: The property of Historic Denver, Inc., a group restoring and preserving old structures in the city, the Molly Brown

House Museum, 1340 Pennsylvania St. (tel. 832-4092), is open Tuesday through Saturday (and in summer on Monday too) from 10 a.m. to 4 p.m., and on Sunday from noon to 4 p.m. (October to March, to 3 p.m.), with an admission charge of $3 for adults, $1.50 for those over 65, and $1 for ages 6 to 18. Designed by Denver architect William Lang, the house was built in 1889 of Colorado lavastone with sandstone trim. The residence of James and Margaret Brown, it served as the governor's mansion in 1902. It was saved from demolition in 1970 by Historic Denver, which restored it to its 1910 appearance. A carriage house at the rear of the house is also open to visitors.

Molly Brown, who broke up with her husband in 1909, became a national heroine in 1912 after the sinking of the *Titanic*. Because of her knowledge of languages, she took charge of a group of immigrant women in a lifeboat from the sinking ship and later raised money for their benefit. She was also the first preservationist of Denver, buying the home of poet Eugene Field in 1930 to present to the city. Today the Molly Brown House has a large collection of turn-of-the-century furnishings and art objects, many the former possessions of the Brown family. A popular fashion show staged in the house is called "Fashions from Molly Brown's Trunk." Elaborate ball and dinner gowns and lingerie dating from 1885 is modeled by volunteers, with piano accompaniment. A narrative describes where garments might have been worn and what was going on in Denver at the time.

Note: Walking tours including the Molly Brown House are held on a summer schedule with guides of **Historic Denver** who show visitors what makes Denver special, with attention to the Victorian houses of the city. The guides, in period costumes, are knowledgeable about the architecture and the history of the time. For information and reservations, call Historic Denver (tel. 534-1858).

UNITED STATES MINT: A tourist attraction exerting a strange fascination is the U.S. Mint, 320 W. Colfax Ave. (tel. 844-3582), which makes six billion coins a year with stamping machines that visitors can watch at work from an overhead walkway. A visitor center later provides visitors with the opportunity to have a blank stamped into a souvenir medal in another stamping machine, as well as to buy various collectors' items in freshly minted coins.

The Denver Mint opened in 1863 originally as an assay office for gold dust and nuggets, and at first did not mint coins. The gold brought in was melted and cast into bars, which were returned to depositors stamped with weight and degree of fineness. Most of that gold came from beds of placer gold from streams that were discovered in 1858, the year of the founding of the city.

In 1904 the assay office moved into new quarters at the present site, and two years later began coinage operations, during the first year turning out $23.8 million in gold coins as well as some in silver. Copper pennies began to be made a few years later. Silver dollars (containing 90% silver) were last manufactured in 1935. In the 1970 coinage law changes, all silver was eliminated from dollars and half dollars; they are made of an alloy of copper and nickel.

Coins are made from prefabricated rolls of metal supplied by private dealers to the mint, which concentrates on the blanking function and on the stamping of the actual coins. It takes 40 tons of pressure to stamp a penny or a dime, 60 tons for a nickel, 80 tons for a quarter, 110 tons for a 50¢ piece, and 80 tons for a $1 coin. Coins are distributed through Federal Reserve banks on shipping orders from the Bureau of the Mint in Washington. Those banks distribute coins to their member banks in turn. The small "D" on coins means they were made here.

From the upstairs gallery visitors watch coin metal first stamped into coin blanks and then edge-rolled to make a raised rim. In a single stroke both sides of the coins are stamped with their designs and legend. The next step is inspection, weighing, counting, and bagging, before being stored in vaults to await shipment.

Inside the front entrance to the mint are murals representing the concepts of commerce, mining, and manufacturing. A mosaic representing the Great Seal of the United States is embedded in the floor of the vestibule; an earlier metal seal, worn nearly smooth by generations of visitors' feet, now hangs on a wall of the Gold Hall. Here there is a display of gold bars, each weighing 27½ pounds. Gold purchases were discontinued in 1968.

Tours of the mint are free of charge; last 20 minutes, and depart every half hour Monday through Friday from 8 a.m. to 3 p.m. in summer, 8:30 a.m. to 3 p.m. in winter, but the mint is closed for lunch daily from 11:30 a.m. to 12:30 p.m.

DENVER ART MUSEUM: This ten-story, 28-sided structure at 100 W. 14th Pkwy. (tel. 575-2793) is open from 10 a.m. to 5 p.m. Tuesday through Saturday. It is also open from noon to 5 p.m. on Sunday; closed Monday. Admission is $3 for adults, $1.50 for students and seniors, free Saturday to noon. Its outside is covered with a million shimmering glass tiles. Inside is one of the country's great collections of artworks by American Indians, a large collection of western art, and 35,000 other art objects in seven curatorial departments. The twin towers of the facility are connected by a central core and house the major art resource of the West inland of the West Coast. The galleries are in seven levels and display artworks that date back, some of them, to the origins of the institution as the 1893 Artists' Club.

The main floor is the site of changing exhibits. On floors above are major collections of African, Oceanic, American Indian, and early New World art. There are pre-Columbian artifacts, Spanish Colonial arts, some Spanish Peruvian works, and a group of southwestern *santos* in the New World category. A solid representation of European artists includes works by Van Dyck, Tintoretto, Rubens, Veronese, Monet, Pissarro, Renoir, Matisse, Utrillo, Modigliani, Degas, Chagall, and Toulouse-Lautrec. There are period rooms of art in French Gothic, English Tudor, and Spanish baroque styles, and Oriental works from China, Japan, and India. At the top of the gallery floors is an exhibit of textiles and costumes from around the world.

The pride of the museum is the largest collection of American Indian art in any art museum in the U.S., consisting of 20,000 pieces from 150 tribes of North America. Covering a time span of some 2,000 years, the collection has been valued at over $25 million. (The works have always been collected for their value as works of art rather than for their anthropological value only). Begun in 1925, the Denver collection is thus the oldest of its kind anywhere in the world. Says Richard Conn, curator of Native Arts: "We must make a distinction between art museums and museums of natural history. Museums collecting for anthropological reasons usually seek large numbers and multiple examples of artifacts. Art museums look for artistic excellence and significance. In this collection the museum has selected carefully for esthetic quality among tribes from every North American region."

Among masterpieces here is the Shakes screen, a carved, painted wood screen depicting the family crest of the Shake family of Wrangell, Alaska; basketry of Elizabeth Hickox of the Wiyot tribe; a water jar by Maria Martinez of the San Ildefonso Pueblo in New Mexico. Instead of glass showcases, displays are laid out in open vistas in an area of 22,000 square feet, works arranged geographically in ten areas. Broad platforms in different forms and colors make backgrounds that try to capture an out-of-doors atmosphere. Among recent acquisitions are totem-pole-like house posts originally used as cornerstones for a Northwest Indian house. The 12-foot posts weighing 1,500 pounds each were brought in from Alert Bay, B.C., having been commissioned as artwork by the museum to be made by Doug Cranmer of the Nimkish band.

The collection was displayed in its new, expanded setting for the first time in 1988 and will play an even more important part in the museum's overall appeal to the public. Conn is adding to the collection of Indian art not only by acquiring historic pieces but also by commissioning and locating works by contemporary Indian artists working in all styles, both traditional and modern.

Guided tours are available, and there are performing arts events scheduled. A gift shop has unusual replicas of certain treasures displayed among the various collections, as well as many books on art subjects and southwestern lore. Also sold are posters, southwestern-style jewelry, and postcards. A restaurant has an open patio for warm-weather lunches.

DENVER MUSEUM OF NATURAL HISTORY: This rambling three-story museum at Colorado and Montview Boulevards (tel. 370-6363) is the seventh-largest natural history museum in the U.S. and one of the greatest in the world. Exquisitely fashioned human and animal figures in over 90 dioramas picture life around the world in various eras. Of particular local interest is the **Coors Hall of Minerals,** displaying the beauties of stones, some semiprecious, of the Southwest, including the state's largest chunk of gold. Note, also, the beadwork on leather garments of Great Lakes Indians made a century ago, showing a mastery of design and ebullient color combinations. There are also some unforgettable century-old photographs of Sioux Indians.

The first floor has displays on ancient old-world cultures and prehistoric American peoples, and others showing articulated skeletons of mammals 50 million years old, and those of extinct marine reptiles and dinosaurs. The second floor has a butterfly exhibit area, and sections devoted to Colorado wildlife, North American bears and sea life, and the ecology of Australia. This floor also has rooms showing artifacts of early American Indian tribes from Alaska to Florida.

The third-floor exhibits include displays of South American wildlife and the habitats of Botswana. Traveling exhibits further enrich the experience of a visit here, and the **Charles C. Gates Planetarium** schedules frequent sky shows. Museum admission is $3.50 for adults, $1.50 for children under 13; hours are 9 a.m. to 5 p.m. daily.

DENVER BOTANIC GARDENS: These indoor and outdoor gardens at 1005 York St. (tel. 575-2547) appeal both to professional botanists and amateur plant lovers. Native plants are displayed with educational information, and there are plantings of exotic flowers, shrubs, and trees too. There is a real Japanese tea house in the Japanese garden, and thousands of plants blooming make a kaleidoscope of color in the rock Alpine Garden. Special interests are served in the tropical conservatory and in the orchid-bromeliad pavilion. Altogether there are over a score of outdoor gardens occupying 20 acres. The high dome-shaped concrete-and-Plexiglass conservatory houses 800 species of tropical and subtropical plants. The gardens are open every day from 9 a.m. to 4:45 p.m. Admission is $3.

FOUR MILE HISTORIC PARK: This restoration area has Denver's oldest house, built in 1859. At 715 S. Forest St. (tel. 399-1859), the park is open Tuesday through Sunday from 11 a.m. to 5 p.m., and occupies 12 acres four miles from downtown. The oldest house, called **Four Mile House,** is set up as the centerpiece of an educational display showing how the vacant prairie land of Cherry Creek Valley was turned into productive farmland by the pioneers who came here in the last century. The "phased interpretive plan," as it is called, traces the historical development of the immediate area by showing some pristine prairie, a part of a stock ranch, a stagecoach stop (the house was on the Cherokee Trail), a dryland farm, and finally an irrigated farm—each representing an era in the development of the land here.

The house, built by a family named Brantner, was originally a two-story log structure, the center of what became one of the state's oldest farms. A widow from Wisconsin bought the place in 1860 for a wayside inn and stagecoach stop, which she ran for four years until a flood damaged the inn. Levi Booth was the next owner of the 160-acre farm, which he also used as a stage stop and tavern. He added 500 acres to his estate and developed an irrigation system, taking water from Cherry Creek. His family continued to occupy the farm until 1946. The original log house has a brick addition and a frame wing that were added to it in 1883. Outbuildings recently reconstructed were made with old hand tools of the period. The restoration and construction is the work of a group called Four Mile Historic Park, a nonprofit organization.

Tours on the hour, the last one departing at 4 p.m., along with admission, cost $2 for adults, $1 for senior citizens, and 50¢ for children ages 6 to 15.

ELITCH GARDENS: This venerable amusement park at 4620 W. 38th St. (tel. 455-4771) is open weekends beginning in May, and every day starting in June. It has a nationally famed roller coaster among its many rides and concessions, elaborate gardens, a log flume ride, outdoor concerts, and the country's oldest summer-stock theater. There is a 53-lane Skee Ball casino, a scooters-in-the-round attraction, and a realistic Cinema-180 show. There is a miniature golf course and a choice among 11 restaurants and snackbars. Miniature Madness is a child/adult-participation area with rides and attractions mainly designed for the kids, with a maze, an outdoor children's theater, a suspension bridge, and many special rides. Gates open at 10 a.m., and daily operation continues to Labor Day.

OTHER DENVER ATTRACTIONS: The Forney **Transportation Museum,** 1416 Platte (tel. 433-3643), has the world's largest steam locomotive, *Big Boy,* among its attractions, which include 250 items: cars, trucks, cycles, steam engines, rail coaches, and airplanes. Among its treasures are Amelia Earhart's Gold Bug Kissel, Aly Khan's Rolls-Royce, an 1899 Locomobile, Teddy Roosevelt's parade car, and a 25-foot wheelbase Hispano-Suiza. The museum is open all year, Monday through Saturday from 10 a.m. to 5 p.m., on Sunday from 11 a.m. to 5:30 p.m.

The **Denver Zoo,** in City Park on 23rd Avenue (tel. 575-2754), has 1,700 animal specimens representing 400 species: tigers, bears, giraffes, an island of monkeys, and rides on camels and elephants. Full meals with beer and wine are offered at the Hungry Elephant, a restaurant near the entrance, within the zoo, that has an outdoor eating area; food is served cafeteria style. Just outside the entrance there is a picnic area with tables and grills. Native and exotic waterfowl and American flamingoes are among occupants of the zoo's several ponds, and there are 300 species of birds in the natural-habitat area called Bird World. A new attraction that opened in 1988 is the 3½-acre Northern Shores complex that offers underwater views of both the polar bear pool and the sea lion pool. A rubber-tired train called the Zooliner tours all zoo paths during the months from spring through fall. There is also a miniature railroad available for rides around the

Children's Zoo. The zoo is open every day: from 10 a.m. to 6 p.m. in summer, to 5 p.m. the rest of the year. Admission is $4, for adults, $2 for children.

The **Museum of Western Art**, 1717 Tremont Pl. (tel. 296-1880), is a new establishment installed in bright, modern surroundings in a three-story Victorian brick house that was originally Denver's most notorious bordello and gambling casino. Through three galleries museum visitors follow the history of western art from a portrait of an Indian woman done by the Swiss artist Carl Bodmer in 1833 to Georgia O'Keeffe's *Cow's Skull on Red*. There are classic western scenes by Remington and Russell, and landscapes by Bierstadt and Thomas Moran, among the 125 paintings and sculptures shown. The museum is open Tuesday through Saturday from 10 a.m. to 4:30 p.m. Admission is $4.

The **Buffalo Bill Memorial Museum** (tel. 526-0747), on Lookout Mountain, reached via exit 256 from I-70 west, has memorabilia from the life and legend of Buffalo Bill Cody, the Pony Express rider, buffalo hunter, army scout, showman, and entrepreneur. It is open daily from 9 a.m. to 5 p.m. Admission is $4.

The **Colorado History Museum**, 1300 Broadway (tel. 866-3682), is the home of the Colorado Historical Society and has a museum with permanent and changing exhibits related to state history. One permanent display, called "The Coloradans," relates the story of the people of the state from its founding. Another, the Broadway School Classroom, shows student life at the turn of the century. There is a miniature Denver of 1860 in fine detail, an early log house, and dioramas. The museum is open Monday through Saturday from 10 a.m. to 4:30 p.m., and on Sunday from noon to 4:30 p.m. Admission is $3.

The **Colorado Railroad Museum**, 17155 W. 44th Ave. in Golden (tel. 279-4591), occupies a railroad depot of the 1880s. There are historical exhibits of early Colorado, an old narrow-gauge locomotive, and some railroad cars and trolleys. It is open year round from 9 a.m. to 5 p.m. daily; admission is $3.

The **Denver Firefighters Museum**, 1326 Tremont Pl. (tel. 892-1436), occupies Denver's Firehouse No. 1, a downtown landmark. Antique firefighting equipment and memorabilia are displayed. It is open Monday through Friday from 11 a.m. to 2 p.m. Admission is $2.

The **Children's Museum**, 2121 Crescent Dr. (tel. 433-7444), reached by car via the 23rd Avenue exit of I-25, offers kids such innovative exhibits as a sea of 80,000 plastic balls, a face-painting tent, and a miniature Safeway supermarket where small fry take the roles of shoppers and checkout clerks. Another experience shows just what it feels like to be handicapped physically in various ways. Open from 9 a.m. to 5 p.m. Tuesday through Sunday, the museum charges $2 for admission.

ART GALLERIES: Besides the Denver Art Museum, the city has a number of other centers for the visual arts. Among co-op and nonprofit galleries are the **Colorado Craft Center**, 14th and Curtis; **CORE—New Art Space**, 3147 Larimer St; the **Emmanuel Gallery of the Auraria Campus**, 10th and Lawrence, showing works in exhibits by students of several regional universities; **Pirate, a Contemporary Art Oasis**, 3659 Navajo (open weekends); **Spark**, 3300 Osage St. (also open weekends); and the **YWCA Gallery**, 535 16th St., showing works by women artists.

Commercial premises include: **Art Exchange/Colors**, 1936 Market St., exhibiting works by members of the Art Students League; **Artyard**, 1251 S. Pearl, with sculpture, wall hangings, and monumental outdoor pieces; the **Inkfish Gallery**, 949 Broadway, showing sculptures, paintings and works on paper; the **Joan Robey Gallery**, 939 Broadway, with works in three-dimensional formats in ceramics, glass, and mixed media; the **Brigitte Schluger Gallery,** 929 Broadway, for Eskimo and Northwest Indian sculpture and carvings; the **Cydney Payton Gallery,** 2544 15th St., offering avant-garde works in various media; **Gallery One,** 1512 Larimer St., with works by regional and nationally recognized artists; the **Reiss Gallery,** 429 Acoma St., exhibiting original art in many forms; the **Carol Siple Gallery,** 1401 17th St., showing works by both established and emerging artists; and the **Turner Gallery,** 300 University Blvd., the city's oldest, specializing in traditional art forms.

SPECIAL TOURS: Back-road mountain tours departing from Denver to remote areas reached on half-day and full-day trips by four-wheel-drive vehicles show visitors ghost towns, old mining camps, historic wagon trails, and other historic sites. Star treks on mountaintops at night can be arranged, as well as overnight camping and fishing trips. For information, contact **Colorado Adventure Network,** 3585 Arthur Court, Boulder, CO 80302, (tel. 303/444-0952).

A good, informative tour is offered free at the **Coors Brewery,** 13th and Ford Streets, in Golden (tel. 277-6363), Monday through Saturday from 8:30 a.m. to 4:30 p.m.

Guided tours are offered free around the Boettcher Concert Hall and the Helen G. Bonfils Theater complex at the **Denver Center for the Performing Arts,** 14th and Curtis Streets (tel. 893-4000), every noon on weekdays.

Guided walking tours of historic areas, and others involving transport by van, are offered by **Historic Denver, Inc.,** 1340 Pennsylvania (tel. 863-1398). Reservations are needed.

5. PERFORMING ARTS AND NIGHTLIFE

Denver has a full complement of orchestras and other musical groups, and theaters of various levels and aims. There is the Denver Symphony and the Colorado Ballet, the Denver Center Theater Company and the complex of the Center for the Performing Arts, where various spaces have further inspired regional performers in the arts. The statistically youthful Denver population and boom-town atmosphere contributes to a proliferation of nightspots of every kind.

CLASSICAL AND THEATRICAL: The **Arvada Center for the Arts and Humanities** (tel. 422-8050) presents regular programs of concert music, theater, and dance in its auditorium at 6901 Wadsworth Blvd.

The **Denver Symphony** (tel. 592-7777) has a full season at the Boettcher Concert Hall, 950 13th St.

The **Colorado Ballet** (tel. 298-0677), the city's sole professional resident company, has programs at the Denver Center for the Performing Arts.

Theater

Theater groups include the **Arvada Center Theater Company,** 6901 Wadsworth Blvd. (tel. 422-8050), the **Avenue Theater,** 2119 E. 17th Ave. (tel. 377-1720), and the **Victorian Theater,** 4201 Hooker St. (tel. 433-5050).

Plays and one-person appearances in drama make up the program of **Center Attractions** (tel. 573-7151) at the Denver Center for the Performing Arts.

Twenty original productions every year is the boast of the **Changing Scene Theater,** at 1527½ Champa St. (tel. 893-5775), with performances Thursday through Sunday.

The **Denver Center Theater Company** (tel. 893-4100) at the Denver Center for the Performing Arts is a professional repertory company with evening performances Monday through Saturday and additional matinees on Wednesday and Saturday.

The **Germinal State,** at 44th and Alcott (tel. 455-7108), is a 132-seat theater presenting plays by modern playwrights such as Brecht, Albee, and Pinter.

The **University of Denver Theater,** South University Boulevard at East Evans Avenue (tel. 871-2518), welcomes the public to its plays.

Film

Cinema is also provided for serious moviegoers at several locations. The **Denver Center Cinema** (tel. 892-0987) at the Denver Center for the Performing Arts shows about 500 films a year in a 260-seat cinema in the Helen Bonfils Theater complex.

The world's largest movie-projection system is put to good use at the **Phipps Imax Theater** in the Museum of Natural History (tel. 370-6300) in City Park. A 441-seat theater has a screen 4½ stories high and 6½ stories wide.

ENTERTAINMENT IN CLUBS AND LOUNGES: The Denver area offers nighttime entertainment to please almost any taste.

Jazz

Jazz is heard in several Denver establishments, such as the **Bay Wolf,** 231 Milwaukee in Cherry Creek (tel. 388-9221), with a bar open seven nights a week, and music seven nights too, starting at 8:30 p.m., with no cover charge.

The **Betty Rose,** 1404 Larimer (tel. 623-8619), has jazz groups nightly.

Sunday jazz by various regional groups like the Boom Town Stompers or the All Star Jazz Band is heard at the **Bull & Bush,** a re-creation of a famous London pub, at 4700 S. Cherry Creek Dr. (tel. 759-0092).

Small jazz groups play weekday afternoons and every night (except Monday) at the **Burnsley Hotel,** 1000 Grant (tel. 830-1000). Jazz quartets are on hand nightly at **City Spirit,** 1434 Blake (tel. 575-0022).

Groups from around the country and locally too are heard nightly at **El Chapultepec,** 1962 Market (tel. 295-9162). Wednesday through Saturday, duos and other small combos play at **Gabriel's,** 1475 S. Colorado Blvd. (tel. 757-7731).

Groups like the Rich Reno band perform at **La Primavera,** 1444 Arapahoe (tel. 892-9200). A Touch of Clazz is one of the groups appearing at the **Parkside Café,** 1875 York (tel. 322-6700).

The Joe Lukasik Trio plays for jazz fans at the **Sheraton Hotel,** 360 Union in Lakewood (tel. 987-2000). Nightly except Sunday the **Stuffed Shirt Lounge** of the Regency Hotel, 3900 Elati (tel. 458-5555), offers jazz combos.

Rock Music

Grease Lightning may be on hand at **Sgt. Pepper's Nightclub,** 10245 E. Colfax Ave. (tel. 361-6408). **The Hi-Lo,** 47th at the Diagonal in Boulder (tel. 444-6666), presents such ensembles as Big Head Todd and the Monsters.

Timothy P. and the Rural Route Three sometimes perform at **Max's,** at Wadsworth and Bowles (tel. 979-9179). Various rock groups hold forth most nights at **Cricket on the Hill,** 1209 E. 13th Ave. (tel. 830-9020).

Basin's Up, 1427 Larimer (tel. 623-2104), is a well-established downtown rock emporium with music most nights. Sound and Fury regularly appears at the **Garage at XXIII Parish,** 2301 Blake (tel. 296-6628). Dick and the Chicks are among possible entertainers at **Herman's Hideaway,** 1578 S. Broadway (tel. 778-9916).

Country and Bluegrass

A favorite meetingplace of bluegrass buffs on the first and third Thursdays of each month is **Ralph's Top Shop,** 2890 S. Zuñi (tel. 762-1330), where jam sessions start at 7:30 p.m. and both pickers and listeners are welcome.

The Dave Toland Z-Bar Band operates seven nights a week at the lively **Zanza-Bar,** 10601 E. Colfax Ave. (tel. 344-2510). Gary "Guitar" Reynolds is usually on the podium evenings at the **Buck Snort Saloon,** 15921 Elk Creek Rd., in Pine (tel. 838-0284).

The Stardust Lounge House Band is heard nightly, where else, but at the **Stardust Lounge,** 52nd and Marshall (tel. 424-9987). Various fiddlers and strummers entertain nightly at the **Urban Cowgirl Saloon,** 9575 W. 57th (tel. 420-4444).

Comedy

Thursday is comedy night at **Heatley's Teahouse,** 266 S. Downing (tel. 777-1991).

Comedy buffs flock to the **Comedy Works,** 1226 15th St. (tel. 595-3637), which has various improvisation nights and new talent nights during the Monday and Tuesday slots and touring guest acts Wednesday through Sunday. There is also an adjoining café, Gibson's.

Would-be and professional comics also perform at the **Comedy Club,** 10013 E. Hampden Ave. (tel. 758-5275), open nightly except Monday. Tuesday is new talent night and Wednesday is improvisational comedy time; headliners appear Wednesday to Sunday.

6. OUTDOORS AROUND DENVER

Denver's proximity to the Rocky Mountains makes it possible for residents or visitors to take a day of skiing, snowmobiling, horseback riding, hiking, river running, fishing, sailing, hunting, mountain climbing, or rockhounding—and be back in the city by nightfall. Within Denver itself there are 85 miles of paved bicycle paths, 100 or more free tennis courts, and a score of golf courses. The city also boasts the world's largest sporting goods store—Garts Sports Castle on Broadway.

The city has at least 300 days of sunshine every year to encourage sports of every kind. Campsites are easily reached from Denver, as are sites suitable for hang-gliding and hot-air ballooning. Among the 120 tennis courts, 49 are lit for night playing, the most popular being in City Park, Washington Park, and Sloans Lake. For information on **tennis courts,** call 575-2552 in Denver. Seven city-operated **golf courses** augment a longer list of privately owned ones open to the public. Within the entire state there are no fewer than 144 full-size 18-hole courses. For information on golfing, call 575-2227 in Denver.

Joggers also use the paved **bikeways,** a favorite stretch being the ten miles along the bank of the Platte River. Other paths link the mind-boggling total of 169 city parks that Denver boasts of, making it the most-parked city in the world. But city streets are marked with bike lanes in many places too, making it relatively simple to cross Denver from almost any point to another across town.

Campers enjoy many parts of the state, where half the land is in the public domain. Near Denver there is camping in Cherry Creek State Recreation Area, Golden Gate Canyon State Park, the Indian Peaks Wilderness, and a variety of privately owned campgrounds. Sailing is popular within the city at Sloans Lake and on the small lake at Washington Park. Cherry Creek Reservoir in southeast Denver also offers boating, and the Platte River is clear for many miles of river running in rafts, kayaks, and canoes.

Denver has pro teams playing basketball, football, hockey, and baseball. **Mile High Stadium** is the scene of home games of both the Broncos, of the National Football League, and the Denver Zephyrs, the minor-league baseball team. The stadium is part of a sports complex reached at exit 210B of I-25, at 17th Avenue. **McNichols Sports Arena** is the scene of home games of the Nuggets of the National Basketball Association, and of the Rockies of the National Hockey League.

DENVER MOUNTAIN PARKS: Land in the mountains near Denver was acquired and set aside for recreational use by the city as early as the 1900s. These are great areas for hiking, picnicking, birdwatching, taking the kids out to use the playgrounds, golfing, or lazing in the grass in the sun.

Bell Park, two miles southeast of Evergreen on Colo. 73, has picnic tables and hiking trails.

Bergen Park, 26 miles from Denver on Colo. 74, has fireplaces, picnic tables, and a shelter house.

Colorow Point Park, two miles west of Lookout Mountain on Lookout Mountain Road is a scenic overlook.

Corwina Park, 22 miles west of Denver on Colo. 74, has playgrounds, fireplaces, picnic tables, and a shelter house.

Daniels Park, with 1,000 acres, is 23 miles south of Denver, via County Line Road and County Road 29, and has a buffalo enclosure, a scenic overlook, playgrounds, fireplaces, picnic tables, and a shelter house.

Dedisse Park is two miles west of Evergreen on Colo. 74, with playgrounds, fireplaces, tables, a golf course, a clubhouse, and a shelter house.

Dillon Park is a mile south of Evergreen on Colo. 73 to Brook Forest Road, then right to Colo. 78. It has playgrounds, fireplaces, picnic tables, and hiking trails.

Echo Lake Park, with 617 acres, is 47 miles west of Denver on Colo. 103, and has playgrounds, fireplaces, tables, picnic grounds, a shelter house, hiking trails, and rooms in the Echo Lake Lodge.

Fillius Park is 25 miles west of Denver on Colo. 74, and has playgrounds, fireplaces, picnic tables, and a shelter house.

Genesee Park is the largest of the parks, with 2,400 acres, 20 miles west of Denver on I-70 at the Genesee Park exit, with playgrounds, fireplaces, picnic tables, an elk and buffalo enclosure, a softball field, a scenic overlook, and a shelter house.

Little Park is 21 miles southwest of Denver on Colo. 74 and has fireplaces and picnic tables.

Lookout Mountain Park, with 66 acres on a promontory, is 17 miles west of Denver via I-70 to the Lookout Mountain Road exit. It offers a scenic overlook, the Buffalo Bill museum and Bill Cody's grave, fireplaces, picnic tables, and a shelter house.

O'Fallon Park, 23 miles southwest of Denver on Colo. 74, has fireplaces and tables in picnic grounds, and hiking trails over 860 acres.

Pence Park is two miles southeast of Kittredge on Indian Hills Road, and offers fireplaces in a picnic ground.

Red Rocks Park is a mile northwest of Morrison via an access road from Colo. 74, and has a cactus garden, spectacular geological formations, a botanical study area, and picnic grounds with tables and a shelter house. The Red Rocks Theater here presents musical programs in the summer.

Summit Lake Park, 62 miles west of Denver on Colo. 103 at the foot of Mount Evans, has a botanical study area, a picnic ground, and a shelter house.

Turkey Creek Park is 23 miles southwest of Denver on U.S. 285 and has a picnic ground.

For additional information on Denver Mountain Parks, get in touch with **Denver Parks and Recreation** at 1445 Cleveland Pl. (tel. 575-2227).

STATE PARKS NEAR DENVER: Several state parks and state recreation areas are within a half-hour drive of Denver and offer a variety of outdoor experiences.

Barr Lake State Park, 13401 Picadilly Rd. in Brighton (tel. 659-6005), is 18 miles northeast of Denver via I-76. A wildlife sanctuary, it consists of a prairie reservoir of 1,937 acres lined with stands of cottonwood, marshes, and aquatic plants, which make the heart of this 2,500-acre park. The southwestern part of the lake is a protected wildlife preserve sheltering a large number of birds of various species, as well as other animals. The recreational uses of the park are those that harmonize with the aim of wildlife protection. Thus motors are not allowed on boats, but visitors may sail, fish, paddle canoes, row boats, or ride horses on adjoining trails. There is picnicking, and in winter nature study groups meet here. There is also snowshoeing and cross-country skiing in the wintertime.

Barr Lake has been a resort since the 1880s, once famed as having the best fishing in the West. But pollution of the lake spoiled that until the damage was reversed in recent years by pollution-control projects on the South Platte River. Water from Barr Lake is still used, however, for irrigation, as it has been from the time of the earliest pioneers in the area.

A fascinating treat for lovers of wildlife is a boardwalk into the marsh to view great blue herons. Other birds often seen are white pelicans, cormorants, egrets, ducks, grebes, gulls, owls, eagles, falcons, and hawks. Swimming is not permitted, but there is fishing for carp, channel catfish, small- and large-mouth bass, perch, trout, crappie, and bluegill—all stocked here by the Division of Wildlife.

Besides the birds, foxes, deer, and other mammals are also protected within the park. A nine-mile trail for hikers and bicyclists circles the lake, and there are shorter walks on the boardwalks extending over the lake. The trails in the park connect with others leading all the way into Denver along the South Platte River via the O'Brian Canal. A nature trail starting from the south parking lot leads to a good view of the heron rookery. There are also bird blinds along this trail for the study and picture-taking of wildlife.

Admission to the park is $3 per vehicle. There are two picnic areas with tables and grills in the park. A commercial campground has camping facilities opposite the park entrance.

Castlewood Canyon State Park (tel. 688-5242) is 30 miles south of Denver on Colo. 83 to Franktown, then west on Colo. 86 a quarter mile to Douglas County Road 51, then south three miles to the park entrance. The park is open from sunrise to sunset year round, with an admission fee of $3 per car. The small park of 873 acres has steep canyons, a meandering stream, a waterfall, lush vegetation, considerable wildlife, and views of Denver to the north and Pike's Peak to the south. The remains of Castlewood Canyon Dam can be seen here; built for irrigation in 1890, it collapsed in 1933 and killed two people. The park has picnic facilities and hiking trails.

Chatfield State Recreation Area is eight miles southwest of Denver at 11500 N. Roxborough Park Rd., Littleton (tel. 797-3986), reached from Denver via U.S. 85 south. Main attraction is Chatfield Reservoir, with a 26-mile shoreline, providing swimming, water sports, boating, and fishing. Occupying 5,600 acres of prairie against a backdrop of the steeply rising Rocky Mountains, the park is named for a farmer who worked this land over a century ago. The reservoir was formed by a dam built in 1975. There are 153 pull-through campsites here, with showers and a laundry as well as a dump station. Various sites offer picnicking facilities. Fishing is mainly for trout, channel cat, bass, crappie, bluegill, and sunfish. An observation area on the south side of the park gives visitors a view of a 27-acre grove designated as a nature study area, site of the park's heronry. The area is closed during nesting season. Rangers give guided interpretive walks and evening programs on nature subjects. Wildlife also includes mule and whitetail deer, hawks, eagles, owls, and waterfowl of other varieties, as well as beaver, muskrat, rabbits, and other small mammals. Hunting is not permitted. The area is also provided with 25 miles of paved bicycle trails, as well as hiking and horseback-riding paths, maps of which are given out at the park entrance. The area has the special attraction, also, of a model airplane field, complete with paved runways, south of the campground. There are corrals where visitors may leave their horses overnight while camping in the park. Wintertime action includes ice fishing and cross-country skiing. Daily admission is $3 per car, plus camping fees of $7. Reservations for camping may be made from anywhere in the U.S. by telephoning toll free 800/824-2267.

Cherry Creek State Recreation Area, 4201 S. Parker Rd. in Aurora (tel. 690-1166), is at the Denver city limits, just southeast of the city at the Parker Road exit of I-225. In the past Cherry Creek, which is the central attraction of the park, has flooded Denver—until Cherry Creek Dam was built in 1953 to prevent that. The resulting reservoir has become a nearby recreation area for the residents of the city: a million and a half visitors per year. A daily permit costs $3 per car, plus $7 daily for use of the 102 campsites, which include showers, a laundry, and interpretive programs, as well as a dump station, but not water or electric hookups. Many lakeshore sites have picnic tables with grills. Water sports include swimming, waterskiing, boating, and fishing for trout, walleye, bass, crappie, pike, and carp. A nature trail a mile and a half in length is offered for students of the great outdoors, who may also partake of evening nature programs in an amphitheater or on ranger-guided nature walks. There is a special observation area for the prairie dog colony. A fitness trail attracts exercisers and there is a dog training area. Horses are rented for rides on ten miles of bridle trails. There is a rifle range, a pistol range, and a trap-shooting area for shotguns. Six miles of paved bike trails circle the reservoir. In wintertime there is ice boating and ice fishing as well as skating on the reservoir, and cross-country skiing when there is adequate snow. Besides the 880-acre lake, the park has grounds of 3,900 acres.

Eldorado Canyon State Park (tel. 494-3943) is eight miles southwest of Boulder, and is reached from Denver via the Boulder Turnpike to the Eldorado Springs exit, then Colo. 170 to the park entrance. An internationally famed area for technical rock climbing, the 272-acre park has sheer sandstone walls in Eldorado Canyon that reach heights of 850 feet. The main attraction is climbing these walls or watching climbers scale them; there is also picnicking, hiking, and fishing, but no camping. A daily pass to the park costs $3 per vehicle.

Golden Gate Canyon State Park (tel. 592-1502) in Golden is reached from Denver via I-70 west to Colo. 58 (Golden exit), then west on Colo. 58 to U.S. 6, and U.S. 6 west 11 miles to Colo. 119. Follow 119 north 12 miles to Colo. 46 and turn right for the park entrance. Gold miners, lumberjacks, and homesteaders made the trails now marked and followed by hikers—they are between two and six miles in length and give day hikers a lot of variety. Their evocative names are Coyote, Black Bear, Blue Grouse, Horse, Mule Deer, Elk, Mountain Lion, Burro, Eagle, Snowshoe Hare, Raccoon, and Buffalo Trails, and at their heads are symbols marking them as easy (for horses too), moderate, or difficult. The Panorama Point Overlook, reached by car, gives a view of 100 miles of the Continental Divide.

There are two campgrounds available by vehicle for $6 nightly, plus the $3-

per-vehicle park entry fee: the 106-site Reverend's Ridge Campground for RVs, with showers, toilets, and a laundry; and the Aspen Meadow, for tents only. Backcountry camping is free of charge (except for vehicle entrance fee if applicable) but permits must be taken out at the visitor center. Horse campers may use Aspen Meadow or the remote Deer Creek campsites, the latter requiring a backcountry permit. Scenic picnic spots are along Ralston Creek, at Ole Barn Knoll, Panorama Point, Bootleg Bottom, and at Kriley and Slough Ponds.

Ralston Creek and the park ponds are stocked with trout by the state Division of Wildlife. In the wintertime there is cross-country skiing, sledding, tubing, snowshoeing, and ice skating in the park. There are open hunting seasons in the park on mule deer and other quarry. Wildlife often met include coyotes, porcupines, beaver, muskrat, ground squirrels, hawks, and Canadian jays. Nature programs are given during the summer at Reverend's Ridge Campground, and there is an ecological and historical display in the visitor center, open daily year around. The nearest store is at Colorado Sierra, a mile and a half from Reverend's Ridge.

OTHER OUTDOOR ATTRACTIONS: Denver City Park, East 17th Avenue between York Street and Colorado Boulevard, has playgrounds, boating, tennis courts, picnic areas, athletic fields, and an 18-hole municipal golf course. Band concerts are a summertime attraction in the park, site of both the zoo and natural history museum (see Section 4, above).

Summer evenings (except Sunday) at 8:15 p.m. there is parimutuel greyhound racing at the **Mile High Kennel Club,** East 62nd Avenue and Colorado Boulevard (tel. 288-1591), with 50¢ admission, or reserved clubhouse seats at $3. There are also matinee races on Monday, Wednesday, and Saturday at 1:30 p.m.

A mile and a half west of the city at exit 259 of I-70 is the **Mother Cabrini Shrine,** a 22-foot-high statue of Christ reached by 373 stairs in the foothills of the Rockies. Also here is the Mother Cabrini Convent, which operates a souvenir shop.

Third week of January is the time for the **National Western Stock Show and Rodeo** in the Denver Coliseum, the largest stock show in the country. For information, call 623-1166.

7. TRIPS OUT OF DENVER

A number of towns with special character lie within easy reach of Denver and make likely destinations for day trips. There is a trip to three old gold- and silver-mining towns that offers the opportunity to enter gold mines, pan for gold, ride a narrow-gauge railroad, and see some of the best-preserved Victorian architecture in the West. Central City is a National Historic District and keeps its century-old look today, in the middle of what was known as "the richest square mile on earth," from which half a billion dollars in precious metals was extracted. There are mine tours, museums, and many shops and restaurants in oldtime structures. The "Oh My God Road" winds dangerously to Idaho Springs, site of the first gold strike in Colorado, in 1859, where today visitors try their luck at panning for what gold may still remain, and also tour a gold mill. Georgetown has some 200 restored Victorian buildings, some open to visitors, including an old inn, and is the departure point for steam trains on the summer trips on the Georgetown Loop.

The highest paved car highway in the country takes visitors to Evergreen, which has a pioneer museum, and to the beautiful mountain environs of the alpine Echo Lake beyond the town. Only a pass between China and Pakistan is higher anywhere in the world than the Mount Evans summit road. The town of

Golden, nearer Denver, offers brewery tours and a Buffalo Bill museum. The small city of Boulder, home of the University of Colorado, has a delightful mall open to people but not cars.

BOULDER: This city of 82,000 is 30 miles northwest of Denver, reached via the Boulder Turnpike (U.S. 36) by car or by **buses** running frequently in service of the Regional Transportation District (tel. 778-6000).

Car rentals in Boulder include **Hertz,** 1760 14th St. (tel. 443-3520); and **National,** 2960 Center Green Court South (tel. 442-5110). Boulder **Yellow Cab** is at 442-2277 (24-hour service).

For travel-service information, don't be put off by the name of the information office: **Boulder Bureau of Conference Services and Cultural Affairs,** at 2440 Pearl, Boulder, CO 80302 (tel. 303/442-1044).

Sights and Attractions

The University of Colorado, familiarly called CU, or Colorado University, influences the youthful spirit of the city by its numbers—20,000 students—and by its cultural and sports events. The original inhabitants of Boulder Valley were Arapahoe Indians, nomads who followed the trails of the buffalo herds. The first pioneers arrived in 1858 and six years later killed the Arapahoe chief in a massacre—there is a bust of him (Niwot) in Court House Square. A gold strike at Gold Hill in 1859 started a boom era in Boulder, bringing in 5,000 prospectors, but two years later there were only 200 people left in the little community when the early gold vanished. But a bigger, longer-lasting gold strike came about in the early 1870s, after which the town became a supply point for miners and a railhead for a narrow-gauge supply line. The town was also the site of an early Chautauqua, one of three still operating in the U.S. Besides students, Boulder residents include many scientists and employees of technological industries. Average age is only 25.

The **University of Colorado Henderson Museum,** just east of Broadway on the campus between 15th and 16th Streets (tel. 492-6892), is open free of charge Monday through Friday from 9 a.m. to 5 p.m., on Saturday to 4 p.m., and on Sunday from 10 a.m. to 4 p.m. It was established in 1902 to display materials on the Rocky Mountain region, and has collections in archeology, anthropology, ethnology, history, geology, mineralogy, paleontology, botany, entomology, zoology, and the arts. The main gallery has special displays changing through the year.

The **Boulder Historical Society Museum,** at 1019 Spruce St. (tel. 449-3464), occupies the oldest residential structure in town, the Squires-Tourtellot House, and is open from 10 a.m. to 4 p.m. Tuesday through Friday, 1 to 4 p.m. on Saturday, and noon to 4 p.m. on Sunday.

Self-guided tours may be taken at the **National Center for Atmospheric Research,** 1850 Table Mesa Dr. (tel. 497-1140), between 8 a.m. and 5 p.m. weekdays.

Art galleries of the **Boulder Center for the Visual Arts,** 1750 13th St. (tel. 443-2122), are open from 11 a.m. to 5 p.m. Tuesday through Saturday, and 1 to 5 p.m. on Sunday.

Where to Stay

Decidedly the most interesting lodging place in Boulder is the **Hotel Boulderado,** 2115 13th St., Boulder, CO 80302 (tel. 303/442-4344, or toll free 800/433-4344), a restored five-story luxury hotel near the pedestrian mall, in the middle of the city, that was built by a consortium of proud citizens in 1908. There is a glowing glass canopy two stories above the lobby that sets the tone of subdued sparkle and warm tones of polished wood paneling, with more rich woodwork in balusters and columns. Richly upholstered armchairs and settees add to the welcome in public areas of the main-floor lobby and in more secluded niches along the second-floor balcony above it. The oyster bar is a busy place of an afternoon, and there are three restaurants and three cocktail bars and lounges. The Mezzanine Lounge is proud of its eight-page drink list and its live music nightly. There is also Winston's Seafood Restaurant, the Steak Porch, and Franco's Pastaria—a "pasta bar" with six various sauces going into 30 selections. A traditional drinking place below stairs is the Catacombs Bar.

All the rooms are individually furnished, no two alike, in real turn-of-the-century antiques from the period of the hotel's origin. Views of the nearby Rockies are a bonus from the windows of most of the rooms. Rates are $69 to $79 double, $10 for additional persons.

The **Briar Rose,** 2151 Arapahoe Ave., Boulder, CO 80302 (tel. 303/442-3007, or toll free 800/458-0882), is a country-style bed-and-breakfast guest home with 11 rooms, all with period furniture, fresh fruit and flowers, feather comforters, and bedside candies and books; some have fireplaces. The morning repast is a good continental breakfast. Rates are $68 to $98 double.

Double rates at $35 to $40 are offered in quite luxurious log cabins at the **Foot of the Moutain Motel,** 200 W. Arapahoe, Boulder, CO 80303 (tel. 303/442-5688). There is cable service on the television and great mountain scenery just outside the door.

Where to Eat

Boulder's youthful hi-tech workers and the thousands of college students and faculty constitute a population that likes eating out, so restaurants flourish in considerable numbers for the size of the city.

English atmosphere pervades the **Broker Inn,** 555 30th St. (tel. 444-3330), serving three meals daily as well as a Sunday brunch. A free shrimp bowl accompanies dinner.

Crystal Springs Grille, in the Clarion Harvest House, 1345 28th St. (tel. 443-3850), has continental dishes, fresh seafood, and Colorado beef.

Jose Muldoon's, 1600 38th St. (tel. 449-4543), offers an array of Mexican specialties, some created at a "build-your-own" tostada bar at lunchtime Monday through Saturday and at Sunday brunch. Fresh seafood dishes are also on the menu. There is food and drink to be had on the outdoor patio during the day and night too, in warm weather, and there is live entertainment Thursday through Monday nights. Lunches and dinners are served seven days a week.

GOLDEN: This small city only 12 miles west of the center of Denver (via U.S. 6 or I-70 and Colo. 58) is famous for its main industry, the largest U.S. brewery, **Adolph Coors Company,** employing 10,000 people. It conducts free tours for visitors from its headquarters at 13th and Ford Streets daily except Sunday from 8:30 a.m. to 4:30 p.m. (with free samples of the beer). For information, dial 277-6363.

Travel service information is available at the **Golden Area Chamber of Commerce,** 611 14th St., Golden, CO 80402 (tel. 303/279-3113).

Sights and Activities

The **Foothills Art Center,** 809 15th St., is a center of regional art that may be purchased as well as admired on the premises. The center, open Monday through Saturday from 9 a.m. to 4 p.m., and 1 to 4 p.m. on Sunday, sponsors various exhibitions during the year, including the annual Rocky Mountain

Watermedia Exhibition and the Golden Sidewalk Art Show; for dates and times, call 279-3922. Installed in a disused Gothic church and its adjoining parsonage dating from 1872, the center developed out of the sidewalk show when winners realized they needed space to exhibit their works for long periods of time. The church, after renovation, served the purpose, and the center opened for the first time in 1968. Work on the building has been done mainly by volunteers, most of them local artists who show their works here. Activities also include the seven-week Holiday Art Market in November or December showing work by 200 artists and crafts people. The **Roundel Gallery** gift shop is stocked year round with articles of local artisans and artists. Artists exchange ideas at meetings of Fine Arts Focus; there are talks scheduled on other subjects as well, and a poetry competition goes on every year.

Other yearly events in Golden include a quarter-horse show, an antique show, an old car show, and a dog show, all at the Jefferson County fairgrounds in June; a **Festival of the West and Buffalo Bill Days** in July; and the **County Fair and Highland Games** of the St. Andrew Society in August.

The **Colorado Railroad Museum,** 17155 W. 44th Ave., near exit 265 of I-70 (tel. 279-4591), is open from 9 a.m. to 5 p.m. daily; admission is $2 for adults, $1 for children under 16. It occupies a replica of an 1880 railroad depot, and has artifacts, papers, old books, and photographs on railroading. Outdoors is a collection of early locomotives and cars dating back to the 1870s.

Heritage Square (tel. 277-0040), on U.S. 40 three-quarters of a mile south of U.S. 6, is a re-creation of an imaginary Colorado town of 1880, with shops that produce goods made on the premises, an ice-cream parlor, a beer garden, and an opera house presenting melodramas. A 1½-mile train ride takes visitors aboard a miniature model of a period locomotive and passenger cars. Other rides include go carts, bumper boats, a waterslide, and in summer, the use of a 2,350-foot-long ski run as an Alpine slide with bobsled-style carts ($4 a ride). Shops are open daily from 10 a.m. to 9 p.m. Memorial Day through Labor Day and Thanksgiving through Christmas; the rest of the year hours are 10 a.m. to 6 p.m. Admission is free.

Red Rocks Park has a natural outdoor amphitheater surrounded by colorful formations of red stone; called **Red Rock Amphitheatre,** it is at the Red Rocks exit of I-70 south of Golden and presents evening concerts of popular entertainers as well as a noted annual Easter sunrise service.

The Allen Mine Lamp Collection is one of the special treasures of the **Geology Museum** of the Colorado School of Mines, at 16th and Maple (tel. 273-3815), open from 9 a.m. to 4 p.m. weekdays and 1 to 4 p.m. on Sunday; closed Saturday. Admission is free of charge. Exhibits of mining through history include a fluorescent metal exhibit, a replica of a gold mine, and a gemstone display. Mineral specimens and books are sold in a small shop here.

An early frontier hotel open to viewers is the **Astor House Hotel Museum,** at 12th and Arapahoe (tel. 278-3557), the oldest stone hotel in the state, built in 1867. The $1 admission fee includes a guided tour, held Monday through Saturday from 10 a.m. to 4 p.m. in summer, to 2 p.m. in winter.

The **Pioneer Museum,** 911 10th St. (tel. 279-3331), in the Golden Civic Center, is open free of charge weekdays from 10 a.m. to 5 p.m. in summer, and 1 to 5 p.m. in winter, with guns, clothing, photographs, furniture, and newspapers from the early West all displayed by members of the D.A.R., which runs the museum.

The **Buffalo Bill Museum,** on Lookout Mountain at the Lookout Mountain exit of I-70 (tel. 526-0747), has the grave of William Frederick Cody, best known of all western scouts, who rode for the Pony Express, organized buffalo hunts for foreign royalty, and toured with his Wild West show all over the world. It is open daily except Monday from 9 a.m. to 5 p.m. in summer, to 4 p.m. in winter. Admission is $2.

Also on Lookout Mountain is the **Jefferson County Nature Center,** 900 Colorow Rd. (tel. 526-0855), a 110-acre estate with an English Tudor-style mansion used for conferences, and a nature trail through Ponderosa pine and mountain meadows. Hours are 9 a.m. to 5 p.m. Monday through Saturday; free of charge.

Buildings of interest in Golden include the **Armory,** at 13th and Arapahoe, the largest cobblestone structure in the U.S., having been built with 3,300 wagonloads of stone and quartz. The **Territorial Capitol,** at 12th and Washington, dating from 1861 is the Loveland Building, where the legislature met between 1862 and 1867 when Golden was the Colorado capital. The **Rock Flour Mill Warehouse,** at 8th and Cheyenne Streets, dating from 1863, is the oldest commercial structure in town, built of red granite from nearby Golden Gate Canyon. It has original cedar beams and wooden floors, and today houses some antique shops.

Where to Stay

Holiday Inn-Denver West, 14707 W. Colfax Ave. (at exit 262 of I-70), Golden, CO 80401 (tel. 303/279-7611), has 228 rooms, doubles from $58, with an indoor pool, health club, fun center, putting green, dining room, coffeeshop, and lounge.

A pleasant Victorian bed-and-breakfast lodging is the **1889 Dove Inn,** 711 14th St., Golden, CO 80401 (tel. 303/278-2209). A full home-cooked breakfast goes with double rooms at $34.

The **Golden Motel,** 510 24th St., Golden, CO 80401 (tel. 303/279-5581), has 15 rooms, some with kitchenettes, at $26 to $34 double.

Where to Eat

Briarwood Inn, at the junction of Colo. 58 and U.S. 6 (tel. 279-3121), has American and continental dishes and a bar, and serves lunch and dinner daily; dinners run $15 to $25.

A menu of Mexican and American dishes is offered at lunch and dinner daily except Sunday at the **Golden Eagle,** 1305 Washington Ave. (tel. 279-5257).

GEORGETOWN: A pretty village of restored Victorian-era houses and stores, Georgetown, 45 miles west of Denver on I-70 at an elevation of 8,500 feet, is named for a gold camp established here in 1860. After the gold played out, the place experienced a rebirth with a silver strike four years later, and the town was nicknamed the Silver Queen. Some of the best Victorian architecture in the West graces many of the 200 structures saved and restored in Georgetown, including the Hamill House, the Hotel de Paris, and the Bowman-White House. Three early firehouses, a courthouse, and several churches are also of interest.

Sights and Attractions

The **Hamill House,** at 3rd and Argentine Streets (tel. 569-2840), is in the style of country Gothic Revival and dates to 1867 when it was the town's most ambitious residence, owned by a silver speculator, William Hamill. Additions to the house in the 1880s include a dining room, solarium, and rear wing, and the installation of new central heating, gas lighting, walnut woodwork, and bay windows. A carriage house and office that occupy two stone structures behind the main house look as if they might have graced the courtyard of a French château, with their uncoursed stone façades and steep pitched roofs topped with little towers. A delicately carved outhouse had two parts, one for the family and the other for servants. When acquired by the Georgetown Society (a nonprofit local organization dedicated to preserving historic structures here) the house had its woodwork, fireplaces, and wallpapers and ceiling papers still in place. Original wallpapers have been repainted to their former brilliance. Restoration to complete the entire property will continue into the 1990s. Admission is $2.50.

The **Georgetown Silver Plume Mining Area** was declared a National Historic Landmark District in 1966. The town has provided other properties as a challenge to the Georgetown Society, including the Tucker-Rutherford House and the Old Cabin. Hours for visitng Society buildings that are open to the public are 9:30 a.m. to 6 p.m. in summer, every day; and in winter, noon to 4 p.m. (closed Monday). Admission to the Hamill House and Hotel de Paris is $1.50 for each.

The **Hotel de Paris** (tel. 569-2311) houses a historic museum run by the National Society of Colonial Dames of America, whose members serve tea and coffee in the courtyard daily in warm weather. The builder of the hotel, Louis Dupuy, once wrote an explanation of his desire to build a French inn so far away from his homeland: "I love these mountains and I love America, but you will pardon me if I bring into this community a remembrance of my youth and my country. . . . My friends, this house will be my tomb—and if, in after years, someone comes and calls for Louis Dupuy, show them this little souvenir of Alençon which I built in America, and they will understand."

The hotel opened in 1875 and soon became famous for its French provincial luxuriousness. Today the hotel is embellished with objects gathered into the museum: Haviland china, diamond-dust mirrors, a big pendulum clock, paintings and etchings of the past century, carved walnut furniture, lace curtains and draperies of tapestry, as well as Dupuy's considerable library. An antique stove and other cooking equipment occupies the kitchen. The wine cellar has some early wine barrels, with their labels still in place, and a display of old bottles and food containers. Dupuy, who was a baker and a master chef, but who had no training in the construction field, also won some renown for the innovations he designed into his hotel, such as steam heat and hot and cold running water.

Also being restored in town is the **Lebanon Mine and Mill** complex, with an adjoining charge room, office, and mine shed. Guided tours are offered daily during the summer. The miner's cottage known as the **Tucker-Rutherford House** has four small rooms recently restored to the 1890s period, painted white with green window sash. Also recently rebuilt is an 1884 railroad bridge serving the restored **Georgetown Loop Railroad,** which runs daily trips in summer between Georgetown and Silver Plume ($11 for adults, $5.75 for children under 16, including the mine tour, with half a dozen runs daily; for times, call 279-6101). Though the direct distance between the terminals is 2.1 miles, the loop trackage covers 4.5 miles, climbing 638 feet in curves and switchbacks. Passengers may make round trips from either end, the whole taking about two hours, including a walking tour of the mine.

Other structures in Georgetown to note are the 1867 **courthouse,** now used as a tourist information office, and the **old jail** across the street, both on Argentine Street; the **Bowman-White House** and trapper's cabin of 1892, at Rose and 9th Streets; the **Alpine Hose Co. No. 2** of 1874, on 5th Street between Rose and Taos Streets; the 1867 **Grace Episcopal Church** on Taos Street; the **Star Hook & Ladder Bldg.** of 1870 on 6th Street; the **Old Missouri Hose Co.** of 1870 at 10th and Taos Streets; and the 1879 **Presbyterian Church** and **Our Lady of Lourdes Church,** both on Taos Street.

Special events during the year in Georgetown include a Fasching **winter carnival** in February, an **antique fair** and **Swedish festival** (midsummer's day) in June, an **auction** in Hamill House in July, **house tours** of private homes in August, an **aspen festival** in September, and a **Christmas market** with seasonal foods, folk dancing, a Santa Lucia procession, and carolers.

For all information on attractions and travel services, get in touch with the **Georgetown Society** (tel. 303/569-2840).

Where to Stay and Eat

Georgetown accommodations include rooms or entire "unhostessed homes" in historic houses booked centrally by **Georgetown Baehler Resort Services,** at 410 3rd St., Georgetown, CO 80444 (tel. 303/569-2665). Rates vary from house to house, but average $120 double, plus damage deposit.

Large sunny rooms are offered at the **Georgetown Motor Inn,** 1100 Rose St., Georgetown, CO 80444 (tel. 303/569-3201), which has 32 units and a pool open in summertime, with double rates of $45.

Among restaurants, of special interest is the **Alpine Inn,** 1106 Rose St. (tel. 893-2480), with its Victorian-era dining room installed in the original Georgetown Loop Depot. There are western paintings by artist Raphael Lilywhite.

Crêpes, waffles, original soups, and home-baked bread are offered at the **Happy Cooker,** 412 6th St. (tel. 569-3166), which also serves cheesecakes and quiches, and is open from 8 a.m. to 6 p.m. daily in summer, to 4 p.m. in winter.

IDAHO SPRINGS/CENTRAL CITY: These towns, along with Golden and

Georgetown, noted above, make up the fabled **Gold Circle of Colorado.** The first big gold strikes came nearly simultaneously in 1859 when John Gregory found gold near Central City and George Jackson struck gold near Idaho Springs. The Gold Circle towns boomed and died, and rose again in the silver boom.

Idaho Springs

Idaho Springs, 35 miles west of Denver on I-70, is a starting point for a scenic drive past some of those old mines. Today lesser metals provide miners their work in these hills: uranium, tungsten, zinc, molybdenum, and lead are worked, and there is a five-mile-long tunnel linking some of these mines a third of a mile below ground.

Colo. 5 is the highway leading up to the summit of **Mount Evans,** which is reached from Idaho Springs by taking Colo. 103 along Chicago Creek to Echo Lake Park—here there are playgrounds, fireplaces, hiking trails, and a shelter house.

The **Indian Springs Resort** offers mineral water baths and swimming in Idaho Springs.

Central City

Central City, 35 miles west of Denver off U.S. 6, arose after the discovery of gold by John Gregory here in 1859—"the richest square mile on earth." Hub of the area was a miners' trading post, and the town grew to become the most important trade and cultural center of the central Rockies by the 1870s. After a decline at the turn of the century, an **Opera Festival,** started in the 1930s, revitalized the town—its first year was 1932, opening in the Central City Opera House with Lillian Gish in the role of Camille. Today the festival continues during July and August with a summer festival of musicals and operas. For information, call 571-4435.

The route to Central City from Denver goes via U.S. 6 through Clear Creek Canyon to Colo. 119, leading north to the community of **Black Hawk,** home of the best example of carpenter Gothic architecture in the U.S. in the restored **Lace House.** A mile beyond Black Hawk, through Gregory Gulch, lies Central City.

The tours of mines and museums in Central City are open year around. In June there is **Madam Lou Bunch Day** honoring the sporting life of the last century. The day involves a bed race on Main Street and a **Madam and Miners Ball** in the evening. After the July opera festival, there is an August **jazz festival.** At the Christmas season there is the **March of the Singing Children,** led by a Santa on horseback, and a **Festival of Lights.**

For all information on attractions and travel services in Central City, get in touch with the **director of public relations,** at city hall (tel. 303/573-0247).

A **walking tour** of Central City begins on Spring Street with the narrow-gauge railroad exhibit. Just beyond is the **Central Gold Mine and Museum,** occupying an 1868 structure that survived the great fire of 1874. Beginning in the Chinese quarter of Dostal Alley, the fire burned up to Eureka Street and, according to legend, was stopped by the fireproof **Teller House and Masonic Temple.** Stone and brick construction were used exclusively after the fire, resulting in the solid buildings standing today in most of the town.

On lower Lawrence Street, next to the old grade school, visitors may enter the **Gilpin County Historical Museum,** formerly a high school, now housing artifacts out of the mining era and some antiques. Another nearby example of Cornish stone masonry is **St. Paul's Episcopal Church.** The granite **Raynold's Building** withstood the 1874 fire when the proprietor hung wet blankets over the windows and doors, thus saving a store of blasting powder in the cellar from blowing up the town. It was later called the Beehive because of the busy activity it saw as a refuge for many of the other burned-out businesses in town.

West of the volunteer fire department is the **Golden Rose Hotel,** at 102 Main St., Central City, CO 80427 (tel. 303/582-5060). It knew a long era of prosperity as a gambling hall and saloon a century ago. It is now completely restored, with 26 rooms all elegantly furnished in 19th-century antiques. There is a spacious lobby with a fireplace, Victorian bathrooms in the rooms, a hot tub and sauna, continental breakfast, and a dining room serving continental cuisine. It is open all year, charging $44 to $96 for rooms or suites.

West on Eureka Street is the **Register-Call Building,** oldest commercial building still in use in town, housing the oldest newspaper in the state, a weekly. There are interesting murals on the walls of the **Masonic Temple** on the third floor of this building. Another old building is the one housing the law office of **Henry M. Teller,** who built the 1872 Teller House described below. The oldest **city hall** in Colorado was built originally of logs in 1862 by the county sheriff, and it has been used as jail and courthouse in the past. The second floor houses the **Gilpin County Art Gallery,** where an annual art exhibition is held. Farther west on Eureka Street is the **Gilpin County Courthouse,** and beyond this is the **Lost Gold Mine,** offering visitor tours.

On the south side of Eureka Street is the famous **Opera House** in all its original splendor, dating from 1878, when it was built by public subscription. It has walls of native granite four feet thick and inside are so-called three-dimensional murals lighted by a great crystal chandelier. Hickory chairs are inscribed with the names of historic Colorado characters and actors from all over the world who appeared on the Opera House stage. Foremost in the gold-and-silver theatrical circuit of the early West, the Opera House went into a gradual decline with the end of mining, being used for minstrel shows, wrestling matches, high school graduations, and finally silent movies before being shuttered for a time. But the efforts of descendants of those early Coloradans who built the house were successful in reopening it for the first annual festival in 1932.

Next to the Opera House is the **Teller House,** at 110 Eureka St., once the most elegant hotel between Chicago and San Francisco. Visitors see President Grant's room, Baby Doe's gold-plated suite, and rare antique furniture. Tours of the Opera House and the Teller House cost $2.75 for both, and are held from 10 a.m. to 5 p.m. in summer, from 11 a.m. to 4 p.m. Thursday through Monday the rest of the year. The **Teller House bar,** incidentally, is home of the famous "face on the barroom floor," recalling a poem about an artist's ill-fated love for a woman "with eyes that petrified me brain, and sunk into my heart." The truth of the drawing is less romantic—it was done as a joke by a Denver newspaper illustrator in 1936.

Main Street also has some old buildings worth the visitor's attention: the **Toll Gate Saloon** was originally a funeral parlor; the **Old Gold Coin,** oldest bar in town, remains quite the way it looked a century ago. Jazz bands are frequent entertainers in the **Glory Hole Tavern,** location of the annual Central City Jazz Festival. On South Main is another old opera house—oldest in the state, in fact—now the **Belvidere Theater.**

EVERGREEN: Evergreen, 30 miles west of Denver via I-70, has a wooded setting and a main attraction in **Evergreen Lake,** where there is fishing and ice skating in winter and regular water sports and boating at other times. A public 18-hole golf course, and hiking and bridle trails, are other attractions. The 70-piece **Colorado Philharmonic** (tel. 674-5161) gives 20 concerts here every summer. Visitors are welcome at the **Hiwan Homestead Museum,** 4208 Timbervale Dr. (tel. 674-6262), for free guided tours of a historic 17-room mountain lodge with historical exhibits. It has towers and a chapel built into the structure, open Tuesday through Sunday from noon to 4 p.m. On Upper Bear Creek Rd., the **International Bell Museum** (tel. 674-3422) shows 3,500 bells from 10 a.m. to 5 p.m. Tuesday through Sunday, in summer only.

Accommodations in Evergreen include **Bauer's Spruce Island Chalets,** 5987 S. Brook Forest Rd., Evergreen, CO 80439 (tel. 303/674-4757), offering small furnished houses with fireplaces and two one-bedroom apartments for a total of just six units. They are heated by furnace for year-round occupancy and have access to two ponds and a creek for fishing. There is a picnic area, and access to hiking trails. Recreation nearby includes lawn games, gold panning, riding, golf, and swimming. Daily rates are $35 to $65 double, and there are weekly rates.

The oldest hotel in Colorado is the Peck House in the small community of Empire, also within the Golden Circle. The **Peck House,** at 83 Sunny Ave., Empire, CO 80438 (tel. 303/569-9870), is 40 miles west of Denver on U.S. 40, just off I-70, at an altitude of 8,600 feet. Established in 1862, it was originally a stagecoach house, and today has 11 guest rooms furnished in oak, walnut, and maple, some dating to the first days of its opening. A wide porch makes a fine place for contemplating the Empire Valley. Hikers often take the old wagon road over Empire Pass, through spectacular scenery, to Georgetown. The dining room has lithographs of scenes out of the mining era. There is a lounge with a Franklin stove and a bar with a spectacular mountain view from its wide windows. In spring and summer the alpine wildflowers bring out hummingbirds in the meadowland around the inn. The dining room is open to the public year round, seven days a week, with Sunday brunch a local tradition. Some rooms have private bath, some share a bath, and some use hall bathrooms. Double rates are $35 to $60.

CHAPTER XV

COLORADO SKI AREAS

□ □ □

Ten million skiers flock into Colorado every year to take to the slopes of 28 resorts, and at more modest altitudes to cross-country trails. There are enough ski runs for downhill addicts in the state to reach all the way from Vail Mountain to Dallas. If all the lift cables were put together into one, it would be long enough to send chairs from Los Angeles to San Diego.

The various Colorado resorts have differing styles, from the international chic of Vail to the Old West atmosphere of Steamboat, or the historic scenes around Breckenridge, or the family-style casualness at Winter Park. Colorado ski slopes use the worldwide system of marking slopes for difficulty: a green circle for easiest, a blue square for more difficult, and a black diamond for most difficult.

Most Colorado resorts provide nursery services and children's lessons that eventually get the kids up on the slopes and also permit parents some freedom for skiing on their own. Older folk are invited to meet others over 50 in the Over the Hill Ski Gang, where they meet others interested in skiing and other sports. For information, contact the **Over the Hill Gang Ski Team International,** 288 Clayton St., Denver, CO 80206 (tel. 303/355-5050, or toll free 800/922-5050).

A cooperative information system among the ski resorts, called **Colorado Ski Country,** operates reception centers at Stapleton International Airport in Denver and at Walker Field in Grand Junction. Current ski information and resort details are available. The system also has current taped snow reports including snow depth at mid-mountain, new snowfall in the past 24 hours, and surface conditions at all the ski areas (tel. 303/831-SNOW). Another number has a tape on conditions throughout the state for cross-country skiers (tel. 303/573-SNOW). State weather and road reports are also available by telephone: 639-1515 for weather, 639-1111 for road conditions west of Denver.

Bookings from a wide selection of ski packages, with thousands of options in resorts in all price categories, may be made through a computerized system that can also arrange air transportation to Colorado and within the state. The service is **Colorado Vacation Travel,** and can be reached at 5335 W. 48th Ave., Denver, CO 80212 (tel. toll free 800/523-2569, or 800/523-3398 in Colorado).

Information on scheduled bus service reaching most of the ski areas is available through a centralized telephone (tel. 303/398-LIFT).

1. ASPEN

Aspen, named for the cover of trees on the mountainsides around the city, was originally a silver-mining town, with hundreds of mines in the area a century ago. In 1885 miners petitioned the city council to allow the stacking of silver ore in the streets because houses and warehouses were all full. The world's largest piece of silver, weighing 1,840 pounds, came out of the Smuggler Mine nearby. But when silver was demonetized in 1893, the mines closed here and elsewhere in the Southwest and Aspen began a decline that lasted to the late 1930s, when the population had dwindled to 500. Then trails and shelters for public skiing were built in a WPA project that after World War II blossomed into a burgeoning international ski resort. In winter there are four ski areas around Aspen operating at full tilt. Summer activities include outdoor sports and the famous Aspen Music Festival that presents weekly concerts all summer in the outdoor amphitheater.

Aspen is 180 miles west of Denver, reached by car via I-70 west to Glenwood Springs and Colo. 82 southeast to the city. **Greyhound/Trailways** buses make scheduled runs between Denver and Aspen (tel. 292-6111). **Amtrak** passengers may reach Aspen on passenger trains from Chicago and Denver, descending at Glenwood Springs, 40 miles from Aspen; or from San Francisco and points west, passengers may get off at Grand Junction. Train information is available by calling toll free 800/872-7245. Air service on an hourly schedule between Aspen and Denver is provided in winter by **Aspen Airways** (tel. 241-6522) and **Rocky Mountain Airways** (tel. toll free 800/525-0280).

Taxi service is by **Mellow Yellow** (tel. 925-2282) and **High Mountain Taxi** (tel. 925-8294). Car rentals are available from **Aspen Auto Rentals** (tel. 925-6110), **Drive-a-Bargain** (tel. 925-2128), and **Roaring Fork Jeep Rental** (tel. 925-8574).

Skiers buses run frequently during the season from Rubey Park in Aspen up to the slopes of the various ski areas.

ASPEN SKI AREAS: Aspen Mountain is the original area in the Aspen complex, one of the most challenging anywhere for expert skiers; intermediates also find slopes they can manage, but not beginners. The season here runs from late November to mid-April. There is a vertical rise of 3,370 feet, and two quad- and six double-chair lifts with an hourly uphill capacity of 8,675 skiers. The Silver Queen gondola carries 2,000 skiers per hour, from base to summit in 13 minutes. Reservations for private instruction start at 8 a.m. at the bottom of Little Nell Slope and at 11 a.m. at the Sundeck Restaurant at the top of the mountain. Daily class lessons meet at 11 a.m. at the Sundeck, for intermediate and advanced skiers only.

Aspen Highlands, the peaks next door to Aspen Mountain, is a popular area for skiers of all talents, with nine double-chair lifts and two Poma lifts with an overall capacity of 10,000 skiers per hour. Along with expert and intermediate trails are a number suitable for beginners, a quarter of the terrain in the latter category. A special attraction here, when the weather permits, is the opening of the lofty Highlands Bowl to guided tours into a rare slope of deep powdered snow—only for expert skiers. From the deck of a lofty eating place called Cloud Nine skiers can take a break and watch daily performances of the ski-jumping ski patrol. The area is the home of the Graduated Length Method of ski instruction, and lessons here come with a money-back guarantee: if you don't make the run from mid-mountain to the base lodge on the fourth day of lessons, your money is "cheerfully refunded." The area has an innovative pricing system for families: lift tickets for all at $72 per day, and "there is no limit to the number of children." For information on skiing and lessons, call 925-5300. Red, green, and yellow jellybean buses make free trips between Aspen and the slopes here, running every quarter hour. Lunch and lift tickets are included in charges for all-day children's teaching programs, 9:30 a.m. to 4 p.m., called the Snow Puppies.

Buttermilk Mountain is known as "a great teaching mountain" although it has 20% of its trails restricted to experts. But half of them are indeed beginners' trails. There is a vertical rise here of 2,030 feet, reached via six double-chair lifts with an hourly capacity of 6,300 skiers. Buttermilk opens in mid-December and runs to April 1. There is a snowmaking system covering 80 acres. Reservations for private instruction start at 8 a.m. daily (tel. 925-4444). Shuttle-bus service is provided between Aspen and Buttermilk Mountain daily from 8 a.m. to 4:30 p.m. free of charge.

The Buttermilk West Restaurant at the bottom of lift no. 3 has outdoor tables and serves wine and beer. A cafeteria with a sundeck and wine and beer service is at the Cliffhouse between lifts nos. 2 and 5. A full bar and cafeteria are open in the Main Buttermilk Restaurant at the bottom of lift no. 1, and Romeo's is still another cafeteria, with a sundeck, at the base of lift no. 4.

Snowmass, the farthest area from town, is open late November to mid-April, and has a vertical rise of 3,596 feet, with 16 chair lifts, giving an hourly capacity of nearly 15,000 skiers. A fifth of the trails are expert, and most of the rest intermediate. The area has a wide variety of instruction. Beginners are taught the basic-turn approach, while more advanced skiers may enroll in mountain masters classes, which are four-day clinics with instruction aimed at individual needs. Children's classes for ages 5 to 12 meet daily at the ski school youth center at 9:30 a.m. Teenagers have separate clinics. Private instruction is also available. For information on lessons, call 925-4444.

Restaurants at the slopes include Elk Camp, at the bottom of lift no. 10, with a bar, sundeck, fireplace and cafeteria; High Alpine, at the top of lift no. 8, with tables for dining, a sundeck, outdoor grill, full bar, and fireplace; Sam's Knob, at the top of lift no. 3, with a sundeck and cafeteria, as well as a full bar; and Ullrhof, at the base of lift no. 4, with a cafeteria, sundeck, and wine and beer available.

Though it is farthest from town, Snowmass, established in 1967, draws more skiers than the other three Aspen-area mountains combined. One reason is the complex of housing and eating places in **Snowmass Village,** adjoining the slopes. There is a mall with 20 restaurants and many shops. A big reason skiers flock here, however, is that the slopes are not very difficult, which seems to appeal to entire families out for a skiing week or weekend. Residents of the lodgings here can ski from their door to the nearby slopes—and it's easy to run home for a lunch break and even a siesta while putting in most of the day skiing anyway. Besides skiing, families especially like the dogsled rides in which they are tugged across the snow by a team of a dozen dogs on a 12-mile trail where herds of elk and mule deer are easily spotted in the white-floored, silent forest. Hot-air early-morning balloon rides are another attraction. There are 25 miles of trails for cross-country skiing, over which guided trips are organized daily. There is also tennis, squash, and racquetball.

LIFT RATES: Rates for all lifts are $30 for a full day, $16 for children under 13 and for adults over 65, at Aspen Highlands, $35 and $16 at Aspen Mountain, and $32 and $16 at Snowmass. Passes or coupon books for three mountains cost $96 for three days, $180 for a week. All information on skiing is available from **Aspen Skiing Co.** (tel. 925-1220), which runs Aspen Mountain, Buttermilk Mountain, and Snowmass; and from **Aspen Highlands** (tel. 925-5300).

WHERE TO STAY: Snowmass Village has several hotels and lodges besides numerous condominium accommodations rented for short periods. All the inns and lodges are within short distances of the ski area. To book, call **Snowmass Resort Association** (tel. 303/923-2010).

Specializing in ski-vacation rentals at Snowmass in a wide variety of studios and apartments, accommodating from two to eight persons, is **Village Property Management** (tel. 303/923-4350, or toll free 800/525-9402); there are also entire vacation houses available. Many of the accommodations have fireplaces and all are of modern construction set off by handsome contemporary furnishings. Free shuttle service takes skiers to the slopes nearby, although many of the lodgings are within a short walk—or ski—of the slopes. Kitchens are fully equipped, and swimming pools and Jacuzzis are available. Motel-style maid service goes with the rentals. Rates go from $60 to $75 nightly, or $340 to $400 weekly, for a studio for two persons, up to $90 to $160 per night for three-bedroom layouts accommodating four or five people. Laundry facilities, game rooms, and many units with private balconies are additional features of the various sites.

In Aspen, the **Mountain Chalet,** 333 E. Durant Ave., Aspen, CO 81611 (tel. 303/925-7797), is only a block or two from the chair lifts and also within a few minutes' walk of Aspen's busy shops, restaurants, and lounges. A bus stop for transport to the other ski areas locally is right across the street. Winter rates include a hearty all-you-can-eat breakfast, and there is always free coffee and tea to be had, as well as hot chocolate and hot cider après-ski. There is also a popular weekly Gluhwein party, on Monday after the slopes have closed. The chalet has 44 rooms, many with superb views of Aspen Mountain, and all have baseboard heat, telephones, radios, and baths; many also have television sets and refrigerators. Among choices of accommodations are two-bedroom apartments with a living-dining room with fireplace and full kitchen, suitable for six people; these rent for $192 in the high season, half that price in the summertime. Other rooms go for $60 to $70 in the early part of the skiing season, $82 to $94 at peak times (Christmas to New Year's, and the period from January 25 to April 4). Dinners are available nightly in the dining room, and there is free use of sauna, heated pool, ice machines, and ski lockers. Coin-operated laundry facilities and a game room are also on hand.

Bed-and-Breakfast
A historic bed-and-breakfast lodge near the Aspen Mountain lift is the **Little Red Ski Haus,** 118 E. Cooper, Aspen, CO 81611 (tel. 303/925-3333), with three lounges, a fireplace, a full complimentary breakfast, wine parties, and ski movies. Rates are $72 to $78 double.

Aspen Central Reservations (tel. 303/925-9000) arranges package rates including six days of skiing and seven nights' lodging, with lift and lesson privileges interchangeable on Aspen Mountain, Buttermilk Mountain, and Snowmass Mountain. There are reductions in cost for skiing packages in the low seasons (late November to mid-December and early April to the end of skiing). The organization books lodgings in many condominiums as well as in lodges, inns, and motels. The telephone number for other **visitor information** is 303/925-1940.

WHERE TO EAT: Aspen has some 60 restaurants offering a wide variety of food from various American and foreign traditions. French haute cuisine, fresh seafood, chili dogs, and sushi—and there are eggs Benedict at the Sunday brunch and blue-corn tortillas to go with the carne asada.

A tradition for three decades, which is a very long time in Aspen, the **Copper Kettle** is at the base of Aspen Mountain off Galena Street (tel. 925-3151), offering the candlelit atmosphere of an old mining operation. There is a new special every evening from an international repertoire, as well as such regular entries as prime rib, veal, lamb, steaks, seafood, and chicken. It is open for dinner nightly, and there's live music in the piano bar.

For good, simple dining, **The Shaft,** on Cooper Street (tel. 925-1483), serves dinner only in a mining-town atmosphere, specializing in barbecued ribs, chicken, steaks, and daily specials, as well as homemade linguine with clam sauce, and every night there is a chicken or beef pot au feu served with homemade Italian-style bread. Full bar service is available.

2. CENTRAL COLORADO

BRECKENRIDGE: Another community founded with a gold strike is Breckenridge, 80 miles west of Denver, reached via I-70 west to Frisco and Colo. 9 south. The town was named for John C. Breckinridge, who was vice-president of the U.S. when the town was founded in 1860. But when he joined the Confederate forces in the Civil War, the residents changed the name of the town—by one letter—to Breckenridge, in a show of Union patriotism.

Western whimsy was rife from the earliest times. An 1867 report in the Denver *Rocky Mountain News* described the town as "a pretty site for a city with the Blue River running by, suggesting a spacious wharf and a line of piers to ape the institutions of New York, Boston, and those other little down east towns." This was all it needed for wags to found the Breckenridge Navy in 1869, commanded by Capt. Sam Adams, who claimed still to be exploring for a passage from the east to the Pacific. In any case he had one advantage, for Breckenridge, at 9,600 feet, had a downhill shot to the ocean to the west all the way. Four boats were outfitted with equipment and crews and launched in the Blue River, supposedly heading for California.

During the mining boom of the 1870s, a 21-mile-long flume was built to bring in water for hoses used to wash away riverbanks in order to expose lodes of quartz and gold ore. Nozzles of those great hoses are displayed today on the courthouse grounds.

Sons of Breckenridge who attained a certain fame were Edwin Carter, a naturalist whose stuffed-bird collection became the nucleus of a permanent exhibit of native fauna at the Museum of Natural History in Denver (his museum here stands on Ridge Street), and Fr. John L. Dyer, the Snowshoe Itinerant, who traveled all year into mining camps, even during the rough winter, to bring religion to the miners. He figures in one of the stained-glass portraits in the State Capitol rotunda in Denver. The biggest hunk of gold ever found in the U.S., weighing 13 pounds 7 ounces, called Tom's Baby, came out of the Gold Flake Mine in 1887, the find of Breckenridge miners Tom Groves and Jerry Lytton, who celebrated the good luck by inventing the Tom and Jerry in a local bar room.

The famous Breckenridge Navy was fated to be reborn in 1898 when Commander Ben Revitt's North American Gold Dredging Co. sent out a fleet of nine dredgers in the Blue River and adjoining streams. They ripped up river bottoms to pull up rock from which ore was separated by an Australian machine, and continued in operation until the onset of World War II. After the war life was very quiet in the town, which nevertheless continued its role as county seat. The modern era as a resort started when the ski area opened in 1961.

A historical walking tour of **Breckenridge Historic Park** begins at the visitor information center. The park has the old Tiger assay office and a miner's cabin from the 1880s. The office was moved here from its site in Tiger and has a period assay laboratory. Miners' tools and period furnishings are of interest in the cabin. A simulated mine and a Victorian house are being added to the attractions in the park, on French Street between Lincoln and Washington.

A scenic driving trip on Boreas Pass Road goes along an old grade of a narrow-gauge railroad, the Denver, South Park & Pacific, which climbed through 11,482-foot **Boreas Pass** and was the highest narrow-gauge line in the U.S. Many overlooks give great views of the town and the Blue River Valley below. Baker's tank is a restored relic of the railroading days; there is a picnic table at the site. At a point 1.8 miles farther, just below the timberline, is a wooden ore tipple identifying the site of the old 7:40 Mine. Remains of old snow sheds that protected the track are seen at the summit of Boreas Pass, once the site of the highest U.S. post office (no longer in existence). The legend is that a circus train, failing to make the grade here, unloaded its elephants, and the beasts were then put to work pulling the train through the pass.

To make a circle tour, continue to U.S. 285 past the village of **Como,** then southwest to **Fairplay,** site of the world's only monument to a burro (a miner's beast named Prunes). During the last weekend of every July a pack burro race up to the Continental Divide honors the animal's memory. North of Fairplay on Colo. 9 is the town of **Alma,** highest town in the U.S., near the remains of old mining camps to the west: Buckskin Joe, Park City, and New London. A mile and a half north of Alma on the slopes of Mount Bross is an ancient stand of bristlecone pines over 1,000 years old. A detailed map of this trip is available in an "explorer's kit" given free at the visitor center in Breckenridge.

Travel Services

Police emergency number is 911. . . . For sleigh rides, get in touch with **Alpine Adventures** at the Peak 9 base area (tel. 453-0111). . . . For horseback riding, apply at **Breckenridge Inn Stables,** 600 S. Ridge St. (tel. 453-2333). Taxi service is provided by **Summit Taxi** (tel. 453-6464). . . . **Resort Express** (tel. 668-3856) buses make daily connections between Breckenridge and Stapleton International Airport. . . . **Road condition** and weather reports are had by calling 453-1090. For snow reports, call 900/410-SNOW.

For all travel services information, get in touch with the **Breckenridge Resort Co.** (tel. 303/453-4422).

Breckenridge Ski Area

There are three mountains at the Breckenridge Ski Area (tel. 453-2368): **Peak 8, Peak 9,** and **Peak 10,** with 107 runs on 50 miles of trails, making it one of the largest areas in the Rockies. Top-to-bottom novice and intermediate trails offer beginners skiing on the entire mountain, not just the lower slopes. The front and back bowls offer challenges to expert skiers, and there are three other mountains included in the lift tickets: Copper Mountain, Keystone, and Arapahoe (see following entries). Three four-person detachable chair lifts are among a total of 14 that carry 22,000 skiers an hour; they have the advantage of detaching at the beginning and end of rides, so they can be slowed down for safe, easy loading and unloading. The management here, a subsidiary of Aetna Insurance, also owns the Aspen Mountain, Buttermilk, and Snowmass areas in Aspen.

Elevations are 12,000 feet for Peak 8, 11,460 feet for Peak 9, and 11,607 feet for Peak 10, the first with a vertical drop of 2,390 feet, the second with 1,803 feet, and the third with 1,389 feet. The longest run on Peak 8 is two miles; on Peak 9, 2.6 miles; on Peak 10, 1.5 miles. Beginners' and intermediates' trails make up half the area, with the remaining 50% in expert runs. Snowmaking equipment called "snoguns" assures a snow cover from the opening of the season in mid-November to the close at mid-April, covering 153 acres of the terrain from bottom to top. Annual snowfall here is 225 inches.

Lift rates are $30 for a full day for adults, $13 for children under 13 and for adults over 60. Weekly rates are $126. Ski-school classes meet from 10:15 a.m. to 12:15 p.m. and from 1:45 to 4 p.m., with full-day rates of $30; half day, $21. Beginner lesson includes a lift ticket. Ski rentals are $6 to $15 daily.

The **Nursery** at Peak 8 (tel. 453-2368) accepts children of all ages.

Food at the ski areas is had at the **Bergenhof** at the Peak 8 base, the **Peak 8 Restaurant** midway, the **Maggie Base Restaurant** at Peak 9, and the **Peak 9 Restaurant** at the top.

Cross-country skiing is organized at the **Nordic Ski Center** (tel. 453-6855) on Ski Hill Road near the Peak 8 base, a mile from town, with access to 15 miles of groomed trails. There are rental skis, a ski shop, and instruction available.

Where to Stay

Breckenridge has nearly 100 condominium complexes renting accommodations by day, weekend, week, or longer to skiers and vacationers. They are in all price categories, and can be booked along with lift tickets, ski school, ski rental, and transportation with the "one-call system" set up by the **Breckenridge Resort Co.** (tel. 303/453-4422).

A few lodges and inns in Breckenridge include the **Beaver Run Resort,** at the base of chair lift D, Breckenridge, CO 80424 (tel. 303/453-6000, or toll free 800/525-2253), open all year, with an on-site commercial center of shops, restaurants, and a nightclub, an indoor-outdoor pool, saunas, Jacuzzis, hot tubs, and an exercise room. Over 600 rooms and over 200 condominium apartments are available; rooms range from $95 double in winter, $70 in summer. Moss rock fireplaces, in-room movies and cable television, private balconies, and immediate access to two ski lifts are visitor attractions. There are also tennis courts, an indoor golf course, and a ski shop.

Blue River Condominiums, at 580 Colo. 9, Breckenridge, CO 80424 (tel. 303/453-2260), is open all year and has 36 units in a setting of aspen and spruce five miles south of town, offering two-bedroom apartments with dishwashers, dryers, and television at $130 in season.

Where to Eat

Wild game dishes are the thing at the **Briar Rose,** 109 E. Lincoln St. (tel. 453-9948). Appetizers here might be escargots, crab stuffed mushrooms, or frogs' legs, and there is a separate menu for "aged steaks cut in our own kitchen." Quail, rabbit, and Canadian walleye compete with such specialties as elk, venison, antelope, and buffalo, when available. The prime rib, cooked to allow the flavor of the rib cap to melt through the full roast, may be used up early in the evening because "this method limits the number of ribs that we can cook nightly," according to the management. A favorite dessert here is the chocolate Bavarian cream pie.

German cuisine is the attraction at **Weber's,** 200 N. Main St. (tel. 453-9464), where choices include sauerbraten, wienerschnitzel à la Holstein (with egg, anchovies, and capers), kassler rippchen, and bratwurst, each served with a hearty German soup, bread with sweet cream butter, tossed green salad, red cabbage or sauerkraut, and egg noodles or potato—and dessert with coffee too.

CRESTED BUTTE: Lying 230 miles southwest of Denver via U.S. 285, U.S. 50, and Colo. 135, **Crested Butte Mountain Ski Area** (tel. 303/349-2222, or toll free 800/525-4220) has eight chair lifts and a T-bar lift reaching the top of slopes with a 2,150-foot vertical drop. Runs, the longest being two miles, are nearly equally divided among novice, intermediate, and expert categories. An additional 350 acres called "the outer limits" draws expert powder-snow skiers when conditions are right. Snowfall averages 23 feet per year at altitudes ranging from 9,000 to 11,250 feet. There are 42 maintained downhill trails.

Lift tickets are $28 for adults, $15 for children. The American Teaching Method is used at the ski school, which costs $30 for a full day. A three-level proficiency rating called the Star Test is also available to skiers who want their skiing judged by experts. Gold, silver, or bronze Star Test pins go to those who complete it. Ski rental is $10.50 daily, $7.50 for children. **Buttetopia** is a day-care center for children, where for $35 a day they get a day of skiing with lunch and equipment, and looking-after while parents ski by themselves. Cross-country skiing is done on six miles of maintained trails where there are regular moonlight tours. Professional guides also lead treks through national forest trails all the way to Aspen, 20 miles to the north, on overnight bivouacs.

Travel Services

Crested Butte has access by air via **Gunnison County Airport,** 30 miles south, with daily nonstop flights to Dallas and Chicago via American Airlines. United makes flights between Denver and Gunnison every day of the year. Gunnison is also served by **Greyhound/Trailways** bus service from Denver.

In spite of this proximity to air transport, **Mount Crested Butte** is far less frequented than other major ski resorts, and waits of over five minutes in line at the lifts are practically unknown. Instead of the artificial Bavarian architecture found at Vail and Aspen and other resorts, the town of Crested Butte is satisfied with its authentic Victorian image—it has been declared a National Historic District. Among rarities is the mounted head of the world-record elk shot in these mountains, now displayed in a Crested Butte gas station.

All travel service information for Crested Butte and area is available from the **Crested Butte Chamber of Commerce** (tel. 303/349-6438).

Where to Stay

Crested Butte accommodations include **Crested Butte Lodge,** on the slopeside at 21 Emmons Rd., Crested Butte, CO 81224 (tel. 303/349-7555, or toll free 800/282-2013, 800/521-5970 in Colorado), with an indoor pool, saunas, a Jacuzzi, shops, a restaurant, and 97 units, rooms and apartments with kitchens and fireplaces, open winter and summer (but closed spring and fall). Winter rates for doubles run $74 to $140.

A Victorian bed-and-breakfast inn offers a warm welcome to skiers a couple of miles from the slopes at the **Claim Jumper,** 704 Whiterock, Crested Butte, CO 81224 (tel. 303/349-6471). One of the houses open for seasonal visits to unique sites in the Crested Butte National Historic District, the inn has a cheerful parlor furnished with antiques and a sunny breakfast room, as well as three bedrooms with brass beds. There are two full-size bathrooms, in one of which the original claw-foot tub still stands. In a separate room is a redwood hot tub and a full sauna. The inn is across the street from the Town Park, a center of various activities throughout the year, and just 100 yards from the departure point of the free shuttle bus to the ski slopes.

The hosts, Jim and Nancy Harlow, have named all the rooms for local places and characters: the Annie Perko Room is named for an aging former miner, a local woman known for using a ski pole as a walking cane. This room, done in mauve wallpaper and gray carpeting, has a rosewood dresser with a bevelled mirror. Another room, Poverty Gulch, gets its name from a wilderness area near town; its color scheme is a soft blue, set off by a bright patchwork quilt on the bed. Oh-Be-Joyful is a hiking area near town that is due to become designated as a wilderness tract; the town's Baptist church also shares this name. This room has wallpaper in a hunter's green, with beige carpeting that sets off the white iron bed and a school desk that belonged to Jim Harlow's grandfather. The hot-tub room is named the Red Lady for its view of the Red Lady Bowl, 2,000 feet above the town; the sauna room is named the Jokerville for an early mine.

Small children are not accepted, nor is smoking allowed. Rates are $80 to $100 double, including breakfast for two.

Where to Eat

Best in Crested Butte is the **Soupçon,** 127A Elk Ave. (tel. 349-5448), a French restaurant serving such specialties as escargots Monaco, roast duckling, and veal piccata. It is open nightly for dinner only from 6 p.m.

ARAPAHOE BASIN–KEYSTONE MOUNTAIN: The Arapahoe Basin
is the highest ski area on the continent served with ski lifts, at a summit elevation of 12,450 feet, and has half its terrain above the timberline to provide a good deal of open-bowl skiing. It is located 75 miles west of Denver via I-70 to the Dillon exit, then on U.S. 6 up to the Basin. Both Arapahoe and Keystone Mountain are ski areas operated by the Keystone Resort. For snow reports, call 468-4111.

Arapahoe is noteworthy for its long season, opening in mid-November and continuing into June. It has a vertical drop of 1,670 feet, with 10% beginners' slopes, 50% intermediate, and 40% expert. The West Wall and Pallavacini trails are famous challenges for powder hounds and mogul masters. Free shuttle buses run between lodges and both ski areas. There are also free bus runs morning and afternoon to the nearby ski areas of Copper Mountain and Breckenridge (see entries in this section).

Keystone Mountain has a 2,340-foot vertical drop, from its top at 11,640 feet to its base at 9,300 feet. It opens early, in mid-October, and stays open to late April. It has the largest snowmaking system in the Rockies, covering 75% of the mountain from top to bottom. The longest run on Keystone is three miles long. Some 25% of the runs here are novice class, 50% intermediate, and 25% expert. It has nine chair lifts and a Poma, as well as the world's fastest gondola.

North Peak, directly behind Keystone Mountain, is reached by the River Run gondola or any of the Keystone chair lifts, and has a 1,600-foot vertical drop. Two triple-chair lifts reach North Peak at an elevation of 11,660 feet. Thirteen runs, covering 200 acres, are open on North Peak for lighted night skiing, to 10:30 p.m. every night. Night lift tickets good from 4 to 10:30 p.m. cost $22. Night-skiing information may be had by calling 468-4173. Skiers are warned to stay on lighted trails: "Night skiers found skiing unlighted runs will be prosecuted to the full extent of the law."

Lift rates are interchangeable between Keystone Mountain, North Peak, and Arapahoe Basin. A full day costs $26; children under 13, $10. Adults aged 60 to 69 are charged $16; those over 70 ski free. Equipment rental is $15, $10 for children. "Performance" rentals of racing equipment are $25.

A **Children's Center** cares for kids up to age 12 at $28 daily (except infants, who cost $32). A "snow play" program including ski equipment for kids 3 years of age and older costs $32 daily. Keystone has four restaurants or snackbars at the base or on the slopes. Arapahoe has a restaurant at the base and a barbecue at the midway point.

The **cross-country touring center** (tel. 468-4188) provides cross-country and telemark lessons, as well as tours by day and by moonlight for both novice and experienced skiers over 20 miles of maintained trails in the Arapaho National Forest. A moonlight tour with a snack is $36, and a full-day tour with lunch, $34. For all ski school information, call 468-4170.

Other activities include **ice skating** at the outdoor skating center, the largest such facility in the U.S., boasting a Zamboni ice-grooming machine (open December to March). Sessions from 9 a.m. to 5 p.m. or 6 to 10 p.m. are $4, plus $2 skate rental. Sleigh-ride dinners to the **Soda Creek Homestead** include a steak dinner at $36.

Where to Stay

Keystone Resort (tel. 303/468-4242, or toll free 800/222-0188) operates a hotel and condominiums rented short-term. The complex has 20 restaurants, some nightspots, shops, an ice skating area, ten swimming pools, saunas, indoor tennis courts, and Jacuzzis. A Keystone charge card, issued to all guests, allows them to charge all purchases and activities in the resort. Children under 12 stay free.

The hotel has 152 rooms, most with private balconies and all with cable television. Some also have sitting rooms and loft bedrooms. Within the lodge are three restaurants and two bars. There are also 900 one- to four-bedroom condos available. A three-level pedestrian mall in Keystone Village has a variety of arts-and-crafts shops and ski-tog emporia; it is open year round.

Rates for rooms in the lodge run $144 double in winter; lower rates are in force in summer.

To book rooms, get in touch with **Keystone Central Reservations**, P.O. Box 38, Keystone, CO 80435 (tel. 303/468-4242).

Where to Eat

Restaurants at Keystone Resort offer a considerable variety. Continental dining is had in the **Garden Room** (tel. 468-2316 for reservations), overlooking Keystone Lake. The **Bighorn Steakhouse** offers steaks, seafood, and a big salad bar. A coffeehouse, the **Edgewater Café,** is open for breakfasts, lunches, and dinners.

At the base of Keystone Mountain there is **Gassy's,** for lunches, snacks, and bar drinks; the **Greatest Crêpe Wagon,** for desserts and crêpes; the **Last Lift Bar,** for snacks and bar drinks; and the **Mountain House Cafeteria,** for breakfasts, lunch, and snacks.

At the top of Keystone Mountain is the **Barbecue at the Summit,** an indoor-or-outdoor eating place; the **High Noon Café,** for cafeteria breakfasts and lunches; and **Soup's On,** for soup and quiches.

At Arapahoe Basin, the **Alpenglow Cafeteria** has breakfasts and lunches, and barbecue at the **Alpine Hut.**

Travel Services

Resort Express provides rides between Stapleton and Keystone by reservation (tel. 468-4200), with runs departing about every two hours all day during the winter skiing season.

COPPER MOUNTAIN RESORT: "The most nearly perfect ski mountain in the United States" is the description of this sports area by officials of the U.S. Forest Service—the resort lies within the Arapaho National Forest. The 290-acre Spaulding Bowl was added in 1985. There are 1,180 acres of skiing used by some 10,000 skiers daily in this area reached via I-70, 75 miles west of Denver. The telephone number for the **Copper Mountain Resort Ski Area** is 303/968-2882; for **snow reports**, 968-2100; and for reservations, call **Copper Mountain Central Reservations** (tel. toll free 800/458-8386).

A planned village provides accommodations, restaurants, and shops at the base of the mountain, and there is skating on a lighted lake and cross-country skiing on 20 miles of maintained trails. The season is early November to late April.

Copper Mountain has a 2,760-foot vertical drop between a 9,600-foot base and a 12,360-foot summit. The longest of the 75 trails is 2.8 miles; they are divided into 25% for novices, 40% for intermediates, and 35% for experts. Trails are served by nine double-chair lifts, six triple-chair lifts, and four surface lifts. Six trails covering 200 acres are served when necessary by snowmaking equipment. Open bowl and glade skiing is offered in Spaulding Bowl, near the older runs.

Lift rates are $27 for adults, $12 for children; adults over age 62 pay $14. A newcomer package at $37 includes equipment rental, lessons, and a lift ticket. Otherwise, ski rental is $12 daily. American Training Method lessons at $30 for a full day meet at 9:45 a.m. and 12:45 p.m. Nursery care for children is available from 8 a.m. to 4:30 p.m.

For **restaurants,** there is a Base Cafeteria, a cafeteria at Union Creek, a bar and deli in Jacques Loft, and a deli at Solitude Station at mid-mountain. Food is also served in the "B" Lift Clubhouse, in the Columbine Café in the Village Square, in the Plaza Restaurant in Mountain Plaza, and at Rackets in the Copper Mountain Racquet and Athletic Club.

Resort Express operates a van between Stapleton International Airport in Denver and Copper Mountain; for reservations, call **Apex Travel** (tel. toll free 800/231-3425). **Rocky Mountain Airways** serves nearby Avon STOLport from Stapleton. **Greyhound/Trailways** buses make daily runs between Stapleton and Copper Mountain. Free **shuttle buses** run around the village every quarter hour through the skiing season from 7:30 a.m. to 10 p.m. **Bus service** between Copper Mountain and other nearby ski areas (Keystone, Breckenridge, Arapahoe Basin) leaves daily, morning and afternoon, from Mountain Plaza.

For **cross-country** skiers there are ten instructors available with classes meeting daily at 10:30 a.m. and 1:30 p.m. Rates are $18; ski rental is $9, or $6 for children. Information is available from the **Cross Country Center** (tel. 968-2882).

DILLON: Somewhat less expensive winter accommodations for skiers at Breckenridge, Keystone, and Copper Mountain are available in the little resort town of Dillon, 75 miles west of Denver via I-70, on the shore of a high-altitude lake with a 25-mile shoreline, **Lake Dillon,** where there are all water sports in the summer and hiking in nearby mountains and primitive areas of **Arapaho National Forest.**

Where to Stay

Dillon Super 8 Motel, 808 Little Beaver Trail, Dillon, CO 80435 (tel. 303/468-8888, or toll free 800/843-1991), is open year round near the exit of I-70, a mile from the lake, with direct bus service to the ski areas. Rates are $44 double in winter, $32 in summer.

Holiday Inn, at the I-70 interchange, Dillon, CO 80435 (tel. 303/668-5000, or toll free 800/HOLIDAY), has 202 units, tennis courts, and a Holidome indoor recreation area with swimming pool, whirlpool, sunbathing, and a fireplace in the lounge, a cocktail bar, a game room, and a restaurant. Rates are $74 to $96 in winter, $35 to $50 in summer.

For central lodging reservations in and around Dillon and Silverthorne, get in touch with **Lake Dillon Resort Assoc.,** P.O. Box 446, Dillon, CO 80435 (tel. 303/468-6222, or toll free 800/525-9824).

3. STEAMBOAT SPRINGS

A vast mountain with a 10,500-foot elevation, **Steamboat Ski Area** (tel. 303/879-6111) has 78 runs and glades blanketed with the finest champagne powder, over a huge area of 1,400 acres and a 3,600-foot vertical drop. Uphill capacity with 20 lifts is 27,030 skiers per hour. It is located 160 miles northwest of Denver via I-70 to exit 205, then Colo. 9 and U.S. 40 to the mountain.

The area includes **Sunshine Peak, Storm Peak, Thunderhead Peak,** and **Christie Peak** in an entire mountain range that is part of the area. The longest run, High Noon, is 2½ miles. Trails are divided into three categories: beginner, intermediate, and expert. Snowfall averages 325 to 350 inches annually, with the skiing season on from the last week of November to the third week of April. Heaviest snowfall comes in January and February, with the sunniest winter weeks during March and April.

Lift tickets are $29 for adults, $18 for children; those over 65 years of age, free. In "low-season" weeks lift tickets are $27 for adults and $16 for children. American Training Method instruction classes in various levels of ability meet at 8:45 a.m., 11:15 a.m., and 1:45 p.m. Rates are $32 for a full day, $34 (with lunch) for children. Various ski shops rent equipment averaging $12.50 daily. Shops at the area are **Sport Stalker** (tel. toll free 800/332-5530) and **Storm Hut** (tel. 879-1645). **Nursery ski school** is $34 daily, including care and lessons.

Among special events at Steamboat are spectacular **torchlight parades** conducted by ski instructors holding torches and skiing down the slopes en masse after dark—seven such events scheduled through the winter. Also famous in Steamboat is the **winter carnival,** held since the early part of this century—the oldest such carnival in the U.S. Besides skiing events, there are balloon races, sled races, a parade, and fireworks; it takes place over a whole week of early February.

Cross-country skiing is taught by seven instructors of the **Steamboat Touring Center** (tel. 879-8180), with lessons morning or afternoon at $15.75 for an hour and a half. Trail pass is $5; equipment rental, $8.50.

Cross-country has a long tradition here, beginning back in 1914 when a Norwegian named Carl Howelson led local folk on a ski tour, resulting in the establishment of the **Steamboat Springs Winter Sports Club,** which today runs a number of competitions in alpine, nordic, and freestyle skiing.

TRAVEL SERVICES: Direct air service from Stapleton International Airport in Denver to Steamboat Springs airport (three miles from the ski area) is via

Rocky Mountain Airways (tel. toll free 800/525-0280) which makes flights daily. **Alpine Taxi** (tel. 879-2800) meets all incoming flights. Two round trips daily between Denver and Steamboat Springs are provided by **Greyhound/Trailways,** which also runs a separate express service out of Stapleton.

In the village of Steamboat Springs, city buses run between town and mountain on the half hour from about 7 a.m. to 1 a.m.; fare is 50¢. For details, call 879-3717.

Car rentals in Steamboat Springs include **Hertz** (tel. 879-8644) and **National** (tel. 879-0800).

For all **police emergency** purposes, dial 911.

For all travel service and other information, get in touch with the **Chamber/Resort Association,** on Lincoln Avenue (in Steamboat Villa mall), Steamboat Springs, CO 80487 (tel. 303/879-0740, or toll free 800/332-3204 in Colorado).

WHERE TO STAY: The **Overlook Hotel,** 1¼ miles east of town on U.S. 40, Steamboat Springs, CO 80487 (tel. 303/879-2900), has 117 rooms, some with two or three interconnected, some with kitchens. There is a heated pool, sauna, whirlpool, two tennis courts, and a laundry, plus a restaurant and a lounge. Rates are $48 to $57 double.

The **S Bar S Ranch,** 44285 Routt County Rd., Steamboat Springs, CO 80487 (tel. 303/879-0788), on the Elk River, is open all year with modest, low-cost accommodations on a working cattle ranch. Rooms have propane heat, linens, and equipped kitchens, and there is riding and free trout fishing in season. Rates are $26 to $34 double, depending on season.

Sheraton Steamboat Resort, 2200 Village Inn Court, Steamboat Springs, CO 80487 (tel. 303/879-2220, or toll free 800/848-8878), near the gondola at the ski lift, has 292 units, with ski-in and ski-out facility, two restaurants, two lounges, and an 18-hole golf course. There are tennis courts, two heated pools, saunas, and hot tubs. There are rooms as well as housekeeping units of one to four rooms, many with fireplaces and balconies. There is a coin laundry. Rates are $80 to $120 double in winter, $49 to $69 in summer.

The **Vista Verde Ranch,** P.O. Box 465, Steamboat Springs, CO 80477 (tel. 303/879-3858), on Seedhouse Road in nearby Clark, offers old-fashioned hand-hewn log cabins along with three meals per day if wanted—"good food and lots of it" is the claim. The place, 25 miles north of Steamboat, is open year around but is a special favorite of skiers. The ranch is bordered by the Routt River and adjoins the million-acre Routt National Forest, scene of countless cross-country skiing trails. Other activities around the ranch are snowshoeing, ice fishing, and riding in a horse-drawn sleigh.

Cabins sleep six and have fireplaces, carpeting, and kitchens for guests who want to do their own cooking. At the main-lodge house there are regular wine-and-cheese parties at the end of the day. This is a working ranch with various live-stock, including Belgian draft horses which pull the feed sled into the snowy fields. Fox, coyote, and elk abound in the area; the ranch provides guided tours traveling by dogsled into the national forest lands. The ranch gets an average of 400 inches of snow yearly.

Fresh-baked breads and pastries are served at breakfast, while lunches may be had at the lodge or packed to go. Home-raised beef supplies many of the dinners. Meals are served family style by the fireplace in the main lodge by hosts Mr. and Mrs. Frank Brophy.

The spa building occupies a hilltop nearby, overlooking the Hinman Valley, and houses a 12-person whirlpool, a sauna, a cold tub, showers, and an exercise room. A wide sundeck invites sunbathing or rolling in the snow between dips in the warm whirlpool.

Rates include use of all ski trails on and adjoining the property, all facilities in the spa building, and snowshoes and sleigh rides. Regular winter season rates for two people in a cabin are $95, $10 for each additional person; add $25 per guest for three meals a day. All-day guided ski tours cost $20; ski rental, $8; and ski lessons, $8.

4. VAIL

Vail is the largest single mountain ski area on the American continent, with 60 miles of runs, two great powder bowls, 18 lifts (among which are the world's only high-speed detachable quad lifts), and 260 acres of snowmaking capacity on the mountain. It is located 100 miles west of Denver via I-70 and is open from the last week in November to the last week of April. It has a vertical drop of 3,150 feet between its 8,100-foot base and 11,250-foot summit. The longest run is 3.75 miles; trails are tagged 30% novice, 40% intermediate, and 30% expert.

Originally land of the Utes, the Gore Valley, as it was named for its European explorer in 1854, was the scene of "spite fires" in which the forests were set alight by Indians angry at the invasions of gold seekers in the 1860s. These burnings created wide, open ski terrain on the ridge and back bowl of Vail Mountain that has made Vail famous.

A few sheep ranchers were the only inhabitants until U.S. 6 was built through Vail Pass in 1939, the pass named for a highway engineer. When the war started the U.S. Army established Camp Hale 20 miles from Vail for the training of the only mountain units that saw action in the war. Among those young ski troopers were several who returned after the war to establish the new ski area of Vail. Development of the mountain land, within the White River National Forest, began in 1962, and history was made after a fashion when an entire ski resort was completed and ready to open within a year—by December 1963. It has the first U.S. gondola lift that took skiers to a skiing bowl in North America.

It was already among the three largest in the U.S. when it opened, and in its first season played host to the U.S. Olympic ski training camp, and held an Olympic qualifying event, the Vail Trophy Race. (In 1989 Vail is host to the World Alpine Ski Championships.) By 1964 additional ski-lift capacity made Vail the largest ski area in the U.S. A sister resort, Beaver Creek, ten miles away in a secluded valley, uses interchangeable lift tickets with Vail.

Lift rates are $30 daily, $20 for children. American Training Method instruction is given from 9:45 a.m. to 3:45 p.m. daily for all abilities at $35 for a full day. Ski-equipment rental is $12 for adults, $9 for children. Nursery care for ages 3 to 6, including lunch, is $35 daily. Several eating places are located at the base and at the summit of the ski area.

TRAVEL SERVICES: Transportation to Vail by air is via **Rocky Mountain Airways** to Avon from Denver, with two to five flights daily; for flight information, call toll free 800/525-0280. **Greyhound/Trailways** buses (tel. 303/476-5137) serve Vail daily from Denver. For transportation around Vail, call **Summit Taxi** (tel. 476-6816).

Rental cars are available from **Hertz,** in the Vail Village Transportation Center, 241 S. Frontage Rd. (tel. 476-5133), and from **National,** also in the Vail Village Transportation Center (tel. 476-6634).

The **Vail Resort** telephone is 476-1000. **Ski reports** on snow conditions in Vail are available in Vail (tel. 476-4888) and Denver (tel. 571-VAIL).

To make reservations, and for all travel service information, call the **Vail Resort Association** (tel. 303/476-1000, or toll free 800/525-3875).

WHERE TO STAY: Regular rates apply in Vail over the Christmas holidays and in February and March. Reduced rates are in effect up to December 19, and during most of January and April.

Luxury Accommodations Near the Slopes

Sonnenalp, 20 Vail Rd., Vail, CO 81657 (tel. 303/476-5656), 300 yards from the Vista Bahn and chair lift no. 1, is a resort encompassing three properties called the Bavaria Haus, the Swiss Chalet, and the Austria Haus, with a total of 185 rooms. There are three restaurants and three lounges in the complex, all offering entertainment. Rates begin at $135 double.

The **Lodge at Vail,** 174 E. Gore Creek Dr., Vail, CO 81657 (tel. 303/476-5011, or toll free 800/231-0136), in the heart of Vail Village at the base of chair lift no. 1 and the Vista Bahn, is Vail's original deluxe hotel. There is dining in both the Café Arlberg and in the Wildflower Inn. There is also a lounge, Mickey's, as well. Rates here begin at $160.

A bit farther (about half a mile away) from the gondola is the **Westin Hotel,** 1300 Westhaven Dr., Vail, CO 81657 (tel. 303/476-7111, or toll free 800/228-3000), in Lions Head. It has 148 units, and a private "skiway" return ski run to bring skiers back to the hotel from the slopes. There is formal dining in Alfredo's restaurant, casual fare in the Café, and relaxing in the Lobby Lounge. Rates are $135 to $195 double.

Moderately Priced Accommodations At or Near the Slopes

Holiday House (the Holiday Inn at Vail), 13 Vail Rd., Vail, CO 81657 (tel. 303/476-5631, or toll free 800/HOLIDAY), is a remodeled mountain lodge 300 yards from the Vista Bahn and chair lift no. 1 in Vail Village. It has 116 hotel rooms and four suites. There is nightly entertainment in the 1800s Bar, and dining in two restaurants, the Fondue Stube and the Gold Rush Dining Room. Rates start at $79, and there's no charge for children staying with their parents.

Lion Square Lodge, 660 W. Lions Pl., Vail, CO 81657 (tel. 303/476-2281, or toll free 800/525-5788), in Lions Head, is 25 yards from chair lift no. 8 and the gondola. In a prime location on Gore Creek, next to Vail Mountain, the lodge has 28 hotel rooms and 90 condominiums, plus dining and a bar in the K. B. Ranch Company restaurant. Hotel rooms begin at $85 double.

Manor Vail Lodge, 595 E. Vail Valley Dr., Vail, CO 81657 (tel. 303/476-5651, or toll free 800/525-9165), has 123 suites and condominiums at the base of Golden Peak on the east side of the village, 50 yards from chair lifts nos. 6 and 12. The Lord Gore restaurant is open for breakfast and dinner. Rates begin at $76.

The Mark, at 715 W. Lions Head Circle, Vail, CO 81657 (tel. 303/476-4444, or toll free 800/228-9290), 200 yards from the gondola in Lions Head, a Marriott resort, has 350 hotel rooms and 50 suites. The resort has two restaurants—Windows, for luxury dining and Center Court, for family fare—and three lounges. Room rates begin at $80.

Montaneros, 641 W. Lions Head Circle, Vail, CO 81657 (tel. 303/476-2491, or toll free 800/523-6327), has 42 condominiums of various sizes located within 50 yards of the gondola and chair lift no. 8 in Lions Head. There are also one-bedroom units, each with a private balcony overlooking the ski runs, renting at $95 double.

Tivoli, 386 Hanson Ranch Rd., Vail, CO 81657 (tel. 303/476-6515), is 200 yards from chair lifts nos. 1 and 6 and the Vista Bahn in Vail Village. Hot breakfasts are served in the dining room, and there's the Après Ski Bar. This European-style guesthouse has 38 rooms with rates starting at $78 double.

Vail Village Inn, 100 E. Meadow Dr., Vail, CO 81657 (tel. 303/476-5622, or toll free 800/445-4014), is 250 yards from the Vista Bahn in Vail Village, with 62 hotel rooms and eight suites. The Village Inn Pancake House is on the premises, as well as the Ambrosia restaurant for luxury dining and the Alpenrose for plainer fare. Room prices start at $75.

BEAVER CREEK: A relatively new area 110 miles west of Denver via I-70, Beaver Creek Ski Area (tel. 303/949-5750) is open from Thanksgiving to mid-April and has a 3,340-foot vertical drop, from a summit at 11,440 feet to a base at 8,100 feet. The longest run is 2¾ miles. Runs are tagged 25% novice, 40% intermediate, and 35% expert. There are five triple- and three double-chair lifts. Rates are the same as at Vail: $30 daily, $20 for children. Ski-school, rental equipment, and nursery ski school facilities are also similar to those at Vail. Thirteen trails, covering 158 acres, are served by snowmaking machines. There are two restaurants at the ski area base. Transportation is free to the village via Beaver Creek Transit.

Nordic ski terrain along the Beaver Creek golf course and on return trails in the ski area is open to cross-country skiers.

Accommodation at Beaver Creek is mostly in condos; for information and reservations, contact **Beaver Creek Central Reservations,** P.O. Box 915, Avon, CO 81620 (tel. 303/949-5750, or toll free 800/525-2257). Beaver Creek village lodges and other facilities are still being built and will all be completed, it is said, by 1990, by which date it is expected the ski area will have 65 trails open.

5. WINTER PARK

WINTER PARK: Winter Park, 70 miles west of Denver via I-70 and U.S. 40, is another major Colorado ski area with two complexes of trails in Winter Park Mountain and Mary Jane Mountain totalling 56 ski trails. Open from mid-November to late April, the area has a 2,120-foot vertical drop from its 11,125-foot summit, and 14 chair lifts. The longest run is two miles. The slopes are graded beginner level, intermediate, intermediate-expert, and expert. Eleven of the trails involving 200 acres are served by snowmaking machinery.

One of the delights for visitors departing from Denver—and for regular skiers who live in the Denver area, of course—is the **ski train** that takes carloads of happy skiers to Winter Park on Saturday and Sunday only on a spectacular and cheery ride on the **Denver & Rio Grande Railroad** (tel. 629-5533). Though the 56-mile trip takes 2½ hours, not breaking any speed records, it is nevertheless the only exclusive ski train operating in the U.S., and besides the scenery, travelers much enjoy the convivial atmosphere aboard.

Starting at 7:30 a.m. from Union Station in downtown Denver at an altitude of one mile above sea level, the ski train winds its way through the foothills of the Rockies, crossing canyons and ravines, clinging to narrow ledges above ice-crusted rivers, and shooting through 27 tunnels as it climbs into the mountains to the east portal of the Moffat Tunnel. Here, at an elevation of 9,185 feet, it enters the sixth-longest tunnel in the world to emerge six miles beyond on the west side of the Continental Divide—at the base of the Winter Park ski area.

The ski train has been running since the early 1950s, originally operating daily with 22 cars, but now reduced to weekend service only with nine somewhat funky yellow Pullman coaches built in 1915. In spite of the curtailed service, space aboard is in great demand. Tickets go on sale at 6:30 a.m. in Union Station in Denver on the Monday before the weekend departure, and sometimes are all sold out, for both the Saturday and Sunday runs, by noon Monday. For railroad buffs and lovers of scenic adventure the ride is a must at $18 round trip. Weekends in late February and March are times of eased demand.

Twenty miles west of Denver the train reaches a spot called Fireclay, where a so-called ghost train of rusting gondola cars loaded with boulders is stationed on the west side of the track. Its purpose is to keep high winds from blowing the ski train off its track. Two miles beyond, the train crosses a bridge into Coal Creek Canyon, from which point the twisting, narrow trackbed cuts through those 27 tunnels, ranging in length from 78 to 1,730 feet.

The railroad was the grand plan of a local financier, David Moffat, who in 1902 determined to make Denver into a major industrial center by providing it with a rail connection to the west, which it then lacked. Although there was train service via long detours to the north and south, there was nothing that cut through the wall of the Rockies directly to the west of the city. The Continental Divide made a strong barrier to railroad building, with its 30-foot snowdrifts, spring floods, and 4,000-foot elevation differential to be overcome between Denver and those heights.

Moffat's plan was to pierce through the mountains with tunnels, and then hang the rail line along the edge of canyons. Thus he could protect the line from the elements and make it run straight through to the West Coast. His enterprise nearly succeeded, working its way 128 miles into the Rockies, but the money was used up before there was a final success. The tracks ended 69 miles from the nearest railhead to the west at Steamboat Springs, and Moffat died a pauper.

But the line was completed a decade later by new investors. Its major drawback was Hell Hill, a formidable 23-mile stretch over Rollins Pass that would need 15 tons of coal to push a locomotive all the way to the summit. Moffat's original plan had to be fulfilled—piercing tunnels. Eighteen lives were lost in the drilling and digging, but in 1928 a tunnel 32,810 feet long—over six miles —was completed all the way through. Today the Moffat Tunnel is the high point of the trip, literally and figuratively, negotiated by the ski train during 12 minutes of darkness.

Lift ticket rates at Winter Park are $26 for adults, $12 for children; over age 70, free. Class lessons are $26 a day. Children's ski school, including lunch and all-day care, runs $38. Day care alone for kids 1 to 8 years costs $30. Equipment rental is $10 for adults, $8 for children.

There is scheduled express service between Stapleton International Airport in Denver and Winter Park several times daily in skiing season, at $12 one way. Reservations can be made by calling **Winter Park Central Reservations** (tel. 303/726-5587).

National Rental Car offers skierized cars at the Denver airport with dropoff service at Winter Park (tel. toll free 800/525-5225, 800/332-0530 in Colorado). **Trailways** buses (tel. 980-0730) make regular runs to and from Denver daily. For **train** information, call toll free 800/872-7245.

Restaurants at the ski areas include the West Portal Station at the base of Winter Park and the Snoasis Cafeteria midway; and at Mary Jane there is the Cafeteria and the Club Car, both at the base.

Reports on **highway conditions** west of Denver are available at 639-1111.

For all travel service information, get in touch with the **Winter Park Resort Chamber of Commerce** (tel. 303/726-8334).

SILVER CREEK: About 15 miles from Winter Park on U.S. 40, Silver Creek (tel. 303/887-3384, or toll free 800/526-0590) opened in 1982 with 16 trails on 150 acres of downhill terrain equipped with advanced snowmaking machines. The vertical drop is 970 feet from a 9,300-foot summit, and trails are

judged 30% beginner, 50% intermediate, and 20% expert. It is open from Thanksgiving to Easter.

There are four chair lifts, and **lift rates** are $18 per day, $9 for children, free for those over age 60. Ski-school rates are $22 daily, including lift tickets. Nursery care for kids goes for $25 daily. The lodge at the base has a saloon and restaurant.

The **Inn at Silver Creek,** on U.S. 40, Silver Creek, CO 80446 (tel. 303/ 887-2131), has 342 rooms, all with private decks, wet bars with sinks, and fireplaces. The inn also has three restaurants—the Deli, the Sunlight Café, and the Remington Room—as well as two lounges, the Black Bear and the Winchester Saloon. Rooms range in price from $56 to $110 double, depending on room size and season.

Train service is via the **Amtrak** (tel. 893-3911 in Denver, or toll free 800/ 421-8320) long-distance train, the *California Zephyr,* which stops here on its way between Chicago and the West Coast. **Greyhound/Trailways** (tel. 292-6111) makes two trips daily from Denver. The Silver Creek **shuttle bus** provides free service to Winter Park, as well as to Granby, Snow Mountain Ranch, and Grand Lake.

6. OTHER COLORADO SKI AREAS

As if the fabled sky-high powdered snows of the great mountain slopes of Aspen, Breckenridge, Steamboat, Vail, Winter Park, and their satellite areas were not already an overwhelming challenge for skiers of every skill and inclination, the state has still another two dozen ski areas to take care of those millions of skiers who flock here every winter from every part of the U.S. Though it would take half a lifetime to try out all the slopes in Colorado, the special advantages and attractions of the various resorts are noted in the entries to follow, to give some grasp of the variety in store for sportsfolk.

BERTHOUD PASS: The state's oldest ski area, Berthoud Pass, near Idaho Springs, is 60 miles west of Denver via I-70 and U.S. 40 at the top of Berthoud Pass, where the *base* of the skiing is already at 11,000 feet in altitude, and the summit 1,000 feet higher. Because of this height there is a long season for natural snowfall, with skiing from mid-October to mid-June. There is a good deal of powder snow offered in these heights—an annual average of 365 inches—with considerable areas best used by experts. Operations are restricted to Wednesday through Sunday. The longest run is 6,000 feet, and the trails are judged 90% advanced and 10% expert. There is a double-chair lift and a T-bar. Rates are $22 daily for lift tickets. Ski-school classes meet at 10 and 11 a.m. and 1:30 p.m., costing $18 for the full day. Ski rental is $10; for children, $7.

Direct bus connections are made on **Greyhound/Trailways** buses to and from Denver, making stops at Berthoud Pass. Accommodation is available at **Berthoud Pass Lodge** (tel. 303/572-8014), a rustic lodge with hostel-type lodging and a restaurant and lounge on the premises. Full travel services are available 12 miles north via U.S. 40 at Winter Park.

BROADMOOR: Five minutes' drive from the famous Broadmoor resort hotel in Colorado Springs is the Broadmoor ski area (tel. 303/578-6027), which has the Winter House restaurant and lounge at its base. A double-chair lift takes care of 600 skiers hourly over a length of 3,000 feet and a 600-foot drop from the 6,800-foot summit. There is snowmaking machinery in use when required. The area is only four miles from downtown Colorado Springs via U.S. 85/87 and Colo. 122.

The season runs from November to March. Of the trails, 60% are for novices, 20% for intermediates, and 20% for experts. Lift rates are $13. Ski classes meet morning and afternoon by reservation at $8 per hour. Ski rental is $10; for children, $7. Snacks and drinks are offered at the Winter House; elegant dining is available at the nearby Broadmoor Hotel (see the Colorado Springs section in Chapter XVIII). There is a free shuttle bus to and from the Broadmoor from the ski area, with connections to other points in the city on city buses.

CONQUISTADOR:
This small ski area in the San Isabel National Forest, six miles west of Westcliffe in south-central Colorado, has 15 trails marked from beginner to expert leading down from a 10,100-foot summit to a base 1,200 feet below. There is instruction in downhill and nordic skiing, and a restaurant and bar at the base. Conquistador is located 150 miles south of Denver via I-25, Colo. 115, Colo. 67, and Colo. 96. It is open daily from December to April. Its longest run is two miles, and its trails are graded as 25% for beginners, 50% for intermediates, and 25% for experts. There are three chair lifts and two Poma lifts. Lift rates are $16 daily, $9 for children, $13 for students and military personnel, free for those over 65. Lessons are $14 per session. Ski rental is $10; for children, $7. Almost the entire area is served by snowmaking machinery. Cross-country skiers have ten miles of maintained trails at the base area, and there are overnight ski tours and cookouts organized at the **Conquistador Nordic Center** (tel. 783-9206).

Castile Lodge, at the base of Conquistador Resort, Westcliffe, CO 81252 (tel. 303/783-9701, or toll free 800/325-4682), within walking distance of the slopes, has hotel rooms with satellite television, telephone, and equipped kitchenette, plus a lobby with a fireplace. Rates are $72 double, and discount lift tickets are offered with lodging packages.

There are several small motels and lodges in the Westcliffe area, including the **Antler Motel,** at the junction of Colo. 96 and 69S, Westcliffe, CO 81252 (tel. 303/783-2426), with doubles for $28; and the **Westcliffe Inn,** Colo. 68 and Hermit Road, Westcliffe, CO 81252 (tel. 303/783-9277), with doubles at $39. Both are within three to five miles of Conquistador.

For further information on the ski area, contact the **Conquistador Resort** (tel. 303/783-9206). For travel information, call the **Custer County Chamber of Commerce** (tel. 303/783-9163).

COOPER:
Ski Cooper is a small, expanding ski area ten miles north of Leadville, an interesting and historic mountain mining town, 100 miles from Denver via I-70 to Colo. 91 and U.S. 24. Within San Isabel National Forest, Cooper has good skiing for both alpine and telemark skiers in many glades and groomed trails, with views extending out over both sides of the Continental Divide. The summit here is at 11,700 feet, with a drop to the base of 1,200 feet. Operations go on daily from 9 a.m. to 4 p.m. The longest run is 1⅛ miles, with 30% judged for beginners, 40% for intermediates, and 30% for experts. There are two chair lifts and two surface lifts. Day lift rates are $16 for adults; children, $9. Full-day ski school costs $20. Ski rental is $9; for children, $7. Nursery care for children aged 2 to 6 is $15 daily. There is a restaurant at the base and full services in Leadville.

Cooper Ski Area telephone is 719/486-2277. For all travel service information, see the **Leadville Chamber of Commerce,** 809 Harrison Ave., Leadville, CO 80461 (tel. 719/486-3900).

Where to Stay
All accommodations for Cooper are down at Leadville, where there are a dozen inns, motels, and guesthouses.

The most interesting lodgings in town are at the recently reopened **Delaware Hotel,** 700 Harrison Ave., Leadville, CO 80461 (tel. 719/486-1418), a century-old hostelry in the middle of town with a fine three-story façade, windows decorated with stone arches, and fancy gingerbread carving along the roofline. Shops occupying space in the old building include a Victorian lounge, an ice-cream parlor, a poster shop, a clothing shop, an arts-and-crafts store, an artists' gallery, a fabric shop, and a photo shop. Double rooms rent for $38 to $50.

Another historic site is the **Mountain Mansion,** 129 W. 8th St., Leadville, CO 80461 (tel. 719/486-0655), a bed-and-breakfast establishment in a former state governor's house in which bedrooms and suites have fireplaces and are furnished with antiques. There is one suite available with cooking facilities, and the hostess, Ana Maria Nezol, originally from Argentina, offers Spanish lessons to anyone staying for more than a day or so. She also presides over Argentine cooking seminars. Rates are $48 double.

CUCHARA VALLEY: Located in the Cuchara Valley of southern Colorado, this resort (tel. 303/742-3163, or toll free 800/227-4436) is 185 miles south of Denver via I-25 south, U.S. 60 west, and Colo. 12 south to the town of Cuchara. A big attraction is skiing in the three glades of powder snow just off the mile-long chair lift no. 3. Two-thirds of the slopes are served by snowmaking machinery, and the season runs from November to April. This is the area in Colorado most accessible to visiting skiers from Texas, Oklahoma, and Kansas. It has a 1,562-foot vertical drop from its 10,800-foot summit, with its longest run 2½ miles. The terrain is 25% for beginners, 50% for intermediates, and 25% for experts. There are two chair lifts and a Poma lift. Rates are $18. Children pay $8, those aged 60 and over ski free. Ski-school lessons, two hours long in groups, cost $12. Ski rental is $12; for children, $8. There is food available at a base lodge.

Greyhound/Trailways service from Denver and Colorado Springs serves the town of La Veta, 14 miles distant, twice daily. Nearest air connection is via Pueblo or Alamosa, both 70 miles distant, via Rocky Mountain Airways.

Lodging may be reserved through **Cuchara Valley Resort Reservations,** P.O. Box 10, Cuchara, CO 81055 (tel. 303/742-3163, or toll free 800/227-4436). Rooms are available at **Aspen Leaf Village,** Panadero Avenue in Cuchara, offering units with kitchens and fireplaces; also at Sun Mountain and Sunwatcher.

ELDORA: Night skiing Wednesday through Saturday is one of the special attractions of this relatively small area 45 miles northwest of Denver via I-25, Colo. 36, and Colo. 119. The modest prices and 30 miles of cross-country trails draw many students from the University of Colorado at Boulder, just 20 miles away. There is a drop of 1,100 feet measured vertically from the 10,500-foot summit, served by four chair lifts. The season goes from mid-November to the first of April, and skiing goes on to 10 p.m. under the lights. The longest run is a mile, the terrain being judged as beginner's level, 16%; intermediate, 64%; and expert, 20%. A separate slope, the **Corona Area,** is open for experts only, as conditions and weather permit. Lift tickets are $18, half price for children and those aged 55 to 69; over-69s ski free. Full-day ski-school lessons are $20. Ski rental is $12; for children, $8. There is a nursery for kids up to 5 years of age at $12 a day. Fifteen trails are covered by snowmaking equipment, and there is a cafeteria in a rustic lodge at the base with daily hot specials; best bargain is the skier's breakfast. There is also the Alpenhorn bar on the upper level of the lodge for ski watching.

Accommodations are in Boulder, 20 miles away (see Chapter XIV). Cross-country tours are organized by **Tour Eldora** (tel. 303/447-8013). You can get skiing information by calling **Lake Eldora Ski Area** (tel. 303/447-8013); **snow reports** are at 447-8013. There are three RTD buses daily between Boulder and Eldora, with easy connections via the same city line on to Denver.

SKI ESTES PARK: Two mountain areas near Estes Park make up this complex (tel. 303/586-8173), the lower mountain with gentle runs and intermediate slopes, and the upper mountain served by a T-bar with a variety of conditions including challenges to the expert in five bowls and the big basin. Located ten miles west of Estes Park in Rocky Mountain National Park, it is open daily from November to April, and has a 2,000-foot vertical drop from a summit at 11,500 feet. Its longest run is 1¼ miles. The terrain is divided among beginner slopes, 30%; intermediate, 40%; and expert, 30%. There are two T-bars and two Poma lifts. Lift tickets are $12 daily, $10 for children. Ski instruction is given in classes morning or afternoon at $15. Ski rental is $12; for children, $8. A nursery ski school for kids aged 4 to 7, from 9 a.m. to 4 p.m., costs $15 including lunch. Three trails are covered by snowmaking machines. The main lodge at the base has a cafeteria.

For information on accommodations and restaurants, see the listings for Estes Park in Chapter XVI, Section 1. All information may be had from the **Estes Park Area Chamber of Commerce** (tel. 303/586-4431, or toll free 800/631-5888).

GENEVA BASIN: Just over an hour's drive from Denver, 65 miles west via U.S. 285 to Grant, continuing on Guanella Pass Road to the base, Geneva Basin (tel. 303/838-5007) is open daily from Thanksgiving to Easter, and has a 1,250-foot vertical drop from its summit at 11,750 feet. The longest run is one mile. Terrain is divided thus: beginners, 25%; intermediates, 45%; and experts' slopes, 30%. There are two chair lifts and two Poma lifts. Rates are $18. Children under 12 pay $10; under 6, free. Those over 60 also ski free. Lessons go for $20, with two-hour sessions starting at 11 a.m. and at 2 p.m. Ski rental is $10, $5 for children. There is a nursery from 8:30 a.m. to 4 p.m., charging $14, including lunch, for children aged 1 to 11. A breakfast or lunch is available in the base cafeteria.

Accommodations are in the small communities of **Grant** and **Bailey,** 10 to 15 miles to the south of the ski area on U.S. 285. About the same distance north, just off I-70 in the historic town of **Georgetown,** are more lodging places.

Up at Georgetown, the **Georgetown Motor Inn,** 1100 Rose St., Georgetown, CO 80444 (tel. 303/569-3201), is open all year with 32 units at $42 double.

LOVELAND: Loveland Basin and Valley (tel. 303/569-2288) is 56 miles west of Denver via I-70 to exit 216, with plenty of early snow for skiing from mid-October through May, open daily. It has a 1,430-foot vertical drop from a summit at 12,430 feet. The longest run is 1½ miles, and trails are tagged 25% beginner, 50% intermediate, and 25% expert. There are seven chair lifts and one Poma lift. Rates are $21. Children pay $9; over 65, $5; over 70, free. Full-day instruction at the ski school costs $20. Rental costs $10 for adults, $6 for children. A nursery for children ages 1 to 11 costs $12 daily, and there is additionally a nursery ski school. Seven trails are covered by snowmaking machinery.

There are restaurants, a cafeteria, and a bar at the area base, and a dozen eating places in **Georgetown,** 12 miles distant. There's easy transport from Denver on the ski-lift bus; for information, dial 398-LIFT. For information on accommodations, get in touch with the **Georgetown Society** (tel. 303/569-2840). See also Chapter XIV.

MONARCH: Monarch Ski Resort near Garfield, Colorado (tel. 303/539-3573, or toll free 800/525-9390), is 160 miles southwest of Denver via U.S. 285 and U.S. 250, and is open daily from November to April with a base 11,000 feet up in the San Isabel National Forest on the Continental Divide, the summit soaring 1,000 feet higher. There are 43 trails on 700 subalpine acres, and an average snowfall of 300 inches that provides a lot of fresh powder prized by expert skiers. Forty instructors are employed in the ski school, which uses the American Teaching Method.

The longest run at Monarch is 1½ miles, and trails are divided into 20% for beginners, 52% for intermediates, and 28% for experts, served by four double-chair lifts. Lift tickets are $18 daily; kids, $10; over-62s, $5. A full day of ski lessons in group classes costs $18. Ski rental is $9, $6 for children.

Greyhound/Trailways buses make connections to Garfield, three miles from the ski area, with Denver, Colorado Springs, or Grand Junction. **American** and **Trans Colorado** airlines fly to Gunnison, 47 miles from the area.

Accommodations nearby include the **Monarch Lodge,** Garfield, CO 81227 (tel. 303/539-2581, or toll free 800/525-9390), three miles east of the ski area. It has 100 rooms, a dining room, two lounges with live entertainment nightly, and a health spa with tennis, racquetball, a sauna, Jacuzzi, indoor heated pool, exercise room, and an 11-station Nautilus fitness area. There is a pro shop, gift shop, and game room. Rooms for one to four people are available for $55 to $85, depending on dates. Other Garfield rooms are available at the **Amen Chalet,** Garfield, CO 81227 (tel. 303/539-4634); the **Garfield Cabin,** Garfield, CO 81227 (tel. 303/539-2581); and the **Snow Shoe Inn,** Garfield, CO 81227 (tel. 303/539-4684).

For travel service information in the area, get in touch with the **Salida Chamber of Commerce,** 406 W. Rainbow Blvd., Salida, CO 81201 (tel. 303/539-2068). For **snow reports** locally, call 539-3573.

POWDERHORN: Located on the northern slopes of the Grand Mesa National Forest, Powderhorn (tel. 303/245-5343) is 250 miles west of Denver via I-70 and Colo. 65, and 40 miles east of Grand Junction via I-70 and Colo. 65. It is open daily from Thanksgiving to mid-April. There is a 1,600-foot vertical drop from a 9,800-foot summit, with the longest run two miles. The terrain is divided into categories: 14% for beginners, 59% for intermediates, and 27% for experts. There are two double-chair lifts and two Poma lifts. Lift rates are $22. Children and those over 60, $11. A full day of ski classes costs $32. Rentals are $12.50; for children, $9. A children's ski school for ages 3 to 9 costs $19 daily. Three of the trails are covered by snowmaking machinery. The Powderhorn Inn and Le Chalet restaurant, with bar and lounge, are located at the base.

A shuttle bus from the ski area meets flights at Grand Junction, served by four airlines from Denver. There is **Greyhound/Trailways** bus service to Grand Junction from Denver and Colorado Springs daily. A **Powderhorn bus** runs between the area and Grand Junction.

For accommodations and eating places, see the listings for Grand Junction in Chapter XVI, Section 3. Some lodgings may be reserved with **Powderhorn Central Reservations** (tel. 303/245-5343, or toll free 800/233-9882).

All area travel service information is available from **Grand Junction Chamber of Commerce,** 360 Grand Ave., Grand Junction, CO 81501 (tel. 303/242-3214).

PURGATORY: An uncrowded resort in southwestern Colorado, Purgatory (tel. 303/247-9000, or toll free 800/525-0892) is near the town of Durango,

348 miles from Denver via I-25, U.S. 160, and U.S. 550, in the San Juan Mountains, part of San Juan National Forest. With annual snowfall over 300 inches there is usually good powder for the expert runs. It is open daily from late November to the end of the first week of April. There is a vertical drop of 2,022 feet from a summit at 10,822 feet. Longest run is two miles, and 20% of the slopes are for beginners, half for intermediates, and 30% for experts. There is a separate beginner slope of seven acres. Nine chair lifts move skiers to the tops. Rates are $27 a day; children, $12; over- 65s, $12. A full day of class instruction in the ski school is $29. Ski rentals are $13, $8 for kids. A nursery takes care of kids aged 2 to 6 for $25 daily; nursery ski school is $30. Twenty-one trails are served by snowmaking machinery. Helicopter skiing is available in distant heights, for intermediate and advanced skiers only. There is also cross-country skiing, sledding, and skating.

At the ski area, the Powderhouse restaurant serves home-style specials. Dante's restaurant, on the backside of the mountain, has a cafeteria and dining room.

Air transportation to Durango is provided from Denver by four airlines. America West Airlines serves Phoenix and California. The **Lift Air & Ski Shuttle** takes skiers directly to the slopes. **Greyhound/Trailways** serves Durango from Denver, Colorado Springs, Grand Junction, and Albuquerque. **Shuttle bus** service (tel. 259-4818) between Durango and Purgatory costs $8 round trip.

For information on accommodations and eating places, see the listings for Durango in Chapter XVIII, Section 2.

For all travel service information, get in touch with the **Durango Chamber of Commerce,** 111 S. Camino del Rio, Durango, CO 81301 (tel. 303/247-0312). Reservations for accommodations and ski packages can be made through **Purgatory-Durango Central Reservations,** 546 Main Ave., Durango, CO 81301 (tel. 303/247-8900, or toll free 800/525-0892).

SUNLIGHT: Located in White River National Forest ten miles from Glenwood Springs, the Sunlight Ski Area (tel. 303/945-7491) is 170 miles west of Denver via I-70, Colo. 82, and County Rd. 117. It is open daily from late November to mid-April. It has a 2,000-foot vertical drop from its 9,850-foot summit, with the longest run at 2½ miles. A fifth of the terrain is for beginners, 58% for intermediates, and 22% for experts. There are two chair lifts and two surface lifts. Lift rates are $20 daily for adults, $10 for children and those over 60. Double sessions at daily ski school are $25. Equipment rental is $10, $7 for children. A day nursery for kids 6 months to 6 years old costs $20, including lunch.

The Sunlight Inn and the Base Lodge, both at the ski area, provide food and drinks.

The area is served by **Greyhound/Trailways** (tel. 292-6111) and by **Amtrak** trains (tel. toll free 800/872-7245) to Glenwood Springs from Denver to the east and Grand Junction to the west. Nearest **airport** is Grand Junction. A courtesy **shuttle bus** makes runs between hotels and motels in Glenwood Springs and the ski area (for times, call 945-7491).

Accommodations and eating places are numerous in Glenwood Springs. See the listings for this city in Chapter XVI, Section 3.

For all travel service information, get in touch with the **Glenwood Springs Chamber of Commerce,** at 1102 Grand Ave., Glenwood Springs, CO 81601 (tel. 303/945-6589).

TELLURIDE: The Telluride Ski Resort (tel. 303/728-4424), which opened in 1972, is in the Uncompahgre National Forest in the southwestern Colorado Rockies, with 24 miles of trails served by six double-chair lifts. It is 335 miles from Denver, 300 miles from Albuquerque. It has an exceptional 3,000-foot vertical drop from its 11,800-foot summit, as well as "the best beginner slope in the country," in the opinion of *Ski* magazine. It is open from late November to April 1, with its longest run at 2.8 miles. A new quad lift goes two miles, and 1,800 feet vertically, in 11 minutes. The terrain is 15% for beginners, half for intermediates, and 35% for experts. Rates for adults are $28 daily; ages 12 and under, $13. Skiers 70 and over ski free. Full-day classes at the ski school are $32. Rental of skis is $12; for children, $10. A full-day nursery for kids aged 1 to 7 is $28, including lunch.

The base area offers other winter activity for the outdoors-minded, such as skating, cross-country skiing, snowshoeing, ice climbing, ice fishing, winter mountaineering, and backcountry skiing. Cross-country instruction and tours are organized by the **Telluride Nordic Center** (tel. 728-4424). There are also telemark clinics here, at $22 daily, from 11 a.m. to 2 p.m.

There is a free town loop van **shuttle** between the slopes and Telluride. The Dalodge bar and restaurant is at the base of the Meadows lift, the Verandah restaurant is at the base of Coonskin lift, and midway on the mountain skiers may eat or drink at the Gorrono Ranch Restaurant and Saloon.

Direct **air service** to the new airport serves Denver and Albuquerque.

Information on accommodations and eating places in Telluride is listed in Chapter XVIII, Section 3. Bookings, including ski packages, may be made with **Telluride Central Reservations,** P.O. Box 1009, Telluride, CO 81435 (tel. 303/728-4431, or toll free 800/525-3455). For all travel service information, get in touch with the **Telluride Chamber Resort Association,** 323 W. Colorado Ave., Telluride, CO 81435 (tel. 303/728-3041). Phone 728-3614 for a snow report.

WOLF CREEK:
Claiming the most snow in Colorado—465 inches (almost 40 feet)—Wolf Creek (tel. 303/731-5605) has some of the world's best powder skiing. Located in southern Colorado in Rio Grande National Forest, it is 270 miles from Denver via I-25 and U.S. 160, open mid-November to mid-April. It has a vertical drop of 1,125 feet from a summit at 11,775 feet, and its longest run is 1.3 miles. The runs are 30% for beginners, 40% for intermediates, and 30% for experts. There are two chair lifts and three surface lifts. Lift rates are $20 for adults; children and over-65s, $10. A full day at the ski school is $20. Ski rental is $9.50, $7.50 for kids.

There are also scenic **sleigh rides** departing in season from the ski area base. There is a snackbar and picnic room at the base. **Pagosa Springs,** nearby, has numerous restaurants, bars and lodging.

For all travel service information, call the **Pagosa Springs Chamber of Commerce** (tel. 303/264-2360). The only car-rental service here is **Pagosa Rent-a-Car** (tel. 731-2179).

Where to Stay
Fairfield Pagosa Resort, three miles west of town on U.S. 160, Pagosa Springs, CO 81147 (tel. 303/731-4141, or toll free 800/523-7704), has 100 units, a restaurant, lounge, and pool. Double rates are $65 to $85.

The **Inn at the Pass,** near the ski area 14 miles east of town on U.S. 160, Pagosa Springs, CO 81147 (tel. 303/264-5385), has ten units, a lounge and restaurant, and rates of $45 to $58 double.

A natural hot mineral-water pool is an attraction at the **Spa Motel,** downtown, Pagosa Springs, CO 81147 (tel. 303/264-5910), with 19 rooms, some with kitchens, at $36 to $40 double.

CHAPTER XVI

NORTHERN COLORADO

□ □ □

1. ROCKY MOUNTAIN NATIONAL PARK
2. CITIES AT THE GATES OF THE ROCKIES
3. DESTINATIONS NORTH BY WEST

Stopping along the highway in August to make snowballs out of drifts edging the road is one of the delights of Rocky Mountain National Park, where one road reaches an altitude of 12,183 feet and the visitor center itself is only a few hundred feet lower down. A booming summertime vacation town is Estes Park just to the east of the national park, while at the southwestern edges are a couple of lakes that also draw recreationists of all kinds.

Growing cities to the east along the Rocky Mountain front at the western extremity of the Great Plains are Greeley, Loveland, and Fort Collins. Hundreds of miles of wilderness and national forest land lie west of the national park boundaries, and at the western extremity of the state is a repository of dinosaur fossils. Serving these huge areas in the western part of the state are the cities of Glenwood Springs and Grand Junction.

1. ROCKY MOUNTAIN NATIONAL PARK

Rocky Mountain National Park's eastern entrance is 65 miles from Denver via U.S. 36, and is the site of one of the country's great alpine highways, **Trail Ridge Road,** crossing the park from east to west. At its highest point it reaches 12,183 feet in an environment that at this height resembles that of the Arctic. Depending on snowfall, it is open from Memorial Day to mid-October. The 50-mile scenic drive ought to be done in no less time than three or four hours, with stops at the numerous scenic outlooks. Glacier-carved peaks on every side are open to view here above the treeline. Exhibits at the **Alpine Visitor Center at Fall River Pass,** 11,796 feet in elevation, explain life of the alpine tundra.

The **Fall River Road** is the original trail crossing these mountains, running up to the pass from **Horseshoe Park Junction.** The part of this road west of the Endovalley picnic area is one way uphill, and as you negotiate its gravelly switchbacks you get a clear idea of very early auto travel in the West. This road, too, is closed in the winter.

One of the few paved roads in the Rockies into a high mountain basin is **Bear Lake Road,** which sees crowded traffic conditions in the summer. To avoid crowds, the answer is simple: hike or ride a horse. Horses with guides can be hired at two locations inside the park on the east side or from liveries just outside the east and west entrances in summer. But some trails are closed to horses.

Rocky Mountain is really a park for hikers. More than 300 miles of trails take hikers to remote parts of the park to get away from the crowds in the parking areas and on the car roads, and to find spots where you have streams, meadows, and mountains all to yourself. The visitor center has U.S. Geological Survey topographic maps and guidebooks for sale, and rangers will be happy to suggest trails that are lightly used, for even some of the footpaths get heavy hiker use. Among them are self-guiding interpretive trails with folders describing natural flora and geological formations.

These trails include **Bear Lake Nature Trail,** around an alpine lake, half a mile long; **Never Summer Ranch,** to some turn-of-the-century ranch buildings, a mile long; **Longs Peak Trail,** to the highest peak in the park (14,225 feet), a 16-mile trek; **Lulu City,** a 7-mile hike to a mining ghost town; **Moraine Park Nature Trail,** a quarter mile long; **Sprague Lake Five Senses Trail,** half a mile in length, especially for wheelchair visitors; **Tundra World** trails, leading short distances to canyon overlooks; and a 16-mile round-trip hike into **Wild Basin,** an area of glaciated valleys, streams, and waterfalls.

Longer hikes that take overnight campouts require the backpacker to take out a free permit at park headquarters or any ranger station; camping in backcountry is limited to one week during the busy June to September season.

The high country was set apart as a park particularly because so much of it lies above the treeline. It was first traversed by settlers in 1859 when Joel Estes and his son, Milton, rode into the valley that bears their name ("park" means "valley" in these parts). There were, however, few settlers in this rugged, wild land. Around the turn of the century a naturalist and writer named Enos Mills began to try to have this pristine area preserved. He succeeded, and the national park was established in 1915.

A special attraction to botanists and other students of various parts of the ecology is the fact of the widely varying differences in flora and fauna that go with the changes in altitude. Pine and juniper grow on lower slopes that get the direct sun, while Douglas fir grows on the cooler north slopes. Along the streams are blue spruce mixed with stands of lodgepole pine. There are great masses of wildflowers in the spring in valleys and meadows. Above 9,000 feet, forests of Engelmann spruce and subalpine fir take over, with wildflower patches in open spaces, full of blue Colorado columbine. Toward the upper limits, twisted trees hug the ground, and above them is the alpine tundra where one-quarter of all plants surviving can also be found in the Arctic.

Dawn and late evening just before dark are the best time to catch glimpses of the elusive wapiti. The symbol of the park, bighorn sheep, are sometimes seen in **Horseshoe Park** near Sheep Lakes at a natural mineral lick. **Moraine Park** and Horseshoe are also home to the coyote and the yellow-bellied marmot, which suns itself on rocks. Beaver are usually easily seen around their ponds and lodges in the evening; they begin work after sunset and continue long after dark.

Campfire talks and other visitor center programs begin in early June and continue into September. Besides headquarters, open all year, the **Alpine and Moraine Park visitor centers** are open in the summertime and into October. The fall is thought to be the best time for visits, especially for avoiding crowds— the magnificent high country in the park draws three million visitors a year.

The park has five **campgrounds:** Moraine Park, Glacier Basin, Aspenglen, Longs Peak, and Timber Creek. Camping is limited to three days at Longs Peak and seven days at the other sites. In summer they are all filled to capacity early in the day. There are no hookups in the campgrounds, and one of them, Longs

Peak, is for tent camping only. Campgrounds have grates for fires, and wood must be brought in or purchased.

Four species of trout are fished in streams and lakes: brown, rainbow, brook, and cutthroat. A state **fishing** license is required, and use of live bait is not permitted. Bear Lake is closed to fishing, as are some lakes and streams at the east side of the park where the greenback cutthroat trout is being reintroduced to its native habitat.

A concession has a technical **climbing school** and guide service within the park. Permits are not required for day hikes; Longs Peak can be reached by those without climbing experience via the Keyhole. The north and east faces, however, are for technical climbing only. The Longs Peak trip is a long and rather hard one at this elevation, over a rise of 4,700 feet at 10,000 to 14,000 feet in altitude. The round trip takes about 12 hours, and starts should be made before 6 a.m. to avoid thunderstorms around the summit in the afternoon. Longs Peak information is available from the ranger station (tel. 586-4975).

There is wintertime **cross-country skiing** in the lower valleys and mountaineering in the heights. There is also **downhill skiing** at Hidden Valley, seven miles from the Fall River entrance. Access roads from the east are kept open. Campgrounds open all winter are Aspenglen, Longs Peak, and Timber Creek, but they do not have water supplies in winter. Overnight backcountry permits are available in winter at headquarters or the West Unit office; some areas are closed because of the danger of avalanche.

ESTES PARK: The major site for accommodations and travel services for visitors to Rocky Mountain National Park is the city of Estes Park at the eastern gateway, which also provides popular and classical music, rodeos, and other attractions throughout the summer largely for regaling vacationers.

Sights and Attractions

The **Estes Park Area Historical Museum,** at U.S. 36 and 4th Street (tel. 586-6256), is open daily free of charge with displays of pioneer artifacts and furnishings from families who homesteaded here to raise cattle, beginning in the 1870s. It was soon after these beginnings that the first intrepid tourists began to find their way to Estes Park and the trails into the Rocky Mountains just to the west. An English tourist named Isabella Bird was one of the first to reach Evans Ranch in 1873, determined to climb Longs Peak; though she failed in the climb, she got a book out of her adventures here: *A Lady's Life in the Rocky Mountains.* Among objects displayed in the museum are her book, early tools, early photos, kitchen implements, and an old Victrola. May through September hours are 10 a.m. to 5 p.m. Monday through Saturday and 1 to 5 p.m. on Sunday; closed Sunday and Monday from October to May. The museum has guided historical walking tours, also free of charge, through downtown Estes Park, taking in such sights as **Grubb's Livery,** the site of the old **Josephine Hotel** (now occupied by the Wheel Bar), the building that was once the **Hupp Hotel** (built in 1906), the 1877 **Elkhorn Lodge,** one of the state's earliest resorts, and the first school, dating back to 1886. Another old hotel, built in 1905 by the inventor of the Stanley Steamer, F. O. Stanley, is the **Stanley Hotel,** open year round (see "Where to Stay").

Roosevelt National Forest offers trails for four-wheel-drive vehicles and motorbikes, and for horseback riding and hiking. There are day hikes from Estes Park into **Homestead Meadows** or to **Lily Mountain,** and backpacking trips to be made into **Signal Mountain** or the **Comanche Peak Wilderness.** The **Estes-Poudre Ranger District** office, 161 2nd St. (tel. 586-3440), has maps and information.

Trips into remote areas of the national forest are also made by six-wheel former army trucks in which groups of convivial vacationers load up and visit beaver country, elk meadows, and virgin forest land, and have a sizzling-steak cookout with cowboy music provided and a sing-along around the campfire. For information, contact **American Wilderness Tours,** 481 W. Elkhorn Ave. (tel. 586-4237). **Estes Park Bus Co.,** at 205 Park Lane (tel. 586-8108), operates tours on regular car roads into the national park as well as daily service to and from Denver.

Horseback riding on jaunts of various lengths, including breakfast and cookout rides, are offered at various stables, including **Elkhorn Stables,** at 650 W. Elkhorn Ave. (tel. 586-3291), "operated by a Christian family," according to the ads; **National Park Village Stables** (tel. 586-5890), at the north park entrance on the Fall River Road (religion of horses not stated); and **Sombrero Stables,** two miles east of town on U.S. 34 (tel. 586-4577).

For an easy way to get around town, the **Estes Park Trolley** (tel. 586-8866) is a good choice, operating daily in the summer season on four routes from 8 a.m. to 10 p.m. for a $1 fare, including one reboarding. The trolleys all intersect on the hour and the half hour at the Transit Center at the corner of Elkhorn and MacGregor Avenues, and serve nearly all the motels, hotels, and camping areas in and around town.

Those who might like to challenge themselves to climbing 14,255-foot Longs Peak will find good advice at **Colorado Wilderness Sports,** 358 E. Elkhorn Ave. (tel. 586-6548), which provides information on trails as well as climbing guides, maps, and equipment. The enterprise also organizes white-water rafting trips down three nearby rivers—the Colorado, the Poudre, and the Arkansas—one-day trips priced at $42 to $56.50, two days at $115 to $125; there are also longer trips on the Green, Yampa, and Dolores Rivers. Also offered are kayak lessons for eventual runs down the Big Thompson River.

Day hikes with llamas carrying the food and gear are organized by **Walkabout Llama Hikes** (tel. 586-5940), which lets hikers lead their own llamas, following guides Jane and Jerry Boudreaux. A day's outing of up to eight miles costs $45, including food but not including a $5 entrance fee to the national park.

A chuckwagon dinner and western show are the attraction nightly at the **Western Odyssey,** 1½ miles east of town on U.S. 34 (tel. 586-5371), where for just $9 guests regale themselves with sliced beef simmered in Lazy-B ranch sauce, baked potatoes, beans, biscuits, peaches, spiced cake, and lemonade or coffee (no alcoholic drinks). Dinner at 7 p.m. is followed by country music from Tom Justin and the Lazy-B Wranglers.

Shopping

Souvenirs of the West are in such great supply that even with three million visitors a year it seems impossible they will all ever be sold, but there are more where these came from to go into the over 200 gift shops, western-style clothing and souvenir emporia, and jewelry stores on Elkhorn Avenue.

There are half a dozen antique stores and some art galleries, notably those of **Greg Steiner,** a local artist whose original technique is the use of transparent oils, located in the Courtyard; and **Ed Herrmann,** on Moraine Avenue.

Where to Stay

With such a great influx of summertime visitors—and a growing number in winter too—it's not surprising to find Estes Park, in spite of its modest-sized permanent population of about 3,000, to have some 120 motels, lodges, and cabin establishments. The **Estes Park Area Chamber of Commerce** (tel. 303/586-4431, or toll free 800/44-ESTES) has a visitor center at the junction of U.S.

36 and U.S. 34 east of town where you can get all the information and help you need for vacation planning, starting with choice of accommodations available.

The **Black Canyon Inn,** 800 MacGregor Ave., Estes Park, CO 80517 (tel. 303/586-8113), overlooks the Black Canyon and the grassy meadows of the historic MacGregor Ranch, yet is within walking distance of the town center. Massive stone fireplaces set a rustic tone in the lodge restaurant. There is a lounge, pool, and hot tub. Rates in season are $60 to $90 double, with breakfast, and lower in winter.

The **Stanley Hotel,** 333 Wonderview Ave., Estes Park, CO 80517 (tel. 303/586-3371, or toll free 800/ROCKIES), is a fine rambling old resort hotel equipped with all modern conveniences. Built in 1909 by F. O. Stanley, the inventor of the Stanley Steamer car, the premises offer Gay '90s elegance and a luxurious dining room, the MacGregor Room. The Dunraven Grille provides entertainment and dancing nightly in season—the hotel is open all year. In summer free weekly concerts are given in the Music Room, and there is nightly dinner theater. Tennis, volleyball, and horseshoes are all available on the site, as well as a huge outdoor pool. Rates are $65 to $110 double.

The **YMCA of the Rockies,** on Colo. 66 west of town (P.O. Box 578), Estes Park, CO 80517 (tel. 303/586-3341), was established in 1907 as a family vacation lodge, and provides a variety of space, from cabins small and large to lodge rooms, all at reasonable cost. In the shadow of the Front Range of the Rockies, the site offers spectacular scenery and easy access to hiking and horse riding trails—there are stables on the premises. Rocky Mountain National Park property bounds the area on three sides. Guest memberships in the YMCA are issued for $5 per family, $3 for individuals, good for any length of stay. A variety of programs is offered during the summer season, such as symphony concerts, jazz performances, modern dance presentations, outdoor cookouts, and square dancing; there are also guided hikes and family campfires. The Estes Park Center also maintains the Lula W. Dorsey Museum, showing documents, photos and memorabilia concerning the history of the YMCA of the Rockies since its founding.

The Estes Park Center offers amenities not generally expected in budget-priced lodgings: babysitters, baggage storage, the Pine Room restaurant serving three meals, a grocery store, an infirmary, a laundry, a Rustic Room snackbar, and telephones in some lodge rooms. Cabins that sleep four cost $36 a night, or $220 a week; bunk beds in lodges cost $20 to $28; private double rooms in the Alpen Inn go for $44. Modified American Plan rates are available (breakfast and dinner provided) at $15 additional. Advance reservations may be made by mail by writing to YMCA of the Rockies, 2515 Tunnel Rd., Association Camp, CO 80511.

Eight cabins situated on 14 acres of woodland at the entrance to the national park welcome guests to **Streamside Cabins,** 1260 Fall River Rd., Estes Park, CO 80517 (tel. 303/586-6464). Cabins with one or two bedrooms have tile baths, carpeting, king- and queen-size beds, cable television, and fireplaces with wood supplied. Kitchens are fully equipped with new electric frying pans and microwave ovens, and free gas grills are on the outdoors decks. Daily newspapers are delivered free, and there is access to all facilities of the Estes Park Health Club for an additional $3.50 daily. Rates for up to four persons in a cabin are $45 to $85.

Open during the summer season only, the **Baldpate Inn,** 4900 S. Co. 7, Estes Park, CO 80517 (tel. 303/586-6151), claims that its display of keys—over 20,000 of them—is the world's largest. The inn, constructed in 1917, was named for the novel *Seven Keys to Baldpate,* in which each of seven hotel guests believes he or she possesses the only key to the place. Guests here are advised: "You can become part of the legend joining a stellar cast of guests who have added their own special key to this collection." Rooms here have views of Longs

Peak from a 9,000-foot-high site on the side of Twin Sisters Mountain. Seven miles from the center of town, the lodge also offers lunches and dinners, as well as complimentary breakfast that goes with the room. There is a soup and salad bar, and fresh baked breads and pies are served. Guests can fish for trout in Lily Lake adjoining the property. Board games or reading from a selection in the inn's library draw guests around a great stone fireplace on cool evenings. Daily rates for two people are $55 to $70.

A pretty eight-room bed-and-breakfast inn at the end of a lane on 27 acres of woodland, **River Song Inn,** P.O. Box 1910, Estes Park, CO 80517 (tel. 303/586-4666), is off Mary's Lake Road. There is a trout stream on the property as well as a gazebo by a pond, and an easy hiking trail with stone benches along the way. Elk, deer, raccoons, eagles, and owls are often seen. Fresh breads and rolls are ready for breakfasters. The inn, open year round, is the choice of cross-country skiers and other winter-sports enthusiasts. The inn has no television; smoking is not permitted, nor are children under 12 years of age. The rooms offer a rare variety: the Faerie Primrose has treetop views and an iron-and-brass bed; the Shooting Star has an antique Jenny Lind bed; Forget-me-Not has great mountain views; Pasqueflower is a cottage with a woodstove, antique tub, and log bed; Mountain Rose has a see-through fireplace; Cowboy's Delight is a rustic space in a carriage house with a four-poster bed and an outside deck; Indian Paintbrush has a queen-size "swing bed"; and Chiming Bells is a suite with sunken tub and fireplace. Rates for two people are $50 to $89.

Where to Eat

P. S. Flowers, 247 W. Elkhorn Ave. (tel. 586-5735), has a motto: "If it's not going to be good, and fun, one should stay home and eat oatmeal." Serving both lunches and dinners, the restaurant also does well with its "last great American happy hour" from 4:30 to 5:30 p.m. daily, inviting the public to "come and enjoy good adult fun before it is outlawed!" A lunch selection might be a fresh trout sandwich deep-fried with lettuce and tomato, Fall River fries, and coleslaw; fish and chips, bratwurst, and Mexican specialties are also served. For dinner the place is known for its beef Stroganoff, its rack of lamb, and its fettuccine; crab legs and barbecued ribs are on order too. A full dinner with wine costs $14 to $16. An outdoor beer garden specializes in copious drafts called Yard-of-Ale.

A good restaurant for hearty, traditional American fare is the **Old Plantation,** 128 E. Elkhorn Ave. (tel. 586-2800), run by members of the Burgess family for going on 60 years. The place is known for its Yankee pot roast, roast duckling, and a standby, the sizzling steak. Veal dishes and fresh trout are always served too, and the soups and desserts are all homemade. The Coat of Arms Tavern is a pleasant, solid lounge for a cocktail or cooling beer. A full dinner here costs up to $20 with wine.

For the price-conscious there's a good beef-barbecue address in town, **Sgt. Pepperwood's,** at Bighorn and Cleave Streets (tel. 586-6317), which makes up orders for take-out and serves lunches and dinners on the premises as well. There is a popular low-priced breakfast buffet. A barbecue dinner with fixings costs around $6.

GRAND LAKE: The other center for tourists visiting Rocky Mountain National Park is the village of Grand Lake at the southwestern entrance, a town with board sidewalks and still a few horses being ridden along the main drag. At an altitude of 8,370 feet it has deep forest trails leading out into the mountains, around the two pristine lakes, Grand and Shadow Mountain; another, larger body, Granby Lake, is only a few miles south.

There are nightly productions by a theater-in-the-round company in the village all summer, and the 18-hole golf course is inordinately proud of having on its ninth hole a "fox hazard." The park entrance is just a mile to the north. The many hiking and riding trails in the area are taken over by snowmobilers in winter, of which this village claims to be the capital; cross-country skiers also use the vast network of trails on federal land in the area.

The town can be reached in summer by crossing the national park or, all year, 100 miles from Denver, via I-70 east to Empire, U.S. 40 north to Granby, and finally U.S. 34 north. The village has the highest altitude yacht club in the world, Grand Lake Yacht Club, organized in 1902, when sailboats were converted from rowboats. There is a summer regatta yearly, in mid-August, in which **Regatta Week** is climaxed by the Lipton Cup race, given since 1912.

Adams Falls, on the slopes of Baldy Mountain, is a favorite target for amateur picture takers; it is reached by a quarter-mile foot trail near the east shore of Grand Lake.

Grand Lake, which reaches a depth of 400 feet, is the largest natural lake in the state, and is linked by a channel to **Shadow Mountain Lake.** The third of these "great lakes of the Rockies" is man-made **Lake Granby;** water from the three is pumped under the mountains to Lake Estes for use in irrigation. **Shadow Mountain National Recreation Area** has various recreational opportunities including boating, fishing, picnicking, hiking, horseback riding, cross-country skiing, and camping. There's fishing for Kokanee salmon, and Mackinaw, rainbow, brown, and cutthroat trout. Salmon snagging season is October to December 31 each year.

The **Kaufman House** on Pitkin Avenue is an early residence, a log structure used as the museum of the Grand Lake Historical Society, open to the public. A restaurant surviving since 1880, the **Corner Cupboard Inn** is on Grand Avenue, which has photos of the early days of the village on its dining room walls. The public square facing Grand Avenue between Pitkin and Garfield Avenues is the site of a buffalo barbecue during the second week of July, to which the public is welcome.

For information on playing golf, call **Grand Lake Golf Course** (tel. 627-8328). For information on in-the-round **theater** productions on the Boardwalk, call 627-3380. Boat rentals are available at **Lake Kove Marina** (tel. 627-3605) on Shadow Mountain Lake, and **Trail Ridge Marina** (tel. 627-3586) and **Grand Lake Marina** (tel. 627-3401) on Grand Lake.

Tours for visitors are held at the **Holzwarth Ranch,** an early homestead, and at the **Granby Pumping Plant.** Among annual events, tourists like the lighted **boat parade** in July and the mid-month **September Festival.**

For all information on events and travel services, get in touch with the **Grand Lake Chamber of Commerce** (tel. 303/627-3402).

Where to Stay

Grand Lake has about three dozen motels and lodges with cabins that appeal to visitors and vacationers. A good one that stays open all year is the **Driftwood Lodge,** three miles south of town on U.S. 34, Grand Lake, CO 80447 (tel. 303/627-3654), where the center attraction is the pine-walled lobby with its fieldstone fireplace and stuffed animal trophies—moose, antelope, Canada goose, and even a polar bear (presumably taken somewhere far to the north). The lodge is just three miles from the entrance to Rocky Mountain National Park. Rooms are electrically heated, a bonus on cold nights in the early summer or fall. There is a grassy golf course and nearby trout fishing, hiking, and horseback trails. The outdoor pool is heated and there are horseshoes and other lawn games, a playground, and picnic tables. Winter occupancy offers cross-country skiing and snowmobiling from the grounds—you can rent a Ski-Doo snowmobile right here. A whirlpool and sauna room is popular with skiers after a day on the slopes at nearby Winter Park. Rates are $31 to $62 double, depending on season.

Where to Eat

Grand Lake has about a dozen eating places, about half open year around, including the **Chuck Hole Café** (tel. 627-3509), a family restaurant for breakfast and lunch only at the end of Grand Avenue; and the **Mountain Inn** (tel. 627-3385), at the west end of Grand Avenue. The historic **Corner Cupboard Inn,** on Grand Avenue (tel. 627-3813), has aged prime meats cut on the premises.

2. CITIES AT THE GATES OF THE ROCKIES

In the prairie country of a basin drained by the Big Thompson, the Cache La Poudre, and the South Platte Rivers, looking up at the eastern wall of the Rockies are the small cities of Loveland, Fort Collins, and Greeley. They are departure headquarters for recreational ventures of vacationers, offer all travel services, and also have busy lives of their own.

LOVELAND: The first settler in the Big Thompson Valley was Mariano Modina, who moved here with his family in 1858 from Taos, New Mexico, to build a trading post near the present site of Loveland, which he named Namaqua. It became a station on the overland stage line. More settlers arrived after the Civil War and laid out a town plan, called Winona, which grew into a small community around a flour mill on the river. Loveland, a few miles to the west, stole Winona's thunder by becoming the site of a station for a new railroad, the Colorado Central between Cheyenne and Golden. The station was at first just a tent, but Loveland had its start, and by 1890 there was a population of 698; presently it is well over 40,000. Named for the railroad company president, the town has become famous as Sweetheart City; tens of thousands of Valentine cards are sent here every February for remailing with the Loveland postmark. Besides a busy post office, Loveland is the center of an agricultural area producing alfalfa, hay, beets, corn, beans, and wheat, as well as ranking fifth in livestock production among Colorado counties.

Loveland is 50 miles north of Denver via I-25, and is served by **Greyhound/Trailways** buses (tel. 292-6111). Taxi service is from **Loveland Taxi** (tel. 667-5859).

Scenic Drives from Loveland

Besides trips to the east into Rocky Mountain National Park, Loveland makes a likely base for trips to special area destinations such as **Cache la Poudre Canyon,** a pyramid built in memory of two railroad builders, an irrigation project on a grand scale, and beautiful river and lake country.

1. An off-the-beaten-path drive from Loveland is over unpaved roads for about half its length. Go west from the city on U.S. 34, and about six miles along, turn north at County Rd. 27 for five miles to a T junction where you turn left into primitive **Buckhorn Canyon.** This is still County Rd. 27, but pavement ends. At a junction, take County Rd. 44H for eight miles to County Rd. 131, and follow this to Colo. 14 in Cache la Poudre Canyon. Turn left (west) on Colo. 14 ten miles to a resort area called **Rustic.** Here, turn north on County Rd. 69, then after three miles, left on County Rd. 162. Go eight miles past the pretty **Bellaire Lake** to the **Red Feather Lakes** vacation area. To get back to Loveland, go east from here on County Rd. 74E to U.S. 287, then south on through Fort Collins. The trip covers about 130 miles and takes a full day.

2. A trip up across the Wyoming line to visit the only American pyramid starts north on I-25 all the way to **Cheyenne,** capital of Wyoming (the last week of July is the time of **Frontier Days,** Wyoming's biggest celebration). Go west on I-80 to **Laramie,** on the way stopping at the **Ames Monument,** a 45-foot pyramid put up as a tribute to two brothers who saved the Union Pacific from folding, during its construction. From Laramie the route is U.S. 287 south to Loveland, passing on the way a turnoff to the **Virginia Dale Stage Station,** one of perhaps only two original stagecoach stops still on their original sites. The day-long trip covers 188 miles on paved highways.

3. An irrigation project ride starts west from Loveland on U.S. 34 for two miles, then south on County Rd. 19E. Across the Big Thompson River is the site of the first area settlement, **Fort Namaqua Historical Wayside Park,** where the Modina family is buried. Continue to a T junction and go west on County Rd. 20 four miles to County Rd. 29, turn left on 29, go half a mile, and take a right on County Rd. 18E to the top of **Bald Mountain.** There is a great view of the **Big Thompson Valley** from the summit here. Beyond is **Pinewood Reservoir,** part of the Colo-Big T water project. After going down the mountain the way you came up, go to **Flatiron Reservoir** for a tour of the power plant (for information on tours in Loveland, call the U.S.B.R. administration office: 667-4410). After the visit, continue east on 18E to a T junction with County Rd. 31, which leads all around the shore of **Carter Lake** and out at the southern end via County Rd. 8E and Colo. 56 into **Berthoud.** From here take U.S. 287 back to Loveland. The whole 40-mile trip, all on paved highways, takes only about two hours' driving time—but you should allot time for touring, looking at the views, and possibly a picnic along the lake shore or at the mountaintop.

4. A trip to **Horsetooth Reservoir** starts by heading west from Loveland on U.S. 34 for seven miles to County Rd. 29; then turn north on 29 a mile to the dam and falls on the Big Thompson River. Cross the river on the bridge; then, continuing on County Rd. 29, enter a pretty valley, **Green Glade,** and a little farther along, **Missouri Canyon,** which opens into **Buckhorn Valley.** Here turn north on County Rd. 27 and follow a sandstone ridge, passing some quarries. At a T intersection in the hamlet of Masonville, turn east on County Rd. 38E, following along the south end of **Horsetooth Reservoir,** a good place for boating and fishing. The road goes past **Spring Canyon Dam** for a view of the city of Fort Collins in the distance. Continue to U.S. 287 and follow this south back to Loveland. This can be an afternoon drive, and the reservoir has picnic areas.

5. A trip to "lonesome high country" starts out north through Fort Collins and La Porte on U.S. 287 to Colo. 14; turn left on 14 heading west into the beautiful Cache la Poudre Canyon and follow it and its fast-flowing stream for 51 miles to **Chamber's Lake.** Here, take Forest Service Rd. 190 north along the **Laramie River** for 21 miles to a junction with County Rd. 80C—there is a tiny post office at this point (Glendevey, Colorado). Take 80C east to a Y about 1½ miles along, bear left on Sand Creek Pass Road, and continue for 50 miles in high, lonesome, untrampled countryside, half of it Forest Service land and the rest used for grazing. Eventually you return to U.S. 287 on this road; turn south to Loveland, 35 miles distant. The 175-mile trip, with 75 miles of it on gravel roads, makes a good all-day jaunt; this is the perfect trip for picnicking.

6. Stove Prairie and Rist Canyon are other areas reachable by car from Loveland by traveling west on U.S. 34 six miles to the Big Thompson School, then go north five miles on County Rd. 27 to the Masonville store. Turn west, still on 27, for 11½ miles through **Buckhorn Canyon** to the junction with County Rd. 44H, but stay on 27 and you climb out of the canyon to the pretty meadow called **Stove Prairie** on a ridge. No. 27 continues north; at the Stove Prairie Schoolhouse turn east on County Rd. 52 to go over the shoulder of **Buckhorn Moun-**

tain. From this the descent is into the lovely, wooded **Rist Canyon.** Eleven miles along is the community of **Bellevue.** Turn right at the village store, to the south on County Rd. 23, and go eight miles along the east shore of **Horsetooth Reservoir** to a junction with County Rd. 38E at the south end of **Spring Canyon Dam.** Here turn east on 38E and follow it to U.S. 287, and from there south to Loveland. The 56-mile circle trip, half of which is paved, is a half-day excursion.

For all travel information, see the **Loveland Chamber of Commerce,** 114 E. 5th St., Loveland, CO 80537 (tel. 303/667-6311).

Where to Stay

The **University Park Holiday Inn,** 425 W. Prospect Rd., Loveland, CO 80537 (tel. 303/482-2626), is a big, modern, cheerful motel with 259 units and a large recreation area including a pool, sundeck, sauna, and whirlpool. There is a pleasant atrium sheltering the Park Place restaurant; a second eating place is named John Q's. Beethoven's Lounge offers dancing nightly, and the Fountain Court is a piano bar. Rates are $46.50 and up, double.

The **Coach House Resort,** 5542 E. U.S. 34, Loveland, CO 80537 (tel. 303/667-7810), offers modern amenities at modest rates of $26 double: king- and queen-size beds, indoor and outdoor pools, satellite television, tennis court, whirlpools, a game room, a barbecue area, and a restaurant and lounge.

Where to Eat

Jerry Bobs, 770 W. Eisenhower Blvd. (tel. 669-0891), is open 24 hours daily with sandwiches as well as a full breakfast, lunch, and dinner menu. There is live entertainment on weekends, and the bar is open daily to 2 a.m. (to midnight on Sunday).

South-of-the-border specialties are prepared at **La Cocina,** 330 N. Lincoln Ave. (tel. 669-0211).

FORT COLLINS: During the Civil War, Rebel prisoners of the Union forces were sent west to protect the stage routes, including the overland trail through the edge of the plains at the foothills of the Rockies. When the Rebels deserted they were replaced by the 11th Ohio Volunteer Cavalry commanded by Col. William O. Collins, who named a fort here. Since the Indian wars, Fort Collins has become a farming and ranching center with a population of 75,000. It lies 65 miles north of Denver on I-25. It is the home of Colorado State University, established in 1879, known for its veterinary and forestry science schools. Fort Collins is the home of accurate time, broadcast by the National Bureau of Standards on a short-wave frequency and accurate to within a millisecond. The bureau adds a "leap second" every year. For time signals, call 499-7111.

The **Fort Collins Museum,** 200 Matthews St., is open free of charge Tuesday through Saturday from 10 a.m. to 5 p.m. and noon to 5 p.m. on Sunday. It has a Folsom Indian display, one of the state's oldest log cabins, and a building from the original military post, as well as memorabilia of the early days of the town. The town is also a likely shopping center for travelers heading in any direction, for it has no fewer than 20 shopping centers within the city limits. The town is one of the fastest growing in the U.S.

Arts in Fort Collins are centered in the **Lincoln Center,** dating back only to 1978, which is home to the **Fort Collins Symphony,** the **Foothills Civic Theater,** the **OpenStage Theater,** the **Larimer Chorale,** the **Canyon Concert Ballet,** and the **Children's Theater.**

The city has 48 historic sites, among them the **Avery House** (for locations, inquire at the Fort Collins Chamber of Commerce). The town is served by **Greyhound/Trailways** buses from Denver; there is in-city transport on

Transfort buses. A restored 1919 **trolley** car runs on its original track from City Park down Mountain Avenue Sherwood Street.

For further travel information, contact the **Fort Collins Chamber of Commerce,** 225 S. Meldrum St., Fort Collins, CO 80521 (tel. 303/482-3746).

Where to Stay

The **Holiday Inn,** 3836 E. Mulberry, Fort Collins, CO 80524 (tel. 303/484-4660), has 190 units at the junction of I-25, with a domed recreation area (the Holidome), heated pool, laundry, sauna, wading pool, whirlpool, a dining room open for three meals daily (dinners from $8 to $15), and a cocktail lounge with nightly entertainment. Rates are $39 double.

A budget choice is **El Palomino Motel,** 1220 N. College Ave., Fort Collins, CO 80524 (tel. 303/482-4555), which has a pool, its own restaurant, and rooms with kitchen facilities. Rates are $24 double.

Where to Eat

Fort Collins has a superabundance of chain-operated fast-food establishments, possibly drawn to the area by its booming population growth. At the same time a variety of ethnic cooking persists in a few eating places.

A sampling of the latter includes **Canino's Italian Restaurant,** 613 S. College Ave. (tel. 493-7205); **China Palace,** 117 S. College Ave. (tel. 221-0448); and **Spanish Manor,** 6324 S. College Ave. (tel. 226-5986).

GREELEY: The city of Greeley, 55 miles north of Denver via U.S. 85, with a population of nearly 60,000, was founded as a sort of farmland Utopia by Nathan C. Meeker, a columnist for the New York *Tribune* who was supported by his publisher, Horace Greeley, in his idea for a planned colony in the West. In 1869 a location for the Union Colony, as it was first called, was chosen at the confluence of the South Platte and Cache La Poudre Rivers at the feet of the Rockies. Within a year there were 350 farmsteads and a population of 1,000. City lots were laid out surrounded by farms. Each colonist contributed a membership fee, giving the right to a farm parcel and an option on a town lot, and lots had to be improved within one year for the claim to continue valid. Proceeds from the sale of town lots went for projects for "the common good," such as a school and a town hall; the planning of street layout, irrigation, and the planting of trees were all part of the overall project. The city has been growing steadily since that beginning on a base of agriculture carried on in the surrounding prairie, but a number of industries have also moved into the city within the past ten years.

The satellite town of **Evans,** adjoining Greeley to the south, was originally a station for the Denver & Pacific Railroad, and was first named Stage after a brakeman named Bill Stage. Evans served as a safety valve to staid, conservative Greeley, a Bible-belt town that sprang up out west with no alcohol tolerated. Evans, however, had four saloons. The two towns squabbled over which was to become county seat over a century ago—and Greeley eventually won. Today Evans's population is around 7,000.

Centennial Village, on North 14th Avenue at Island Grove Park (tel. 353-6123), is a collection of buildings showing life around Greeley between 1860 and 1920, open May to September weekdays from 10 a.m. to 6 p.m. and weekends from 1 to 5 p.m., free of charge, with guided tours scheduled hourly. Visitors enter the complex through an old railroad depot and then visit a prairie church and a one-room schoolhouse.

The **Municipal Museum,** 919 7th St. (tel. 353-6123), in the east wing of the Civic Center, shows historical items about the city; there are tools, clothing, and household goods of the pioneer times.

Free tours of the **Kodak Colorado** plant (tel. 686-7611), ten miles east of the city, are held from mid-June to mid-August on weekdays at 9:30 a.m. and 1:30 p.m. A visitor center at a major cattle feedlot operation, **Montfort of Colorado** (tel. 356-2323), has an observation deck and also presents a film explaining the installation. It is open daily from 8 a.m. to 4 p.m. at its location ten miles northeast of the city.

Greeley buses provide in-town transportation; for schedules, call 353-6123, ext. 345. **Yellow Cab** is reached at 353-5151. **Police emergency** number is 911.

Annual events in the city include an **arts picnic** in Lincoln Park, 9th Street and Tenth Avenue, during the third week of July. There are programs given by the Greeley Philharmonic Symphonette, the Greeley Chorale, the Greeley Chamber Orchestra, and by popular and country music groups and dance groups. For information, call 353-6123, ext. 390. Free tickets to watch a scrimmage of the **Denver Broncos** professional football team, who work out on the campus of the University of Colorado, can often be obtained by calling 352-3566.

Island Grove Park at 14th Avenue and A Street is the scene of the annual **Independence Stampede** the first week of July, with the biggest Fourth of July rodeo in the country. Nationally known entertainers perform during the six days of festivities, and there are pancake breakfasts, a carnival, barbecues, street dances, a parade, and theatrical performances. The park is also the site of the **Weld County Fair** (tel. 356-4000) in August.

A three-day **jazz festival** goes on at the university campus in late April or early May; for details, call 351-2200. Cultural programs scheduled by the university are also open to the public; for information on them, call 351-2265.

Greeley has a mild summer climate, the many summer days just right for outdoor recreation. Locals and visitors, too, take advantage of this small city's 33 public parks, 26 tennis courts, three swimming pools, and public golf courses.

Greeley is served by **Greyhound/Trailways** buses to Denver's Stapleton International Airport as well as to downtown Denver. **Greeley Commuter** has frequent flights between Greeley and Denver.

For all travel service information, contact the **Greeley Convention and Visitors Bureau,** P.O. Box CC, Greeley, CO 80632 (tel. 303/330-0902).

Where to Stay

The **Holiday Inn,** 609 Eighth Ave., Greeley, CO 80631 (tel. 303/356-3000, or toll free 800/HOLIDAY), has a heated pool, in-room movies, free local telephone calls, a dining room and lounge, and 100 rooms at $55 double.

Town and Country, 615 26th St., Greeley, CO 80631 (tel. 303/352-8531), has a tanning salon, a dining room, and 26 guest rooms at $25 double.

Where to Eat

Both **Carlson's Hut,** 3007 S. Eighth Ave. (tel. 356-9664), in a serene atmosphere, and **Eastwood's Ebony Room,** 3313 S. 11th Ave. (tel. 339-5241), serve steaks and seafood for lunch and dinner, daily except Sunday.

In nearby LaSalle, the **Armadillo,** 111 S. 1st St. (tel. 284-6560), serves authentic Mexican specialties at lunch and dinner seven days a week.

Live Entertainment

The **Greeley Philharmonic** orchestra has a season running from October to May with about ten performances at Foundation Hall (tel. 351-2200). A combination of professionals and drama students makes up the casts of productions of the **Little Theater of the Rockies** (tel. 351-2200), which has five summer-stock productions each season, including a musical and an opera. The university Garden Theater (tel. 351-2200) is the scene of **Concerts Under the Stars** in July and August presented by the Colorado Philharmonic Orchestra, the Greeley Summer Symphonic Band and Festival Choir, and other performers. The **Greeley Civic Theater** (tel. 330-3261) produces four to six plays every year.

3. DESTINATIONS NORTH BY WEST

West of the Continental Divide, the small city of Grand Junction serves as the gateway to Colorado for travelers heading east from the West Coast, in a fabulous land of spires and towers of weathered rock that is protected near town in a national monument. Fourteen species of dinosaurs can be seen in fossils in another national monument in this part of the state. In this remote country the wild canyons are mostly accessible only by river raft through white-water trips. This remote, open range country is big for sheep raising in land that once was best used as hideouts for bandits.

GRAND JUNCTION: On the western slopes of the Rockies 250 miles west of Denver on I-70, this city of 30,000, at the confluence of the Colorado and Gunnison Rivers, has a mild, breezy climate at an altitude of 4,500 feet, with summertime temperatures ranging from 60° to 90°; in winter, from 20° to 40°. Founded as a rail center in 1882, the town is a center of peach production in local orchards that benefit from a long growing season. It was also a center of the uranium boom in the 1950s. The city is famous for its 1962 shopping mall that became a model for urban redevelopment throughout the U.S.

The **Museum of Western Colorado,** at 4th and Ute Streets (tel. 242-0971), is open Monday through Saturday from 10 a.m. to 4:45 p.m., free of charge. The historical span ranges from the actual formation of the crust of the earth, through fossil life, into the story of various human inhabitants of the region, including the Anasazi, Fremont, and Uncompahgre peoples. Modern Indians who have lived in the area—Utes, Hopis, and Navajos—are also portrayed by their crafts. Dioramas and habitats show the flora and fauna of the land, and there is material about early explorers and the pioneer settlers.

Also run by the museum is an exhibit of fossils and skeletons called **Dinosaur Valley,** at 4th and Main Streets (tel. 243-DINO), where six animated dinosaur replicas go through their paces. It's open every day but Monday from 9 a.m. to 5 p.m. Admission is $2.50 for adults, $1.50 for children.

Another museum project is **Cross Orchards Living History Farm,** at 3079 F Rd. (tel. 242-0971), with farm machines running, historic buildings, and live animals. There is also a fruit orchard and a program of summertime activities. It is open May to October, Wednesday through Saturday from 10 a.m. to 4 p.m.

Also of interest downtown is the restored **railroad depot,** now housing commercial enterprises, at 1st and Pitkin. The **Western Colorado Center for the Arts,** at 7th Street and Orchard Avenue, shows the works of the cowboy artist Harold Bryant. **Lincoln Park,** a 140-acre recreation area east of 12th Street between North and Gunnison Avenues, has a golf course, stadiums, a swimming pool, and lighted tennis courts, as well as picnic tables.

For all travel service information, contact the **Grand Junction Area Chamber of Commerce,** 360 Grand Ave., Grand Junction, CO 81501 (tel. 303/242-3214).

Where to Stay

The **Holiday Inn,** 755 Horizon Dr., Grand Junction, CO 81506 (tel. 303/243-6790, or toll free 800/HOLIDAY), has 294 units, a laundry, a Holidome with a pool, a sauna, a whirlpool, and a playground. A dining room, coffeeshop, and cocktail lounge with nightly entertainment are on the premises. Rates are $45 to $65 double.

Howard Johnson's, 752 Horizon Dr., Grand Junction, CO 81506 (tel. 303/243-5150), has 100 units, a laundry, heated pool, dining room, and a coffeeshop open 24 hours a day in summer, from 6 a.m. to 1 a.m. in winter. There's also a cocktail lounge. Doubles are $38 to $48.

Best Value Inn, 718 Horizon Dr., Grand Junction, CO 81506 (tel. 303/243-5080), has 142 rooms, a heated pool, a separate wading pool, sauna, dining room, coffeeshop, and bar, with double rates at $22.

Where to Eat

The Winery, 642 Main St. (tel. 242-4100), has a setting of rustic early Colorado Territorial décor for serving its steaks and seafood, with an unusually wide selection of wines. Cocktails and other drinks are also on hand from the bar.

Sweetwaters, 336 Main St. (tel. 243-3900), specializes in northern Italian cuisine using imported pasta, and serves fresh fish, steaks, and daily specials as well. There is a sunny deck for warm-weather dining, and full bar service. Closed Sunday.

COLORADO NATIONAL MONUMENT:
This area of canyons and rock formations 15 miles from Grand Junction is reached via I-70 to Fruita and Colo. 340 to Rim Rock Drive. A 35-mile circuit can be made across the park on **Rim Rock Drive** and back to Grand Junction on Colo. 340.

One day is enough to see the exhibits at the visitor center, open all year, and to make the Rim Rock Drive tour, with an afternoon hike and a picnic too. Most of the canyons are accessible to hikers. There are maintained trails and old deer trails crisscrossing the north-facing slopes. The marked trails enter the canyons in switchbacks, straightening out when they reach the canyon floor.

It gets hot in the canyons in the summer and the animals that live here seek the shelter of junipers and piñon pines on the lower slopes. Each layer visible in the striations of the canyon walls marks a time in the history of the land. Great volumes of rocks have been worn away over the millennia, and it is the remnants of the rock that make the spectacular, strange forms in the park. There are rounded slopes, sheer cliffs, towers, and pinnacles, and the park was established to preserve them for the future. Fossils permit scientists to date these rocks— here most were formed during the Mesozoic Era of 225 to 65 million years ago, a time when dinosaurs dominated animal life. The animals living here today come out at dawn or dusk—mule deer and elk among them. There are some mountain lions, and buffalo are protected within the park. Many of the foot trails marked here today were blasted out of the rock by the park's first caretaker, John Otto, who hoped to open up the area for people to see. The Rim Rock Drive, completed by the Civilian Conservation Corps, was a fulfillment of his ideas.

Otto made these canyons and rocky heights his home for 30 years, and launched a one-man letter-writing campaign to stir interest in making the place a national park. He succeeded when President Taft established the monument in 1911. He has lived on as a local legend since his death in 1952.

Entombed within the rock layers here are remains of dinosaurs, fish and shellfish, early mammals, and other creatures that lived over a span of 100 million years. A combination of upward lifts and erosion, along with volcanic eruptions, caused the chaos of formations. Early people who managed to make a living in this rough terrain were of the prehistoric Fremont culture. After them, in around A.D. 1200, came ancestors of the modern Ute Indians.

The park is open in winter as well as in summer, and the cool weather is sometimes more pleasant than the hot days of August. The **Liberty Cap Trail** particularly is a likely one for cross-country skiing when the snow has fallen. Among sights to be looked for in various parts of the monument are petroglyphs depicting human figures, animals, and cryptic symbols.

The **visitor center** is near Saddlehorn, four miles from the west entrance near Fruita. Here there is a campground with tables, grills, and rest rooms, with a $5 fee collected during the summer only. Interpretive and campfire programs are held daily in summer, less frequently during the rest of the year. The visitor center shows a slide program and has exhibits explaining the geology and history of the monument. There are also maps and publications on these subjects for sale.

There are short walks to be made along canyon rims following **Window Rock, Canyon Rim, John Otto,** and **Coke Oven** trails. **Serpents Trail,** 2½ miles, winds through rock layers along 54 switchbacks that once formed the original road into the high country. **Monument Canyon** and **Liberty Cap** trails make longer hikes. Overnight backpackers should register at the visitor center.

DINOSAUR NATIONAL MONUMENT: This National Park Service area extends over part of northwestern Colorado into Utah, with a visitor center 140 miles north of Grand Junction (via I-70 west to Loma, Colo. 139 north to Rangely, Colo. 64 west to Dinosaur, and U.S. 40 west to Jensen, Utah, with an access road from Utah 149 north). Park headquarters is on U.S. 40 just east of Dinosaur, Colorado.

This fascinating monument is a sort of time capsule from the world of the dinosaurs. The **Dinosaur Quarry** here has revealed many long-disappeared species through fossil remains left behind over the millennia. There are fossils of sea creatures two to three times older than those of the dinosaurs in the rocks here. Some of these have been thrown upward in volcanic upheavals and then cut through by rivers that exposed the fossils.

Thus the Age of Dinosaurs is only part of a longer story. About 145 million years ago a suitable habitat for dinosaurs developed in this region: a low plain crossed by wide rivers and many streams where ferns, mosses, and tall conifers grew. Such dinosaurs as brontosaurus, diplodocus, stegosaurus, and other vegetarians, as well as the sharp-toothed carnivores such as allosaurus, all lived here and died here. Most of their skeletons decayed and disappeared, but in at least one spot here floodwaters washed a lot of dinosaur carcasses onto a sandbar where they were preserved in sand—along with turtles, crocodiles, clams, and other residents. The layer itself was not thick, but more sediment piled up thousands of yards deep on top of it as the sea came in and departed. Dissolved silica percolating through the strata turned the old riverbed into hard sandstone and mineralized the animal bones into the permanent fossil forms we can see today.

When the Rockies began rising to the east, the land here rose with it, the forces squeezing the layers from the sides, warping and tilting them, cracking and shifting them along fault lines. Weathering wore away layers of the upper strata to reveal the older rocks and eventually the fossils.

Drawings were carved into these cliffs about 1,000 years ago by the prehistoric Fremont people. The ridge where the fossils were found is near the **Green River,** down which fur trader William H. Ashley floated in 1825, the same route explorer John Wesley Powell took in 1869. But it was not until Earl Douglass (a paleontologist from the Carnegie Museum in Pittsburgh) looked closer at the ridge in 1908 that he suspected it might contain fossils, and in a diary entry in 1909 he wrote: "At last in the top of the ledge . . . I saw the tail bones of a Brontosaurus in exact position. It was a beautiful sight."

The quarry site became a national monument in 1915. Douglass kept digging, but although he brought out thousands of bones, including several almost complete dinosaur skeletons, he left much still to be taken out. The remainder of this bone-bearing layer forms a wall of the Quarry Visitor Center, the only place in the park where bones can be seen by visitors. Bones are undergoing the process of being exposed in the sandstone cliff.

Besides the quarry, the monument has two spectacular, remote, little-visited canyons of the **Green and Yampa Rivers.** Land exposed here was once the floor of a sea where corals and shellfish lived; today the climate is semi-desert. Temperatures can vary as much as 155° between January and July in the park.

The desert-like land of the park supports sagebrush, saltbush, and grease-wood, at higher elevations graduating into "pygmy forests," as they are called, of piñon pine and juniper. Such plants are adept at conserving water and resisting extremes of temperature, as well as living in poor soil.

Along the riverbanks are oasis-like borders of cottonwoods and box elders, making vivid greens to contrast with the sandy dryness beyond. Canada geese may suddenly take wing from a stretch of water in a canyon, and there are big-horn sheep to be spotted in the rocky cliff heights. At some points the river rushes into loud, rock-tumbling rapids, an odd sight in a desert.

The **Quarry Visitor Center,** seven miles north of Jensen, Utah, is open daily throughout the year. Because of limited parking, a shuttle bus (in summer only) takes visitors from the main parking area to the quarry. At the park headquarters two miles east of Dinosaur, Colorado, there is a slide program on the area. It is open daily in summer, weekdays only during the winter. Schedules of summer-time interpretive programs are posted at both centers.

The **Harpers Corner Scenic Drive** gives visitors views of the great canyon country within the park, a round trip of about two hours, with several stops at overlooks. **Harpers Corner** has a trailhead for a walk of two hours that gives great views of the rocky depths. Other scenic points accessible by car include **Gates of Lodore** and **Deerlodge Park,** where the Green and Yampa Rivers enter the canyons; and **Jones Hole,** an oasis-like tributary of **Whirlpool Canyon** with a hiking trail along a rushing stream. Other roads suitable for high-clearance vehicles go into the backcountry. Most spectacular of these is the 13-mile **Echo Park Road.**

Split Mountain and **Echo Park Campgrounds** have space for RVs, with dump stations but no hookups. There is firewood for sale. Primitive **campgrounds** are at Echo Park, Gates of Lodore, Deerlodge, and Rainbow Park. There is drinking water at Echo Park and Lodore.

GLENWOOD SPRINGS:

This century-old spa 160 miles west of Denver on I-70 has been world-famous for its mineral hot springs for just a century. The world's largest hot springs pool stretches for two blocks in the center of the pretty mountain town, which has a population of 5,500 and an altitude of 5,700 feet.

There is daily bus service from Denver and Grand Junction via **Greyhound/ Trailways** (tel. 292-6111). **Amtrak** (tel. 893-3911, or toll free 800/872-7245) passenger trains stop daily from Chicago and Denver to the east and San Francisco to the west. **Budget** car rentals have a dropoff here (tel. 945-8990).

The **Sunlight Ski Area** is ten miles southwest of town (see Chapter XV, Section 6).

The hot-springs pool, 405 feet long, has circulating mineral waters at 90°, while a smaller therapy pool has water at 104°. An underground complex of caves circulating warm steam is another venerable attraction that legendarily brought Indians here long before the arrival of the first European explorers in these mountains.

The pool is accessible through the **Hot Springs Lodge** (tel. 945-6571), which also provides an athletic club with facilities for such sports as handball, racquetball, and swimming. There is a weightlifting machine and a jogging area, as well as bikes for rent.

At the east end of the pool, the water bubbles in naturally at 130°, and is cooled with spring water mixed as it is pumped into the main areas. There is swimming to 10 p.m. all year round with the exception of a few days each fall, winter, and spring when it is closed for maintenance.

Just east of the pool are the **Vapor Caves,** where baths, massages, and facials are given by appointment (tel. 945-5825). Three caves are heated by the mineral hot springs to 115° at 100% humidity—a natural steambath, consisting of lying on marble benches over a stream of hot mineral water, from which the rising vapors are said to be helpful in treating arthritis, asthma, and the like. A soak-and-steam for half an hour is followed by some relaxing in a solarium. A simple vapor bath costs $6, while a bath with massage, facial, and foot reflexology costs $45. Hours are 9 a.m. to 9 p.m. for the caves.

Among annual events in town are an **arts festival** the last week of September and the state's longest-running festival, **Strawberry Days,** during the second week of June. Organized originally in 1898 to celebrate the local strawberry harvest, the celebration still has plenty of free strawberries and ice cream for everybody attending. There is a parade, arts-and-crafts fair, band concert, square dancing, and food stands.

For all travel service information, stop at the **Glenwood Springs Chamber of Commerce** at 1102 Grand Ave., Glenwood Springs, CO 81601 (tel. 303/945-6589).

Where to Stay

A major pleasure in traveling in the West is finding fancy old hotels that have survived and are restored to their early glamour, like the **Hotel Colorado,** at 526 Pine St., Glenwood Springs, CO 81601 (tel. 303/945-6511), famous as the spring White House of Pres. Theodore Roosevelt in 1905. Completed in 1893, the hotel was the fanciest in the state after the Brown Palace in Denver, being a copy of the Villa Medici in Rome and costing $850,000. Constructed of Roman brick and peachblow sandstone, it had 200 rooms, a formal dining room, a ballroom, a waterfall, and a huge outdoor fountain. There were not only the hot springs in "the warmest pool in the world," as it was advertised then, but also big-game hunting and gambling for international aristocracy.

In spite of the collapse of the silver market, which was originally responsible for Colorado's boom times, in 1893, the hotel succeeded when Teddy Roosevelt made it his base for a bear hunt. The legend is that although he did shoot ten bears and three lynxes during his stay, one day he returned from the hunt empty-handed and the maids made him a stuffed bear and hung it in the lobby for him. This was Teddy's bear, model for the subsequently famous "teddy bear" toys. A later president, William Howard Taft, was also a guest here in 1909. But the hotel went downhill during the Depression. During World War II it was used as a center for rehabilitation of wounded soldiers.

The recent restoration has brought back the old luxury to interior and exterior as well, with Victorian rooms, elegant restaurants, a fountain courtyard and café, and a spectacular grand lobby. There are 130 rooms with double rates of $45 to $55.

The **Hot Springs Lodge,** 401 N. River Rd., Glenwood Springs, CO 81601 (tel. 303/945-6571), noted above, has 73 rooms in the lodge by the huge hot-water pool. Rates are $49 to $70 double.

Riverside Cottages, 1287 County Rd. 154, Glenwood Springs, CO 81601 (tel. 303/945-5509), two miles south of town, has 1,200 feet of frontage on the

Roaring Fork River and 14 housekeeping cabins at $41 to $60. There is fishing in the river, and picnic tables and gas grills.

Where to Eat

Buffalo Valley Inn, 3637 U.S. 82 (tel. 945-5297), two miles south of town, has an Old West décor and such specialties as smoked pork barbecue, steaks, and prime rib. It's open daily for lunch and dinner.

Penelope's, 2525 Grand Ave. (tel. 945-7003), has fresh seafood, duck, veal, beef Wellington, and other entrees, with homemade breads. Open for dinner only, the restaurant overlooks the Roaring Fork River.

Sopris Restaurant, five miles south of town on U.S. 82 (tel. 945-7771), specializes in veal dishes like veal parmesan and lemon veal, rack of lamb, and a variety of steaks and fresh seafood. It's open daily for dinner, year round.

CHAPTER XVII

SOUTHWESTERN COLORADO

□ □ □

1. MESA VERDE
2. FOUR CORNERS
3. MOUNTAIN TOWNS
4. GUNNISON COUNTRY

High, beautiful mountain, valley, and plateau country remote from the rest of the U.S., southwestern Colorado has some of the nation's best outdoors areas for hiking, camping, and fishing; a few spectacular high-country ski areas (one with nearly 40 feet of snow annually); and the irreplaceable, unique treasures of the ancient cliff dwellers whose ruins are preserved in Mesa Verde National Park and in Hovenweep National Monument. This Four Corners Area, the only U.S. point where four states meet at a common point, has a wealth of archeological treasure in public lands nearby in adjoining sections of Utah, New Mexico, and Arizona.

Western mining towns, all restored and decked out in Victorian-era finery, draw the visitors' admiration, along with forgotten ghost towns where the attraction is a certain nostalgia in the air brought on by a crumbling mine shaft or overgrown ore tailing, rusting machinery the only hint of boom times that briefly made little beehive cities of these remote mountains. There is a great chasm with a fishing lake at its bottom, Gunnison Canyon, its beauties protected in a national monument. The land is wide and open—there are no big cities, only pleasant clear-skied high-altitude towns where every citizen will tell you he believes life is as good as it can get here: Cortez, Durango, Montrose. It is rodeo country, county fair country, and Indian country too: the Ute nation has land in Colorado and nearby across the Utah line is part of the huge Navajo reservation. There are restored railroad lines providing the most spectacular views seen from any trackage in the country—one of them runs daily all year long under steam power. Millions of acres of national forest land provide protected wilderness for lovers of the quiet empty spaces and the woods, and there are scores of primitive campsites for getting away from it all, most accessible by passenger car. The Ute Mountain Range in the very southwest corner seems to come alive out of its rocky fastness in the form of the Sleeping Ute, a human form on the horizon, a giant lying on his back with a feathered headdress outlined sharply from his head; his arms are folded peacefully upon his chest, and legs, feet, even his toes are sharply outlined.

To the east the sinuous barrier of the San Juan Mountains makes a wavering route northward out of New Mexico to form the Continental Divide that continues on up north to Canada, traversed here in Four Corners country by mountain passes nearly 11,000 feet in height. Up here even in summer there is a sweet mountain coolness, while down below there is desert heat in the valleys. It is a country that requires time and curiosity for proper exploring.

1. MESA VERDE

Mesa Verde National Park, with an entrance off U.S. 160 ten miles east of Cortez, is the site of thousands of ruins in one of the country's major archeological sites, where visitors may enter many of the cliff houses, perhaps to sense the immediacy of a moment in which they share in their minds the life of a people who disappeared 600 years ago. The wealth of ruins, most visible beyond the overhanging cliffs when seen from vantage points at the edges of several canyons, seems so fantastic that the place has been nicknamed the "Disneyland of American Archeology." From a distant perspective, the apartment complexes of three and four stories, with stepped-back roofs forming porches for the dwellings above, look like dollhouses. Half a century ago the author Willa Cather described village as "pale little houses of stone nestling close to one another. . . . In sunlight it was the color of winter oak leaves. A fringe of cedars grew along the edge of the cavern, like a garden. They were the only living things. Such silence and stillness and repose—immortal repose. That village sat looking down into the canyon with the calmness of eternity."

The earliest site at Mesa Verde dates from A.D. 608, about 800 years later than the oldest Anasazi ruins elsewhere in the Four Corners region. Until the 12th century the Indians lived on top of the mesa (named Verde for its green woods) in pit houses, simple cellar-like dugouts, and later adobe and stone huts. Not until the last century of their lives here did they build the elaborate structures of painstakingly shaped stone—skilled craftsmanship that could compare with modern masonry—within the shadowy depths of the great caves high in canyon walls. Then in the 13th century they disappeared. Where they went is the subject of many theories, but it seems clear that some of their descendants still live around the Four Corners area.

Mesa Verde is the largest archeological preserve in the country, but was unknown in modern times until a couple of ranchers, Charles and Richard Wetherill, chanced on some of the ruins in 1888. More or less uncontrolled looting of artifacts followed the discovery, and in 1891 a Swedish archeologist, Gustaf Nordenskiold, shipped more than 600 pieces back to Sweden. A New York *Daily Graphic* reporter named Lucy Peabody, who came west to write stories about the newly discovered historic villages, aroused national interest in protecting the site, and in 1906 the 52,000-acre site was made a national park.

Within Mesa Verde, known as the only park in the U.S. devoted to the works of man, there is a self-guided quarter-mile walk to the most elaborate ruin in the Southwest, **Cliff Palace,** an intriguing assemblage of towers, masonry façades with shadowy square windows, and *kivas,* large circular rooms used for spiritual ceremonies.

To reach the inside of another major ruin, **Balcony House,** visitors must climb a 32-foot ladder. Although the 12-mile **Ruins Road** makes a number of pit houses and cliffside overlooks easily accessible by car, two of the ruins, **Step House** and **Long House,** both on **Wetherill Mesa,** can be visited only by a free park bus that leaves from the visitor center every half hour during the summer months. Rangers lead tours to **Spruce Tree House,** another of the major cliff-dwelling complexes, only in the winter, when other park facilities are closed.

Some of the tiny rooms in ruins in high caves seen from various roads in the park are still a mystery, for they were too small for living quarters and too inaccessible to have served for food or other storage uses. Though some of these tiny rooms had windows, there is, and evidently was, no other way to reach them than by being lowered to them at the end of a rope. One theory of archeologists is that they might have served as jail cells—once in, a person would have no way out. It is estimated that there are 10,000 to 12,000 ruins in the canyons of Mesa Verde, many never excavated and others probably not even discovered yet. The rock of the house construction matches that of the cliff walls so well that they can be seen only at certain times of day when the sunlight lets them stand out. Although none of the trails to the ruins is strenuous, the altitude of 8,000 feet makes them tiring for visitors just up from the lower country outside.

Besides the fascinating architecture of the hidden villages in the cliffsides, the park has other treasures in its museum, established to house artifacts and specimens related to the prehistory or the history of the site or nearby sites (such as Hovenweep National Monument, a few miles to the west). A wide variety of natural science specimens is displayed. The open-air exhibits have examples of remarkable evidence of prehistoric behavior in the cliff dwellings and mesa-top ruins. The sites are documented in excavation reports and site survey records, and in fact the stone structure of the headquarters building itself is considered worthy of inclusion in the National Register of Historic Sites.

The dry climate and cliff overhangs have preserved artifacts that would have deteriorated elsewhere. Basketry, bone, cordage, and cloth have provided scientists with remains of this prehistoric culture that are uncommon in other regions of the country. Although many of the artifacts were taken from these sites before the park was established, in recent years scientific institutions around the country have succeeded in collecting many of them from private sources and returning them to public view. Holding important collections of Mesa Verde materials today are, for example, the Colorado Historical Society in Denver, the Field Columbian Museum of Natural History in Chicago, the Robert H. Lowie Museum of Anthropology in Berkeley, and the University Museum of the University of Pennsylvania in Philadelphia. The treasures taken by Nordenskiold, noted earlier, are displayed in the Finnish National Museum in Helsinki, the first Mesa Verde collection put together in a scientific manner. Early digs conducted by the National Park Service in the early part of the century, after the park had been established, were supervised by Dr. Jesse Walter Fewkes of the Bureau of Ethnology; most of the artifacts recovered in those early years are today in the Smithsonian Institution in Washington.

The artifacts shown here are in a museum that was originally opened in 1917 in the ranger's former residence cabin, and it was the first museum established in a park by the National Park Service. Besides exhibits in the museum on **Chapin Mesa**—now housed in a stone structure that replaced the cabin in 1936 —some museum artifacts are also shown at the newer **Far View Visitor Center,** where visitors begin their tours of the park. (These prehistoric westerners and their artifacts exert a strong fascination on Europeans, especially Germans— there are more German visitors at Mesa Verde than visitors from just across the state line in New Mexico.)

Those early Anasazi people, named so by the Navajo word for "old ones," who occupied these sites have been labeled Basketmakers by archeologists for the skill shown in this craft, which outshone their talents at pottery making, though they did also make ceramic ware. Their earliest dwellings were the pithouses seen most easily from several of the turnouts on the Ruins Road. These are fairly simple rectangular pits dug into the ground so that the walls became the sides of the house, pits grouped in little villages of a dozen or so residences usually situated atop a mesa, but sometimes within a cave. The pits were roofed over with *vigas*—

slender wood beams—and the cracks filled in with grass and mud. In the rich soil atop the mesa they grew crops of beans, corn, and squash. Their only domestic animals were dogs and turkeys, the latter raised for their feathers that were woven into winter blankets.

By the middle of the 8th century these people began building above-ground houses that eventually took the form of the Indian pueblo community, like those still occupied to the south in New Mexico. First poles were set into the ground to form the outline of the house, and then sticks were woven between the poles to begin walls, and to form a roof. A thick coat of mud then made the place weather-proof, in principle. The structures were built against one another in a long curving row. Sometimes pit houses were also built out front, thought to be forerunners of the later *kiva*—the circular underground ceremonial chamber still seen in modern pueblos today.

Around A.D. 1000 stone masonry began displacing the pole-and-mud construction, and compact apartment-like buildings went up, showing exceptional skill in masonry by the 12th century. They had as many as three stories and could contain 50 rooms or more. But near the end of the 12th century the people began abandoning these apartments in order to move down into the cliffs in cave dwellings we find today. These were hard to get into and out of, but something—no one knows what—impelled them to move to these awkward spots, especially dangerous, one would suppose, for old folk and children. The best guess may be that they were protecting themselves from invaders. In any case they remained in these cliffside houses for less than a century before disappearing from Mesa Verde altogether. An extended drought at the end of the 13th century is often cited as a probable reason; a more recent idea is that they simply used up all the available wood, lost the usual cycle of replenishment of topsoil, and found they could no longer grow food here: a sort of ecological suicide. It is thought they may have been the ancestors of some of the pueblo dwellers in present-day New Mexico. It is also noted that in the remote, rarely visited fastnesses of the Copper Canyon, which reaches 1,000 miles in various branches, some 750 miles to the south in the Mexican state of Chihuahua the Tarahumara Indians, numbering around 30,000, still live today in stone-walled houses with sooty ceilings within caves in the canyon walls.

Chapin Mesa, site of park headquarters, the archeological museum, and a post office, is 21 miles from the park entrance on U.S. 160. Just four miles in from the entrance is Morfield Campground, and 15 miles in is the **Far View Visitor Center.** The center, open in summer only from 8 a.m. to 5 p.m., has maps of the park and detailed booklets on the various ruins. These are also available at the Chapin Mesa Museum, open daily year round. In summer rangers organize nightly campfire programs on various subjects associated with the lore of the park.

Morfield Campground, open May 1 to October 31, has campsites for tents and RVs with tables and grills and a dump station. The campground has a small grocery store and there are toilets and showers.

Accommodations are available within the park at the **Fair View Motor Lodge** (tel. 303/529-4421), at the visitor center area, open May to October, offering rooms with private baths and balconies at $46 double. The main lodge has a dining room open for three meals daily, a cocktail lounge, a gift shop selling Indian-made crafts, and a theater for interpretive programs in the evening. A smaller restaurant is open May to October in **Spruce Tree Terrace,** where there is also a shop selling groceries and Indian crafts, near the museum at Chapin Mesa.

In winter the Ruins Road and museum remain open, but other facilities are closed. In winter the only guided tours available, depending on weather conditions, go to Spruce Tree House. Two hiking trails lead into Spruce Tree Canyon;

hikers must register at the ranger's office before taking them. There are picnic areas at the Spruce Tree Terrace area and at pullouts along Ruins Road.

2. FOUR CORNERS

Four Corners, marked by a bronze plaque, where four states—Arizona, Utah, Colorado, and New Mexico—meet at a single point, is reached via U.S. 160, 40 miles southwest of Cortez in the Ute Mountain Indian Reservation. Tourists love to get down on all fours with hands touching two states and knees in two other states. The traveling newspaper columnist Ernie Pyle once made a long detour here in the 1930s just to sit in four states at one time, and think a few long thoughts—all duly reported in that day's dispatch. In what may be a sort of four-state land grab, the neighboring Navajos have set up a toll booth to collect $1 from each car entering the site, and have also put up a long row of Indians arts-and-crafts stands. Besides Mesa Verde, the area also offers Hovenweep National Monument and the high, sunny town of Cortez, where Indian crafts in several trading posts interest visitors. (Four Corners attractions in New Mexico and Arizona nearby are dealt with in separate sections in chapters for those states.)

HOVENWEEP NATIONAL MONUMENT: This remote area, in contrast to Mesa Verde which is jammed with traffic all summer, gets only handfuls of visitors even in the high tourist season of summer. Its 500 acres of ruins are in several pueblos, four in Colorado and two across the border in Utah. **Headquarters** is reached via U.S. 160 south and McElmo Canyon Road west, a total distance of 40 miles from Cortez. There is a spacious campground here, rarely ever full—a turnout of ten campers is considered average.

In this desert serenity the stark isolation emphasizes the mystery of 20-foot-high sandstone towers believed to have been built by the same people, or their cousins, who lived in Mesa Verde. Like them, the people who lived here at Hovenweep were originally nomadic hunters who settled in caves about 2,000 years ago and started farming in the bottoms of canyons. They later built stone huts and here built cliff dwellings and the strange towers not seen elsewhere. These have small windows up and down their masonry sides and are still very solid. They continue to baffle archeologists, who suggest they possibly functioned as guard towers for springs at the heads of canyons, or lookout towers, or signal towers, or celestial observatories, or water towers, or granaries, or ceremonial structures, or early high-rise apartments. None of these conjectures has been proved, and the ranger on duty is happy to entertain guesses—he's making a collection of them. There are six clusters of the towers scattered over the wide area.

The monument got its name from its first visitor in modern times, the intrepid photographer of the West, William H. Jackson, who came upon the abandoned ruins in 1874 and called them by the Ute name for "deserted valley": Hovenweep. But there is life here: an easy trail, **Tower Point Loop,** leads visitors past a number of mostly useful plants that were known to the original inhabitants in these houses. Utah juniper, the only tree growing atop the mesa here, was used for house building and for firewood; the shaggy bark made insulation for winter moccasins and leggings and for bedding, or for diapers. The juniper berries flavored food—and are used in making gin today. Seeds inside the berries make necklaces and bracelets. The cliff rose has cream-colored sweet-smelling flowers in the early summer, and in the fall whitish plumes emerge from the flowers. The Hopis use the leaves and twigs to induce vomiting and as a healing agent for wounds or sores. Navajos use the wood of the plant for arrow shafts and prayer sticks.

Mormon tea looks like upside-down whisk brooms with its clusters of green stems, growing to about a yard in height. Tea made from boiling the stems is supposed to cure many ailments, including headache, coughs, colds, and impurities in blood. Its high tannin content makes it a diuretic. Sagebrush has gray-green wedge-shaped leaves and dominates the whole area; it makes good fuel with a pleasantly aromatic quality that Navajos use traditionally to absorb bad smells, such as that of a skunk. The bark makes padding and insulation or can be woven into rope or sandals. Narrowleaf yucca was another plant useful to the Anasazi, who ate the banana-like fruit raw, roasted, dried, or baked as a kind of bread. The leaves make fiber useful as rope or in baskets or sandals. Hopi potters today use the tip of a yucca leaf in painting sharply outlined designs on their work (the tip also makes a serviceable sewing needle). The pulverized root of yucca makes soap or shampoo, and the flower stalk has a high sugar content something like sugarcane.

The squawbush, up to six feet in height, has three-lobed leaves and sticky dark-red berries that make a good summer drink with sugar and water. Pemmican, a mixture of dried meat, dried fruit, and fat, also had squawbush berries in the recipe. The stems are used in basketry. Four-wing saltbush grows to five feet in height and has narrow, densely growing leaves and strange four-lobed fruits that dry out to a white papery form. Leaves and shoots are eaten as salad or in soup—our domestic spinach is a relation of this plant. Local Indians and Hispanics grind the seeds, add water and sugar, and make a drink called pinole. A yellow dye used by the Navajos is made from the dried twigs and leaves also. Utah serviceberry has good-smelling white flowers in the spring, with roundish serrated leaves, and a sweetish berry used in jellies and jams, or in pemmican. Carrying baskets were once made of the straight branches by the Apaches.

The prickly pear cactus known all over the Southwest, with its spiny pads shaped like beavertails, is in fact a cousin of the beavertail cactus. Its bright-yellow flowers appear in mid-May to June, followed by the appearance of purple fruit used in jam or jelly. Rock lichens make colorful splotches on slick rock everywhere, the only plant that can live on bare rock. It consists of both a fungus and an alga. The fungus makes a home for the alga and absorbs minerals and water from the rock. As a green plant the alga makes food for the fungus. The lichen actually breaks down the rock in tiny portions by excreting a mild acid, the first step in soil formation. Then when the lichen finally dies, it disintegrates and adds a bit of organic matter to the soil it has begun to make. Dyes are made out of various colored lichens scraped off rock and ground into powder.

Hovenweep National Monument is open year round, with access by graded dirt roads that become muddy in wet weather. Rainstorms may make them temporarily impassible.

CORTEZ: A small city of 8,000 people in the Montelores Valley, Cortez is a center for visits to Mesa Verde and the surrounding region, including the **Dolores River Valley,** reached along Colo. 145 to the northeast. An antique railroad locomotive, the *Gallopin' Goose,* and a trout hatchery are stops on the way. **Rico,** high up, is an old mining town still showing signs of life; next you come to a scenic beauty spot in the **San Juan National Forest,** the **Meadows.** There are campsites and picnic areas maintained by the Forest Service. Along this route, incidentally, is some of the best fishing in the Southwest, at **Summit Reservoir,** reached from the village of Dolores (on Colo. 145) south on Colo. 184 for 7½ miles. The **Dolores River** is another trout area. Other fishing places near Cortez are **Lake Narraguinnep,** 15 miles distant, reached via U.S. 666 north and Colo. 147 east; and **Totten Reservoir,** four miles to the east.

The **Cortez Municipal Golf Course** has 18 holes over 6,870 yards, and is located 12 miles northeast of town on Colo. 145, with great views from the greens of the La Plata Mountains and the Sleeping Ute. Its fairways are interspersed with two lakes, several ponds, many trees, and some sand traps; visitors are welcome. **City Park** has barbecue grills and picnic tables, a playground, and the municipal swimming pool open to visitors. A block north are night-lighted municipally owned tennis courts. Cortez also offers visitors stock-car races, summertime rodeos, bowling, softball, and square dancing. The **Montezuma County Fair** is held here every August.

For all travel information, get in touch with the **Cortez Chamber of Commerce** visitor center, 808 E. Main St., Cortez, CO 81321 (tel. 303/565-3414).

Sights

Mancos Canyon Indian Park, 14 miles south of Cortez on U.S. 160, is the site of daily auto tours of ruins on the **Ute Mountain Indian Reservation,** in which visitors take their own car and provide themselves with picnic lunches (and plenty of water!). The all-day trip starts at 9 a.m. Another Indian-run enterprise on the same highway a bit closer to the city is the **Ute Mountain Homelands Arts & Crafts** shop, 12 miles south of town at the Towaoc turnoff, where visitors may tour the workshops and watch artisans and artists ply their trades. There is bingo here nightly as well. East of Cortez two miles on U.S. 160 is another Indian workshop where potters of the Ute, Navajo, Zuñi, and Yaqui nations make original ceramic pieces, each signed by the maker. Anasazi designs like those on thousand-year-old pots found at Mesa Verde nearby are popular on gracefully designed low-necked bowls, for example, and there are beer mugs with similar motifs that look both modern and ancient somehow. The pottery is glazed twice with lead-free materials to become watertight; the pottery shop, called **Mesa Verde Pottery,** is open daily from 8 a.m. to 5 p.m. **Notah Dinah** is an Indian trading post with more crafts, Indian made, displayed for sale, at 309 N. Broadway. Indian craftsmen also work with traditional design in silver and gold pieces at **Cortez Silver & Gold,** east of town on U.S. 160.

Ten miles north on the scenic highway Colo. 145 in the village of Dolores, the small **Dolores Star Museum** has pioneer artifacts out of the Territorial days.

Hiking trails provide some of the most scenic mountain experiences in the West from trailheads near Cortez. The **Wilson Mountain Primitive Area** can be reached only on foot by two trails in the San Juan National Forest and by others in the Uncompahgre National Forest. The **Lizard Head Trail** begins northwest of Cortez, two miles below Lizard Head Pass from Colo. 145. The **Navajo Lake Trail** begins eight miles in from Colo. 145 along the narrow road to Dunton. **Silver Creek Trail** leading to a range of peaks east of Rico is accessible to the hiker from its start off Colo. 145 three miles south of Lizard Head Pass. Other trails, some requiring several days to complete, that lead off this mountain highway (Colo. 145) are **Horse Gulch Trail, Burnett Creek Trail,** which lead into the area of Eagle Peak, Storm Peak, and Calico Peak; and **Calico Trail** and **Priest Gulch Trail,** leading out from the Priest Gulch campground 22 miles north of Dolores. There is also **Bear Creek Trail,** leading off from Colo. 145 two miles west of the campground.

Where to Stay

The **Far View Lodge,** on Navajo Hill, Mesa Verde National Park, CO 81330 (tel. 303/529-4421), 15 miles inside the park, has the considerable advantages of terrific views of the high Mesa Verde country and a quiet location within easy reach of the main cliff dwellings visible from roads or trails. The Far

View Terrace offers breakfast, lunch, and dinner entrees; the breakfast special here is the fresh baked Navajo taco. Navajo and Ute Indians demonstrate their crafts here daily from 10 a.m. to 2 p.m. There is bar service on the terrace too, for a margarita after a day's rock climbing and cliff-house viewing. A multimedia show on the subject of the area's lore, entitled *Anasazi* after the early residents of these cliffside apartments, is shown during the evening. A large gift shop offers authentic Indian-made wares, and there is also a national park visitor center and bus stop for mesa tours (visited only by bus or on foot) adjacent to the lodge site. The lodge, open from May to late October, charges $69 to $72 for double rooms.

In town, the **Ramada Inn,** 666 S. Broadway, Cortez, CO 81321 (tel. 303/565-3773), has 87 rooms, a pool, and a lounge and restaurant. Double rates here are $48 to $65.

The **Bel Rau Lodge,** 2000 E. Main St., Cortez, CO 81321 (tel. 303/565-3738), has 16 units, six of them with kitchens, and a playground and heated pool. Rates start at $35 double.

Where to Eat

The **Pony Express Restaurant,** 603 E. Main (tel. 565-3475), has a full menu for lunch and dinner as well as a popular buffet; its day starts with breakfast at 6 a.m. with such specialties as eggs Benedict or eggs burrito.

Nero's Italian Restaurant, at 303 W. Main (tel. 565-7366), has a décor enhanced by art done by local artists. Its specialties include lasagne, veal marsala, shrimp Parmesan, scampi, linguine with clam sauce, and chicken Florentine. Nightly specials also offer steak and fish dishes, and there is full bar service and a good wine list.

DURANGO: A railroad town founded in 1880 when a spur line was built into the mountain country to serve the gold and silver mines in the area, Durango is a delight to tourists for its extensive restoration of Territorial buildings covering an area of several blocks downtown, including inns and eating places. The narrow-gauge Durango-Silverton rail line that originally established the town has also been restored and runs daily all year. At an elevation of 6,500 feet, the small city of 15,000 is on the Animas River (site of a major trout hatchery) and has a horizon to the north picked out with peaks in the 13,000- and 14,000-foot range, while to the south and west lies desert country. Rainfall is under 20 inches a year (but thunderstorms are frequent on summer afternoons, and prudent hikers obey the local adage: "Be on top by noon"). About five feet of snow is average for a Durango winter. Average temperatures for January are 25° to 45°, and for July, 67° to 83° —a cool, sunny climate that gets chilly even on summer evenings.

Transportation is provided by city buses called **The Lift** (tel. 259-LIFT) at 50¢ per ride. There are no bus stops, and a note on the bus map urges travelers: "You must wave enthusiastically at the driver to let him know you would like a lift!" Taxis are provided by **Durango Transportation** (tel. 259-4818).

Intercity bus service is on **Greyhound/Trailways** (tel. 292-6111).

Aspen Airways (tel. toll free 800/525-0256) has daily direct flights to La Plata Airport in Durango from Denver. **Trans-Colorado Airlines** (tel. toll free 800/525-1455, 800/332-4907 in Colorado) has direct flights daily from Denver. **America West Airlines** (tel. 247-9597) has service to Phoenix and the West Coast.

Car rentals include **Avis** (tel. 247-9761), **Thrifty** (tel. 259-3504), and **Hertz** (tel. 247-3933).

For all travel service information, contact the **Durango Chamber Resort**

Association, 111 S. Camino del Rio, Durango, CO 81301 (tel. 303/247-0312, or, for reservations only toll free 800/525-8855).

Recreation In and Around Durango

Fisherfolk impatient with the uncertainty of fly casting in fast-flowing mountain streams can always count on a good catch at the local so-called trout ranches, where trout are raised and sold by the pound to anyone who wants to drop in a line. Two such establishments here are **Twin Buttes Trout Ranch,** on Lightner Creek off U.S. 160 west of town, and **Silver Streams Lodge,** at Vallecito Lake. Tackle and bait are provided free and all the fisherperson pays is $3 a pound for the fish.

Horseback riding is a major activity in this spectacular cool mountain and forest country, and there are still plenty of spots in the rugged San Juan Mountains and elsewhere in the region that are best reached on a horse. The **Bar D Riding Stables,** nine miles north of Durango on East Animas Road (tel. 247-5755), offer breakfast rides and scheduled one- and two-hour rides daily. Horses are rented also at **Meadowlark Ranch,** Vallecito Lake (tel. 884-2966).

White-water rafting down the Animas River is provided by several outfits in Durango. Oldest local outfitter is **Colorado River Tours,** 1523 Main Ave. (tel. 259-0708), offering free transportation to the river edge from local lodging places. Trips on the Animas River have a barbecue included. There is parking at the outfitter's office. **Rocky Mountain Outpost,** at 1111 Camino del Rio (tel. 259-4783), offers raft, kayak, and canoe trips with guides, meals, and passenger participation in the paddling. Raft or canoe trips are also made on the San Juan River.

Wild Goose Adventures (tel. 259-4453) has 2½-hour trips three times daily leaving from Schneider Park across the Animas River from the Holiday Inn, going downriver 11 miles and returning by bus. **Four Corners Marine,** 360 S. Camino del Rio (tel. 259-3893), across from the Centennial Mall south of town, offers kayak, dory, and raft instruction, with daily lessons and three-day sessions.

Water sports, fishing, and boating are popular with locals and visitors at **Navajo Lake,** 40 miles southeast of Durango via U.S. 160 east, Colo. 172, and Colo. 151 to Arboles. The 37-mile-long lake spans the Colorado–New Mexico line. At Arboles, Colorado, is a marina with rental boats and ramps, and a marine equipment store. All facilities at **Arboles Marina** may be reserved by calling 883-2343.

Durango has a **jogging** trail just under a mile in length beginning in Memorial Park, 32nd Street at West Third Avenue, following the bank of the Animas River south to Rank Park at the high school. Rim Drive on the campus of Fort Lewis College is also used by joggers.

Racquetball enthusiasts may use courts at the **Court Club of Durango,** 1600 Florida Rd. (tel. 259-2579), which also has a swimming pool, steamroom, Jacuzzi, and Nautilus center. Visitors are charged $5 for court use.

The **Purgatory Alpine Slide** at the Purgatory Ski Area, 27 miles north of town on U.S. 550 (tel. 247-9000), is open all summer from 10 a.m. to 5 p.m.

Open daily is the 18-hole **Hillcrest Golf Course** on Fort Lewis College Mesa (tel. 247-1499), overlooking the city, open from 7 a.m. with a fee. Golf equipment and carts are available, and there are a driving range, practice green, and practice sand trap.

Durango is a rodeo town, with **rodeos** three times a week all summer, on Monday, Wednesday, and Friday at 8 p.m. at the **La Plata County Fairgrounds,** 25th Street and Main Avenue. All standard rodeo events are performed by amateurs.

Bicycle racing comes to town every Memorial Day in the **Iron Horse Classic,** in which riders race the narrow-gauge train over two mountain passes from Durango to Silverton. The bikers always beat the train. Other stages of the event include lap races in town and a 55-mile round-trip circuit to Bayfield and back.

One of the best scenic drives, all on paved roads, in the Southwest is the all-day **Circle Drive** out of Durango, doing 225 miles over four mountain passes. Departing north from town on U.S. 550, the Million Dollar Hwy. (named for all the gold that passed over it), the route goes over Coalbank and Molas Passes into the old mining town of Silverton, and continues over Red Mountain Pass and along the cliffside into Ouray. Eleven miles north of Ouray, at Ridgeway, take Colo. 62 southwest over Dallas Divide to Placerville, from which there is a four-mile side trip to Telluride. Then from Placerville take Colo. 145 south over Lizard Head Pass to Dolores. The route then is Colo. 184 to Mancos and U.S. 160 back to Durango.

The **Durango & Silverton Narrow Gauge Railroad Co.** operates trains May through October with coal-fired locomotives and 1880-style coaches over 45 miles of mountain wilderness between Durango and Silverton. The Alamosa parlor car has a full bar open during the trips, which take three hours each way; there is a two-hour stopover in Silverton before the return trip. Trains leave at 7:30, 8:30, 9:30, or 10:15 a.m. The round-trip fare is $32.25 to Silverton and back, or $55.50 in the bar car. Children aged 5 to 11 are charged $16.25. Ticket office in Durango is at the terminal at 479 Main Ave. (tel. 247-2733). A parking lot at the terminal charges $4 daily for cars, $5 for RVs.

A new service on the train is the Railcamp, a boxcar refurbished to serve as a recreational vehicle that is "spotted" on a secluded siding each Monday, and is then picked up and returned to Durango each Friday.

Where to Stay Around Durango

The **Strater Hotel,** 699 Main Ave., Durango, CO 81301 (tel. 303/247-4431), ranks among the finest Victorian inns of the West, with an elegant façade of red brick emphasized by white outlining woodwork in bay windows and fancy roofline. Authentic Victorian antiques in walnut, including some beds with ornate carved canopies, furnish the 94 rooms that have been welcoming guests without a break since the place opened in 1887. Everywhere the charm of old woodwork and fixtures draws the eye; even the safe in the reception area is decorated with a finely painted Colorado scene of lake and pinnacle. Chandeliers and carved wooden fancywork embellish the ceiling overhead in the lobby; the brightly polished brass railings welcoming you up the entrance steps from outside set a tone of warm elegance.

Among the most impressive rooms is the bridal suite (no. 322) in red velvet under valances, with a bed with storks on it carved in relief under the canopy. In spite of the other-century finery the rooms have telephones, air conditioning, and television, but each has a special quality with unique antiques, wall coverings ranging from flocked gold or burgundy papers or white paint to plain brick and wood paneling. Ornate gilt frames hold old photographs or oil paintings. The rooms also have private baths, some of the old claw-footed-tub variety.

There are two restaurants in the hotel. The Opera House has Tiffany-style lamps, stained-glass windows, and a buffet with a great antique mirror. Gold-trimmed mirrors and brass candelabras on marble-topped walnut sideboards characterize the more formal Columbian Room. Colorado sautéed trout, veal, homemade pasta, and good steaks cut thick are specialties of the Strater kitchen. More Gay '90s décor is found in the Diamond Belle Saloon, with barmaids in costume, bartenders in sleeve garters, and sexy nudes reclining in oil paintings, the scene further enlivened by the sounds of a honky-tonk piano. Melodrama and other period drama is performed during the summer nightly in the Diamond Circle Theatre.

Winter rates (October 15 to June 1) are $54 to $56 double; summer rates run $56 to $60 double.

Another fine old hotel, also in the downtown historic district of restored structures, is the **General Palmer House,** 567 Main Ave., Durango, CO 81301 (tel. 303/247-4747, or toll free 800/523-3358, 800/824-2173 in Colorado), named for the builder of the Denver & Rio Grande Railroad (of which the Silverton-Durango section, still running, was a part). Built in 1898, the inn was remodeled in 1982, with rooms offering such Victorian reproductions as armoires, lace-canopied beds, and chevelle mirrors. All rooms have private baths, telephones, and televisions. The lobby is of interest for its Tiffany chandeliers and lamps. Rates are $52 to $75 double in winter, $60 to $85 in summer.

The **Durango Inn,** 21382 U.S. 160 West, Durango, CO 81301 (tel. 303/247-3251), has 56 units, an outdoor pool, hot therapy tub, sauna, playground, and 57 acres of grounds along Lightner Creek. A cocktail lounge and the Atrium Restaurant are also on the premises. Winter rates are $39 double; summer rates, $56 double.

Guest Ranches

Colorado Trails Ranch, 12 miles from town on County Rd. 240, Durango, CO 81301 (tel. 303/247-5055), is open June to September on a 525-acre layout. It has swimming, waterskiing, tennis, and evening entertainment, as well as plenty of horseback riding including overnight pack trips and breakfast rides. Modern cabins with baths accommodate 75 guests, at rates of $650 to $860 per week *per person,* American Plan.

Wilderness Trails Ranch, 776 County Rd. 300, Durango, CO 81301 (tel. 303/247-0722), has a big two-story gable-roofed log ranch house and roomy cabins with open-front porches in the Pine River Valley. A fieldstone fireplace in the lodge is an evening gathering spot for sing-along singers and guitar players. There is waterskiing on Vallecito Lake. Regular cookouts and a weekly overnight pack trip are part of the program of rides. Morgan horses are raised and sold at the ranch. There is live western music for the weekly Saturday-night dance; the staff puts on a musical show on other nights, and there is a magic show too. A stocked pond provides trout fishing. Rates, *per person,* double, are $567 to $630 weekly, American Plan, including horse for the week.

Where to Eat in Durango

Home-cooked German food is the attraction at **Edelweiss Motel and Restaurant,** across from the Community Hospital on County Rd. 203 (tel. 247-5685). Wienerschnitzel and sauerbraten are always on the menu. It is open for breakfast and for dinner daily, and has full bar service. Dinners run $7 to $16.

Francisco's, a block north of the train depot at 619 Main Ave. (tel. 247-4098), has fresh, homemade authentic Mexican dishes: enchiladas, chiles rellenos, tamales, and sopaipillas among them. Natillas, flan, and cheesecake are for dessert. Margaritas are served by the glass or pitcher.

Honey-marinated flank steak (with famous locally made honey) is a special of **Katie O'Brien's,** Abbey Square at 152 E. 6th St. (tel. 247-2626), where dinners range from $9 to $24. Special prices apply for a prime rib dinner for two. Abbey scallops sauté and chicken teriyaki are other choices.

A traditional Durango restaurant is the **Ore House** at 147 E. 6th St. (tel. 247-5707), in a western-style décor aimed at being "rustic and casual," according to the management, which runs a similar enterprise in the nearby city of Cortez. Steaks and seafoods are the mainstay and there is a salad bar and full bar service. Open daily for dinner.

3. MOUNTAIN TOWNS

In the heights of the San Juan Mountains and in adjoining valleys and canyons are a few small communities that come alive in summer as headquarters for visitors exploring the wilderness of forest, stream, pond, and mountain. Some have active winter-visitor business as well. Among them are Silverton, Ouray, and Telluride.

SILVERTON: At the northern terminus of the Durango & Silverton Narrow Gauge Railroad, Silverton, at an altitude of 9,300 feet, has a population of 850 and calls itself "the mining town that never quit." Around the little town are peaks of mountains reaching 12,000 and 13,000 feet. One local mine still going is Colorado's largest gold producer, Sunnyside Gold, which opened in 1874. Blair Street was a notorious area of saloons and brothels a century ago, today housing more sedate restaurants and shops in the original buildings. The whole town is a Registered Historic Landmark.

Trains on the **D&SNGR** depart from Silverton at 12:45, 2, 3, and 3:45 p.m. daily in summer for the 45-mile trip to Durango, and in fall trains leave once daily at 1:45 p.m. There is no service between late October and early May. For ticket information in Silverton, call the depot at 387-5416.

Located on U.S. 550 about 50 miles north of Durango, the town is a departure point for hikers and cross-country skiers in the surrounding **San Juan National Forest.** Admirers of Territorial architecture also like Silverton well enough to spend a few hours admiring the old structures along Blair Street, Main Street, and cross streets. Open in the summer is the **San Juan County Historical Society Museum** (tel. 387-5838), in the old 1902 county jail. The courthouse with its gold-domed clock tower is one of the best in Colorado. A National Park Service grant has helped in the restoration of the 1909 Town Hall. One of the oldest buildings in the region is the 1880 Posey & Wingate Building, while the Silverton Standard Building houses the oldest continuous business in western Colorado. An ornate structure is the Olde Livery, a barn built in the 1890s.

An information booth on Greene Street has all travel service information, or telephone the **Silverton Chamber of Commerce** (tel. 303/387-5654).

Where to Stay and Eat

The **Grand Imperial Hotel,** on Greene Street, Silverton, CO 81433 (tel. 303/387-5527), used to house the Hub Saloon, where the old song "There'll Be a Hot Time in the Old Town Tonight" was written. Dating from 1883, the great stone façade, decked out with red, blue, and gold wood trim, makes an imposing presence today as it did in the past. It still houses the cherrywood bar from that early Hub Saloon, the bar having survived being painted over during Prohibition —it has been scraped down to its original condition again. There is a tin mansard roof that gleams in the sun, and inside, restored pressed-tin ceilings bring back the good old days. The hotel has 40 Victorian guest rooms with private baths and the **Gold King dining room.** Rooms have hand-printed wallpaper and brass beds, at double rates of $38 to $45.

A quiet lodging with good food available is the **Teller House Hotel,** 1250 Greene St., Silverton, CO 81433 (tel. 303/387-5423), with bed-and-breakfast for two at $28. The **French Bakery Restaurant** on the premises, open every day for breakfast and lunch, and for dinners Friday through Monday, makes the hotel a pleasurable experience at any time of year.

OURAY: This historic town, 70 miles north of Durango on U.S. 550, is reached over the beautiful Red Mountain Pass from the south. Named for a Ute Indian leader, it was another of the many gold- and silver-mining camps that became established towns in the area. A copper mine nearby is still producing, but from a high of 2,000 people a century ago the population is less than half that today. The **Ouray County Historical Museum** is open daily in the summer and provides a printed guide to a walking tour of historic buildings in the small town. Also of interest to visitors is a very large swimming pool fed by natural mineral hot springs. Victoriana buffs will admire the Beaumont Hotel, Wright's Opera Hall, the Western Hotel, and the Elks' Lodge, among other examples of Queen Anne, Greek Revival, and Romanesque architecture.

A Walking Tour

A walking tour of old structures begins at the historical museum at 5th Street and Sixth Avenue, and goes next to the **McCoy Home** of 1895, at 510 Fifth Ave. The spindles and stained glass, and the tower with its lightning-rod cap, are typical of the Queen Anne architecture of the period. The 1888 **Ashley House** at 4th Street and Fifth Avenue highlights Queen Anne details in contrasting colors that emphasize the stained-glass windows, patterned shinglework, fancy brackets, floral relief, and spindled porch supports. At the same intersection is another late Queen Anne-style residence, the **Hurlburt House** of the 1880s. Cornish stonemasons built the oldest church in Ouray, **St. John's Episcopal,** dating from 1880, also at 4th Street and Fifth Avenue. A block over, at 4th Street and Fourth Avenue, the 1890 **Presbyterian Church** was restored after a fire in the 1940s. At 4th Street and Third Avenue, the rambling **Tanner House** of 1896 has curved bay windows with prismatic Italian glass and an interesting stamped-metal wreath design in the front porch pediment. The first lodge on the Western Slope was the 1904 **Elks Club,** designed by an amateur architect who was a grocer by trade. Leaded and flashed stained-glass windows in wood mullions adorn transoms, and the tower clock always reads 11 o'clock, in Elks tradition.

A decorative iron front embellishes the 1888 **Opera House** at 5th and Main, which has cast-iron piers supporting the pressed-metal front of the second floor. A showpiece a century ago the **Beaumont Hotel** of 1886, also at 5th and Main, in a French-influenced architecture with multiple façades, is undergoing restoration. An elaborate false façade embellishes the all-wood **Western Hotel** of 1892 at 220 Seventh Ave., one of the few old wood structures not to have been destroyed by fire over the years. Classic dormers, bay windows, and gables decorate the **Story House** of 1895 at 4th Street and Seventh Avenue, in the Queen Anne style. Complex geometry went into the asymmetrical **Louis King House,** built in the 1880s, with complicated overhangs, porches, and roof planes. At 4th Street and Sixth Avenue, the **Ouray County Courthouse** has a large upstairs courtroom lighted by arched windows in an Italianate structure with a mansard-capped cupola and triple archway and balustrade. Imitation oak-grained pine lines the walls inside the building.

Other Sights and Activities

Visitors taking the tour of the **Bachelor-Syracuse Mine** in Ouray see a real gold and silver operation in progress here for a century. Guides take visitors aboard a mine train over half a mile into Gold Hill to view silver veins and other mineral deposits. There is a lesson given in gold panning: "Try to pay for your vacation" is the advice. In any case you "keep what you pan." There is a shop selling ore specimens and jewelry of gold and silver. Tours are scheduled between May 15 and October 15; for times, call 325-4500.

Backcountry exploration by four-wheel-drive vehicle can be arranged with full mapping instruction provided at two rental establishments in Ouray, **Jeeps Ouray** (tel. 325-4154) and **Switzerland of America Jeep Rentals** (tel. 325-4484). Tours with a driver who knows where all the old mines are located can be booked on half-day or full-day trips with **San Juan Scenic Jeep Tours,** at Main and 5th Streets (tel. 325-4444).

For all travel service information, get in touch with the **Ouray Chamber of Commerce** (tel. 303/325-4746).

Where to Stay

Of historic interest in Ouray is the **St. Elmo Hotel,** 426 Main St., Ouray, CO 81427 (tel. 303/325-4951), in an art deco style that has been a landmark in town since it opened in 1898. The spacious, old-fashioned lobby is a meeting place for locals and guests alike. Its rooms still contain many original furnishings. The place was initially put up as an adjunct to the popular Bon Ton Restaurant, also still in operation on the premises (see "Where to Eat," below). There are 11 rooms, seven with private bath, and double rates from $38 to $62, including a breakfast of homemade breads and muffins.

Wiesbaden Spa & Lodgings, 625 5th St., Ouray, CO 81427 (tel. 303/325-4347), has a vapor cave with a natural mineral-water pool at 106°; there is massage available as well as acupuncture, facials, and salt rubs. Some units have kitchenettes and fireplaces. Double rates are $49 to $78.

A pleasant, inexpensive lodging, with breakfast included at $30 for two, is the small **Baker's Manor Guest House,** 317 2nd St., Ouray CO 81427 (tel. 303/325-4574).

Where to Eat

Of historic interest is the **Bon Ton Restaurant,** at 426 Main St. in the St. Elmo Hotel (tel. 325-4951), which has a traditional Italian menu as well as steaks and a daily seafood selection, usually a crêpe. There is a varied wine list. It's open year round for dinner daily and a weekend brunch on an outdoor patio in good weather.

The Coachlight, 118 W. Seventh Ave. (tel. 325-4361), occupies an old 1887 hotel building and has stained-glass windows and period oil paintings. On the menu is Colorado beef, steaks, lamb, seafood, trout, chicken, and lasagne. There is a soup bar, a salad bar, and homemade breads, and house specialties are spinach fandango and French chocolate silk pie. Dinner only is served May to mid-October.

The **Outlaw Bar & Steakhouse,** 610 Main St. (tel. 325-9996), has an oldtime bar with a sculptured metal ceiling and a specialty of aged Colorado beef. There is a good wine list. Summer special is chuckwagon steak barbecues. The restaurant is open all year, daily for dinners.

TELLURIDE: Another small mining town classified as a National Historic Landmark, Telluride has become famous in the past decade as a ski resort (see Chapter XV). A number of old hotels and brothels out of the Territorial era have been restored to house restaurants and drinking places today, and there are year-round recreational opportunities in the fabulous San Juan Mountains.

At a distance of 335 miles from Denver (reached via I-70 and U.S. 550 south to Ridgway, and Colo. 62 and Colo. 145), the town occupies a majestic site at an

8,750-foot altitude at the head of a glacier-made valley surrounded by peaks in the 13,000- and 14,000-foot range. Butch Cassidy made the town his hideout in 1889 soon after it was founded, and it remains separated from the rest of civilization by a great stretch of the **San Juan National Forest** of alpine meadows, trout streams, fir forest, and massive mountain peaks. In summer, visitors enjoy exploring the four-wheel-drive and hiking trails, the streams and the ponds, and the life of the town that includes a music festival and a film festival.

Originally dubbed by miners the City of Gold, Telluride had a bustling mining-camp population of 5,000 at the turn of the century, with electric lights, brick buildings, a famous gaming and sporting-house district, and some luxurious hotels and restaurants. Miners worked extracting gold and silver through the winters here in mines at heights of 12,000 feet. They lived with a robust spirit the townsfolk try to recapture in life here today: there are over 1,000 permanent residents.

A Walking Tour

A walking tour of Telluride takes in a number of interesting sites within a few downtown blocks. The 1887 **San Miguel County Courthouse** is built of materials from an earlier structure destroyed by fire. The *Galloping Goose,* an auto-engine-powered locomotive, ran on the old Rio Grande Southern Railway until 1953, and is displayed near the courthouse. The **Sheridan Hotel,** built in 1895, was the site of William Jennings Bryan's famous "Cross of Gold" speech. Also interesting for their architectural detail are the **First National Bank Building,** the **Zia Sun Building** (scene of a Butch Cassidy bank robbery in 1889), and the **Olympic Sports Building.** The red-light district had 26 houses and 175 prostitutes in its heyday; each house paid a weekly $150 license fee to City Hall. **The Cribs** and other structures on Pacific Street remain from that era. One brothel, the **Senate,** now a restaurant, has an original roulette wheel and poker tables from the early days. Another, the **San Juan Bordello,** is now open for tours from noon to 6 p.m. daily.

Memorabilia of the mining life a century past is displayed in the **San Miguel County Museum** (tel. 728-3344), originally the Miners' Hospital; it is open daily May 1 to November 1 for an admission of $3. Other buildings to be noted are the **Town Hall** (1883), originally the town's first school, and the **L. L. Nunn House.**

Other Sights and Activities

Besides the summertime film festivals, there are annually a wine festival, a bluegrass and country music festival, a rock festival, a jazz festival, a chamber music festival, a dance festival, and at the end of August a **mushroom festival**—in which workshops on identification of mushrooms and "the social aspects of psychoactive mushrooms" are held. A unique event is the annual **Ideas Festival** in mid-August. Programs of political debate vie with music, theater, and films. For information, call 728-4981. In September, there is a running marathon over a 13,000-foot mountain pass and a hang-gliding championship competition.

Among sights in the area are **Bridal Veil Falls,** Colorado's highest at 450 feet, at the spur end of Colo. 145, with access on foot or by four-wheel-drive, and the **Bridal Veil Hydroelectric Plant,** a National Historic Landmark atop the falls at the point where the San Miguel River emerges from the Bridal Veil Basin and enters the Telluride Valley. Built in 1904, it generated power for nearby mining operations. Some 3,000 feet above Telluride was another mining community called Tomboy that produced millions of dollars' worth of gold until 1935, when it closed. Ruins of mines are in this area. Near the timberline the **Alta Lakes** provide good trout fishing; there are more mine ruins and a national forest campground. Three of the highest and most spectacular mountain passes in Colorado are also nearby: **Ophir Pass, Black Bear Pass,** and **Imogene Pass.** A one-way mountain track, for four-wheel-drives only, is negotiable from Red Mountain to Telluride, crossing the famed **Ingram Falls.**

Concerts, cabaret theater, or films are shown in the historic **Sheridan Opera House** (tel. 728-3642), built in 1913, another local structure on the National Register of Historic Places. There is an ornate theater bar, and drinks may be taken to tables in the upper balcony. The bar opens nightly at 8 p.m. and shows begin at 8:30.

For all travel service information, see the **Telluride Chamber Resort Association,** 323 W. Colorado Ave., Telluride, CO 81435 (tel. 303/728-3041). Lodging is booked by **Telluride Central Reservations** (tel. 303/728-4431, or toll free 800/525-3455).

Where to Stay

Manitou Hotel, on the San Juan River three blocks south of Main Street, Telluride, CO 81435 (tel. 303/728-4311), has 29 units, some with refrigerators and some also with kitchens. Rates are $85 to $95 double in ski season, and $50 to $70 in summer.

The **New Sheridan Hotel,** 231 W. Colorado Ave., Telluride, CO 81435 (tel. 303/728-4351), dates to 1895 and was the pride of the bustling little city at the turn of the century. It has been completely restored to its Victorian elegance by a renovator of historic buildings from Ohio, Walter McClellan. The bedrooms have brass beds, oak furniture, and stained-glass lamp fixtures, but also, in some, the convenience of modern, private bathrooms. A long cherrywood bar made in Austria is the centerpiece of the Victorian lounge on the first floor. Julian's Restaurant also occupies the hotel. Backgammon is regularly played in the back room, and there is a patio popular in good weather for lunch and cocktails. The hotel is only three blocks from the Coonskin ski lift. Rates are $38 to $70 double, depending on the season.

Where to Eat

A streak of whimsey enlivens the scene at the **T-Ride Country Club,** 333 W. Colorado (tel. 728-6344), a country club without a golf course or members—it is in fact simply a restaurant open to the public. But the public is asked to do its own cooking. What you do is choose a raw steak—an 8- or 12-ounce New York cut for $7 or $9, a one-pound T-bone for $13, or a shish kebab for $8—and you grill it yourself over the charcoal broiler. The proprietors aver that this "concept provides for a casual, relaxed atmosphere which results in fun, conversation, and perfectly prepared food." That perfection does, of course, depend on the diner's personal cooking skills, yet the restaurant is well attended and its customers are pleased with the food. What helps, of course, are the servings of dark rye bread and whipped butter and the all-you-can-eat choices among 30 fresh items in a salad bar, not to mention fresh corn on the cob and huge baked potatoes with sour cream, as well as baked beans. There is a modest wine list too.

A casual spot for drinks or for breakfast, lunch, or dinner is the **Coyote Lounge,** 666 W. Colorado (tel. 728-6912), which claims to serve Colorado's best prime rib, and has some good vegetarian dishes as well. There is a sundeck for warm-weather dining, and full bar service.

The restored New Sheridan Hotel, 231 W. Colorado Ave., is the site of **Julian's** (tel. 728-3839), serving various kinds of spaghetti (with tomato sauce, or with fresh white clam sauce), shrimp (in various sauces), or veal dishes.

The **Senate Bar & Restaurant,** 123 S. Spruce (tel. 728-3201), has such specials as wienerschnitzel, Austrian rib steak, salmon in parchment, and beef tenderloin in mushroom sauce. Seafood mornay crêpes are a favorite. Dinner is served seven nights a week.

4. GUNNISON COUNTRY

A narrow canyon cut half a mile deep called the Black Canyon of the Gunnison is a major attraction in the plateau country of southwestern Colorado between the towns of Montrose and Gunnison, the latter town serving a major ski area, Crested Butte (see Chapter XV). Also part of the Gunnison River basin is Curecanti National Recreation Area with three adjoining lakes formed by Blue Mesa Dam, the three known simply as Blue Mesa Lake.

BLACK CANYON OF THE GUNNISON NATIONAL MONUMENT:

"No other canyon in North America combines the depth, narrowness, sheerness, and somber countenance of the Black Canyon," wrote Wallace Hansen, who mapped the geology of the region for the U.S. Geological Survey in the 1950s. Although 53 miles in length, just 12 miles are within the national monument— the deepest and most spectacular part, where slanting rays of sunlight penetrate the canyon floor for only short periods. The walls are almost always in dark shadows, giving the place its name. Its depths range from 1,730 to 2,700 feet, and its width at the Narrows is only 1,100 feet at the rim and 40 feet down at the river. The elevation above sea level, at the rims, is around 8,000 feet.

The canyon is one of the few remaining unspoiled areas of its kind in the country, and only foot trails go into the wilderness from the end of an access road winding down into the bottom of the canyon. A main road also follows along near the line of the south rim, where short paths lead to locations where informational signs explain the geology of the canyon. **Cedar Point,** on the south rim, has a self-guiding trail. A printed guidebook is available for hikes along **High Point Trail,** which departs from the end of the road. Near the **South Rim Campground** in summer, campfire programs are given nightly. During the day nature walks are also conducted by rangers. The deep slash in the earth looks as if it must have been caused in some cataclysmic violence, but it actually took two million years of erosion to form it, a process still going on, although slowed because of the damming of the Gunnison River above the park.

Stone islands and pinnacles in the eastern area of the park were also created by slow processes of erosion. The sheer walls between **Chasm View** and **High Point** are carved from a gray rock called quartz monzonite, and surfaces of schist, gneiss, and granite, streaked by the elements, add varieties of color.

Along the rims there is a cover of mountain brush that is mostly Gambrel oak and serviceberry. Piñon and juniper grow in the higher elevations, and some of these gnarled old trees outline themselves with a certain dignity of timelessness along the sharp rim of the canyon. It is estimated some of them may be seven centuries old. Fendlerbush, wild rose, mountain mahogany, rock spirea, snowberry, gooseberry, chokecherry, and wax currant are also common. There are numerous mule deer, coyotes, bobcats, and gray foxes; smaller animals include marmots, squirrels, chipmunks, and wood rats. Porcupines sleep under rocky ledges in the day; most of the other animals are also nocturnal. Birds are more easily seen, however: juncos, chickadees, scrub jays, eagles, magpies, vultures, hawks. There are a few small snakes and lizards.

In spite of the lack of sunlight some trees grow in the bottom of the canyon, Douglas fir and aspen among them, and there are lichens and mosses. The river has brown trout, rainbow trout, squawfish, and flannel-mouth sucker; fishing is permitted with a state license.

The canyon is named for an army captain, John W. Gunnison, who led an expedition through this country after it became U.S. territory following the war with Mexico in 1848—but he avoided the canyon altogether, bypassing it to the south. The canyon was avoided by early Spanish explorers too, and only in modern times has it had regular human visitors, many of them nowadays rock climbers who like the challenge of the sheer canyon walls. The first survey of the canyon did not take place in fact until 1882–1883, when the Denver & Rio Grande Railroad sent an engineer to determine whether the line could be extended downstream below Cimarron. Bryan H. Bryant and a crew worked along the canyon bottom as far as they could go, climbed out, then descended again at the next draw, thus completing the survey from Cimarron to Grizzly Gulch. It was decided not to build the railroad here.

Float trips are dangerous and blocked in many places by rocks, and rafters who have tried it agree they mainly do rock climbing and scrambling instead of running the river. Three upriver dams for irrigation and electricity production have changed the nature of the river in the canyon bottom to some extent, modifying its flow and its temperature; the accumulated talus is no longer flushed out by sporadic floods.

There are campgrounds on both the north and south rim with a restricted water supply hauled in by truck; there are tables and grills, and wood or charcoal should be brought in. Snacks and souvenirs are sold at the **Rim House** on the south rim in the summer season. The rims are both open to cars, the south rim all year and the north closed in winter. The south rim entrance is 11 miles from Montrose via U.S. 50 and an access road. The north rim is reached from Colo. 92 east of Crawford over a 14-mile graded access road.

CURECANTI NATIONAL RECREATION AREA:
The upstream dams just east of Black Canyon have formed **Crystal Lake, Morrow Point Lake,** and **Blue Mesa Lake,** making the centers of a recreation area affording all water sports, fishing, boating, and boat tours. Most of the action is around Blue Mesa Lake. Morrow Point Lake is reached only by the Pine Creek Trail and any boats have to be carried in by hand. In the summer the boat tour weaves near the canyon-like walls of the lake, narrated by a park ranger (for times, call 641-0403); access to the trail to Crystal Lake is at the east end of the lake below Morrow Point Dam.

A slide program at **Elk Creek Visitor Center** shows all the recreational opportunities in the area, which start at the visitor center all summer—hikes, bird walks, and demonstrations. Evening campfire programs are held at the **Elk Creek** and **Lake Fork** campgrounds. **Elk Creek Marina** has rental boats and equipment for fishing and waterskiing—a state fishing license is required.

Dirt roads north of Blue Mesa Lake into the **West Elk Mountains** are passable when dry but treacherous when wet. Three basins of Blue Mesa Lake are good, wide stretches of water for sailboats; swimming is done anywhere in the lakes, although there are no beaches or lifeguards. In winter ice fishermen go out onto the lakes, and campgrounds are kept open for them until blocked in by snow. Snowmobilers also run on the lake ice in winter.

When filled to capacity Blue Mesa Lake is the largest lake in Colorado. The other lakes are like fjords within their deep crevices, and the boat tours on Morrow Point Lake show the sculpting work of time and the river on the steep walls, where the effects of millions of years of eroding forces are sharply seen.

Curecanti is named for a Ute chief who hunted this territory. The main season here is May to October, and fishermen are drawn by the thousands to try for Kokanee salmon, and rainbow, brown, and Mackinaw trout. The largest browns are caught in May and early June, and some Mackinaw too, but the mainstay is the rainbow trout year round. Trollers find rainbows and Kokanee throughout the season, with the salmon best in mid- and late summer. The spawning runs of the salmon occur in October. In winter from December to March there is also cross-country skiing in the area, and with rangers' permission, hang-gliding enthusiasts and scuba-divers, as well as rock climbers, ply their sports here.

Hunting is permitted in season. Elk wander into campgrounds in winter, and there are many chipmunks, squirrels, cottontails, marmots, and prairie dogs around in the summer. Rarer are weasels, coyotes, bobcats, and even bears. Beavers sometimes build their dams on tributary streams. There are eagles, red-tailed hawks, ravens, magpies, eared grebes, seagulls, and great blue herons. Winter can get terribly cold—to 37° below zero—and summer days up to 80°, nights in the 30° to 40° range. A burst of wildflowers comes with the melting snows in the spring. Yellow swaths of rabbitbrush tint meadows otherwise dominated by purplish sagebrush. Slopes above the valley have growths of low scrub oak, and there are cottonwoods and willows in the canyon bottoms. Here and there on the mesa tops are Douglas-fir copses. On winter mornings you can see herds of elk or deer numbering up to 40, along U.S. 50; in the summer they move into the heights of the West Elk Mountains.

Lava deposits show volcanic action that once wiped out all life on the earth in these parts, covering the surface with 1,000 feet of molten rock. The layered sandstones and shales seen west of Dry Gulch on U.S. 50 are the same geological formations found in Dinosaur National Monument, although fossils have not yet been found here—but hikers keep searching for them. As for human habitation in the area, recent finds show traces of prehistoric man dating to 8144 B.C. More recently the Ute Indians came here to the mountain in the summertime.

CRAWFORD STATE RECREATION AREA: A mile south of Crawford on Colo. 92, 14 miles north of the Black Canyon, a 400-acre reservoir makes the center of a camping, boating, picnicking, and fishing area also used in winter for ice fishing, skating, and snowmobiling. The park office phone is 921-5721; a daily $2 pass is required for each vehicle.

There are 63 campsites for tents and RVs, with tables and grills and water supply; camping costs $6 nightly plus entrance fee. There is also a dump station. Waterskiing goes on all summer, and scuba-diving is also permitted. The reservoir is stocked with rainbow and brown trout and catfish. Record yellow perch have been taken also. The reservoir is a stopping place for migratory waterfowl, including western grebes and Canada geese. With an elevation of 6,600 feet, there is a mild climate all summer.

MONTROSE AREA: Besides serving as a travelers' center for trips to the Black Canyon and the recreation areas nearby, Montrose is a departure point for car trips into some especially beautiful high Colorado country. It is also central to three great national forests—the **Uncompahgre, Gunnison,** and **Grand Mesa** —where there are uncrowded areas for outdoor adventure and exploring.

Four-wheel-drive trips into the San Juan Mountains at $35 per person are run June to October out of Montrose by **Mountain Top Scenic Tours** (tel. 249-6644). Four miles south of town on U.S. 550 the **Ute Indian Museum** is open daily June to September for a $1 admission, as a memorial to Chief Ouray and his wife, Chipeta. Ute history is described through artifacts, photographs, maps, and dioramas.

An 85-mile trip to **Owl Creek Pass** goes out of Montrose south on U.S. 550 for 23 miles to a turnoff to the left to Owl Creek Pass, marked by a U.S. Forest Service sign. A gravel road follows Cow Creek for seven miles to Debbie's Park, where the actress Debbie Reynolds once made part of a movie. The next eight miles in **Uncompahgre National Forest** rise to the crest of Owl Creek Pass, at 10,114 feet. Fifteen miles in from the pass is 325-acre **Silverjack Reservoir,** with good fishing and pretty hikes along the shore.

Beaver Lake is also nearby, a peaceful area with a campground. From here it is 18 miles down to U.S. 50 alongside the Cimarron irrigation canal. At Cimarron is an old narrow-gauge train on an original trestle over Cimarron Creek. Nearby at **Morrow Point Dam** in Curecanti National Recreation Area there is a half-hour self-guided tour of the underground powerplant in operation here. The return to Montrose via **Cerro Summit** is another 20 miles.

The **Grand Mesa** trip takes motorists to the world's largest flattop mountain, 10,000 feet high, from which views extend far over into Utah and to the north and south in Colorado. The 40-mile width of the mesa has some 200 lakes and reservoirs, and there is the **Powderhorn Ski Area** (see Chapter XV).

The route goes north on U.S. 50 from Montrose to Delta, then right on Colo. 92 four miles and left on Colo. 65 to Cedaredge and Grand Mesa. Cedaredge is the heart of apple-orchard country, the **Surface Creek Valley,** where three-quarters of the state's apple crop is grown and there is an October apple festival. In season there are also pick-your-own roadside orchards where you may take fresh peaches, apricots, pears, and cherries, as well as plenty of apples for your ride.

The route back to Montrose can be the reverse trip again, or instead turn off near the top of the mesa on **Land's End Road** for a hair-raising gravel-road ride down 55 hairpin curves to the bottom of the west side of the mesa to meet U.S. 50 eight miles south of Whitewater. Here, turn left on U.S. 50 and, 19 miles south, look for the sign to **Escalante Canyon** for a short side trip. After returning from the canyon, turn right for a 32-mile return ride to Montrose.

The **Paradox Valley** is so named because the Dolores River runs across it instead of logically along its length—paradoxically. A trip into this country departs from Montrose via U.S. 550 south 23 miles to Ridgeway, turning right at Colo. 62 into the beautiful **Pleasant Valley** and on over the 8,970-foot **Dallas Divide.** There is a good view of the 14,500-foot peak of Mount Sneffles to the left. Then follow the **San Miguel River** to the communities of Placerville, Norwood, and Redvale, to the confluence with the Dolores River outside Nucla. At Naturita, turn right at the junction of Colo. 97 for a side trip to this little town of **Nucla.** Then return and continue on Colo. 141 to Uravan, where the hanging flume is to be seen—an early-day water system built along the wall of the canyon here. Continue alongside the Dolores River to Gateway to the north, and then along through the **Unaweep Canyon** to Whiteriver. From here it's 52 miles back to Montrose via U.S. 50 south.

Where to Stay

The **Red Barn,** 1417 E. Main St., Montrose, CO 81401 (tel. 303/249-4507), has 70 units, an outdoor heated pool, a spa, hot tub, sauna, and weight room, and the adjoining Red Barn Restaurant. There is also a cocktail lounge. Rates are $38 to $41 double.

The **Chief Motel,** 1150 N. Townsend (tel. 303/249-4595), has 21 units, some with kitchenettes, and a playground, with double rooms at $26 to $30.

GUNNISON: This small city 200 miles southwest of Denver, reached via U.S. 285 and U.S. 50, lies at the eastern end of the Curecanti National Recreation Area and makes a center for vacationers and outdoors lovers there, in the Black Canyon, up at Crested Butte Ski Area (see Chapter XV), and in Gunnison National Forest to the north, and in areas of Rio Grande and San Isabel National Forests.

A historic landmark is an 1881 railroad tunnel that can be reached by car from Gunnison by going 12 miles east on U.S. 50 to Parlin, then 19 miles north to the **Denver, South Park & Pacific Railroad** line trackbed. At the eastern city limits of Gunnison is a **Pioneer Museum,** part of which occupies an old schoolhouse. There is also an entire narrow-gauge railroad train. Farm implements and old wagons are shown, and the museum is open, for 50¢ admission, daily from Memorial Day to Labor Day. Gunnison is famous for its annual **Cattlemen's Day's Celebration and Rodeo** in mid-July, with horse racing, a parade, a beef sale, and barbecues. During early August there is also an annual arts festival in nearby Crested Butte.

Gunnison Airport is served daily by Trans-Colorado Airlines and also in winter by American Airlines. **Greyhound/Trailways** buses run between Denver and Gunnison.

For all travel service information, see the **Gunnison Country Chamber of Commerce,** at 500 E. Tomichi Ave., Gunnison, CO 81230 (tel. 303/641-1501).

Where to Stay

The **Mountain View Lodge,** 117 N. Taylor Gunnison, CO 81230 (tel. 303/641-1799), has a garden, sundeck, and barbecue area that give a countrified feeling to a center-of-town location. Lodgings here come with one or two bedrooms, and some have kitchens as well. Rates in season are $45 to $58 double, lower in summer.

Free coffee and rolls around a great fireplace make a cheery attraction at the **Nordic Inn,** in nearby Mount Crested Butte, CO 81225 (tel. 303/349-5542). Balconies provide superb mountain views and a deck for good suntans. Double rates are $43 to $56 in the summer, $48 to $102 in winter.

The **Gold Creek Inn,** on Gold Creek in nearby Ohio City, CO 81237 (tel. 303/641-2086), has large rooms with a double bed and two single beds in each, all furnished with antiques. The rustic house also shelters a restaurant serving choice entrees where diners are warmed at a blazing fire in the grate, Wednesday through Saturday evenings year round. The Sunday brunch is a tradition here, and room rates begin at $20.

Where to Eat

Cattlemen Inn, 301 W. Tomichi Ave. (tel. 641-1061), has two dining rooms, a bar and cocktail lounge, with the Beef 'n' Barrel Restaurant downstairs, open for breakfast, lunch, and dinner.

The **Epicurean Restaurant,** 110 N. Main (tel. 641-2964), has such rare breakfast specials as ebelskivers and wild-rice pancakes, as well as omelets and soufflés. There is a full bar, a good wine list, and three meals are served daily.

CHAPTER XVIII

SOUTH-CENTRAL COLORADO

□ □ □

The frontal range of the Rockies continues south of Denver in a formidable wall blocking the great spread of the prairieland reaching out 1,000 miles from the east. Running north-south below the wall at the edge of the prairie is I-25, traversing the population centers of Colorado Springs, Pueblo, and farther south, Walsenburg and Trinidad. Rangeland, cornfields, and wheatfields stretch out into the featureless country to the east, while up in the mountains the twisting highways and back roads lead to recreation areas in the national forests, to high plateaus and ski areas, to old mining camps and ghost towns. Manitou Springs, home of the cog railway to the top of Pikes Peak, is the starting point for various races to the famous summit, including an auto competition. There are narrow-gauge train rides nearby too.

1. COLORADO SPRINGS

This resort is home of the United States Air Force Academy and of the famous Broadmoor resort. Colorado Springs and nearby Manitou Springs offer a variety of tourist attractions, plus a wide variety of travel and vacation accommodations, and serve as a base for trips into mountain country to the west. Situated 70 miles south of Denver on I-25, the city, founded in 1871, became an internationally known health resort in the late 1800s.

Note: The **telephone area code** for much of this region is 719.

TRANSPORTATION: Airlines serving the city are **America West** (tel. toll free 800/247-5692), **American** (tel. 632-7760), **Continental** (tel. 473-7580), **TWA** (tel. 599-4400), and **United** (tel. 635-0570).

Greyhound/Trailways is at 229 E. Pikes Peak Ave. (tel. 635-1505). **Colorado Springs Bus Service** operates buses on city routes for 50¢ fares daily from 6 a.m. to 6 p.m. (for information, call 475-9733); service to Manitou Springs is also provided. **Yellow Cab** is reached at 635-9907.

Car-rental agencies include **Budget** (tel. 574-7402), **Hertz** (tel. 596-1863), **Payless** (tel. 471-4444), and **Thrifty** (tel. 574-2472).

Reports on highway conditions are available by calling 633-6622.

Bus tours to the top of Pikes Peak and to other tourist attractions are operated by **Gray Line** (tel. 633-1747) and **Pikes Peak Tours** (tel. 633-1181).

SIGHTSEEING: The **U.S. Air Force Academy,** 12 miles north of the city, reached via exit 150 of I-25, has a visitor center (tel. 472-2555) open daily year round, where information is given on visiting this 18,000-acre campus, including self-guiding tour maps. Films on cadet life are shown and there is a gift shop. A memorable architectural feature of the grounds is the modern chapel with 17 spires, suggesting a series of tepee façades, a structure housing separate inner chapels for the major faiths. It is open to visitors. Free programs are shown at the **Academy Planetarium** twice or more often daily all year. Sports events at the huge fieldhouse, big enough for indoor football, are also open to the public. The complement of 4,500 cadets goes through four years of training here to become air force officers.

The **Pro Rodeo Hall of Champions and Museum of the American Cowboy** is also north of the city at exit 147 of I-25 off Rockrimmon Boulevard (tel. 593-8847), and is open from 9 a.m. to 5 p.m. in summer, from 9 a.m. to 4:30 p.m. Tuesday through Saturday and noon to 4:30 p.m. on Sunday during the winter. Admission is $3 for adults, free for children. It is operated as a non-profit organization "to preserve the legacy of the cowboy" in a variety of displays of cowboy gear. A multimedia theatrical presentation first sketches the history of cowboys and rodeos in the West. Special displays on the development of ropes, saddles, chaps, and boots are to be seen in Heritage Hall. A special film technique gives viewers a realistic, jouncing ride atop a wild brahma bull in a film sequence shown in Theater II. Showcases of trophies, buckles, and memorabilia honor rodeo champions in the Hall of Champions.

North of the city, at exit 156A of I-25, at 1025 Northgate Rd., is the **Western Museum of Mining and Industry,** another nonprofit museum established to preserve historical artifacts, in this case those from the legacy of the mining industry. There is restored machinery from the early days of hard-rock mining. In the summer there are tours of an operating gold and silver ore mill, and visitors may pan for gold in a trough. An operating Corliss steam engine is a special attraction. The museum is open from 9 a.m. to 4 p.m. daily year round; admission is $3. For information, call 598-8850.

The **Colorado Springs Fine Arts Center,** 30 W. Dale St. (tel. 634-5581), is open free of charge Tuesday through Saturday from 10 a.m. to 5 p.m. and on Sunday from 1 to 5 p.m., and was the first facility in the U.S. built for the purpose of combining performing arts and visual arts: there are two museums, a theater, and a concert hall. Two art collections have made the center noted: one of American art, spanning work from the 19th and 20th centuries, and another of Hispanic and Indian art of the Southwest. The American artworks include western art, bronzes by Charles Russell, and paintings by Albert Bierstadt and Nicholai Fechin. Other paintings by John Singer Sargent, Walter Kuhn, Phillip Pearlstein, and Georgia O'Keeffe are shown. The **Taylor Museum,** housing the southwestern arts, shows crafts as well, such as Indian baskets, pottery, and textiles. The Alice Bemis Taylor Collection of Spanish Colonial Folk Art makes the base of the museum's treasures, one of the largest such collections in the world. Saintly images called *santos* are displayed in an adobe chapel. Three-dimensional objects are displayed in an "eyes of the mind" gallery for the blind; there are descriptive notes in Braille. Performing arts are also involved in the center's full schedule of programs: theater by the **Play Factory** and the **Young Actors Theater,** as well as dance programs and concerts.

Wildlife World Museum, 18725 Monument Hill Rd. (tel. 488-2460), reached from exit 163 of I-25 north of the city, is another nonprofit corporation organized to preserve particular treasures, in this case paintings, carvings, and sculptures of wildlife. A number of stuffed animals, work of the taxidermist's art, are also on display. Probably most admired in the collections are the carvings of birds out of wood, usually basswood, a skill that evolved from the making of duck decoys. There are over 2,000 specimens of these carved birds. The museum is open from 8 a.m. to 5 p.m. daily year round, with a small admission fee charged.

Somewhat similar in appeal is the **National Carvers Museum,** north of the city on Baptist Road at exit 158 of I-25 (tel. 481-2656), open daily from 9 a.m. to 5 p.m. year round with an admission fee of $2. There are over 5,000 wood-carvings shown, and a carver is on hand to demonstrate the art. Free wooden nickels are given out at a small gift shop.

Cheyenne Mountain Zoo (tel. 475-9555) is three miles west of the city center on Cheyenne Boulevard and has over 600 animals of all kinds in the cool lower slopes of Cheyenne Mountain, at an elevation of 6,800 feet. It is open daily year round, charging adults $4; children aged 3 to 11, $2. The Cheyenne Mountain Hwy. continues from the zoo entrance on up to the **Shrine of the Sun,** a memorial to Will Rogers, which is open daily.

Open during the summer only is the **Doll and Carriage Museum,** 218 Beckers Lane, Manitou Springs, with an entrance fee of $2 to see a collection of 1,500 old dolls and 150 carriages that date back as far as 1858. Near the Broadmoor on Lake Avenue are more old carriages and other wheeled vehicles from the past, including a Conestoga wagon, at the **Carriage House Museum.** Admission is free, year round, Tuesday through Sunday from 10 a.m. to noon and 1 to 5 p.m.

Miramont Castle, 9 Capitol Hill Ave. (tel. 685-1011), is a museum in a strange structure built in at least nine identifiable architectural styles, among them Gothic, Romanesque, Tudor, and Byzantine. It is open from 10 a.m. to 5 p.m. daily, in summer only, with an admission fee of $2. There is a Queen's Parlour tea room and a children's museum.

An area of strange rock formations is a city park called the **Garden of the Gods,** with a visitor center at 1400 Glen Ave. (tel. 578-6933). A Registered National Landmark, the park was a wintering place of Ute Indians until a century ago. The site was given to the city in 1907 by a railroad tycoon and now has over 1,300 acres in an area where the plains meet the forest, providing a variety of plant communities. Oldest survivors in the park are some ancient, twisted junipers; one, with a five-foot-diameter trunk, is nearly 1,000 years old. The strangest animals in the park are honey ants, which gorge themselves with honey like living honey pots to feed a colony of ants for the winter. Hiking trails can be followed with the help of maps available at the visitor center, open daily in summer and weekends to the end of October. There are displays on the history, geology, plants, and wildlife of the park. Twice a day in summer there are half-hour guided walks through the garden area, and afternoon patio programs of naturalist talks, demonstrations, and slide shows are also held.

Also in the park is the **White House Ranch** (tel. 578-6777), with an admission fee of $1.50 for adults, 75¢ for children 6 to 17, which has an 1860s homestead in a working ranch and a general store. Demonstrations of activities of early ranch life are presented.

A nickelodeon playing a cheery dancehall tune welcomes you to **Pikes Peak Ghost Town,** 400 S. 21st St. (tel. 634-0696), a museum in the form of a collection of old western buildings such as a saloon, blacksmith shop, general store, livery stable, and rooming house. It is open during the summer daily for an admission fee of $2.50 for adults, $1.25 for children under 12.

McAllister House, 423 N. Cascade Ave., is listed in the National Register of Historic Places, and is a property of the Colonial Dames of America. Open Thursday through Saturday in winter from 10 a.m. to 4 p.m. and on Sunday from noon to 4 p.m., (also on Wednesday in summer), there is an admission fee of $2 for adults, 75¢ for children 6 to 13. Built in 1873, the Gothic cottage was constructed of brick when the builder, an army major named Henry McAllister, learned that the local wind (called the chinook) was of such force as to have blown a train off the tracks nearby; the walls are nearly two feet thick. A fine touch came in the three marble fireplaces; the house was ahead of its time out here, also, with the installation of running water.

More historic buildings are to be seen in the part of town originally established as **Colorado City,** along Colorado Avenue between 21st and 31st Streets. Founded in 1859, Colorado City boomed in the 1880s when the railroad came through. Tunnels led from the respectable side of town to the saloon and redlight district so that city fathers could carouse without being seen going or coming back—or so the legend goes.

Of special interest is the nonprofit **Museum of the American Numismatic Association,** 818 N. Cascade Ave. (tel. 632-2646), with eight galleries of coins from around the world and a collectors' library as well, open free of charge year round Tuesday through Saturday from 8:30 a.m. to 4 p.m.

Also one-of-a-kind is the **World Figure Skating Hall of Fame,** 20 1st St. (tel. 635-5200), open year round from 10 a.m. to 4 p.m. Monday through Saturday, with free admission. Memorabilia of great skaters is displayed, and there is a library of books and documents about ice skating, as well as an exhibit of medals and trophies. The famous skate collection of Eddie H. Shipstad is shown, and there is a gift shop.

Over in Manitou Springs, at 135 Manitou Ave., the **Colorado Car Museum** (tel. 689-5996) is open daily May to October. Admission is $2.50 for adults; children under 12, $1.25. There are presidential limousines, and a 1900 steamer famous as the first car to climb Pikes Peak.

The **Pikes Peak Highway** starts 12 miles west of the city at Cascade, reached via U.S. 24, and leads 18 miles to the 14,000-foot summit, where there is a lunchroom and gift shop. It is open from May to late October, depending on the amount of snowfall, at a toll of $3 per adult, 50¢ for kids under 12.

The **Pikes Peak Cog Railway,** 515 Ruxton Ave. in Manitou Springs (tel. 685-5401), is an easier way to get to the top, making round trips in 3½ hours daily between May and October, with more frequent departures in the summer, at a cost of $15 for adults, $7 for children under 12. Next to the cog railway depot is another tourist ride on the **Mount Manitou Scenic Incline Railway** (tel. 685-9086), the world's longest of its kind, which takes visitors to the top of Mount Manitou daily all summer from 9:30 a.m. to 9 p.m. at $5 for adults, $2 for children under 12.

Pikes Peak is also the scene of the famous New Year's Eve climb by members of the AdAmAn Club, founded in 1922. Traditionally they set off fireworks from the summit at midnight to welcome in the New Year. There is also a venerable auto race up the toll road every summer, as well as the Pikes Peak Marathon, an annual foot race. Among showoffs climbing Pikes Peak was a man who pushed a wheelbarrow to the top and another who took three weeks to nudge a peanut all the way to the summit with his nose.

Manitou Springs, with its garish welcome sign arching Main Street, might vie with Estes Park as the quintessential tourist-trap town, but the souvenir selling and tourist catching is all done with a sort of cheerful humor, and the Rockies all around you, at least, are real. Manitou used to be called the Saratoga of the West a century ago when long trips to "take the waters" at the mineral springs were more the style in Victorian vacationing. Famous back then was Manitou Ginger Champagne, made with the local naturally active mineral water and a secret recipe including ginger. But a fire burned down the bottling plant and the recipe was lost—ending this era in soft-drink history. There is word, however, that the brand may reappear in stores before long.

Travel information is available from **Colorado Springs Convention and Visitors Bureau,** 104 S. Cascade Ave., Colorado Springs, CO 80903 (tel. 719/635-1632, or toll free 800/88-VISIT). The bureau has 60-minute cassettes to go with self-driven tours of Cripple Creek, Pikes Peak, the Air Force Academy, and Manitou Springs. The **Fun Fone** for local events info is 635-1723.

WHERE TO STAY: The Broadmoor, Lake Circle (at Lake Avenue), Colorado Springs, CO 80906 (tel. 719/634-7711), is a Colorado Springs institution and a tourist attraction in its own right, as well as a sprawling resort complex with handsome period architecture in its original buildings and modern innovations in additional structures recently added. The resort began as a utopian community that was the dream of a German nobleman-farmer who in 1885 landscaped a dairy farm here at the foot of Cheyenne Mountain in order to make it into a sort of American Monte Carlo. By 1891 he had built a Georgian casino on the rim of a lake here. The German, Count James de Pourtales, and his wife, Berthe, hoped to draw an international elite to the new community, which he called Broadmoor after the name of the original farm. There was a great hotel planned across the lake from the casino, with covered walks to connect them along the shore; trolley lines were laid all the way out from the center of Colorado Springs to the casino, some five miles distant. But the plan foundered, the hotel was not built, and the casino burned in 1897.

Two decades later, however, a successful local goldminer and entrepreneur named Spencer Penrose fulfilled the count's dream by building the Broadmoor Hotel on the site of the burned casino; it opened in 1918, built in the Italian Renaissance style. A golf course, tennis courts, swimming pools, a skating arena, a rodeo stadium, and a ski run were added. Details of the hotel construction included an Italian marble staircase, Della Robbia tile, hand-painted beams, and a chandelier—all still visible today. The first names entered on the guest register were those of John D. Rockefeller, Jr., and his party, who were inspecting coal mines in the West. Plaster latticework ceilings were made by Italian workmen brought in especially for this job—one of these is visible today in the ballroom corridor of the mezzanine. The main lounge in the mezzanine also still has its handsome, intricately hand-painted ceiling.

Today the Broadmoor is an entire community, with 560 units for guests, and gourmet-level cuisine in four dining rooms, with food also served in six other eating places, including a couple of golf clubhouses. There is a popular English-style pub called the Golden Bee. The original hotel is now styled Broadmoor Main, where you can find the Tavern, decorated with original Toulouse-Lautrec lithographs; the tropical Garden Room; and the elegant main dining room. The modern Broadmoor South has an enclosed rooftop dining room with great mountain views and Edwardian furnishings called the Penrose Room. Also complete within itself is Broadmoor West, with its own tennis and swimming facilities, and the Charles Court dining room decorated in Oriental art dating back to the Ming Dynasty. Among recreational attractions is Ski

Broadmoor (see Chapter XV, Section 6). Also on the 500 acres of grounds are saunas, beauty shops, bike trails, and a movie theater, and there are rowboats and canoes rented for the little lake on the site. Rates are seasonal, $105 to $195 double.

The **Hearthstone Inn,** 506 N. Cascade Ave. Colorado Springs, CO 80903 (tel. 719/473-4413), is a rambling 25-room turn-of-the-century structure with many gables, roof peaks, dormers, and chimneys looking out on a broad tree-lined avenue just north of the center of the city. On the National Register of Historic Places, the century-old house was originally the home of a local paperbag manufacturer. In 1977 two women named Williams (but not related) named Ruth and Dot restored the building, mostly by their own hands; they had help from Ruth's mother, who made new curtains for all 146 windows. The women used up 792 rolls of wallpaper in doing the job. Breakfast here, served between 8 and 9 a.m., to 10 a.m. on weekends, is a hearty feast of fruit and fresh baked goods; a cheese soufflé, German pancakes, or quiche frequently appear on the table. (The innkeepers have published a cookbook entitled *From the Kitchen of the Hearthstone Inn.*) Dining room fireplaces are alight on cold days and evenings and there is always free coffee to be taken from the coffeepot. Hand-cranked ice cream is a summertime specialty, and the place comes to life in a special way in its Christmas decorations, set off by a 24-foot-high tree bedecked in popcorn.

Rooms have their own names, characters, and prices. The Gable Room, for example, is a small attic hideaway; the Terrace Suite has an enclosed porch; the Mountainside has a fine view of Pikes Peak. All but two of the rooms have private baths. Rates range between $60 and $95 double.

The **Sheraton Inn,** 8110 N. Academy Blvd., Colorado Springs, CO 80920 (tel. 719/598-5770, or toll free 800/325-3535), has 203 units, an indoor pool, some suites, in-room movies, and a restaurant and nightclub. Rates are $65 to $75 double.

The **Blue Fox Motel,** 5056 N. Nevada Ave., Colorado Springs, CO 80907 (tel. 719/598-7793), with 50 units, has an outdoor pool and the usual amenities—TV and telephones—at $34 double.

In Manitou Springs

El Colorado Lodge, 23 Manitou Ave., Manitou Springs, CO 80829 (tel. 719/685-5485), has 31 units, some cottages with kitchens and fireplaces, a heated pool, playground, and large patio, with double rates at $32 and up.

The **Silver Saddle Motel,** 215 Manitou Ave., Manitou Springs, CO 80829 (tel. 719/685-5611), has a heated outdoor pool and cable television, mountain views from balconies, and 55 rooms at $26 to $38 double.

Bed-and-Breakfast

Bed & Breakfast–Rocky Mts., P.O. Box 804, Colorado Springs, CO 80901 (tel. 719/630-3433), lists over 100 bed-and-breakfast lodgings in Colorado, New Mexico, Wyoming, Montana, and Utah, at rates from budget to luxury ($25 to $95 double). Information can be had by telephone or by sending $3 for a directory.

WHERE TO EAT: Flying W Chuckwagon Suppers, 3330 Chuckwagon Rd.
(tel. 719/598-4000, or toll free 800/638-1313 in Colorado), provides a western show with steaks served ranch style every night at 5 and 8 p.m. during the summer, at $10 per person. The Winter Steak House is open on Friday and Saturday evenings during the rest of the year (except January and February) for cowboy-style steaks.

Bolero's, 2886 S. Circle Dr. (tel. 576-5900), serves lunch weekdays and dinner seven nights in an elegant atmosphere with views of the Front Range of the Rockies. Special menu selections are prepared tableside, and there is a salad bar. There is also dancing to live music Thursday through Saturday evening, and a champagne brunch with an elaborate all-you-can-eat buffet and omelets-to-order on Sunday.

Greenstreets, 505 Popes Bluff Trail (tel. 599-7727), is open every day for lunch and dinner with great salads and soups, big hamburgers, ribs, and the locally notorious buffalo chips. There is a seafood buffet on Friday evening, a jazz buffet on Saturday with all-you-can-eat prime rib and crab, and a champagne brunch on Sunday with no limit on the bubbly.

Modest prices for authentic Tex-Mex specialties are asked at **La Casita Patio,** 1331 S. Nevada Ave. (tel. 633-9616), open 24 hours for drive-through take-out orders, or for casual dining indoors or outside.

FLORISSANT FOSSIL BEDS NATIONAL MONUMENT: Located on a high mountain plateau 35 miles west of Colorado Springs via U.S. 24 to Florissant and Teller County Rd. No. 1, half a mile from Florissant, is a recently acquired National Park Service property that preserves fossils and petrified wood. Tree stumps are visible in two places within the park, and there are shale deposits seen by taking a nature trail. There is an 11-foot-high petrified sequoia stump, 10 feet in diameter, the largest known.

The fossils here are preserved in rocks of ancient Lake Florissant, which existed here 38 to 26 million years in the past, being formed when lava flows dammed nearby streams, forming the 12-mile-long lake. Over a period of half a million years volcanoes showered millions of tons of ash and dust into the air to settle around the lake, trapping plants and animals. Some of these settled into the bottom of the lake where they were embedded in layers of ash and became fossilized as the ash formed shale, a sedimentary rock formed in thin layers.

Mud flows also buried forests during this long period of time, and petrified the trees where they stood. Eventually the lake was filled with volcanic materials that preserved the shale. Upon them are what scientists see as a fossil handwriting —detailed, exquisite impressions of insects and leaves. They are here in such profusion that Florissant Fossil Beds are the most extensive record of this kind in the world. Impressions of dragonflies, beetles, ants, butterflies, spiders, fish, some mammals and birds, and many species of insects are perfectly preserved from the time of their lives as long ago as 35 million years. Leaves from birches, willows, maples, beeches, and hickories, and needles from fir trees and sequoias are plentiful, and there are palm trees to show how the climate has changed since those ancient times eons ago. A display of these fossil impressions is shown at the visitor center.

The fossils here were discovered by Dr. A. C. Peale of the U.S. Geological Survey in 1874, and since that time scientists from all over the world have dug into the shale to remove some 80,000 specimens. Among insects, 11,000 species have been identified, including all the fossil butterflies of the New World. There have also been 140 plants and many species of fish, birds, and mammals, as well as the petrified tree stumps excavated.

The valley here is named "florissant" from the French for "flowering." There are plenty of wildflowers here in the spring, but the pioneer who named it was actually an immigrant from Florissant, Missouri. At an altitude of 8,200 to 8,800 feet, the park has rolling, grassy hills and ridges covered with Ponderosa pine, Douglas fir, and blue spruce. The aspens, with their brilliant leaf colors in the fall, contrast with the evergreens. Wildflowers are Indian paintbrush, loco weed, senecio, scarlet gilia, wild iris, shooting stars, and columbines, among many. Mountain bluebirds, warblers, juncos, red-tailed hawks, killdeer, nuthatches, chickadees, and golden eagles also live here; and there are squirrels, prairie dogs, coyotes, badgers, rabbits, porcupines, mule deer, and a few antelope, elk, cougars, and bears.

An extra attraction in the park is the homestead of Adaline Hornbek, who pioneered the land here with her three sons in 1878. The park is open daily from 8 a.m. to 4:30 p.m., in summer to 7 p.m.

2. CRIPPLE CREEK

This famous old mining-camp town, 45 miles up in the Rockies to the west of Colorado Springs (via U.S. 24 west to Divide and Colo. 67 south), was known as the world's greatest gold camp after gold was first discovered up here in 1890. Until mining ceased in 1961 there was some $600 million worth of ore taken from the surrounding hills.

By the turn of the century the town had a population of 25,000, and its neighboring community of Victor, five miles away, had 18,000; there were 11 other towns in the area. There were 15 newspapers published in all these places, eight of them in Cripple Creek; one, the *Colored Tribune,* sold to the black population.

The center of action throughout the mining district was Bennett Avenue in Cripple Creek, five blocks long, with department stores and shops of all kinds. It is said today that the streets of nearby Victor really were paved with gold—the poorer grades of ore not fit for the mills, yet containing gold, were used for paving. Between the two towns there were 35 restaurants and 150 saloons, scores of them lining Myers Avenue, the street of dancehalls, theaters, brothels, and cribs. The big gambling houses were on Bennett Street. Other communities included Altman (at 10,620 feet in altitude the highest city in the world), Goldfield, Cameron, Independence, Elkton, Anaconda, and Gillett.

Cripple Creek has known some famous folk over the years. Lowell Thomas was a newspaper reporter in nearby Victor, and Jack Dempsey fought his first fight in the Gold Coin Club in Victor. Bernard Baruch was a telegrapher at the Midland terminal depot, and Texas Guinan, the New York burlesque queen, started showbiz as a church organist in Anaconda. Groucho Marx, stranded here, drove a grocery wagon in Cripple Creek for a time.

The **Cripple Creek District Museum,** in the old Midland depot at the east end of Bennett Avenue (tel. 689-2634), has three floors of relics of the good old days. There is a floor of Victorian rooms, a floor of mining and transportation objects, and two adjacent buildings, one an assay office where fire assay testing of local ores is carried on, the other a so-called heritage gallery containing a natural history display and old photographs and paintings. The museum is open with a small admission fee, daily in the summer from 10 a.m. to 5 p.m., and weekends the rest of the year.

Also open to visitors is a former brothel, the **Old Homestead,** 353 E. Myers Ave., open daily in the summer from 11 a.m. to 5 p.m. with a $2 admission fee. Considered the most luxurious brothel in the gold camp, it is an 1896 two-story structure where, on the ground floor, three parlors have mannekins dressed in the fancy dresses of the Victorian era. There are crystal alcohol lamps over a fireplace and a gambling table from a neighboring emporium. One parlor has a grand piano and an Edison phonograph. Five bedrooms upstairs have spindle beds with patchwork quilts, marble-top dressers, and satin dresser scarves.

There are tours 1,000 feet underground into the Mollie Kathleen gold mine during the summer only, from 9 a.m. to 5 p.m. every day. The mine was worked until 1961, when the operation began losing money. A cage takes visitors to the lower levels where mining equipment is still in place; there is a small museum of mining artifacts on display.

The **Imperial Hotel,** on 3rd Street, Cripple Creek, CO 80813 (tel. 719/ 689-2922), is the only original Cripple Creek hotel still standing, dating from 1896, just after the great fire that razed the town. Except for a time during World War II it has been in operation continuously and now offers melodramas twice daily except Monday throughout the summer, with tickets ranging from $5 to $8, $3.25 for children. There is a century-old bar in the Red Rooster saloon and an original roulette wheel from a long-gone gambling house. Buffet or à la carte lunches and dinners are served in three dining rooms, and there are 50 rooms at $30 to $40 double.

For travel service information, get in touch with the **Cripple Creek Two Mile High Club,** 347 E. Bennett St., Cripple Creek, CO 80813 (tel. 719/689- 2594).

VICTOR: Five miles from Cripple Creek at the feet of Battle and Squaw Mountains, Victor was called the City of Mines—it had 450 mines working at one time. The decline of Victor and Cripple Creek came after a bitter confrontation between unionized mine workers in the Western Federation of Miners and mine owners in 1903. Union men were arrested and shipped out of the state on flatcars to Kansas and banned from Colorado Territory. Although the union was broken, the boom days had ended.

A scenic drive here is the **Phantom Canyon** route along the old trackbed of the Florence–Cripple Creek narrow-gauge railroad. **Gold Camp Road** leads from Victor down to Colorado Springs, for another exciting ride, and there is also the run on **County Rd. 64** from Victor to Gillett, continuing to Divide, along the old roadbed of the Midland Railroad. A four-wheel-drive scenic route is the **Shelf Road** to Canon City.

Operating daily in summer are steam trains of the **Cripple Creek & Victor Narrow Gauge Railroad,** pulled by an old 15-ton 0-4-0 steam locomotive of the 1900s. A round trip takes visitors to the ghost mining camp of Anaconda.

ROYAL GORGE: Canon City, 45 miles from Colorado Springs via Colo. 115 south and U.S. 50 west, is next door to the 1,055-foot-deep Royal Gorge, spanned by the world's highest bridge. An aerial tramway also moves across the sky over this chasm to thrill tourists riding in it.

A drive across the bridge costs $3 for each adult car passenger, $1.50 for children. It is open year round, and so is the aerial tramway, giving rides at $6, $4 for children. It is boarded from a visitor center at the cliff edge overlooking the Arkansas River over 1,000 feet below. There is a gift shop here, a post office, and a viewing balcony. Operating summers from the far side of the huge parking lot is a miniature railway that gives rides over three miles of track through Royal Gorge Park, inhabited by a herd of tame deer. There is also an inclined railway sliding down into the canyon.

Royal Gorge raft trips are organized over varying lengths of the river, some involving rough white-water passages. Full-day trips cost $40 and up and there are two-day trips including cookouts along the way. Two outfitters are **Royal Gorge Rafting,** 45045 U.S. 50 (tel. 275-5161), west of Canon City; and **Arkansas Adventures** (tel. 275-3229), on U.S. 50, 20 miles above Royal Gorge.

Where to Stay
Royal Gorge Motel, 1925 Fremont Dr., Canon City, CO 81212 (tel. 719/ 275-3377), has 68 units located eight miles from Royal Gorge. There is a heated swimming pool, a trout pond, and a restaurant and lounge. Rates are $50 double.

Park Lane Motel, 1401 Main St., Canon City, CO 81212 (tel. 719/275-

7240), has 14 modest rooms, some with kitchens, a playground, and a heated pool, at $26 double.

Where to Eat

Besides the motel dining rooms noted above, the **Bavarian Inn,** eight miles west of Canon City on U.S. 50 at the junction of Royal Gorge Road (tel. 269-3594), offers German cooking. It is open, with full bar service, daily for lunch and dinner.

3. PUEBLO AND SOUTH

PUEBLO: An early gateway to the Rockies on the Arkansas River, Pueblo stands on the site of a log cabin built here in 1806 by Capt. Zebulon Pike. Mormon immigrants from Missouri built a settlement here in 1846, a church, and a row of log cabins in one of which the first white child of Colorado was born. Fort Pueblo was built next, in 1860, to protect settlers and stage lines from Indian attacks. Today the city has a variety of industry as well as being an agricultural center and site of the University of Southern Colorado.

A **visitor information center** is open daily May to September in a railroad caboose at the junction of U.S. 50 and I-25 at exit 101 (tel. 719/543-1742). The **police emergency** number is 911. The **Pueblo Chamber of Commerce** provides information all year at its office at 302 N. Santa Fe Ave., Pueblo, CO (tel. 719/542-1704).

Sightseeing

Rosemount Victorian House Museum, 419 W. 14th St. (tel. 545-5290), is located in the historic Thatcher house, Rosemount, dating from 1891. The lower two floors remain as originally decorated, and the top floor has the McClelland Collection of curiosities from around the world. The carriage house has a tea room. Admission is $2, and it is open daily except Monday all year, except during January.

El Pueblo State Historical Museum, 905 S. Prairie Ave. (tel. 564-5274), has a full-size reproduction of an early trapping fort, Fort Pueblo.

The Showroom, 102 S. Oneida (tel. 546-1825), is a museum of Pueblo memorabilia and has some vintage cars, as well as serving as the home of a theatrical group called the Impossible Players.

On B Street at Victoria is the old **Union Depot,** once the hub of the rail system of the entire region. The **Goodnight Barn,** 1½ miles west of the city on Colo. 96, is the last remaining building of the notorious Charles Goodnight cattle kingdom. Cattle trails throughout the area bear the Goodnight name. A replica of the **stockade** that Zebulon Pike built here in 1806 on his mapping expedition of the Arkansas River is to be seen on South Elizabeth Street. A restored county courthouse at 10th and Main has historical murals and paintings inside, while other turn-of-the-century buildings, **City Hall** and **Memorial Auditorium,** on Union Avenue, are also the pride of local residents.

Aircraft from World War II to modern times are shown at the **Weisbrod Airplane Museum,** at the airport six miles east of town on U.S. 50, where the free exhibits include a Flying Boxcar, a Skyhawk attack bomber, a Boeing Stratojet, and a futuristic high-speed ground research vehicle from the U.S. Department of Transportation. There is also a new **Fire Museum** at 102 Broadway. A scenic park, likely spot for picnics nearby, **Pueblo/Puebla Plaza,** is named for the sister-city arrangement with Puebla, Mexico. Federal government publications of every kind are sold at the **Government Printing Office Bookstore,** 720 N. Main, locally known as "the bookstore that put Pueblo on the map."

Art shows and theater productions are held at the **Sangre de Cristo Arts Center,** 210 N. Santa Fe Ave. The two-week **Colorado State Fair,** running through late August into September, involves hundreds of exhibits, a midway, entertainment, and horse racing, at the fairgrounds on Beulah Avenue.

Outdoors enthusiasts find recreation at **Pueblo Dam and Reservoir,** seven miles west of the city off U.S. 50, where there are water sports including boating and fishing as well as a wildlife preserve and a campground. More wildlife is seen at the **Audubon River Trail and Nature Center,** on the site of an old pioneer ranch, 3900 W. 11th St.

Where to Stay

The **Holiday Inn,** 4001 N. Elizabeth St., Pueblo, CO 81008 (tel. 719/543-8050), has 191 rooms, an indoor pool and sauna, and a restaurant and cocktail lounge with live entertainment. Doubles are $44 to $52.

The **Pueblo West Inn,** 201 S. McCulloch Blvd., Pueblo, CO 81007 (tel. 719/547-2111), has 80 rooms and some individual lanais, a heated pool, and four lighted tennis courts. There is a restaurant and cocktail lounge. Doubles are $32.

Budget accommodations in cheery surroundings are had at **Motel 6,** 4103 N. Elizabeth St., Pueblo, CO 81008 (tel. 719/543-6221). Located near I-25, the motel has a good pool, free local telephone, and double rates at $22.

Where to Eat

Noted for good fried chicken is the **Black Swan,** 209 W. 7th St. (tel. 542-0858).

Steaks, seafood, Italian dishes, and reasonably priced buffets are offered at the **Holiday Inn,** 4001 N. Elizabeth St. (tel. 543-8050), open daily from 6 a.m. to 10 p.m.

HUERFANO COUNTY: Fifty miles south of Pueblo on I-25 is the small city of **Walsenburg,** seat of Huerfano County, another gateway between the prairie to the east and the Frontal Range to the west.

Three miles from Walsenburg is **Lathrop State Park** (tel. 719/738-2376), comprising a wildlife area, a public golf course, two lakes with boat access, and picnic grounds and campsites. Set in high-plains grassland with piñon and juniper trees in the higher elevations, the park has a starkly beautiful horizon in the Spanish Peaks that reach 13,610 and 12,669 feet, and were named Huajatolla by local Indians. They compared the peaks to two women's breasts that gave sustenance to all living things of the earth. The clouds were born there, without which there would be no life-giving rain. The two campgrounds can accommodate tents or RVs, and there are dump stations. Night fishing is permitted from boats equipped with proper running lights. High winds that may be dangerous for small craft also bring out the sailing enthusiasts. Zones are set aside for swimming, fishing, and waterskiing. Fish stocked are rainbow trout and channel catfish.

Hikers have two short trails here departing from the parking lot to the foot of the Hogback. One, of a distance of 1¾ miles, continues to the top of the Hogback for views of the Greenhorn Mountains, Huerfano Butte, and Pikes Peak. Murals on the history of the area are to be seen in the visitor center, the work of local artist Paul Busch.

La Veta, a small town 17 miles west of Walsenburg, gives a better view of the Spanish Peaks and makes a gateway to Huajatolla Canyon and the Cuchara Valley. **Fort Francisco Museum** has artifacts of the pioneer era. The town is famous for a two-day fair around the Fourth of July.

Within San Isabel National Forest is the little town of **Cuchara,** 26 miles southwest of Walsenburg on Colo. 12, a mountain vacation hideout for plains-bound Kansans, Texans, and Oklahomans who stream here in the summertime. There is good trout fishing and endless hiking in the unspoiled mountain country. Another community, **Gardner,** is famous for its **Chuckwagon Days,** held in late August in commemoration of the traditional cattle roundup. Stews are served to hundreds of visitors from heavy iron kettles that once saw service in pioneer times.

TRINIDAD: This historic end-of-the-plains town 200 miles south of Denver on I-25 is only about ten miles above Raton Pass on the New Mexico line, and has long been a traveler's stopping place since the time of the Indians, and the Spanish explorers, trappers, and settlers who followed. It was on a mountain branch of the Santa Fe Trail, over which travelers were at various times Kit Carson, Ceran St. Vrain, the Bent brothers, Uncle Dick Wooton, and Bat Masterson, Trinidad's marshal for a time.

Main Street, which was part of the Santa Fe Trail in the past, has streets made of red brick crossing it, and brick streets are part of the town's old traditions. This paving was put in during the early 1900s and now there are exactly 7.6 miles of brick streets, mostly around the Baca House, the Bloom Mansion, and the Pioneer Museum complex.

Sights and Activities
The main visitor attraction is the block of old buildings. The **Baca House,** built in 1869, is a two-story adobe in Greek Revival style, owned by a sheep rancher, Felipe Baca. His descendants lived here until the 1920s and the house has still most of its original furnishings. Wooden floors have hand-woven wool rugs and mattresses are stuffed with raw wool. Dried herbs and vegetables hang in the kitchen in the style current before the advent of refrigeration. A kettle of handmade soap sits in a corner by a cookstove. Gourds and earthen pots used for carrying drinking water hang nearby. Handmade toys are shown in a children's room upstairs—cracked marbles, a wooden top, a cloth doll in a faded dress. The State Historical Society operates the house as part of the **Pioneer Museum** (tel. 846-7217), and also has open to the public the **Bloom House,** a rococo Victorian mansion embellished with much fancy woodcarving and ornate ironwork. Inside there is flamboyant wallpaper, heavy carved furniture, and plenty of bric-a-brac, with lace curtains at the windows and fancy doilies on chair arms. Cut-glass bowls and porcelain figurines decorate tables and shelves. Silk-embroidered crazy-quilts embellish the carved bedroom sets. The study has a chair fashioned of Texas longhorn steer horns, a favored item of décor in its day. Outbuildings of the Baca House shelter collections of tools, carts, wagons, and workaday artifacts from the last century, as well as some wonderful old photographs from the 1880s and 1890s. There are guns and a buckskin coat once belonging to Kit Carson. The museum complex is open daily from Memorial Day to Labor Day: Monday through Saturday, with guided tours on the half hour from 10 a.m. to 5 p.m., and on Sunday from 1 to 5 p.m., at a $2 admission charge.

Other interesting sights include the **Children's Museum,** 314 N. Commercial St., in Firehouse No. 1, with a retired 1937 fire engine and an old fire pole. The **A. R. Mitchell Museum of Western Art,** 131 W. Main St., has original western works by Harvey Dunn, Harold von Schmidt, Nick Eggenhofer, Ned Jacob, and of course, A. R. Mitchell, the native son who painted most of his works on local subjects, many of which appeared as magazine-cover illustrations half a century ago. Mitchell kept many of his works, refusing to sell them, with the result that the museum here has about 100 original Mitchell works shown.

There is also a section devoted to Mitchell's personal collections of Indian crafts, and at one end of a balcony is the Malcolm Erickson Collection of Hispanic Folk Religious Art, shown in a *morada,* originally a meeting room for the Penitente sect. *Santos* and *bultos*—paintings and statues—include a depiction of a figure of Death wielding an axe rather than the familiar scythe. The museum is open during the summer only, mid-May to mid-September, free of charge, from 10 a.m. to 4 p.m. daily except Sunday.

Trinidad State Recreation Area, on Colo. 12 west of town (tel. 719/846-6951), has 2,300 acres including an 800-acre lake for boating, waterskiing, and fishing for rainbow and brown trout, largemouth bass, and channel catfish. Swimming is not allowed. There is a campground with 62 sites for RVs, with hookups, showers, toilets, a laundry, and a dump station (camping is $7, plus $1.50 for hookups if needed). Two short hiking trails lead from the camping area, one, fairly steep, to **Carpios Ridge,** where there are views of the reservoir and Fishers Peak. The **Levsa Canyon Trail** loops to the west, also above the reservoir.

For all travel information, see the **Trinidad Chamber of Commerce** at 212 Nevada Ave., Trinidad, CO 81082 (tel. 719/846-9285).

Where to Stay

The **Holiday Inn,** two miles south of town at exit 11 of I-25, Trinidad, CO 81082 (tel. 719/846-4491, or toll free 800/465-4329), has an indoor pool, restaurant, and lounge, and 113 rooms at $50 and up, double.

The **Derrick Motel,** also at exit 11 of I-25, Trinidad, CO 81082 (tel. 719/846-3307), has 17 rooms and cable television on a site away from traffic. Double rooms are $24.

Where to Eat

Besides the restaurants in the motels, choice spots in town include **Arturo's,** 400 E. Main St. (tel. 846-6060), serving Mexican and Chinese dishes for lunch and dinner daily in the De Dia room downstairs, and evenings (except Monday) upstairs in the De Noche Room, specializing in steaks and seafood.

El Capitan, 321 State St. (tel. 846-9903), serves not only Mexican foods but also authentic Italian dishes, including pizza; there is a salad bar and a lounge, all open daily for lunch and dinner, except Sunday.

4. SAN LUIS VALLEY

Known by the Indians as the land of the blue-sky people, the broad, high San Luis Valley has mountains all around it that assure cool summers, yet its latitude makes for winters milder than those in the heights farther north in the state. There are millions of acres of forest land reserved in national forests and other public preserves, including the fabulous Great Sand Dunes, and there are small towns providing all travel services, notably Alamosa and Monte Vista. There is also a spectacular narrow-gauge train ride that runs over the mountains across into New Mexico. The valley is in parts of Alamosa, Conejos, Costilla, Mineral, Rio Grande, and Saguache Counties, comprising some of the most spectacular remote high country in the West, in the longest valley in the U.S.

ALAMOSA: At the center of the San Luis Valley, Alamosa is 230 miles from Denver (via I-25 south to Walsenburg and U.S. 160 west), and is situated on the Navajo Trail (U.S. 160), the shortest route across the U.S. from east to west. Temperatures average 16° in January, 64° in July. The town is served by **Continental Airlines** with daily service to and from Denver out of Alamosa Municipal Airport, and by **Greyhound/Trailways** buses.

Founded in 1878 with the extension of a narrow-gauge railroad into the valley, the town was named for the Spanish word for cottonwood tree, the species found growing along the banks of the Rio Grande here. Soon rails reached out in all directions from the town, which became a thriving farm center and supply depot for mines. The valley, as large as the state of Delaware, lies at an average altitude of 7,500 feet and has the Continental Divide in the San Juan range to the west and the sharp-ridged Sangre de Cristo range, which reaches on down into New Mexico, to the east. The floor of the valley is nearly a desert, receiving only eight inches of rainfall annually.

At the east entrance to Alamosa is **Cole Park,** on the Rio Grande, where there are camping and picnic grounds. **Splashland,** on Colo. 17 north of the center of town, is a natural artesian warm-water pool open to the public. The town also runs a public golf course, with water and sand hazards along the bank of the **Rio Grande.**

For all travel service information, stop at the **Alamosa Chamber of Commerce** in Cole Park (tel. 303/589-6531).

Where to Stay

The **Alamosa Inn,** 1819 Main St., Alamosa, CO 81101 (tel. 303/589-2567), has 143 rooms, an indoor pool and sauna, and a restaurant with cocktail lounge, as well as a gift shop. Doubles run $44.

The **Holiday Inn,** 333 Santa Fe Ave., Alamosa, CO 81101 (tel. 303/589-5833, or toll free 800/465-4329), has 125 units, an indoor recreation center, a game room, a pool, restaurant and cocktail lounge, and a gift shop. Double rooms are $50 to $60.

The **Walsh Hotel,** 617 6th St., Alamosa, CO 81101 (tel. 303/589-6641), has 55 units, some hotel rooms and some motel units, and a restaurant and cocktail lounge. There is also a youth hostel on the premises. Doubles are $32.

Where to Eat

Besides a dozen fast-food establishments, Alamosa has a couple of likely steak restaurants: the **Sirloin Steak House,** 513 La Due (tel. 589-6391), and **Salazar's,** 1406 Main St. (tel. 589-3838).

GREAT SAND DUNES NATIONAL MONUMENT: This 46,000-acre expanse of fine sand lies 32 miles northeast of Alamosa, reached from the south over U.S. 160 and Colo. 150, or from the west over Colo. 17 and County Six Mile Lane. The **visitor center** (tel. 378-2312) is open from 7 a.m. to 8 p.m. in summer and 8 a.m. to 5 p.m. the rest of the year. Near the dunes are fire grates and picnic tables in an area also used for camping in the winter. **Pinyon Flats Campground** is open May to October. Backcountry hikers may camp in the park after taking out a permit, issued free of charge. A four-wheel-drive-only route to Medano Pass on the **Medano Primitive Road** requires reduced air pressure in tires to negotiate soft sand. (Tire air for reinflating tires is available in the maintenance yard at the park entrance.) Tours are run through the sand dunes in four-wheel-drive vehicles by a concessioner in nearby Mosca called **Great Sand Dunes Oasis** (tel. 378-2222). Further information is available from the visitor center.

The best way to get the surrealistic experience of losing yourself in a sandy scene of unsure dimensions is simply to walk into the dunes on foot. Although the mountains that made the sand are within view in the far distance, it is not so clear where you are or where you have been once you are wandering in this strange desert. It is not at all a question of being lost—just feeling in an extremely strange environment that has a special visual effect. It may make you feel very small.

The wind is always at work here, blowing grains off the crests of the dunes. They began forming as the last Ice Age ended when streams of water melting from glaciers carried rocks, gravel, sand, and silt down from the mountains. The lighter materials were carried out onto the floor of the valley. From the San Juan Mountains it was the Rio Grande that moved material onto the floor of the valley, and as the river shifted its course over the millennia vast deposits of sand were exposed to the wind. The mountains across the valley to the east, the Sangre de Cristos, tower 4,000 feet above the valley floor, forming a barrier in its northerly range to winds blowing in from the southwest. But in its southern part the range parallels the wind and shoots it into a pocket where the mountains change their direction. Here the wind is funneled through three low passes, bouncing and rolling the old river sand toward the mountain barrier. There the wind drops its power and leaves the sand behind, making this sea of sand 150 square miles in area. Caught in a wind trap, the main dune field of 50 square miles is stable, but the surfaces of the dunes are always changing with the winds. Medano Creek washes sand at the leading edge of the dunes back into the valley, from which it is again blown onto the dunes. So-called reversing winds from the mountains pile the dunes back upon themselves and build them higher and higher, the highest dunes in North America. Some are 700 feet in height. They seem steeper than they are because of deceptive shadows; physicists know that sand cannot be piled any steeper than 31°, but to visitors the dunes sometimes seem to look like sheer walls. In summer, incidentally, they always wear shoes to protect their feet from the hot sand—it gets as hot as 140°. Climbing dunes is fun, but at this 7,500-foot altitude, somewhat tiring, especially when your steps slide back into the soft sand at every effort. But you can climb to the top of your own particular little mountain and discover your own valley—never to reappear exactly like this after the winds have reshaped the surfaces again, and yet again. The sands appear gold, pink, tan, sometimes bluish. Highest of all the dunes is one right near the visitor center—getting to the top and back down takes about three hours, and from it you can see the whole sea of sand and much of the Sangre de Cristos. A special feeling of freedom comes in heading off in any direction: there are no paths, of course, in this ever-changing landscape. A destination of the vehicle tours on primitive roads is the **Ghost Forest**—a section of Ponderosa pines that were buried by the sands and eventually uncovered by the wind.

Among the specialized animals able to survive in this weird environment are the Ord kangaroo rat, a creature that never drinks water; and the giant sand treader camel cricket, that lives nowhere else on earth. These animals and the surrounding flora in the mountain foothills are discussed in evening programs and guided walks during the summer season, and there is a self-guided nature trail open all year. The entrance fee is $1 per car.

SAN JUAN ART CENTER: A rare opportunity to watch craftspeople in the Hispanic tradition of folkloric design at work is afforded visitors to a former church in the hamlet of Garita, reached via a turnoff to the west of U.S. 285 halfway between the towns of Saguache and Monte Vista. The church, **La Sapilla de San Juan Bautista,** is on the National Register of Historic Sites, and is open all summer, weekdays from 9 a.m. to 4 p.m. and weekends from 1 p.m. For times of opening during the winter, call 734-3191. The artisans are all members of a group called **Artes del Valle.** There are weavers at work, potters at a pottery wheel, an expert in the colcha embroidery stitch, sculptors working in wood and clay. There is a sales and display area.

SAN LUIS: Colorado's oldest town, 42 miles southeast of Alamosa, via U.S. 160 east and Colo. 159 south, was founded in 1851 and retains a number of original structures from its early days, made of adobe brick. One of these is the 1860 **Church of the Precious Blood.** The **San Luis Museum,** open year round, has artifacts from the early life of the region. There is also an outdoor theater where programs go on during the July festivals of Santa Ana and Santiago. The museum is part of a cultural center complex surrounding a pretty plaza worth a visit; for information on dates and times of activities, call the museum, at 672-3372. Also of interest in town is the 1883 San Luis **courthouse.** The town still keeps an area of 633 acres reserved as a public common.

North of town 16 miles via Colo. 159 is **Fort Garland,** once commanded by Kit Carson and now restored as a museum open to visitors.

MONTE VISTA: At a distance of 210 miles southwest of Denver via U.S. 285, this town of 5,000 population on the Navajo Trail at an altitude of 7,600 feet is a center for growing potatoes, lettuce, and barley, as well as range animals. The town is known for its annual **Ski Hi Stampede,** over three days in late July, which, it is claimed, is the oldest rodeo in Colorado, and also involves horse races, street parades, a carnival, and western-style dancing.

Another visitor attraction are the migratory waterfowl viewed in season in **Monte Vista National Wildlife Refuge,** just south of town on Colo. 15.

Where to Stay

Monte Villa Inn, 925 First Ave., Monte Vista, CO 81144 (tel. 303/852-5166), has 39 rooms, a coffeeshop, a restaurant specializing in Mexican dishes, and a cocktail lounge. Doubles run $50.

The **Woods Motel,** 25 Broadway, Monte Vista, CO 81144 (tel. 303/852-3516), has 15 rooms at $38 double.

Where to Eat

A local hangout is the Pirate's Cave upstairs in the **High Country Steak House,** 819 First Ave. (tel. 852-5866).

CUMBRES & TOLTEC SCENIC RAILROAD: Open summers and early fall are 64-mile trips over the spectacular Cumbres & Toltec Scenic Railroad, the best remaining trackage of a network of narrow-gauge lines that connected mining towns in the Southwest. Originating in 1880 as an extension of the Denver & Rio Grande Railway, the C&TS was originally a branch serving mining camps in the San Juan Mountains around Silverton, Colorado. At the time, the Rio Grande company had a plan to connect its Denver headquarters with Mexico City, and the tracks did get as far south as Santa Fe. But the gold and silver strikes in the Rockies turned attention to the mining interests to the west.

Leaving the San Luis Valley main line at Antonito, Colorado, the line angles to the southwest through rolling mesa land, climbing into the forested foothills of the San Juan range. It passes through groves of pine and aspen and past weird rock formations, then winds through the fabulous Toltec Gorge of the Los Piños River. Its highest point is at 10,015-foot Cumbres Pass, from which it drops down at a grade of 4% into Chama, New Mexico.

The famous traveler and railroad buff Lucius Beebe called this part of the line "the most awesomely spectacular example of mountain railroading in North America." It is owned today jointly by the states of New Mexico and Colorado, and is a Registered National Historic Site. Two trains run on the line, starting at opposite ends, and going as far as Osier, Colorado, before turning back to their points of departure. The *Colorado Limited* leaves Antonito daily at 10 a.m., and travels 38 miles via Sublette, New Mexico, to Osier, arriving at 1 p.m. It leaves Osier at 2 p.m., returning to Antonito at 4:45 p.m. From the New Mexico end of the line the *New Mexico Express* departs from Chama daily at 10:30 a.m., makes a stop at Cumbres Pass between 11:40 a.m. and noon, and arrives at Osier in time to meet the *Colorado Limited* at 1 p.m. Passengers are thus free to change trains and make an entire round-trip over all the trackage in two days, or to make the whole trip one way and return to their departure point by van, returning to Antonito this way by 5:30 p.m. It is also possible to leave Antonito by van at 9:15 a.m., cross over to Chama, board the *New Mexico Express* there, change to the return run of the *Colorado Limited,* and be back in Antonito again by 5 p.m.

Regular excursions cost $27 for adults, $10 for children, or through trips with van return, $41.50 for adults, $20 for children. Through trips with no return are $37; children pay $17.50. Overnight specials, including hotel room, dinner, and breakfast, go from $121. For reservations from the Colorado side call the C&TS office in Antonito at 376-5483; the New Mexico terminal phone is 505/756-2151.

5. PAGOSA SPRINGS

Just to the west of the Continental Divide from the San Luis Valley, 270 miles from Denver via U.S. 285 south and U.S. 160 west, Pagosa Springs is named for its local hot springs from a Ute Indian word for "healing water." The site was the original 1879 emplacement of Fort Lewis, which served to protect settlers from Indians. The town was incorporated in 1891 and became a lumbering center when a railroad was built into the area in 1900.

Mineral baths are given at several of the motels as well as at thermal establishments. Winter ice fishing and spring trout casting are good at **Echo Lake,** five miles south of town on U.S. 84. Northeast 16 miles on U.S. 160 at the foot of Wolf Creek Pass is **Treasure Falls,** tumbling 100 feet down the side of **Treasure Mountain,** which legendarily hides a treasure of $5 million in gold bars. Just east of the summit at the Continental Divide there is a hiking route called **Treasure Mountain Trail** that may lead to the cache. Other spectacular hikes can be made in a day or less: to **Four Miles Falls, Opal Lake, Piedra Falls, Williams Creek, Piedra River,** and **Quartz Lake,** among them.

A fascinating area is **Chimney Rock National Archeological Area,** containing ruins of the prehistoric Anasazi culture. Tours of the ruins are provided by rangers of the U.S. Forest Service during the summer on Wednesday and Friday mornings. Reservations are made at the Pagosa Ranger District Office in Pagosa Springs (tel. 264-2268). The entrance to the ruins is reached by going west on U.S. 160 from Pagosa Springs for 19 miles to Colo. 151, and south on 151 about 3¼ miles to the gate. Located within San Juan National Forest, the Chimney Rock area was designated a Peregrine falcon aerie in 1974 and was closed to the public for a time. The birds are thriving, however, to the extent that guided groups can make limited tours without bothering them during nesting and fledgling times. In the summer, the falcons can be seen in flight, and when hatchery birds are released as fledglings, they can be seen learning to fly. The area has a total of 3,160 acres, 960 of which contain ruins on the mesa top, not only from the Anasazi culture, but also from the indigenous Chaco culture. Of the former there are 65 sites with 217 structures. The Chacoan structures include a *kiva,* an underground ceremonial room, and a pueblo. Datings by tree-ring cuttings and by judging the periods of ceramics in the ruins show that the Anasazi occupied the area for about two centuries beginning around A.D. 925. The Chaco occupation occurred during the latter half century of this period. Twin pinnacles are thought to have been symbolic of the twin war gods known in Pueblo Indian mythology.

Besides scheduling the twice-weekly summer guided tours, rangers may schedule tours at other times of year on request.

For information on accommodations and restaurants, see the listings for the Wolf Creek Ski Area in Chapter XV. For travel service information, call the **Pagosa Area Chamber of Commerce** in Pagosa Springs (tel. 303/264-2360).

6. BENT'S OLD FORT

One of the rare travelers' stops in the flat prairie country of southeastern Colorado is a National Historic Site on Colo. 194 eight miles east of La Junta and 15 miles west of Las Animas. Bent's Old Fort on the Arkansas River was once the hub from which American trade moved south into Mexico and west into the Great Basin and on to the Pacific, as well as north into Wyoming. Completed in 1833–1834 by the brothers Charles and William Bent and Ceran St. Vrain, it became the most important outpost of U.S. life between Missouri and Santa Fe. A traveler in 1840 described it thus: "Although built of the simple prairie soil, made to hold together by a rude mixture with straw and the plain grass itself, the fort is constructed with all the defensive capacities of a complete fortification. The dwellings, the kitchens, the arrangements for comfort are all such as to strike the wanderer with the liveliest surprise, as though an 'air-built castle' had dropped to earth before him in the midst of the vast desert."

The trade the fort was involved in was three-cornered: U.S.-made goods were hauled over the Santa Fe Trail from Missouri, and some were left here while others were taken on down into Mexican territory and sold by St. Vrain and Charles Bent in Taos and Santa Fe. Goods took the reverse route, some Mexican and Navajo products being stored in the fort and some continuing on back east to Missouri. The third corner of the trading triangle consisted of Plains Indians who traded their buffalo robes for goods available at the fort. The fort also sold goods to the mountain men who brought in beaver pelts from the north for trading for equipment and supplies. The Bents and St. Vrain ran a vast commercial empire out here for 17 years. A historian sees them as men "whose will was prairie law, who could sway whole tribes, who knew Indians and Mexicans as few others did."

The influx of U.S. soldiers in the Mexican War in 1846 began the end of this private empire; they were soon joined by settlers, adventurers, and later, gold seekers who used up the precious wood and fouled the watering places, frightening off the buffalo that was the lifeblood of the Indian. Bent, St. Vrain and Co. was caught between the invading whites and the resentful Indians. When the Indians began serious warfare in 1847 the era of rich trading was over. Then Charles Bent was killed in a revolt in Taos and St. Vrain departed for New Mexico, leaving William Bent on his own to maintain operations, but an epidemic of cholera spreading through the Indian tribes in 1849 was the final blow to the enterprise. Disillusioned, Bent moved his family and employees out as the fort burned. No one knows whether Bent himself or the Indians set fire to it.

By skill and subtleness the partners, especially William Bent, achieved greater influence among the Indians than any of their rival traders. The most important of the tribes trading with them was the Southern Cheyenne, on whose hunting grounds the fort itself was built. William Bent treated the Indians fairly and demanded that his employees do the same, and he restricted the use of whisky in bartering with the Indians. To strengthen his ties with them, he married Owl Woman, the daughter of a Cheyenne priest named Gray Thunder. Because the Indians' wars among themselves were bad for business, Bent also encouraged peace among the various tribes. Because of his influence deadly enemies among the Indians could meet and trade at his fort in peace.

The fort today is reconstructed as accurately as possible to its appearance in 1845–1846, when the Bent brothers and St. Vrain were at the height of their powers commercially and politically. Both antiques and reproductions furnish the rooms. There is a kitchen with adjoining pantry, cook's room and dining room; a trade room with robes, pelts, and blankets in stock; blacksmith and carpenter shops; William Bent's office and bedroom; quarters for Mexican laborers, trappers, and soldiers; and a billiard room. There is the room Susan Magoffin used on her trip through to Santa Fe with her husband in 1846—her meticulous diary entries give us our best descriptions of the fort at the time.

Index

NOW, SAVE MONEY ON ALL YOUR TRAVELS!
Join Frommer's™ Dollarwise® Travel Club

Saving money while traveling is never a simple matter, which is why, over 27 years ago, the **Dollarwise Travel Club** was formed. Actually, the idea came from readers of the Frommer publications who felt that such an organization could bring financial benefits, continuing travel information, and a sense of community to economy-minded travelers all over the world.

In keeping with the money-saving concept, the annual membership fee is low—$18 (U.S. residents) or $20 U.S. (Canadian, Mexican, and foreign residents)—and is immediately exceeded by the value of your benefits which include:

1. The latest edition of any TWO of the books listed on the following pages.

2. A copy of any Frommer City Guide.

3. An annual subscription to an 8-page quarterly newspaper *The Dollarwise Traveler* which keeps you up-to-date on fastbreaking developments in good-value travel in all parts of the world—bringing you the kind of information you'd have to pay over $35 a year to obtain elsewhere. This consumer-conscious publication also includes the following columns:

> **Hospitality Exchange**—members all over the world who are willing to provide hospitality to other members as they pass through their home cities.
>
> **Share-a-Trip**—requests from members for travel companions who can share costs and help avoid the burdensome single supplement.
>
> **Readers Ask . . . Readers Reply**—travel questions from members to which other members reply with authentic firsthand information.

4. Your personal membership card which entitles you to purchase through the club all Frommer publications for a third to a half off their regular retail prices during the term of your membership.

So why not join this hardy band of international Dollarwise travelers now and participate in its exchange of information and hospitality? Simply send $18 (U.S. residents) or $20 U.S. (Canadian, Mexican, and other foreign residents) along with your name and address to: Frommer's Dollarwise Travel Club, Inc., Gulf + Western Building, One Gulf + Western Plaza, New York, NY 10023. Remember to specify which *two* of the books in section (1) and which *one* in section (2) above you wish to receive in your initial package of member's benefits. Or tear out the next page, check off your choices, and send the page to us with your membership fee.

FROMMER BOOKS
PRENTICE HALL PRESS
ONE GULF + WESTERN PLAZA
NEW YORK, NY 10023

Date_____

Friends:
Please send me the books checked below:

FROMMER'S™ $-A-DAY® GUIDES

(In-depth guides to sightseeing and low-cost tourist accommodations and facilities.)

☐ Europe on $30 a Day $14.95
☐ Australia on $30 a Day $12.95
☐ Eastern Europe on $25 a Day $12.95
☐ England on $40 a Day $12.95
☐ Greece on $30 a Day $12.95
☐ Hawaii on $50 a Day $13.95
☐ India on $25 a Day $12.95
☐ Ireland on $30 a Day $12.95
☐ Israel on $30 & $35 a Day $12.95
☐ Mexico (plus Belize & Guatemala)
   on $25 a Day $13.95

☐ New Zealand on $40 a Day $12.95
☐ New York on $50 a Day $12.95
☐ Scandinavia on $50 a Day $12.95
☐ Scotland and Wales on $40 a Day $12.95
☐ South America on $30 a Day $12.95
☐ Spain and Morocco (plus the Canary Is.)
   on $40 a Day $13.95
☐ Turkey on $25 a Day $12.95
☐ Washington, D.C., & Historic Va. on
   $40 a Day $12.95

FROMMER'S™ DOLLARWISE® GUIDES

(Guides to sightseeing and tourist accommodations and facilities from budget to deluxe, with emphasis on the medium-priced.)

☐ Alaska $13.95
☐ Austria & Hungary $14.95
☐ Belgium, Holland, Luxembourg $13.95
☐ Brazil $14.95
☐ Egypt $13.95
☐ France $14.95
☐ England & Scotland $14.95
☐ Germany $13.95
☐ Italy $14.95
☐ Japan & Hong Kong $13.95
☐ Portugal, Madeira, & the Azores $13.95
☐ South Pacific $13.95
☐ Switzerland & Liechtenstein $13.95
☐ Bermuda & The Bahamas $13.95
☐ Canada $13.95
☐ Caribbean $13.95

☐ Cruises (incl. Alask, Carib, Mex, Hawaii,
   Panama, Canada, & US) $14.95
☐ California & Las Vegas $14.95
☐ Florida $13.95
☐ Mid-Atlantic States $13.95
☐ New England $13.95
☐ New York State $13.95
☐ Northwest $13.95
☐ Skiing in Europe $14.95
☐ Skiing USA—East $13.95
☐ Skiing USA—West $13.95
☐ Southeast & New Orleans $13.95
☐ Southwest $14.95
☐ Texas $13.95
☐ USA (avail. Feb. 1989) $15.95

FROMMER'S™ TOURING GUIDES

(Color illustrated guides that include walking tours, cultural & historic sites, and other vital travel information.)

☐ Australia $9.95
☐ Egypt $8.95
☐ Florence $8.95
☐ London $8.95

☐ Paris $8.95
☐ Thailand $9.95
☐ Venice $8.95

TURN PAGE FOR ADDITIONAL BOOKS AND ORDER FORM.

FROMMER'S™ CITY GUIDES

(Pocket-size guides to sightseeing and tourist accommodations and facilities in all price ranges.)

☐ Amsterdam/Holland $5.95	☐ Montreal/Quebec City. $5.95
☐ Athens. $5.95	☐ New Orleans. $5.95
☐ Atlantic City/Cape May $5.95	☐ New York $5.95
☐ Boston. $5.95	☐ Orlando/Disney World/EPCOT $5.95
☐ Cancún/Cozumel/Yucatán. $5.95	☐ Paris $5.95
☐ Dublin/Ireland $5.95	☐ Philadelphia $5.95
☐ Hawaii. $5.95	☐ Rio $5.95
☐ Las Vegas. $5.95	☐ Rome. $5.95
☐ Lisbon/Madrid/Costa del Sol $5.95	☐ San Francisco $5.95
☐ London $5.95	☐ Santa Fe/Taos (avail. May 1989) $5.95
☐ Los Angeles $5.95	☐ Sydney (avail. Feb. 1989) $5.95
☐ Mexico City/Acapulco. $5.95	☐ Washington, D.C. $5.95
☐ Minneapolis/St. Paul $5.95	

SPECIAL EDITIONS

☐ A Shopper's Guide to the Caribbean. .$12.95	☐ Motorist's Phrase Book (Fr/Ger/Sp) . . .$4.95
☐ Beat the High Cost of Travel $6.95	☐ Paris Rendez-Vous $10.95
☐ Bed & Breakfast—N. America $8.95	☐ Swap and Go (Home Exchanging). . . .$10.95
☐ Guide to Honeymoon Destinations	☐ The Candy Apple (NY for Kids). $11.95
(US, Canada, Mexico, & Carib). $12.95	☐ Travel Diary and Record Book $5.95
☐ Manhattan's Outdoor Sculpture $15.95	☐ Where to Stay USA (Lodging from $3
	to $30 a night) $10.95

☐ Marilyn Wood's Wonderful Weekends (NY, Conn, Mass, RI, Vt, NH, NJ, Del, Pa) $11.95
☐ The New World of Travel (Annual sourcebook by Arthur Frommer previewing: new travel trends, new modes of travel, and the latest cost-cutting strategies for savvy travelers). $12.95

SERIOUS SHOPPER'S GUIDES

(Illustrated guides listing hundreds of stores, conveniently organized alphabetically by category)

☐ Italy. $15.95	☐ Los Angeles $14.95
☐ London $15.95	☐ Paris $15.95

GAULT MILLAU

(The only guides that distinguish the truly superlative from the merely overrated.)

☐ The Best of Chicago (avail. April 1989)$15.95	☐ The Best of New England (avail. April
☐ The Best of France (avail. July 1989) . .$15.95	1989) $15.95
☐ The Best of Italy (avail. July 1989). . . .$15.95	☐ The Best of New York $15.95
☐ The Best of Los Angeles $15.95	☐ The Best of San Francisco $15.95
	☐ The Best of Washington, D.C. $15.95

ORDER NOW!

In U.S. include $1.50 shipping UPS for 1st book; 50¢ ea. add'l book. Outside U.S. $2 and 50¢, respectively. Allow four to six weeks for delivery in U.S., longer outside U.S.

Enclosed is my check or money order for $_____

NAME _____

ADDRESS _____

CITY _____ STATE _____ ZIP _____